**To Judy,
Craig, Jeanne, and Lynne**

CONTENTS

PREFACE

While retaining the general outline and model development of the previous editions, numerous changes have been made in this third edition of *Macroeconomics*. With regard to organization, the chapter on international economics now precedes the chapter on economic growth. The classical view is treated in Chapter 11, rather than in an appendix. The IS–LM model with the government budget constraint, previously covered in Chapter 9, is considered in an appendix.

With regard to content, the most important changes are as follows. Chapter 2 now includes a discussion of gross domestic product (GDP) plus an expanded discussion of the underground economy. Chapters 3 and 4 have been reduced in length. Discussions of the life cycle hypothesis, the effect of a liquidity constraint on consumption, and government debt and the tax-discounting hypothesis have been incorporated into Chapter 5. Chapter 6 now includes a discussion of the q theory of investment.

In Chapter 7, the definition of the money supply and description of the money creation process have been updated. New emphasis has been placed on the difficulty that the Federal Reserve has in controlling the money supply in the short run. Chapter 8 now includes a discussion of the stability of the demand for money function (the "missing money" puzzle). Chapter 9 contains a new application of the IS–LM model, the policy mix, as well as an expanded discussion of the interest rate as an indicator of the thrust of monetary policy.

Chapter 11 now consists of expanded and refined discussions of the classical and monetarist views, while Chapter 12 consists of expanded discussions of the rational expectations and supply-side views. Previously, the classical view was discussed in an appendix while the other views were covered in a single chapter. Chapter 13 has been substantially revised to put more emphasis on inflation as a monetary phenomenon. It also includes discussions of inflation from the classical,

Keynesian, monetarist, rational expectations, and supply-side perspectives. Chapter 14 has been substantially rewritten so as to make it more understandable.

Two sections, the appreciation of the dollar: 1980–85 and rising protectionism, have been added to Chapter 16. Chapter 18 now includes a discussion of the budgetary process and the Gramm–Rudman–Hollings Act, plus an expanded discussion of the impact of budget deficits and the public debt on the economy. A discussion of financial innovations and their impact on monetary policy has been incorporated into Chapter 19. The appendix on productivity growth (by Ronald L. Moomaw) has been rewritten and expanded.

To provide additional insights and to smooth the transition from chapter to chapter, a "concluding remarks" section has been included in virtually all of the chapters. The *Instructor's Manual* has been revised and a *Study Guide* is now available.

The author wishes to acknowledge the many helpful comments of Jack E. Adams, University of Arkansas at Little Rock; David G. Bivin, Indiana University–Purdue University at Indianapolis; G. Geoffrey Booth, Syracuse University; Donald Elliott, Southern Illinois University; Carl E. Enomoto, New Mexico State University; George C. Georgiou, Towson State University; Yoo Soo Hong, Ronald L. Moomaw, Kent W. Olson, John D. Rea, Andreas Savvides, and Larkin B. Warner, all of Oklahoma State University; and Barbara M. Yates, Seattle University. I also wish to thank my wife, Judith J. Edgmand, and one of my daughters, Jeanne E. Edgmand, for their assistance. Finally, I wish to thank Laura J. Davis for typing part of the revised manuscript.

Michael R. Edgmand

1

INTRODUCTION

Our economy is periodically beset by unemployment, inflation, low economic growth rates, and balance of payments deficits. During the Great Depression of the 1930s, unemployment was widespread. In the 1940s, inflation replaced unemployment as the major economic problem. During the late 1950s and early 1960s, the economy experienced relatively high rates of unemployment, low rates of economic growth, and balance of payments deficits. In the late 1960s, inflation again moved to the forefront.

In the 1970s, inflation was rampant. In the early 1980s, the inflation rate declined dramatically. At the same time, however, the unemployment rate increased significantly. Since then, the unemployment rate has declined and the growth rate has risen. Despite the improvement in the nation's economic performance, the United States has experienced record balance of payments deficits. The following chapters deal with the causes of these economic problems and means for coping with them.

This chapter begins with a discussion of microeconomics and macroeconomics. After briefly describing the Keynesian revolution, we consider the role of economic models. Next, the comparative statics approach is illustrated in the context of a simple price determination model. The goals of macroeconomic policy are then described; a preview of the book follows.

MICROECONOMICS AND MACROECONOMICS

There are two main branches of economic theory, microeconomics and macroeconomics. *Microeconomics* deals with individual units in the economy, usually households or firms. Microeconomics is concerned, for example, with how a household allocates its income among expenditures for various goods and services. Similarly, microeconomics is concerned with the determination of a firm's profit-maximizing level of production.

In some instances, microeconomics deals with units as large as an industry. For example, if the demand for a particular industry's product increases, microeconomics attempts to trace the impact of the increase upon the price of the product and the industry's level of production.

In contrast, *macroeconomics* deals with the economy as a whole. It ignores individual units and many of the problems which they face. By concentrating on the economy in the aggregate, macroeconomics is concerned with the total output of the economy and the general price level, not the output and price levels of a single firm or industry.

Methodologically, there is also a distinction between microeconomics and macroeconomics. In microeconomics, it is generally assumed that the total output and the general price level of the economy are given; microeconomics then tries to explain how the outputs and prices of individual products are determined. Macroeconomics assumes the constancy of the distribution of output and relative prices. It treats total output and the general price level as variables and attempts to explain how they are determined.

In practice, this sharp distinction between microeconomics and macroeconomics is difficult to maintain. Changes in the microeconomic variables may well affect the macroeconomic variables, and vice versa. For example, during the 1973 oil embargo, the oil shortage—a microeconomic problem—helped depress the activity of the economy. Nevertheless, the distinction between microeconomics and macroeconomics is meaningful.

ECONOMIC THEORY AND THE KEYNESIAN REVOLUTION

Before the 1930s, microeconomics rather than macroeconomics absorbed the attention of economists. The primary reason was the assumption that full employment prevailed except for temporary disruptions. If full employment prevails, the nation's output is constant in the short run. With aggregate output assumed constant, economists devoted their time to microeconomics with its emphasis on the determination of the prices and output levels of individual products. In the 1930s, however, two events stimulated the development of macroeconomics. First, the Great Depression demonstrated that the assumptions of full employment and constant aggregate output were untenable. In 1929, the unemployment rate was 3.2 percent. By 1933 it had reached 24.9 percent. Real gross national product, a measure of the nation's output of goods and services, fell from $709.6 billion in 1929 to $498.5 billion in 1933, a decline of approximately 30 percent. When economists recognized that the unemployment rate and aggregate output were variables, they saw the obvious desirability of studying the forces which determine them.

Second, in 1936, John Maynard Keynes published *The General Theory of Employment, Interest, and Money*.[1] In this book, Keynes presented a theory which showed that unemployment could exist for long periods of time or even indefinitely. Many economists received Keynes's theory, or *Keynesian economics* as it was later called, enthusiastically. In fact, the publication of his book and subsequent adoption of his views are often referred to as the *Keynesian revolution*. Although Keynes's theory may not have been truly revolutionary, his book did have a profound effect upon economists and economic theory.

ECONOMIC MODELS

Most of this text is devoted to the development of a theoretical model of the economy. A *model* is a set of relationships representing the economy or one or more of its parts. It may be expressed in words, tables, graphs, and/or mathematical equations. By abstracting from detail and focusing attention on the essential relationships, a model simplifies reality so that we can understand it.

Although economic models or theories are often criticized as unrealistic, they should be judged in terms of their explanatory power rather than their realism. For one thing, models cannot be fully realistic. The world is too complex to be described in complete detail. For another, one of the main purposes of economic theory is explanation. Therefore, the adequacy of the model or theory should be judged in these terms. If a model helps us to understand reality, it is a "good" model. If a model leads to misunderstanding, it is inadequate and we seek alternative models. For example, before Keynes, full employment was considered to be the normal state of affairs on the basis of the prevalent macroeconomic model, the classical model.[2] Unemployment, if it existed, was considered to be only temporary. But substantial unemployment existed during the 1930s and showed few signs of disappearing; consequently, economists were ready to drop or to revise the classical model. According to Keynes's theory, unemployment could exist for prolonged periods. Since actual experience seemed to be more in line with predictions based on Keynes's theory, the classical model was abandoned in favor of Keynes's theory.

COMPARATIVE STATICS AND DYNAMICS

Economic theory is used to predict the results of certain actions. For example, economic theory can predict or explain the consequences of an increase in the supply of money. Similarly, it can predict the impact of a reduction in federal tax rates. In making these predictions, we use the comparative statics method almost exclusively. That is, we compare equilibrium positions corresponding to two or more sets of external circumstances. To illustrate the method and its shortcomings, we develop the following example from microeconomics. At the same time, some of the concepts and terms used later in the text are introduced.

Suppose we are concerned with the market for meat. First, assume that the quantity of meat that consumers wish to buy per period depends upon, or is a function of, the price of meat and the per capita income of consumers. In equation form, the demand for meat is

$$\textbf{(1.1)} \qquad\qquad D = f(p, y),$$

where D is the quantity of meat demanded, p is the price of meat, and y is per capita income. Suppose also that the amount demanded varies inversely with price and directly with per capita income. Thus, the lower the price, the greater the amount demanded; the higher the level of per capita income, the greater the amount demanded.

Second, assume that the quantity of meat that producers or suppliers will make available per period varies directly with the price of meat. Thus, as the price of meat increases, the amount of meat supplied increases. In equation form, the supply of meat is

$$\textbf{(1.2)} \qquad\qquad S = g(p),$$

where S is the quantity of meat supplied and p is the price of meat.

Equations (1.1) and (1.2) are *behavioral equations* because they describe the "behavior" of demanders and suppliers. Prospective purchasers buy more meat at lower prices, whereas suppliers offer more meat for sale at higher prices.

Third, the market for meat is in equilibrium when the amount of meat demanded per period equals the amount of meat supplied per period:

$$\textbf{(1.3)} \qquad\qquad D = S.$$

Equation (1.3) is the *equilibrium condition* because it specifies the condition necessary for the market for meat to be in equilibrium.

Equilibrium exists when there is no net tendency for the variables in question to change. In this case, it occurs at the price at which the quantity of meat demanded equals the quantity of meat supplied. At any other price, the quantity demanded will either be greater or less than the quantity supplied. In either instance, the price of meat will change; it will rise if the quantity demanded exceeds the quantity supplied and fall if the opposite occurs.

Suppose per capita income, y, is constant so that

$$y = y_0.$$

Given y and the three equations, the equilibrium values of the three variables, p, D, and S, can be determined either algebraically or geometrically. Algebraically, the equilibrium price is determined by substituting the behavioral equations into the equilibrium condition. The equilibrium quantity is then found by substituting the equilibrium price in either the demand or supply equation, since the quantity demanded is equal to the quantity supplied when the market is in equilibrium.

Geometrically, the equilibrium combination of price and quantity may be determined by plotting the demand and supply curves and locating their intersection. Since the quantity demanded is inversely related to price, the demand curve, drawn for a given level of per capita income y_0 in Figure 1.1, is negatively sloped. The supply curve is positively sloped since the quantity supplied is directly related to price.

According to Figure 1.1, the equilibrium price is p_0 and the equilibrium quantity is D_0 (both demanded and supplied). So long as the underlying conditions remain unchanged, the equilibrium price and quantity will remain p_0 and D_0, respectively.

Before continuing, we note that the three variables, p, D, and S, are called the *endogenous* variables of the model, meaning that they are variables whose values are determined within the model. In this case, they are determined by the interaction of the demand for, and supply of, meat. The variable y is an *exogenous* variable: its value is determined outside the model (by external forces).

The use of the model may be extended by considering what happens if the exogenous variable, y, changes or if a shift occurs in either the demand curve or the supply curve. For example, suppose that the level of per capita income increases from y_0 to y_1. The amount of meat demanded at each price increases so that the

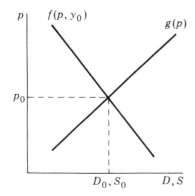

FIGURE 1.1

The demand for and the supply of meat

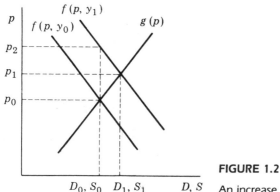

FIGURE 1.2 An increase in the demand for meat

demand curve in Figure 1.2 shifts to the right. As a consequence, the new equilibrium price is p_1 and the new equilibrium quantity is D_1. Hence, an increase in per capita income is predicted to increase both the price of meat and the amount sold.

The sizes of the increases depend on various factors. The greater the increase in per capita income or the greater the responsiveness of consumers to increases in per capita income, the greater the increase in demand and, hence, the greater the increase in the price of meat. Similarly, the more responsive suppliers are to an increase in the price of meat, the smaller will be the increase in the price of meat.

This analysis is an example of *comparative statics*. It involves the comparison of equilibrium positions corresponding to two sets of circumstances. Specifically, it indicates the changes in the equilibrium values of the endogenous variables when there is a change in an exogenous variable or in a functional relationship.

Despite the widespread usage of comparative statics, the approach has limitations. First, it does not describe the process or path by which the variables move from one equilibrium position to another. In the context of the example, does the price of meat rise from the original equilibrium price, p_0, to p_2 and then fall to p_1, or does it increase steadily to p_1? Since comparative statics involves only a comparison of initial and final equilibrium positions, we do not know. Second, the approach does not indicate how long it takes for the variables to move from one equilibrium position to another. How long does it take for the price of meat to adjust to an increase in demand? A week? A month? A year or more? The comparative statics approach cannot answer such questions.

Third, the comparative statics method does not even provide assurance that the new equilibrium position will be reached. It may be that the variables move away (diverge) from the new equilibrium position; in this case, an *unstable* equilibrium exists. If the equilibrium is unstable, the comparative statics method produces erroneous results since the new equilibrium position is not attained. On the other hand, if the variables move toward the new equilibrium position, a *stable* equilibrium exists.

If the system is stable, the comparative statics method yields valid predictions; however, it still does not indicate the time path of the variables, nor does it indicate how long the variables will take to reach their new equilibrium values. To avoid the shortcomings of comparative statics, dynamic analysis may be used. Dynamic analysis or *dynamics*, in cases where it can be applied, permits the study of the time path of the variables regardless of whether the equilibrium is stable or not.

Despite the advantages of dynamic analysis, it is rarely used in basic macroeconomic texts for at least two reasons. First, all but the very simplest dynamic models involve the use of differential or difference equations. Second, a generally accepted theory of income determination based on dynamic analysis does not exist. Hence, the comparative statics method is used almost exclusively in this text, despite its limitations.

THE GOALS OF MACROECONOMIC POLICY

Economic theory attempts to explain why problems arise in the economy and how these problems can be dealt with. It is, therefore, indispensable in formulating and conducting economic policy. But before studying macroeconomic theory and policy, one must state the macroeconomic goals of the economy. After all, without definite goals there is little point in formulating policy.

Full Employment

Economists often cite four macroeconomic goals: full employment, price stability, economic growth, and external balance. Although disagreement about these goals exists, all, or almost all, economists agree on the desirability of full employment. Indeed, such a goal has legislative mandate. In the Employment Act of 1946, Congress declared "that it is the continuing policy and responsibility of the Federal Government to use all practicable means . . . to promote maximum employment. . . ." More specific goals are listed in the Humphrey–Hawkins Full Employment and Balanced Growth Act, which was passed in 1978.

Full employment is favored because the greater the level of employment, the greater the amount of goods and services available to society. As noted earlier, the unemployment rate rose from 3.2 percent in 1929 to 24.9 percent in 1933. At the same time, real gross national product declined by approximately 30 percent. With the dramatic increase in unemployment and corresponding reduction in real gross national product, society lost goods and services it would have had if full employment had prevailed.

Full employment is also desired because the burden of unemployment and loss of goods and services falls disproportionately on people without jobs. Although part of the burden is offset by unemployment insurance benefits and various transfer payments, it still exists.

With regard to full employment, the Humphrey–Hawkins Act lists an unemployment rate of 4.0 percent (3.0 percent for adults) as an interim goal. (The full employment goal and its relationship to the unemployment rate are discussed at greater length in Chapter 15.)

Price Stability

The argument for price stability is not as straightforward as the argument for full employment. With inflation or at least unanticipated inflation, some people are adversely affected, but others benefit. Those that benefit include persons whose incomes rise more rapidly than prices and persons who were able to borrow at relatively low interest rates prior to the inflation. The latter benefit because they are able to repay their low-interest loans with dollars that are worth less than those they borrowed. Persons that are adversely affected include those whose incomes rise less rapidly than prices and those who made loans at relatively low interest rates prior to the inflation. The latter lose because they are repaid with dollars that are worth less than those they lent. Thus, with inflation or at least unanticipated inflation, some people gain and some lose so that a redistribution of income and wealth occurs. But, so long as full employment is maintained, it is not clear that society as a whole is worse off since the same amount of goods and services are available to it.

If the foregoing argument is correct, why should society be concerned with inflation? One view is that the price level should be constant to prevent the redistribution of income and wealth that occurs with inflation. Another view is that inflation has an adverse effect on the economy so that, over time, relatively fewer goods and services are available to society. To illustrate, it is claimed that inflation discouraged investment in plant and equipment in the 1970s. As a consequence, output and employment grew less rapidly than they would have with price stability. (This and other arguments relating to the desirability of price stability are outlined and critically evaluated in Chapter 13.)

Economic Growth

A third goal often cited is economic growth. If society's real output increases more rapidly than its population, economic growth is occurring. With economic growth, society has more goods and services at its disposal and a correspondingly higher standard of living. This does not imply that all members of society benefit or benefit equally from economic growth. But a growing "economic pie" should make it easier to redistribute income.

In the late 1960s and early 1970s, many people questioned the desirability of further economic growth. They noted that growth is often accompanied by increased pollution and a more rapid depletion of natural resources. With the reduction in the nation's growth rate in the 1970s, more emphasis has been placed on economic growth as an economic goal in recent years. (The pros and cons of economic growth are discussed in more detail in Chapter 17.)

External Balance

A fourth and final macroeconomic goal is external balance. The *balance of payments* is a summary of all economic transactions between households, firms, and government agencies of one country and the rest of the world during a given period of time. The transactions include exports, imports, and various capital flows. In the United States balance of payments, exports are recorded as plus items since they give rise to dollar inpayments. Imports are recorded as minus items since they require dollar outpayments. When capital flows from the United States to the rest of the world, the flows are recorded as minus items since the flows represent outpayments. Capital flows from the rest of the world to the United States are recorded as plus items since they represent inpayments.

If the sum of the transactions recorded as minus items (outpayments) exceeds the sum of transactions recorded as plus items (inpayments) in the relevant portion of the balance of payments, a balance of payments deficit exists. This deficit is financed (or balanced) by a corresponding flow of gold, foreign exchange, or other means of payment. A balance of payments deficit may continue over a number of years; however, no country can experience a balance of payments deficit indefinitely. It will, sooner or later, be forced to take corrective action or forego the gains from international trade. Consequently, external balance is often listed as an economic goal. (This goal is considered in more detail in Chapter 16.)

Concluding Remarks

During the 1960s, many economists were optimistic about the use of economic policy to achieve these macroeconomic goals. The events of the 1970s shattered this optimism, and today much disagreement exists as to which policies will work best in achieving them. For this reason, we shall be concerned not only with the Keynesian perspective, but with the monetarist, rational expectations, and supply-side perspectives as well.

PREVIEW OF THE BOOK

Chapter 2 is devoted to national income accounting. In that chapter, various national income accounting concepts are defined and discussed, along with some of the problems in compiling and interpreting national income statistics. These statistics are indispensable for a variety of tasks, including policy making.

Chapter 3 introduces a simple model of the economy. In later chapters, more complex models are presented. In Chapter 4, the government sector is added to the model of Chapter 3. The consumption and investment functions are discussed in Chapters 5 and 6, respectively. At the end of Chapter 6, a new investment function is incorporated into the model of Chapter 4, and equilibrium in the product market is examined.

Chapter 7 deals with the supply of money; Chapter 8 discusses the demand for money and equilibrium in the money market. Chapter 9 integrates the money market into the model. Chapter 9 also deals with determinants of the relative effectiveness of monetary and fiscal policy. Aggregate supply is explicitly considered in Chapter 10. The nation's output and price level are then shown to be determined by the forces of aggregate demand and supply.

The models developed in Chapters 3 to 10 are Keynesian in nature. In Chapters 11 and 12, alternative approaches are outlined and critically evaluated. Chapter 11 deals with the classical and monetarist models; Chapter 12 treats the rational expectations and supply-side theories.

Chapters 13, 14, and 15 are devoted to inflation. In Chapter 13, inflation is defined and its causes and effects are considered. In Chapter 14, the inflationary process is outlined and various views of the inflation–unemployment tradeoff are examined. The U.S. experience is also discussed. Chapter 15 deals with policies designed to reduce inflation and unemployment. Indexation, a means for coping with inflation rather than reducing it, is also considered.

Chapter 16 explores the relationship between the domestic economy and foreign trade, including protectionism. Chapter 17 outlines and evaluates several theories of economic growth. It also discusses the desirability of economic growth.

Chapters 18, 19, and 20 are devoted to policy. Fiscal policy is considered in Chapter 18; monetary policy is discussed in Chapter 19. A third approach, incomes policy, is outlined and critically evaluated in Chapter 20.

NOTES

1. John Maynard Keynes, *The General Theory of Employment, Interest, and Money* (New York: Harcourt, Brace and Company, 1936).

2. Generally, those economists (mainstream) who lived from 1750 to 1870 are referred to as *classical* economists. They include Adam Smith, Thomas Robert Malthus, David Ricardo, and John Stuart Mill.

REVIEW QUESTIONS

1. Define and briefly discuss microeconomics and macroeconomics. Illustrate by citing two applications for each.

2. Why was macroeconomics neglected, for the most part, before the 1930s? What happened in the 1930s to spark interest in macroeconomics?

3. What is an economic model? Should we be concerned if a model is not as detailed as it could be? Why? Why not?

4. Describe the comparative statics approach and list its advantages and disadvantages.

5. Define each of the following terms: behavioral equation, equilibrium condition, endogenous variable, exogenous variable.

6. List and briefly discuss the macroeconomic goals of society.

SUGGESTED READING

BAUMOL, WILLIAM J., *Economic Dynamics* (3rd ed.). New York: The MacMillan Company, 1970.

Economic Report of the President. Washington, D.C.: Government Printing Office, annually.

FRIEDMAN, MILTON, "The Methodology of Positive Economics," in M. Friedman, *Essays in Positive Economics,* pp. 3–43. Chicago: University of Chicago Press, 1953.

KEYNES, JOHN MAYNARD, *The General Theory of Employment, Interest, and Money.* New York: Harcourt, Brace and Company, 1936.

KOOPMANS, TJALLING C., "The Construction of Economic Knowledge," in Koopmans, *Three Essays on the State of Economic Science*, pp. 127–66. New York: McGraw-Hill Book Company, 1957.

LEKACHMAN, ROBERT, *The Age of Keynes.* New York: Vintage Books, 1966.

PAPPS, IVY, and WILLIE HENDERSON, *Models and Economic Theory.* Philadelphia: W.B. Saunders Company, 1977.

SMITH, WARREN L., *Macroeconomics*, Chap. 1, pp. 1–21. Homewood, Ill.: Richard D. Irwin, Inc., 1970.

2

NATIONAL
INCOME ACCOUNTING

Over the years, economists and noneconomists alike have been interested in our nation's economic performance. Before the 1930s, however, national income and other data essential to the task of evaluating the nation's performance were not available. In 1932, Congress directed the Department of Commerce to prepare data, and the first estimates of national income were published in 1934. Since 1934, additional data have been forthcoming with the development of a system of national income accounting. This chapter treats the basic national income accounting framework.[1]

National income accounting data allow us to assess the economy's performance and to make projections about its future course. If the economy's performance is viewed as poor, the monetary and fiscal authorities may wish to enact policies designed to improve its performance. The data also provide invaluable aid to firms in forecasting future demand for their products and to economists in constructing and testing economic models. Indeed, national income accounting data are indispensable in measuring the performance of the economy, facilitating economic forecasting, and providing a basis for policy making.

GROSS NATIONAL PRODUCT

Various measures of the nation's income or output exist, but the most frequently cited measure is gross national product (GNP). *Gross national product* is the total market value of all final goods and services produced in the nation's economy in one year. As seen in Table 2.1, the nation's gross national product was $3,989.1 billion in 1985. To prevent double counting, the figure includes only final goods and services; intermediate products are excluded. If, for example, the total market value of both the steel and automobile industries were counted, some of the nation's output would be counted twice, since part of the output of the steel industry is used in producing automobiles. To aggregate over the range of final goods and services, the market value of each final good or service is compiled and the individual market values summed. Aggregation in value terms is necessary because it is not meaningful to aggregate the wide range of goods and services in terms of quantities. Since GNP is a measure of production rather than sales, goods produced during the year are counted as part of GNP whether they are sold or added to business inventories.

Since GNP is a measure of (current) production, many market transactions are excluded. Transactions involving used (secondhand) goods are excluded since these goods were counted earlier. Purchases of stocks and bonds are also excluded since they involve only an exchange of assets, rather than production of goods and services. Commissions based on the transactions, however, are included in GNP since they represent payments for services. Capital gains and losses are excluded since they do not result from current production. Even though illegal activities may involve production of goods and services, their market value is not included in GNP because they are illegal. Of course, even if national income accountants were to attempt to include their market value, it would be impossible to obtain accurate data.

In some cases, national income accountants must *impute* or estimate the value of production which is not reflected in market transactions.[2] This *imputation* or estimate is then counted as part of GNP. For example, a value is imputed to food produced and consumed on farms. If this imputation were not included in GNP, the nation's output would be underestimated. Although only a few imputations are made, the approach could be extended to a wide range of activities. For example, if a person hires a mechanic to repair his or her car, the payment for the mechanic's services is counted as part of the nation's GNP. But if the owner repairs his or her own car (or a friend does it for free), no imputation is made and the activity is not counted as part of GNP, even though the same services may have been performed. No imputations are made in this and many other instances because of the difficulties in estimating market values for them.

Prior to discussing the various components of GNP, we shall briefly consider another concept, gross domestic product, which is very closely related to GNP. Gross national product is a measure of the output of goods and services of the country regardless of whether that labor and those factors of production are located in that country or abroad. This implies that the output of U.S. citizens working in other countries is included in U.S. GNP while the output of non-U.S. citizens working in the United States is excluded. To measure domestic production, national income accountants use another concept, gross domestic product (GDP). *Gross domestic product* is the total market value of all final goods and services produced in one year by factors of production located within the country.

To calculate GDP, national income accountants first subtract the income earned by labor and other factors of production owned by the country's residents and located in other countries and then add the income earned by labor and other factors of production owned by residents of foreign countries and located in the country. If the residents of a given country are earning more abroad than the residents of other countries are earning in that country, GNP exceeds GDP. This has been the case for the United States in recent years.

For many countries, including the United States, the difference between GNP and GDP is small, in relative terms, and, for that reason, it makes little or no difference whether we focus on GNP or GDP. For other countries, the difference is large and more emphasis is usually placed on GDP because it is a better measure of the market value of final goods and services produced within those countries.

As shown in Table 2.1, gross national product is divided into four major

TABLE 2.1 United States gross national product, 1985 (billions of current dollars)

Gross national product				3,989.1
Personal consumption expenditures			2,582.1	
Durable goods		361.1		
Nondurable goods		912.3		
Services		1,308.8		
Gross private domestic investment			668.6	
Fixed investment		661.4		
Nonresidential	475.8			
Structures	170.3			
Producers' durable equipment	305.5			
Residential	185.6			
Change in business inventories		7.2		
Nonfarm	10.7			
Farm	−3.5			
Government purchases of goods and services			815.3	
Federal		355.0		
National defense	262.0			
Nondefense	93.0			
State and local		460.3		
Net exports of goods and services			−76.9	
Exports		370.2		
Imports		447.0		

Source: Department of Commerce, *Survey of Current Business*, 66, no. 2 (February 1986), 2.

categories: personal consumption expenditures, gross private domestic investment, government purchases of goods and services, and net exports of goods and services. These categories correspond to the four sectors of the economy: household, business, government, and foreign trade.

Personal consumption expenditures equal the total market value of goods and services purchased by households and nonprofit institutions and the value of goods and services received by them as income in kind. The former includes purchases of food, clothes, refrigerators, medical services, and haircuts. Income in kind includes the portion of crops retained by farmers for personal consumption. Although not "purchased" by farmers, a value is imputed to the amounts retained and included in the national income accounts under personal consumption expenditures.

Personal consumption expenditures, or *consumption*, is divided into three categories: durable goods, nondurable goods, and services. For the most part, goods that last more than a year are classified as durable goods; those that last less than a year are considered nondurable goods. Refrigerators and furniture are durable goods; food and clothing are nondurable goods. Dry cleaning, shoe repair, and public transportation are classified as services.

Consumption, the largest component of GNP, amounted to $2,582.1 billion or 64.7 percent of GNP in 1985. Services accounted for 50.7 percent of the total, with nondurable goods accounting for 35.3 percent.

Gross private domestic investment or *gross investment* is the total market value of purchases of newly produced structures and producers' durable equipment, plus the value of the change in the volume of inventories held by business. Thus, gross investment includes construction of plants and purchase of new business equipment. It also includes the construction of residential housing; thus, the purchase of a newly constructed home is classified as investment rather than consumption. Finally, gross investment includes changes in the volume of business inventories. Changes in business inventories are included in GNP since it is a measure of production, not sales. In 1985, gross investment was $668.6 billion or 16.8 percent of GNP.

Since a portion of gross investment is devoted to replacing structures and equipment that have worn out or been destroyed during the year, net private domestic investment or *net investment* is also estimated. Net investment is obtained by subtracting capital consumption allowances from gross investment. *Capital consumption allowances* consist of depreciation, a measure of the deterioration of the economy's structures and equipment, and an allowance for accidental damage to the nation's structures and equipment. Thus, gross investment was $668.6 billion in 1985, but net investment was only $230.1 billion, obtained by subtracting capital consumption allowances of $438.5 billion from gross investment. Net investment is important as a measure of the *net* increase in the nation's capital stock.

Government purchases of goods and services consist of purchases by various government units, federal, state, and local. These purchases include the procurement of military hardware for national defense and the salaries of government employees. In 1985, government purchases amounted to $815.3 billion or 20.4

percent of gross national product. State and local units accounted for 56.5 percent of the purchases; the federal government accounted for the remainder. Almost three-fourths of the federal total went for national defense.

It should be emphasized that not all government spending is included in gross national product. The principal exclusion is *government transfer payments*. Government transfer payments include social security benefits, unemployment compensation, and payments to retired military personnel. Like government purchases of goods and services, transfer payments involve payments by the government, but unlike the former, they involve no exchange of goods and services. Without such exchange, there is no economic production; hence government transfer payments are excluded from GNP.

Net exports of goods and services represent the value of exports of goods and services minus the value of imports of goods and services. Since GNP is a measure of production, exports are clearly a part of GNP. Perhaps it is less clear why imports are deducted. Imports are counted as part of the other components of GNP. Consequently, they must be subtracted from the sum of those components to ensure that GNP reflects only domestic production. For example, the purchase of a new Fiat is included under consumption. Since Fiats are not produced in this country, the value of the Fiat must be subtracted in order to make sure only domestic automobile production is included in GNP. In 1985, exports totaled $370.2 billion while imports amounted to $447.0 billion. Consequently, net exports equaled − $76.9 billion. Thus, although exports accounted for 9.3 percent of GNP and imports 11.2 percent, net exports were only 1.9 percent of GNP.

NET NATIONAL PRODUCT

Net National Product (NNP), another measure of the nation's output, is the total market value of the economy's net output of final goods and services. As shown in Table 2.2, NNP is derived by subtracting capital consumption allowances from

TABLE 2.2 Gross national product, net national product, and national income, 1985 (billions of current dollars)

Gross national product	3,989.1
Less: Capital consumption allowances with capital consumption adjustment	438.5
Equals: Net national product	3,550.6
Less: Indirect business tax and nontax liability	328.4
Business transfer payments	19.3
Statistical discrepancy	0.7
Plus: Subsidies less current surplus of government enterprises	9.9
Equals: National income	3,212.0

Source: Department of Commerce, *Survey of Current Business*, 66, no. 2 (February 1986), 3.

GNP. Since GNP and capital consumption allowances were $3,989.1 billion and $438.5 billion, respectively, in 1985, net national product equaled $3,989.1 billion minus $438.5 billion, or $3,550.6 billion. Subtracting capital consumption allowances leaves net national product as the sum of personal consumption expenditures, government purchases of goods and services, net exports of goods and services, and *net* private domestic investment. Gross national product is, of course, the sum of the first three plus *gross* private domestic investment. Net national product is important because it is a measure of the nation's *net* output, the goods and services available to society after replacement of structures and equipment that have worn out or been destroyed during the year. Despite its importance from a conceptual standpoint, NNP is rarely cited or used because of the difficulties inherent in measuring capital consumption allowances.

NATIONAL INCOME

National income, also a measure of the economy's output, is the total of the earnings of labor and other factors of production which arises from the current production of goods and services in the economy. As indicated by Table 2.2, national income may be obtained from net national product by making the following subtractions and additions. First, subtract *indirect business tax and nontax liability*. Indirect business taxes include sales, excise, and business property taxes; nontax liabilities include inspection fees, special assessments, and various fines and penalties. The total liability is subtracted from net national product, since the receipts accrue ultimately to the government rather than being available to pay factors of production. In 1985, the indirect business tax and nontax liability amounted to $328.4 billion. Next, subtract business transfer payments. *Business transfer payments* are payments by business to individuals and nonprofit institutions; however, business receives no goods or services in return, at least in the year in which the payments are made. Business transfer payments include corporate gifts to various nonprofit institutions, including universities; they also include allowances for consumer bad debts. Business transfer payments are subtracted from net national product because they represent a "drain" on the resources of business and, hence, are not available for payment to the various factors of production. In 1985, business transfer payments equaled $19.3 billion. Finally, *subsidies minus current surplus of government enterprises* are added to net national product. *Subsidies* are monetary grants made by the government to business. They increase the resources of firms, thereby making more income available for factor payments. *Current surplus of government enterprises* is the difference between sales receipts and current operating expenses of government enterprises. The current surplus is subtracted from subsidies because these resources were not distributed to the factors of production. These two items— subsidies and current surplus of government enterprises—are shown as a single item because of the difficulties in separating subsidies by government agencies from other transactions of the same agencies. In 1985, the amount was $9.9 billion.

After making these adjustments to net national product, national income is obtained. In 1985, net national product was $3,550.6 billion. If we subtract the indirect business tax and nontax liability of $328.4 billion and business transfer payments of $19.3 billion from net national product and add subsidies less current surplus of government enterprises of $9.9 billion to it, we find that national income is $3,212.7 billion. This result differs from the total shown in Table 2.2 for national income by $0.7 billion, the amount shown as the statistical discrepancy. We shall show how this statistical discrepancy arises later.

As shown in Table 2.3, national income is divided into five types of income: compensation of employees, corporate profits, proprietors' income, rental income of persons, and net interest. *Compensation of employees* consists of wages and salaries plus supplements to wages and salaries, such as employer contributions to pension plans and the social security system. An imputation is included for room, board, and other payments in kind furnished to employees as part of their compensation. The imputation is made and included in order to maintain comparability between such employees and those who receive their wages entirely in monetary form. Compensation of employees is by far the largest component of national income. It equaled $2,372.4 billion or 73.9 percent of national income in 1985.

Corporate profits constitute a second type of national income. In 1985, corporate profits, as reported by firms, amounted to $225.0 billion (the sum of profits tax liability and profits after tax in Table 2.3). This amount has been adjusted, however, since the accounting practices of firms often differ from those required

TABLE 2.3 National income by type of income, 1985 (billions of current dollars)

National income					3,212.0
Compensation of employees				2,372.4	
Wages and salaries			1,960.2		
Supplements to wages and salaries			412.2		
Corporate profits with inventory valuation and capital consumption adjustments				296.2	
Corporate profits with inventory valuation adjustment and without capital consumption adjustment		224.4			
Profits tax liability		85.5			
Profits after tax		139.5			
Dividends	83.5				
Undistributed profits	56.0				
Inventory valuation adjustment		−0.6			
Capital consumption adjustment			71.8		
Proprietors' income with inventory valuation and capital consumption adjustments				242.3	
Rental income of persons with capital consumption adjustment				14.0	
Net interest				287.2	

Source: Department of Commerce, *Survey of Current Business*, 66, no. 2 (February 1986), 4.

for the national income accounts. Thus, in 1985, corporate profits with inventory valuation and capital consumption adjustments equaled $296.2 billion or 9.2 percent of national income.

With regard to inventories, the accounting valuation of inventories often differs from current replacement costs when prices are changing. Since current replacement cost is the relevant concept for the national income accounts, the accounting valuation or book value may give a misleading impression of changes in business inventories and profits. To illustrate, assume that a firm's initial inventory of its product consists of 100 units valued at $10 per unit. Suppose the firm purchases (or produces) 30 units during the accounting period at $15 per unit and sells 30 units. If the firm uses the first-in, first-out (FIFO) method of inventory valuation, inventories are charged to sales in the order of their acquisition. This means that the book value of the inventory is reduced by $300 with the sale of the 30 units from the initial inventory. On the other hand, the book value of the firm's inventory is increased by $450 with the purchase (or production) of 30 units valued at their cost of acquisition. For the period, the book value of the inventory increased by $150. Under the FIFO method, the $150 increase in book value is shown as part of the firm's profits.

From a national income accounting standpoint, the firm's profits are overstated by $150. In the example, the firm sold 30 units from its inventory. These units were valued at $10 per unit although their replacement cost was $15 per unit. The firm treats the difference between the initial value, $10 per unit, and current replacement cost, $15 per unit, as income and profits. In the context of national income accounting, however, the difference is similar to a capital gain and, as a consequence, not part of national income. In the national income accounts, $5 per unit or $150 is deducted from the firm's profits to approximate more closely the firm's profits from current productive activity. The $150 which is subtracted from the firm's profits is called the *inventory valuation adjustment*. In 1985, corporate profits before taxes equaled $225.0 billion, whereas the inventory valuation adjustment equaled $0.6 billion. Thus, corporate profits with inventory valuation adjustment and without capital consumption adjustment were $224.4 billion.

The reason for the *capital consumption adjustment* is similar to that for the inventory valuation adjustment. Since accounting practices vary with regard to depreciation, national income accountants estimate depreciation based on current prices and a consistent set of accounting procedures relating to the depreciation formula and the service lives of assets. Since profits depend, in part, on depreciation and since the national income accounts estimate of depreciation usually differs from the estimate based on corporate income tax returns, corporate profits must be adjusted to reflect the difference. In 1985, corporate profits with inventory valuation adjustment equaled $224.4 billion. The capital consumption adjustment, however, equaled $71.8 billion, so corporate profits with inventory valuation and capital consumption adjustments equaled $296.2 billion.

Proprietors' income is the income of unincorporated enterprises: sole proprietorships, partnerships, and producers' cooperatives. Like corporate profits, proprietors' income is subject to inventory valuation and capital consumption adjustments. In 1985, proprietors' income with adjustments equaled $242.3 billion or 7.5 percent of national income.

Rental income of persons includes rental income of those not primarily engaged in the real estate business, the rental income imputed to owner-occupied nonfarm homes, and royalties received by persons from patents, copyrights, and rights to natural resources. An imputation for the rental value of owner-occupied homes is made in order to provide comparable treatment between rented and owner-occupied housing. If a person pays rent, the amount enters the national income accounts. If the person were to buy the house and no imputation were made, rental payments would stop and national income would fall even though the same amount of housing is available. To prevent changes in national income due merely to trends toward rental or owner-occupied housing, national income accountants treat home ownership as a business producing housing services which are sold to the homeowner in his or her capacity as tenant. The amount is based on the sum for which the particular type of home could be rented; the expenses for the home owners, repair and maintenance particularly, are deducted to obtain imputed net rent. The gross amount is included in GNP as consumption. In 1985, the rental income of persons, with capital consumption adjustment, equaled $14.0 billion or 0.4 percent of national income.

The final type of national income is net interest. *Net interest* consists of interest paid by business minus interest received by business plus net interest received from abroad. Interest paid both by government (federal, state, and local) and by consumers is excluded. Government interest is excluded because it does not represent income arising from current economic production. For example, the federal government pays interest on the public debt. Since most of the debt was incurred in the past, the interest payments are not closely tied to current activities of government. Interest paid by consumers is also excluded because it does not represent income arising from current economic production. Interest paid by consumers is also excluded from consumption. In 1985, net interest equaled $287.2 billion or 8.9 percent of national income.

THE PRODUCT AND INCOME APPROACHES TO GNP, NNP, AND NATIONAL INCOME

The three measures of the nation's output—gross national product, net national product, and national income—may be obtained in two different ways. Gross national product may be compiled by summing the market values of all final goods and services. Net national product and national income may then be derived by making the appropriate subtractions and additions. This approach, discussed earlier in the chapter, is called the *product* approach. Alternatively, national income may be compiled by summing the different types of factor incomes. Net national product and gross national product may then be derived by making the necessary additions and subtractions. The additions and subtractions are in the reverse order because the derivation now runs from national income to gross national product. For example, instead of subtracting business transfer payments from net national product, they are added to national income. This approach is called the *income* approach. The two approaches are summarized in Table 2.4 on page 22.

In deriving GNP using the product and income approaches, a discrepancy usually arises from the two estimates. This discrepancy, called the *statistical discrepancy* in the national income accounts, reflects the difference between gross national product measured with the product approach and gross national product measured with the income approach. It arises because of errors in the estimates. To reconcile gross and net national products as estimated using the product approach and national income as estimated by the income approach, the statistical discrepancy is subtracted from net national product.

PERSONAL INCOME, DISPOSABLE PERSONAL INCOME, AND PERSONAL SAVING

Personal income, disposable personal income, and personal saving are also important national income accounting concepts. For example, personal income or disposable personal income, although not measures of the nation's output, may be more relevant for a marketing study than gross national product or national income. As shown in Table 2.5, to obtain personal income, first, subtract corporate profits with inventory valuation and capital consumption adjustments, net interest, contributions for social insurance, and wage accruals less disbursements. Second, add government transfer payments to persons, personal interest income, dividend income, and business transfer payments. The result is *personal income.* By these subtractions and additions one seeks to deduct from national income all income earned in current production but not received by persons and to add to it the payments received by persons but not earned in current production. For example, contributions for social insurance are included in national income as part of compensation of employees, but are deducted from national income in deriving personal income because those contributions are income that is not received by persons. Government and business transfer payments are added to national income because they add to personal income even though the payments are excluded from national income. Corporate profits, with inventory valuation and capital consumption adjustments, are subtracted, but personal dividend income is added to ensure that only the portion of corporate profits actually paid to persons is included in personal income. Net interest is subtracted and personal interest income is added for the same reason. (Personal interest income is defined as net interest plus interest paid by consumers to business plus interest paid by government to persons and business minus interest received by government.) Finally, the excess of wage accruals over

TABLE 2.4 National income and product account, 1985 (billions of current dollars)

	Compensation of employees	2,372.4		Personal consumption expenditures	2,582.1
Plus:	Corporate profits with inventory valuation and capital consumption adjustments	296.2	Plus:	Gross private domestic investment	668.6
Plus:	Proprietors' income with inventory valuation and capital consumption adjustments	242.3	Plus:	Government purchases of goods and services	815.3
Plus:	Rental income of persons with capital consumption adjustment	14.0	Plus:	Net exports of goods and services	−76.9
Plus:	Net interest	287.2			
Equals:	National income	3,212.0			
Less:	Subsidies less current surplus of government enterprises	9.9			
Plus:	Statistical discrepancy	0.7			
Plus:	Business transfer payments	19.3			
Plus:	Indirect business tax and nontax liability	328.4			
Equals:	Charges against net national product	3,550.6			
Plus:	Capital consumption allowances with capital consumption adjustment	438.5			
Equals:	Charges against gross national product	3,989.1	Equals: Gross national product		3,989.1

Source: Department of Commerce, *Survey of Current Business*, 66, no. 2 (February 1986), 2–4.

TABLE 2.5 National income, personal income, disposable personal income, and personal saving, 1985 (billions of current dollars)

	National income	3,212.0
Less:	Corporate profits with inventory valuation and capital consumption adjustments	296.2
	Net interest	287.2
	Contributions for social insurance	354.9
	Wage accruals less disbursements	−0.2
Plus:	Government transfer payments to persons	465.2
	Personal interest income	456.0
	Personal dividend income	78.9
	Business transfer payments	19.3
Equals:	Personal income	3,293.4
Less:	Personal tax and nontax payments	492.7
Equals:	Disposable personal income	2,800.7
Less:	Personal outlays	2,671.5
Equals:	Personal saving	129.1

Source: Department of Commerce, *Survey of Current Business*, 66, no. 2 (February 1986), 3, 6.

disbursements is subtracted to guarantee that only income that is disbursed is included in personal income. As seen in Table 2.5, personal income was $3,293.4 billion in 1985.

By subtracting *personal tax and nontax payments* from personal income, another national income accounting concept, *disposable personal income*, is obtained. Personal taxes include income, estate and gift, and personal property taxes; nontaxes include passport fees, fines and penalties, and donations. In 1985, personal tax and nontax payments equaled $492.7 billion. Since personal income equaled $3,293.4 billion in 1985, disposable personal income equaled $2,800.7 billion in that year. Disposable personal income or disposable income is a very important concept since it measures "take home" or after-tax income.

Finally, disposable personal income may be divided into personal outlays and personal saving. *Personal outlays* consist of personal consumption expenditures, interest paid by consumers to business, and net personal transfer payments to foreigners. In 1985, personal consumption expenditures were $2,582.1 billion, interest paid by consumers equaled $87.4 billion, and net personal transfer payments to foreigners equaled $2.1 billion. *Personal saving* was $129.1 billion, 4.6 percent of disposable personal income.

Gross national product, net national product, national income, and the other national income accounting concepts are measured on a calendar year basis, but quarterly data are available. The data are adjusted to eliminate the influence of seasonal factors and multiplied by 4 to obtain an estimate of the annual rate.

National income accounting data can be found in the *Survey of Current Business* (especially the July issue) and various other publications.

STOCK AND FLOW VARIABLES

Gross national product, net national product, and the other national income accounting concepts just discussed are flow variables. A *flow variable* is a quantity that can be measured only in terms of a specified period of time. For example, GNP was $3,989.1 billion in 1985. This means that $3,989.1 billion worth of final goods and services were produced during 1985. In stating flow variables, it is important to be specific about the *time period* in question. For example, it is meaningless to say that a person's salary is $2,000, because it is unclear whether the income is $2,000 per week, per month, or per year.

In contrast, a *stock variable* is a quantity measured at a specified point in time. For example, the capital stock of the economy is a stock variable. It is a certain amount at a specified point in time. Similarly, the money supply is a stock variable, a definite amount on a specific date. In stating stock variables, both the amount and *point in time* must be clearly stated or implied.

Flow and stock variables are related. For example, the capital stock of the economy (a stock variable) increases when net investment (a flow variable) is positive. The *capital stock* of the economy is the accumulated stock of structures, producers' durable equipment, and business inventories. Gross investment is the amount of newly produced structures and producers' durable equipment plus changes in inventories. Since part of gross investment simply replaces structures and equipment that wear out or are destroyed during the year, only net investment adds to the capital stock of the economy. For example, gross investment was $668.6 billion in 1985. The capital stock of the economy increased during 1985 but by less than $668.6 billion because part of the capital stock, $438.5 billion (as indicated by the capital consumption allowances entry in Table 2.2), wore out or was destroyed during the year. Consequently, the capital stock increased by only $230.1 billion, the difference between gross investment and capital consumption allowances, from January 1, 1985, to January 1, 1986. Since the difference between gross investment and capital consumption allowances is net investment, the increment to the capital stock, $230.1 billion, equals net investment. So long as net investment is positive, the capital stock of the economy grows. Should net investment become negative, the capital stock of the economy would decline; negative net investment means that more of the capital stock is wearing out than is being replaced.

In studying macroeconomics, it is important to distinguish between stock and flow variables. For example, students commonly confuse personal saving or saving and personal savings or savings. *Personal saving*, the difference between disposable personal income and personal outlays, is a flow variable. *Personal savings*, the sum of current and past saving, is a stock variable. As saving occurs, savings increase.

Similarly, students confuse income and money. The former is a flow variable; the latter, a stock variable.

THE MEASUREMENT OF REAL OUTPUT
AND THE PRICE LEVEL

A main purpose of national income accounting is the measurement of the nation's output of goods and services. In compiling gross national product, market prices are used since it is not meaningful to aggregate physical quantities of different goods. Use of market prices, however, creates a problem in comparing GNP in different years, since both prices and real output tend to change over time.[3] To illustrate the problem and to show how it is resolved, consider the following hypothetical example, involving, for simplicity, only two goods, shirts and sweaters, and two periods, 1975 and 1985. The necessary data are shown in Table 2.6.

By multiplying price times quantity for each good and summing the products, we obtain measures of production analogous to GNP in the two years. For example, 1 million shirts were produced in 1975 at an average market price of $10 per shirt. Thus, the market value of shirt production amounted to $10 million. The corresponding market value of sweater production is $1 million; the total market value of the two commodities is $11 million. In a similar manner, the total market value of the two commodities may be calculated for 1985; it is $33 million.

Since the market value of output has increased from $11 million to $33 million, it appears that output tripled from 1975 to 1985. The figures are deceptive, however, in that they reflect not only increases in output but also price increases. To obtain figures which reflect only the increase in output, we assume that 1975 prices prevailed in both 1975 and 1985. With prices assumed constant, the difference in real output between the two years will be revealed. The data are shown in Table 2.7.

In terms of 1975 prices, the total market value of production is $11 million in 1975 and $22 million in 1985. Accordingly, production appears to have doubled from 1975 to 1985. Examination of the production figures for the individual goods

TABLE 2.6 Hypothetical data for computation of gross national product (measured in current prices)

	1975 Output	1975 Prices	1975 Output Measured in 1975 Prices	1985 Output	1985 Prices	1985 Output Measured in 1985 Prices
Shirts	1 million	$10	$10 million	2 million	$15	$30 million
Sweaters	50,000	20	1 million	100,000	30	3 million
Total			$11 million			$33 million

TABLE 2.7 Hypothetical data for computation of gross national product (measured in constant, 1975, prices)

	1975 Output	1975 Prices	1975 Output Measured in 1975 Prices	1985 Output	1975 Prices	1985 Output Measured in 1975 Prices
Shirts	1 million	$10	$10 million	2 million	$10	$20 million
Sweaters	50,000	20	1 million	100,000	20	2 million
Total			$11 million			$22 million

indicates that this is so. Shirt production increased from 1 million to 2 million shirts; sweater production increased from 50,000 to 100,000.

Gross national product compiled on the basis of constant prices is called GNP as measured in constant or real dollars or, for short, *real* GNP. This concept is to be distinguished from GNP as measured in current or nominal dollars or, alternatively, money or *nominal* GNP.

The distinction between the two concepts is important. For example, if prices are increasing, GNP measured in current dollars will increase more rapidly than GNP measured in constant dollars, as the former reflects increases in both quantities and prices, whereas the latter reflects only the increases in quantities. For example, in 1985, nominal GNP increased by 5.7 percent. But real GNP increased by only 2.3 percent, with the remainder of the increase in nominal GNP resulting from the price increases which occurred in 1985. Thus, in 1985, both nominal and real GNP increased, with the former increasing more rapidly because of price increases. With prices changing, nominal and real GNP may even change in opposite directions. For example, in 1982, nominal GNP increased and real GNP decreased. The divergence occurred because prices increased significantly in 1982 while the real output of final goods and services decreased. The price increases more than offset the quantity decreases so that nominal GNP increased and real GNP decreased. GNP as measured in constant dollars is the more relevant concept because it more closely reflects the total amount of final goods and services produced in the economy.

Gross national product in both current and constant (1982) dollars for 1929–85 is shown in Table 2.8 on pages 28 and 29. Over the period, real GNP increased at an average annual rate of 3.2 percent. It did not increase steadily, but grew more rapidly in some years and less rapidly or even decreased in others. Since years of rapid increases in real GNP are often followed by years of small increases or decreases, the economy is said to be subject to *business cycles*. The National Bureau of Economic Research (NBER), a private research organization, dates these cycles.

An alternative method of calculating real GNP is to compute nominal GNP and price index numbers for the years in question. Real GNP is then obtained by dividing nominal GNP by the corresponding price index number. In the foregoing example, suppose prices in 1975 are represented by 100, an index number. The price of shirts increased from $10 in 1975 to $15 in 1985, a 50 percent increase. The price of sweaters increased from $20 to $30 over the same period, also a 50 percent increase. Since prices increased by 50 percent from 1975 to 1985, the appropriate index number for 1985 is 150. Had prices increased (decreased) by 100 percent (25 percent), the appropriate price index for 1985 would be 200 (75). Since index numbers are percentages, prices in 1975 are 100 percent of the 1975 level. If the appropriate index number is 150 in 1985, prices in 1985 are 150 percent of their 1975 level.

In the example cited, real GNP in 1975 may be derived by dividing or deflating nominal GNP in 1975, $6 million, by the price index for 1975, 100. Since index numbers are percentages, real GNP in 1975 equals $11 million divided by 1.00, which equals $11 million. Similarly, real GNP in 1985 may be calculated by dividing nominal GNP in 1985, $33 million, by the price index for 1985, 150. Thus, real GNP in 1985 is $33 million divided by 150 percent or 1.50, which equals $22 million. These estimates of real GNP are the same as those obtained earlier by calculating GNP in 1975 and 1985 in terms of 1975 prices.[4]

For the economy, the relevant price index is the *implicit price deflator for gross national product*. In equation form, the relationship between real GNP, nominal GNP, and the implicit price deflator for GNP is

$$\text{Real GNP} = \frac{\text{Nominal GNP}}{\text{Implicit price deflator for GNP}}.$$

Thus, real GNP equals nominal GNP divided by the implicit price deflator for GNP. Alternatively, the relationship is

$$\text{Implicit price deflator for GNP} = \frac{\text{Nominal GNP}}{\text{Real GNP}},$$

which implies that the implicit price deflator equals the ratio of nominal GNP to real GNP.

To obtain real GNP, national income accountants construct price indexes for the various components of GNP. The nominal value of each component is divided or deflated by its corresponding price index to obtain the real value of the component. The real values of the components are then summed to obtain real GNP. After obtaining real GNP, the implicit price deflator is derived by dividing nominal GNP for the year by real GNP in the same year. The price deflator is called the *implicit* price deflator because it is obtained by dividing nominal GNP by real GNP, rather than by taking a weighted average of the price indexes for the various components of GNP. The implicit price deflator for gross national product is an important concept because it is a measure of the price level of all final goods and services. Data for the implicit price deflator for 1929–85 are presented in Table

TABLE 2.8 Gross national product in current and constant (1982) dollars and the implicit price deflator for gross national product, 1929–85

Year	Gross National Product (billions of current dollars)	Percentage Change from Preceding Period, Gross National Product (billions of current dollars)	Gross National Product (billions of constant, 1982, dollars)	Percentage Change from Preceding Period, Gross National Product (billions of constant, 1982, dollars)	Implicit Price Deflator for Gross National Product	Percentage Change from Preceding Period, Implicit Price Deflator for Gross National Product
1929	103.9		709.6		14.6	
1933	56.0		498.5		11.2	
1940	100.4		772.9		13.0	
1945	213.4		1,354.8		15.8	
1946	212.4	−0.5	1,096.9	−19.0	19.4	22.9
1947	235.2	10.8	1,066.7	−2.8	22.0	13.9
1948	261.6	11.2	1,108.7	3.9	23.6	7.0
1949	260.4	−0.5	1,109.0	0.0	23.5	−0.5
1950	288.3	10.7	1,203.7	8.5	24.0	2.0
1951	333.4	15.7	1,328.2	10.3	25.1	4.8
1952	351.6	5.5	1,380.0	3.9	25.5	1.5
1953	371.6	5.7	1,435.3	4.0	25.9	1.6
1954	372.5	0.2	1,416.2	−1.3	26.3	1.6
1955	405.9	9.0	1,494.9	5.6	27.2	3.2
1956	428.2	5.5	1,525.6	2.1	28.1	3.4
1957	451.0	5.3	1,551.1	1.7	29.1	3.6
1958	456.8	1.3	1,539.2	−0.8	29.7	2.1

Year						
1959	495.8	8.5	1,629.1	5.8	30.4	2.4
1960	515.3	3.9	1,665.3	2.2	30.9	1.6
1961	533.8	3.6	1,708.7	2.6	31.2	1.0
1962	574.6	7.6	1,799.4	5.3	31.9	2.2
1963	606.9	5.6	1,873.3	4.1	32.4	1.6
1964	649.8	7.1	1,973.3	5.3	32.9	1.5
1965	705.1	8.5	2,087.6	5.8	33.8	2.7
1966	772.0	9.5	2,208.3	5.8	35.0	3.6
1967	816.4	5.8	2,271.4	2.9	35.9	2.6
1968	892.7	9.3	2,365.6	4.2	37.7	5.0
1969	963.9	8.0	2,423.3	2.4	39.8	5.6
1970	1,015.5	5.3	2,416.2	-0.3	42.0	5.5
1971	1,102.7	8.6	2,484.8	2.8	44.4	5.7
1972	1,212.8	10.0	2,608.5	5.0	46.5	4.7
1973	1,359.3	12.1	2,744.1	5.2	49.5	6.5
1974	1,472.8	8.3	2,729.3	-0.5	54.0	9.1
1975	1,598.4	8.5	2,695.0	-1.3	59.3	9.8
1976	1,782.8	11.5	2,826.7	4.9	63.1	6.4
1977	1,990.5	11.7	2,958.6	4.7	67.3	6.7
1978	2,249.7	13.0	3,115.2	5.3	72.2	7.3
1979	2,508.2	11.5	3,192.4	2.5	78.6	8.9
1980	2,732.0	8.9	3,187.1	-0.2	85.7	9.0
1981	3,052.6	11.7	3,248.8	1.9	94.0	9.7
1982	3,166.0	3.7	3,166.0	-2.5	100.0	6.4
1983	3,401.6	7.4	3,277.7	3.5	103.8	3.8
1984	3,774.7	11.0	3,492.0	6.5	108.1	4.1
1985	3,989.1	5.7	3,571.0	2.3	111.7	3.3

Source: Department of Commerce, *Survey of Current Business*, 66, no. 2 (February 1986): 18, 20, 22.

2.8. Price indexes for the various components are available in the national income accounts. Two other price indexes, the consumer and producer price indexes, are discussed in Chapter 13. Both are important, but neither is a measure of the general price level.

GNP AND THE UNDERGROUND ECONOMY

In recent years, many people have become concerned that measured GNP may drastically underestimate the nation's level of economic activity because of the existence of an underground economy. The *underground economy* consists of economic activity that avoids official detection and measurement. The activities are either inherently illegal or not reported for tax avoidance purposes.[5] Examples of the former include traffic in illegal drugs, bookmaking, and prostitution. Examples of the latter include the nondeclaration of receipts by owners or managers of restaurants, bars, and various retail establishments and the failure to report income from tips and casual or part-time work. Although an underground economy has always existed, many believe that it is much larger now than in the past because of the increased tax burden, greater government regulation, and widespread dissatisfaction with government. In this regard, marginal tax rates are important; however, people's perceptions of the fairness of the tax system and the extent to which people believe that others are complying with the system are also important.

How large is the underground economy? No one knows for sure. In one of the first studies of the underground economy, Peter M. Gutmann estimated that economic activity in the underground economy totaled $176 billion in 1976, about 10 percent of measured GNP.[6] Since Gutmann's study, many other studies have been conducted.[7] Some of the estimates are lower than Gutmann's, but most are higher and some are much higher. Based on various surveys, participation in the underground economy is common; 20 to 25 percent of those interviewed admit at least some degree of noncompliance with the nation's tax laws. Other surveys indicate that one of five households has at least one member participating in the underground economy on either a full- or part-time basis.

Because of the nature of the problem, it is impossible to obtain precise estimates. Even so, we can conclude that the underground economy is large. To put it into perspective, we had in 1976 (based on Gutmann's estimate) a covert economy about the size of the U.S. economy in 1941 existing within the official economy.

Although the existence of the underground economy casts doubt on the validity of the statistics on GNP and the other national income accounting concepts, the data would still be useful if the official and underground economies were growing at the same rate. But this is not the case. Most studies suggest that the underground economy is both large *and* growing more rapidly than the official economy. Consequently, the official data may be very misleading. To illustrate, suppose real GNP appears to be growing more slowly than in the past. Policy makers may react by instituting more expansionary monetary and fiscal policies. If economic activity is expanding at the same rate as in the past but with relatively more of it occurring in the underground economy, the more expansionary policies are likely to result in more inflation, not increased economic activity.[8]

The existence of a large underground economy has other implications. It implies that a disproportionate share of the tax burden is carried by those who are not participating in the underground economy. If those who participate in the underground economy were taxed, tax rates could be reduced significantly without loss of tax revenue. In addition, the underground economy may be less efficient. The various activities must be carried out covertly, which often precludes the most efficient means of production and distribution. Moreover, because of the nature of the underground economy, it is difficult for participants to obtain information which would be helpful to them. Also, most or all transactions must be conducted with cash, which is disadvantageous in many instances. These factors, however, are offset to some degree by the greater flexibility, including part-time and at-home work, afforded by the underground economy.

Various suggestions have been made to reduce the size of the underground economy. These include reducing tax rates, making the tax system more equitable, devoting more resources to law enforcement, and increasing the penalties for participating in the underground economy. It must be recognized, however, that with existing tax rates (or even lower ones) a strong economic incentive exists for persons to participate in the underground economy. Moreover, given its shadowy nature, one cannot be optimistic about reducing its size by devoting more resources to law enforcement. For these reasons, a large underground economy is likely to persist for the foreseeable future. Consequently, we must be much more cautious in the use of GNP and other national income accounting data in the future than we have been in the past.

GNP AND WELFARE

Real GNP is sometimes regarded as a measure of the nation's well-being or welfare, but, as we shall see, it is, at best, an imperfect measure. As just discussed, the official estimates of GNP do not take account of the existence of a large and growing underground economy. Also, it is necessary to take account of population growth, since an increase in real GNP which is offset or more than offset by an increase in population probably does not mark an improvement in society's welfare

Although per capita real GNP is a better measure of welfare, per capita NNP and consumption are probably even better. Part of real GNP is used to replace structures and equipment that wear out or are destroyed during the year; only net output is available for consumption and other purposes. Consequently, per capita real NNP is a better measure of society's welfare than per capita real GNP. This argument may be carried further.

Net national product consists of consumption, net investment, government purchases, and net exports. An increase in net investment increases society's productive capacity, thus making possible greater consumption in the future. In the short run, however, increased net investment is likely to be at the expense of consumption. Similarly, increased food production and increased expenditures for police protection both add to net national product. If the increased expenditure for police protection is merely to keep pace with a rising crime rate, it is not clear that society's welfare has improved. The same argument could be made in regard to other government purchases. Finally, exports are added to net national product and imports are subtracted to obtain a measure of society's production. Yet, from society's standpoint, exports are not available for domestic consumption but imports are. Because of these considerations, many, if not most, economists believe that per capita real consumption is a better guide to welfare than either per capita real GNP or NNP.

So far, the criticisms of gross national product as a measure of welfare have resulted in changing the measure to only a portion of gross national product, consumption, and dividing by population to adjust for population changes. Other problems are more difficult to resolve. For example, leisure is not included in real GNP or the other national income accounting concepts. If an increase in per capita consumption is accompanied by a significant reduction in leisure, it is not clear that society is better off. Also, many environmentalists argue that increases in real GNP are likely to be accompanied by more pollution and a more rapid depletion of natural resources. Therefore, they believe that an increase in per capita real GNP or consumption may not signal an increase in society's welfare.

In an attempt to approximate more closely society's welfare, William Nordhaus and James Tobin have devised a *measure of economic welfare* (MEW).[9] Among other things, they rearranged various items in the national income accounts and included imputations for leisure, household production and consumption—such as meals, cleaning, and repairs—and various disamenities of urbanization including pollution, litter, congestion, noise, and insecurity. Nordhaus and Tobin then concluded that per capita MEW increased from 1929 to 1965 but at a slower rate, 1 percent, than per capita net national product, 1.7 percent.

Despite the admirable attempt by Nordhaus and Tobin, their measure remains a gauge of consumption, not welfare. Society's welfare depends not only on income or consumption but also on its distribution. An increase in per capita income or consumption may not indicate an increase in welfare if it is accompanied by a redistribution of income from the poor to the rich. Indeed, some "radical economists" believe that redistribution of income should have a much higher priority than continued economic growth. Also, little or no correlation may exist between material abundance and happiness. Our ancestors' income did not approximate ours nor did they have access to today's variety of goods and services. Yet, they may have been as happy or even happier.

Given the various problems in measuring society's welfare, it should be clear that, at best, there is only a loose association or correlation between real GNP and society's welfare. (The relationship between real GNP and welfare in the growth context is examined in more detail in Chapter 17.)

CONCLUDING REMARKS

In order to concentrate on the theory of income determination in the following chapters, we shall use a simplified version of the national income accounts. We assume that capital consumption allowances, indirect business taxes, business transfer payments, and subsidies less current surplus of government enterprises are equal to zero. This means that gross national product, net national product, and national income are equal and that gross private domestic investment equals net private domestic investment. Since GNP equals the sum of consumption (C), investment (I), government purchases (G), and exports (X) minus imports (M), and since national income (Y) is now assumed to equal GNP, Y is also equal to the sum of C, I, G, and $X - M$ or, symbolically,

$$Y = C + I + G + X - M.$$

It is also assumed that contributions to social insurance, wage accruals less disbursements, and net personal transfer payments to foreigners are equal to zero and that net interest equals personal interest income. If all corporate profits are distributed as dividend income, national income (Y) also equals consumption (C) plus saving (S) plus personal taxes (Tx) minus government transfer payments (Tr) or, symbolically,

$$Y = C + S + \text{Tx} - \text{Tr}.$$

This relationship, as well as the preceding relationship, will be utilized in the following chapters.

National income is the sum of society's expenditures on goods and services; in other words, it equals society's output. National income is also equal to the sum of the incomes of labor and other factors of production; it, therefore, equals society's income. Since society's output is equal to society's income, we shall use the terms output and income interchangeably.

Finally, all variables—unless otherwise specified—will be measured in terms of real or constant dollars.

NOTES

1. The conceptual framework of the national income accounts is outlined in U.S. Department of Commerce, Office of Business Economics, *National Income, 1954 Edition* (Washington, D.C.: Government Printing Office, 1954). Since 1954, the framework has been modified in various ways. These changes are discussed in Department of Commerce, Office of Business Economics, *U.S. Income and Output* (Washington, D.C.: Government Printing Office, 1958); and Department of Commerce, *Survey of Current Business* (Washington, D.C.: Government Printing Office, various issues).

2. In general, only activities resulting in market transactions are defined as economic

production and included in GNP. This rule, though convenient, imparts a bias when comparing the outputs of countries at different stages of development or when analyzing the output trend in a single country. As a country develops economically, less is produced for home consumption and more is produced for sale. Consequently, even if total production does not increase, measured output increases as more market transactions take place. For example, breadmaking, once a common household activity in this country, is rare today. Yet even if no more bread is made today than in the past, the national income accounts will show that more is being produced.

3. There are other problems in comparing GNP in different years. New goods appear; others disappear. Changes in quality occur. Comparing GNP between countries presents still other problems.

4. In the example, both shirt and sweater prices increased by 50 percent. If prices (and quantities) change by different percentages, a new problem—the index number problem—arises. (For a discussion, see Appendix 1.)

5. Income from activities that are inherently illegal accounts for 25 to 50 percent of unreported income. This income, even if reported, would not be included in GNP.

6. Peter M. Gutmann, "The Subterranean Economy," *Financial Analysts Journal*, 33 (November–December 1977), 26–27 and 34.

7. These studies are outlined and critically evaluated in Carol S. Carson, "The Underground Economy: An Introduction," *Survey of Current Business*, 64 (May 1984), 21–37, and (July 1984), 106–18; Bruno S. Frey and Werner Pommerehne, "The Hidden Economy: State and Prospects for Measurement," *Review of Income and Wealth*, 30 (March 1984), 1–23; and Richard D. Porter and Amanda S. Bayer, "A Monetary Perspective on Underground Economic Activity in the United States," *Federal Reserve Bulletin*, 70 (March 1984), 177–90.

8. With an underground economy, GNP, NNP, and national income are understated. Various economists claim that the same is true of employment, personal saving, and productivity. They also claim that unemployment and the unemployment rate are overstated. The implicit price deflator for GNP and, therefore, the recorded inflation rate are affected, but disagreement exists about the direction. Finally, the statistics on income distribution and the balance of payments are affected. For discussions, see Carson, *ibid.*; Edward F. Denison, "Is U.S. Growth Understated Because of the Underground Economy? Employment Ratios Suggest Not," *Review of Income and Wealth*, 28 (March 1982), 1–16; and Richard J. McDonald, "The 'Underground Economy,' and BLS Statistical Data," *Monthly Labor Review*, 107 (January 1984), 4–18.

9. William Nordhaus and James Tobin, "Is Growth Obsolete?" in *Economic Growth*, Economic Research: Retrospect and Prospect, Fiftieth Anniversary Colloquium V (New York: National Bureau of Economic Research, 1972).

REVIEW QUESTIONS

1. Gross national product, net national product, and national income are measures of the nation's output. Yet, from a conceptual standpoint, they differ. Briefly explain what each attempts to measure.

2. In estimating GNP, why is it important to count only those goods and services defined as final goods and services? Discuss in the context of a specific example.

3. Distinguish between GNP and GDP.

4. In regard to the national income accounts:

   a. Explain why a rental value is imputed to owner-occupied homes.

   b. Explain why no rental value is imputed to owner-driven automobiles.

5. The government receives accounting data from business firms relating to depreciation and changes in inventories. Explain why national income accountants adjust these data.

6. Indicate whether each of the following is included or excluded from GNP and the reasons for its inclusion or exclusion:

   a. Government transfer payments

   b. Rental income of owner-occupied homes

   c. Changes in inventories

   d. Services of homemakers

   e. Indirect business taxes

   f. Exports of goods and services

   g. Imports of goods and services

   h. Business transfer payments

7. Indicate whether each of the following is included or excluded from national income and the rationale for its inclusion or exclusion:

   a. Undistributed corporate profits

   b. Proprietors' income

   c. Fringe benefits

   d. Capital gains

   e. Indirect business taxes

   f. Net interest paid by government

   g. Wages and salaries paid in kind

   h. Interest paid by consumers to business

8. It is said that gross national product, net national product, and national income may be calculated by either the product or the income approaches.

   a. Show and explain how to calculate them using the product approach.

   b. Show and explain how to calculate them using the income approach.

   c. Suppose the two estimates of GNP differ. Explain how the estimates are reconciled.

9. Given the following national income accounting data:

Entry	Amount (Billions of Current Dollars)
Personal consumption expenditures	500
Personal taxes	170
Indirect business taxes	20
Dividends	110
Imports of goods and services	80
Contributions to social insurance	60
Net private domestic investment	40
Interest paid by consumers to business	20
Business transfer payments	40
Exports of goods and services	70
Net personal transfer payments to foreigners	10
Government transfer payments	150
Corporate profits with inventory valuation and capital consumption adjustments	180
Government purchases of goods and services	200
Gross private domestic investment	100

Calculate gross national product, net national product, national income, personal income, disposable personal income, and personal saving.

10. Given the following national income accounting data:

Entry	Amount (Billions of Current Dollars)
Personal consumption expenditures	580
Rental income of persons	100
Indirect business taxes	60
Proprietors' income with inventory valuation and capital consumption adjustments	100
Contributions for social insurance	60
Net interest	50
Personal taxes	260
Compensation of employees	500
Capital consumption allowances with capital consumption adjustment	50
Corporate profits with inventory valuation and capital consumption adjustments	200
Dividends	100
Wage accruals less disbursements	10
Net interest paid by government	20
Government transfer payments	50
Subsidies less current surplus of government enterprises	10

Calculate gross national product, net national product, national income, personal income, disposable personal income, and personal saving.

11. Explain why it is important to distinguish between nominal GNP (GNP measured in current dollars) and real GNP (GNP measured in constant dollars).

12. Explain the relationship between real GNP, nominal GNP, and the implicit price deflator for GNP.

13. Explain why nominal GNP decreased more rapidly than real GNP from 1929 to 1933.

14. What is the underground economy? What accounts for its present size? What are the implications of a large and growing underground economy?

15. Suppose real GNP increases by 10 percent. Does this mean that society is now 10 percent better off? In other words, has society's welfare increased by 10 percent? Defend your answer.

SUGGESTED READING _____

BAILEY, MARTIN J., *National Income and the Price Level* (2nd ed.), Chap. 12, app., pp. 247–74. New York: McGraw-Hill Book Company, 1971.

Economic Indicators. Prepared for the Joint Economic Committee by the Council of Economic Advisers. Washington, D.C.: Government Printing Office, monthly.

Economic Report of the President. Washington, D.C.: Government Printing Office, annually.

SMITH, WARREN L., *Macroeconomics*, Chaps. 2, 3; pp. 25–65. Homewood, Ill.: Richard D. Irwin, Inc., 1970.

SOMMERS, ALBERT T., *The U.S. Economy Demystified*. Lexington, Mass.: Lexington Books, 1985.

TANZI, VITO (ed.), *The Underground Economy in the United States and Abroad*. Lexington, Mass.: Lexington Books, 1982.

U.S. Department of Commerce, Bureau of Economic Analysis, *Business Conditions Digest*. Washington, D.C.: Government Printing Office, monthly.

———, *Survey of Current Business*. Washington, D.C.: Government Printing Office, monthly.

3

Introduction to the Theory of Income Determination

Although national income accounts measure the nation's output, they do not explain why output is at a certain level or why it increases more rapidly in some years than in others. To discover the determinants of the level of economic activity, we must use economic theory.

This chapter presents a simple Keynesian model of income determination. In order to concentrate on the basic model, the government and foreign trade sectors are omitted. The government sector is incorporated into the model in Chapter 4; the foreign trade sector, in Chapter 16. In addition, the price level is assumed to be constant. This assumption is relaxed in Chapter 10.

The theories of income determination presented in this and most of the other chapters are short-run theories. Among other things, they ignore the effects of investment and technological progress on the nation's productive capacity. In the short run (two or three years or less), the effects are small enough to be ignored. In the long run, however, these effects are very important. Long-run theories of income determination are called *growth theories*. Chapter 17 deals with these theories.

THE MODEL

This chapter focuses on consumption and investment. As discussed later, aggregate demand—the sum of society's expenditures on consumption and investment—determines the equilibrium level of income. Should aggregate demand change, the equilibrium level of income also changes. Thus, aggregate demand plays a key role in the model.

The Consumption Function

Many different factors, including tastes, income, and interest rates, determine consumption. For example, if the income of one household is greater than the income of another, the former is likely to consume more. Even if their incomes are the same, however, they will spend different amounts on consumption if their attitudes toward thrift differ. Similarly, households may vary their consumption in response to changes in interest rates.

Although many factors affect consumption, aggregate income is the most important by far. Consequently, we shall concentrate on the relationship between consumption and income, *the consumption function,* in this chapter and postpone more detailed discussion of the determinants of consumption until Chapter 5.

In our version of the consumption function, consumption is assumed to vary directly with income. Specifically, consumption is assumed to increase as income increases, with the increase in consumption being less than the increase in income. In equation form, the consumption function is

$$C = a + bY \quad (a > 0, 0 < b < 1),$$

where C and Y represent real consumption and real income, respectively. The equation indicates that consumption is a linear function of income. Linearity is assumed, for the most part, because the empirical evidence suggests that the function is linear or approximately so. In the equation, a and b are constants, called *parameters.* Consumption, C, and income, Y, are variables.

The parameter b, called the *marginal propensity to consume* or *MPC*, is the slope of the consumption function. If ΔY denotes a change in income and ΔC denotes the change in consumption associated with the change in income, b, the MPC, equals $\Delta C/\Delta Y$. For example, if income increases by $200 billion and, as a result, consumption increases by $150 billion, the MPC is $150 billion divided by $200 billion or 0.75. In postulating our consumption function, we assumed that consumption increases as income increases, but by a smaller amount. This implies that b, the MPC, must be between 0 and 1, an assumption which is in accord with the empirical evidence.

The parameter a is the portion of consumption which does not vary with income, or, to put it differently, a represents the consumption which would occur if income were 0. Short-run studies of the consumption function suggest that a is positive.

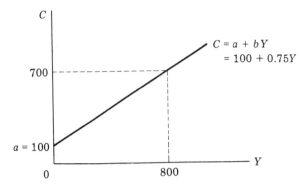

FIGURE 3.1

The consumption function

The consumption function may be depicted graphically by specifying various levels of income, determining the corresponding levels of consumption, and then plotting the combinations of income and consumption. To illustrate, suppose the consumption function is $C = 100 + 0.75Y$. If Y equals \$800 billion, C equals \$700 billion, obtained by solving the equation $C = 100 + 0.75 (800)$. This combination of Y and C is plotted as a point on the consumption function $C = 100 + 0.75Y$ in Figure 3.1. Other points on the consumption function can be obtained in the same manner.

An alternative way to plot the consumption function is to recognize that a is the intercept and b the slope. The intercept and slope completely determine a straight line. For example, if a equals 100 and b equals 0.75, the function will start at $a = 100$ and have a slope, b, equal to 0.75. Should a change, the consumption function will shift so that the new function is parallel to the old. Should b change, the function will rotate about the intercept, a.

The Saving Function

Since the decision on how much income to consume implies a decision on how much to save, a saving function may be derived with the aid of the consumption function. With no government and foreign trade sectors, income equals, by definition, consumption plus saving, S:

$$Y = C + S.$$

But C is equal to $a + bY$. Consequently, after substituting, rearranging terms, and factoring, the saving function is found to be

$$S = -a + (1 - b)Y \qquad (0 < (1 - b) < 1),$$

where S and Y represent real saving and real income, respectively.

The parameter $1 - b$, referred to as the *marginal propensity to save* or *MPS*, is the slope of the saving function. If ΔY denotes a change in income and ΔS denotes the change in saving associated with the change in income, $1 - b$, the MPS, equals $\Delta S/\Delta Y$. For example, if income increases by \$200 billion and, as a consequence, saving increases by \$50 billion, the MPS is \$50 billion divided by \$200 billion or 0.25. Since b, the MPC, is assumed to be between 0 and 1, $1 - b$, the MPS, is also between 0 and 1, which implies that saving increases as income increases, but by a smaller amount.

The saving function may be plotted in the same manner as the consumption function. To show the relationship between the consumption and saving functions, however, we shall consider an alternative approach. Suppose, in Figure 3.2, the scales are the same on both axes of the graph of the consumption function. Next, assume that income is plotted on both axes and that a 45° line is drawn through the origin. At all points on the 45° line, income on the vertical axis is equal to income on the horizontal axis since the scales are the same on both axes. Given the 45° line and the consumption function, we can now derive the saving function graphically. Since income equals consumption plus saving, saving is the difference between income and consumption. Therefore, to find saving at each level of income, consumption is subtracted from income. Graphically, saving is the vertical distance between the income line, the 45° line, and the consumption function, saving being

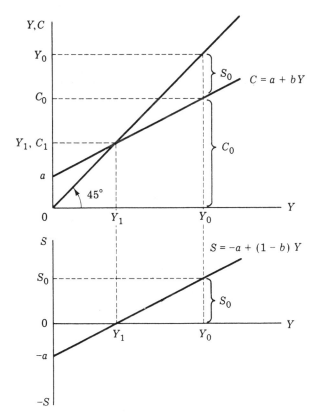

FIGURE 3.2

The graphical derivation of the saving function

positive (negative) when income is greater (less) than consumption. Consider income Y_0 in Figure 3.2. At income Y_0, consumption equals C_0; consequently, saving equals S_0, obtained by subtracting C_0 from Y_0. Therefore, one point on the saving function is the point $Y = Y_0$, $S = S_0$.

Select another level of income, say, Y_1 where the consumption function intersects the 45° line. At that level of income, consumption equals C_1, which also equals Y_1. Therefore, at $Y = Y_1$, S_1 equals 0, since S_1 equals $Y_1 - C_1$ and C_1 equals Y_1. Consequently, another point on the saving function is the point $Y = Y_1$, $S = 0$. Finally, suppose income is 0. At that level of income, consumption equals a. Hence, saving equals $-a$, obtained by subtracting $C = a$ from $Y = 0$. Thus, a third point on the saving function is the point $Y = 0$, $S = -a$. The remainder of the points may be obtained by considering other levels of income. As an exercise, the reader might repeat the procedure using the consumption function just discussed, $C = 100 + 0.75Y$, and income levels 800, 400, and 0.

In Figure 3.2, saving is positive at income levels greater than Y_1 since income exceeds consumption at those levels of income. Saving is negative at income levels less than Y_1 since consumption exceeds income. Negative saving, *dissaving*, occurs if individual households consume more than their income. They may do so by spending part of their savings or by borrowing. For society as a whole, dissaving is unlikely although it did occur during 1932 and 1933.

The Investment Function

From the consumption and saving functions, we turn to the investment function. Like consumption, investment depends on many variables, including interest rates. For the present, however, investment is assumed to be a constant. (The determinants of investment are examined in detail in Chapter 6.)

Since investment is assumed to be constant at, say, the I_0 level, the investment function is

$$I = I_0 \qquad (I_0 > 0),$$

where I represents real investment and I_0 represents a given, positive level of investment. Suppose I_0 equals $50 billion. With investment on the vertical axis and income on the horizontal, the investment function is plotted as the horizontal line in Figure 3.3, indicating that investment does not vary with the level of income.

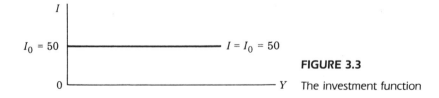

FIGURE 3.3

The investment function

Summary

Restating the model, the consumption and investment functions are

(3.1) $$C = a + bY \quad (a > 0, 0 < b < 1),$$

(3.2) $$I = I_0 \quad (I_0 > 0).$$

These equations are behavioral equations, as defined in Chapter 1, because they purport to explain the behavior of consumers and investors.

To complete the model, we must specify an equilibrium condition, that is, a condition necessary for a particular level of income to be an equilibrium level. The equilibrium condition may be specified as

(3.3) Aggregate supply $=$ Aggregate demand.

Thus, for income (or output since the terms may be used interchangeably) to be an equilibrium level, aggregate supply must equal aggregate demand. This approach, the *aggregate supply–aggregate demand approach*, to the determination of the equilibrium level of income is discussed in the next section. The equilibrium condition may also be specified as

(3.4) $$I = S.$$

Thus, for income to be an equilibrium level, investment must equal saving. This approach, the *investment–saving approach*, and its relationship to the aggregate supply–aggregate demand approach are discussed later.

EQUILIBRIUM INCOME: THE AGGREGATE SUPPLY–AGGREGATE DEMAND APPROACH

Using the aggregate supply–aggregate demand approach, we can now determine the equilibrium level of income. Aggregate supply represents the nation's output of goods and services, and aggregate demand represents society's demand for those goods and services. The essence of this approach is that the nation's output of goods and services must equal the demand for those goods and services for income to be at its equilibrium level. If the nation's output equals the demand for goods and services, firms will be able to sell their entire output. Consequently, no incentive exists for them to alter their production and income remains at the equilibrium level.

If the nation's output exceeds the demand for goods and services, firms are unable to sell their entire output and experience a buildup in their inventories. An incentive exists, therefore, for them to reduce production. As a result, output falls until it equals the demand for goods and services. Similarly, if the nation's output is less than the demand for goods and services, firms sell more than they are producing and experience a depletion of their inventories. An incentive exists, therefore, for them to increase production. As a result, output rises until it equals the demand for goods and services.

The aggregate supply–aggregate demand approach is developed graphically in Figure 3.4. Aggregate supply, the output of goods and services, is depicted by the 45° line. With the same scales on both axes, output on the vertical axis equals output or income on the horizontal axis for all points on the 45° line. The 45° line is not a "true" aggregate supply curve. For example, it indicates that any amount, from 0 to infinity, may be produced. This is not possible; production is limited by the nation's resources and its technology. Nevertheless, in the development of the model, it is helpful to think of the 45° line as an aggregate supply curve.

Aggregate demand represents society's demand for goods and services. With no government and foreign trade sectors, it consists of the demand for consumer goods and services and the demand for investment goods. The consumption function represents the demand for consumer goods and services since it shows the level of consumption for each level of income. Similarly, the investment function represents the demand for investment goods. Together, the two functions represent the aggregate demand for goods and services. Consequently, aggregate demand is equal to $C + I$, which, by substitution, equals $a + bY + I_0$. Graphically, the aggregate demand line is the vertical summation of the C and I lines or, to put it differently, it is the C line plus the constant I_0. The $C + I$ line is depicted in Figure 3.4.

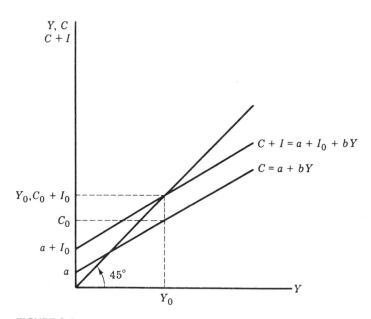

FIGURE 3.4

Aggregate supply, aggregate demand, and the equilibrium level of income

With the 45° line representing aggregate supply and the $C + I$ line representing aggregate demand, the equilibrium level of income is Y_0. Income level Y_0 must be the equilibrium level since it is the only level for which aggregate supply equals aggregate demand. At income levels greater than Y_0, aggregate supply (represented by the 45° line) is greater than aggregate demand (represented by the $C + I$ line), and income falls as firms cut output in response to inventory accumulation. At income levels less than Y_0, aggregate supply is less than aggregate demand, and income rises as firms expand output in response to inventory depletion.

To illustrate, suppose the consumption and investment functions are

$$C = 100 + 0.75Y,$$

$$I = 50.$$

The consumption and consumption plus investment functions are plotted in Figure 3.5. Graphically, the equilibrium level of income is given by the intersection of the aggregate supply curve (the 45° line) and the aggregate demand curve (the $C + I$ line).

Algebraically, the equilibrium level of income may be obtained by substituting the consumption and investment functions into the equilibrium condition:

$$\text{Aggregate supply} = \text{Aggregate demand.}$$

Since aggregate supply represents output, Y, and aggregate demand represents the demand for goods and services, $C + I$, then Y and $C + I$ may be substituted for them to obtain

$$Y = C + I.$$

If C equals $100 + 0.75Y$ and I equal 50,

$$Y = 100 + 0.75Y + 50$$

and
$$Y = 600.$$

Thus, the equilibrium level of income is $600 billion.

Once the equilibrium level of income is determined, the equilibrium level of consumption may be determined by substituting the equilibrium level of income into the consumption function. In the example, the equilibrium level of consumption is $550 billion, obtained by substituting $Y = \$600$ billion into the consumption function $C = 100 + 0.75Y$.

Since investment is $50 billion, the aggregate demand for goods and services at the equilibrium level of income is $600 billion, obtained by summing the demand for consumer goods and services, $550 billion, and the demand for investment

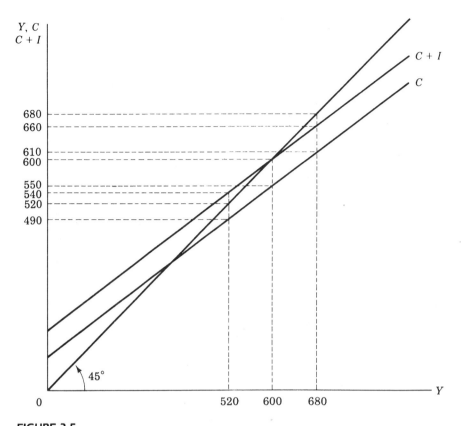

FIGURE 3.5

Aggregate supply, aggregate demand, and the equilibrium level of income:
A numerical example

goods, $50 billion. Since aggregate supply is also $600 billion, aggregate supply equals aggregate demand at the $600 billion level. Since society is willing to purchase all the nation's output at that income level, firms can sell their entire output. Thus, no tendency exists for them to alter their production, and $600 billion is the equilibrium level of income.

In Figure 3.5, the equilibrium level of income is $600 billion. If income is at another level, it gravitates to the equilibrium level. Suppose managers believe they can sell $680 billion worth of goods and produce accordingly. Aggregate supply is $680 billion. Given this level of output (income), consumption is $610 billion, obtained by substituting income equal to $680 billion into the consumption function $C = 100 + 0.75Y$. Since investment is $50 billion, aggregate demand is $660 billion.

Although aggregate supply is $680 billion, aggregate demand is only $660 billion. Hence, only $660 billion worth of goods and services are sold. The remaining $20 billion worth of goods are added to business inventories. If production were to continue at the $680 billion level, managers would find that their inventories would continue to increase. Therefore, firms reduce production.

Suppose managers cut back production to, say, $640 billion. At that level of output, consumption is $580 billion and investment is $50 billion; consequently, aggregate demand is $630 billion. Since aggregate supply is $640 billion, aggregate supply exceeds aggregate demand once again. In this case, society purchases only $630 billion worth of goods and services while the remaining $10 billion worth of goods is added to business inventories. Thus, with income equal to $640 billion, inventory accumulation occurs, although at a slower rate. The inventory accumulation provides managers with an incentive to reduce production.

At this point, managers might reduce production to $600 billion. If they do, they will be able to sell their entire output and there will be no tendency for them to alter production. For illustration, however, suppose production is reduced to $520 billion. At that level of output, consumption is $490 billion and investment, $50 billion; therefore, aggregate demand is $540 billion. To sell $540 billion of output with production of only $520 billion, managers will have to sell $20 billion from inventories. Since aggregate demand and sales exceed production, managers will find that their inventories are being depleted. This is a signal for them to produce more, and income tends to increase.

By this time, the main points should be clear. If aggregate supply exceeds aggregate demand, income tends to fall because of the buildup in inventories. If aggregate demand exceeds aggregate supply, income tends to increase because of the depletion in inventories. Thus, income is at its equilibrium level only when aggregate supply equals aggregate demand. Finally, since income tends to fall when aggregate supply exceeds aggregate demand and to rise when aggregate demand exceeds aggregate supply, income moves to its equilibrium level.

EQUILIBRIUM INCOME: THE INVESTMENT–SAVING APPROACH

Earlier, an alternative approach to equilibrium was suggested, the investment–saving approach. Confusion sometimes arises with regard to this approach because, by definition,

$$Y = C + I$$

and
$$Y = C + S.$$

The former implies that investment is the difference between income and consumption; the latter implies that saving is the difference between income and consumption. Since both investment and saving equal the difference between income and consumption by definition, investment equals saving by definition. Consequently, how can $I = S$ be a condition necessary for a level of income to be an equilibrium level when the condition holds at *every* level of income?

As discussed later, one must distinguish intended from realized investment. Realized investment equals saving at every level of income. Intended investment, however, equals saving only at the equilibrium level of income. Consequently, for $I = S$ to be an equilibrium condition, investment must be interpreted as intended investment.

Intended or *ex ante investment* is the amount of investment which firms intended or planned to invest; its magnitude is indicated by the investment function, $I = I_0$. *Unintended investment* is the change in business inventories due to a discrepancy between aggregate supply and aggregate demand. As discussed earlier, if aggregate supply exceeds aggregate demand, production exceeds sales and business inventories increase. The increase in inventories is treated as investment in the national income accounts. Geometrically, unintended investment is represented by the vertical distance between the 45° line (aggregate supply) and the $C + I$ line (aggregate demand). *Realized* or *ex post investment* is the sum of intended and unintended investment. Since national income accountants cannot distinguish between intended and unintended investment, no distinction is made between them in the national income accounts.

In terms of the example, consider the equilibrium level of income, $600 billion. At that income, consumption equals $550 billion; therefore, saving, the difference between income and consumption, equals $50 billion. Intended investment, as indicated by the investment function, is $50 billion. Since aggregate supply equals aggregate demand at the equilibrium level of income, unintended investment is 0. Thus, at the equilibrium level of income, both intended and realized investment equal saving.

Next, consider $680 billion, a disequilibrium level of income. At that income, consumption equals $610 billion, which implies that saving equals $70 billion. Intended investment is only $50 billion, but with aggregate supply $20 billion greater than aggregate demand, unintended investment (unintended inventory accumulation) is $20 billion. Thus, although intended investment does not equal saving, realized investment does.

Finally, suppose income is $520 billion. Since consumption is $490 billion, saving equals $30 billion. As before, intended investment is $50 billion. In contrast to the previous case, however, unintended investment (unintended inventory accumulation) is negative, −$20 billion. Unintended investment is negative because, with income equal to $520 billion, aggregate demand ($540 billion) exceeds aggregate supply ($520 billion), and inventories are depleted by $20 billion. The reduction in inventories enters the national income accounts as negative investment. Realized investment, the sum of intended ($50 billion) and unintended (−$20 billion) investment, is $30 billion. Thus, although intended investment fails to equal saving, realized investment equals saving.

Summing up, realized investment equals saving regardless of the level of income. Intended investment equals saving only at the equilibrium level of income.

Intended investment is either greater than or less than saving at all other income levels. Consequently, $I = S$ can serve as an equilibrium condition, but only if I represents intended investment. Thus, for income to be an equilibrium level, intended investment must equal saving.

The equilibrium level of income can be determined either algebraically or geometrically with the investment–saving approach. To determine the equilibrium level of income algebraically, investment and saving may be substituted into the equilibrium condition

$$I = S.$$

As in the earlier example, suppose that investment is \$50 billion and consumption is $100 + 0.75Y$. Since saving (S) is the difference between income (Y) and consumption (C), saving is $-100 + 0.25Y$. Thus, upon substitution,

$$50 = -100 + 0.25Y,$$

or, upon rearranging terms and simplifying,

$$0.25Y = 150.$$

Finally,

$$Y_0 = 600.$$

Thus, the equilibrium level of income is \$600 billion, the same as obtained earlier with the aggregate supply–aggregate demand approach. The equilibrium level of saving is \$50 billion, obtained by substituting the equilibrium level of income, \$600 billion, into the saving function, $-100 + 0.25Y$.

The equilibrium level of income may also be determined geometrically. In Figure 3.6, the saving function is derived from the 45° line and the consumption function using the procedure outlined earlier. The investment function, from Figure 3.3, represents intended investment. Since income is at its equilibrium level when intended investment equals saving, the equilibrium level of income is given by the intersection of the investment and saving functions. In this case, the equilibrium level of income is \$600 billion.

The relationship between the aggregate supply – aggregate demand and investment – saving approaches is illustrated in Figure 3.6. If intended investment equals saving, aggregate supply equals aggregate demand and income is at its equilibrium level. If saving exceeds intended investment, however, aggregate supply exceeds aggregate demand, and income is at a disequilibrium level. With aggregate supply greater than aggregate demand, inventories accumulate and income falls. Similarly, if intended investment exceeds saving, aggregate demand exceeds aggregate supply. With aggregate demand greater than aggregate supply, inventories

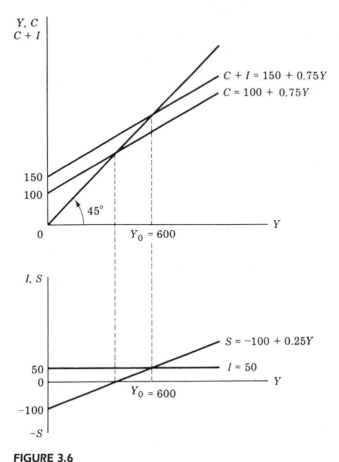

FIGURE 3.6

Investment, saving, and the equilibrium level of income

are depleted and income rises. Thus, when saving exceeds intended investment, income falls, and when intended investment exceeds saving, income rises. Under these circumstances, income will move to the equilibrium level where intended investment equals saving.

For the model just described, the equilibrium level of income may represent a full employment level. That is, full employment may exist at the equilibrium level of income. But it may not. Unemployment may exist at the equilibrium level of income because, for the model in question, the equilibrium level of income is merely the level where intended investment equals saving or, alternatively, aggregate supply equals aggregate demand. In Chapter 10, we develop a more sophisticated model which will show the level of employment corresponding to each level of income. In this chapter, we assume that unemployment exists so that increases in aggregate demand result in increases in production.

INVESTMENT AND THE EQUILIBRIUM LEVEL OF INCOME

Thus far we have established how to determine the equilibrium level of income and demonstrated how income gravitates to that level. The next step is to show how shifts in the consumption and investment functions alter the equilibrium level of income. Since the consumption function is usually regarded as stable (because it does not shift or shifts only infrequently), we shall concentrate mainly on shifts in the investment function.

Suppose, initially, that the relevant investment and consumption plus investment functions are I and $C + I$ in Figure 3.7. The equilibrium level of income, given by the intersection of the 45° line and the $C + I$ line, is Y_0. Next, suppose business decides to invest more. In Figure 3.7, if investment increases from I_0 to I_1, the investment and consumption plus investment functions shift to I' and $C + I'$, respectively, and the equilibrium level of income increases from Y_0 to Y_1. Income level Y_1 must be the new equilibrium level because it is the only level of income which now equates aggregate supply and aggregate demand. The explanation for the increase in income is straightforward. If business invests more, the aggregate demand for goods and services increases. With this increase, aggregate demand exceeds the original level of aggregate supply. As a consequence, inventories are depleted. The reduction in inventories signals firms to produce more, and output increases to the new equilibrium level.

With the change in investment, we find that a change in income occurs. Mathematically, a relationship between the change in income, ΔY, and the change in investment, ΔI, can be obtained; this relationship is called the *investment multiplier*. To derive the multiplier, k, first substitute the behavioral equations into the equilibrium condition in order to determine the equilibrium levels of income corresponding to investment levels I_0 and I_1. The equilibrium condition is

$$\text{Aggregate supply} = \text{Aggregate demand}.$$

Aggregate supply, Y, and aggregate demand, $C + I$, may be substituted into the equilibrium condition to obtain

$$Y = C + I.$$

Since C equals $a + bY$ and $I = I_0$, another substitution yields

$$Y = a + bY + I_0.$$

After rearranging terms, factoring, and dividing both sides of the equation by

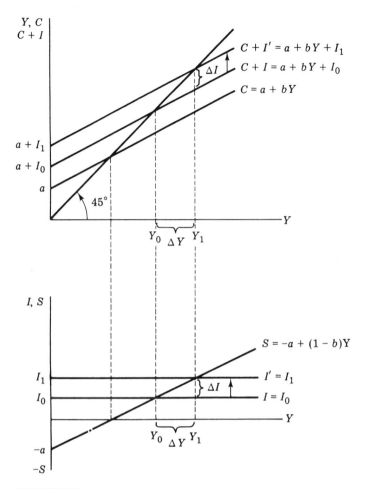

FIGURE 3.7

Equilibrium income and a shift in the investment function

$(1 - b)$, the equilibrium level of income is

$$(3.5) \qquad Y_0 = \frac{a}{1 - b} + \frac{I_0}{1 - b}.$$

It is the equilibrium level of income associated with investment level I_0 in Figure 3.7.

If investment increases to I_1, a new, higher equilibrium level of income results. To determine the new equilibrium level, the procedure is repeated with investment level I_1 in place of I_0. The new equilibrium level is

(**3.6**)
$$Y_1 = \frac{a}{1 - b} + \frac{I_1}{1 - b}.$$

It is the equilibrium level of income associated with investment level I_1 in Figure 3.7.

The next step is to subtract equation (3.5) from equation (3.6) to obtain

$$Y_1 - Y_0 = \frac{I_1 - I_0}{1 - b} = \frac{1}{1 - b}(I_1 - I_0).$$

Since $Y_1 - Y_0$ equals ΔY and $I_1 - I_0$ equals ΔI, we obtain, upon substitution,

$$\Delta Y = \frac{1}{1 - b} \Delta I = k\Delta I.$$

Thus, the investment multiplier, k, equals $1/(1 - b)$, the reciprocal of the marginal propensity to save.

The multiplier analysis shows that a change in investment will give rise to a change in income greater than the increase in investment. With b and hence $1 - b$ between 0 and 1, the multiplier is greater than 1. For example, suppose b equals 0.75, implying an investment multiplier of $1/(1 - 0.75)$ or 4. If investment increases by \$20 billion, the increase in income is 4(\$20) or \$80 billion. The change in income, \$80 billion, is greater than the change in investment, \$20 billion.

Disbelief is sometimes registered when it is claimed that income changes by an amount greater than the change in investment. By definition,

$$Y = C + I.$$

Consequently, it is argued that the change in income should equal the change in investment. As will be demonstrated, however, the change in income is greater because the change in investment results in changes in consumption in the same direction. Consequently, the change in income consists of changes in both consumption and investment so that the change in income is greater than the change in investment.

To determine why the increase in income is greater than the increase in investment, consider the following example. Suppose the marginal propensity to consume is 0.75 and investment increases by \$20 billion. With the increase in investment, income increases by \$20 billion. Since consumption is a function of income, consumption also increases. The increase in consumption equals \$15 billion, obtained by multiplying the marginal propensity to consume, 0.75, by the change in income, \$20 billion. The \$15 billion increase in consumption constitutes an increase in income. Consequently, consumption increases again. In this instance, consumption increases by $11.25 billion, found by multiplying 0.75 by the change in income, $15 billion. This increase in consumption, hence income, generates another increase in consumption. In this case, the increase in consumption is $8.4375 billion, obtained by multiplying 0.75 by $11.25 billion. This increase in consumption, hence income, triggers still another increase in consumption. In fact, this process—the *multiplier process*—continues indefinitely. But since the increases in consumption become progressively smaller, the total increase in income is finite. If the marginal propensity to consume is 0.75, the investment multiplier is 4 and the ultimate increase in income corresponding to a $20 billion increase in investment is $80 billion.[1] Of the $80 billion increase in income, only $20 billion is accounted for by the increase in investment. The remaining $60 billion is accounted for by increases in consumption which occur during the multiplier process.

The multiplier process is symmetric; it occurs for both increases and decreases in investment. As before, suppose the marginal propensity to consume is 0.75. Instead of assuming that investment increases by $20 billion, suppose it decreases by $20 billion. With the decrease in investment, income decreases by $20 billion. Since consumption is a function of income, consumption also decreases; it decreases by $15 billion, found by multiplying the marginal propensity to consume, 0.75, by the change in income, −$20 billion. The decrease in consumption, hence income, results in another decrease in consumption. This time, the decrease in consumption is $11.25 billion obtained by multiplying 0.75 by the change in income, −$15 billion. These decreases in consumption continue until income has decreased by $80 billion, obtained by multiplying the investment multiplier, 4, by the change in investment, −$20 billion.

The multiplier analysis suggests that the greater the change in investment, the greater will be the change in income. Similarly, the analysis suggests that the greater the marginal propensity to consume, the greater will be the change in income for a given change in investment. If the marginal propensity to consume increases, the marginal propensity to save decreases. Since the investment multiplier is the reciprocal of the marginal propensity to save, the multiplier increases in value, indicating a larger change in income for any given change in investment. The larger change in income occurs because consumption now changes by a greater amount at each stage of the multiplier process. For example, if the marginal propensity to consume is 0.8, a $20 billion increase in investment triggers a $16 billion increase in consumption. Previously, with a marginal propensity to consume of 0.75, the increase in consumption was only $15 billion. Thus, the greater marginal propensity to consume results in a greater increase in consumption. With the greater increases in consumption at this and succeeding stages, the ultimate increase in income is greater. With a marginal propensity to consume of 0.8, the investment multiplier is $1/(1 - 0.8)$ or 5. Thus, the increase in income corresponding to a $20 billion increase in investment is 5($20) or $100 billion. Of the increase, $20 billion is accounted for by the increase in investment, with the remaining $80 billion accounted for by the increases in consumption. In contrast, if the marginal propensity to consume is 0.75, the multiplier is 4 and income increases by only $80 billion with the same increase in investment.

The multiplier analysis applies to shifts in the investment function and the resulting changes in income. It also applies to shifts in the consumption function. A $20 billion (upward) shift in the consumption function has the same impact on aggregate demand as a $20 billion increase in investment. Consequently, the increase in income is the same, which implies that the multipliers are the same. If the marginal propensity to consume is 0.75, the multiplier is $1/(1 - 0.75)$ or 4. Consequently, a $20 billion increase in consumption results in an increase in income equal to 4($20) or $80 billion. The ultimate increase in income is greater than the initial increase in consumption, because the initial increase in consumption, hence income, causes an additional increase in consumption and income. The increases in consumption and income continue until the multiplier process has run its course and income is at its new equilibrium level. In this case, the increase in income is composed entirely of increases in consumption.

Multiplier analysis has at least three uses. First, it shows that a change in spending has an impact on the economy greater than the initial impact. Second, by comparing multipliers derived from different models, one can compare various implications of the underlying models. The use of multiplier analysis for this purpose is illustrated in the next chapter. Third, by estimating multipliers for various fiscal and monetary variables, it is possible to estimate the effectiveness of fiscal and monetary policy. Some estimates are reported in Chapters 18 and 19.

CONCLUDING REMARKS

In this chapter, we considered a simple theory of income determination, one in which aggregate demand plays a key role. Although formulation of this model is only a first step in formulating more sophisticated models, the model does provide some useful insights. The model helps to explain, for example, why economic forecasters and policymakers are very interested in the amounts that households and firms plan to spend. Similarly, the model suggests that one of the first effects of a change in aggregate demand is a buildup or depletion of business inventories, the normal state of affairs.

In the next chapter, we incorporate the government sector into the model. By doing so, we will be able to gain additional insights and discuss fiscal policy. As we shall see, however, the essential properties of the model are unchanged.

NOTES

1. Mathematically, the increase in income equals $20 + 15 + 11.25 + 8.4375 + \cdots$, which equals $20 + 0.75(20) + 0.75(0.75)(20) + 0.75(0.75)(0.75)(20) + \cdots$, which also equals $20[1 + (0.75) + (0.75)^2 + (0.75)^3 + \cdots]$. The expression in brackets represents

the sum of a convergent geometric series. Based on the formula for the sum of such a series, it equals $1/(1 - 0.75)$ or 4. Thus, the increase in income is $20(4)$ or $80 billion. In general, the change in income equals $\Delta I + b\Delta I + b(b\Delta I) + b^2(b\Delta I) + \cdots$ or $\Delta I(1 + b + b^2 + b^3 + \cdots)$. Since b is assumed to be between 0 and 1, $(1 + b + b^2 + b^3 + \cdots)$ is the sum of a convergent geometric series. This sum equals $1/(1 - b)$, which implies that the change in income equals $\Delta I/(1 - b)$.

REVIEW QUESTIONS

1. Suppose we have the following model:

$$C = a + bY = 50 + 0.8Y,$$

$$I = I_0 = 50.$$

   a. What is the condition necessary for a level of income to be an equilibrium level?

   b. Determine the equilibrium levels of income, consumption, and saving.

   c. Suppose the level of income is $450 billion. In terms of the example, explain why income tends to change until the equilibrium level of income is achieved.

   d. Is the equilibrium level of income necessarily a full employment level? Why? Why not?

   e. Suppose investment increases by $10 billion. Find the resulting changes in income, consumption, and saving.

2. Find and plot the saving function implicit in the model of question 1.

3. Explain the unintended investment concept. How is it useful in explaining why a particular level of income is an equilibrium level?

4. It is said that a single individual may save more by consuming less, but if everyone tries to save more by consuming less, they may end up saving no more than before or even less. Is this statement true? Why? Why not?

5. It is said that an increase in investment causes an increase in income greater than the initial increase in investment. In this context, explain the logic of the multiplier process.

6. Derive the multiplier for a, the intercept term of the consumption function.

7. Suppose the consumption function is nonlinear. If consumption increases as income increases, but at a diminishing rate,

   a. how is the equilibrium condition affected?

   b. how is the investment multiplier affected?

8. In the short run, it makes no difference whether consumption increases (the consumption function shifts upward) or whether investment increases (the investment function shifts upward). In the long run, it makes a difference. Explain.

SUGGESTED READING _____

HEILBRONER, ROBERT L., and LESTER C. THUROW, *Understanding Macroeconomics* (8th ed.). Englewood Cliffs, N.J.: Prentice-Hall, Inc., 1984.

KEYNES, JOHN MAYNARD, *The General Theory of Employment, Interest, and Money*. New York: Harcourt, Brace and Company, 1936.

SAMUELSON, PAUL A., "The Simple Mathematics of Income Determination," in Lloyd A. Metzler and others, *Income, Employment, and Public Policy*, pp. 133–55. New York: W.W. Norton & Co., Inc., 1948.

4

GOVERNMENT
AND THE THEORY
OF INCOME DETERMINATION

The activities of government, federal, state, and local, exert an influence on the level of economic activity in a variety of ways. If a more vigorous antitrust program were pursued, lower prices and greater output might result. On the other hand, if new legislation granted labor unions greater bargaining power, wages and prices might increase. Similarly, passage of a strict antipollution law would affect the level and direction of economic activity, as would a new multilateral trade agreement to reduce international trade barriers. The level of economic activity may also be altered by changing the levels of government spending and taxes. In this text, we concentrate almost entirely on the levels of government spending and taxes and their impact on the economy. The other activities of government are important, but they are considered elsewhere in the study of economics.

Government spending includes transfer payments as well as purchases of goods and services. Both involve payments by government, but transfer payments are made without receipt of goods and services, at least in the year in which the payments are made. Since taxes are payments to government without receipt of goods and services, taxes are the reverse of transfer payments. In view of this relationship, we shall be concerned with only *net* taxes, the difference between taxes and transfer payments. The federal government's budget and the budgetary process are discussed in more detail in Chapter 18.

Government purchases may exceed net taxes since government may borrow or, in the case of the federal government, issue money. Later, we shall see that the method of financing a budgetary deficit is important in determining the impact of, say, an increase in government purchases.

The model of Chapter 3 contained only two sectors: the household and business sectors. In this chapter, we introduce the government sector. Specifically, government purchases and net taxes are incorporated into the model. The implications are then examined. Like the variables in the previous chapter, government purchases and net taxes are defined in real terms.

GOVERNMENT PURCHASES
AND THE EQUILIBRIUM LEVEL OF INCOME

First, we shall introduce government purchases into the model. We assume that government purchases, G, are an exogenous variable whose value is determined by the administrative and legislative branches of government; therefore,

$$G = G_0.$$

This means that, as a first approximation, the level of government purchases is constant until action is taken by government to change it. With government purchases on the vertical axis and income on the horizontal, the government purchases function is parallel to the income axis at the G_0 level in Figure 4.1. Thus, the level of government purchases, G, is independent of the level of income.

The model with government purchases is

$$C = a + bY,$$

$$I = I_0,$$

$$G = G_0.$$

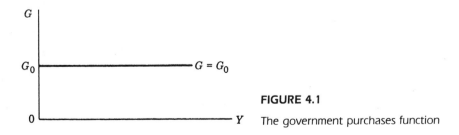

FIGURE 4.1

The government purchases function

The equilibrium condition is

$$\text{Aggregate supply} = \text{Aggregate demand}$$

or, alternatively,

$$I + G = S.$$

The model is similar to the model of Chapter 3. As before, the equilibrium level of income is determined by aggregate supply and aggregate demand. However, the aggregate demand for goods and services now includes government purchases of goods and services, since these purchases reflect the demand for goods and services by government. In Figure 4.2, the line representing aggregate demand is $C + I + G$; it is the vertical summation of the consumption and investment lines of the previous chapter and the government purchases line of Figure 4.1.

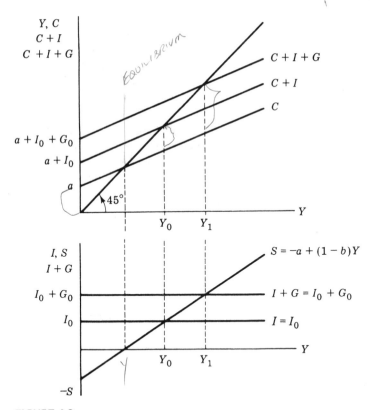

FIGURE 4.2

Government purchases and the equilibrium level of income

The equilibrium level of income is now given by the intersection of the aggregate supply line, the 45° line, and the aggregate demand line, $C + I + G$. In Figure 4.2, the equilibrium level of income is Y_1. For income levels greater than Y_1, aggregate supply exceeds aggregate demand. Hence, output exceeds sales and business inventories increase. As a result, firms will reduce their output. For income levels less than Y_1, aggregate demand exceeds aggregate supply. Therefore, output is less than sales and business inventories decrease. Consequently, firms will increase their output. Since aggregate supply equals aggregate demand at income level Y_1, output equals sales and firms have no incentive to change their output. Therefore, Y_1 is the equilibrium level of output. Since government purchases represent an addition to the aggregate demand for goods and services, the equilibrium level of income Y_1 is greater than the original equilibrium level, Y_0.

The equilibrium level can also be determined through the investment–saving approach. With this approach, $I + G$ must equal S for income to be an equilibrium level. Investment and government purchases are summed because they enter the model in the same manner. Both are components of aggregate demand, and an increase in government purchases has the same effect on aggregate demand and income as an increase in investment.[1] In Figure 4.2, the investment plus government purchases line is $I_0 + G_0$, obtained by summing investment, I_0, and government purchases, G_0. The saving line is $-a + (1 - b)Y$. Consequently, the equilibrium level of income is Y_1.

To gain familiarity with the model, consider the following example. Suppose consumption equals $100 + 0.75Y$, investment equals $50 billion, and government purchases equal $20 billion. The equilibrium level of income may be determined by substituting the behavioral equations into the equilibrium condition and solving for income. Since the equilibrium condition is aggregate supply equal to aggregate demand, and since Y equals aggregate supply and $C + I + G$ equals aggregate demand, we obtain, upon substitution,

$$Y = C + I + G = 100 + 0.75Y + 50 + 20$$

or, solving for income,

$$Y = 680.$$

Thus, the equilibrium level of income is $680 billion. With aggregate supply equal to $680 billion, consumption equals $610 billion, found by substituting income, $680 billion, into the consumption function $C = 100 + 0.75Y$. With investment equal to $50 billion and government purchases equal to $20 billion, aggregate demand, $C + I + G$, equals $680 billion. Since aggregate supply equals aggregate demand at the $680 billion level, $680 billion must be the equilibrium level of income. Saving, the difference between income and consumption, is $70 billion. Since investment equals $50 billion and government purchases equal $20 billion,

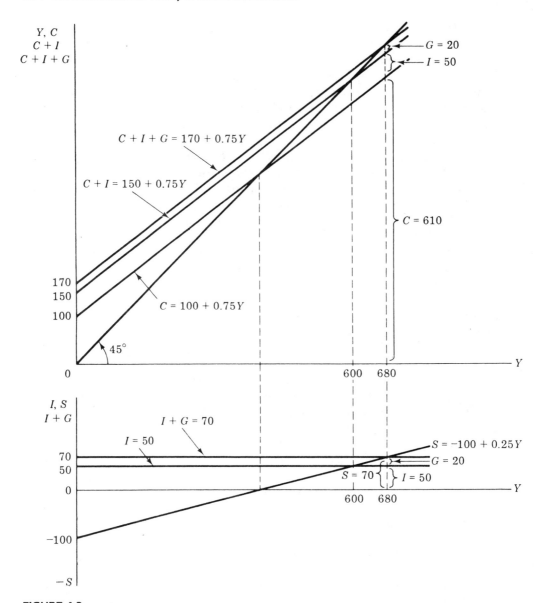

FIGURE 4.3

Government purchases and the equilibrium level of income: A numerical example

investment plus government purchases equals saving. These amounts are shown in Figure 4.3.

With government purchases equal to $20 billion, the equilibrium level of income is $680 billion. If government purchases are 0, the equilibrium level of income, obtained in Chapter 3, is only $600 billion. The increase in income is attributable to the increase in government purchases. Consequently, an increase in government purchases may be expected to result in an increase in income.

TAXES AND THE EQUILIBRIUM LEVEL OF INCOME

Next, we shall introduce net taxes or, for short, taxes. Taxes enter the model in a different way; they enter through the consumption function. A large part of national income accrues to government in the form of tax revenue. Consequently, consumption is now taken to depend on after-tax or disposable income. Disposable income, Y_d, is obtained by subtracting taxes, T, from income, Y; hence, disposable income equals income minus taxes or $Y_d = Y - T$. For the present, taxes are assumed to be exogenous. Thus, the tax function is

$$T = T_0.$$

This assumption is relaxed later.

The model is now as follows:

$$C = a + bY_d \quad \text{(where } Y_d = Y - T\text{)},$$

$$I = I_0,$$

$$G = G_0,$$

$$T = T_0.$$

The equilibrium condition is

$$\text{Aggregate supply} = \text{Aggregate demand}$$

or, alternatively,

$$I + G = S + T.$$

The model is similar to the previous model. The equilibrium level of income is determined by aggregate supply and aggregate demand. Taxes, however, are reflected in aggregate demand. If taxes are introduced, disposable income decreases and, as a result, consumption decreases. Since consumption is a component of aggregate demand, aggregate demand also decreases. Consequently, the consumption and aggregate demand functions of Figure 4.2 shift downward and the equilibrium level of income decreases. Thus, the analysis suggests that a tax increase results in a decrease in the equilibrium level of income. As discussed later, the equilibrium level of income is also determined by the $I + G$ and $S + T$ functions. Taxes are added to saving since taxes enter the model in a manner similar to saving.

To illustrate, suppose we continue with the earlier example but with taxes assumed to equal $20 billion. To find the equilibrium level of income, we again substitute into the equilibrium condition and solve for income. Since consumption equals $100 + 0.75Y_d$, investment equals $50 billion, government purchases equal $20 billion, and taxes equal $20 billion, and the equilibrium condition is aggregate supply equal to aggregate demand, we obtain, upon substitution,

$$Y = C + I + G = 100 + 0.75(Y - 20) + 50 + 20$$

or $\qquad Y = 620.$

Thus, the equilibrium level of income is $620 billion. With aggregate supply equal to $620 billion, consumption equals $550 billion, found by substituting income, $620 billion, and taxes, $20 billion, into the consumption function $C = 100 + 0.75Y_d$. With investment equal to $50 billion and government purchases equal to $20 billion, aggregate demand also equals $620 billion. Consequently, $620 billion must be the equilibrium level of income. With taxes in the model, saving, S, is no longer the difference between income, Y, and consumption, C; it is the difference between *disposable* income, Y_d, and consumption. At the equilibrium level of income, disposable income, the difference between income and taxes, is $600 billion. Since consumption is $550 billion, saving is $50 billion. Saving may also be determined by substituting income and taxes into the saving function implicit in the model, $S = -a + (1 - b)(Y - T)$. The various amounts are shown in Figure 4.4.

The new equilibrium level of income, $620 billion, is less than the previous equilibrium level, $680 billion, the level which prevailed when taxes were assumed equal to 0. With the tax increase, disposable income decreases, thereby reducing consumption. With the decrease in consumption, aggregate demand decreases; hence, the equilibrium level of income decreases. Thus, unlike an increase in government purchases, a tax increase reduces the equilibrium level of income.

Since the effect of a tax increase tends to offset the effect of an increase in government purchases, it appears, at first glance, that equal increases in government purchases and taxes have no net effect on the equilibrium level of income. As illustrated in the example, this is not so. With government purchases and taxes equal to 0, the equilibrium level of income, obtained in Chapter 3, is $600 billion. With government purchases and taxes equal to $20 billion, the equilibrium level of income is $620 billion. Thus, with the $20 billion increase in government purchases and taxes, there is a net increase in income.

The net increase in income occurs because a change in government purchases has a greater impact on aggregate demand than an equivalent change in taxes. With an increase in government purchases from 0 to $20 billion, the aggregate demand line shifts upward by $20 billion. If taxes increase from 0 to $20 billion, the immediate effect is to reduce disposable income at each level of income by $20 billion. If disposable income decreases by $20 billion, consumption decreases by $15 billion, obtained by multiplying the marginal propensity to consume, 0.75, by

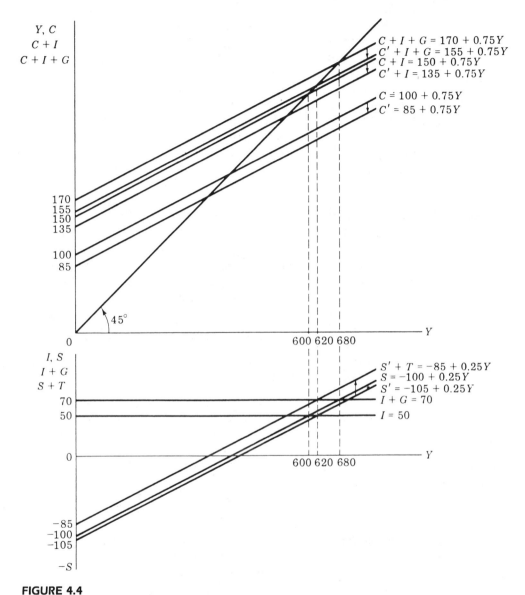

FIGURE 4.4

Taxes and the equilibrium level of income: A numerical example

the change in disposable income, $20 billion. Since consumption is $15 billion less at each level of income, aggregate demand is also $15 billion less, and the consumption and aggregate demand lines in Figure 4.4 shift downward by $15 billion. Since there is a net increase in aggregate demand, there is also a net increase in income.

As shown in Figure 4.4, the same result is obtained with the $I + G$ and $S + T$ functions. With an increase in government purchases from 0 to $20 billion, the $I + G$ function shifts upward by $20 billion. With an increase in taxes from 0 to $20 billion, disposable income is reduced by $20 billion at each level of income. With a marginal propensity to save of 0.25, saving decreases by $5 billion and the saving function shifts downward by that amount. Since the new equilibrium condition is $I + G$ equal to $S + T$, we must add $T = $20 billion to the new saving function. Consequently, the $S + T$ function is $15 billion above the original saving function.[2] The $S + T$ function intersects the $I + G$ function at the new equilibrium level of income.

THE GOVERNMENT PURCHASES AND TAX MULTIPLIERS

As just discussed, an increase in government purchases increases income, whereas a tax increase has the opposite effect. To estimate the change in income resulting from a change in one of these variables, we can derive multipliers for them. To derive the *government purchases multiplier*, for example, we use the procedure outlined in the previous chapter. The first step is to determine the equilibrium level of income corresponding to government purchases level G_0. This income level is obtained by substituting the behavioral equations into the equilibrium condition: aggregate supply equal to aggregate demand. Thus,

$$Y = C + I + G = a + bY_d + I_0 + G_0$$
$$= a + b(Y - T_0) + I_0 + G_0,$$

or, solving for income,

(**4.1**) $$Y_0 = \frac{a - bT_0 + I_0 + G_0}{1 - b}.$$

The equilibrium level of income, designated as Y_0 since it corresponds to government purchases level G_0, is shown in Figure 4.5.

Repeating the procedure for government purchases level G_1 yields

(**4.2**) $$Y_1 = \frac{a - bT_0 + I_0 + G_1}{1 - b}.$$

The equilibrium level of income is designated as Y_1 since it corresponds to government purchases level G_1. It too is shown in Figure 4.5.

Next, subtract equation (4.1) from equation (4.2) to obtain

$$Y_1 - Y_0 = \frac{G_1 - G_0}{1 - b}.$$

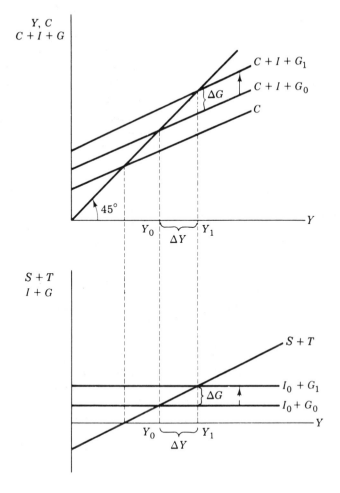

FIGURE 4.5

Equilibrium income and a change in government purchases

With $Y_1 - Y_0$ equal to ΔY, and $G_1 - G_0 = \Delta G$, we have

$$\Delta Y = \frac{1}{1 - b} \Delta G = k_G \Delta G.$$

The government purchases multiplier, k_G, is $1/(1 - b)$, the reciprocal of the marginal propensity to save. This multiplier is the same as the investment multiplier derived in Chapter 3. The investment multiplier is also $1/(1 - b)$ for this model.

If the marginal propensity to consume, b, is 0.75, the government purchases multiplier is $1/(1 - 0.75)$ or 4. Under these circumstances, a $20 billion increase in government purchases leads to an $80 billion increase in income. Thus, like an increase in investment, an increase in government purchases results in an increase in income greater than the initial increase in spending. The reason is that the increase in government purchases constitutes an increase in income, thereby triggering successive increases in consumption, which also constitute increases in income.

To illustrate, suppose the marginal propensity to consume is 0.75 and government purchases increase by $20 billion. The increase in government purchases constitutes an increase in income of $20 billion. With the increase in income, disposable income also increases by $20 billion. Since consumption is a function of disposable income, consumption increases. The increase in consumption is $15 billion, obtained by multiplying the marginal propensity to consume, 0.75, by the change in disposable income, $20 billion. Since the $15 billion increase in consumption represents an increase in income, disposable income increases, generating another increase in consumption. The increase in consumption is $11.25 billion, found by multiplying 0.75 by the increase in disposable income, $15 billion. The increase in consumption and income triggers still another increase in consumption. With an increase in disposable income of $11.25 billion, the increase in consumption is $8.4375 billion. These increases in consumption continue until the multiplier process has run its course. Since the increase in income is $80 billion and $20 billion of it is accounted for by the increase in government purchases, the remaining $60 billion is accounted for by the increases in consumption.

Before discussing the tax multiplier, we note that, in the model, government purchases are assumed to be noncompetitive with private spending. If they are competitive, the government purchases multiplier must be multiplied by the net change in spending, not the change in government purchases. For example, if government purchases increase by $20 billion and $10 billion of the increase replaces private spending, the net increase in spending is $10 billion. If the multiplier is 4, the resulting increase in income is $40 billion, not $80 billion. The possibility that government spending may "crowd out" private spending is discussed in subsequent chapters.

The *tax multiplier,* k_T, may be derived in the same manner as the government purchases multiplier; it is $-b/(1 - b)$. If the marginal propensity to consume, b, is between 0 and 1, the tax multiplier is negative and, in absolute terms, one less than the government purchases multiplier. For example, if b is 0.75, the tax multiplier is $-0.75/(1 - 0.75)$ or -3. In contrast, the government purchases multiplier is $1/(1 - 0.75)$ or 4. The minus sign indicates that a change in taxes causes a change in income in the opposite direction. Thus, a tax multiplier of -3 implies that a $20 billion *increase* in taxes results in a *decrease* in income of $60 billion; this result is obtained by multiplying the tax multiplier, -3, by the change in taxes, $20 billion.

The example indicates that a tax increase causes a decrease in income with the change in income being greater than the change in taxes. To illustrate, note that a $20 billion tax increase implies a $20 billion reduction in disposable income. If the marginal propensity to consume is 0.75, consumption decreases by $15 billion, found by multiplying 0.75 by the change in disposable income, $20 billion. With the decrease in consumption, hence income, disposable income decreases by $15 billion, which results in another decrease in consumption. These decreases in consumption continue until the multiplier process is complete. Since the decreases in consumption due to the tax increase are the same, except for sign, as in the government purchases example, the decreases in consumption total $60 billion. Since a tax increase alters only disposable income initially, the total decrease in income is $60 billion

Since the tax multiplier is, in absolute terms, smaller than the government purchases multiplier, a change in taxes will cause a smaller change in income than a change in government purchases of the same magnitude.

THE BALANCED BUDGET MULTIPLIER

Suppose government purchases and taxes change by the same amount. To determine the resulting change in income, we add the change in income due to a change in government purchases, $k_G \Delta G$, and the change in income due to a change in taxes, $k_T \Delta T$. In equation form,

$$\Delta Y = k_G \Delta G + k_T \Delta T$$

$$= \frac{1}{1 - b} \Delta G + \frac{-b}{1 - b} \Delta T.$$

Since the change in government purchases, ΔG, is assumed equal to the change in taxes, ΔT, we obtain, upon substitution,

$$\Delta Y = \left(\frac{1}{1 - b} - \frac{b}{1 - b} \right) \Delta G$$

$$= \frac{1 - b}{1 - b} \Delta G$$

$$= 1(\Delta G) = \Delta G.$$

Consequently, the change in income equals the change in government purchases. As an illustration, recall the earlier numerical example. When government purchases and taxes were 0, the equilibrium level of income was $600 billion. When government purchases and taxes were $20 billion, the equilibrium level of income was $620 billion. Consequently, the change in income was equal to the change in government purchases. The reason for the net increase in income was discussed earlier. However, the increase in income may also be explained in terms of the multiplier analysis. Earlier, we showed that a $20 billion increase in government purchases resulted in an $80 billion increase in income. Of the increase in income, $20 billion was accounted for by the increase in government purchases and $60 billion was accounted for by increases in consumption. We also showed that a $20 billion tax increase resulted in a $60 billion decrease in income. The $60 billion decrease was accounted for by decreases in consumption. Consequently, if a $20 billion increase in government purchases is financed by a $20 billion increase in taxes, the increases in consumption due to the increase in government purchases are offset by the decreases in consumption due to the tax increase. Since the increase in government purchases constitutes an increase in income, income increases by $20 billion, the amount of the increase in government purchases.

Thus, when government purchases and taxes change by the same amount, income changes by an amount equal to the change in government purchases. Since the change in income due to the change in government purchases and taxes equals the change in government purchases, the multiplier is 1. This multiplier is called the *balanced budget multiplier*. In this context, *balanced budget* means that the change in government purchases is matched by a change in taxes, not that government purchases equal taxes.

TAXES AS A FUNCTION OF INCOME

Earlier, taxes were assumed to be exogenous and, thus, independent of the level of income. Some taxes may be of this type; most are not. For example, the personal income tax, the most important source of tax revenue at the federal level, is not independent of the level of income. As personal income increases, personal tax liabilities also increase. Thus, it is necessary to relax the assumption that taxes are exogenous and assume that they vary positively with the level of income. For simplicity, we shall assume that taxes are a linear function of income. Consequently, the new tax function is

$$T = T_0 + tY \qquad (0 < t < 1).$$

The tax function implies that, as income increases, taxes increase but not by as much as income.[3] For example, suppose t, the marginal tax rate, is 0.20. If income increases by $10 billion, taxes increase by $2 billion.

The new model is

$$C = a + bY_d \qquad \text{(where } Y_d = Y - T\text{)},$$

$$I = I_0,$$

$$G = G_0,$$

$$T = T_0 + tY.$$

The equilibrium condition is

$$\text{Aggregate supply} = \text{Aggregate demand}$$

or, alternatively, $\qquad\qquad I + G = S + T.$

With taxes a function of income, the equilibrium condition is unchanged, but the multipliers and the slopes of several of the functions are altered.[4] The multipliers, which may be derived using the procedure outlined earlier, are

$$k_I^* = k_G^* = \frac{1}{1 - b + bt} = \frac{1}{1 - b(1 - t)},$$

$$k_{T_0}^* = \frac{-b}{1 - b + bt} = \frac{-b}{1 - b(1 - t)}.$$

The tax multiplier is for a change in the constant term, T_0, and may be used to determine the change in income due to a parallel shift in the tax function.[5]

With the addition of the bt term in the denominator, the multipliers are smaller (in absolute terms) than those derived previously. With taxes assumed to be exogenous, the investment and government purchases multipliers equaled $1/(1 - b)$. Therefore, if the marginal propensity to consume is 0.75, the multiplier is $1/(1 - 0.75)$ or 4. If taxes vary with income, the corresponding multiplier is $1/(1 - b + bt)$. If the marginal propensity to consume is 0.75 and the marginal tax rate, t, is 0.20, the new multiplier is $1/(1 - 0.75 + 0.75(0.20))$ or 2.5. Consequently, with a $20 billion increase in investment or government purchases, income increases by $50 billion, rather than $80 billion.

To see why the increase in income is less when taxes vary with income, consider an earlier example. With a marginal propensity to consume of 0.75, a $20 billion increase in investment generated a $15 billion increase in consumption, which, in turn, triggered a $11.25 billion increase in consumption, and so on. Ultimately, the increases in consumption totaled $60 billion, and with the $20 billion increase in investment, income increased by $80 billion. If taxes vary with income, however, the increases in consumption are less. With a marginal tax rate, t, of 0.20, taxes increase by $4 billion with the $20 billion increase in investment. With the $4 billion increase in taxes, disposable income increases by $16 billion, not $20 billion. With a $16 billion increase in disposable income, consumption increases by $12 billion, obtained by multiplying the marginal propensity to consume, 0.75, by the change in disposable income, $16 billion. The $12 billion increase in consumption is less than the $15 billion increase which occurred when taxes were assumed exogenous. With the $12 billion increase in consumption and income, taxes increase by $2.4 billion. Consequently, the increase in disposable income is only $9.6 billion. The resulting increase in consumption is $7.2 billion, obtained by multiplying 0.75 by the change in disposable income, $9.6 billion. The increase in consumption, $7.2 billion, is less than the increase in consumption, $11.25 billion, which occurred when taxes were assumed exogenous. Thus, because of the tax increase which occurs when income increases, each increase in consumption is less than the corresponding increase with taxes assumed exogenous. Consequently, the total increase in consumption is less when taxes vary with income, which implies that the total increase in income is less. In this example, the total increase in income is $50 billion. Of the increase, $20 billion is accounted for by the initial increase in investment, which implies that the remaining $30 billion is accounted for by increases in consumption. With taxes exogenous, the total increase in income is $80 billion and consists of a $20 billion increase in investment and a $60 billion increase in consumption.

With a reduction in the size of the multipliers, fluctuations in income due to fluctuations in investment or, more generally, spending, are smaller.[6] Because they reduce fluctuations in income and because they do so without action on the part of policy makers, taxes and transfer payments which vary with income are examples of *automatic stabilizers*. To illustrate the nature of these automatic stabilizers, suppose the level of economic activity declines. With reductions in output and employment, tax revenue falls and transfer payments increase. These changes prevent disposable income and, hence, consumption from decreasing as much as they would in the absence of these automatic stabilizers. Consequently, the decline in economic activity is not as severe as it otherwise would be.

FISCAL POLICY

As discussed earlier, government purchases and taxes have an impact on the aggregate demand for goods and services. Consequently, they may be altered to attain some of society's economic goals. The use of government purchases and taxes to achieve certain macroeconomic goals is called *fiscal policy*. As an example, suppose unemployment exists. Government purchases may be increased or taxes reduced so as to increase aggregate demand. With the increase in aggregate demand, income increases and unemployment decreases.

If unemployment exists, government purchases or taxes may be altered to achieve full employment. The necessary change in government purchases or taxes can be estimated with the aid of multiplier analysis. To illustrate, suppose aggregate demand is $C + I + G$ in Figure 4.6. The equilibrium level of income is Y_0. If the full employment level of income is Y_1, policy makers may wish to undertake policies designed to attain that income level.

Suppose policy makers wish to increase government purchases in order to attain income level Y_1. The first step in determining the necessary increase in government purchases is to specify the desired increase in income, ΔY. This increase in income is the difference between Y_1 and Y_0. Next, the desired increase in income, ΔY, is substituted into the relationship:

$$\Delta Y = k_G^* \Delta G.$$

Solving the equation for ΔG yields the change in government purchases necessary to achieve the desired change in income, namely $\Delta Y/k_G^*$. This change is represented by the vertical distance between the 45° line and the aggregate demand line, $C + I + G$, at income level Y_1 in Figure 4.6

To illustrate, suppose Y_0 is $750 billion and Y_1 is $800 billion. The desired

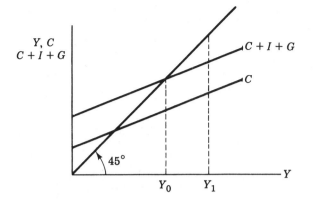

FIGURE 4.6

Fiscal policy and full employment

increase in income is $50 billion. If the marginal propensity to consume is 0.8 and the marginal tax rate is 0.25, the government purchases multiplier is 2.5. Consequently, the necessary increase in government purchases, ΔG, is $50/2.5 or $20 billion.

Instead of increasing government purchases, policy makers could reduce taxes. To achieve the desired increase in income, the necessary change in taxes must be determined. The procedure is the same as before except that the tax multiplier is used in place of the government purchases multiplier. As before, suppose ΔY is estimated to be $50 billion. If the marginal propensity to consume is 0.8 and the marginal tax rate is 0.25, the tax multiplier is -2.0. Consequently, the necessary change in taxes, ΔT, is $50/(-2.0) or $-$25 billion. Thus, taxes must decrease by $25 billion to achieve the desired increase in income. Since the tax multiplier is smaller, in absolute terms, than the government purchases multiplier, the change in taxes must be greater than the change in government purchases to achieve the same change in income. In the two examples, the changes in taxes and government purchases are $25 billion and $20 billion, respectively.

In the previous example, aggregate demand was initially less than the full employment level of output, Y_1, and unemployment existed at the equilibrium level, Y_0. Next, suppose aggregate demand is greater than the full employment level of output, Y_1, as shown in Figure 4.7. Even though aggregate demand exceeds the full employment level of output, Y_1, and the indicated equilibrium level of income is Y_0, real output cannot exceed Y_1, because Y_1 is the most that can be produced, given the nation's resources and technology. With aggregate demand greater than the full employment level of output, the price level, assumed constant in the model, has a tendency to increase. To eliminate the excess aggregate demand through fiscal policy, government purchases may be reduced or taxes increased. As before, the necessary changes in government purchases and taxes may be determined with the aid of multiplier analysis.

For example, suppose the indicated equilibrium level of income, Y_0, is $850 billion and the full employment level of income, Y_1, is $800 billion. If the marginal

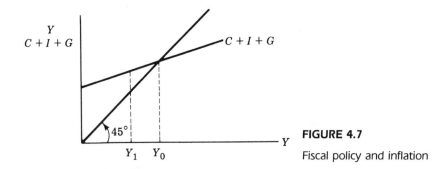

FIGURE 4.7

Fiscal policy and inflation

propensity to consume is 0.8 and the marginal tax rate is 0.25, the government purchases multiplier is 2.5 and the necessary decrease in government purchases is $20 billion. If taxes are to be increased, the necessary increase is $25 billion, given the difference between the government purchases and tax multipliers. But the $25 billion tax increase is sufficient only if the level of government purchases remains constant. If government purchases were to increase by the amount of the increase in taxes, aggregate demand would increase rather than decrease and add to the upward pressure on the price level. If government purchases were to increase at all, taxes would have to increase by more than $25 billion to offset the effect of the increase in government purchases.

In conclusion, if the level of aggregate demand is less than the full employment level of income, *expansionary* fiscal policy—an increase in government purchases or a reduction in taxes—may be used to increase aggregate demand. With the increase in aggregate demand, income and employment increase. If the level of aggregate demand is greater than the full employment level of income, *contractionary* fiscal policy—a reduction in government purchases or a tax increase—may be used to decrease aggregate demand. With the reduction in aggregate demand, the tendency for the price level to rise is alleviated. For reasons to be discussed at the end of this chapter and in Chapter 18, providing a satisfactory level of aggregate demand is more difficult than has just been described.

GOVERNMENT SURPLUSES AND DEFICITS AS A MEASURE OF FISCAL RESTRAINT

It is sometimes suggested in the press and elsewhere that budgetary deficits and surpluses show that fiscal policy is expansionary or contractionary, with a deficit indicating an expansionary policy and a surplus a contractionary policy. Since taxes and transfer payments vary automatically with income, however, deficits and surpluses are misleading as measures of fiscal restraint. For example, during a recession, tax revenue decreases and government transfer payments increase, usually creating a budgetary deficit or making the existing deficit larger. Consequently, the deficit may be due to the recession, not to expansionary fiscal policy.

To provide a better measure of the thrust of fiscal policy, another concept—the full employment budget surplus—has been developed. The *full employment budget surplus* is an estimate of what the budget result would be with given spending and tax programs at the full employment level of income. Thus, the measure is designed to be independent of the level of economic activity so that the effect of income on taxes and transfer payments is eliminated.

The full employment surplus is not as misleading as the actual budget surplus with regard to the measurement of fiscal restraint. For example, a budget deficit is likely to occur during a recession because of the effect of the automatic stabilizers. To some, the deficit signals that fiscal policy is expansionary. But because of the effects of the automatic stabilizers, we cannot be certain. With the calculation of the full employment surplus, the effects of the automatic stabilizers are eliminated and the spending and tax policies of the government are revealed. If government's spending and tax policies are expansionary, the full employment budget, like the actual budget, shows a deficit. If the government's policies are contractionary, the full employment budget shows a surplus. In this case, the full employment budget surplus is more reliable as a measure of fiscal restraint since it shows that fiscal policy is contractionary. Thus, the full employment surplus is a better guide to the thrust of fiscal policy than the actual surplus or deficit.

Although the full employment budget surplus is useful, it too is misleading for a variety of reasons. For example, suppose the full employment budget surplus is zero at a particular level of spending and taxation. Next, assume both government purchases and taxes increase by the same amount so that the full employment budget surplus remains zero. The full employment budget surplus is zero at both levels of spending, indicating the same degree of budget restraint in both cases. Yet our study of the balanced budget multiplier shows that this is not so. Even though both budgets are balanced at full employment, the budget with the greater level of government purchases is more expansionary. There are still other criticisms of the full employment surplus concept which suggest that it is of limited use. (The concept is discussed in more detail in Chapter 18.)

CONCLUDING REMARKS

In this chapter, the government sector was introduced. By varying government spending and taxes, it is possible to alter the level of aggregate demand and, hence, the equilibrium level of income. For example, if aggregate demand is insufficient to provide for full employment, government spending may be increased or taxes reduced so as to increase aggregate demand. Moreover, by using the analysis presented earlier, the amounts of spending and taxation necessary to achieve or maintain full employment may be estimated.

Unfortunately, the achievement or maintenance of full employment through fiscal policy is not as easy as it appears. First, the multipliers associated with government spending and taxes are not known with certainty. Disagreement exists about the size of the government purchases and tax multipliers, implying disagreement about the potency of fiscal policy. Some economists believe that the multipliers are large, which implies that fiscal policy is powerful. Others believe that the multipliers are small or zero, which implies that fiscal policy is impotent. This issue is discussed in subsequent chapters, and various estimates of the multipliers are given in Chapter 18.

Second, fiscal policy must be timely in order to be stabilizing. Suppose, for example, unemployment develops. By the time new legislation is approved and the new program has an impact on the economy, the problem may be inflation rather than unemployment. If so, the new program will add to the problem and thus serve to destabilize the economy rather than stabilize it. The possibility that fiscal policy (and discretionary policy in general) is destabilizing is discussed in Chapters 18 and 19.

In later chapters, government purchases, G, are assumed to be exogenous. In contrast, taxes, T, are assumed to be endogenous, with taxes varying with income in the manner described earlier. Unless otherwise stated, government purchases and taxes are defined in real terms.

NOTES

1. In the long run, the distinction between investment and government purchases is important because investment adds to or helps maintain the nation's capital stock, whereas government purchases, for the most part, do not. In this context, the distinction is not important.

2. The saving function was $-100 + 0.25Y$ originally. If taxes increase from 0 to $20 billion, the new saving function is $-100 + 0.25(Y - 20)$ or $-105 + 0.25Y$. The saving plus tax function is $-105 + 0.25Y + 20$ or $-85 + 0.25Y$.

3. Like taxes, government transfer payments vary with income, but unlike taxes, they vary inversely. One reason is that transfer payments include unemployment compensation, and as income falls, unemployment increases and more compensation is paid. In the model, the marginal tax rate, t, is assumed to reflect the responsiveness of both taxes and transfer payments to changes in income.

4. The new consumption function is $C = a + b[Y - (T_0 + tY)]$ or, after rearranging terms and factoring, $C = a - bT_0 + b(1 - t)Y$. If t is between 0 and 1, $(1 - t)$ is between 0 and 1 and the slope of the new consumption function, $b(1 - t)$, is less than the slope of the original consumption function, b. Since investment and government purchases are independent of income, the slope of the aggregate demand function is also $b(1 - t)$. With taxes a function of income, the saving and saving plus tax functions are $-a - (1 - b)T_0 + (1 - b)(1 - t)Y$ and $-a + bT_0 + [1 - b(1 - t)]Y$, respectively, If t is between 0 and 1, the slope of the new saving function, $(1 - b)(1 - t)$, is less than the slope of the original function, $(1 - b)$, and the slope of the new saving plus tax function, $[1 - b(1 - t)]$, is greater than the slope of the original function, $(1 - b)$.

5. With taxes a function of income, the balanced budget multiplier is equal to 1, but only if the ultimate change in taxes is constrained to equal the change in government purchases.

6. These fluctuations are even smaller under a progressive tax system. With a pro-

gressive tax system, the marginal tax rate increases as income increases. Consequently, the increases in consumption generated by an increase in investment are smaller, implying that the ultimate increase in income is less.

REVIEW QUESTIONS

1. Suppose we have the following model:

$$C = a + bY_d = 40 + \frac{2}{3}Y_d,$$

$$I = I_0 = 150,$$

$$G = G_0 = 70,$$

$$T = T_0 = 60.$$

a. What is the condition necessary for a level of income to be an equilibrium level?

b. Determine the equilibrium levels of income, consumption, and saving.

c. Suppose income is $600 billion. In terms of the example, explain why income tends to change until the equilibrium level is achieved.

d. Is the equilibrium level of income necessarily a full employment level? Why? Why not?

e. Suppose the full employment level of income is $690 billion.

    (1) If government wishes to achieve full employment by increasing government purchases, what is the necessary increase?

    (2) If government wishes to achieve full employment by decreasing taxes, what is the necessary decrease?

    (3) If government wishes to achieve full employment by increasing government purchases with the increase being financed by tax increases, what is the necessary increase?

2. In question 1, does intended investment equal saving at the equilibrium level of income? Why? Why not?

3. Explain how an increase in government purchases results in an increase in income greater than the initial increase in government purchases.

4. Assuming taxes are exogenous, derive the tax multiplier. Explain (in terms of economics, not mathematics) why the multiplier is

a. negative.

b. smaller, in absolute terms, than the government purchases multiplier.

5. Explain the effects of an increase in taxes, assuming

a. government purchases are constant.

   b. the increase in tax revenue results in an equal increase in government purchases.

6. Suppose government transfer payments increase and the increase is financed by a tax increase. What will be the effect on income? On the distribution of income? Under what circumstances will the change have an impact on income?

7. Suppose we have the following model:

$$C = a + bY_d = 60 + \frac{3}{4}Y_d,$$

$$I = I_0 = 160,$$

$$G = G_0 = 260,$$

$$T = T_0 + tY = 80 + \frac{1}{3}Y.$$

   a. Which variables are exogenous? endogenous?

   b. What is the condition necessary for a level of income to be an equilibrium level? Is the condition different from the condition in the model of question 1? Why? Why not?

   c. Determine the equilibrium levels of income, consumption, and saving.

   d. Show that the equilibrium condition is satisfied at the equilibrium level of income.

   e. Suppose investment increases by $10 billion. Find the resulting changes in income, consumption, and saving.

8. Explain why the government purchases (and investment) multiplier is less when taxes are a function of income than when taxes are exogenous.

9. What is fiscal policy? Explain how the multiplier analysis is useful in formulating fiscal policy.

10. Suppose the government, through fiscal policy, can provide for full employment. Does it automatically follow that it should? Defend your answer.

11. Suppose government purchases are $200 billion and the tax function is $60 + 0.2Y$. Determine the level of income at which the government's budget is balanced. Explain the effect of a change in income upon the government's budgetary position.

12. Explain why a budgetary deficit may be misleading with regard to the measurement of the thrust of fiscal policy.

SUGGESTED READING

BLINDER, ALAN S., *Fiscal Policy in Theory and Practice*. Morristown, N.J.: General Learning Press, 1973.

————, and ROBERT M. SOLOW, "Analytical Foundations of Fiscal Policy," in Alan S. Blinder and others, *The Economics of Public Finance*, pp. 3–115. Washington, D.C.: The Brookings Institution, 1974.

Economic Report of the President. Washington, D.C.: Government Printing Office, annually.

MUSGRAVE, RICHARD A., and PEGGY B. MUSGRAVE, *Public Finance in Theory and Practice* (4th ed.). New York: McGraw-Hill Book Company, 1984.

SALANT, WILLIAM A., "Taxes, Income Determination, and the Balanced Budget Theorem," *Review of Economics and Statistics*, 39 (May 1957), 152–61.

U.S. Department of the Treasury, *Treasury Bulletin*, Washington, D.C.: Government Printing Office, monthly.

5

CONSUMPTION

So far, we have assumed that consumption is a function of disposable income. It is, however, a function of other variables as well. In this chapter, we consider these variables. Before doing so, we shall consider two alternative explanations of the relationship between consumption and income. One explanation, the permanent income hypothesis, stresses that consumption is a function of permanent income, a long-run concept, while the other, the life cycle hypothesis, emphasizes that consumption is a function of net worth, current nonproperty income, and expected annual nonproperty income.

KEYNES AND THE CONSUMPTION FUNCTION

The consumption function, the relationship between consumption and income, is largely a Keynesian contribution. Before the 1930s, most economists stressed the relationship between consumption (or saving) and the interest rate, a relationship discussed later. Keynes postulated that consumption depends mainly on income.[1]

In regard to the relationship, he argued that consumption increases as income increases but by an amount less than the increase in income. Thus, Keynes assumed that the marginal propensity to consume is greater than zero and less than unity. Keynes also argued that the *average propensity to consume,* the fraction of income consumed, decreases as income increases. For example, in Figure 5.1, the average propensity to consume, or APC, at income level Y_1 equals C_1 divided by Y_1. If C_1 equals $600 billion and Y_1 equals $800 billion, the APC is 0.75.

Mathematically, the APC equals C/Y. The APC also equals the slope of a line drawn from the origin to the combination of income and consumption in question. For example, at income level Y_1, the APC equals C_1/Y_1 or, alternatively, the slope of 0A, a line drawn from the origin to point (Y_1, C_1). If income increases to Y_2, the APC equals C_2/Y_2 or, alternatively, the slope of 0B. Since the slope of 0B is less than that of 0A, the APC at income level Y_2 must be less than the APC at income level Y_1.

The MPC and APC are often confused. The MPC equals $\Delta C/\Delta Y$; the APC equals C/Y. Thus, the MPC is the slope of the consumption function, whereas the APC is the slope of the line drawn from the origin to the combination of income and consumption in question. In Figure 5.1, the MPC is constant and less than the APC. Moreover, as income increases, the APC declines. In general, the MPC is not equal to the APC. Assuming the consumption function to be linear, the MPC equals the APC if and only if the consumption function passes through the origin.

The consumption function in Figure 5.1 reflects Keynes's assumptions about the relationship between consumption and income. Specifically, the function is drawn so that the marginal propensity to consume is positive but less than 1 and the average propensity to consume decreases as income increases.

Early Keynesians were enthusiastic about Keynes's innovation for two reasons. First, if a stable relationship between consumption and income exists, the amounts of investment, government purchases, and taxes necessary to provide for full employment may be determined. For example, suppose Y_2 represents the full

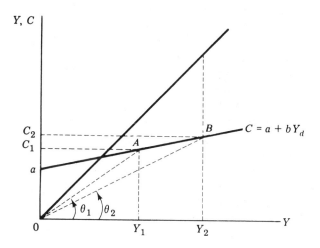

FIGURE 5.1

The consumption function and the full employment level of income employment level of income in Figure 5.1, and $C = a + bY_d$ represents the consumption function for a given level of taxes. The amounts of investment and government purchases necessary to achieve the full employment level of income Y_2 are represented by the distance between the 45° line and the consumption function. As a consequence, these amounts can be estimated. Policy makers can then take steps to achieve those levels.

Second, early Keynesians were enthusiastic because the initial empirical studies appeared to confirm the relationship. These early tests were based on cross-sectional budget studies. For groups of families, data were collected on size and disposition of income for a given period of time. Almost without exception, these budget studies show a relationship between family consumption and family income like that which Keynes postulated for the economy. A straight line fitted to the data by regression analysis or some other statistical technique intersects the vertical axis at a positive level of consumption and has a slope ranging from 0.6 to 0.8. Thus, the consumption–income relationship derived on the basis of budget studies appears to be consistent with the relationship postulated by Keynes.

Despite this evidence, it is not altogether clear that we can transfer estimates based on budget study data to the aggregate consumption function in which Keynes was interested. The cross-sectional data show how family consumption varies as family income varies. Keynes's hypothesis, however, relates to how aggregate consumption varies as aggregate income varies. Since aggregate income is constant for the time span considered by budget studies, the budget studies shed little or no light on how aggregate consumption varies in response to variations in aggregate income. In fact, the aggregate relationship will mirror the budget studies relationship only under certain restrictive conditions. Even so, the same type of relationship appears in the aggregate data, provided that the study is confined to several decades or less.

After World War II, several occurrences cast some doubt on the usefulness and validity of the Keynesian consumption function. First, economists using Keynesian consumption functions were unsuccessful in predicting postwar consumption. Their estimates were much less than the actual amounts. Second, in 1946, Simon Kuznets published data for the United States between 1869 and 1938 which showed the function to be linear; however, the line was of the form $C = b^*Y$.[2] In other words, a was approximately zero, contrary to the earlier assumption, which implies that the consumption function passes through the origin. Moreover, b^* was approximately 0.9, decidedly higher than reported earlier. This implies that the new function is steeper than originally assumed.

Thus, based on the empirical evidence, there appear to be two consumption functions: (1) the *short-run* or *cyclical consumption function* based on budget study data and short-run aggregate data; and (2) the *long-run* or *secular consumption function* based on Kuznets's data. The short-run consumption function, shown in Figure 5.2, intersects the vertical axis at a positive amount of consumption and is relatively flat. The long-run consumption function, also shown in Figure 5.2, passes through the origin and is relatively steep. In both cases, the marginal propensity

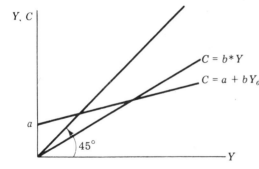

FIGURE 5.2

The short- and long-run consumption functions

to consume is constant. In the case of the short-run consumption function, the average propensity to consume decreases as income increases, whereas in the case of the long-run consumption function, the average propensity to consume is constant.

A number of hypotheses have been offered to explain consumer behavior and, at the same time, to reconcile the short- and long-run consumption functions. We now examine the two hypotheses: the permanent income and life cycle hypotheses.

THE PERMANENT INCOME HYPOTHESIS

Keynes argued that current consumption depends on current income. From a theoretical standpoint, however, consumption depends on more than current income. According to the *permanent income hypothesis*, as developed by Milton Friedman, current consumption depends on current and anticipated future income.[3] This view is intuitively plausible. For example, if a household receives current income which is appreciably less than it anticipates in the future, the household is likely to consume more than is suggested by the level of its current income.

Friedman's permanent income hypothesis is based on three fundamental propositions. First, a household's actual income, y, and consumption, c, in a particular period may be separated into permanent and transitory components. In other words,

$$y = y_p + y_t$$

and

$$c = c_p + c_t,$$

where the subscripts p and t stand for permanent and transitory, respectively.

According to Friedman, *permanent income* is the amount a household can consume while keeping its wealth intact. By *wealth*, Friedman means the present value of the income expected to accrue to the household in the future. Since permanent income is, in part, based on the household's anticipated future income, it is a long-run concept.

Since permanent income depends on future income, it cannot be measured directly. In his empirical work, Friedman regards permanent income as a weighted average of current and past incomes, with the current year weighted more heavily and prior years weighted less and less heavily. Since permanent income is a weighted average of current and past incomes, it is less variable than current income.

Transitory income may be interpreted as unanticipated income; it may be either positive or negative. For example, farmers may receive more income than anticipated because of unusually good weather, or they may receive less income because of exceptionally bad weather. Similarly, an individual may earn less than anticipated because of illness. If a household's transitory income is positive, its actual income exceeds its permanent income. On the other hand, if its transitory income is negative, the reverse is true. By its nature, transitory income is regarded as temporary.

According to Friedman, a household's actual consumption may also be divided into permanent and transitory components. *Permanent consumption* is consumption determined by permanent income. *Transitory consumption* may be interpreted as unanticipated consumption, such as unexpected doctor bills, unusually high (or low) heating bills, and the like. Transitory consumption, like transitory income, may be either positive or negative. If it is positive, a household's actual consumption is greater than its permanent consumption. If it is negative, the opposite is true. Like transitory income, transitory consumption is regarded as temporary.

Second, Friedman assumes that permanent consumption is a constant proportion, β, of permanent income. In equation form,

(5.1) $$c_p = \beta y_p \qquad (0 < \beta < 1).$$

Although β is independent of the absolute level of permanent income, it depends on the interest rate and a number of other variables which will be discussed.

Third, Friedman assumes that there is no relationship between transitory and permanent income, between transitory and permanent consumption, and between transitory consumption and transitory income. The first assumption implies that transitory income is random with respect to permanent income; the second implies that transitory consumption is independent of permanent consumption. The last assumption—that transitory consumption is random with respect to transitory income—implies that the marginal propensity to consume from transitory income is zero. This means that a household fortunate enough to receive positive transitory income will not alter its consumption (which is based on permanent income). Instead, the household will save the additional income. Similarly, if a household is unlucky enough to receive negative transitory income, it will not reduce its consumption. Rather, it will reduce its saving.[4]

Based on the three propositions, a household is assumed to plan its consumption on the basis of its permanent income with permanent consumption equal to a constant proportion, β, of its permanent income. Consequently, under the permanent income hypothesis, the basic relationship between consumption and income is depicted by the long-run consumption function. In the short run, however, the basic relationship is obscured by transitory consumption and transitory income. In fact, in the short run, the relationship between consumption and income appears to be that of the short-run consumption function discussed earlier.

To reconcile the short- and long-run consumption functions using the permanent income hypothesis, consider the economy over the business cycle. As discussed earlier, the nation's output increases over time. But output does not grow at a steady rate; it often reaches a peak and then declines. These fluctuations in output and economic activity in general are called *business cycles*. When output is at its highest level, the business cycle is said to be at its *peak*. When output is at its lowest level, the business cycle is at its *trough*.

Since permanent income is a long-run concept, it does not vary to the same degree as actual income over the business cycle. Consequently, when the business cycle is at its peak, actual income is greater than permanent income. Since actual income is greater than permanent income, transitory income is positive. Since the marginal propensity to consume from transitory income is zero, households do not alter their expenditure plans. Consequently, consumption is not proportional to actual income at the peak; it is less than proportional, thereby producing a point on the short-run consumption function which is below the long-run consumption function. To illustrate, suppose Y' in Figure 5.3 represents income at the peak of the business cycle. With permanent income less than actual income at the peak, assume that Y'_p represents the corresponding level of permanent income. Since

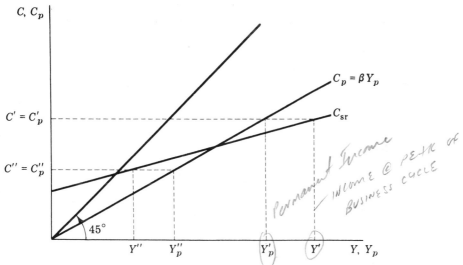

FIGURE 5.3

The permanent income hypothesis and the consumption function consumption is determined by permanent income, consumption is $C' = C'_p$ at permanent income Y'_p.[5] Inasmuch as the short-run consumption function is based on actual consumption and income, (Y', C') is a point on the short-run consumption function.

At the trough, the situation is reversed. Actual income is less than permanent income. Since actual income is less than permanent income, transitory income is negative. Since the marginal propensity to consume from transitory income is zero, households do not reduce their consumption. Instead, they reduce their saving. As a result, consumption is more than proportional to actual income, thereby producing a point on the short-run consumption function which is above the long-run consumption function. To illustrate, suppose Y'' and Y''_p represent the actual and permanent levels of income, respectively, at the trough. Since consumption is determined by permanent income, consumption is $C'' = C''_p$ and (Y'', C'') is another point on the short-run consumption function.

In simplest terms, the short-run consumption function, a relationship between actual consumption and actual income, exists because of deviations between actual and permanent income. Since permanent income is a long-run concept, actual income varies to a greater degree than permanent income. Inasmuch as consumption is based on permanent income, consumption varies to a smaller degree than actual income. These smaller variations in consumption produce the relatively flat consumption function that is observed in the short run.

THE LIFE CYCLE HYPOTHESIS

The *life cycle hypothesis*, as postulated by Albert Ando and Franco Modigliani, assumes that the welfare of an individual consumer is a function of his current and future consumption.[6] The individual acts to maximize his welfare; in doing so, however, he is constrained by the resources at his disposal which consist of the individual's net worth, current nonproperty income, and discounted value of future nonproperty income. For the individual, current consumption will be a function of his resources and the interest rate, with the exact nature of the relationship depending on the age of the individual. To obtain an aggregate consumption function, Ando and Modigliani first aggregate over all individuals of a given age and then over all ages.

By making various assumptions, Ando and Modigliani arrive at the following (aggregate) consumption function:

(5.2) $$C_t = \alpha_1 A_{t-1} + \alpha_2 Y_t + \alpha_3 Y_t^E.$$

The variable C_t is consumption in time period t; it consists of the rental value of the stock of consumer durable goods and expenditures on nondurable goods and services. (Consumption is defined in the same manner in the permanent income hypothesis.) With regard to the other variables, A_{t-1} represents net worth in period

$t-1$; Y_t, nonproperty income in period t; and Y_t^E, expected annual nonproperty income. All variables are measured in nominal terms.

Ando and Modigliani estimate this relationship. Since the variable Y_t^E, expected annual nonproperty income, is not observable, they could not estimate the parameters directly. Ando and Modigliani use several (indirect) approaches. In their most elementary formulation, they assume that expected annual nonproperty income, Y_t^E is the same as, or proportional to, current nonproperty income, Y_t. Under this formulation, equation (5.2) becomes

(5.3) $$C_t = \alpha_1 A_{t-1} + \alpha Y_t.$$

Ando and Modigliani estimate α_1 and α to be about 0.06 and 0.7, respectively. These results indicate that consumption is positively related to net worth, current nonproperty income, and, by implication, expected annual nonproperty income.

As in the case of the permanent income hypothesis, the life cycle hypothesis may be used to explain the relationship between the short- and long-run consumption functions. As before, assume that expected annual nonproperty income is the same as, or proportional to, current nonproperty income. Under this assumption, equation (5.3) is the relevant consumption function. This relationship, with net worth assumed constant, is depicted in Figure 5.4. For example, net worth in period 1 is A_0 so that the intercept of the relevant consumption function, $C = \alpha_1 A_0 + \alpha Y_1$, is $\alpha_1 A_0$. Should income vary in period 1, consumption will also vary

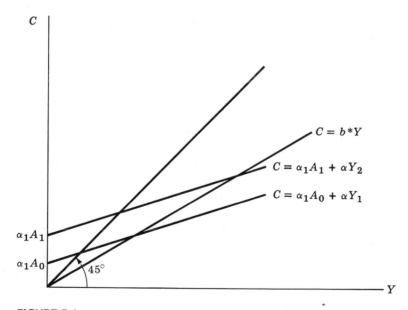

FIGURE 5.4

The life cycle hypothesis and the consumption function

as shown by a movement along the relatively flat consumption function, $C = \alpha_1 A_0 + \alpha Y_1$.

As households save, however, net worth increases. Consequently, net worth in period 2 will be A_1 and, with the increase in the intercept from $\alpha_1 A_0$ to $\alpha_1 A_1$, the relevant consumption function becomes $C = \alpha_1 A_1 + \alpha Y_2$. Once again, should income vary in period 2, consumption will also vary as shown by a movement along the relatively flat consumption function, $C = \alpha_1 A_1 + \alpha Y_2$. Thus, with net worth constant, the relevant consumption function is the short-run consumption function. As time passes, however, net worth increases and it is these increases, combined with the normal increases in income that occur over time, that trace out the long-run consumption function.

POLICY IMPLICATIONS OF THE PERMANENT INCOME AND LIFE CYCLE HYPOTHESES

The implications of the permanent income and life cycle hypotheses differ from those of Keynes's hypothesis, which makes no distinction between permanent and transitory income or between current and expected annual nonproperty income. Consequently, households are assumed to react in the same manner regardless of the type of increase in income. According to the permanent income hypothesis, households base their consumption on permanent rather than actual income. Consequently, they will react in different ways, depending on whether they regard an increase in income as permanent or transitory. If households receive an increase in income which they interpret as an increase in permanent income, they will increase their consumption by an amount proportional to the increase in income. On the other hand, if households interpret the increase in income as transitory, they will not increase their consumption at all. In terms of multiplier analysis, this means that since the marginal propensity to consume from permanent income is high (Friedman estimated it to be 0.88), the multipliers (assuming the change is viewed as permanent) will be relatively large, larger in fact than suggested by the short-run consumption function. Similarly, since the marginal propensity to consume from transitory income is zero, the multipliers (assuming the change is viewed as temporary) will be small or even zero.

If Keynes's view is correct, it makes no difference whether a change in taxes is permanent or temporary. A tax rebate or a temporary change in taxes may be desirable in order to provide prompt and temporary stimulus or restraint to the economy. For rebates or temporary tax changes to be effective, however, a relatively large change in consumption must occur within a short time span following the rebate or change in taxes. The Keynesian consumption function satisfies both requirements. The permanent income and life cycle hypotheses, on the other hand, predict a small and slow adjustment.[7]

In the United States, the fiscal authorities have used tax rebates and income tax surcharges on several occasions. In 1975, a tax rebate was given. The rebate was designed to increase consumption, thereby stimulating the economy. In 1968, a temporary 10 percent income tax surcharge was imposed. The tax increase was designed to reduce consumption or at least slow its rate of increase, thereby reducing inflation. Tax rebates have been proposed upon other occasions.

Franco Modigliani and Charles Steindel have examined the effects of the 1975 tax rebate upon consumption.[8] In general, they found that the rebate resulted in appreciably smaller increases in consumption than those associated with a permanent tax reduction of equivalent size. They also found that the increases in consumption occurred less rapidly.

Modigliani and Steindel also considered the effects of the 1968 income tax surcharge upon consumption. They believe that the surcharge, in effect for most of the 1968–70 period, reduced consumption. The reduction, however, was appreciably less than would have occurred with a permanent tax increase of equivalent size. As a result, the surcharge was relatively ineffective in curbing inflation.[9]

Thus, the permanent income and life cycle hypotheses and the empirical evidence suggest that rebates and temporary changes in taxes are relatively ineffective in altering consumption and hence aggregate demand. Since the empirical evidence also suggests that rebates and temporary tax changes are not completely ineffective, such actions may play a useful role in stabilizing the economy. For one thing, Congress may be more willing to legislate temporary tax changes than permanent changes. For another, the smaller multipliers associated with rebates and temporary tax changes can be offset by making the rebates or tax changes larger.

CONSUMPTION AND OTHER VARIABLES

Income plays a very important role in theories of consumer behavior; it is the principal determinant of consumption. Consumption is, however, determined by other factors as well. In this section, we consider the most important of these other factors.

Tastes

Individuals differ in their attitudes toward thrift. In part, the differences may be traced to differences in age, family composition, and the like; these differences are discussed later. Even among similar individuals (same age, and so on) with identical incomes, some consume more than others because of differences in their attitudes toward thrift.

Despite differences in individual attitudes, an aggregate consumption function may be derived for the economy. This function will be based on a given set of consumer attitudes. If people suddenly change their attitudes toward thrift, the aggregate consumption function will be altered. For example, if people decide to save a larger proportion of their income, the consumption function will shift downward.

There is little or no evidence to suggest that individual attitudes toward thrift change appreciably over time. True, society occasionally experiences fads, such as the hula hoop and skateboard crazes. These fads are usually shortlived and involve items that account for only a small fraction of family budgets. Consequently, they do not represent changes in individuals' attitudes toward thrift.

Socioeconomic Factors

Consumption is also influenced by a host of socioeconomic factors, including age, education, occupation, and family composition. In regard to age, individual and family income characteristically rises from the youngest age groups to a peak in the middle age groups and then fall in the older age groups. The proportion of income saved displays a similar pattern. It increases from the youngest age groups to a maximum in the middle age groups and then declines in the older age groups. This implies that the proportion of income consumed is relatively high for those in the youngest and oldest age groups and low for those in the middle age groups.

Besides consuming a higher proportion of their income, those in the youngest age groups also buy a different collection of goods and services than those in other age groups. For example, people in the youngest age groups generally spend more for consumer durables than those in older age groups.

Despite the differences in consumption patterns, an aggregate consumption function may be obtained by summing over the various age groups. This aggregate relationship will be based on a given age distribution for the population, and should the age distribution change, the aggregate relationship will be altered.

In the short run, the age distribution is constant or approximately so. In the long run, that may not be true; it depends, for example, on birth rates. All other things equal, a high birth rate implies a relatively young population. Should birth rates decline as they have in the United States, the average age of the population will increase. Given the difference in proportion of income consumed between age groups, the increase in the average age of the population alters the aggregate consumption function. The increase in average age will also increase the demand for some goods and services and reduce the demand for other goods and services owing to the differences in consumption patterns between age groups.

Although changes in the age distribution of society have important implications, we need not concern ourselves since the age distribution changes very little in the short run, and we are concentrating on short-run theories of income determination.

The effects of other socioeconomic variables, such as education and occupation, on consumption may be considered in much the same way as the effects of age, but since these factors do not vary appreciably in the short run, they are not important short-run determinants of consumption. Consequently, we go on to consider other determinants of consumption.

Wealth

Wealth, either explicitly or implicitly, is often included in the aggregate consumption function as a determinant of consumption. For example, it plays several roles in Friedman's permanent income hypothesis. First, permanent income is defined in reference to wealth. As discussed previously, permanent income is the amount a household could consume while maintaining its wealth intact. Consequently, although wealth does not appear explicitly in Friedman's consumption function, $C_p = \beta Y_p$, it is included implicitly in the permanent income variable.

Second, wealth, or rather the ratio of permanent income derived from nonhuman wealth to permanent income, helps to determine the ratio, β, of permanent consumption to permanent income. According to Friedman, people save in part to provide a reserve for emergencies, and some forms of wealth are better suited as a reserve than others. In particular, he believes nonhuman wealth (tangible assets) is a better reserve than human wealth (which reflects the individual's prospective earnings from labor) because it is easier to borrow on the basis of nonhuman wealth than prospective earnings. Consequently, the greater the fraction of permanent income derived from nonhuman wealth, the less need there is to save, and therefore the greater the ratio, β, of permanent consumption to permanent income. In the short run, the fraction of permanent income derived from nonhuman wealth is constant or approximately so.

Wealth, or net worth, is also an important determinant of consumption according to the life cycle hypothesis. As postulated by Ando and Modigliani, net worth (defined so as to exclude human wealth) is one of the variables appearing in the consumption function. Based on their estimate of $\alpha_1 = 0.06$, a \$100 increase in net worth will result in an increase in consumption of \$6.00.

Some economists have included *liquid assets*, a component of wealth, rather than wealth in their consumption function. The inclusion is often justified on the grounds that liquid assets are a proxy (substitute) variable for wealth and that data on liquid asset holdings are easier to obtain than data on wealth. Arnold Zellner, D. S. Huang, and L. C. Chau attempt to justify the inclusion of liquid assets along different lines.[10] They state that liquid assets are a barometer for many short-run factors which affect consumption. For example, a household may plan to buy a durable good requiring a large expenditure. The household may accumulate liquid assets in anticipation of the purchase. If it does, the buildup of liquid assets foreshadows the actual expenditure. On the basis of their empirical results, Zellner and the others conclude that liquid assets play an important role in determining consumption.

More recently, some economists have argued that liquid assets, or rather the lack of them, act as a constraint on consumer spending.[11] The permanent income and life cycle hypotheses imply that if households experience a temporary reduction in income, they will dissave or borrow if necessary to maintain their spending. If they do, little or no reduction in consumption will occur. On the other hand, some households, particularly low-income ones, may lack the necessary liquid assets to dissave or to serve as collateral when borrowing. If a large number of households face such a liquidity constraint, consumption will decrease significantly even if the reduction in income is temporary. This implies that tax rebates or temporary tax changes will have a greater impact on consumption and, hence, aggregate demand than implied by the permanent income and life cycle hypotheses. Unfortunately from the standpoint of both the theory of consumer behavior and policy, no general agreement exists as to the importance of the liquidity constraint.[12]

Government Debt

Many economists believe that (interest-bearing) government debt is part of the nation's wealth or net worth. If it is, an increase in government debt brought about by, say, a reduction in taxes will stimulate consumption, hence, aggregate demand. This view has been challenged by Robert J. Barro, among others.[13] Barro argues that the increase in (interest-bearing) government debt necessary to finance the deficit which occurs as a result of a tax cut implies an equal and offsetting increase in tax liabilities. As the federal government issues debt (borrows), it is obligated to pay interest on the debt and to pay off the debt as it matures. Thus, if people correctly perceive the increase in tax liabilities, no increase in wealth will occur with the increase in government debt because the increase implies an equal and offsetting increase in tax liabilities.

If people believe that an increase in government debt generates an equal and offsetting increase in tax liabilities, a change in taxes will have no impact on consumption, contrary to the model of Chapter 4. According to that model, a tax cut (for example) will increase consumption through its impact on disposable income. On the other hand, if the tax cut is financed by issuing government debt and households perceive that the debt generates an equal and offsetting increase in tax liabilities, they will believe that they are no better off than before and no increase in consumption will occur. Thus, according to this view, a tax cut, financed in the manner described, has no impact on consumption and, hence, aggregate demand. If this view is correct, fiscal policy will be much less powerful than the analysis of Chapter 4 suggests. (We shall return to the implications of this view for fiscal policy in Chapter 18.)

Because of its implications for consumer behavior, various economists have tested the extent to which households perceive government debt to be wealth. Unfortunately, the results of these studies differ. Some studies, including those by Levis A. Kochin, J. Ernest Tanner, John J. Seater, Roger C. Kormendi, and John J. Seater and Roberto S. Mariano, support the view that households, in whole or part, perceive that an increase in government debt generates an equal and offsetting increase in tax liabilities.[14] Other studies, including those by Jess B. Yawitz and

Laurence H. Meyer, Willem H. Buiter and James Tobin, Martin Feldstein, and Marcelle Arak, support the opposite view.[15] Thus, despite the importance of the issue, no consensus has emerged.

Capital Gains

It has been argued that capital gains (or losses) affect aggregate consumption. Presumably, a capital gain, by increasing the individual's net worth, would induce additional consumption, whereas a capital loss would reduce consumption. A number of economists have investigated the relationship with mixed results. John J. Arena found no relationship between aggregate consumption and stock market capital gains and losses over the period 1946–64.[16] He reached this conclusion although stock market prices fluctuated considerably over the period, producing large capital gains and losses, with capital gains predominating. Arena argued that there is no relationship between aggregate consumption and capital gains because most stock is held by people with high incomes and their consumption is insensitive to short-term movements in stock prices.

In contrast, Kul B. Bhatia found a significant relationship between aggregate consumption and capital gains.[17] Bhatia's study included capital gains from the stock market, real estate, and livestock. His results indicate a positive relationship between aggregate consumption and capital gains, both accrued and realized.

Barry Bosworth also found a positive relationship between consumption and capital gains.[18] He argued that the relationship is weak, however, and that only a relatively large change in stock market prices would appreciably alter consumption. Bosworth believes that the decline in stock market prices in 1973 and 1974 reduced consumption, thereby adding to the recessionary pressures in those years.

Frederic Mishkin has found evidence of a stronger relationship between consumption and stock prices.[19] He also found that declining stock prices contributed significantly to the severity of the 1973–75 recession. Mishkin estimated that about half of the reduction in aggregate demand which occurred during the period was due to declines in stock prices.

Despite recent studies which purport to show that consumption is related to stock prices, there is disagreement about the importance of the relationship. Perhaps consumption and stock market prices are both related to a third variable (for example, consumer confidence). If so, no relationship exists between consumption and stock prices. In view of this possibility, there is more uncertainty about the relationship than is suggested by the recent studies.

The Interest Rate

The classical economists assumed that consumption was a function of the rate of interest. In particular, they believed that an increase in the interest rate encourages saving and discourages consumption. Later economists have been skeptical on both theoretical and empirical grounds. An increase in the interest rate may encourage saving, thereby discouraging consumption, but it may have the opposite effect. If an individual saves in order to have a fixed amount at retirement or at some other time, she will find that, at a higher rate of interest, she can save less of her current income and still reach her goal because, with a higher interest rate, her savings will earn a higher return and thus grow more rapidly. Consequently, she can afford to consume more of her current income. If society is composed primarily of "target" savers, an increase in the rate of interest will reduce saving and increase consumption, contrary to the view of the classical economists.

Empirically, the relationship between consumption and the interest rate is also unclear. Michael J. Boskin found a relatively strong relationship between consumption and the interest rate.[20] In terms of the relationship between saving and the interest rate, he believes that the interest elasticity of saving is about 0.4, implying that a 10.0 percent increase in the interest rate results in a 4.0 percent increase in saving. Although he used a variety of equations, estimation techniques, and definitions of the relevant variables, he obtained approximately the same results.

In a subsequent study, E. Philip Howrey and Saul H. Hymans offered various criticisms of Boskin's study, including his definitions of the appropriate variables.[21] To illustrate, they object to his definition of the real after-tax rate of return. (In determining how much to save, the relevant variable is the expected real after-tax rate of return, not merely the interest rate.) For this and other reasons, they argue that Boskin's results are unreliable. Based on their empirical work, Howrey and Hymans conclude that no relationship exists between saving and the interest rate.

Various other studies of the relationship between saving and the interest rate have been published with some supporting the view that saving is positively related to the interest rate and with others supporting the view that saving is unrelated to the interest rate. In addition to presenting new empirical evidence, Thorvaldur Gylfason has surveyed many of these studies and concludes that the bulk of them (including his own) support the view that saving is positively related to the interest rate.[22]

The Price Level

In Chapter 4, it was assumed that real consumption is a function of real income. Therefore, an increase in nominal income accompanied by an equal increase in the price level will not alter real consumption. If, in fact, households do not alter their real consumption when faced with equiproportionate increases in nominal income and the price level (with real wealth assumed constant), they are said to be *free of money illusion*. On the other hand, if they do alter their real consumption, they are said to be *experiencing money illusion*.

For years, economists assumed that consumers were free of money illusion, partly because, from a theoretical standpoint, money illusion implies irrationality and partly because early empirical studies found little evidence of money illusion. In 1969, however, William H. Branson and Alvin K. Klevorick published a study which purported to show that money illusion exists in regard to the consumption function.[23] Using quarterly data for 1955–65, they found that the price level plays a significant role in determining the level of per capita real consumption in the United States. In particular, they found that real consumption increases when the consumer price index rises with real income and wealth constant. This suggests that when prices and the nominal values of income and wealth increase proportionately, households pay more attention to the increase in the nominal value of income and wealth and increase their consumption more than proportionately. In another study, Raymond M. Johnson found evidence of money illusion in the United States, but for only part of the 1940–69 period, implying that the Branson–Klevorick result does not hold for all time periods.[24]

In a related study, F. Thomas Juster and Paul Wachtel considered the effects of anticipated and unanticipated inflation on consumption.[25] From a theoretical standpoint, if households anticipate inflation, they should increase current consumption. Juster and Wachtel found evidence to the contrary. They conclude that anticipated inflation has a small negative effect on consumption, whereas unanticipated inflation has a large negative effect. Juster and Wachtel believe their results support the view that a rise in prices (anticipated or not) will adversely affect consumer confidence and hence consumption. Subsequent studies indicate that the relationship between consumption and inflation is more complex (and ambiguous) than just indicated.[26]

CONCLUDING REMARKS

We have surveyed a number of determinants of consumption. Of these, income (or some variant thereof) is clearly the most important. Consequently, we shall concentrate on the relationship between consumption and income in the following chapters. We shall, however, have occasion to consider further the relationship between consumption and wealth. Also, we shall assume the basic relationship between consumption and income to be the consumption function outlined in Chapter 4. We do so because of the complexity involved in incorporating the permanent income or life cycle hypotheses into the theoretical framework.[27] At the same time, we must keep in mind that this version of the consumption function has a number of shortcomings. In Chapter 17, which deals with economic growth, we use the long-run consumption function since growth is a long-run concept.

NOTES _____

1. John Maynard Keynes, *The General Theory of Employment, Interest, and Money* (New York: Harcourt, Brace and Company, 1936), p. 96. Keynes also discussed other determinants of consumption.

2. Simon Kuznets, *National Product since 1869* (New York: National Bureau of Economic Research, 1946), p. 119. See also Simon Kuznets, "Proportion of Capital Formation to National Product," *American Economic Review*, 42 (May 1952), 507–26.

3. Milton Friedman, *A Theory of the Consumption Function* (New York: National Bureau of Economic Research, 1957).

4. Empirically, much evidence suggests that the marginal propensity to consume from transitory income is positive. At the same time, this evidence also suggests that the marginal propensity to consume from transitory income is less than the marginal propensity to consume from permanent income. Consequently, it is useful to distinguish between the two types of income.

5. The existence of transitory consumption further obscures the true relationship. Since transitory consumption is random, however, there is no reason to take account of it in the explanation.

6. Albert Ando and Franco Modigliani, "The 'Life Cycle' Hypothesis of Saving: Aggregate Implications and Tests," *American Economic Review*, 53 (March 1963), 55–84. See also Modigliani and Richard Brumberg, "Utility Analysis and the Consumption Function: An Interpretation of Cross-Section Data," in *Post-Keynesian Economics*, ed. Kenneth K. Kurihara (New Brunswick, N.J.: Rutgers University Press, 1954), pp. 388–436; and Modigliani, "The Life Cycle Hypothesis of Saving Twenty Years Later," in *Contemporary Issues in Economics*, ed. Michael Parkin (Manchester: Manchester University Press, 1975), pp. 2–36. These and other articles on the life cycle hypothesis authored or coauthored by Modigliani are reprinted in Andrew Abel (ed.), *The Collected Papers of Franco Modigliani*, vol. 2 (Cambridge, Mass.: The MIT Press, 1980).

7. As indicated by equation (5.2), a larger change in consumption occurs when both current and expected annual nonproperty income change than when only current nonproperty income changes.

8. Franco Modigliani and Charles Steindel, "Is a Tax Rebate an Effective Tool for Stabilization Policy?" *Brookings Papers on Economic Activity,* no. 1 (1977), 175–203. See also Alan S. Blinder, "Temporary Income Taxes and Consumer Spending," *Journal of Political Economy*, 89 (February 1981), 26–53.

9. This conclusion is widely shared by economists. See, for example, Robert Eisner, "What Went Wrong?" *Journal of Political Economy,* 79 (May–June 1971), 632. Arthur M. Okun has argued to the contrary. See Okun, "The Personal Tax Surcharge and Consumer Demand, 1968–70," *Brookings Papers on Economic Activity,* no. 1 (1971), 167–212. For comments on Okun's view, see William L. Springer, "Did the 1968 Surcharge Really Work?" *American Economic Review,* 65 (September 1975), 644–59. See also, Okun, "Did the 1968 Surcharge Really Work?: Comment," *American Economic Review,* 67 (March 1977), 166–69; and Springer, "Did the 1968 Surcharge Really Work?: Reply," *American Economic Review,* 67 (March 1977), 170–72.

10. They define *liquid assets* as consumers' holdings of currency, demand and time deposits, savings and loan association shares, and U.S. saving bonds. A. Zellner, D. S. Huang, and L. C. Chau, "Further Analysis of the Short-run Consumption Function with Emphasis on the Role of Liquid Assets," *Econometrica,* 33 (July 1965), 573.

11. See, for example, James Tobin, *Asset Accumulation and Economic Activity* (Chicago: University of Chicago Press, 1980), pp. 57–58.

12. For a recent study and references to earlier ones, see Fumio Hayashi, "The Effect of Liquidity Constraints on Consumption: A Cross-Sectional Analysis," *Quarterly Journal of Economics,* 100 (February 1985), 183–206.

13. Robert J. Barro, "Are Government Bonds Net Wealth?" *Journal of Political Economy,* 82 (November–December 1974), 1095–1117.

14. Levis A. Kochin, "Are Future Taxes Anticipated by Consumers?" *Journal of Money, Credit, and Banking,* 6 (August 1974), 385–94; J. Ernest Tanner, "Empirical Evidence on the Short-Run Real Balance Effect in Canada," *Journal of Money, Credit, and Banking,* 2 (November 1970), 473–85; Tanner, "Fiscal Policy and Consumer Behavior," *Review of Economics and Statistics,* 61 (May 1979), 317–21; John J. Seater, "Are Future Taxes Discounted?" *Journal of Money, Credit, and Banking,* 14 (August 1982), 376–89; Roger C. Kormendi, "Government Debt, Government Spending, and Private Sector Behavior," *American Economic Review,* 73 (December 1983), 994–1010; and John J. Seater and Roberto S. Mariano, "New Tests of the Life Cycle and Tax Discounting Hypotheses," *Journal of Monetary Economics,* 15 (1985), 195–215.

15. Jess B. Yawitz and Laurence H. Meyer, "An Empirical Investigation of the Extent of Tax Discounting," *Journal of Money, Credit, and Banking,* 8 (May 1976), 247–54; Willem H. Buiter and James Tobin, "Debt Neutrality: A Brief Review of Doctrine and Evidence," in *Social Security versus Private Saving,* ed. George M. von Furstenberg (Cambridge, Mass.: Ballinger Publishing Co., 1979), pp. 39–63; Martin Feldstein, "Government Deficits and Aggregate Demand," *Journal of Monetary Economics,* 9 (January 1982), 1–20; and Marcelle Arak, "Are Tax Cuts Stimulatory?" *Review of Economics and Statistics,* 64 (February 1982), 168–69.

16. John J. Arena, "Postwar Stock Market Changes and Consumer Spending," *Review of Economics and Statistics,* 47 (November 1965), 379–91.

17. Kul B. Bhatia, "Capital Gains and the Aggregate Consumption Function," *American Economic Review,* 62 (December 1972), 866–79. See, however, Michael B. McElroy and J. C. Poindexter, "Capital Gains and the Aggregate Consumption Function: Comment," *American Economic Review,* 65 (September 1975), 700–703.

18. Barry Bosworth, "The Stock Market and the Economy," *Brookings Papers on Economic Activity,* no. 2 (1975), 257–90. See also Irwin Friend and Charles Lieberman, "Short-Run Asset Effects on Household Saving and Consumption: The Cross-Section Evidence," *American Economic Review,* 65 (September 1975), 624–33.

19. In his study, Mishkin emphasized the importance of considering the various items of the consumer's balance sheet separately. Frederic S. Mishkin, "What Depressed the Consumer? The Household Balance Sheet and the 1973–75 Recession," *Brookings Papers on Economic Activity,* no. 1 (1977), 123–64. Joe Peek provides evidence showing that (net) capital gains play an important role in determining (recent) personal saving. He concludes that capital gains are important in the consumption/saving decision. Peek, "Capital Gains and Personal Saving Behavior," *Journal of Money, Credit, and Banking,* 15 (February 1983), 1–23.

20. Michael J. Boskin, "Taxation, Saving and the Rate of Interest," *Journal of Political Economy,* 86 (April 1978), S3–S27.

21. E. Philip Howrey and Saul H. Hymans, "The Measurement and Determination of Loanable-Funds Saving," *Brookings Papers on Economic Activity,* no. 3 (1978), 655–85.

22. Thorvaldur Gylfason, "Interest Rates, Inflation, and the Aggregate Consumption Function," *Review of Economics and Statistics,* 63 (May 1981), 233–45.

23. William H. Branson and Alvin K. Klevorick, "Money Illusion and the Aggregate Consumption Function," *American Economic Review,* 59 (December 1969), 832–49.

24. Raymond M. Johnson, "The Empirical Question of Money Illusion in the United States: Its Implications for a Patinkin-Type Model" (unpublished doctoral dissertation, Oklahoma State University, 1973).

25. F. Thomas Juster and Paul Wachtel, "Inflation and the Consumer," *Brookings Papers on Economic Activity,* no. 1 (1972), 71–114; and "A Note on Inflation and the Saving Rate," *Brookings Papers on Economic Activity,* no. 3 (1972), 765–78.

26. In this regard, see Gylfason, "Interest Rates, Inflation, and the Aggregate Consumption Function," and Paul Wachtel, "Inflation and the Saving Behavior of Households: A Survey," in *The Government and Capital Formation,* ed. George M. von Furstenberg (Cambridge, Mass.: Ballinger Publishing Co., 1980), pp. 153–74.

27. There have been several attempts to incorporate the permanent income concept into a macroeconomic framework. See David Laidler, "The Permanent-Income Concept in a Macro-economic Model," *Oxford Economic Papers,* 20 (March 1968), 11–23; and Barry Schecter and John Pomery, "Permanent Income in a Macro-economic Model: A Correction," *Oxford Economic Papers,* 23 (November 1971), 456–57; or Fred R. Glahe, "A Permanent Restatement of the IS-LM Model," *American Economist,* 17 (Spring 1973), 158–67.

REVIEW QUESTIONS _____

1. From the *Economic Report of the President* or other sources, collect data on real consumption and real GNP for a ten-year period. Plot the data and "fit" a line to the observations.

2. Since the rich apparently consume a smaller fraction of their income than the poor, it has been suggested that income be redistributed from the rich to the poor in order to increase consumption. Critically evaluate the argument. If the argument is fallacious, does it mean that redistribution of income is undesirable?

3. In regard to the consumption function:

    a. Outline the differences between the short- and long-run consumption functions.

    b. Show how to reconcile the two versions of the consumption function using

    (1) the permanent income hypothesis.

    (2) the life cycle hypothesis.

4. Compare and contrast the permanent income and life cycle hypotheses.

5. According to the permanent income and life cycle hypotheses, how is consumption defined? How does this definition differ from the national income accounting definition?

6. What are the implications of the permanent income and life cycle hypotheses for temporary changes in taxes? How are the implications changed if households face liquidity constraints?

7. Discuss the role of wealth in the permanent income hypothesis.

8. Why is it important to determine whether households regard government debt as wealth?

9. From a theoretical standpoint, what is the relationship between consumption and the interest rate? What does the empirical evidence suggest?

SUGGESTED READING _____

ANDO, ALBERT, and FRANCO MODIGLIANI, "The 'Life Cycle' Hypothesis of Saving: Aggregate Implications and Tests," *American Economic Review,* 53 (March 1963), 55–84.

BOWLES, DAVID C., "Consumption and Saving through the 1970s and 1980s: A Survey of Empirical Research," in Thomas M. Havrilesky (ed.), *Modern Concepts in Macroeconomics*, pp. 15–26. Arlington Heights, Ill.: Harlan Davidson, Inc., 1985.

DOLDE, WALTER, "Temporary Taxes as Macroeconomic Stabilizers," *American Economic Review*, 69 (May 1979), 81–85.

FERBER, ROBERT, "Consumer Economics, A Survey," *Journal of Economic Literature*, 11 (December 1973), 1303–42.

FRIEDMAN, MILTON, *A Theory of the Consumption Function.* New York: National Bureau of Economic Research, 1957.

KEYNES, JOHN MAYNARD, *The General Theory of Employment, Interest, and Money.* New York: Harcourt, Brace and Company, 1936.

KOTLIKOFF, LAURENCE J., "Determinants of Saving," *NBER Reporter* (Spring 1984), 5–8.

6

INVESTMENT
AND EQUILIBRIUM
IN THE PRODUCT
MARKET

Like consumption, investment depends on a number of variables. Most of this chapter discusses these variables and various theories of investment behavior. At the end of the chapter, equilibrium in the product market is considered and a relationship between the market rate of interest and the equilibrium level of income is derived. This relationship, called the *IS curve*, is useful in subsequent chapters.

In the national income accounts, investment is divided into nonresidential structures and producers' durable equipment, residential structures, and change in business inventories. To keep the topic manageable, the ensuing discussion deals almost exclusively with investment in nonresidential structures and producers' durable equipment or, for short, plant and equipment.[1]

INVESTMENT AND THE PRESENT VALUE
OF A FUTURE INCOME STREAM

Presumably, managers invest in new plant and equipment because they believe it to be profitable. The return to investment in plant and equipment is spread over a number of years. For example, a manager may expect profits from a particular project to accrue over a five-year span. This complicates making decisions about investment because profits received in the near future are worth more than profits received in the more distant future. Profits received in the near future may be loaned at the market rate of interest; they are, therefore, more valuable. Consequently, managers cannot simply add profits for the various years and compare total profits with the cost of the investment project. They must use a more complicated approach to determine whether a project is profitable.

To obtain a formula for determining the *present value* of income which accrues over a number of years, consider the following example. Suppose an individual is to receive $1,100 in one year. If the market rate of interest is 10 percent, what is the $1,100 worth today? In other words, if the market rate of interest is 10 percent, what is the present value of the $1,100 payable in one year? In simplest terms, the present value of the $1,100 payable in one year is the amount an individual would have to lend for a year at the market rate of interest in order to have $1,100 at the end of the year. In this case, the present value is $1,000, since an individual can lend $1,000 at the market rate of interest, 10 percent, and have, at the end of one year, $1,100 (the initial amount, $1,000, plus the interest earned during the year, $100).[2]

The present value of the $1,100 payable at the end of one year must be $1,000. Suppose the individual wishes to sell his claim to $1,100 payable in one year. If he attempts to do so, he will find that no one is willing to pay more than $1,000. For example, suppose he tries to sell the claim for $1,050. If the market rate of interest is 10 percent, he will find no buyers, since prospective purchasers can lend $1,050 for a year and have, at year's end, $1,155 (the initial amount, $1,050, plus the interest earned during the year, $105). If someone were to purchase the claim, the purchaser would have only $1,100 at the end of the year. Consequently, it is not in the financial interest of potential buyers to purchase the claim for $1,050, or indeed, for any amount greater than $1,000 because, with a 10 percent interest rate, they may lend $1,000 and have $1,100 at the end of the year.

Similarly, it is not in the financial interest of the owner to sell the claim for less than $1,000. Suppose the owner were to sell the claim for $950 and lend the proceeds at the 10 percent interest rate. At the end of the year, he would have $1,045 (the initial amount, $950, plus the interest earned during the year, $95). If he had kept the claim, he would have received $1,100. Consequently, it is not in his financial interest to sell the claim for $950 or, for that matter, for any amount less than $1,000.

Since no one is willing to purchase a claim to $1,100 payable in one year for more than $1,000 if the market rate of interest is 10 percent and the owner is unwilling to sell for less than $1,000, the present value of the claim must be $1,000. Similarly, its market value or price must be $1,000.

We can now move from this simple example to develop a general formula for calculating the present value of a future income stream. By *future income stream*, we mean a series of incomes accruing over time. Assume an individual has an initial amount, P_0, to lend at the market rate of interest, i. If the individual lends her initial amount, P_0, at the market rate of interest, i, she will have P_1 dollars at the end of one year, where P_1 equals the initial amount P_0 plus the interest earned during the year, iP_0. Mathematically,

(6.1) $$P_1 = P_0 + iP_0 = P_0(1 + i)^1.$$

Suppose the individual lends the amount she has at the end of the first year for another year. At the end of the second year, she will have P_2 dollars, where P_2 equals the amount she had at the end of the first year, P_1, plus the interest earned during the second year, iP_1. In symbols,

$$P_2 = P_1 + iP_1 = P_1(1 + i)^1.$$

Since P_1 equals $P_0(1 + i)$ in equation (6.1), we obtain by substitution

(6.2) $$P_2 = P_0(1 + i)(1 + i) = P_0(1 + i)^2.$$

Similarly, suppose the individual lends the amount she has at the end of the second year for another year. At the end of the third year, she will have P_3 dollars, where P_3 equals the amount she had at the end of the second year, P_2, plus the interest earned during the third year, iP_2. Mathematically,

$$P_3 = P_2 + iP_2 = P_2(1 + i).$$

Since P_2 equals $P_0(1 + i)^2$ in equation (6.2), we obtain by substitution

(6.3) $$P_3 = P_0(1 + i)^2(1 + i) = P_0(1 + i)^3.$$

Now we can establish a general formula for determining the amount P_n an individual will have at the end of n years if she lends an initial amount P_0 at the market rate of interest i for n years. Note that equations (6.1) through (6.3) contain the terms P_0 and $(1 + i)$. This suggests that the general formula should contain those terms. Note also that when n equals 1 in equation (6.1) the term $(1 + i)$ is raised to the first power. Similarly, when n equals 2 in equation (6.2), the term $(1 + i)$ is raised to the second power, and when n equals 3 in equation (6.3), the term $(1 + i)$ is raised to the third power. Therefore, based on the pattern displayed in equations (6.1) through (6.3), the general formula is

(6.4) $$P_n = P_0(1 + i)^n.$$

Present Value

Thus, if an individual lends P_0 dollars for n years at the market rate of interest i, she will have P_n dollars at the end of n years.

The present value of income to be received after n years equals the amount an individual would have to lend at the market rate of interest i for n years in order to receive the given amount, P_n. Thus, equation (6.4) can be used to determine the present value of income to be received at some future date. Suppose that the individual is to receive P_n dollars in n years, and that the market rate of interest is i. Solving equation (6.4) for P_0, the present value of the future income equals P_n divided by $(1 + i)^n$. In equation form,

(6.5)
$$P_0 = \frac{P_n}{(1 + i)^n}.$$

Thus, in general, if an individual is to receive P_n dollars in n years, she must *discount* the future income by applying equation (6.5) in order to determine its present value.

To illustrate, suppose we reconsider the earlier example. If an individual is to receive $1,100 in one year and the market rate of interest is 10 percent, we have

$$P_0 = \frac{\$1,100}{(1 + 0.10)^1} = \frac{\$1,100}{1.1} = \$1,000.$$

Thus, we obtain the same answer obtained earlier using an intuitive approach.

Equation (6.5) indicates an inverse relationship between the present value, P_0, of future income and the market rate of interest, i. Thus, if the market rate of interest decreases, the present value of future income increases. Suppose, in terms of the example, the market rate of interest is 5 percent rather than 10 percent. This implies that the present value of the $1,100 payable in one year is $1,047.62, obtained by applying equation (6.5) with $P_1 = \$1,100$, $n = 1$, and $i = 0.05$, rather than $1,000. Thus, with the lower rate of interest, the claim to the $1,100 payable in one year is more valuable than before. With the lower interest rate, a prospective purchaser must lend a greater amount, $1,047.62, to have $1,100 at the end of the year. Consequently, the claim to $1,100 payable at the end of one year is worth more than before.

With equation (6.5), the present value of income accruing at a specified date in the future may be calculated. Suppose there is a series of incomes payable at future dates: P_1 at the end of the first year, P_2 at the end of the second year, and so forth. We may calculate the present value of the income stream accruing over n years by applying equation (6.5) to each income and then adding the results. The present value of P_1 is $P_1/(1 + i)^1$; the present value of P_2 is $P_2/(1 + i)^2$; and so forth. After adding, we find that the general formula for determining the present value of an income stream is

(6.6)
$$PV = \frac{P_1}{(1 + i)^1} + \frac{P_2}{(1 + i)^2} + \cdots + \frac{P_n}{(1 + i)^n},$$

where PV is the present value of the income stream, P_1 represents income payable at the end of the first year, P_2 income payable at the end of the second year, P_n

income payable at the end of the nth year, i the market rate of interest, and n the time span in question.

As an application, consider the present value of a particular type of bond. Suppose the owner of the bond receives R dollars at the end of each year for n years. In addition, suppose the owner receives P dollars when the bond matures at the end of the n years. If the market rate of interest is i, the present value of the bond is obtained by applying equation (6.6); it is

$$PV = \frac{R}{(1 + i)^1} + \frac{R}{(1 + i)^2} + \cdots + \frac{R}{(1 + i)^n} + \frac{P}{(1 + i)^n}.$$

The terms $R/(1 + i)^1$, $R/(1 + i)^2$, and $R/(1 + i)^n$ represent the present values of the R dollars payable at the end of the first, second, and nth years, respectively; the term $P/(1 + i)^n$ represents the present value of the P dollars payable at the bond's maturity in n years. The present value of the bond is the sum of these individual terms.

As before, there is an inverse relationship between the present value of the bond, PV, and the market rate of interest, i. Should the market rate of interest decline, the present value of the bond increases. This relationship prevails because, with a lower interest rate, an individual must loan a greater amount of money to generate an equivalent income stream. Consequently, the bond owner finds that the bond is worth more. All other things equal, the greater the time span to maturity, the greater the change in the present value of the bond for a given change in the interest rate. This implies that long-term bonds should experience greater fluctuations in price than short-term bonds, the normal state of affairs.

THE INVESTMENT DECISION

Suppose someone is considering the purchase of a particular bond. To decide whether to purchase the bond, the prospective buyer will presumably calculate the present value of the income stream associated with the bond and compare it with the cost of the bond. If this estimate of the present value of the bond exceeds the cost of the bond, it appears profitable to purchase the bond and the prospective buyer will presumably do so. If the estimate of the present value of the bond is less than its cost, the prospective buyer will not buy the bond.

The decision to invest in plant and equipment involves the same sort of analysis. The prospective investor must calculate the present value of the income stream associated with the investment project and compare it with the cost of the project. The process is, however, more difficult because of the uncertainty associated with the investment project. In regard to bonds, estimation of the income stream is little or no problem since the required information is usually printed on the face of the bond. On the other hand, it is difficult to estimate the income stream associated with an increase in productive capacity. It requires year by year estimates of the increase in output associated with the increase in productive capacity, the price or prices at which this additional output can be sold, and the operating costs associated with the project. After obtaining these estimates, net income is found by subtracting operating costs associated with the increase in productive capacity in each year from the revenue associated with the project in the corresponding year. Only then will the prospective investor have an estimate of the (net) income stream associated with the project.

After obtaining an estimate of the (net) income stream, the prospective investor can calculate its present value and compare the result with the cost of the project. If the present value of the income stream associated with the project is greater than its cost, the prospective investor should undertake the project. If the present value of the income stream associated with the project is less than its cost, the prospective investor should not undertake the project.

In the investment decision-making process, the market rate of interest plays an important role. The interest rate is used to discount the future income stream associated with the project. The present value of the future income stream is then compared with the cost of the project in order to make the investment decision. If the interest rate changes, the present value of the income stream is altered. As a consequence, investment projects which were profitable at the old interest rate may be unprofitable at the new rate, and vice versa. Thus, investment, in part, depends on the market rate of interest, i.

There is an alternative view of the investment decision-making process which clearly stresses the importance of the market rate of interest. Under the present value approach, the comparison is between the present value, PV, of the future income stream associated with the investment project and the cost of the project, Q. Under the alternative approach, the comparison is between the marginal efficiency of investment, r, and the market rate of interest, i. The *marginal efficiency of investment* is the rate of interest which equates the cost of the project and the discounted value of the future income stream associated with the project. The general formula for calculating the present value of a future income stream is

$$\text{PV} = \frac{P_1}{(1 + i)^1} + \frac{P_2}{(1 + i)^2} + \cdots + \frac{P_n}{(1 + i)^n}.$$

To calculate the marginal efficiency of investment, r, we obtain estimates of the cost of the project, Q, and the future income stream associated with the project, $P_1, P_2, \ldots, P_n$. These values are substituted into the general formula to obtain

$$Q = \frac{P_1}{(1 + r)^1} + \frac{P_2}{(1 + r)^2} + \cdots + \frac{P_n}{(1 + r)^n},$$

which must then be solved for the unknown, r. The marginal efficiency of investment is often referred to as the internal rate of return.

After calculating the marginal efficiency of investment, r, the prospective investor must compare it with the market rate of interest, i. If the marginal efficiency of investment is less than the market rate, the investment project is unprofitable or at least less profitable than the alternative, lending the money at the market rate of interest. Consequently, the prospective investor should not undertake the project. On the other hand, if the marginal efficiency of investment, r, is greater than the market rate of interest, i, the investment project is profitable or at least more profitable than lending the money at the market rate of interest. Consequently, the prospective investor should undertake the project even if he has to borrow all or part of the necessary funds at the market rate of interest.

To illustrate, suppose the marginal efficiency of investment on a particular project is estimated at 10 percent. If the market rate of interest is 12 percent, the prospective investor should not undertake the project. If the interest rate were to drop to 8 percent, the project is now profitable. Consequently, the prospective investor should undertake the project.

In the investment decision-making process, the market rate of interest plays an important role. If the interest rate is too high (greater than the marginal efficiency of investment), the project is unprofitable. On the other hand, if the interest rate is sufficiently low (less than the marginal efficiency of investment), the project is profitable. Thus, whether investment in the project occurs or not depends on the market rate of interest. Consequently, economists often specify that investment depends on, or is a function of, the market rate of interest. Thus, we may write the investment function as

$$I = I(i),$$

where I represents investment, measured in real or constant dollars, and i represents the market rate of interest. Presumably there is an inverse relationship between investment and the market rate of interest. With a decline in the market rate of interest, investment increases as projects which were not profitable at the higher rate of interest become profitable and, hence, are undertaken.

THEORIES OF INVESTMENT

Keynes and the classical economists generally assumed that investment is a function of the interest rate. Starting in the late 1930s, however, economists became increasingly skeptical about the importance of the interest rate as a determinant of investment. Indeed, early empirical studies indicated that investment is relatively insensitive to changes in the interest rate.[3] As a consequence, a number of alternative theories of investment were offered. We shall consider four of these theories: accelerator, internal funds, neoclassical, and q. We start with the accelerator theory.

The Accelerator Theory of Investment

The *accelerator theory of investment*, in its simplest form, is based upon the notion that a particular amount of capital stock is necessary to produce a given output. For example, a capital stock of $400 billion may be required to produce $100 billion of output. This implies a fixed relationship between the capital stock and output.

The relationship, x, may be written as

$$x = \frac{K_t}{Y_t}, \quad \text{ECONOMY'S CAP STOCK / OUTPUT}$$

where K_t is the economy's capital stock in time period t and Y_t is output in time period t. It can also be written as

(6.7) $$K_t = xY_t.$$

If x is constant, the same relationship held in the previous period; hence,

(6.8) $$K_{t-1} = xY_{t-1}.$$

By subtracting equation (6.8) from equation (6.7), we obtain

$$K_t - K_{t-1} = xY_t - xY_{t-1} = x(Y_t - Y_{t-1}).$$

Net investment, $K_t - K_{t-1}$, equals the difference between the capital stock in time period t and the capital stock in time period $t - 1$. It also equals gross investment, I_t, minus capital consumption allowances or depreciation, D_t, or $I_t - D_t$. Thus,

$$I_t - D_t = K_t - K_{t-1} = x(Y_t - Y_{t-1}) = x\Delta Y,$$

where ΔY represents the change in output. Thus, net investment equals x, the *accelerator coefficient*, multiplied by the change in output. Since x is assumed constant, net investment is a function of changes in output. If output increases, net investment is positive. If output increases by a greater amount, net investment will be a larger amount.

From an economic standpoint, the reasoning is straightforward. According to the theory, a particular amount of capital is necessary to produce a given level of output. For example, suppose $400 billion worth of capital is necessary to produce $100 billion worth of output. This implies that x, the ratio of the economy's capital stock to its output, equals 4. If aggregate demand is $100 billion and the capital stock is $400 billion, output is $100 billion. So long as aggregate demand remains at the $100 billion level, net investment will be zero, since there is no incentive for firms to add to their productive capacity. Gross investment, however, will be positive, since firms must replace plant and equipment that is deteriorating.

Suppose aggregate demand increases to $105 billion. If output is to increase to the $105 billion level, the economy's capital stock must increase to the $420 billion level. This follows from the assumption of a fixed ratio, x, between capital stock and output. Consequently, for production to increase to the $105 billion level, net investment must equal $20 billion, the amount necessary to increase the capital stock to the $420 billion level. Since x equals 4 and the change in output equals $5 billion, this amount, $20 billion, may be obtained directly by multiplying x, the accelerator coefficient, by the change in output. Had the increase in output been greater, (net) investment would have been larger, which implies that (net) investment is positively related to changes in output.

In this crude form, the accelerator theory of investment, or acceleration principle, is open to a number of criticisms. First, the theory assumes that a discrepancy between the desired and actual capital stocks is eliminated within a single period. If industries producing capital goods are already operating at full capacity, it may not be possible to eliminate the discrepancy within a single period. In fact, even if the industries are operating at less than full capacity it may be more economical to eliminate the discrepancy gradually.

Second, since the accelerator theory assumes no excess capacity, we would not expect it to be valid in recessions, as they are characterized by excess capacity. Based on the theory, net investment is positive when output increases. But if excess capacity exists, we would expect little or no net investment to occur, since net investment is made in order to increase productive capacity.

Third, even if no excess capacity exists, firms will invest in new plant and equipment in response to an increase in aggregate demand only if demand is expected to remain at the new, higher level. In other words, if managers expect the increase in demand to be temporary, they may maintain their present levels of output and raise prices (or let their orders pile up) instead of increasing their productive capacity and output through investment in new plant and equipment.

Fourth, the accelerator theory assumes a fixed ratio between capital and output. This assumption is occasionally justified, but most firms can substitute labor for capital, at least within a limited range. As a consequence, firms must take into consideration other factors, such as the interest rate.

Finally, the theory explains net but not gross investment. For many purposes, including the determination of the level of aggregate demand, gross investment is the relevant concept. In view of these and other criticisms of the accelerator theory of investment, it is not surprising that early attempts to verify the theory were unsuccessful.

Over the years, more flexible versions of the accelerator theory of investment have been developed. Unlike the version of the accelerator theory just presented, the more flexible versions assume a discrepancy between the *desired* and *actual* *capital stocks* is eliminated over a number of periods rather than in a single period.

As a consequence,

$$K_t - K_{t-1} = \lambda(K_t^* - K_{t-1}) \qquad (0 < \lambda < 1),$$

where K_t is the actual capital stock in time period t, K_{t-1} is the actual capital stock in time period $t - 1$, K_t^* is the desired capital stock, and λ is a constant between 0 and 1. The equation suggests that the actual change in the capital stock from time period $t - 1$ to time period t equals a fraction of the difference between the desired capital stock in time period t and the actual capital stock in time period $t - 1$. If λ were equal to 1, as assumed in the initial statement of the accelerator theory, the actual capital stock in time period t equals the desired capital stock.

According to the accelerator model, the desired capital stock, K_t^*, is determined by output. In the crude version of the accelerator model, the desired capital stock is proportional to a single level of output. In the more flexible versions of the accelerator model, the desired capital stock is specified as a function of both current and past output levels. Consequently, in these versions, the desired capital stock is determined by long-run considerations.

Finally, the crude version of the accelerator model may be modified so that it explains gross as well as net investment. Since net investment, $I_t - D_t$, equals the change in the capital stock, $K_t - K_{t-1}$, we have

$$I_t - D_t = K_t - K_{t-1} = \lambda(K_t^* - K_{t-1}).$$

To determine gross investment, it is common to assume that replacement investment is proportional to the actual capital stock.[4] Thus, we assume that replacement investment in time period t, D_t, equals a constant δ multiplied by the capital stock at the end of time period $t - 1$, K_{t-1} or

$$D_t = \delta K_{t-1} \qquad (0 < \delta < 1).$$

For example, if δ equals 0.05, then 5 percent of the economy's capital stock at the beginning of time period t wears out or is destroyed during the period.

Since net investment, $I_t - D_t$, equals $\lambda (K_t^* - K_{t-1})$, we have, upon substitution,

$$I_t - \delta K_{t-1} = \lambda(K_t^* - K_{t-1}),$$

or

(6.9) $$I_t = \lambda(K_t^* - K_{t-1}) + \delta K_{t-1},$$

where I_t represents gross investment, K_t^* the desired capital stock, and K_{t-1} the actual capital stock in time period $t - 1$. Thus, gross investment is a function of the desired and actual capital stocks.

As we have just demonstrated, it is possible to modify the crude version of the accelerator theory so as to overcome many of its shortcomings. Consequently, it is not surprising that attempts to verify the more flexible versions have been much more successful than the earlier attempts to verify the crude version. Some of this empirical evidence is discussed later.

Before discussing this evidence, however, we shall consider the alternative theories of investment behavior. In doing so, we shall see that they differ primarily in terms of the determinants of the desired capital stock.

The Internal Funds Theory of Investment

Under the *internal funds theory of investment,* the desired capital stock and, hence, investment depends on the level of profits. Several different explanations have been offered. Jan Tinbergen, for example, has argued that realized profits accurately reflect expected profits.[5] Since investment presumably depends on expected profits, investment is positively related to realized profits.

Alternatively, it has been argued that managers have a decided preference for financing investment internally.[6] Firms may obtain funds for investment purposes from a variety of sources: (1) retained earnings, (2) depreciation expense (funds set aside as plant and equipment depreciate), (3) various types of borrowing, including sale of bonds, (4) the sale of stock. Retained earnings and depreciation expense are sources of funds internal to the firm; the other sources are external to the firm. Borrowing commits a firm to a series of fixed payments. Should a recession occur, the firm may be unable to meet its commitments, forcing it to borrow or sell stock on unfavorable terms or even forcing it into bankruptcy. Consequently, firms may be reluctant to borrow except under very favorable circumstances. Similarly, firms may be reluctant to raise funds by issuing new stock. Management, for example, is often concerned about its earnings record on a per share basis. Since an increase in the number of shares outstanding tends to reduce earnings on a per share basis, management may be unwilling to finance investment by selling stock unless the earnings from the project clearly offset the effect of the increase in shares outstanding. Management may also fear loss of control with the sale of additional stock. For these and other reasons, proponents of the internal funds theory of investment argue that firms strongly prefer to finance investment internally and that the increased availability of internal funds through higher profits generates additional investment.

Thus, according to the internal funds theory, the desired capital stock and investment are determined by profits. According to the accelerator theory, however, they are determined by output. Since the two theories differ with regard to the determinants of the desired capital stock, they also differ with regard to policy. If the accelerator theory is valid, expansionary fiscal policy (increasing government purchases and/or reducing personal income taxes) will result in higher levels of output, thereby increasing the desired capital stock and investment. On the other hand, a reduction in corporate income taxes is unlikely to increase the desired capital stock and investment. The reduction in corporate income taxes would increase the availability of internal funds but, according to the accelerator theory, the desired capital stock depends on output, not the availability of internal funds.

If the internal funds theory is valid, however, reducing corporate income taxes will result in significant increases in the desired capital stock and investment. In contrast, expansionary fiscal policy will have little or no direct effect on the desired capital stock because it affects output, not the availability of internal funds. Expansionary fiscal policy may have some indirect effect because profits tend to rise as output increases.

Before turning to the neoclassical and q theories, it should be acknowledged that the proponents of the internal funds theory recognize the importance of the relationship between the desired capital stock and output, especially in the long run. Nevertheless, they maintain that internal funds are an important determinant of the desired capital stock, particularly during recessions.

The Neoclassical Theory of Investment

The theoretical basis for the *neoclassical theory of investment* is the neoclassical theory of the optimal accumulation of capital. Since the theory is both long and highly mathematical, we shall not attempt to outline it.[7] Instead, we shall briefly examine its principal results and policy implications. According to the neoclassical theory, the desired capital stock is determined by output and the price of capital services relative to the price of output. The price of capital services depends, in turn, on the price of capital goods, the interest rate, and the tax treatment of business income. As a consequence, changes in output or the price of capital services relative to the price of output alter the desired capital stock, hence, investment.

As in the case of the accelerator theory, output is a determinant of the desired capital stock. Thus, increases in government purchases or reductions in personal income tax rates stimulate investment through their impact on aggregate demand, hence, output. As in the case of the internal funds theory, the tax treatment of business income is important. According to the neoclassical theory, however, business taxation is important because of its effect on the price of capital services, not because of its effect on the availability of internal funds. Even so, policies designed to alter the tax treatment of business income affect the desired capital stock and, therefore, investment.

In contrast to both the accelerator and internal funds theories, the interest rate is a determinant of the desired capital stock. Thus, monetary policy, through its effect on the interest rate, is capable of altering the desired capital stock and investment. This was not the case in regard to the accelerator and internal funds theories.

The q Theory of Investment

According to the *securities valuation* or *q theory of investment*, the desired capital stock and, hence, investment are positively related to q, the ratio of the market's valuation of the firm to the replacement cost of the firm's assets.[8] The market value of the firm is obtained by summing the market values of the firm's common and preferred stock and its (net) debt. (Each of these items represents a claim upon the firm's earnings.) The firm's (physical) assets consist mainly of plant, equipment, and inventory.

The rationale for this relationship is most easily seen in the context of housing. Suppose the market price of housing rises above the replacement cost of housing. Builders will have an incentive to construct more houses. Similarly, suppose the market value of a firm rises above the replacement cost of its assets. The firm will have an incentive to issue additional shares of stock or more bonds and use the proceeds to buy additional capital stock. The result would be an increase in the net value of the firm.

If the q theory of investment is valid, monetary policy will have a significant impact on the desired capital stock and investment. If the interest rate decreases, the market valuation of the firm will rise because of the inverse relationship between bond prices and the interest rate. (To the extent that stock prices rise when the interest rate falls, the firm's market value will also increase for that reason.) The increase in the firm's market valuation increases q, resulting in an increase in the desired capital stock and investment. Changes in the tax treatment of business income will also alter q.[9] Lowering the corporate income tax, for example, will raise q, thereby increasing the desired capital stock and investment.

As just discussed, the policy implications of the various theories of investment differ. It is important, therefore, to survey the empirical evidence in order to determine which theory best explains investment behavior.

THE EMPIRICAL EVIDENCE

There is considerable disagreement concerning the validity of the accelerator, internal funds, neoclassical, and q theories of investment. Much of the disagreement arises because the various empirical studies have employed different sets of data. Consequently, several economists have tried to test the various theories or models of investment using a common set of data. At the aggregate level, Peter K. Clark considered five models: a generalized accelerator model, an internal funds model, two versions of the neoclassical model, and a q model.[10] Based on quarterly data for 1954–73, Clark concluded that the accelerator model provides a better explanation of investment behavior than the alternative models.

At the industry level, Dale W. Jorgenson, Jerald Hunter, and M. Ishag Nadiri tested four models of investment behavior: an accelerator model, two versions of the internal funds model, and a neoclassical model.[11] Their study covered 15 manufacturing industries and was based on quarterly data for 1949–64. Jorgenson, Hunter, and Nadiri found, like Clark, that the accelerator theory is a better explanation of investment behavior than either of the two versions of the internal funds models. Unlike Clark, however, they concluded that the neoclassical model was better than the accelerator model.

At the firm level, Jorgenson and Calvin D. Siebert tested a number of investment models, including an accelerator model, an internal funds model, and two versions of the neoclassical model.[12] The study was based on annual data for 15 large corporations and covered 1937–41 and 1949–63. Jorgenson and Siebert concluded that the neoclassical models provided the best explanation of investment behavior and the internal funds model the worst.[13] Their conclusions are consistent with those of Jorgenson, Hunter, and Nadiri and, with regard to the internal funds theory, with those of Clark. Clark concluded, however, that the accelerator model was better than the neoclassical model.

In short, these studies suggest that the internal funds theory does not perform as well as the accelerator and neoclassical theories at all levels of aggregation.[14] The evidence, however, is conflicting with regard to the relative performance of the accelerator and neoclassical models, with the evidence favoring the accelerator theory at the aggregate level and the neoclassical model at other levels of aggregation.

In an important survey article, Jorgenson has ranked different variables in terms of their importance in determining the desired capital stock.[15] Jorgenson divided the variables into three main categories: capacity utilization, internal finance, and external finance. Capacity utilization variables include output and the relationship of output to capacity. Internal finance variables include the flow of internal funds; external finance variables include the interest rate. Jorgenson found capacity variables to be the most important determinant of the desired capital stock. He also found external finance variables to be important, although definitely subordinate to capacity utilization variables.[16] Finally, Jorgenson found that internal finance variables play little or no role in determining the desired capital stock.

Jorgenson's conclusion in regard to the capacity utilization variables lends some support to the accelerator model. But he finds external finance variables to be of importance in determining the desired capital stock, which suggests that the neoclassical model is the appropriate theory of investment behavior, since it includes both output and the price of capital services as determinants of the desired capital stock.

THE INVESTMENT FUNCTION:
A GRAPHICAL APPROACH

To obtain a manageable investment function, we shall proceed as follows: Using the neoclassical theory of investment, assume that the desired capital stock is a function of output and the interest rate.[17] By assuming output constant, the relationship between the interest rate and the desired capital stock may be plotted. If the interest rate is plotted on the vertical axis and the desired capital stock on the horizontal, the relationship is shown in the left panel on Figure 6.1. Thus, if the interest rate is i_0, the desired capital stock is K_0^*. Should the interest rate decrease to i_1, the desired capital stock increases to K_1^*, because, with a lower interest rate, it is profitable for firms to employ more capital.

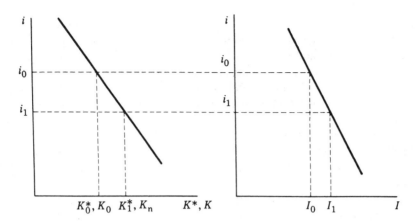

FIGURE 6.1

The interest rate, the desired capital stock, and investment

Suppose the interest rate is i_0 and the desired capital stock is K_0^*. If the actual capital stock, also measured on the horizontal axis, is K_0, there is no discrepancy between the desired and actual capital stocks. Hence, net investment is zero. Gross investment is, however, positive, since firms must invest to replace plant and equipment that has worn out or been destroyed. Consequently, at interest rate i_0, investment is I_0, which according to equation (6.9), equals δK_0. This combination is shown in the right panel of Figure 6.1.

If the interest rate decreases to i_1, the desired capital stock increases to K_1^*. Since the actual capital stock is K_0, the desired capital stock exceeds the actual capital stock, and net investment is positive as firms add to their productive capacity. But firms do not attempt to eliminate the gap between the desired and actual capital stocks in a single period; they do so over a number of periods. For example, suppose the desired capital stock exceeds the actual capital stock by $20 billion. If λ in equation (6.9) equals one-half, net investment equals $10 billion, obtained by multiplying λ by the difference between the desired and actual capital stocks. Consequently, at interest rate i_1, gross investment equals I_1, which consists of net investment, $\lambda(K_1^* - K_0)$, plus replacement investment, δK_0. This combination is depicted in the right panel of Figure 6.1. Since I_1 exceeds I_0, an inverse relationship exists between the market rate of interest, i, and investment, I; as the interest rate decreases, investment increases.

Over time, the discrepancy between the desired and actual capital stocks will be eliminated. For example, suppose the interest rate remains at i_1. So long as net investment remains positive, the capital stock increases, thereby reducing the discrepancy between the desired and actual capital stocks. Since net investment equals λ, a constant multiplied by the discrepancy between the desired and actual capital stocks, investment will be less in succeeding periods, and the investment function of Figure 6.1 will shift to the left.[18] Eventually, the actual capital stock will equal the desired capital stock, and net investment will be zero. Gross investment, however, will be greater than the original equilibrium level, I_0, since the new equilibrium capital stock K_n (equal to K_1^*) is greater than the original level K_0 (equal to K_0^*), and more investment is required for replacement purposes.

Thus, we find that investment, I, is a function of the interest rate, i, and the capital stock, K. It is also a function of output, Y, which has been assumed constant so far. If output increases, the relationship between the interest rate and the desired capital stock is altered. For example, suppose the interest rate is i_0 and output increases from Y_0 to Y_1. Based on the neoclassical theory of investment, the desired capital stock increases to K_2^*. This implies that the interest rate-desired capital stock relationship of Figure 6.1 shifts to the right, as shown in Figure 6.2. Since the new desired capital stock, K_2^*, exceeds the actual capital stock, K_0, net investment is positive; this implies that the investment function of Figure 6.1 shifts to the right, as shown in Figure 6.2. Since only part of the discrepancy between the desired and actual capital stocks is eliminated within the single period, the investment function will shift by a smaller amount than the interest rate-desired capital stock relationship.[19]

This analysis suggests that investment is a function of output, the interest rate, and the actual capital stock. In what follows, we shall assume the capital stock constant, the usual assumption in short-run models of income determination. Thus, investment is assumed to be a function of output and the interest rate. In equation form, we have

$$I = I(Y, i),$$

where I represents (gross) investment, Y output, and i the interest rate. Investment is assumed to be positively related to output and inversely related to the interest rate.

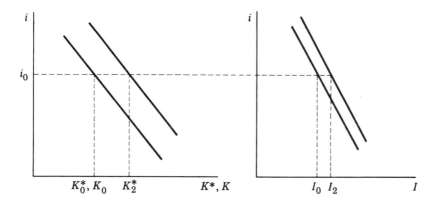

FIGURE 6.2

A change in output and its impact on the desired capital stock and investment

THE IS CURVE

We now examine the implications of the new investment function for equilibrium in the product or commodity market. By *product market*, we mean the market for goods and services. The money and labor markets are considered in later chapters. In Chapter 4, we considered the following model of the product market:

(6.10) $\qquad C = a + bY_d \qquad$ (where $Y_d = Y - T$),

(6.11) $\qquad I = I_0,$

(6.12) $\qquad G = G_0,$

(6.13) $\qquad T = T_0 + tY.$

The equilibrium condition is

(6.14) $\qquad\qquad I + G = S + T.$

In the model, equilibrium in the product market occurs when $I + G$ equals $S + T$. Consequently, the equilibrium level of income, Y_0, is determined by the intersection of the $I_0 + G_0$ and $S + T$ curves in Figure 6.3.

In this chapter, we have assumed that investment varies with output and the interest rate. As a consequence, we must alter the model of Chapter 4 by replacing the original investment function, $I = I_0$, with the new investment function, $I = I(Y, i)$. The rest of the model, including the equilibrium condition, is unchanged.

The new investment function implies that there is no longer a single equilibrium level of income. Instead, an equilibrium level of income exists for each interest rate. This follows from the assumption that for each interest rate there is a different level of investment. The relationship between the interest rate and the equilibrium level of income is called the *IS curve* because it is derived from the $I(+G)$ and $S(+T)$ curves. We now proceed to derive the relationship. For the derivation we

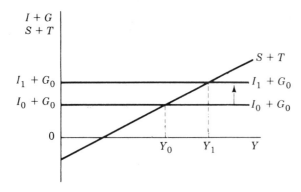

FIGURE 6.3

The investment plus government purchases and saving plus tax functions and the equilibrium level of income

assume that investment is independent of output. (The IS curve with investment a function of both output and the interest rate is derived in Appendix 2.)

In Figure 6.4, the $I + G$ curve is plotted in the northwest quadrant. The $I + G$ curve is obtained by summing investment and government purchases at each interest rate. According to the interest rate-investment relationship of Figure 6.1, investment increases as the interest rate decreases. Since government purchases are independent of the interest rate, the increase in investment plus government purchases accompanying the reduction in the interest rate from i_0 to i_1 in Figure 6.4 is due entirely to an increase in investment. The $S + T$ curve of Figure 6.3 is plotted in the southwest quadrant of Figure 6.4. As income increases, saving plus taxes increase. In the southeast quadrant, a 45° line is plotted so as to translate income from the vertical axis to the horizontal.

To derive the IS curve in the northeast quadrant, we start with interest rate i_0 and investment plus government purchases equal to $I_0 + G_0$. The equilibrium condition requires that saving plus taxes equal investment plus government purchases. As a consequence, the equilibrium level of income is Y_0 (which corresponds to income level Y_0 in Figure 6.3). At any other income level, saving plus taxes is either greater than investment plus government purchases or less than investment

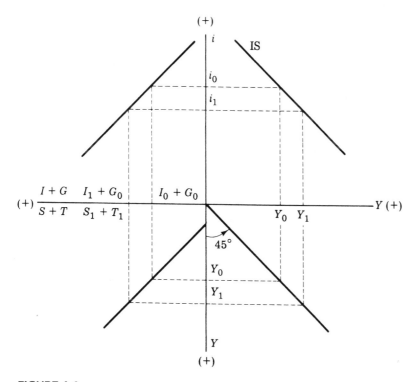

FIGURE 6.4

The derivation of the IS curve

plus government purchases. In either case, income will adjust to its equilibrium level. Consequently, for interest rate i_0, the corresponding equilibrium level of income is Y_0. The point (Y_0, i_0) may, therefore, be plotted in the northeast quadrant.

To obtain other points on the IS curve, we consider other interest rates and proceed in the same manner. For example, suppose the market rate of interest is i_1. At interest rate i_1, investment plus government purchases is $I_1 + G_0$, which is greater than $I_0 + G_0$ because, with a lower interest rate, investment is greater. With the increase in investment, there is an increase in the equilibrium level of income. In this case, the new equilibrium income is Y_1 (which corresponds to income level Y_1 in Figure 6.3), since Y_1 is the only level of income which equates saving plus taxes and investment plus government purchases at the new, higher-level $I_1 + G_0$. Consequently, for interest rate i_1, the corresponding equilibrium level of income is Y_1. This combination of income and the interest rate is plotted in the northeast quadrant as the point (Y_1, i_1).

If other interest rates are considered, the remainder of the IS curve will be traced out. If the $I + G$ and $S + T$ curves are linear, the IS curve is also linear, and only two points are necessary to derive the curve. For convenience, the $I + G$ and $S + T$ curves in Figure 6.4 are assumed to be linear.

This IS curve may also be derived algebraically. If we have

$$C = 100 + 0.75Y_d \qquad \text{(where } Y_d = Y - T),$$

$$I = 125 - 600i,$$

$$G = 50,$$

$$T = 20 + 0.2Y,$$

we can find the equilibrium level of income for each rate of interest. First, we substitute into the equilibrium condition

$$I + G = S + T.$$

If C equals $100 + 0.75Y_d$, S equals $-100 + 0.25Y_d$, and, upon substitution,

$$125 - 600i + 50 = -100 + 0.25[Y - (20 + 0.2Y)] + 20 + 0.2Y$$

or, upon simplification,

(6.15) $$Y = 650 - 1500i.$$

Since equation (6.15) represents the IS curve, different combinations of Y and i can be obtained by substituting various interest rates into the equation and then solving for the corresponding income levels. For example, if the interest rate is 15 percent, we have

$$Y = 650 - 1500(0.15) = 650 - 225 = 425.$$

Thus, for an interest rate of 15 percent, the corresponding equilibrium level of income is \$425 billion; this combination constitutes one point on the IS curve. The combination (\$500 billion, 10 percent) represents another point.

The IS curve consists of equilibrium combinations of income and the interest rate for the product market. Thus, the product market is in equilibrium at any combination of income and interest rate on the IS curve. We have seen that $I + G$ equals $S + T$ at income Y_0 and interest rate i_0. Similarly, $I + G$ equals $S + T$ at income Y_1 and interest rate i_1 and at any other combination of income and interest rate on the IS curve.

By the same token, at any combination of income and interest rate off the IS curve, the product market is not in equilibrium. Income will, however, adjust until the product market is in equilibrium or, in other words, a combination of income and interest rate on the IS curve is attained. For example, suppose income is Y_1 and the interest rate is i_0. At interest rate i_0, investment plus government purchases is $I_0 + G_0$. At income level Y_1, saving plus taxes equals $S_1 + T_1$. Investment plus government purchases is, therefore, less than saving plus taxes and the product market is not in equilibrium. Since, however, investment plus government purchases is less than saving plus taxes, income decreases until the equilibrium level of income is achieved. Since we are primarily concerned with equilibrium income levels, we shall confine the future discussion of the product market to combinations of income and the interest rate on the IS curve.

As drawn in Figure 6.4, the IS curve has a negative slope, indicating that higher levels of income are associated with lower interest rates. The negative slope is a result of the assumption that investment is inversely related to the interest rate. As the interest rate decreases, investment, and hence the equilibrium level of income, increase.

The IS curve is derived from the $I + G$ and $S + T$ curves. As a consequence, if either curve shifts, the IS curve shifts. For example, suppose the tax treatment of business income is altered so as to stimulate investment. With the shift in the investment function, the $I + G$ curve shifts to the left, as shown in Figure 6.5. To derive the new IS curve, we proceed as before; however, we use the new $I + G$ curve rather than the original curve.

At interest rate i_0, the new level of investment plus government purchases is $I_2 + G_0$. This implies that for interest rate i_0 the new equilibrium level of income is Y_2, since Y_2 is the only level of income which equates saving plus taxes to investment plus government purchases at the new, higher-level $I_2 + G_0$. This combination of income and interest rate is plotted as the point (Y_2, i_0) in the northeast quadrant and is a point on the new IS curve, IS_1.

Similarly, at interest rate i_1, the new level of investment plus government purchases is $I_3 + G_0$. Thus, for interest rate i_1, the new equilibrium level of income is Y_3, since Y_3 is the only level of income which equates saving plus taxes to investment plus government purchases at the new, higher-level $I_3 + G_0$. This combination of income and interest rate is plotted as the point (Y_3, i_1) in the northeast quadrant and is another point on the new IS curve, IS_1. Other points may be obtained in the same manner. The new IS curve, IS_1, lies to the right of

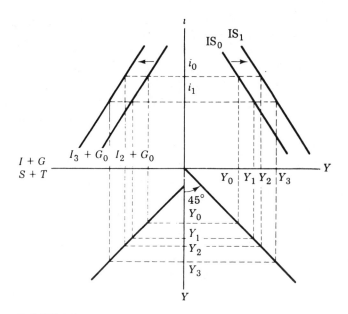

FIGURE 6.5

A shift in the investment function and its impact on the IS curve

the original curve. This is to be expected since, if society invests more at each interest rate, the corresponding equilibrium level of income is greater. Had society invested less, the $I + G$ curve would have shifted to the right, and, as a consequence, the IS curve would have shifted to the left. An increase in government purchases has the same effect on the $I + G$ curve and, hence, the IS curve as a change in the tax treatment of business income which promotes investment.

If investment or government purchases change, the IS curve shifts. The degree to which the IS curve shifts may be predicted with the aid of the multipliers derived earlier. According to Figure 6.4, investment is I_0 at interest rate i_0. If investment increases to I_2, as shown in Figure 6.5, income (at interest rate i_0) increases to Y_2. The change in income from Y_0 to Y_2 due to the change in investment from I_0 to I_2 equals the investment multiplier, $1/(1 - b + bt)$, multiplied by the change in investment. For example, if the investment multiplier is 2.5 and the change in investment is $20 billion, the resulting change in income and, hence, the horizontal shift in the IS curve is 2.5($20) or $50 billion.

The IS curve is also altered if the $S + T$ curve shifts. For example, suppose society decides to save more. If society decides to save more, the saving plus tax curve shifts to the left, as shown in Figure 6.6. The new IS curve is derived in the same manner as before except that the new $S + T$ curve is used rather than the original. The new IS curve is IS_1.

The new IS curve, IS_1, lies to the left of the original, indicating that, at each interest rate, the new equilibrium level of income is less than the original equilibrium level because a decision by society to save more is, at the same time, a decision to consume less. As a consequence, aggregate demand falls; hence, the equilibrium level of income decreases. If society had decided to save less, the $S + T$ curve would have shifted to the right and, as a consequence, the IS curve would have shifted to the right.

If taxes increase, the $S + T$ curve shifts to the left. The $S + T$ curve shifts by an amount less than the increase in taxes since a tax increase reduces saving. As a result of the shift in the $S + T$ curve, the IS curve shifts to the left, indicating that income is less at each interest rate. The degree to which the IS curve shifts in response to the change in taxes may be predicted with the aid of the tax multiplier. For example, if the tax multiplier is -1.5 and taxes increase by \$20 billion, the resulting change in income and, hence, the shift in the IS curve is $-\$30$ billion.

In the model just postulated, investment is a function of the interest rate and consumption is a function of disposable income. Other variables may be added to the investment and consumption functions without significantly altering the IS curve analysis. If investment is a function of both income and the interest rate, the slope of the IS curve is altered. The interpretation of the curve, however, remains the same. (For a discussion of the IS curve with investment a function of both income and the interest rate, see Appendix 2.)

Similarly, if consumption is a function of both income and wealth, the IS curve will shift in response to a change in wealth. For example, suppose the IS curve of Figure 6.4 is derived for a particular level of wealth. Next, suppose wealth increases. The increase in wealth increases consumption and reduces saving. As a consequence, the saving plus taxes curve shifts to the right. This implies that the IS curve also shifts to the right, indicating that income at each interest rate is greater than before. The increase in income occurs because, with an increase in wealth,

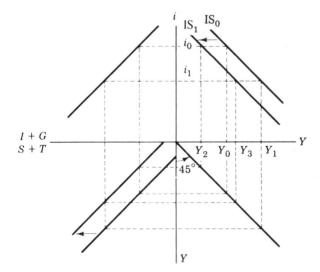

FIGURE 6.6

A shift in the saving function and its impact on the IS curve consumption and, hence, aggregate demand increase. With the increase in aggregate demand, the equilibrium level of income increases at each interest rate.

CONCLUDING REMARKS

In this chapter, we considered various theories of investment as well as equilibrium in the product market. With investment a function of the interest rate, we found that an equilibrium level of income exists for each interest rate. Consequently, the market rate of interest must be known in order to determine the equilibrium level of income. In Chapters 7 and 8, we investigate the money market and derive the LM curve, a relationship between income and the equilibrium interest rate for the money market, which is analogous to the IS curve for the product market. In Chapter 9, we deal with the interaction of the product and money markets and determine the equilibrium values of the interest rate and income.

NOTes _____

1. For discussions of and references to investment in business inventories and residential structures, see John A. Naylor, "A Survey of Post-1970 Empirical Studies of Investment Expenditures," in *Modern Concepts in Macroeconomics*, ed. Thomas M. Havrilesky (Arlington Heights, Ill.: Harlan Davidson, Inc., 1985), pp. 27–55.

2. For simplicity, we assume that interest is not compounded semiannually or more often. Similarly, we assume that there is a single market rate of interest; this problem is addressed in the next chapter.

3. The early studies are summarized in John R. Meyer and Edwin Kuh, *The Investment Decision* (Cambridge, Mass.: Harvard University Press, 1957).

4. By *replacement investment*, we mean investment intended to replace plant and equipment that is wearing out or has been destroyed. For references and a survey of the empirical evidence, see Dale W. Jorgenson, "Econometric Studies of Investment Behavior: A Survey," *Journal of Economic Literature*, 9 (December 1971), 1138–41.

5. Jan Tinbergen, *Statistical Testing of Business-Cycle Theories* (Geneva: League of Nations, 1938). For an alternative expected profit approach, see Yehuda Grunfeld, "The Determinants of Corporate Investment," in *The Demand for Durable Goods*, ed. Arnold C. Harberger (Chicago: University of Chicago Press, 1960), pp. 211–66.

6. Meyer and Kuh, *The Investment Decision*; James S. Duesenberry, *Business Cycles and Economic Growth* (New York: McGraw-Hill Book Company, 1958); W.H. Locke Anderson, *Corporate Finance and Fixed Investment: An Econometric Study* (Cambridge, Mass.: Harvard University Press, 1964); and John R. Meyer and Robert R. Glauber, *Investment Decisions, Economic Forecasting, and Public Policy* (Cambridge, Mass.: Harvard University Press, 1964).

7. See, for example, Dale W. Jorgenson, "The Theory of Investment Behavior," in *The Determinants of Investment Behavior*, ed. Robert Ferber (New York: National Bureau of Economic Research, 1967), pp. 129–55.

8. James Tobin, "A General Equilibrium Approach to Monetary Theory," *Journal of Money, Credit, and Banking*, 1 (February 1969), 15–29; and Tobin and William C.

Brainard, "Asset Markets and the Cost of Capital," in *Economic Progress, Private Values, and Public Policy*, eds. Bela Balassa and Richard Nelson (Amsterdam: North-Holland Publishing Company, 1977), pp. 235–62.

9. For a discussion of the impact of tax changes upon investment using the q theory approach, see Lawrence H. Summers, "Taxation and Corporate Investment: A q Theory Approach," *Brookings Papers on Economic Activity*, no. 1 (1981), 67–127.

10. Peter K. Clark, "Investment in the 1970s: Theory, Performance, and Prediction," *Brookings Papers on Economic Activity*, no. 1 (1979), 73–113. Charles W. Bischoff and Richard W. Kopcke conducted similar studies. Using quarterly data for 1953–68, Bischoff concluded that the accelerator and neoclassical models explain investment about equally well and both provide better explanations of investment behavior than the internal funds and q models. Based on quarterly data for 1956–79, Kopcke asserts that the internal funds and neoclassical models are superior to the accelerator and q models. Bischoff, "Business Investment in the 1970s: A Comparison of Models," *Brookings Papers on Economic Activity*, no. 1 (1971), 13–58; and Kopcke, "The Determinants of Investment Spending," Federal Reserve Bank of Boston, *New England Economic Review*, (July–August 1985), 19–35.

11. Dale W. Jorgenson, Jerald Hunter, and M. Ishag Nadiri, "A Comparison of Alternative Econometric Models of Quarterly Investment Behavior," *Econometrica*, 38 (March 1970), 187–212.

12. Dale W. Jorgenson and Calvin D. Siebert, "A Comparison of Alternative Theories of Corporate Investment Behavior," *American Economic Review*, 58 (September 1968), 681–712.

13. J.W. Elliott conducted a study similar to that of Jorgenson and Siebert but for a much larger (184) sample of firms. His results, based on the 1953–67 period, suggest that the internal funds model performs better than the accelerator theory which, in turn, out-performs the neoclassical model. Elliott, "Theories of Corporate Investment Behavior Revisited," *American Economic Review*, 63 (March 1973), 195–207.

14. The q theory does not fare well in the studies surveyed here. The same is true in George M. von Furstenberg's study. von Furstenberg, "Corporate Investment: Does Market Valuation Matter in the Aggregate?" *Brookings Papers on Economic Activity*, no. 2 (1977), 347–97. Studies supporting the q theory include those by Tobin and Brainard; John H. Ciccolo, Jr.; Burton G. Malkiel, von Furstenberg, and Harry S. Watson; Nicholas Oulton; and Henry W. Chappell, Jr. and David C. Cheng. For the most part, however, these studies do not compare alternative theories using a common set of data. Tobin and Brainard, "Asset Markets and the Cost of Capital,"; Ciccolo, "Four Essays on Monetary Policy" (Ph.D. Dissertation, Yale University, 1975); Malkiel, von Furstenberg, and Watson, "Expectations, Tobin's q, and Industry Investment," *Journal of Finance*, 34 (May 1979), 549–61; Oulton, "Aggregate Investment and Tobin's Q: the Evidence from Britain," *Oxford Economic Papers*, 33 (July 1981), 177–202; and Chappell and Cheng, "Expectations, Tobin's q, and Investment: A Note," *Journal of Finance*, 37 (March 1982), 231–36.

15. Jorgenson, "Econometric Studies of Investment Behavior."

16. For supporting evidence with regard to the interest rate, see Robert E. Hall, "Investment, Interest Rates, and the Effects of Stabilization Policies," *Brookings Papers on Economic Activity*, no. 1 (1977), 61–103; and John C. Warner, "Unfulfilled Long-Term Interest Rate Expectations and Change in Business Fixed Investment," *American Economic Review*, 68 (June 1978), 339–47.

17. We assume that technology, the tax treatment of business income, and the other determinants of the desired capital stock are constant.

18. If net investment is $10 billion in the initial period, the capital stock increases by $10 billion, thereby reducing the gap between the desired and actual capital stocks from $20 billion to $10 billion. Net investment in the next period is $5 billion, found by multiplying

λ equal to one-half by the gap between the desired and actual capital stocks, $10 billion.

19. As net investment occurs, the capital stock increases and the gap between the desired and actual capital stocks is reduced. Since net investment is positively related to that gap, net investment decreases and eventually equals zero when the gap is eliminated. This suggests that the investment function of Figure 6.2 shifts to the left as capital accumulation occurs.

REVIEW QUESTIONS

1. Explain why it is necessary to discount a future income stream to determine its present value.

2. Suppose you have $1,000 and the opportunity to purchase an asset which yields $585 at the end of the first year and $585 at the end of the second year (and zero thereafter). If the market rate of interest is 10 percent, is it to your advantage to purchase the asset? Why? Why not?

3. Company A is considering the purchase of a machine which costs $2,000, will last for two years, and is expected to produce 1,000 units of output per year. During the first year, each unit of output is expected to sell for $2 per unit; labor and raw material costs are expected to be $0.90 per unit (other operating costs are assumed to be negligible). During the second year, each unit of output is expected to sell for $2.50 per unit; labor and raw material costs are expected to be $1.00 per unit; and maintenance cost is expected to be $290 (other operating costs are assumed to be negligible). Assume no scrap value for the machine and all revenues and costs concentrated at the end of each year.

   a. Calculate net income for each of the two years.

   b. If the interest rate is 12 percent, calculate the present value of the income stream associated with the use of the machine. Should Company A buy the machine? Why? Why not?

   c. If the interest rate is 10 percent, calculate the present value of the income stream associated with the use of the machine. Should Company A buy the machine? Why? Why not?

   d. If the interest rate is 8 percent, calculate the present value of the income stream associated with the use of the machine. Should Company A buy the machine? Why? Why not?

   e. Calculate the marginal efficiency of investment associated with the machine.

4. Suppose Company A is considering an expansion in its productive capacity and has estimated the marginal efficiency of investment to be 8 percent.

    a. If the market rate of interest is 10 percent, should the firm undertake the project if it has to borrow the money? Why? Why not?

    b. If the market rate of interest is 10 percent, should the firm undertake the project if the firm has the necessary funds on hand? Why? Why not?

    c. If the market rate of interest is 6 percent, should the firm undertake the project? Why? Why not?

5. Suppose a company is considering the purchase of a machine with an anticipated marginal efficiency of investment of 8 percent. Explain how and, briefly, why the marginal efficiency of investment is altered by the following:

    a. An *increase* in the cost of the machine.

    b. An *increase* in the expected price (or prices) for which the product produced by the machine may be sold.

    c. An *increase* in the expected operating costs associated with the machine.

    d. An *increase* in the corporate tax rate.

6. Outline and critically evaluate the crude version of the accelerator theory of investment. How does the more sophisticated version of the accelerator theory differ from the crude version?

7. Compare and contrast the accelerator, internal funds, neoclassical, and q theories of investment with regard to

    a. the determinants of the desired capital stock.

    b. their policy implications.

8. Briefly review the empirical evidence relating to the four theories of investment behavior.

9. Suppose the model is

$$C = 130 + 0.5Y_d \quad \text{(where } Y_d = Y - T),$$

$$I = 200 - 600i,$$

$$G = 112,$$

$$T = 20 + 0.2Y.$$

Determine the equilibrium level of income corresponding to each of the following interest rates:

Interest Rate (i), Percent	Income (Y), $ Billions
15	————
10	————
5	————

10. Suppose the IS curve is as follows:

Interest Rate (i) Percent	Income (Y), $ Billions
20	600
15	700
10	800
5	900

a. Is the product market in equilibrium at $i = 10$ percent and $Y = \$800$ billion? Why? Why not? If not, explain why Y tends to change until equilibrium is established. (Assume i remains equal to 10 percent).

b. Is the product market in equilibrium at $i = 15$ percent and $Y = \$800$ billion? Why? Why not? If not, explain why Y tends to change until equilibrium is established. (Assume i remains equal to 15 percent.)

11. Define the IS curve and explain why income increases as the interest rate decreases (as you move along the IS curve).

12. Explain how the IS curve is altered if

a. government purchases *increase*,

b. taxes *increase*,

c. government purchases and taxes *increase* by the same amount,

d. the interest rate *increases*.

13. How is the IS curve affected if

a. investment is a function of both income and the interest rate.

b. saving is a function of both income and the interest rate.

SUGGESTED READING

CLARK, PETER K., "Investment in the 1970s: Theory, Performance, and Prediction," *Brookings Papers on Economic Activity,* no. 1 (1979), 73–124.

EISNER, ROBERT, "Econometric Studies of Investment Behavior: A Comment," *Economic Inquiry*, 12 (March 1974), 91–104.

————, *Factors in Business Investment.* Cambridge, Mass.: Ballinger Publishing Co., 1978.

JORGENSON, DALE W., "Econometric Studies of Investment Behavior: A Survey," *Journal of Economic Literature*, 9 (December 1971), 111–47.

————, "The Theory of Investment Behavior," in Robert Ferber (ed.), *The Determinants of Investment Behavior*, pp. 129–55. New York: National Bureau of Economic Research, 1967.

NAYLOR, JOHN A., "A Survey of Post-1970 Empirical Studies of Investment Expenditures," in Thomas M. Havrilesky (ed.), *Modern Concepts in Macroeconomics*, pp. 27–55. Arlington Heights, Ill.: Harlan Davidson, Inc., 1985.

TOBIN, JAMES, "A General Equilibrium Approach to Monetary Theory," *Journal of Money, Credit, and Banking*, 1 (February 1969), 15–29.

————, and WILLIAM C. BRAINARD, "Asset Markets and the Cost of Capital," in Bela Balassa and Richard Nelson (eds.), *Economic Progress, Private Values, and Public Policy*, pp. 235–62. Amsterdam: North-Holland Publishing Company, 1977.

7

THE SUPPLY
OF MONEY

In Chapter 6, we examined the relationship between investment and the interest rate. In this and the following chapter, we consider the determinants of the interest rate—the supply of, and the demand for, money. In this chapter, we discuss the money supply, its determinants, and various policy instruments of the Federal Reserve. In the next, we consider the demand for money, its determinants, and equilibrium in the money market. The money market is then incorporated into the model of Chapter 6 to form a more complete theory of income determination.

Before turning to the supply of money, let us consider an unresolved issue. In Chapter 6, we assumed a single market rate of interest, even though a multiplicity of interest rates exist. Interest rates vary by borrower, by type of bond, and by length of loan. To illustrate, the United States Treasury borrows (issues bonds) at relatively low interest rates; large corporations usually borrow at higher rates. Individuals typically borrow at even higher rates. Interest rates or bond yields also vary by type of bond. Tax-exempt bonds usually have lower yields than similar bonds which are not tax exempt. Bonds redeemable at the option of the company or convertible into common stock have yields which differ from bonds that do not have those features. Finally, yields also vary according to the length of time to maturity. For example, yields on short-term bonds usually differ from those on otherwise identical long-term bonds.

Perhaps the most important reason for the diversity of interest rates is risk. The greater the risk of default of promised interest and principal payments, the higher is the interest rate associated with the loan. Differences in tax treatment and other bond characteristics also account for some of the diversity of rates.

Given the diversity of interest rates, one procedure is to incorporate a number of rates into the model, thereby adding to its complexity. Fortunately, this is not necessary since the various interest rates typically rise or fall together. To be sure, the synchronization is not perfect. Long-term interest rates, for example, may fall more slowly than other rates. Yet the movements of the various rates are not dissimilar enough to justify including a number of interest rates in the model.

MONEY AND ITS FUNCTIONS

Money normally serves three functions. It is a unit of account, a medium of exchange, and a store of value. As a *unit of account,* it measures the value of things, thereby providing a common basis for comparison. If one item is priced at $20 and another at $10, people know immediately the relative cost of each item—the first costs twice as much as the second. The unit of account function is important, therefore, for computation, record keeping, and decision making.

Money also serves as a *medium of exchange,* something which can be used to purchase goods and services and pay debts. Hence, money facilitates the exchange of goods and services. In primitive societies, households are largely self-sufficient. There is little trade and little need for a medium of exchange. With the development of industry and trade, a greater need for a medium of exchange emerges. Indeed, it is difficult to imagine a modern economy without a medium of exchange. Barter, the alternative approach, is extremely inefficient. It takes too much time and effort to find persons who both have what you want and want what you have.

Finally, money serves as a *store of value.* Households may hold all or part of their savings in monetary form. Savings may also be held in other forms, such as bonds, common stock, and land. As a consequence, money is not the only store of value. During periods of inflation, the purchasing power of money is eroded. During those periods, therefore, money does not perform its store of value function very satisfactorily.

Perhaps the most common definition of *money* is anything generally accepted as final payment for goods, services, or debt. By this definition, *currency* or *cash* (paper money and coins) and demand deposits are money. *Demand deposits*—checking accounts at commercial banks—are considered money because they are readily accepted as a medium of exchange. By the same definition, savings and time deposits, hereafter referred to as *time deposits,* are not money. Time deposits are not acceptable as a medium of exchange; they must be converted to demand deposits or some other form of money.[1]

THE MONEY SUPPLY

Prior to 1980, the money supply was usually defined as currency and demand deposits held by the nonbank public. With the growth of other checkable deposits in the 1970s, however, this definition became less and less satisfactory. As a result, the definition was modified in 1980 and again in 1982. Today, the *money supply* is usually defined as currency, traveler's checks, demand deposits, and other checkable deposits, including NOW, super NOW, and ATS deposits, credit union share draft balances, and demand deposits at thrift institutions.[2]

Negotiable order of withdrawal (NOW) *deposits* are interest-bearing accounts that permit owners to withdraw or transfer funds by writing negotiable orders of withdrawal (similar to checks) payable to third parties. *Super NOW accounts* are similar to NOW accounts but require a higher minimum balance and pay a higher interest rate. *Automatic transfer service* (ATS) *deposits* provide for automatic transfer of funds from savings deposits to demand deposits to cover checks. *Credit union share draft balances* are the credit union equivalent of NOW accounts. They bear interest and the owners can write credit union share drafts (also similar to checks) on them.

Traveler's checks and other checkable deposits are considered part of the money supply because they are readily accepted as a medium of exchange. This definition of the money supply corresponds to one of the monetary aggregates, M1, published by the Federal Reserve. This aggregate and its components are shown in Table 7.1.

In addition to M1, the Federal Reserve publishes data on three other monetary

TABLE 7.1 M1 and its components, March 1986[1]

	Amount	Percentage
M1	638.4	100.0
Currency	173.9	27.2
Traveler's checks	6.1	1.0
Demand deposits	273.1	42.8
Other checkable deposits	185.3	29.0

[1] In billions of current dollars (seasonally adjusted); average daily figures.

Source: Board of Governors of the Federal Reserve System, *Federal Reserve Bulletin*, 72, no. 6 (June 1986) A13.

aggregates (M2, M3, and L). Current data for M1 and the other aggregates are found in the *Federal Reserve Bulletin* and various other publications. Although we assume for our immediate purposes that M1 is the appropriate definition of the money supply, we shall consider alternative definitions and their implications for monetary policy in Chapter 19.

So far, we have discussed the *nominal money supply*—the dollar value of the nation's money supply. The nominal money supply is very important, but it does not take into account its purchasing power. The *real money supply* reflects both the dollar value of the money supply and the price level. If the nominal money supply is denoted as Ms and the price level (implicit price deflator for GNP) as P, the real money supply is defined as the nominal money supply deflated (divided) by the price level or Ms/P. For example, suppose the nominal money supply in a particular year is \$200 billion and the price level is 100. The real money supply equals \$200 billion divided by 100 percent or \$200 billion. Suppose, in a later year, the nominal money supply is \$400 billion and the price level is 200. If a person were to consider only the nominal money supply, he might conclude, incorrectly, that the money supply can buy a greater amount of goods and services. Since both the nominal money supply and the price level have increased by 100 percent, the real money supply, Ms/P, is unaltered.

In the following chapters, we shall be concerned primarily with the real money supply, since it includes both the nominal money supply and the price level. For the next two chapters, however, we continue to assume that the price level is constant; consequently, in those chapters, a change in the nominal money supply implies an equivalent change in the real money supply.

As a first approximation, we assume that the nominal money supply is determined by the actions of the Federal Reserve. Thus, the nominal money supply, Ms, is an exogenous variable and the nominal money supply function may be written as

$$(7.1) \qquad\qquad Ms = Ms_0.$$

If the nominal money supply is considered "too small," we assume that the Federal Reserve or Fed may take appropriate action to increase it. Similarly, if the money supply is "too large," the Fed may take action to decrease it.

Since the price level is assumed constant at the P_0 level, action by the Fed to alter the nominal money supply also alters the real money supply. Thus, the real money supply function is

$$(7.2) \qquad\qquad \frac{Ms}{P} = \frac{Ms_0}{P_0}$$

and the real money supply is an exogenous variable.

In the remainder of this chapter, we develop a more sophisticated money supply function and examine the various instruments the Federal Reserve has at its disposal to alter the nominal money supply.

THE COMMERCIAL BANKING SYSTEM

Since demand deposits of commercial banks constitute the largest single component of the nation's money supply, we focus primarily on commercial banks and demand deposits in this and the following section.[3] The results are generalized later in the chapter.

Each commercial bank in the United States is organized as a corporation and has a charter authorizing it to engage in banking. As a bank, each offers a variety of services, including the acceptance of demand and time deposits. As of June 30, 1984, there were 14,508 commercial banks in the United States.

Commercial banks may be chartered by either the federal or state governments. Banks chartered by the federal government are known as *national banks*; banks chartered by state governments are called *state banks*. State banks outnumber national banks by a margin of about two to one, but national banks, in general, are larger than state banks.

By law, national banks must belong to the Federal Reserve System. State banks may join if they desire to do so and if they meet the requirements. As of June 30, 1984, only about 11 percent of the 9,684 state banks belonged to the system. Consequently, less than 41 percent of the nation's banks were members of the Federal Reserve System. But these banks, called *member banks*, accounted for over 70 percent of total deposits.

Member banks are subject to the rules and regulations of the Federal Reserve System, including reserve requirements. Member banks must hold a percentage of their deposits as vault cash and noninterest-earning deposits at Federal Reserve Banks. Historically, nonmember banks were required by state law to hold reserves, but these requirements were usually not as restrictive as those for member banks. As a result, nonmember banks had an incentive to remain nonmember banks, and member banks had an incentive to leave the system. With the enactment of the Depository Institutions Deregulation and Monetary Control Act of 1980, however, all banks (as well as all other depository institutions) are subject to the same federally imposed reserve requirements.

COMMERCIAL BANKS AND MONEY CREATION

In this section, we consider the impact of an increase in reserves upon demand deposits and the money supply. In doing so, we assume that commercial banks do not hold excess reserves and that the public does not add to its holdings of cash, traveler's checks, other checkable deposits, and time deposits during the demand deposit expansion process.

A simplified version of a commercial bank's *balance sheet*, a statement of the bank's assets, liabilities, and capital accounts as of a certain date, is shown in Table 7.2. The bank, Bank A, is assumed to be a member of the Federal Reserve System and, as a consequence, maintains deposits at its Federal Reserve Bank. *Assets*

TABLE 7.2 A simplified balance sheet for commercial bank A

Assets	
Cash	$ 200,000
Deposits at Federal Reserve Bank	800,000
U.S. Treasury securities	2,000,000
Loans	3,500,000
Total Assets	$6,500,000
Liabilities	
Demand deposits	$4,000,000
Other checkable deposits	500,000
Nonpersonal time deposits	500,000
Personal time deposits	1,000,000
Total Liabilities	$6,000,000
Capital Accounts	
Common stock	$ 100,000
Surplus	200,000
Undivided profits	200,000
Total Capital Accounts	$ 500,000
Total Liabilities and Capital Accounts	$6,500,000

represent items that the bank owns and include cash and deposits at its Federal Reserve Bank. Since, however, neither cash nor deposits at Federal Reserve Banks earn interest, commercial banks have an incentive to make loans and to purchase assets, such as Treasury securities, which bear interest. The bank's *liabilities* are its debts and include demand and time deposits. The *capital accounts* show the amount originally invested by the stockholders and the modifications that have occurred through profits and losses over the years.

The bank's assets, liabilities, and capital accounts are related. The bank's assets must equal its liabilities plus capital accounts. Moreover, for each transaction affecting the bank's balance sheet, there must be two entries. For example, if the bank should desire more cash, it may obtain more from its Federal Reserve Bank by reducing its deposits at the Federal Reserve Bank. The increase in cash and decrease in deposits at the Federal Reserve Bank will be reflected in the bank's balance sheet.

Rather than reproducing the bank's entire balance sheet each time a transaction occurs, it is convenient to summarize the transaction with a T-account. Assets are recorded on the left side of the T-account, with liabilities and capital accounts on the right side. As before, there will be two entries for each transaction, and equality must be maintained between assets on the one hand and liabilities plus capital accounts on the other. For example, suppose Bank A obtains more cash from its Federal Reserve Bank by reducing its deposits at the Federal Reserve

Bank. If the amount involved is $10,000, the following T-account reflects the transaction:

Commercial Bank A

Assets		Liabilities and Capital Accounts
Cash	+$10,000	
Deposits at Federal Reserve Bank	−$10,000	

As another example, suppose an individual deposits $10,000 in cash in her checking account. Bank A finds that it has a $10,000 increase in assets and a $10,000 increase in liabilities. The transaction is shown in the following T-account:

Commercial Bank A

Assets		Liabilities and Capital Accounts	
Cash	+$10,000	Demand deposits	+$10,000

We now trace the effect of an increase in reserves on demand deposits and ultimately the money supply. As stated earlier, banks are required to maintain reserves against deposits. For simplicity, assume that banks are required to hold reserves equal to 20 percent of their demand, other checkable, and nonpersonal time deposit liabilities. For Bank A, these liabilities total $5 million; hence, Bank A must have vault cash and deposits at its Federal Reserve Bank totaling $1 million. These reserves, shown in Table 7.2, are Bank A's *required* or *legal reserves.* Reserves over and above required reserves are, by definition, *excess reserves.* Excess reserves are crucial to the creation of demand deposits by the banking system.

The monetary authorities may increase the money supply through Federal Reserve purchases of Treasury securities. Suppose the Fed purchases $1,000 of Treasury securities from an individual and pays for the securities with a check drawn on a Federal Reserve Bank. If the individual deposits the check at Bank A, Bank A's demand deposits increase by $1,000; since the Federal Reserve credits Bank A's account at its Federal Reserve Bank, Bank A's deposits at its Federal Reserve Bank also increase by $1,000. The transaction is illustrated in the following T-account:

Commercial Bank A

Assets		Liabilities and Capital Accounts	
Deposits at Federal Reserve Bank	+$1,000	Demand deposits	+$1,000

Since demand deposits are part of the money supply, the $1,000 increase in demand deposits represents a $1,000 increase in the money supply. Bank A's reserves have increased by $1,000. Its required reserves have increased by $200, the product of the required reserve ratio, 20 percent, and the increase in demand deposits, $1,000. Thus, excess reserves have increased by $800.

With the creation of the excess reserves, a further increase in demand deposits and, hence, the money supply is likely to ensue. In fact, our earlier assumptions, that banks do not wish to hold excess reserves and that the public does not wish to add to its holdings of cash, other forms of money, and time deposits, guarantee that the process will continue.

Since reserves earn no interest, Bank A has an incentive to make loans, and we assume that it does. Bank A's loans increase by $800; its demand deposits also increase by $800 as the bank credits the borrower's checking account. This transaction is shown in the following T-account:

Commercial Bank A

Assets		*Liabilities and Capital Accounts*	
Loans	+ $800	Demand deposits	+ $800

Since the borrower presumably obtained the loan for a purpose, he will write a check on the bank. The recipient of the check is likely to deposit the check at Bank B, since Bank A is only one of some 14,500 banks in the country. Bank A's demand deposits are reduced by $800 and Bank B's are increased by $800. Moreover, as the check clears, the Federal Reserve reduces Bank A's deposits at its Federal Reserve Bank by $800 and increases Bank B's by $800. These transactions are shown in the following T-accounts:

Commercial Bank A | | Commercial Bank B | |

Assets	*Liabilities and Capital Accounts*	*Assets*	*Liabilities and Capital Accounts*
Deposits at Federal Reserve Bank − $800	Demand deposits − $800	Deposits at Federal Reserve Bank + $800	Demand deposits + $800

Although Bank A experienced an $800 reduction in demand deposits to offset its $800 increase, Bank B experienced an $800 increase. As a result, demand deposits and, hence, the money supply have increased by $800.

With the reduction in Bank A's reserves and demand deposits, Bank A no longer has excess reserves. As a result of the transaction, however, Bank B now has excess reserves. Bank B has experienced increases in reserves and demand deposits of $800. Since the required reserve ratio is 20 percent, it must hold only $160 as required reserves. Consequently, Bank B has $640 in excess reserves.

As in the case of Bank A, Bank B is assumed to make a loan. As a consequence, its loans increase by $640 and its demand deposits by $640 as the borrower's checking account is credited. These transactions are shown in the following T-account:

Commercial Bank B

Assets		Liabilities and Capital Accounts	
Loans	+ $640	Demand deposits	+ $640

The borrower will write a check on the bank. If the recipient of the check deposits it at Bank C, Bank B's demand deposits are reduced by $640 and Bank C's demand deposits increase by $640. Moreover, Bank B's deposits at its Federal Reserve Bank are reduced by $640 and Bank C's deposits are increased by $640. These transactions are shown in the following T-accounts:

Commercial Bank B		Commercial Bank C	
Assets	*Liabilities and Capital Accounts*	*Assets*	*Liabilities and Capital Accounts*
Deposits at Federal Reserve Bank − $640	Demand deposits − $640	Deposits at Federal Reserve Bank + 640	Demand deposits + 640

Although Bank B loses demand deposits of $640 to offset the initial increase of $640, Bank C gains $640 in demand deposits. With the $640 increase in demand deposits, the money supply increases by $640.

With the increase in demand deposits (and reserves), Bank C now has excess reserves which it can lend. Rather than follow the process further, however, we shall determine the total increase in demand deposits. In the illustration, demand deposits increase by $1,000, then $800, and then $640. As the increase in demand deposits occur, more and more of the initial increase in reserves is required to support demand deposits. Given the assumptions, the increase in demand deposits must continue until no excess reserves exist. Consequently, the initial change in reserves, ΔH, eventually becomes a change in required reserves, ΔR. Thus,

$$\Delta H = \Delta R.$$

The change in required reserves, ΔR, is equal to the ratio of required reserves to demand deposits, r, multiplied by the total increase in demand deposits, ΔD. Thus, upon substitution,

$$\Delta H = r\Delta D.$$

Dividing both sides of the equation by r and rearranging terms, we obtain

$$(7.3) \qquad\qquad \Delta D = \frac{\Delta H}{r},$$

where ΔD represents the total change in demand deposits, ΔH the initial change in reserves, and r the ratio of required reserves to demand deposits.

According to equation (7.3), the total change in demand deposits equals the initial change in reserves multiplied by the reciprocal of the reserve requirement. In the example, the total increase in demand deposits equals \$1,000/0.20 or \$5,000.[4] Since the reserve requirement is 20 percent and the initial increase in reserves is \$1,000, the total increase in demand deposits must be \$5,000 in order that the initial increase in reserves be absorbed as required reserves.

According to equation (7.3), the total change in demand deposits is positively related to the initial change in reserves and inversely related to the reserve requirement. Thus, if the initial increase in reserves is \$2,000, the total increase in demand deposits is \$2,000/0.20 or \$10,000. On the other hand, if the reserve requirement is 40 percent, the same initial increase in reserves results in only a \$5,000 increase in demand deposits.

Since demand deposits are part of the money supply and since the public did not add to its holdings of cash, traveler's checks, and other checkable deposits during the expansion process, the total increase in the money supply equals the total increase in demand deposits.

MONEY CREATION: SOME COMPLICATIONS

The increase in demand deposits and money supply indicated by equation (7.3) represents the maximum possible expansion. Initially, it was assumed that commercial banks do not hold excess reserves and that the public does not add to its holdings of cash, other forms of money, and time deposits during the expansion process. If those assumptions are met, the increase in demand deposits and money supply is indicated by equation (7.3). If the assumptions are not met, the increase in the money supply will be less than indicated by equation (7.3). Hence, it is desirable to develop an equation for determining the increase in the money supply when depository institutions hold excess reserves and the public adds to its holdings of cash, other checkable deposits, and time deposits.

As a first step, we note the Depository Institutions Deregulation and Monetary Control Act of 1980 altered the classification of deposits upon which depository institutions must hold reserves. Prior to the Act, the fundamental distinction was between demand and time deposits; it is now between transaction accounts, nonpersonal time deposits, and personal time deposits.[5] *Transaction accounts* or deposits include demand deposits, NOW accounts, super NOW accounts, ATS accounts, and credit union share draft balances. The same set of reserve requirements apply to all transaction accounts. *Nonpersonal time deposits* include passbook accounts, savings certificates, and certificates of deposits owned by firms and organizations. Depository institutions must hold reserves against nonpersonal time deposits; they are not required to hold them against personal time deposits.

Next, we note that some depository institutions, especially small ones, hold excess reserves. The management of those institutions apparently thinks that required reserves are inadequate to meet potential deposit losses; they hold excess reserves to provide liquidity. This alternative is particularly attractive when interest rates are low because the cost of holding excess reserves is small then.

If depository institutions add to their excess reserves during the expansion process, they will lend smaller amounts and a correspondingly smaller increase in transaction deposits will occur. Excess reserves, therefore, represent a leakage or drain from the deposit expansion process. If depository institutions hold excess reserves in some fixed proportion, e, of their transaction deposits, this drain equals $e\Delta D$, or the proportion, e, multiplied by the change in transaction deposits, ΔD. Therefore, the initial increase in reserves, ΔH, will ultimately be divided into changes in required reserves, ΔR, and excess reserves, $e\Delta D$, or

$$\Delta H = \Delta R + e\Delta D.$$

Since the change in required reserves, ΔR, equals $r\Delta D$, or the reserve requirement for transaction deposits, r, multiplied by the change in transaction deposits, ΔD, we obtain

$$\Delta H = r\Delta D + e\Delta D,$$

by substitution.

Next, suppose the public adds to its holdings of cash during the expansion process. With the increase in cash holdings, depository institutions lose reserves. The reserve losses limit the amounts that depository institutions can lend and, therefore, the increase in transaction deposits. Thus, increases in cash balances represent a drain from the expansion process. If the public holds cash in some fixed proportion, c, of its transaction deposits, this drain equals $c\Delta D$, or the proportion, c, multiplied by the change in transaction deposits, ΔD. In this case, the initial increase in reserves, ΔH, will ultimately be divided into changes in required reserves, $r\Delta D$, excess reserves, $e\Delta D$, and cash held by the public, $c\Delta D$, or

$$\Delta H = r\Delta D + e\Delta D + c\Delta D.$$

Suppose firms and organizations add to their time deposits during the expansion process. Depository institutions will not lose reserves. Since they must hold reserves in support of nonpersonal time deposits, however, part of the initial increase in reserves must be used for nonpersonal time deposits. Consequently, there will be fewer reserves to support transaction deposits and a correspondingly smaller increase in transaction deposits. Thus, increases in nonpersonal time deposits represent a drain from the transaction deposit expansion process. If firms and organizations hold time deposits in some fixed proportion, t, of their transaction deposits, and if r' represents the reserve requirement for nonpersonal time deposits, the drain equals $r't\Delta D$, or the reserve requirement, r', multiplied by the change in nonpersonal time deposits, $t\Delta D$. As a result, the initial increase in reserves, ΔH, will ultimately be split into changes in required reserves for transaction deposits, $r\Delta D$, excess reserves, $e\Delta D$, cash held by the public, $c\Delta D$, and required reserves for nonpersonal time deposits, $r't\Delta D$, or

$$\Delta H = r\Delta D + e\Delta D + c\Delta D + r't\Delta D.$$

To determine the change in transaction deposits, ΔD, corresponding to an initial change in reserves, ΔH, we rearrange terms, factor, and divide both sides of the equation by $r + e + c + r't$. Thus,

(7.4)
$$\Delta D = \frac{\Delta H}{r + e + c + r't}.$$

Equation (7.4) indicates that the change in transaction deposits is a function of the initial change in reserves, the reserve requirements for transaction and nonpersonal time deposits, and the ratios of excess reserves, cash, and nonpersonal time deposits to transaction deposits. Suppose the initial increase in reserves is $1,000; the reserve requirements for transaction and nonpersonal time deposits are 0.20 and 0.10, respectively; and the ratios of excess reserves, cash, and nonpersonal time deposits to transaction deposits are 0.05, 0.15, and 1.00, respectively. By substitution, we obtain

$$\Delta D = \frac{\$1,000}{0.20 + 0.05 + 0.15 + 0.10(1.00)} = \$2,000.$$

In this case, the increase in transaction deposits is $2,000, which is substantially less than the $5,000 first obtained in the previous section. In that section, it was assumed that depository institutions did not hold excess reserves and the public did not add to its holdings of cash and nonpersonal time deposits during the deposit expansion process. If these assumptions are relaxed, the result will be a smaller increase in transaction deposits.

So far, we have concentrated on the increase in transaction deposits. Our primary concern, however, is with the increase in the money supply in response to an increase in reserves. The change in the money supply consists of the changes in transaction deposits and cash held by the public. Since the public holds cash in some fixed proportion, c, of its transaction deposits, the change in cash balances equals $c\Delta D$, or the proportion, c, multiplied by the change in transaction deposits, ΔD. Thus, the change in the money supply, ΔMs, equals the change in transaction deposits, ΔD, plus the change in cash balances, $c\Delta D$, or

$$\Delta Ms = \Delta D + c\Delta D,$$

or $$\Delta Ms = (1 + c)\Delta D.$$

Since $$\Delta D = \frac{\Delta H}{r + e + c + r't},$$

we obtain

(7.5) $$\Delta Ms = \frac{(1 + c)\Delta H}{r + e + c + r't}.$$

Initially, ΔH represented the change in reserves. But if the public adds to its holdings of cash during the expansion process, part of the original increase in reserves drains from the system. Under these circumstances, ΔH must be defined as the change in reserves of depository institutions *and* cash held by the public. In this context, ΔH is referred to as the change in the monetary base. Similarly, the *monetary base*, H, is defined as the reserves of depository institutions and cash held by the public. The monetary base, H, is often called *high-powered money* because each dollar increase in the monetary base can produce an increase of several dollars in the money supply.

The term $(1 + c)/(r + e + c + r't)$ is called the *money multiplier*. It may be used to estimate the change in the money supply resulting from a change in the monetary base. To illustrate, suppose the monetary base increases by \$1 billion. If r equals 0.20, e equals 0.05, c equals 0.15, r' equals 0.10, and t equals 1, the money multiplier equals $(1 + 0.15)/[0.20 + 0.05 + 0.15 + 0.10(1)]$ or 1.15/0.50, which equals 2.3. Thus, the ultimate increase in the money supply is estimated to be \$2.3 billion, obtained by multiplying the increase in the monetary base, \$1 billion, by the money multiplier, 2.3.[6]

If m represents the money multiplier, the change in the money supply, ΔMs, resulting from a change in the monetary base, ΔH, is given by the relationship,

$$\Delta Ms = m\Delta H.$$

This relationship implies a relationship between the money supply and the monetary base; it is

(7.6) $$Ms = mH.$$

Equation (7.6) represents a nominal money supply function. According to the function, the money supply is positively related to both the money multiplier and the monetary base. If the money multiplier is constant, however, we need worry only about the monetary base because it will be the only source of instability with regard to the nominal money supply. In the next section, we shall examine the money multiplier more closely to determine if it can be regarded as a constant.

THE MONEY MULTIPLIER

By changing the monetary base, the Federal Reserve can alter the money supply. Indeed, with a constant money multiplier, the change in the money supply due to a change in the monetary base may be estimated. Yet, the various relationships in the money multiplier are not necessarily constant, and the money multiplier can change.

As discussed earlier, the value of the money multiplier is determined by reserve requirements and the ratios of excess reserves, currency, and nonpersonal time deposits to transaction deposits. The reserve requirements for transaction and nonpersonal time deposits, r and r', respectively, are determined by the Federal Reserve. If reserve requirements are reduced, the money multiplier increases. As discussed later, the Fed may alter the money supply by changing reserve requirements and, hence, the money multiplier, rather than changing the monetary base.

The ratio of excess reserves to transaction deposits, e, is determined by depository institutions. If they hold more excess reserves relative to transaction deposits, e increases and the money multiplier decreases. As a result, the nominal money supply decreases even though the monetary base is unchanged.

The ratio of currency in circulation to transaction deposits, c, is determined by the public. If the public holds more cash relative to transaction deposits, c increases and the money multiplier decreases which implies that the nominal money supply decreases.

The ratio of nonpersonal time deposits to transaction deposits, t, is also determined by the public or, specifically, by firms and organizations. If they decide to increase nonpersonal time deposits relative to transaction deposits, t increases. The increase in t has the same impact on the money multiplier and the nominal money supply as an increase in e or c.

As is evident, the actions of depository institutions and the public affect the value of the money multiplier. The implication is that the money multiplier and, hence, the nominal money supply may vary considerably from week to week or month to month even if the monetary base is constant. The extent of the variation is, of course, an empirical question.

An estimate of the money multiplier may be obtained by taking the ratio of the nominal money supply, Ms, to the monetary base, H. In 1985, this ratio, the money multiplier, was approximately 2.6. The 2.6 is, however, an average. If the money multiplier is calculated on a weekly or monthly basis, the multiplier shows considerable instability, making it virtually impossible for the monetary authorities to adjust the monetary base to compensate for the variation.[7] As a result, the nominal money supply also displays considerable instability on both a weekly and monthly basis. In fact, most economists concede that the Federal Reserve cannot control the money supply closely from week to week or even from month to month. As more time passes, however, the weekly and monthly variations in the money multiplier average out, implying that the Federal Reserve can control the money supply more closely. Indeed, most economists agree that the Federal Reserve can control the nominal money supply closely on a quarter-to-quarter (or longer) basis.

THE MONEY SUPPLY AND THE FEDERAL RESERVE'S INSTRUMENTS OF CONTROL

The Federal Reserve has three instruments to control the money supply: (1) open market operations, (2) changes in reserve requirements, and (3) changes in the discount rate. *Open market operations*, the purchase or sale of U.S. Treasury securities, are used to control the monetary base. If the goal is to increase the money supply, the Fed may do so by purchasing Treasury securities. As illustrated earlier, the Fed pays for these securities with checks drawn on Federal Reserve Banks. These checks will be deposited at commercial banks or other depository institutions. As the checks clear, the Fed will credit the institutions' deposits at Federal Reserve Banks, thereby creating additional reserves for the monetary system. If the goal is to reduce the money supply, the Fed may do so by selling Treasury securities. The purchasers will presumably pay for the securities with checks drawn on commercial banks or other depository institutions. As these checks clear, the Fed will reduce the institutions' deposits at Federal Reserve Banks, thereby reducing the reserves of the monetary system.

The authority to conduct open market operations rests with the Federal Open Market Committee. The committee is composed of the seven members of the Federal Reserve's Board of Governors and the presidents of five of the twelve Federal Reserve Banks. The president of the Federal Reserve Bank of New York is a permanent member of the committee; the presidents of the other eleven banks alternate. Purchases and sales of Treasury securities are conducted through the Federal Reserve Bank of New York.

Purchases and sales of Treasury securities by the Federal Reserve occur almost daily. They occur partly because of Federal Reserve action to expand or contract the money supply and partly to offset changes in the monetary base due to factors beyond the control of the Federal Reserve. Open market operations of the second type are called *defensive operations*. Because the Fed undertakes operations of both types, it is not easy to determine the purpose of its actions. For example, suppose the Fed purchases Treasury securities. The Fed may be acting to increase the money supply. But the Fed's purchases may be designed simply to offset, say, the effects of a decision by the public to hold more cash; if so, the action will maintain the money supply at its original level.

The Federal Reserve may also alter the money supply by *changing the reserve requirements* for depository institutions. As indicated, a change in reserve requirements alters the money multiplier. For a given monetary base, a change in the money multiplier results in a change in the money supply. If the goal is to increase the money supply, the Fed can reduce reserve requirements, thereby increasing the money multiplier and, hence, the money supply. In terms of the monetary system, a reduction in reserve requirements creates excess reserves. For example, Bank A was initially assumed to hold reserves of $1 million with demand, other checkable, and nonpersonal time deposit liabilities of $5 million (see Table 7.2). If the required reserve ratio is 0.20, Bank A has no excess reserves. If the reserve requirement is reduced to 0.15, Bank A has excess reserves of $250,000, a sizable increase. The increase in excess reserves results in an expansion in the money supply. If the goal is to decrease the money supply, the Fed can raise reserve requirements. With an increase in reserve requirements, depository institutions with insufficient reserves must add to them. They may do so by reducing their loans and, thus, the money supply.

Changes in reserve requirements are a potent weapon. Even small changes in reserve requirements result in large changes in the money supply. Nevertheless, changes in reserve requirements have several disadvantages as an instrument of monetary control. They lack the flexibility of open market operations. Open market operations occur more or less continuously and can easily be reversed should the need arise. Frequent changes in reserve requirements are not practical because the changes would make it very difficult for depository institutions to manage their assets and liabilities. Also, increases in reserve requirements are disruptive, especially for depository institutions that are not sufficiently liquid to meet the higher requirements. Similarly, prior to the passage of the Depository Institutions Deregulation and Monetary Control Act of 1980, the monetary authorities were reluctant to raise reserve requirements because such action would worsen the competitive position of member banks relative to nonmember banks, thereby providing member banks with a greater incentive to leave the Federal Reserve System. For these reasons, almost all of the changes in reserve requirements since the Korean War have been reductions. With the passage of the Monetary Control Act, all depository institutions are subject to the same set of reserve requirements. Even so, the dominant view is that reserve requirements will not be changed frequently in the future.

Finally, the Federal Reserve may alter the money supply by *changing the discount rate*, the rate at which depository institutions borrow from Federal Reserve Banks[8]. The board of directors of each Federal Reserve Bank determines the bank's discount rate. The rates must, however, be approved by the Federal Reserve's Board of Governors. If the goal is to expand the money supply, the Federal Reserve reduces the discount rate, thereby encouraging depository institutions to borrow from the Federal Reserve. If they do so, the monetary base and, hence, the money supply increase. If the goal is to reduce the money supply, the Fed increases the discount rate, which discourages borrowing. Thus, by changing the discount rate, depository institutions are given an incentive to alter their borrowings from the Federal Reserve and, therefore, the monetary base and the money supply.

It has been claimed that the announcement of discount rate changes may have desirable psychological effects. For example, if the discount rate is increased, people may believe that monetary policy is becoming less expansionary. Depository institutions might, therefore, become more cautious in making loans, which is desirable if the Fed wishes to pursue a less expansionary policy.

Discount rate changes as a means to alter the money supply present a number of disadvantages. Depository institutions may be reluctant to borrow from the Fed except as a last resort. Consequently, changes in the discount rate may have little or no effect on bank borrowings and, hence, the monetary base. Moreover, the announcement effect may be perverse. Potential borrowers may interpret a rise in the discount rate as a signal that the Fed is pursuing a less expansionary policy. They may therefore attempt to borrow before market interest rates rise. If they are successful, the outcome is the opposite of the result desired.

When the discount rate is altered, it is not clear that the change indicates a new trend in monetary policy. Since depository institutions may borrow from a number of sources, the change in the discount rate may simply be to bring it into line with other interest rates. Thus, even if the announcement effect is favorable, it may be difficult to interpret whether a change in the discount rate marks a change in monetary policy. For these reasons, many, if not most, economists believe that the Fed should peg the discount rate to other interest rates.

In conclusion, the Federal Reserve's most flexible instrument of monetary control is open market operations. It is also the most important and most frequently used instrument. Over the years, reserve requirements have been reduced, allowing for a long-run increase in the money supply. On the other hand, very few increases in reserve requirements have occurred.

GOVERNMENT DEFICITS AND THE MONEY SUPPLY

When government spending exceeds tax and other revenues, government has a budgetary deficit which it must finance. The deficit may be financed by increasing taxes, by borrowing from the public (or depository institutions), or by borrowing from the Federal Reserve. The federal government borrows by issuing Treasury securities. Depending upon the method of financing, the money supply may change.

If the government finances the deficit by increasing taxes, no net change in the money supply occurs. There will be a reduction in the money supply as taxes are collected. As the government spends the tax revenue, however, the money supply increases to its former level.

Similarly, if the government borrows by selling bonds to the public (or depository institutions), there will be no net change in the money supply. With the sale of the bonds, there will be a reduction in the money supply. But as the government spends the proceeds, the money supply increases to its former level.

If the government finances the deficit by selling securities to the Federal Reserve, the result is different; there will be an increase in the money supply. If the securities are sold to the Federal Reserve and the proceeds spent by the government, the money supply increases by an amount equal to the change in the monetary base (which equals the amount of the sales) multiplied by the money multiplier. As we shall see in later chapters, this increase in the money supply has a stimulating effect on the economy. Moreover, the effect is the same as the case where the federal government simply prints the amount of currency necessary to finance the deficit.

CONCLUDING REMARKS

In this chapter, we considered the most common definition of the nation's money supply (M1) and assumed initially that it was an exogenous variable determined by the actions of the Federal Reserve. We then considered a more sophisticated version of the (nominal) money supply function. According to that function, the money supply is determined by the actions of depository institutions and the public, as well as actions of the Federal Reserve. As a result, the money multiplier varies from week to week and from month to month. This instability makes it very difficult, perhaps impossible, to control the money supply closely on a weekly or even a monthly basis. On the other hand, the changes in the money multiplier tend to cancel over longer time spans so that the Federal Reserve can control the money supply closely on, say, a quarterly basis. Consequently, our initial assumption is correct *provided* sufficient time elapses.

In the following chapter, we take up the demand for money with a view to incorporating it and the supply of money into the model of Chapter 6.

NOTES _____

1. Since conversion is relatively easy, some economists have argued that time deposits should be classified as money. See, for example, Milton Friedman and Anna J. Schwartz *Monetary Statistics of the United States: Estimates, Sources, Methods* (New York: National Bureau of Economic Research, 1970).

2. By definition, currency held by banks (as vault cash) and by the Federal Reserve and the U.S. Treasury is excluded. Similarly, checkable deposits of domestic banks, foreign banks and official institutions, and the U.S. government are excluded. Finally, only traveler's checks issued by nonbank companies are included. Traveler's checks issued by banks are excluded because the amount issued is already counted as part of demand deposits.

3. Banks are only one type of depository institution. *Depository institutions* are financial institutions that accept checkable deposits. Other types are savings and loan associations, credit unions, and mutual savings banks.

4. Alternatively, the total increase in demand deposits, ΔD, equals $1,000 + 800 + 640 + 512 + \cdots$, which equals $1,000 + 0.8(1,000) + 0.8(0.8)(1,000) + 0.8(0.8)(0.8)(1,000) + \cdots$, which also equals $1,000[1 + (0.8) + (0.8)^2 + (0.8)^3 + \cdots]$. The expression in brackets represents the sum of a convergent geometric series. Based on

the formula for the sum of such a series, it equals $1/(1 - 0.8)$ or 5. Thus, the increase in demand deposits is $1,000(5) or $5,000. In general, the change in demand deposits equals $\Delta H + (1 - r)\Delta H + (1 - r)^2 \Delta H + (1 - r)^3 \Delta H + \cdots$ or $\Delta H [1 + (1 - r) + (1 - r)^2 + (1 - r)^3 + \cdots]$. Since $1 - r$ is between 0 and 1, $[1 + (1 - r) + (1 - r)^2 + (1 - r)^3 + \cdots]$ is the sum of a convergent geometric series. This sum equals $1/r$, which implies that the total change in demand deposits, ΔD, equals $\Delta H/r$.

5. In the example upon which equation (7.3) is based, the new distinction is not important, since the public was assumed not to add to its holdings of other checkable and time deposits during the expansion process. In the following analysis, the distinction is important.

6. The money multiplier presented ignores some complexities of the financial system. To illustrate, the reserve requirement for transaction accounts varies by the amount of transaction deposits held by the depository institution. Similarly, the reserve requirement for nonpersonal time deposits applies only to deposits with an original maturity of less than one and a half years.

7. The Federal Reserve Bank of St. Louis publishes money multiplier data on a weekly basis. (See *U.S. Financial Data*, prepared by the Federal Reserve Bank of St. Louis, weekly.) Various economists have argued that the Federal Reserve should use sophisticated statistical techniques to predict the value of the money multiplier. This, they claim, would allow the Federal Reserve to adjust the monetary base to compensate for the (predicted) instability. The result would be greater stability in the nominal money supply. In this regard, see James M. Johannes and Robert H. Rasche, "Predicting the Money Multiplier," *Journal of Monetary Economics*, 5 (July 1979), 301–25; and R. W. Hafer, Scott E. Hein, and Clemens J. M. Kool, "Forecasting the Money Multiplier: Implications for Money Stock Control and Economic Activity," Federal Reserve Bank of St. Louis, *Review*, 65 (October 1983), 22–33.

8. Prior to the passage of the Depository Institutions Deregulation and Monetary Control Act of 1980, only member banks could use the "discount window" on a regular basis. Under the Act, all depository institutions have access to the "window."

REVIEW QUESTIONS _____

1. Money is usually defined in terms of its medium of exchange function. What is a medium of exchange? Why was the definition of the nation's money supply broadened in the early 1980s?

2. Explain why a dollar may be "worth" only 25 cents. In this context, can a dollar be "worth" more than a dollar?

3. Although the purchasing power of a dollar is important, it is not crucial with respect to standards of living. Discuss.

4. With the use of T-accounts, describe the impact of a $1,000 sale of Treasury securities by the Federal Reserve. Assume that the reserve requirement for checkable and nonpersonal time deposits is 20 percent. For simplicity, assume that depository institutions do not hold excess reserves and the public does not alter its holdings of cash and nonpersonal time deposits.

5. Under the assumptions of the previous question, determine the ultimate decrease in the money supply.

6. Suppose the legal reserve requirements against checkable and nonpersonal time deposits are 10 percent and 5 percent, respectively. Also, suppose depository institutions hold no excess reserves and the public holds $0.25 in currency and $1.00 in nonpersonal time deposits for each $1.00 of checkable deposits.

   a. Calculate the money multiplier.

   b. Suppose the monetary base increases by $10 billion. Determine the increase in the money supply.

   c. If the monetary base is $100 billion, determine the money supply.

7. How does each of the following affect the money supply? Defend your answers.

   a. A change in the monetary base.

   b. A decision by depository institutions to lend more of their excess reserves.

   c. A switch from demand to other checkable deposits.

   d. A switch from checkable deposits to cash.

   e. A switch from demand to nonpersonal time deposits, assuming that the reserve requirement is lower for the latter.

8. What is the monetary base? Suppose the Federal Reserve does not have complete control of the monetary base. What are the implications?

9. List and briefly discuss the various instruments the Federal Reserve may use to alter the money supply.

10. Critically evaluate the following statement. An increase in the discount rate indicates that the Federal Reserve has decided to reduce the money supply.

11. Explain how the various means of financing a government deficit affect the money supply.

SUGGESTED READING

BALBACH, ANATOL B., "How Controllable is Money Growth?" Federal Reserve Bank of St. Louis, *Review*, 63 (April 1981), 3–12.

BRYANT, RALPH C., *Controlling Money: The Federal Reserve and its Critics*. Washington D.C.: The Brookings Institution, 1983.

Federal Reserve Bulletin, Board of Governors of the Federal Reserve System, monthly.

JORDAN, JERRY L., "Elements of Money Stock Determination," Federal Reserve Bank of St. Louis, *Review*, 51 (October 1969), 10-19.

MALKIEL, BURTON G., *The Term Structure of Interest Rates: Theory, Empirical Evidence, and Applications*. New York: McCaleb-Seiler Publishing Company, 1970.

McNEILL, CHARLES R., "The Depository Institutions Deregulation and Monetary Control Act of 1980," *Federal Reserve Bulletin*, 66 (June 1980), 444-53.

Monetary Trends, prepared by the Federal Reserve Bank of St. Louis, monthly.

Simpson, Thomas D., "The Redefined Monetary Aggregates," *Federal Reserve Bulletin*, 66 (February 1980), 97-114.

Thomas, Lloyd B., Jr., *Money, Banking, and Economic Activity* (3rd ed.). Englewood Cliffs, N.J.: Prentice-Hall, Inc., 1986.

8

THE DEMAND FOR MONEY
AND EQUILIBRIUM
IN THE MONEY MARKET

From the discussion of the supply of money in Chapter 7, we now turn to a discussion of the demand for money. The demand for money concept has a long history. For the most part, however, this chapter is confined to Keynes's analysis and subsequent developments. Since the publication of Keynes's *General Theory* in 1936, economists generally distinguish three major motives for holding money balances or, to put it differently, three different demands for money. They are the transactions, precautionary, and speculative demands for money.

Following the discussion of the demand for money, equilibrium in the money market is considered, and a relationship between income and the equilibrium interest rate is derived. This relationship, called the *LM curve*, is analogous to the IS curve which was derived in Chapter 6 for the product market.

THE TRANSACTIONS DEMAND FOR MONEY

Much money is held or demanded simply to bridge gaps between the receipt of money payments and the making of money expenditures. Individuals are often paid on the first of the month; but they must pay bills and finance day-to-day transactions throughout the month. Consequently, they demand money balances to finance these transactions; these balances are called *transactions balances* and the demand for them, the *transactions demand for money*. For an individual, the average money balance held depends on such things as the number of times per year the person is paid and the extent to which receipts and expenditures coincide. For example, the more often a person is paid, the less money, on average, she will hold. Suppose an individual receives a salary of $1,000 per month payable on the first of each month. If the individual plans to spend her money evenly over the pay period, her average money balance is $500, the average of her initial balance, $1,000, and her balance at the end of the month, $0. If the same individual were paid $500 every two weeks, her average money balance would be only $250, the average of her balances at the beginning and end of each of the two-week periods. Similarly, the greater the coincidence between receipts and expenditures, the less money a person will hold. In fact, if a person were paid on the first of the month and were also able to pay all her bills on the first, she would not need to hold any money at all.

Like individuals and households, firms also demand transactions balances. Firms receive income from the sale of their products or services. They must hold money to pay bills, meet payrolls, and the like. The average money balance held by a firm depends on various factors. Some firms, by the nature of their business, require greater money balances than others. The average money balance held also depends on the number of times a firm pays its employees each year and the extent to which receipts and expenditures coincide. The more often a firm pays its employees, the less money, on the average, the firm holds. Similarly, the greater the coincidence between receipts and expenditures, the less money the firm will require.

In the short run, these determinants of the transactions demand for money are constant. The same is true for other institutional factors which help to determine the transactions demand for money. But the amount of money demanded for transactions is not constant. The amount varies positively with income. For example, as an individual's income increases, so does the amount of money he demands. This relationship is explained as follows: suppose an individual receives an increase in income from $1,000 per month to $1,500 per month. The individual can be expected to make more transactions during the month or at least to increase the amounts involved in his usual transactions. To finance these transactions, the person will hold more money. If he continues to spend his entire income during the pay period, his average monthly balance will be $750, an increase of $250, with the increase in monthly income from $1,000 to $1,500.

The same argument holds for society. If society's income increases, households and firms demand more money to finance the increased volume of transactions, hence, the positive relationship between the amount of money demanded for transactions and income. Before continuing, we should emphasize that we are interested in the real demand for money. In determining their desired money holdings, households and firms are concerned with both the volume of their transactions and the prices at which the transactions are conducted. For example, if prices increase by 10 percent, their nominal money holdings must increase by 10 percent in order to finance the same volume of transactions. Thus, it is real money balances that are important; therefore, we relate the real amount of money demanded to real income.

Actually, the real amount of money demanded for transactions purposes should depend on total real expenditures or transactions rather than real income. Total expenditures is a broader concept than income since it includes the purchase of both intermediate and final products, as well as the purchase of secondhand goods, stocks, and bonds; only final products are included in gross national product and the other measures of the nation's income or output. Since the transactions motive for holding money is based on the need to finance transactions, it is desirable to relate the amount demanded to the total volume of transactions instead of income, but it makes no difference, if the ratio of total expenditures to income is constant.

Suppose the ratio of total expenditures to income were to change. This would be the case if, for example, industry were to become more vertically integrated. The *vertical integration of industries*, that is, the combining in one firm of operations formerly conducted by separate firms in a chain of production, such as the taking over of can production by beer companies, reduces intermediate expenditures relative to income and thus the ratio of total expenditures to income. If the amount of money demanded is related to the total volume of transactions, the relationship will indicate, correctly, the reduction in the amount of money demanded due to the reduction in the volume of transactions. On the other hand, if the amount of money demanded for transactions is related to income, we will conclude that, since income did not change, the amount of money demanded is unaltered. This conclusion is wrong. Since the firm will have fewer transactions to finance, it will require less money.

In the example, if the ratio of total expenditures to income changes, the relevant variable is total expenditures. If the ratio between the two remains constant, either may be used. Since the factors which determine the ratio of total expenditures to income, such as the degree of vertical integration of industry, change only slowly, we can, in the short run, use income as the determinant of the transactions demand for money. Moreover, the income variable is consistent with the other variables in the model, and income estimates are readily available in the national income accounts.

THE TRANSACTIONS DEMAND FOR MONEY AND THE INTEREST RATE

Following Keynes, it was generally assumed that the amount of money demanded for transactions depends only on income (in the short run). In the 1950s, however, William J. Baumol and James Tobin showed that the transactions demand for money also depends on the interest rate.[1] Baumol and Tobin noted that households and firms receive income, all or part of which will be needed at later dates for various expenditures. They emphasized that the units need not hold money for the entire period between the receipt of income and the transactions in question. Instead, households and firms may buy Treasury bills or other interest-bearing assets and sell them prior to the transaction dates. The advantage of this approach is that interest (or a higher rate of interest) is earned on the assets. Because of this option, the amount of money held for transactions depends on the interest rate. The higher the interest rate, the more likely households and firms are to buy Treasury bills or other assets and thus reduce their average money balances.

The basic principle may be explained with the aid of a simple illustration. Although this illustration is based on a transfer of funds from time to demand deposits, it can be generalized to include, say, the purchase and sale of Treasury bills as a means to minimize transactions balances. Suppose a corporation receives T dollars every four weeks and the amount is deposited directly in a time deposit. Also, suppose that this income is spent evenly over the "month" so that ($\frac{1}{28}$)th of it is spent the first day, ($\frac{1}{28}$)th the second day, and so on, until the entire amount is spent by the end of the "month." Since interest is earned on time deposits, the corporation has an incentive to transfer balances to its checking account only when necessary.[2] If there is no cost involved in transferring these balances, the corporation will transfer only small amounts at a time (which will require a large number of transfers) in order to minimize the loss of interest income. Suppose a cost is involved; for simplicity, assume that it is b dollars per transfer regardless of the amount transferred. The cost will limit the number of transfers that occur. In fact, if the cost were to exceed the interest earned, it would not pay the corporation to have the funds deposited in its savings account initially. It would be better to have them deposited directly in its checking account.

Since the corporation spends its income evenly over the period, the amount transferred from time to demand deposits will be the same each time. If C represents the amount transferred and T income, the number of transactions, n, equals T/C. For example, if T equals \$100,000 and C equals \$25,000, n equals 4. Thus, the corporation would transfer \$25,000 from time to demand deposits at the start of each of the four weeks.

In this context, the corporation will try to minimize the cost associated with holding demand deposit balances. This cost has two components: (1) the cost associated with transferring funds from time to demand deposits, and (2) the interest income foregone by holding, on average, some positive amount in its checking account. The cost associated with transferring funds is bn, obtained by multiplying the cost per transfer, b, by the number of transfers, n. This cost also equals $b(T/C)$, since n equals T/C. The cost associated with holding a positive checking account balance is $i(C/2)$, found by multiplying the opportunity cost of holding money (which is the interest rate, i) by the average amount of money held in the checking account, $C/2$. The latter is obtained in the following way. Since C dollars is transferred at the start of the subperiod and is spent during the subperiod, the initial and final balances are C and zero dollars, respectively. Since the funds are spent evenly over the subperiod, the average balance is the average of the initial (C) and final (zero) balances or $C/2$. For example, if C equals \$25,000, the average balance is \$12,500. Since each subperiod is exactly like the others, the average balance for the period is $C/2$, the same as for each subperiod.

If the two costs are summed, we obtain

$$\text{Total cost} = b\left(\frac{T}{C}\right) + i\left(\frac{C}{2}\right).$$

If we differentiate total cost with respect to C, set the result equal to zero, and solve for C, we find that total cost is minimized when

(8.1)
$$C = \sqrt{\frac{2bT}{i}}.$$

Since the average amount of money held equals $C/2$, we can divide both sides of equation (8.1) by 2 to obtain

(8.2)
$$\frac{C}{2} = \sqrt{\frac{bT}{2i}}.$$

Equation (8.2) represents the transactions demand for money based on the illustration. The equation suggests that the amount of money demanded depends on the interest rate, the cost of transferring funds, and income. With a higher interest rate, the corporation (and by implication, society) finds it profitable to transfer funds more often, thereby economizing on the amount of money held for transactions purposes. On the other hand, an increase in the cost of transferring funds will discourage such transfers, resulting in a greater amount of money held for transactions purposes. As postulated earlier, an increase in income results in a greater amount of money held for transactions purposes. One new implication is that economies of scale exist. That is, as income increases, the amount of money held increases, but the increase is less than proportional to the increase in income.

As a practical matter, most households and many, if not most, firms do not find it advantageous to reduce their transactions balances by buying Treasury bills or other interest-bearing assets because their initial balances are relatively small, their planning periods too short, and the costs of buying and selling the assets too great. On the other hand, households and firms with large transactions balances do find it profitable to buy and sell these assets. Consequently, the amount of money demanded for transactions is likely to vary with interest rates. Thus, in the short run, the amount of money demanded for transactions varies directly with income and inversely with the interest rate. In the long run, the amount of money demanded for transactions will also depend on the various institutional arrangements of society.

THE PRECAUTIONARY DEMAND FOR MONEY

With regard to the precautionary demand for money, Keynes argued that society would demand money, over and above the transactions demand, in order to provide for unforeseen contingencies and to take advantage of bargains. This demand is called the *precautionary demand for money* and stems from the precautionary motive for holding money. For example, if a New York family takes a long vacation in California, the family is likely to carry more money than necessary to finance day-to-day transactions; they will want a reserve for protection against unexpected expenses, such as emergency automobile repairs. They may also carry a reserve to buy, for example, fine California wines that they consider bargains.

In the short run, the amount of money demanded for precautionary purposes is determined by income and interest rates in approximately the same manner as the amount of money demanded for transactions. Specifically, the amount of money demanded for precautionary purposes is directly related to income and inversely related to interest rates. This does not mean that the transactions and precautionary demand for money functions are identical.

In the long run, the precautionary demand is probably sensitive to changes in financial and other institutional arrangements. For example, the development and widespread acceptance of credit cards has probably reduced the precautionary demand for money. After all, if credit cards are readily acceptable, little need exists for the New York family to hold more than a minimum amount of money. Since these institutional arrangements change only slowly, the precautionary demand for money depends on income and interest rates in the short run.

THE SPECULATIVE DEMAND FOR MONEY

The classical economists believed that people held money only for transactions purposes. They thought people would not hold money over and above the amount needed to bridge the gap between receipts and expenditures. Keynes introduced two additional motives for holding money, the precautionary and speculative motives. Addition of the precautionary demand for money did not really constitute a radical departure from classical thought because it could be readily assimilated into the transactions demand for money. On the other hand, the *speculative demand for money* was truly an innovation.

To illustrate the nature of the speculative demand for money, consider a person who has the choice of holding bonds which yield interest or money which either yields no interest or a lower amount. Because of the income foregone, the classical economists believed the person would hold no more money than necessary for transactions (and precautionary) purposes. Keynes, however, believed the person would hold additional money if he or she expected the interest rate to go up in the future. By holding money, the person can take advantage of higher interest rates should they occur. For example, suppose the current interest rate is 6 percent but the person expects the rate to rise to 8 percent in the near future. According to Keynes, the person will hold money in anticipation of the higher interest rate. By waiting until the interest rate increases to 8 percent, bonds with higher yields can be purchased. Or, to put it differently, if interest rates rise, bond prices fall and the person is able to purchase bonds at a lower price.

Instead of holding money in anticipation of the increase in the interest rate, suppose the person were to buy bonds currently yielding 6 percent and then attempt to exchange them later for bonds which yield 8 percent. If he were to do so, he would suffer a capital loss due to the inverse relationship between bond prices and interest rates. If a person buys bonds which yield 6 percent and the interest rate subsequently increases to 8 percent, bond prices decrease and he will be unable to exchange the bonds without experiencing a capital loss. Consequently, if a person expects interest rates to go up in the future, he will hold money rather than bonds. Thus, according to Keynes, it is rational for a person to hold money over and above the amount needed for transactions (and precautionary) purposes. If a person expects interest rates to be constant or go down in the future, he will, using the same reasoning, buy and hold bonds.

Since people generally have different estimates of future changes in the interest rate, the aggregate relationship between the speculative demand for money and the interest rate will be an inverse one. At lower and lower interest rates, more and more people expect interest rates to go up in the future. Consequently, at lower interest rates, more and more money will be demanded for speculative purposes. If the interest rate falls sufficiently far below normal, everyone may become convinced that it must rise in the near future. In this situation, the speculative demand for money is perfectly elastic at that low interest rate. This perfectly elastic portion of the demand for money function is called the *liquidity trap*. In the liquidity trap, asset-holders will absorb unlimited quantities of money into idle balances without using any of it to buy bonds and, hence, drive down interest rates. Empirical studies (discussed later) of the interest elasticity of the demand for money provide little or no evidence supporting the existence of a liquidity trap.

Thus, Keynes argued that people will hold money over and above that held for transactions (and precautionary) purposes if they expect interest rates to go up in the future. Tobin criticized Keynes's explanation of the relationship between the speculative demand for money and the interest rate and offered an alternative explanation.[3] Specifically, he argued, first, that Keynes's explanation implies an all-or-none type of behavior on the part of individuals. An individual will hold either all bonds or all money, depending upon her expectations about future movements in the interest rate. If the individual expects interest rates to go up in the future, she will hold only money in order to take advantage of the future increase in the interest rate. Conversely, if she expects the interest rate to be constant or to decline, she will hold only bonds. Empirically, this is not so; individuals appear to hold some of each. Since different individuals have different expectations about future movements in the interest rate, the aggregate relationship is the same as just postulated; the empirical evidence does, however, contradict the hypothesis at the individual level. A second criticism is that if the interest rate remained constant for a long period of time, the speculative demand for money would simply disappear as people would expect the interest rate to remain constant. This is true because Keynes assumed people hold money for speculative purposes only if they expect interest rates to go up in the future.

Tobin derives an inverse relationship between the speculative demand for money and the interest rate with the following argument. First, he assumes the individual may hold money, bonds, or a combination of money and bonds. The bonds yield a fixed amount of income per year, whereas money has no yield. Prospective bondholders are assumed to be uncertain as to the future rate of interest on bonds; consequently, there is a risk of a capital gain or loss. If a prospective bondholder buys a bond and the interest rate declines, bond prices will increase and the bondholder will experience a capital gain. If the interest rate increases, on the other hand, the holder will suffer a capital loss. Thus, buying a bond involves risk of a capital gain or loss, and the greater the proportion of bonds in an investment portfolio, the greater the risk. We also find that the greater the proportion of bonds in an investment portfolio, the greater the expected return. As a result, prospective bondholders can increase their expected return by purchasing relatively large amounts of bonds; by doing so, however, they increase their chances of a large capital loss.

Next, Tobin argues that most people diversify their portfolios. Individuals tend to hold some bonds in order to earn a return on their portfolios and some money so as to avoid the possibility of a large capital loss. Moreover, as the interest rate changes, individuals adjust their holdings. According to Tobin, a rise in the interest rate increases the expected return from bonds and induces prospective bondholders to hold more bonds and less money. An increase in the rate of interest induces individuals to increase their bondholdings because the greater risk that they assume is compensated for by the higher return. If the interest rate decreases, the expected return from bonds decreases and people reduce their bondholdings and increase their money holdings, since the new, lower interest rate fails to compensate adequately for the risk associated with the original level of bondholdings. Thus, an inverse relationship exists between the speculative demand for money and the rate of interest.

According to Tobin, his explanation of the relationship between the speculative demand for money and the interest rate provides a more satisfactory theoretical foundation than Keynes's explanation. Moreover, according to Tobin, his reasoning explains why individuals diversify their portfolios, whereas Keynes's theory implies that individuals hold only one type of asset. But whether we accept Keynes's or Tobin's explanation of the relationship, there appears to be an inverse relationship between the amount of money demanded for speculative purposes and the interest rate.

THE DEMAND FOR MONEY FUNCTION

Following Keynes, many authors discussed his three demands for money and then combined the transactions and precautionary demands in order to simplify the analysis. Moreover, at least in their graphical analysis, they assumed that the combined transactions and precautionary demand for money depended only on income and that the speculative demand depended only on the interest rate. In recent years, these practices have become less common because, as we have seen, both the transactions and precautionary demands, as well as the speculative demand, depend on the interest rate. We shall follow the more recent practice and postulate that the real demand for money depends on, or is a function of, real income and the interest rate. In equation form, the demand for money function is

(8.3)
$$\frac{Md}{P} = L(Y,i),$$

where Md/P represents the real amount of money demanded, Y real income, and i the interest rate. The real amount of money demanded is directly related to real income and inversely related to the interest rate, so an increase in real income increases the real amount of money demanded, whereas an increase in the interest rate has the opposite effect. In the long run, the real amount of money demanded will vary as a result of financial innovations and so forth.

As will be demonstrated in Chapter 9, the interest elasticity of the demand for money is one determinant of the relative effectiveness of fiscal and monetary policy. With this in mind, we shall briefly discuss some of the empirical evidence before plotting the demand for money function.

The many studies of the demand for money differ with regard to the variables considered, the time periods covered, and even the statistical techniques utilized. Consequently, it is difficult to generalize with regard to the interest elasticity of money, but John T. Boorman has done so.[4] Boorman concluded that the interest rate is an important determinant of the demand for money. If the interest rate is the short-term rate, the estimates of the interest elasticity of the demand for money range from -0.07 to -0.20. An interest rate elasticity of -0.20 implies that a 10 percent increase in the interest rate reduces the real amount of money demanded by 2 percent, a relatively small decrease. If the interest rate is the long-term rate, the estimates are higher (in absolute terms); they range from -0.7 to -0.9.

Although the demand for money is sensitive to changes in the interest rate, Boorman concluded that there is little or no evidence that the demand for money is highly interest elastic or that a liquidity trap exists. As discussed earlier, the perfectly elastic portion of the demand for money function (if it exists) is called a liquidity trap.

By plotting the demand for money function, we can conveniently summarize its properties. We have three variables: real amount of money demanded, real income, and the interest rate. To plot the demand for money function on a two

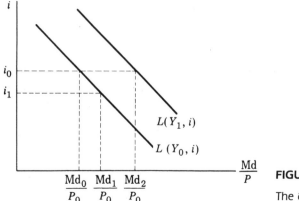

FIGURE 8.1

The demand for money function

dimensional graph, one variable must be held constant. In this case, we put the interest rate on the vertical axis and the real amount of money demanded on the horizontal axis; then we plot the demand for money function, holding income constant. For example, if real income is assumed to be Y_0, the relevant relationship in Figure 8.1 is $L(Y_0, i)$. The relationship indicates that at income level Y_0 and interest rate i_0, the real amount of money demanded is Md_0/P_0. If the interest rate declines to i_1 (with real income constant), the real amount of money demanded increases to Md_1/P_0, illustrating the inverse relationship between the real amount of money demanded and the interest rate.

The relationship $L(Y_0, i)$ was plotted on the assumption that income is constant at the Y_0 level. If income increases from Y_0 to Y_1, the demand for money curve shifts to the right, indicating that at each interest rate more money is demanded. For example, at interest rate i_0, the amount of money demanded increases from Md_0/P_0 to Md_2/P_0, illustrating the positive relationship between the real amount of money demanded and income.

STABILITY OF THE DEMAND FOR MONEY FUNCTION:
THE "MISSING MONEY" PUZZLE

In the 1960s and early 1970s, economists regarded the demand for money function as a stable function. Starting in 1974, however, predictions of the amount of money demanded based on conventional demand for money functions became less and less accurate. Specifically, the actual amounts were less than the predicted amounts and, as time passed, the discrepancy became larger and larger. The problem—the divergence of the actual and predicted amounts—became known as the "missing money" puzzle.[5] The episode implies that the demand for money decreased in the 1970s.

The problem reemerged in the 1980s but in a different form. Starting in late 1981, conventional demand for money functions started underpredicting, rather than overpredicting, the amount of money held, suggesting an increase in the demand for money.

These episodes imply that the demand for money function is not stable. If true, it will be much more difficult for the monetary authorities to pursue policies which stabilize the economy. Although monetary policy will not be discussed in detail until the next chapter, we can briefly indicate the nature of the problem. Suppose the Federal Reserve increases the money supply by a certain amount to stimulate the economy. If the demand for money unexpectedly increases, the increase in the money supply will be too small to achieve the desired stimulus. On the other hand, if the demand for money unexpectedly decreases, the increase in the money supply will be too large, thereby overstimulating the economy.

Various hypotheses have been offered to explain the "missing money" puzzle. These hypotheses may be grouped into two general categories: (1) those that attribute the change in the demand for money to changes in the institutional framework and innovations, including improvements in corporate cash management; and (2) those that emphasize that the conventional approach was flawed from the start. We shall briefly consider each of the approaches.

Various changes in the institutional framework occurred in the mid-1970s. Firms, for example, were permitted to have savings accounts at commercial banks starting in November 1975. Other checkable deposits were becoming more important and, at the time, these deposits were not included in the nation's money supply. In addition to these and other changes in the institutional framework, firms and households were under strong pressure to economize on money holdings because of the high inflation and interest rates which prevailed in the mid-1970s. The evidence suggests that they responded by managing their money balances much more carefully.

Attempts to verify that the instability of the demand for money was due to changes in the institutional framework and innovations, however, have not been particularly successful. Even so, most economists believe that this explanation is more satisfactory than the alternative explanation to which we now turn.

Some economists were dissatisfied with the conventional approach to the demand for money even before the relationship broke down in 1974. Some of them, for example, believed that permanent income, as defined in Chapter 5, is better than GNP in terms of explaining the demand for money. With the failure of the conventional approach to predict the demand for money accurately, these economists were quick to offer alternative demand for money functions. Unfortunately, these alternative functions provide a less satisfactory explanation of the instability than does the institutional change argument.

In conclusion, it appears that institutional changes and innovations were responsible for the instability of the demand for money in the 1970s. Since these changes are likely to continue, the observed instability of the demand for money in the 1970s and 1980s is also likely to persist. For this reason, it will be more difficult for the Federal Reserve to stabilize the economy than it would be if the demand for money were a stable function. At the same time, it should be emphasized that the demand for money is not highly unstable. Indeed, few economists believe that monetary policy should be abandoned for that reason.

THE MONEY MARKET

We can now consider the money market. In Chapter 7, we indicated that, as a first approximation, the nominal money supply, Ms, is an exogenous variable. The nominal money supply, Ms, is given at a particular level, say Ms_0, and will remain at that level until the Federal Reserve takes action to increase or decrease it. Assuming a constant price level, $P = P_0$, the assumption of a constant nominal money supply implies that the real money supply is also constant. Thus, the real money supply function is

$$(8.4) \qquad \frac{Ms}{P} = \frac{Ms_0}{P_0}.$$

This function is plotted in Figure 8.2 with the interest rate on the vertical axis and the real money supply on the horizontal. The curve is perpendicular to the money supply axis at the given level of the real money supply, Ms_0/P_0, since the real money supply is assumed to be unresponsive to changes in the interest rate.

As discussed earlier in this chapter, the real amount of money demanded,

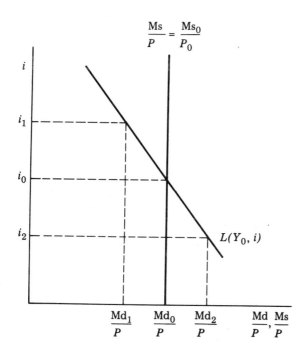

FIGURE 8.2

Equilibrium in the money market

Md/P, varies directly with income and inversely with the interest rate. Thus, the real demand for money function is

(8.5)
$$\frac{Md}{P} = L(Y, i).$$

This function was plotted in Figure 8.1. The demand for money curve for income Y_0 has been reproduced in Figure 8.2.

To complete the model, an equilibrium condition (a condition necessary for the money market to be in equilibrium) must be specified. The equilibrium condition is that the real amount of money supplied must equal the real amount of money demanded. In equation form, this condition is

(8.6)
$$\frac{Ms}{P} = \frac{Md}{P}.$$

If this condition is not fulfilled at a particular combination of income and interest rate, the money market is in disequilibrium and the interest rate tends to change until the money market is in equilibrium. To illustrate, suppose income is Y_0 and the interest rate is i_0 in Figure 8.2. This combination of income and interest rate is an equilibrium combination for the money market since the amount of money supplied, Ms_0/P_0, equals the amount of money demanded, Md_0/P_0. Thus, for income Y_0, interest rate i_0 is the equilibrium rate.

To confirm that i_0 is the equilibrium interest rate, consider alternative interest rates such as i_1 and i_2. At interest rate i_1, the amount of money demanded, Md_1/P_0, is less than the amount of money supplied, Ms_0/P_0; there is an excess supply of money. Under these circumstances, households and firms try to eliminate their excess money holdings by, say, buying bonds. If households and firms, in the aggregate, are buying bonds, bond prices increase. Because of the inverse relationship between bond prices and interest rates, interest rates decrease, increasing the amount of money demanded. In this case, the interest rate declines to i_0, the rate at which the amount of money demanded equals the amount of money supplied. Interest rate i_0 is the equilibrium interest rate since, once this rate is established, there is no tendency for it to change. At interest rate i_2, the amount of money demanded, Md_2/P_0, exceeds the amount of money supplied, Ms_0/P_0, and so an excess demand for money exists. Since there is an excess demand for money, households and firms attempt to add to their money holdings by, say, selling bonds. If households and firms, in the aggregate, are selling bonds, bond prices fall and interest rates rise, reducing the amount of money demanded. In this case, the interest rate increases to i_0, the rate at which the amount of money demanded equals the amount of money supplied. Thus, for income level Y_0, the equilibrium interest rate is i_0.

To summarize, equations (8.4) through (8.6) represent the assumptions concerning the money market. Equations (8.4) and (8.5) are behavioral equations;

equation (8.6) is an equilibrium condition. If the equilibrium condition is not met, the interest rate has a tendency to change until it is met.

THE LM CURVE

We are now in the position to derive a curve for the money market, the LM curve, which is analogous to the IS curve for the product market. Just as the IS curve of Chapter 6 consists of equilibrium combinations of income and the interest rate for the product market, the *LM curve* consists of equilibrium combinations of income and the interest rate for the money market. The LM curve is important because we can use it together with the IS curve to determine the equilibrium combination of income and the interest rate for the economy.

To derive the LM curve, we start with the graphical approach. First, the money supply function from Figure 8.2 is plotted in the right panel of Figure 8.3. Next, the demand for money function from Figure 8.1 is plotted in the right panel of Figure 8.3. A demand for money curve exists for each level of income. For example, if the level of income is Y_0, the demand for money curve is the one labeled $L(Y_0, i)$. If the level of income increases to Y_1, the demand for money curve shifts to the one labeled $L(Y_1, i)$, indicating an increase in the amount of money demanded. Finally, in the left panel of Figure 8.3, the interest rate is plotted on the vertical axis (with the same scale as the interest rate axis in the right panel) and income is plotted on the horizontal axis.

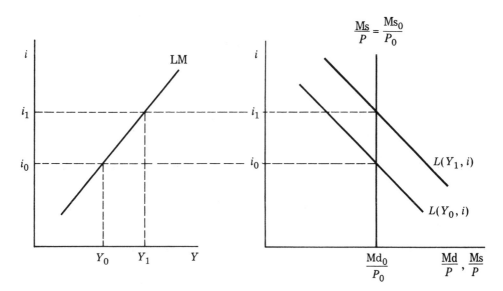

FIGURE 8.3

The derivation of the LM curve

Suppose the initial level of income is Y_0. The relevant demand for money curve is $L(Y_0, i)$. Given the demand for money and the supply of money, the equilibrium interest rate is i_0, for this is the rate of interest which equates the amount of money demanded, Md_0/P_0, with the amount of money supplied, Ms_0/P_0. Since i_0 is the equilibrium interest rate corresponding to income level Y_0, the equilibrium combination (Y_0, i_0) can be plotted in the left panel of Figure 8.3 by first plotting income level Y_0 on the horizontal axis and then extending a horizontal line from interest rate i_0 in the right panel to the left panel. The equilibrium combination (Y_0, i_0) is one point on the LM curve.

Next, consider a higher level of income, say, Y_1. At the higher level of income, Y_1, the relevant demand for money curve is $L(Y_1, i)$. Using the same argument as before, the corresponding equilibrium rate of interest is i_1, which is greater than i_0. Since i_1 is the equilibrium interest rate corresponding to income level Y_1, the equilibrium combination (Y_1, i_1) can be plotted in the left panel of Figure 8.3 in the same manner as before. This combination is another point on the LM curve.

By considering other income levels and determining the corresponding equilibrium interest rates, the remainder of the LM curve may be derived. The curve is designated as the LM curve because it is derived from the *liquidity preference function*, Keynes's term for the demand for money function, and the money supply function. It is positively sloped because at higher levels of income the amount of money demanded is greater, and with a constant money supply, the interest rate must be higher to maintain equilibrium in the money market.

The LM curve may also be derived algebraically. If $Ms/P = 200$ and $Md/P = 135 + 0.25Y - 600\,i$, we can find the equilibrium rate of interest for each level of income. First, substitute into the equilibrium condition

$$\frac{Ms}{P} = \frac{Md}{P}$$

to obtain

$$200 = 135 + 0.25Y - 600i$$

or, upon simplification,

(8.7) $$Y = 2400i + 260.$$

Since equation (8.7) represents the LM curve, different combinations of Y and i can be obtained by substituting various income levels into the equation and then solving for the corresponding interest rates. If income is $500 billion, we have

$$500 = 2400i + 260,$$

which, solving for i, gives the equilibrium interest rate 0.10 or 10 percent. This combination ($500 billion, 10 percent) constitutes one point on the LM curve. If income is $620 billion, the same procedure gives an interest rate of 15 percent. The combination ($620 billion, 15 percent) is another point on the LM curve.

Since the LM curve consists of equilibrium combinations of interest rates and income levels for the money market, the money market is in equilibrium at any point on the curve. However, consider, say, (Y_1, i_0), a point off the LM curve. At that combination of income and interest rate, an excess demand for money exists and households and firms attempt to increase their money holdings by selling bonds. As a result, bond prices decrease and interest rates increase. If income is constant, the interest rate increases to i_1, the equilibrium rate. Next, consider the point (Y_0, i_1). At that combination of income and interest rate, an excess supply of money exists and households and firms try to reduce their money holdings by purchasing bonds. As a consequence, bond prices increase and interest rates decrease. If income is constant, the interest rate will fall to i_0. Thus, if the economy is at a point off the LM curve, the money market is in disequilibrium, and the interest rate tends to change until the market is in equilibrium.

Having derived the LM curve, the next step is to consider changes in the supply of, and demand for, money in order to determine the impact of these changes on the LM curve. Suppose, in Figure 8.4, the initial real money supply is Ms_0/P_0 and the corresponding LM curve is LM_0. Next, suppose that the nominal money supply increases from Ms_0 to Ms_1. With the price level assumed constant, the increase in the nominal money supply results in an increase in the real money supply from Ms_0/P_0 to Ms_1/P_0, and so the real money supply line shifts to the right. To find the new LM curve, the procedure just outlined is applied. The new real money supply line is used rather than the initial line. Thus, at income level Y_0, the new equilibrium interest rate is i_0' rather than i_0, and so (Y_0, i_0') represents a point

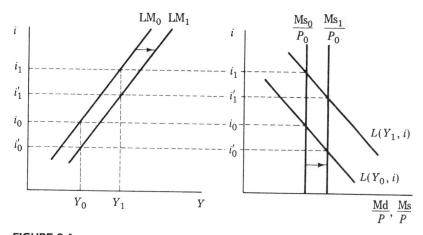

FIGURE 8.4

An increase in the real money supply and its impact on the LM curve on the new LM curve. Similarly, at income level Y_1, the new equilibrium interest rate is i_1' and (Y_1, i_1') is another point on the new LM curve. If other income levels are considered and the corresponding equilibrium levels of the interest rate determined, the new LM curve is found to be LM_1.

The new LM curve, LM_1, lies to the right of the old, indicating that at each level of income the equilibrium rate of interest is now less. For example, at income level Y_0, the new equilibrium interest rate is i_0', which is less than the original interest rate i_0. This is not surprising; with an increase in the nominal and real money supplies, we would expect interest rates to decline. The money market was originally in equilibrium at interest rate i_0 and income level Y_0. With the increase in the money supply, households and firms find themselves with excess money holdings. They attempt to reduce their money holdings by purchasing bonds, and so bond prices increase and interest rates decrease.

If the nominal money supply is reduced (with the price level constant), the real money supply is reduced and the real money supply curve shifts to the left. As a result, the LM curve shifts to the left, indicating that at each level of income, the interest rate is now higher.

We now consider an increase in the demand for money and its effect on the LM curve. Suppose the original demand for money function is designated as $L_0(Y, i)$ and the corresponding demand for money curves as $L_0(Y_0, i)$ and $L_0(Y_1, i)$, as shown in Figure 8.5. If the original real money supply is Ms_0/P_0, the original LM curve is LM_0. Next, suppose the demand for money increases. If the demand for money increases, the family of demand curves shown in Figure 8.5 will shift to the right, indicating that at each level of income (and interest rate) more money is demanded than before. This means that at each level of income the equilibrium

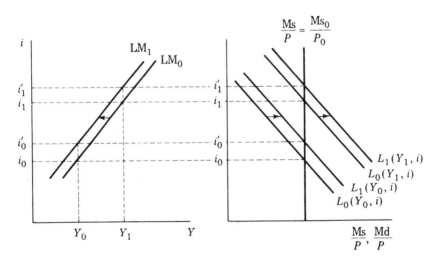

FIGURE 8.5

An increase in the demand for money and its impact on the LM curve rate of interest is greater than before. For example, consider income level Y_0. Previously, at that level of income, the equilibrium rate was i_0. It is now i_0'. Consequently, instead of having a point on the LM curve at (Y_0, i_0), we now have a point on the new LM curve at (Y_0, i_0'). Thus, an increase in the demand for money will shift the LM curve to the left. If the demand for money decreases, the LM curve will shift to the right.

THE LM CURVE WITH THE MONEY SUPPLY AS AN ENDOGENOUS VARIABLE

In Chapter 7, we assumed that the nominal money supply function was

$$Ms = mH,$$

where Ms is the nominal money supply, m is the money multiplier, and H is the monetary base. If the money multiplier is constant, the nominal money supply will change only when the monetary base changes. The money multiplier is not necessarily constant; it may vary systematically, for example, with the interest rate. This would be the case if depository institutions loan more of their excess reserves when the interest rate rises. Assuming that depository institutions reduce the ratio of excess reserves to transaction deposits in response to an increase in the interest rate, the money multiplier and, hence, the nominal money supply will increase.[6] In this case, we may specify the new nominal money supply function as

(8.8)$$Ms = Ms(H, i).$$

According to this specification, the nominal money supply is positively related to both the monetary base and the interest rate.

The new money supply function is plotted in Figure 8.6. Note that as the interest rate increases, the nominal money supply increases, and with the price

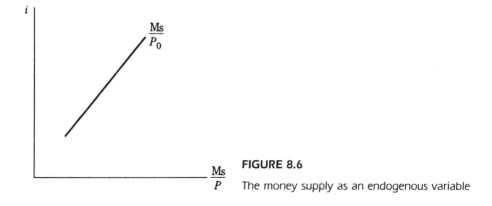

FIGURE 8.6

The money supply as an endogenous variable

level assumed constant, the real money supply also increases. As a result, the new real money supply function is positively sloped.

With the alteration in the slope of the real money supply curve, the slope of the LM curve is also altered. To compare the new LM curve with the original, suppose the original real money supply and LM curves are plotted in Figure 8.7; they are Ms_0/P_0 and LM_0, respectively. Next, suppose that the new money supply function is plotted as Ms/P_0 in Figure 8.7 and, for convenience, that it passes through the point $(Ms_0/P_0, i_0)$. To obtain a point on the new LM curve, assume the income level is Y_0. At that income level, the corresponding equilibrium interest rate is i_0, and so (Y_0, i_0) is a point on the new LM curve. This point is also a point on the old LM curve; consequently, the new LM curve coincides with the old curve at (Y_0, i_0). This occurs because the new money supply function cuts the old money supply function at the point $(Ms_0/P_0, i_0)$. To obtain another point on the LM curve, assume the income level is Y_1. The relevant demand for money curve is still $L(Y_1, i)$. But the new equilibrium rate of interest is i'_1. Interest rate i'_1 is greater than i_0 and less than i_1 because the money supply has increased as income and the amount of money demanded have increased. The increase in the money supply takes some of the upward pressure off the interest rate; consequently, the interest rate does not increase by as much as before. By considering other income levels, the new LM curve may be derived; it is LM_1. Because of the effect of an increase in the interest rate on the nominal money supply, it is more interest elastic than the original LM curve, LM_0.

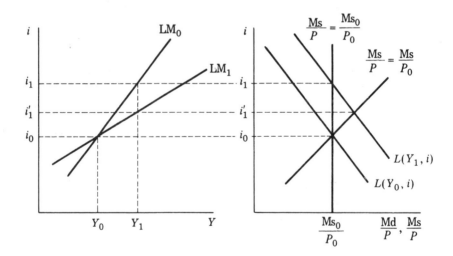

FIGURE 8.7

The LM curve with the money supply as an endogenous variable

CONCLUDING REMARKS

In this chapter, we considered the demand for money. We then discussed the interaction of the demand for, and supply of, money in the money market. Finally, we derived a curve, the LM curve, which depicts equilibrium combinations of interest rates and income levels for the money market. This curve is analogous to the IS curve, which shows equilibrium combinations of interest rates and income levels for the product market. In the next chapter, we shall consider a model of the economy with both a product market and a money market. The equilibrium values of income and the interest rate are given by the intersection of the IS and LM curves.

NOTES

1. William J. Baumol, "The Transactions Demand for Cash: An Inventory Theoretic Approach," *Quarterly Journal of Economics*, 66 (November 1952), 545–56; and James Tobin, "The Interest-Elasticity of Transactions Demand for Cash," *Review of Economics and Statistics*, 38 (August 1956), 241–47.

2. In this example and in general, the crucial point is not whether interest is paid on checkable deposits but whether higher rates are available elsewhere.

3. James Tobin, "Liquidity Preference as Behavior Towards Risk," *Review of Economic Studies*, 25 (February 1958), 65–86. This argument should not be confused with Tobin's earlier argument concerning the interest elasticity of the transactions demand for money.

4. These studies were based on the pre-1980 definition of the money supply. John T. Boorman, "The Evidence on the Demand for Money: Theoretical Formulations and Empirical Results," in *Current Issues in Monetary Theory and Policy*, 2nd ed., eds. Thomas M. Havrilesky and John T. Boorman (Arlington Heights, Ill.: AHM Publishing Corporation, 1980), pp. 315–60.

5. In this regard, see Stephen M. Goldfeld, "The Demand for Money Revisited," *Brookings Papers on Economic Activity*, no. 3 (1973), 577–638; Jared Enzler, Lewis Johnson, and John Paulus, "Some Problems of Money Demand," *Brookings Papers on Economic Activity*, no. 1 (1976), 261–80; and Goldfeld, "The Case of the Missing Money," *Brookings Papers on Economic Activity*, no. 3 (1976), 683–730. Much of the subsequent literature is summarized in John P. Judd and John L. Scadding, "The Search for a Stable Money Demand Function," *Journal of Economic Literature*, 20 (September 1982), 993–1023; and David E. W. Laidler, *The Demand for Money: Theories, Evidence, and Problems*, 3rd ed. (New York: Harper & Row, Publishers, Inc., 1985.

6. A change in the interest rate may also affect the ratios of cash and nonpersonal time deposits to transaction deposits and, therefore, the money multiplier and the nominal money supply. For a discussion of the interest elasticity of the nominal money supply (based on the pre-1980 definition of the money supply), see Robert H. Rasche, "A Review of Empirical Studies of the Money Supply Mechanism," Federal Reserve Bank of St. Louis, *Review*, 54 (July 1972), 11–19.

REVIEW QUESTIONS

1. Discuss the relationship between the transactions demand for money and income. In your answer, be sure to discuss the underlying reasoning. What effect would the increased use of charge accounts have on the transactions demand? Defend your answer.

2. Explain why the transactions demand for money depends, in part, on the interest rate and the cost of transferring funds.

3. What determines the precautionary demand for money in
   a. the long run?
   b. the short run?

4. Discuss the relationship between the speculative demand for money and the interest rate as explained by
   a. John M. Keynes.
   b. James Tobin.

5. What is the "missing money" puzzle? If the demand for money function is unstable, what are the implications for monetary policy?

6. Define the LM curve and explain why the interest rate increases as income increases (as you move along the LM curve).

7. Suppose the LM curve is as follows:

Interest Rate (i), Percent	Income (Y), $ Billion
20	800
15	700
10	600
5	500

   a. Is the money market in equilibrium at i = 10 percent and Y = $600 billion? Why? Why not? If not, explain why i tends to change until equilibrium is established. (Assume Y remains equal to $600 billion.)
   b. Is the money market in equilibrium at i = 10 percent and Y = $700 billion? Why? Why not? If not, explain why i tends to change until equilibrium is established. (Assume Y remains equal to $700 billion.)

8. Suppose the real money supply is $300 billion and the real demand for money is $50 + 0.5Y - 600i$. Determine the equilibrium interest rate corresponding to each of the following income levels.

Income (Y), $ Billion	Interest Rate (i), Percent
560	————
620	————
680	————

9. Explain how the LM curve is altered if

   a. the nominal money supply *decreases*.

   b. the real demand for money *decreases*.

   c. the level of income *increases*.

10. Explain why the LM curve is more interest elastic when the nominal money supply is positively related to the interest rate.

SUGGESTED READING ────────────────────────────────

BOORMAN, JOHN T., "The Evidence on the Demand for Money: Theoretical Formulations and Empirical Results," in Thomas M. Havrilesky and John T. Boorman (eds.), *Current Issues in Monetary Theory and Policy* (2nd ed.), pp. 315–60. Arlington Heights, Ill.: AHM Publishing Corporation, 1980.

JUDD, JOHN P., and JOHN L. SCADDING, "The Search for a Stable Money Demand Function: A Survey of the Post-1973 Literature," *Journal of Economic Literature*, 20 (September 1982), 993–1023.

KEYNES, JOHN MAYNARD, *The General Theory of Employment, Interest, and Money*. New York: Harcourt, Brace and Company, 1936.

LAIDLER, DAVID E. W., *The Demand for Money: Theories, Evidence, and Problems* (3rd ed.). New York: Harper & Row, Publishers, Inc., 1985.

TOBIN, JAMES, "Liquidity Preference as Behavior Towards Risk," *Review of Economic Studies*, 25 (February 1958), 65–86.

9

The Theory
of Income Determination:
The Product and Money Markets

In Chapters 3 and 4, a simple model of income determination was developed. In Chapters 5 and 6, the consumption and investment functions were examined and equilibrium in the product market was discussed. Chapters 7 and 8 dealt with money supply and demand and equilibrium in the money market. This chapter combines the models of the product and money markets to form a more complete theory of income determination.

With a more complete model, we hope to predict more accurately the impact of, say, an increase in government purchases upon the equilibrium level of income. Also, by including additional variables, we can predict the impact upon those variables as well as the variables previously included in the model. Finally, by including the money market, we can discuss monetary policy and the determinants of the relative effectiveness of monetary and fiscal policy.

In this chapter, the model, which now includes the product and money markets, is first summarized. The IS and LM curves are then plotted and the equilibrium values of income and the interest rate determined. Next, changes in government purchases and in the nominal money supply are considered with a view to determining their impact upon the economy. Monetary policy is then discussed, along with some of the determinants of the relative effectiveness of monetary and fiscal policy. Finally, the IS–LM model is applied to the question of the appropriate mix of monetary and fiscal policies.

THE PRODUCT AND MONEY MARKETS: A SUMMARY

With reference to the product market, we have assumed that consumption is a function of disposable income, that investment is a function of the interest rate, that government purchases are exogenous, and that taxes are a function of income. With reference to the money market, we have assumed that the nominal money supply is, as a first approximation, exogenous. Since the price level is assumed constant, the real money supply is also exogenous. The real demand for money is a function of income and the interest rate. For the product market to be in equilibrium, investment plus government purchases must equal saving plus taxes. For the money market to be in equilibrium, the real amount of money supplied must equal the real amount of money demanded.

The assumptions about the product and money markets can be summarized in equation form:

(9.1) $$C = C(Y_d) \qquad (\text{where } Y_d = Y - T),$$

(9.2) $$I = I(i),$$

(9.3) $$G = G_0,$$

(9.4) $$T = T(Y),$$

(9.5) $$\frac{Ms}{P} = \frac{Ms_0}{P_0},$$

(9.6) $$\frac{Md}{P} = L(Y, i).$$

The equilibrium conditions are

(9.7) $$I + G = S + T,$$

(9.8) $$\frac{Ms}{P} = \frac{Md}{P}.$$

Equations (9.1) through (9.4) are for the product market. These equations and equation (9.7), the equilibrium condition for the product market, are summarized geometrically through the IS curve. Equations (9.5) and (9.6) are for the money market; these equations and equation (9.8) are summarized geometrically through the LM curve.

EQUILIBRIUM AND THE IS AND LM CURVES

The model now includes both the product and money markets. In this chapter, we continue to assume that the price level is constant; this assumption is relaxed in the next chapter. To determine the equilibrium combination of income and the interest rate, we superimpose the LM curve on the IS curve in Figure 9.1. The IS curve consists of equilibrium combinations of income and the interest rate for the product market while the LM curve consists of equilibrium combinations of those variables for the money market. Consequently, the product market is in equilibrium only when the actual combination of income and the interest rate is on the IS curve and the money market is in equilibrium only when the actual combination is on the LM curve. For the new model to be in equilibrium, both markets must be in equilibrium. Therefore, the actual combination of income and the interest rate must lie on both curves. This occurs only at the point where the IS and LM curves intersect at income Y_0 and interest rate i_0. Consequently, the equilibrium combination of income and the interest rate for the IS–LM model of Figure 9.1 is (Y_0, i_0).

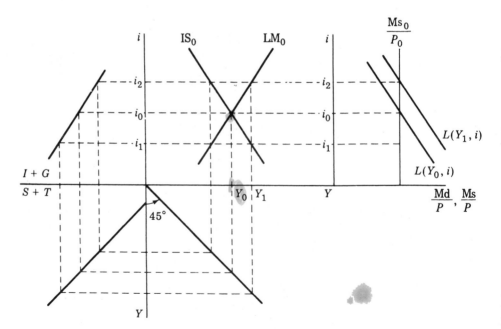

FIGURE 9.1

Equilibrium in the IS-LM model

The equilibrium combination of income and the interest rate can also be determined algebraically by substituting the behavioral equations into the equilibrium conditions in order to find the equations for the IS and LM curves and then solving the set of simultaneous equations for income and the interest rate. To illustrate, we shall use the example developed in Chapters 6 and 8. In Chapter 6, we derived an IS curve algebraically. It was

$$Y = 650 - 1500i.$$

In Chapter 8, we derived an LM curve algebraically. It was

$$Y = 260 + 2400i.$$

To determine the equilibrium combination of income and the interest rate for the product and money markets, we solve the two equations simultaneously. Since Y equals both $650 - 1500i$ and $260 + 2400i$, $650 - 1500i$ equals $260 + 2400i$ or, after rearranging,

$$2400i + 1500i = 650 - 260$$

or $$i = 0.10.$$

Consequently, the equilibrium interest rate is 0.10 or 10 percent. To determine the equilibrium level of income, substitute $i = 0.10$ in either the equation for the IS curve or the equation for the LM curve. If we substitute into the former, we have

$$Y = 650 - 1500(0.10) = 650 - 150 = 500.$$

The equilibrium level of income is $500 billion. Therefore, the equilibrium combination of income and the interest rate is $500 billion, 10 percent.

Returning to Figure 9.1, we see that both the product and money markets are in equilibrium at income Y_0 and interest rate i_0. That is, at income Y_0 and interest rate i_0, investment plus government purchases equals saving plus taxes, and the amount of money supplied equals the amount of money demanded. Suppose we consider a different combination of income and the interest rate, for example, (Y_1, i_1). At income level Y_1 and interest rate i_1, the product market is in equilibrium, but the money market is not. The amount of money demanded is greater than the amount of money supplied. Under these circumstances, households and firms attempt to increase their money holdings by, say, selling bonds. This decreases bond prices and increases interest rates. As interest rates increase, there are repercussions in the product market; investment decreases and, as a consequence, income decreases. If the equilibrium is stable, income and the interest rate change until equilibrium is established in both markets. This occurs only at income Y_0 and interest rate i_0.

Similarly, consider combination (Y_1, i_2). The money market is in equilibrium, but the product market is not. Investment plus government purchases is less than saving plus taxes. Whenever investment plus government purchases is less than saving plus taxes, aggregate demand is less than aggregate supply and income declines. As income falls, there are repercussions in the money market; in particular, the amount of money demanded decreases. This means that the interest rate decreases. If the equilibrium is stable, income and the interest rate change until equilibrium is established in both markets. This occurs only at income Y_0 and interest rate i_0.

Thus, if we are at a point other than (Y_0, i_0), at least one of the markets is in disequilibrium and income or the interest rate or both change. Moreover, as changes in income or the interest rate occur in one market, there are repercussions in the other market. Income and the interest rate, however, will adjust until both markets are in equilibrium. The equilibrium combination for the product and money markets is given by the intersection of the IS and LM curves.

EQUILIBRIUM AND SHIFTS IN THE IS AND LM CURVES

We may use the IS–LM model to determine the impact of an increase in government purchases. As in the previous models, an increase in government purchases causes an increase in the equilibrium level of income. With the assistance of the IS–LM diagram, however, we will find that the increase in income is likely to be less than predicted on the basis of the earlier multiplier analysis. Also, with the assistance of the IS–LM diagram, we are able to determine the impact of the increase in government purchases on the interest rate, a variable absent from the earlier models.

Suppose the initial IS and LM curves are IS_0 and LM_0, respectively, in Figure 9.2, and government purchases increase.[1] With the increase in government purchases, the $I + G$ curve shifts to the left by an amount equal to the increase in government purchases. As a consequence, the relevant IS curve is now IS_1, which is derived from the new $I + G$ curve and the original $S + T$ curve. The new equilibrium combination of income and the interest rate is Y_1 and i_1, given by the intersection of the new IS curve and the original LM curve. Since the new equilibrium levels of income, Y_1, and the interest rate, i_1, are greater than the original equilibrium levels, Y_0 and i_0, we conclude that the increase in government purchases caused an increase in both income and the interest rate. Based on the earlier models, the increase in income is to be expected. With an increase in government purchases, aggregate demand increases and, as a consequence, the equilibrium level of income increases.

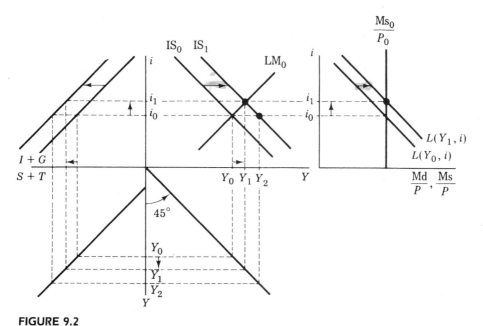

FIGURE 9.2

An increase in government purchases in the IS-LM model

Since the interest rate was absent from earlier models, the increase in the interest rate may have been unexpected. With the increase in income, however, the amount of money demanded increases. In terms of Figure 9.2, the demand for money curve shifts to $L(Y_1, i)$. Since the amount of money supplied is unchanged, the increase in the amount of money demanded results in an increase in the equilibrium interest rate.

Before proceeding, let us consider what happens to the rest of the variables as a result of the increase in government purchases. Both consumption and saving increase. The change in consumption cannot be determined directly from Figure 9.2; we know from equation (9.1), however, that consumption is positively related to disposable income. Since income increases from Y_0 to Y_1, taxes increase; since the marginal tax rate is less than 1, the increase in taxes is less than the increase in income. Disposable income, therefore, increases; as a result, consumption increases. Since saving is also positively related to disposable income, saving increases.

With an increase in the interest rate, investment decreases as a result of the inverse relationship between investment and the interest rate. This can also be determined from Figure 9.2. Note that the $I + G$ curve shifts to the left by an amount equal to the increase in government purchases. Because of the increase in the interest rate, however, the increase in investment plus government purchases is less than the increase in government purchases, implying that investment must have decreased somewhat to partially offset the increase in government purchases.

Because investment varies with the interest rate, the multipliers derived earlier do not apply to the IS-LM model. Earlier, the government purchases multiplier, with taxes a function of income, equaled $1/(1 - b + bt)$. Consequently, the change in income, ΔY, due to the change in government purchases, ΔG, could be determined (predicted) with the aid of the relationship

$$\Delta Y = \frac{1}{1 - b + bt} \Delta G.$$

The IS-LM model suggests that the actual change in income is, in general, less than the change in income predicted on the basis of the preceding relationship. Why is this the case? Earlier, investment was assumed constant, $I = I_0$; in the IS-LM model, investment is a function of the interest rate. With a change in government purchases, the interest rate changes. Since investment is a function of the interest rate, investment also changes and in the opposite direction of the change in government purchases. The change in investment offsets, in part, the change in government purchases, producing a smaller change in income. For example, suppose government purchases increase. As we have seen, an increase in government purchases results in both an increase in the level of income and the rate of interest. As indicated previously, the increase in the interest rate causes investment to decrease, partially offsetting the increase in government purchases. Thus, instead of income increasing to Y_2 in Figure 9.2, as would be the case if investment were constant, income increases only to Y_1.

This particular result occurs not only for the government purchases multiplier but also for the other multipliers, including the balanced budget multiplier. In the IS-LM model, the balanced budget multiplier is less than 1. If government purchases and taxes increase by the same amount, income increases. As income increases, however, the amount of money demanded increases. As a result, the interest rate increases and investment decreases. The decrease in investment, by partially offsetting the increase in government purchases, prevents income from increasing by an amount equal to the increase in government purchases. Therefore, the balanced budget multiplier is less than 1. Thus, in general, the actual change in income is less than predicted on the basis of the multipliers derived in Chapter 4. Within the context of this model, the actual change in income equals the predicted change only if (1) the demand for money function is perfectly interest elastic or (2) the investment function is perfectly interest inelastic. Both cases are considered later in the chapter, as well as in Appendix 2.

To gain familiarity with the model, suppose we consider the effects of increases in the nominal and real money supplies. Based on the earlier discussion of the money market, we expect the interest rate to decrease. Since investment is inversely related to the interest rate, we postulate that investment and, therefore, income will increase. We may verify the analysis with the assistance of the IS-LM diagram. Suppose, in Figure 9.3, the original IS and LM curves are IS_0 and LM_0 so that the original equilibrium interest rate is i_0 and the original equilibrium income level is

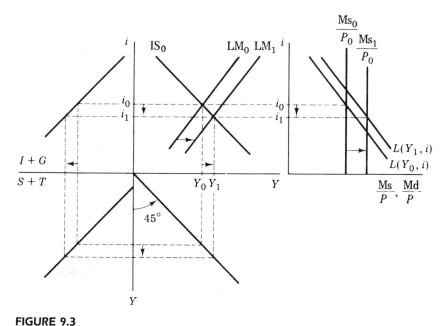

FIGURE 9.3

An increase in the nominal money supply in the IS-LM model

Y_0. If the nominal money supply increases with the price level constant, the real money supply also increases, and the real money supply curve in Figure 9.3 shifts to the right. As a consequence, the LM curve shifts to the right. The new equilibrium combination of income and the interest rate is (Y_1, i_1); this combination is determined by the intersection of the new LM curve, LM_1, and the original IS curve, IS_0. The new equilibrium rate of interest, i_1, is less than the original rate, i_0. Given the inverse relationship between investment and the interest rate, investment increases. Owing to the increase in investment, income increases to its new equilibrium level, Y_1. With the increase in income, taxes increase but by an amount less than the increase in income. Consequently, disposable income increases; hence, consumption and saving increase.

To gain additional familiarity with the model, the reader should consider changes in the other exogenous variables and underlying functional relationships so that he or she may determine the impact of the changes upon the variables in the model. The reader should also be able to explain why the variables change as they do.

MONETARY POLICY

Earlier, fiscal policy was defined as the use of government spending and taxes to achieve certain macroeconomic goals. Monetary policy may be defined in a similar fashion. *Monetary policy* is the use of the money supply to achieve certain macroeconomic goals. If the monetary authorities wish to increase aggregate demand in order to achieve higher levels of income and employment, they may do so by increasing the nominal money supply. If they wish to decrease aggregate demand, they may do so by decreasing the nominal money supply.

Earlier, we saw that government purchases, as a component of aggregate demand, directly influence the equilibrium level of income. If government purchases increase, aggregate demand and, thus, the equilibrium level of income increase. Taxes, on the other hand, are assumed to affect the equilibrium level of income only indirectly through their influence on consumption. If taxes are reduced, disposable income increases. With the increase in disposable income, consumption increases and so does aggregate demand, since consumption is a component of aggregate demand. If aggregate demand increases, so does the equilibrium level of income.

As just shown, an increase in the nominal money supply also affects the equilibrium level of income indirectly. If the nominal money supply increases with the price level constant, the real money supply increases. With the increase in the real money supply, interest rates decrease. As a result, investment increases. Since investment is a component of aggregate demand, aggregate demand increases, thereby increasing the equilibrium level of income. Consequently, monetary policy works indirectly by influencing the interest rate and investment. Monetary policy may also influence other variables. This possibility is discussed later.

Monetary policy has been defined in terms of the money supply, and so it is appropriate to judge whether monetary policy is expansionary or contractionary in terms of changes in the money supply.[2] Yet monetary policy is often judged to be expansionary or contractionary on the basis of changes in the interest rate. For example, if the interest rate declines, the reduction is seen as evidence that the monetary authorities are pursuing expansionary policies. Similarly, an increase in the interest rate is viewed as evidence that the monetary authorities are pursuing contractionary policies.

Interest rates are likely to be a poor indicator of the thrust of monetary policy. Although interest rates tend to fall (rise) when the monetary authorities follow expansionary (contractionary) policies, they also change for other reasons. If government purchases increase or taxes decrease, the interest rate may rise even if the monetary authorities are pursuing an expansionary policy. Suppose, in Figure 9.4, the IS and LM curves are IS_0 and LM_0, respectively, so that the initial equilibrium combination of income and the interest rate is (Y_0, i_0). Next, assume that government purchases are increased or taxes are reduced so that the IS curve shifts to IS_1. At the same time, assume that the Federal Reserve increases the money supply so that the LM curve shifts to LM_1. In this case, the new equilibrium combination of income and the interest rate is (Y_1, i_1), indicating that the interest rate has increased despite the action by the Federal Reserve to increase the money supply. If a person merely looked at the interest rate to determine the thrust of monetary policy, he or she would conclude incorrectly that the Federal Reserve was pursuing a contractionary policy.

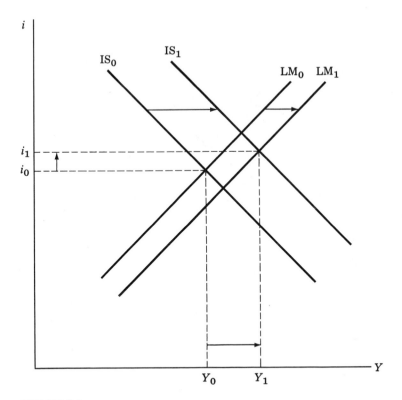

FIGURE 9.4

Shifts in the IS and LM curves and monetary policy: an increase in the interest rate

Similarly, if firms (households) decide to invest (consume) less, the interest rate may fall even if the Federal Reserve is pursuing a contractionary policy. Suppose, in Figure 9.5, the IS and LM curves are IS_0 and LM_0, respectively, so that the initial equilibrium combination of income and the interest rate is (Y_0, i_0). Now assume that firms (households) invest (consume) less so that the IS curve shifts to IS_1. At the same time, suppose the Federal Reserve decreases the money supply so that the LM curve shifts to LM_1. The new equilibrium combination of income and the interest rate is (Y_1, i_1), indicating that the interest rate has decreased despite the action by the Federal Reserve to decrease the money supply. Once again, if a person were concentrating solely on interest rates, he or she would conclude incorrectly that the Federal Reserve was pursuing an expansionary policy.

We could consider other examples but the main point should be clear. The interest rate changes for many reasons. Consequently, one should not rely on the interest rate to determine the thrust of monetary policy. We shall examine the implications of doing this for the conduct of monetary policy in Chapters 11 and 19.

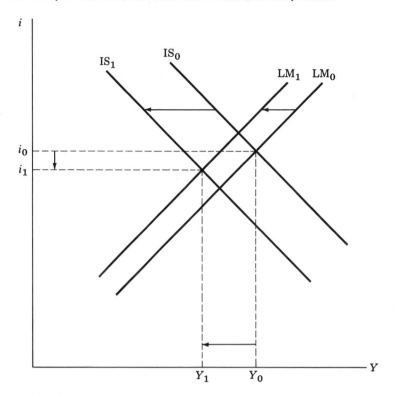

FIGURE 9.5

Shifts in the IS and LM curves and monetary policy: a decrease in the interest rate

THE RELATIVE EFFECTIVENESS OF MONETARY AND FISCAL POLICY

We now consider the determinants of the relative effectiveness of monetary and fiscal policy. We shall measure the effectiveness of monetary and fiscal policy in terms of their ability to produce changes in the equilibrium level of income. Consequently, the greater the change in the equilibrium level of income for a given change in the nominal money supply (government purchases or taxes), the more effective is monetary (fiscal) policy. Some determinants of the effectiveness of monetary and fiscal policy do not appreciably alter the relative effectiveness of the policies. For example, the greater the marginal propensity to consume, the greater is the effectiveness of both monetary and fiscal policy. Monetary policy works through the interest rate and investment. For a given change in investment, the change in income will be larger, the larger the marginal propensity to consume. Similarly, for a given change in government purchases, the change in income will be larger, the larger the marginal propensity to consume.

Other determinants of the effectiveness of monetary and fiscal policy affect the relative effectiveness of those policies. We consider two of the determinants: the interest elasticities of the demand for money and investment.

In the following discussion, we consider the relative effectiveness of the policies when the demand for money is perfectly interest elastic and when investment is perfectly interest inelastic. As discussed in Chapters 6 and 8, neither case is likely. The cases are considered, however, because they make it relatively easy to show the importance of the different elasticities.

The Interest Elasticity of the Demand for Money

First, the more interest elastic the demand for money, the less effective is monetary policy and the more effective is fiscal policy. Monetary policy is assumed to affect the economy through the interest rate and investment. For example, if the money supply increases, the interest rate decreases and investment, hence income, increases. The more interest elastic the demand for money, the smaller will be the decrease in the interest rate and, therefore, the smaller the increases in investment and income. Consequently, monetary policy is said to be less effective. To illustrate, suppose the demand for money curve for income Y_0 is $L_0(Y_0, i)$ in Figure 9.6. If the real money supply is Ms_0/P_0 and income is Y_0, the equilibrium interest rate is i_0. Suppose the monetary authorities takes action to increase the nominal money supply to Ms_1. Since the price level is assumed constant, the real money supply increases to Ms_1/P_0 and the interest rate decreases to i_1.[3] Had the demand for money been more interest elastic, there would have been a smaller decrease in the interest rate. For example, suppose the demand for money curve were $L_1(Y_0, i)$ rather than $L_0(Y_0, i)$. The initial equilibrium interest rate is i_0 as before. With the increase in the nominal and real money supplies, the interest rate

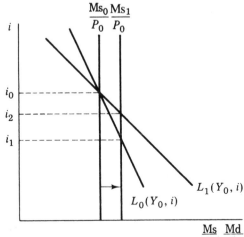

FIGURE 9.6

Monetary policy and the interest elasticity of the demand for money declines to i_2 rather than i_1. With the smaller reduction in the interest rate, there will be smaller increases in investment and income. Since there is now a smaller increase in the level of income for a given change in the nominal money supply, we say that monetary policy is less effective when the demand for money is relatively interest elastic.

Based on the illustration, the more interest elastic the demand for money, the less effective is monetary policy. In fact, monetary policy will not work at all if the economy is in a liquidity trap. As defined in Chapter 8, the liquidity trap is the perfectly elastic portion of the demand for money function. It is shown in Figure 9.7 as the horizontal portion of the demand for money curve $L(Y_0, i)$. If the real money supply is Ms_0/P_0, the equilibrium interest rate is i_0. Suppose the nominal and real money supplies increase. The real money supply line shifts to Ms_1/P_0, but the interest rate remains at the i_0 level. The additional money is absorbed into idle balances because people expect the interest rate to go up in the future. Consequently, they choose to hold money rather than to buy bonds, which would increase bond prices and reduce interest rates. Since the interest rate is unchanged, investment remains at its original equilibrium level. If investment is unaltered, there is no change in the level of income. Thus, if the economy is in the liquidity trap, monetary policy is ineffective.

Unlike monetary policy, the more interest elastic the demand for money, the more effective is fiscal policy. In general, if government purchases increase (or if taxes are reduced), both income and the interest rate increase. As the interest rate increases, however, investment decreases and offsets part of the increase in government purchases. Consequently, income fails to increase by as much as it would if the level of investment were constant. The more interest elastic the demand for money, the smaller the increase in the interest rate and, thus, the decrease in investment. The smaller the reduction in investment, the smaller is the offset to

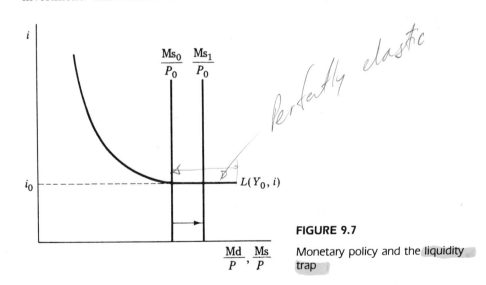

FIGURE 9.7

Monetary policy and the liquidity trap

the increase in government purchases and the larger is the increase in income. Consequently, we find that the more interest elastic the demand for money, the more effective is fiscal policy. In fact, when the demand for money is perfectly interest elastic (the liquidity trap case), fiscal policy is at its peak in terms of effectiveness. If the economy is in the liquidity trap and government purchases increase, income increases. But, since the economy is in the liquidity trap, the interest rate is unaltered; hence, there is no change in investment. Consequently, there is no decrease in investment to offset the increase in government purchases and nothing to reduce the effectiveness of fiscal policy. In this case, income will increase by an amount equal to $1/(1 - b + bt)$ multiplied by the change in government purchases. The term $1/(1 - b + bt)$ is the government purchases multiplier derived in Chapter 4 with investment assumed constant and taxes a function of income. If the economy is in the liquidity trap, there will be no change in the interest rate and, hence, no change in investment. Consequently, we may use the multiplier to predict the change in income.

We have seen that the greater the interest elasticity of the demand for money, the less effective is monetary policy and the more effective is fiscal policy. Consequently, the interest elasticity of the demand for money is a determinant of the *relative* effectiveness of monetary and fiscal policy. In the liquidity trap, monetary policy is at its worst in the terms of effectiveness and fiscal policy is at its best. As more interest inelastic demand for money functions are considered, however, monetary policy becomes more effective and fiscal policy less effective.

The Interest Elasticity of Investment

The interest elasticity of investment is also a determinant of the relative effectiveness of monetary and fiscal policy. The more interest inelastic the investment function, the less effective is monetary policy and the more effective is fiscal policy. Monetary policy is assumed to act through the interest rate and investment. The elasticity of the demand for money determines the responsiveness of the interest rate to changes in the real money supply, whereas the elasticity of investment determines the responsiveness of investment to changes in the interest rate. From the standpoint of monetary policy, it is desirable that investment be highly responsive to a given change in the interest rate, since a relatively large change in investment produces a relatively large change in income. To illustrate, suppose the investment function is $I_0(i)$ in Figure 9.8. If the initial interest rate is i_0, investment is I_0. Suppose the monetary authorities take action to increase the nominal money supply and the interest rate declines to i_1. As a consequence, investment increases to I_1. With the increase in investment, income increases. Had investment been less responsive to the change in the interest rate, the increases in investment and income would have been smaller. Suppose the appropriate investment function is $I_1(i)$, rather than $I_0(i)$. If the interest rate decreases from i_0 to i_1, investment increases from I_0 to I_2, where I_2 is less than I_1. With the smaller increase in investment, a correspondingly smaller increase in income occurs. Since investment function $I_1(i)$

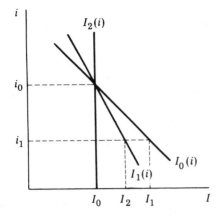

FIGURE 9.8

Monetary policy and the interest elasticity of investment

is more interest inelastic than investment function $I_0(i)$, monetary policy is less effective when investment is relatively interest inelastic.

Based on the illustration, the more interest inelastic the investment function, the less effective is monetary policy. In fact, if the investment function is perfectly interest inelastic, monetary policy does not work at all. Suppose the investment function is $I_2(i)$ and the initial interest rate is i_0. Suppose the monetary authorities take action to increase the money supply and the interest rate declines to i_1. Despite the decrease in the interest rate, there is no increase in investment since investment function I_2 indicates that investment is unresponsive to changes in the interest rate. Since there is no change in investment, there is no change in income and monetary policy is ineffective.

Unlike monetary policy, fiscal policy is more effective if investment is relatively interest inelastic. As we have seen, an increase in government purchases increases both income and the interest rate. Since the interest rate increases, investment decreases, and the decrease in investment partially offsets the increase in government purchases, thereby dampening the increase in income. The more interest inelastic the investment function, the smaller the change in investment and, therefore, the smaller the offset to the change in government purchases and, consequently, the larger the change in income. Thus, the more interest inelastic the investment function, the more effective is fiscal policy. In fact, if investment is perfectly interest inelastic, fiscal policy is at its peak in terms of effectiveness. This occurs because, even if interest rates increase as government purchases increase, investment will be unaltered. Consequently, there is no reduction in investment to offset the increase in government purchases and, therefore, nothing to reduce the effectiveness of fiscal policy. Since investment is constant, the multiplier $1/(1 - b + bt)$ may be used to predict the change in income.

In conclusion, we see that the more interest inelastic the investment function, the less effective is monetary policy and the more effective is fiscal policy. Consequently, like the interest elasticity of the demand for money, the interest elasticity of investment is a determinant of the relative effectiveness of monetary and fiscal policy.

We have seen that the relative effectiveness of monetary and fiscal policy hinges on various elasticities in the model. It is important, therefore, to estimate those elasticities in order to assess the effectiveness of monetary and fiscal policy. Based on the evidence presented in Chapters 6 and 8, it appears that both monetary and fiscal policies are effective. That is, either approach may be used to alter the level of aggregate demand, hence the equilibrium level of income. The main issue to be resolved is the relative effectiveness of the two approaches. Some economists, usually called *monetarists*, claim that monetary policy is much more powerful than fiscal policy. Other economists, while conceding the potency of monetary policy, deny that monetary policy is more powerful than fiscal policy.

MONETARY POLICY: A REEXAMINATION OF THE TRANSMISSION MECHANISM

So far, monetary policy has been assumed to affect income only through the interest rate and investment. Many economists have argued that this view is too narrow. They believe that monetary policy affects income through other variables as well. Moreover, they argue that concentration on the interest rate and investment as the *transmission mechanism*—the process by which the money supply affects income— has resulted in the underestimation of the potency of monetary policy. To broaden our view of the transmission mechanism, we examine two other ways in which monetary policy may affect income in this section. (The transmission mechanism is discussed in more detail in Chapter 11.)

Like investment, consumption may vary with the interest rate. If consumption is inversely related to the interest rate as the classical economists assumed, increases in the nominal and real money supplies result in lower interest rates and more consumption. Since consumption is a component of aggregate demand, aggregate demand increases, thereby increasing the equilibrium level of income. If both consumption and investment increase, income will increase by a greater amount than if only investment increases. Consequently, monetary policy is more effective if consumption is inversely related to the interest rate. Of course, if the demand for money is perfectly interest elastic, monetary policy is ineffective even if consumption varies inversely with the interest rate.

Monetary policy may also affect income by altering net private wealth. For our immediate purposes, we define net private wealth so as to include the nation's money supply.[4] As discussed in Chapter 5, consumption is positively related to net private wealth. If the nominal money supply increases and the price level is constant, the real money supply increases. Since it is one component of real net private wealth, wealth and, hence, consumption increase. With the increase in consumption, both aggregate demand and the equilibrium level of income increase. Moreover, the increases in wealth and consumption occur without regard to changes in the interest rate. Previously, investment (and possibly consumption) increased only if the interest rate decreased, and so monetary policy was ineffective if the demand for money was perfectly interest elastic. If consumption is a function of wealth, consumption and, therefore, aggregate demand increase even if the demand for money is perfectly interest elastic. Consequently, monetary policy is now effective even in the liquidity trap. In general, if consumption is a function of wealth, monetary policy is more effective than postulated earlier.

AN APPLICATION OF THE IS–LM MODEL:
THE POLICY MIX

With the United States experiencing a severe recession in 1981–82, various economists argued that the policy mix was inappropriate. Specifically, they claimed that the prevailing mix resulted in high interest rates which depressed investment and slowed the nation's economic recovery. By pursuing a less expansionary fiscal policy and a more expansionary monetary policy, they asserted that interest rates would fall, thereby stimulating investment. To evaluate this argument, we place it in the context of the IS–LM model.

Suppose, in Figure 9.9, the initial IS and LM curves are IS_0 and LM_0, re-

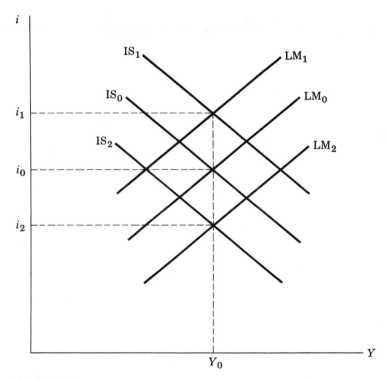

FIGURE 9.9

Alternative policy mixes

spectively, so that the initial equilibrium combination of income and the interest rate is (Y_0, i_0). The same equilibrium level of income can be achieved by pursuing either a combination of expansionary fiscal policy and contractionary monetary policy or a combination of contractionary fiscal policy and expansionary monetary policy. With regard to the first case, suppose government purchases are increased or taxes reduced so that the IS curve shifts to IS_1 and the money supply is reduced so that the LM curve shifts to LM_1. The same level of income (Y_0) prevails; however, the interest rate (i_1) is now higher than it was initially. In the second case, suppose government purchases are reduced or taxes increased so that the IS curve shifts to IS_2 and the money supply is increased so that the LM curve shifts to LM_2. Once again, the same level of income prevails; the interest rate (i_2), however, is lower.

Based on this analysis, the policy mix is not particularly important in determining the equilibrium level of income. Any of the three combinations results in the same equilibrium level of income (Y_0). The combinations do yield different interest rates, however, and this is important, especially in the long run. A lower interest rate results in a greater amount of investment which, in turn, implies a higher rate of capital accumulation. With the more rapid accumulation of capital, the nation's productive capacity grows more rapidly, making possible higher levels of output and consumption in the future.

Because the policy mix affects the interest rate and investment, it is an important consideration, especially in the long run. In view of its importance, we shall return to this issue in Chapter 16. (As emphasized in that chapter, political and other considerations may prevent the optimal combination from being achieved.)

CONCLUDING REMARKS

In this chapter, the money market was added to the model. By doing so, we broadened the scope of the model and presumably improved its predictive ability. Nevertheless, the model is still deficient in several respects. First, we have assumed that any amount can be produced. This cannot be true. In any period, the output that can be produced is limited by the economy's resources and its technology. Second, the price level is assumed constant. In the next chapter, a theory of aggregate supply is developed, thereby enabling explicit consideration of the economy's productive capacity and treatment of the price level as a variable.

NOTES _____

1. The government purchases multiplier is derived in Appendix 2. In the following analysis and in Appendix 2, it is assumed that the government finances the increase in government purchases by selling U.S. Treasury securities to the private sector and that the

sale has no impact on the economy. For an analysis of this and other cases, see Appendix 3, where the government budget constraint is explicitly considered.

2. In this context, we define an *expansionary monetary policy* as an increase in the nominal money supply and a *contractionary monetary policy* as a decrease in the nominal money supply. As discussed in later chapters, monetary policy is usually defined in terms of growth rates of the nominal money supply rather than increases or decreases in the absolute amount.

3. The new equilibrium interest rate is not i_1 since the decrease in the interest rate stimulates investment, hence, income. As income increases, the amount of money demanded increases and the demand for money curve shifts to the right. Consequently, the new equilibrium interest rate is less than i_0 but greater than i_1; it is shown as interest rate i_1 in Figure 9.3. To show more clearly the importance of the interest elasticity of the demand for money, the shift in the demand for money curve due to the increase in income is ignored.

4. Controversy exists about the appropriate definition of net private wealth. For example, checkable deposits should probably be excluded from net private wealth for, although checkable deposits are assets to their owners, they are liabilities to depository institutions, and when the assets and liabilities of the private sector are aggregated to obtain an estimate of net private wealth, they cancel. For a discussion and references, see Y. C. Park, "Some Current Issues on the Transmission Process of Monetary Policy," International Monetary Fund, *Staff Papers*, 19 (March 1972), 3–5.

REVIEW QUESTIONS

1. Suppose the IS and LM curves are as follows:

Interest rate (i) (percent)	Income (Y): The IS curve ($ billion)	Income (Y): The LM curve ($ billion)
20	600	800
15	700	700
10	800	600
5	900	500

   a. Determine the equilibrium interest rate and income level.

   b. Suppose the rate of interest is 10 percent and the level of income, $800 billion. Explain how there is a tendency for the interest rate and income to gravitate to their equilibrium levels.

   c. Suppose the interest rate is 10 percent and the level of income, $600 billion. Explain how there is a tendency for the interest rate and income to gravitate to their equilibrium levels.

2. Suppose the model is

$$C = 130 + 0.5Y_d \quad \text{(where } Y_d = Y - T\text{)},$$
$$I = 200 - 600i,$$
$$G = 112,$$
$$T = 20 + 0.2Y,$$
$$\frac{Ms}{P} = 300,$$
$$\frac{Md}{P} = 50 + 0.5Y - 600i.$$

Determine the equilibrium value of each of the variables in the model.

3. To test your understanding of the IS–LM model, indicate whether each of the following variables increases, decreases, or remains constant.

   a. Suppose firms decide to invest *more*.

   b. Suppose households decide to consume *more*.

   c. Suppose taxes *increase*.

   d. Suppose the demand for money *increases*.

   The variables are income, the interest rate, investment, government purchases, taxes, consumption, saving, and the real amounts of money supplied and demanded.

4. In the context of the IS–LM model, explain why the actual change in income

   a. is likely to be less than predicted on the basis of the multipliers derived in Chapter 4.

   b. equals the predicted change if

   (1) the demand for money is perfectly interest elastic.

   (2) the investment function is perfectly interest inelastic.

   (3) the nominal money supply is perfectly interest elastic.

5. Suppose the economy is experiencing high rates of unemployment. Based on the IS–LM analysis, what policies might be recommended to solve the problem? Explain how each policy works to solve the problem.

6. Explain why changes in the interest rate may be a poor indicator of the thrust of monetary policy.

7. Explain how each of the following helps to determine the relative effectiveness of monetary and fiscal policy.

   a. The interest elasticity of the demand for money.

   b. The interest elasticity of investment.

   c. The interest elasticity of the nominal money supply.

8. Show and explain why fiscal policy is ineffective if the demand for money is perfectly interest inelastic.

9. Suppose consumption is inversely related to the interest rate. Does this make monetary (fiscal) policy more or less effective? Defend your answer.

10. Suppose the demand for money function is unstable. With the aid of the IS–LM diagram, explain how the instability makes the conduct of monetary (fiscal) policy more difficult.

11. Suppose the Federal Reserve does not have complete control of the money supply. What are the implications for monetary policy?

12. Explain why the monetary–fiscal policy mix is important. Why might it be difficult or impossible to achieve the appropriate mix?

SUGGESTED READING

HICKS, JOHN R., "Mr. Keynes and the 'Classics': A Suggested Interpretation," *Econometrica*, 5 (April 1937), 147–59.

LAIDLER, DAVID, "Money and Money Income: An Essay on the 'Transmission Mechanism'," *Journal of Monetary Economics*, 4 (1978), 151–91.

PARK, Y. C., "Some Current Issues on the Transmission Process of Monetary Policy," International Monetary Fund, *Staff Papers*, 19 (March 1972), 1–43.

TOBIN, JAMES, "A General Equilibrium Approach to Monetary Theory," *Journal of Money, Credit, and Banking*, 1 (February 1969), 15–29.

10

THE THEORY OF INCOME DETERMINATION: AGGREGATE SUPPLY AND DEMAND

So far, we have assumed that aggregate supply plays a subordinate role in the model. Specifically, we postulated that output is not limited by resources and technology and that the price level is constant. Although convenient, neither assumption is tenable, and in the first part of this chapter we shall develop a theory of aggregate supply. In the second part of the chapter, we combine the theories of aggregate supply and demand in order to form a more complete theory of income determination. Several applications of the model are considered.

AGGREGATE SUPPLY

To develop an aggregate supply model, we must first consider a number of relationships: the production function, the demand for labor function, and the supply of labor function. From these relationships, we derive an *aggregate supply function*, a relationship between output and the price level. We start with the production function.

The Production Function

A *production function* is the relationship between the rates of input of productive services and the rate of output. In other words, it is a technological relationship between inputs and output. For instance, suppose it takes two units of capital and three units of labor (in fixed proportion) to produce one unit of a particular product. This relationship between inputs and output is an example of a production function. The relationship may be expressed either verbally or mathematically.

Typically, economists are concerned with production functions in a microeconomic context. That is, they study the production function of a single firm or an individual industry. For our purposes, however, we must consider an aggregate production function, a relationship between aggregate inputs and aggregate output. For the economy as a whole, we postulate that, given the nation's land, natural resources, and technology, aggregate output is a function of the economy's capital stock and the amount of labor employed. In equation form, the relationship is

(10.1)
$$Y = f(K, N),$$

where Y represents the economy's output (or income since the terms may be used interchangeably), K the economy's capital stock, and N the amount of labor employed.[1] Output is assumed to be positively related to the capital stock and the amount of labor employed. Diminishing returns are also assumed with regard to the factors of production so that an increase in employment (the capital stock), with the capital stock (employment) constant, increases output but at a diminishing rate.

Since the theory of income determination presented in this chapter is a short-run theory, both the capital stock and technology (as well as the nation's land and natural resources) are assumed constant. If the capital stock is assumed constant, the relationship $Y = f(K, N)$ may be written as

(10.2)
$$Y = f(N)$$

and is plotted in Figure 10.1. In Figure 10.1, output is measured on the vertical axis and employment on the horizontal. The relationship $Y = f(N)$ suggests that output increases as employment increases but at a diminishing rate. For example, if employment is N_0, output is Y_0. As employment increases by equal increments to N_1 and then to N_2, output increases, but the increases in output become smaller.

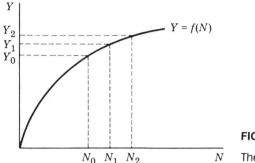

FIGURE 10.1

The production function

The Demand for Labor Function

If we assume a given capital stock and pure competition, we find that the *demand for labor curve* consists of the marginal product of labor curve, which can be derived from the production function.[2] Under pure competition, firms hire workers until the money wage, W, is equal to the price level, P, multiplied by the marginal product of labor, MP_N. In equation form the relationship is

(10.3) $$W = P \cdot MP_N.$$

The *money wage* represents the actual wage paid to labor. For example, the money wage for the economy might be $10,000 per year. The price level is defined as before. The marginal product of labor, MP_N, is the change in output per unit change in the quantity of labor employed, assuming the capital stock constant. For example, if output increases by $10,000 with the employment of an additional worker, the marginal product of labor is $10,000. For the economy as a whole, the marginal product of labor is measured in real or constant dollars.

In the relationship, W represents the cost of hiring an additional worker, and $P \cdot MP_N$ represents the revenue associated with the employment of an additional worker. So long as the cost of hiring an additional worker is less than the revenue gained, firms will hire additional workers. As firms hire additional workers, the marginal product of labor declines. Consequently, employment will increase until the money wage, W, equals the price level, P, multiplied by the marginal product of labor, MP_N. Firms have no incentive to hire additional labor since the cost of hiring an additional worker exceeds the revenue gained.

If both sides of equation (10.3) are divided by the price level, P, one gets the following relationship:

(10.4) $$\frac{W}{P} = MP_N.$$

The wage–price ratio on the left side of equation (10.4) is usually referred to as the *real wage*. It is the money wage deflated by the price level. Consequently, with the capital stock constant and with pure competition, the real wage, W/P, equals the marginal product of labor, MP_N.

To obtain the demand for labor curve, which is the relationship between the amount of labor demanded and the real wage, we use the relationship $W/P = MP_N$ and determine the marginal product of labor from the production function. The marginal product of labor is the change in output per unit change in the quantity of labor employed. If the change in output is ΔY and the change in employment is ΔN, the marginal product of labor is the change in output, ΔY, divided by the change in employment, ΔN, or $\Delta Y/\Delta N$. Consequently, the marginal product of labor, $\Delta Y/\Delta N$, equals the slope of the production function.

In Figure 10.2 the marginal product of labor at employment level N_0 is $(\Delta Y/\Delta N)_0$, the slope of the production function at that level of employment. For illustration, assume that it is $10,000. We may plot this combination of employment and the marginal product of labor in the right panel as the point $(N_0, \$10,000)$. Similarly, at employment level N_1, the marginal product of labor is $(\Delta Y/\Delta N)_1$, the slope of the production function at that level of employment. Since diminishing returns to labor have been assumed, the marginal product of labor at employment level N_1 is less than the marginal product of labor at employment level N_0. Assume that it is $8,000. This combination of employment and the marginal product of labor is plotted as the point $(N_1, \$8,000)$ in the right panel. By considering other levels of employment and the corresponding marginal products of labor, we obtain the relationship, D_N, shown in the right panel of Figure 10.2. The relationship slopes downward and to the right because of diminishing returns to labor.

The relationship, D_N, in the right panel of Figure 10.2 is the demand for labor

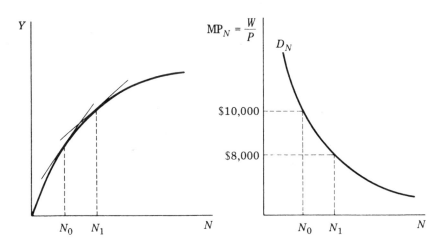

FIGURE 10.2

The production and demand for labor functions

function, because once the real wage is specified, the amount of labor demanded is determined. For example, suppose the money wage is $10,000 and the price level is 100 (percent). This means that the real wage is $10,000 divided by 1.00 or $10,000. Consequently, the amount of labor demanded is N_0. At that real wage, the profit-maximizing level of employment is N_0; firms, therefore, wish to hire N_0 workers. Suppose the money wage were $8,000 rather than $10,000. If the price level is 100, the real wage is $8,000 divided by 1.00 or $8,000. The amount of labor demanded is now N_1. With the lower real wage, firms find it profitable to hire additional workers.

Thus, the amount of labor demanded varies inversely with the real wage. At real wage $(W/P)_0$ in Figure 10.3, the amount of labor demanded is N_0. If the real wage declines, the amount of labor demanded increases. For example, if the real wage declines to $(W/P)_1$, the amount of labor demanded increases to N_1 because, with the lower real wage, firms have an incentive to hire additional workers. Since the amount of labor demanded is a function of the real wage, we specify the demand for labor function as

(10.5)
$$D_N = g\left(\frac{W}{P}\right),$$

where D_N is the amount of labor demanded and W/P is the real wage. The amount of labor demanded is inversely related to the real wage; hence, a decrease in the real wage increases the amount of labor demanded.

Since the marginal product of labor curve is derived from the production function, it shifts if the production function shifts. For example, if the capital stock increases, the production function shifts upward and the demand for labor curve shifts to the right, indicating an increase in the demand for labor. Both changes are shown in Figure 10.4. The demand for labor increases because, with an increase in the capital stock, workers have more equipment. This makes them more productive; if they are more productive, firms wish to hire more of them. Note that

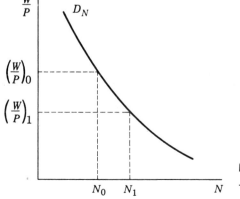

FIGURE 10.3

The demand for labor function

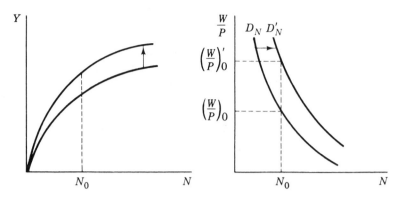

FIGURE 10.4

An increase in the capital stock and its impact on the production and demand for labor functions

we are not necessarily implying that an increase in the capital stock increases the level of employment; we are only arguing that the demand for labor increases. At this point, we do not have sufficient information to determine the impact of an increase in the capital stock on the level of employment.

The Supply of Labor Function

We have a production function and from it, a demand for labor function. We now turn to the *supply of labor function*. As in the case of the demand for labor function, the real wage plays a key role in the supply of labor function. In fact, the amount of labor supplied is assumed to be a function of the real wage. In equation form, the supply of labor function is written as

$$(10.6) \qquad\qquad S_N = h\left(\frac{W}{P}\right),$$

where S_N is the amount of labor supplied and W/P is the real wage. The amount of labor supplied is assumed to be positively related to the real wage so that an increase in the real wage results in an increase in the amount of labor supplied.[3] Graphically, the supply of labor function is depicted in Figure 10.5, with the real wage measured on the vertical axis and the amount of labor supplied on the horizontal. At real wage $(W/P)_0$, the amount of labor supplied is N_0. Should the real wage increase to $(W/P)_1$, the amount of labor supplied increases to N_1.

The impression that the money wage rather than the real wage is the relevant variable in determining the amount of labor supplied is easily refuted. For example, suppose a prospective worker is offered similar jobs in Alaska and Texas. Suppose further that the job in Alaska pays $30,000 per year and the job in Texas pays $20,000. Although it appears that the job in Alaska is preferable on economic

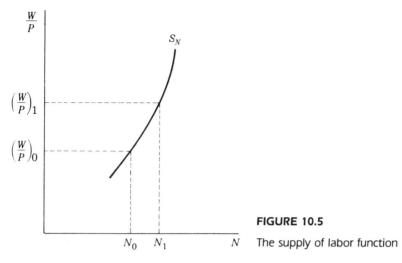

FIGURE 10.5

The supply of labor function

grounds to the job in Texas, this may not be true because the job offers are in terms of money wages. If these money wages are deflated by the appropriate price levels, the job in Texas may be preferable. This would be so if, for example, prices are twice as high in Alaska as in Texas. Consequently, it is the real wage that is relevant.

Just as the real wage is relevant for determining which job to accept, the real wage is relevant in determining whether to seek employment. If the real wage increases, individuals not usually in the labor force may decide to look for jobs. If they do, the amount of labor supplied increases in response to the higher real wage.

We have assumed that the supply of labor is a function of the real wage. Other factors affect the supply of labor by shifting the labor supply curve. For example, if population has been increasing for a number of years, the supply of labor curve will be shifted to the right, indicating that more labor will be supplied at each real wage. Similarly, the supply of labor curve will shift if there is a change in people's attitudes toward work. If students, rather than going to school, find it desirable to seek employment, the supply of labor curve will shift to the right. Consequently, in assuming that the supply of labor is a function of the real wage, other factors are not excluded; they are assumed constant. In the short run, this may be justifiable; in the long run, with a growing population, it is not.

Equilibrium in the Labor Market

So far, the demand for and supply of labor have been assumed to be functions of the real wage. Both functions are plotted in Figure 10.6. For the labor market to be in equilibrium, the amount of labor demanded must equal the amount of labor supplied. In Figure 10.6, the equilibrium combination of the real wage and level of employment is $((W/P)_0, N_0)$, given by the intersection of the demand for

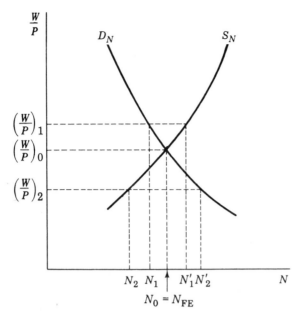

FIGURE 10.6

The demand for and supply of labor functions

labor curve, D_N, and the supply of labor curve, S_N. At real wage $(W/P)_0$, firms wish to hire N_0 workers. Similarly, at real wage $(W/P)_0$, N_0 persons are seeking jobs. Since firms are able to hire the number of employees that they wish and all persons seeking jobs are able to find them, no tendency exists for money and real wages to change and the labor market will be in equilibrium.

Suppose the real wage is $(W/P)_1$. At real wage $(W/P)_1$, the amount of labor demanded is N_1, and the amount of labor supplied is N_1'. Since more labor is supplied than demanded, the labor market is not in equilibrium and a tendency exists for the money wage to change. Since more persons are seeking employment than firms wish to hire, there is a tendency for money wages to fall as prospective workers compete for the limited number of jobs. If the money wage decreases (with the price level constant), the real wage decreases until the equilibrium level is reached. But if the real wage remains at $(W/P)_1$, employment is only N_1, since firms wish to hire only N_1 workers at that real wage. Since the number of persons seeking employment exceeds the number of jobs available at that real wage, unemployment may be said to exist. This unemployment is sometimes referred to as *involuntary unemployment.*

Suppose the real wage is $(W/P)_2$. At real wage $(W/P)_2$, the amount of labor demanded, N_2', exceeds the amount of labor supplied, N_2, and the labor market is not in equilibrium. In this case money wages tend to increase, since the number of persons firms attempt to hire exceeds the number currently seeking employment. If the money wage increases (with the price level constant), the real wage increases until the equilibrium level, $(W/P)_0$, is reached. But if the real wage remains at

$(W/P)_2$, employment is only N_2 since only N_2 persons are willing to work at that real wage.

Thus, at the equilibrium real wage, the amount of labor demanded equals the amount of labor supplied. Since the number of persons seeking jobs equals the number of persons whom firms wish to hire, we define the *full employment level of employment*, N_{FE}, as the level of employment where the amount of labor demanded equals the amount of labor supplied. By this definition, full employment exists at employment level N_0 in Figure 10.6.[4]

The Aggregate Supply Function

We can now derive the aggregate supply curve, which is a relationship between the price level, P, and aggregate output, Y. For the derivation, the production function is reproduced in the southeast quadrant of Figure 10.7. As employment increases, output increases, but at a diminishing rate. The demand for and supply of labor functions are depicted in the southwest quadrant. As the real wage increases, the amount of labor demanded decreases while the amount of labor supplied increases. The average money wage for the economy is depicted in the northwest quadrant. With the real wage, (W/P), measured on the horizontal axis and the price level, P, on the vertical axis, the money wage, W_0, is represented by a rectangular hyperbola.

A rectangular hyperbola is a mathematical relationship of the form

$$xy = \text{constant.}$$

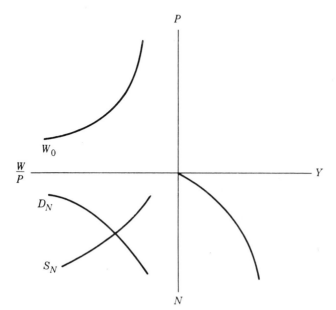

FIGURE 10.7

The derivation of the aggregate supply curve

For illustration, suppose that the constant equals 10. The function, $xy = 10$, may be plotted by assuming various values for x and finding the corresponding values for y. When x equals 10, y equals 1, found by substituting x equal to 10 into the relationship $xy = 10$ and solving for y. Consequently, in Figure 10.8, with x measured on the horizontal axis and y on the vertical, we may plot the point corresponding to x equal to 10 and y equal to 1. Similarly, when x equals 5, y equals 2. This point may also be plotted in Figure 10.8. Other combinations of x and y, such as x equal to 2, y equal to 5, and x equal to 1, y equal to 10, may be plotted. These and other points form the curve labeled $xy = 10$ in Figure 10.8. The main property of this curve is that if we consider any point on the curve and take the corresponding number on the x axis and multiply it by the corresponding number on the y axis, we obtain the constant. Also, note that if we know two of the items in the relationship, $xy = $ constant, we can find the third either algebraically or geometrically. Finally, should the constant increase (decrease), the rectangular hyperbola will shift farther from (closer to) the origin.[5]

Next, assume that x is equal to W/P and y is equal to P. The constant, therefore, is equal to the money wage, W, as xy now equals $(W/P)(P)$. This implies that a money wage may be represented by a particular rectangular hyperbola. The money wage W_0 is represented in Figure 10.7. If the money wage increases, the

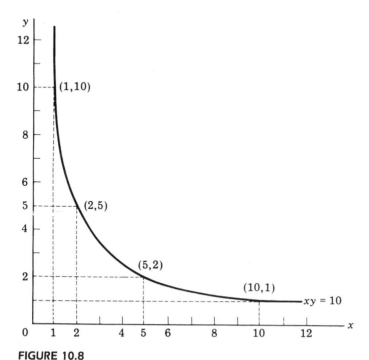

FIGURE 10.8

The rectangular hyperbola $xy = 10$

rectangular hyperbola will shift farther from the origin; but the money wage is the same at any point on a given rectangular hyperbola.

To derive the aggregate supply curve, assume that money wages are *flexible*. This means that money wages are free to rise or fall in response to conditions in the labor market. If the initial price level is P_0 and the money wage is W_0, the real wage is $(W/P)_0$ in Figure 10.9. At real wage $(W/P)_0$, the amount of labor demanded is N_0. Since the amount of labor supplied is also N_0, the level of employment is N_0, the full employment level. The resulting level of output is Y_0, the full employment level. Since Y_0 is the level of output corresponding to price level P_0, the combination may be plotted in the northeast quadrant of Figure 10.9 as the point (Y_0, P_0). This point is one point on the aggregate supply curve, AS.

To obtain additional points, we consider other price levels. For example, suppose the price level is P_1, which is less than P_0. Price level P_1, when combined with money wage W_0, produces a higher real wage, $(W/P)_1$. At real wage $(W/P)_1$, the amount of labor demanded, N_1, is less than the amount of labor supplied, N_1'. Consequently, prospective workers compete for the limited number of jobs, and with money wages flexible, money wages decline until the full employment real wage, $(W/P)_0$, is reestablished. Given the real wage $(W/P)_0$, employment is

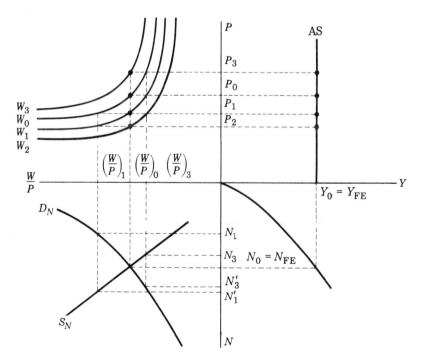

FIGURE 10.9

The derivation of the aggregate supply curve with money wages flexible

N_0 and output is Y_0. This suggests that output level Y_0 corresponds to price level P_1; this combination is plotted as the point (Y_0, P_1) in the northeast quadrant.

Similarly, consider price level P_2, which is less than P_1. Price level P_2, when combined with money wage W_1, produces a real wage greater than the full employment real wage, and there is an excess supply of labor. With money wages flexible, money wages fall in response to the excess supply of labor. Consequently, after money wages adjust, the real wage is $(W/P)_0$, employment is N_0, and output is Y_0. This implies that output level Y_0 corresponds to price level P_2; this combination is plotted as the point (Y_0, P_2).

We could continue this procedure and consider other price levels below P_0, but we would get the same result in each case: money wages adjust until the full employment real wage is established. Therefore, for price levels less than P_0, output is Y_0 and the aggregate supply curve is perfectly inelastic at the full employment level of output.

Suppose we consider price level P_3, which is greater than price level P_0. Price level P_3, when combined with money wage W_0, produces real wage $(W/P)_3$. At that real wage, more labor is demanded, N_3', than supplied, N_3. Firms, therefore, compete for the limited number of workers, and money wages increase until the full employment real wage, $(W/P)_0$, is restored. As a consequence, the real wage is $(W/P)_0$, employment is N_0, and output is Y_0. Thus, for price level P_3, the corresponding level of output is Y_0. This combination is plotted as the point (Y_0, P_3). Other price levels above P_0 may be considered. The result is the same at each price level; with money wages flexible, money wages adjust until the full employment real wage is established. Therefore, for price levels greater than P_0, output is Y_0 and the aggregate supply curve is perfectly inelastic at the full employment level of output.

The aggregate supply curve, labeled AS in Figure 10.9, relates the aggregate supply of goods and services to the price level and should not be confused with the supply of labor curve, S_N, which relates the amount of labor supplied to the real wage. With money wages flexible, the aggregate supply curve is perfectly inelastic at the full employment level of output.

The aggregate supply curve in Figure 10.9 was derived under the assumption that money wages are flexible, free to adjust to conditions in the labor market. Money wages may, however, be *rigid*, at least in the downward direction. By rigid downward, we mean that money wages are not free to fall in response to an excess supply of labor. Money wages may be rigid downward for a variety of reasons. Keynes argued that money wages may not decline at the same rate in all industries. Thus, for workers to protect their position relative to other workers, Keynes claimed that it is in the interest of workers to resist reductions in their money wages. More recently, it has been argued that money wages are rigid downward because of labor union pressure and minimum wage legislation. Labor unions allegedly have the power to increase money wages more rapidly than they would otherwise increase. If unions possess this power, they also have the power to keep money wages from decreasing as rapidly as they should. Similarly, minimum wage legislation provides a floor for money wages in many industries. Consequently, because of reluctance of workers to take wage cuts, labor union pressure, and minimum wage legislation, money wages may be rigid downward. On the other hand, in the absence of wage and price controls, money wages are likely to be flexible upward because there are few barriers (perhaps long-term contracts) to increases in money wages.

If money wages are rigid downward and flexible upward, the aggregate supply curve of Figure 10.9 is altered. Consequently, let us derive the new aggregate supply curve on the assumption that money wages are rigid downward and flexible upward. In Figure 10.10, suppose money wages are rigid downward at the W_0 level and the initial price level is P_0. At price level P_0 and money wage W_0, the real wage is $(W/P)_0$, which means that employment is N_0 and output is Y_0. Since output Y_0 corresponds to price level P_0, we may plot (Y_0, P_0) in the northeast quadrant. This point corresponds to the same point obtained earlier with money wages flexible.

Next, consider price level P_1, which is less than P_0. Price level P_1, when combined with money wage W_0, produces real wage $(W/P)_1$ and results in an excess supply of labor. Previously, money wages decreased in response to the excess supply of labor. With money wages assumed rigid downward, however, they do not fall and real wage $(W/P)_1$ prevails. Consequently, employment is N_1 and the level of output is Y_1. Since output Y_1 corresponds to price level P_1, the new equilibrium combination of output and the price level (Y_1, P_1) may be plotted in the northeast

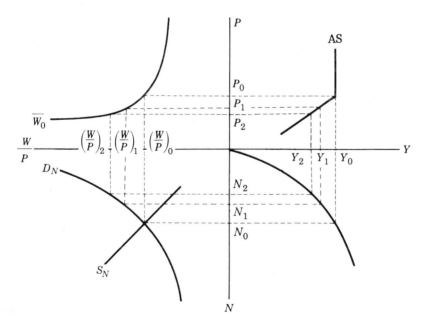

FIGURE 10.10

The derivation of the aggregate supply curve with money wages rigid downward quadrant of Figure 10.10. Similarly, consider price level P_2, which is less than P_1. This price level, when combined with money wage W_0, produces real wage $(W/P)_2$ with an even greater excess supply of labor. With money wages assumed rigid downward, they do not fall, and so employment is N_2 and output is Y_2. Since output Y_2 corresponds to price level P_2, the new equilibrium combination may be plotted in the northeast quadrant of Figure 10.10. If other price levels below P_0 are considered, the points trace out the positively sloped portion of the aggregate supply curve in Figure 10.10. Consequently, with money wages rigid downward at the W_0 level, the aggregate supply curve is positively sloped for price levels less than P_0. Since money wages are assumed flexible upward, the aggregate supply curve will be perfectly inelastic at the full employment level of output, Y_0, for price levels greater than P_0.

AGGREGATE DEMAND

In the previous section, an aggregate supply curve—a relationship between the nation's output and the price level—was derived. This curve is related to the labor market. To determine the equilibrium combination of output and the price level for the economy, an *aggregate demand curve* must be obtained. This curve is similar to the aggregate supply curve but is related to the product and money markets. In this section, the aggregate demand curve is derived from the IS–LM model of Chapter 9.

In the IS–LM model, the price level was assumed constant. With the price level assumed constant at the P_0 level and a given nominal money supply, Ms_0, the equilibrium level of income (output) is determined by the intersection of the IS and LM curves. In Figure 10.11, the initial equilibrium level of output is Y_0. Consequently, output level Y_0 and price level P_0 constitute one combination of Y and P, which equilibrates the product and money markets. This combination, (Y_0, P_0), is plotted in the income–price level quadrant of Figure 10.11 and is one point on the aggregate demand curve, AD.

To obtain another point on the aggregate demand curve, suppose the price level is P_1, which is less than P_0. Price level P_1, when combined with nominal money supply Ms_0, produces real money supply Ms_0/P_1, which is greater than Ms_0/P_0. As a consequence, the real money supply curve of Figure 10.11 shifts to the right. Since the LM curve is derived, in part, from the real money supply curve, the LM curve also shifts to the right. The new equilibrium level of income is Y_1, given by the intersection of the original IS curve, IS_0, and the new LM curve, LM_1. Thus, for price level P_1, the new equilibrium level of income is Y_1; this combination is plotted in the income–price level quadrant as the point (Y_1, P_1). To obtain other points, we could consider other price levels and find the corresponding equilibrium levels of income. A lower price level implies a greater real money supply and a correspondingly lower interest rate. The reduction in the interest rate, in turn, increases investment and, hence, the equilibrium level of income. The lower price

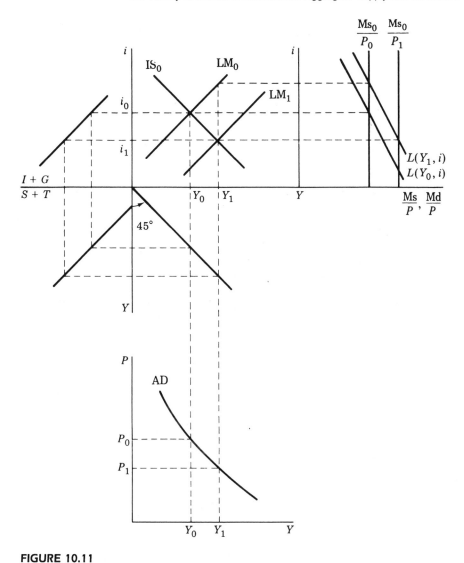

FIGURE 10.11

The derivation of the aggregate demand curve

level implies, therefore, a greater equilibrium level of income. The effect of the lower price level on the real money supply, interest rates, and investment is called the *Keynes effect.*

Thus, by conceptually varying the price level, we may derive the aggregate demand curve, AD, of Figure 10.11. Actually, the curve is not a demand curve in the ordinary sense. Instead, the curve consists of combinations of output and the price level, which provide equilibrium for both the product and money markets.

Since, however, the curve is commonly referred to as the aggregate demand curve, we shall use that term.

THE AGGREGATE SUPPLY–AGGREGATE DEMAND MODEL

To determine the equilibirum combination of output and the price level, the aggregate demand curve may be superimposed upon the aggregate supply curve derived earlier. If money wages are assumed flexible, the aggregate supply curve is AS_0 in Figure 10.12. If the corresponding aggregate demand curve is AD_0, the equilibrium combination of output and the price level is (Y_0, P_0), given by the intersection of the aggregate supply curve AS_0 and the aggregate demand curve AD_0. Price level P_0 must be the equilibrium price level. At any other price level, either an excess demand for goods and services or an excess supply exists. If the price level is less than P_0, aggregate demand exceeds aggregate supply and the price level increases. If the price level is greater than P_0, aggregate supply exceeds aggregate demand and the price level decreases.

If aggregate demand is AD_0, the money wage is W_0, the real wage is $(W/P)_0$, and employment is N_0, the full employment level. Since the equilibrium combination of output and the price level is (Y_0, P_0) in Figure 10.12, the same combination

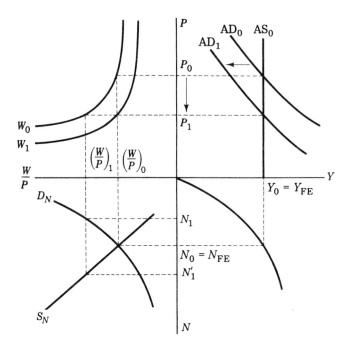

FIGURE 10.12

A reduction in aggregate demand with money wages flexible

must prevail in the IS–LM diagram from which the aggregate demand curve AD_0 is derived (see Figure 10.11). Given price level P_0, the rest of the equilibrium values in the IS-LM diagram may be determined in the same manner as in Chapter 9.

If aggregate supply is AS_0 and aggregate demand is AD_0, full employment prevails. In fact, regardless of the level of aggregate demand, full employment prevails if money wages and prices are flexible. For example, suppose aggregate demand falls to AD_1. With the reduction in aggregate demand, there is downward pressure on prices and, if they are flexible, they decrease to the P_1 level. Price level P_1, when combined with money wage W_0, produces real wage $(W/P)_1$. This creates an excess supply of labor and puts downward pressure on money wages. If they are flexible, they fall to W_1, where once again the full employment real wage, $(W/P)_0$, prevails. This means that the level of employment is N_0 and the resulting level of output is Y_0. Full employment is reestablished but at a lower absolute level of money wages and prices. Of course, these changes occur more or less simultaneously rather than in the order described.

Thus, if money wages and prices are flexible, full employment prevails. If aggregate demand decreases, unemployment may exist temporarily but as money wages and prices adjust, full employment will be restored. The classical economists generally assumed wage and price flexibility. They believed, therefore, that full employment is the normal state of affairs. (The classical model is examined in Chapter 11.)

If money wages are rigid downward, full employment may not exist To illustrate, suppose money wages are rigid downward and aggregate supply is AS_0 in Figure 10.13. If aggregate demand is AD_0, the equilibrium combination of output and the price level is (Y_0, P_0). Since Y_0 represents the full employment level of output, full employment exists. Suppose, however, aggregate demand declines to AD_1. If prices are flexible, the price level decreases to P_1 in response to the decline in aggregate demand. Price level P_1, when combined with money wage W_0, produces real wage $(W/P)_1$. At that real wage, an excess supply of labor exists and money wages should fall. Suppose they are prevented from falling, however, because of labor union pressure, minimum wage legislation, and so on. The real wage remains $(W/P)_1$ and the resulting levels of employment and output are N_1 and Y_1, respectively. Clearly, the level of employment, N_1, is less than the full employment level, N_0, and unemployment exists.

Thus, if money wages are rigid downward, the level of aggregate demand is very important. If aggregate demand is AD_0 (or more) in Figure 10.13, full employment prevails. If aggregate demand is less than AD_0, unemployment exists.

UNEMPLOYMENT AND STABILIZATION POLICY

With money wages rigid downward, unemployment may exist due to inadequate aggregate demand. If it does, expansionary fiscal and/or monetary policy may be used to increase aggregate demand, thereby increasing income and employment.

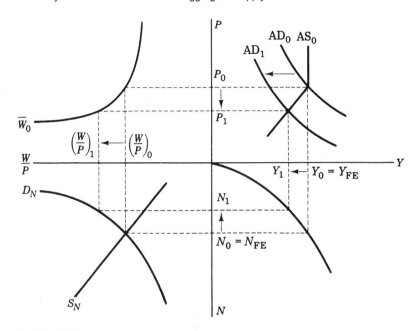

FIGURE 10.13

A reduction in aggregate demand with money wages rigid downward

For example, if taxes are reduced, consumption increases, thereby increasing aggregate demand. The impact of these changes can be determined with the aid of the model.

Suppose, in Figure 10.14, the economy is initially in equilibrium at output level Y_0 and price level P_0. With a tax reduction, the $S + T$ curve shifts to $S + T'$ and, as a consequence, the IS curve shifts from IS_0 to IS_1. At price level P_0, the new level of income is Y_1, given by the intersection of the new IS curve, IS_1, and the original LM curve, LM_0. Therefore, at price level P_0, aggregate demand is now greater than before since Y_1 is greater than Y_0. Consequently, in the income–price level quadrant of Figure 10.14, we plot a point at (Y_1, P_0). This point lies to the right of the point (Y_0, P_0) and is a point on the new aggregate demand curve AD_1. The remainder of the new aggregate demand curve, AD_1, is obtained by conceptually varying the price level (see Figure 10.11).

With the increase in aggregate demand, the new equilibrium combination of income and the price level is (Y_2, P_2), given by the intersection of the new aggregate demand curve AD_1 and the original aggregate supply curve, AS_0. Consequently, with the tax cut, the price level increases to P_2, the real wage decreases to $(W/P)_2$, employment increases to N_2, and output increases to Y_2. With the postulated tax reduction and resulting increase in aggregate demand, employment and output increase to their full employment levels. Had the tax cut been smaller, employment and output would have increased, but not to their full employment levels.[6]

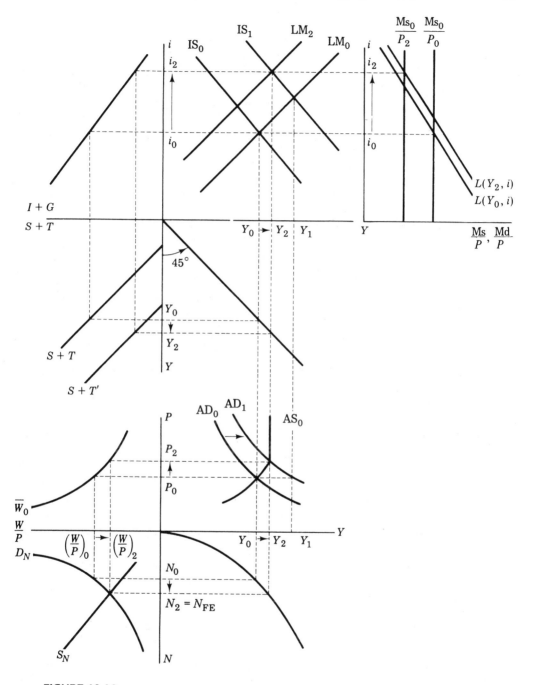

FIGURE 10.14

A tax reduction in the aggregate supply–aggregate demand model

With the increase in the price level to P_2, the LM curve shifts to LM_2 so that final equilibrium in the IS–LM portion of Figure 10.14 is given by the intersection of the new IS curve, IS_1, and the new LM curve, LM_2. Thus, the new equilibrium interest rate is i_2, which implies that interest rates increase as a result of the tax reduction. If interest rates increase, investment decreases. With the tax reduction and increase in income, both consumption and saving increase.

Based on the foregoing analysis, it appears that a tax reduction is a means to stimulate the economy during a recession. Alternatively, an increase in government purchases is a means to stimulate the economy. An increase in government purchases increases aggregate demand, which, in turn, increases the price level, output, and employment. Thus fiscal policy, the use of government spending and taxes to achieve certain economic goals, may be used to achieve full employment.

Similarly, monetary policy, the use of the nominal money supply to achieve certain economic goals, may be used to achieve full employment. To see this and to gain additional experience in using the aggregate supply–aggregate demand model, let us consider the impact of an increase in the nominal money supply. Suppose, in Figure 10.15, the economy is initially at output Y_0 and price level P_0. Suppose the money supply increases from Ms_0 to Ms_1. In the IS–LM portion of Figure 10.15, the real money supply curve shifts to Ms_1/P_0. As a consequence, the LM curve shifts to LM_1. At price level P_0, the new level of income is Y_1, given by the intersection of the original IS curve, IS_0, and the new LM curve LM_1. Thus, at price level P_0, aggregate demand is now greater than before, since Y_1 is greater than Y_0. Consequently, in the income–price level quadrant of Figure 10.15, we plot a point at (Y_1, P_0). This point lies to the right of the point (Y_0, P_0) and is a point on the new aggregate demand curve AD_1. The remainder of the new aggregate demand curve, AD_1, is obtained by conceptually varying the price level.

With the increase in aggregate demand, the final equilibrium combination of output and price level is (Y_2, P_2), given by the intersection of the new aggregate demand curve AD_1 and the original aggregate supply curve AS_0. This means that the price level has increased from P_0 to P_2 and that output and employment have increased from Y_0 to Y_2 and N_0 to N_2, respectively. Since N_2 represents the full employment level of employment, full employment prevails. Had the increase in the nominal money supply been smaller, employment and output would have increased, but not to their full employment levels.

With the increase in the price level to P_2, the real money supply is reduced to Ms_1/P_2. As a consequence, the LM curve shifts to LM_2 so that the final equilibrium combination of income and the interest rate is (Y_2, i_2). With the reduction in the interest rate, investment increases. In fact, it is the reduction in the interest rate and the subsequent increase in investment which increases aggregate demand. With the increase in disposable income, both consumption and saving increase.

Thus, if unemployment exists, expansionary monetary and/or fiscal policy may be used to increase aggregate demand, thereby increasing output and employment. (The relative effectiveness of the two policies is determined by the factors discussed in Chapter 9; hence, no further discussion is required.)

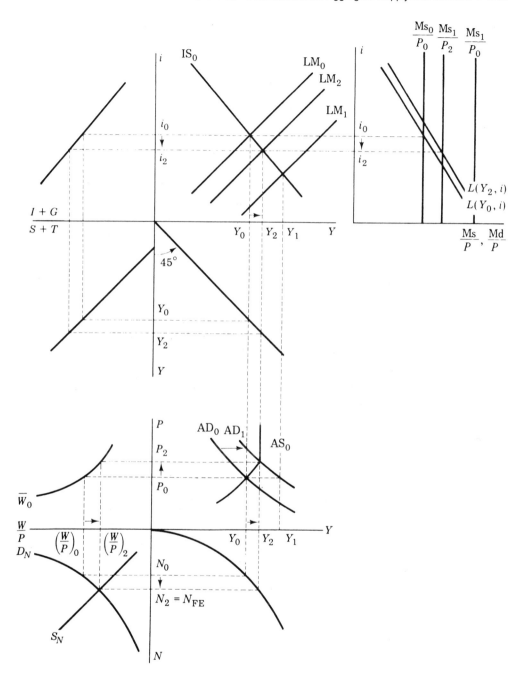

FIGURE 10.15

An increase in the nominal money supply in the aggregate supply—aggregate demand model

Estimates of the government purchases, tax, and money multipliers are presented in Chapters 18 and 19. Various issues related to the application of the policies are also discussed in those chapters.

APPLICATIONS OF THE AGGREGATE SUPPLY– AGGREGATE DEMAND MODEL

The aggregate supply–aggregate demand model may be applied to other problems. To illustrate, suppose managers, fearing a recession, decide to invest less. The impact of their decision may be analyzed with the aid of the model. Suppose the initial equilibrium combination of output and the price level is (Y_0, P_0) in Figure 10.16. If investment is reduced, the investment plus government purchases curve shifts to the right and the IS curve shifts to the left, and income is reduced from Y_0 to Y_1 in the IS–LM diagram (not shown). As a consequence, at price level P_0 in Figure 10.16, the level of income is Y_1 rather than Y_0. By conceptually varying the price level, the rest of the new aggregate demand curve, AD_1, is obtained.

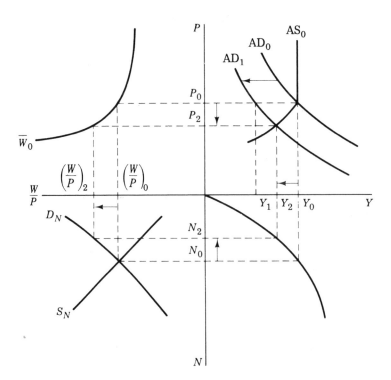

FIGURE 10.16

A decrease in investment in the aggregate supply–aggregate demand model

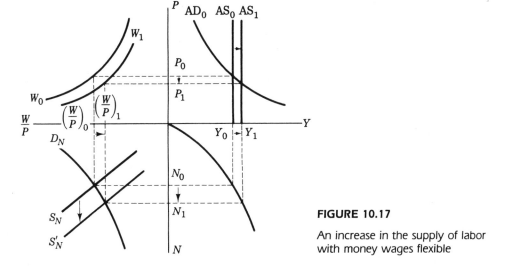

FIGURE 10.17

An increase in the supply of labor with money wages flexible

With the reduction in investment and aggregate demand, the price level, output, and employment decrease (assuming money wages rigid downward). Thus, a reduction in investment has an adverse effect upon output and employment. The effects of the decrease in investment may, however, be offset by the effects of expansionary monetary and/or fiscal policy.

Other applications of the model may be considered. One important application has to do with the supply of labor. Suppose, initially, that money wages are flexible and that the aggregate supply curve in Figure 10.17 is AS_0. With aggregate demand curve AD_0, the initial equilibrium combination of output is (Y_0, P_0). Since Y_0 represents the full employment level of output, full employment prevails. If the supply of labor increases, the supply of labor curve shifts from S_N to S'_N. Since the aggregate supply curve is derived, in part, from the supply of labor curve, the aggregate supply curve also shifts. If the new aggregate supply curve is derived in the same manner as the initial curve, the new aggregate supply curve, AS_1, is found to be perfectly inelastic at the new full employment level of output, Y_1. The new equilibrium combination of output and the price level is (Y_1, P_1), given by the intersection of the aggregate demand curve, AD_0, and the new aggregate supply curve AS_1. Thus, with aggregate demand constant, the increase in aggregate supply results in a lower price level, P_1, a lower money wage, W_1, a lower real wage, $(W/P)_1$, a greater level of employment, N_1, and a greater level of output, Y_1. With money wages (and prices) flexible, these results are not surprising. With an increase in the supply of labor, money and real wages fall. As real wages fall, firms have an incentive to hire additional workers. As employment increases, output increases. With aggregate demand constant, the increase in output reduces the price level. Of course, the greater the increase in the supply of labor, the greater the increases in output and employment.

Output Y_1 represents the new full employment level of output, and so full employment prevails after the increase in the supply of labor. Thus, with money wages and prices flexible, an increase in the supply of labor does not result in an increase in unemployment. With money wages rigid downward, however, unemployment may result. Suppose, in Figure 10.18, the initial aggregate supply and demand curves are AS_0 and AD_0, respectively, so that the equilibrium combination of output and the price level is (Y_0, P_0). If the initial supply of labor curve is S_N, Y_0 represents the full employment level of output and so full employment exists. Next, suppose the supply of labor increases and the supply of labor curve shifts to S'_N. With the shift in the supply of labor curve, the aggregate supply curve also shifts. If the aggregate supply curve is derived on the basis of labor supply curve S'_N rather than S_N, the new aggregate supply curve is AS_1. Note that the new aggregate supply curve, AS_1, coincides with the original aggregate supply curve, AS_0, over part of its range.

The new equilibrium combination of output and the price level is (Y_0, P_0), given by the intersection of the aggregate demand curve and the new aggregate supply curve. This combination is the same as the original combination, and so the price level, money wage, real wage, employment, and output are unchanged. Thus, despite the increase in the supply of labor, no increase in employment occurs.

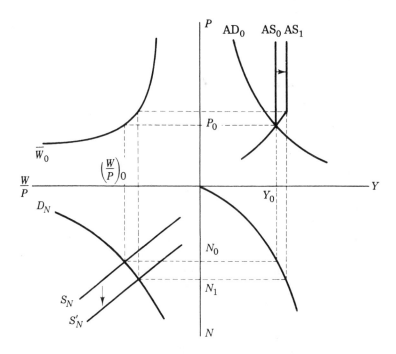

FIGURE 10.18

An increase in the supply of labor with money wages rigid downward

Since the new full employment level of employment is N_1 and employment remains N_0, unemployment has increased.

Thus, the impact of an increase in the supply of labor is quite different if money wages are rigid downward. With money wages flexible, money and real wages decrease, and so firms have an incentive to hire additional workers. Consequently, full employment prevails after the adjustment process has run its course. With money wages rigid downward, however, money wages do not decrease in response to an increase in the supply of labor. Consequently, employers have no incentive to hire additional workers and so employment and output are unchanged. As a result, the increase in the supply of labor merely increases unemployment.

The foregoing application is not purely academic. With a growing population, the supply of labor increases each year. If money wages are flexible, money wages adjust so that employment increases and unemployment remains constant. On the other hand, if money wages are rigid downward, employment remains constant and unemployment increases.[7] Consequently, action must be taken to prevent or alleviate the problem. In this case, expansionary monetary and/or fiscal policy may be used to increase aggregate demand. With an increase in aggregate demand, additional jobs are created for those entering the labor force. The government could undertake policies designed to make money wages and prices flexible. Given the political strength of labor unions and the popularity of minimum wage legislation, this approach is unlikely to be pursued. On the other hand, it is desirable to preserve what wage and price flexibility there is.

CONCLUDING REMARKS

Before concluding this chapter, several precautionary notes are in order. First, the changes we have considered—a tax reduction, an increase in the nominal supply of money, a decrease in investment, and an increase in the supply of labor—were considered separately, with other things held constant. This approach is useful in isolating the effects of the change in question. In applying the model to the economy, however, remember that other things are not constant. During a specified period, the economy is likely to be subjected to a number of forces, some of which are conflicting. Nevertheless, it is useful to consider the impact of a single change, especially when formulating policy.

Second, we have, for the most part, considered only the direction of the change of the variables in the model in response to, say, a tax reduction. But policy makers need to know more than that output and employment increase in response to a tax reduction. They need at least some notion of the magnitude of the tax reduction necessary to achieve full employment. This means that one must empirically estimate the parameters of the model. Indeed, a number of econometric models have been developed for the economy. These models have been used to analyze the impact of various policy changes.

Third, the model employed is, for our purposes, reasonably complex. Nevertheless, it is relatively simple compared to econometric models of the economy. To illustrate, we have deliberately simplified the consumption and investment functions of Chapters 5 and 6. We have done so in order to provide a general view of the economy and to keep the model manageable. This approach has some costs. Some predictions of the model may be inaccurate or even erroneous.

One alternative is to construct a more complex model. Such a model would be less intuitive and less manageable than the somewhat complex model just presented. Hence, we shall not, for the most part, add to the complexity of the model in later chapters. Instead, we shall concentrate on more policy-oriented matters.

NOTES

1. There are a number of problems in constructing and using production functions, especially aggregate functions. Capital and labor are not homogeneous. Some economists question whether the capital stock can even be measured. Moreover, individual (microeconomic) production functions can be aggregated only under special assumptions. For these and other reasons, some economists prefer not to use aggregate production functions. (For a discussion of the Cobb–Douglas production function, see Chapter 17.)

2. For a discussion at the microeconomic level, see Jack Hirshleifer, *Price Theory and Applications*, 3rd ed. (Englewood Cliffs, N.J.: Prentice-Hall, Inc., 1984), pp. 316–24.

3. For a discussion at the microeconomic level, see Hirshleifer, *Price Theory*, pp. 360–65. It has been argued that the supply of labor curve may be backward bending. If this is so, an increase in the real wage will increase the amount of labor supplied up to a point; beyond that point, however, an increase in the real wage will reduce the amount of labor supplied. Although theoretically possible, the supply of labor curve is likely to be positively sloped over the relevant range.

4. Since the amount of labor supplied varies with the real wage, full employment is an ambiguous concept. If the real wage is $(W/P)_0$, full employment may be said to exist at employment level N_0. If, however, the real wage is $(W/P)_2$, full employment may be said to exist at employment level N_2.

5. Suppose the constant increases from 10 to 20. When x equals 10, y equals 2, found by substituting x equal to 10 into the relationship $xy = 20$ and solving for y. Consequently, we have the point $(10, 2)$ on the new rectangular hyperbola. Similarly, when x equals 5, y equals 4, found by substituting x equal to 5 into the relationship $xy = 20$. Consequently, we have the point $(5, 4)$ on the new rectangular hyperbola. In general, the new set of points yields a new rectangular hyperbola, $xy = 20$, which is farther from the origin than the original rectangular hyperbola, $xy = 10$.

6. As in the earlier models, it is possible to derive multipliers which can be used to predict the change in income for a given change in the variable in question. Generally, the multipliers are smaller than the corresponding multipliers in the IS–LM model. For various multipliers based on this model and their derivation, see Harry G. Johnson, *Macroeconomics and Monetary Theory* (Chicago: Aldine Publishing Company, 1972), pp. 187–97.

7. Money wages may not be completely rigid. As a consequence, there may be some increase in employment; there is, however, no guarantee that money wages will be sufficiently flexible to restore full employment in the short run. Similarly, aggregate demand

may increase, especially if the increase in the supply of labor is due to increases in population. If so, there will be some increase in employment; again, however, there is no guarantee that the increase in aggregate demand will be sufficient to provide jobs for those entering the labor force.

REVIEW QUESTIONS

1. What is a production function? List the assumptions made with regard to the production function in the model.

2. Explain the relationship between the production function and the demand for labor function.

3. Discuss the supply of labor function. With reference to the supply of labor curve, explain why it is difficult to define a unique full employment point.

4. Explain why money wages may be rigid downward. Do the same arguments apply with regard to the upward rigidity of money wages? Why? Why not?

5. Explain how to derive an aggregate supply curve assuming that money wages are

   a. flexible.

   b. rigid.

   c. rigid downward and flexible upward.

6. With the aid of the aggregate supply model, show how to calculate the amounts of national income going to labor and (the owners of) the capital stock. Will an increase in the real wage guarantee that labor will receive a greater amount of national income? Why? Why not?

7. With the aid of the IS–LM diagram, show and explain how to derive the aggregate demand curve. Explain in terms of economics why the aggregate demand curve slopes downward and to the right.

8. Suppose consumption is positively related to both income and the real money supply. How is the aggregate demand curve altered?

9. Suppose we have the following data for the production function:

Employment (N) (in millions)	Output (Y) ($ billion)
50	400
60	500
70	580
80	640
90	680

In addition, suppose we have the following data for the supply of labor function:

Real wage (W/P), $	Number of workers seeking employment (N) (in millions)
10,000	100
8,000	90
6,000	80
4,000	70

a. Based on these data, determine the equilibrium level of output corresponding to each of the following price levels. (Assume that money wages are flexible.)

Price level (P)	Output (Y) ($ billion)
150	_____
100	_____
75	_____
60	_____

b. Based on the data, determine the equilibrium level of output corresponding to each of the following price levels. Assume that money wages are rigid downward at $6,000 per year but are flexible upward.

Price level (P)	Output (Y) ($ billion)
150	_____
100	_____
75	_____
60	_____

c. Suppose the aggregate demand schedule is as follows:

Price level (P)	Output (Y) ($ billion)
150	460
100	520
75	580
60	640

Find the equilibrium value of each of the following variables assuming that

(1) money wages are flexible and (2) money wages are rigid downward at $6,000 but flexible upward.

	(1)	(2)
(1) the price level		
(2) the money wage		
(3) the real wage		
(4) employment		
(5) output		

d. Suppose the aggregate demand schedule is as follows:

Price level (P)	Output (Y) ($ billion)
150	580
100	640
75	700
60	760

Find the equilibrium value of each of the following variables assuming that (1) money wages are flexible and (2) money wages are rigid downward at $6,000 but are flexible upward.

	(1)	(2)
(1) the price level		
(2) the money wage		
(3) the real wage		
(4) employment		
(5) output		

e. Based upon the analysis in parts c and d, what two general approaches are available to attain full employment?

10. The classical economists generally assumed that money wages and prices are flexible. What implications does this have for the levels of output and employment? How were the implications contradicted by the events of the Great Depression of the 1930s?

11. Suppose unemployment exists. Within the context of the model, explain how the unemployment may be alleviated. Explain how each policy works to alleviate the problem.

12. For each of the following changes, indicate whether the equilibrium value of each of the variables listed increases, decreases, or remains constant. Assume that money wages are rigid downward and flexible upward, that less than full employment exists, at least initially, and that the aggregate supply curve does not shift.

a. An *increase* in government purchases.

b. A decision by households to save *more*.

c. An *increase* in the supply of money.

d. A *decrease* in the demand for money.

The variables are the price level, the money wage, the real wage, employment, unemployment, output, the interest rate, investment, consumption, saving, the real amount of money supplied, and the real amount of money demanded.

13. For each of the following changes, indicate whether the equilibrium value of each of the variables listed in the previous question increases, decreases, or remains constant. (Assume that the aggregate demand curve does not shift.)

a. An *increase* in the capital stock (assume money wages flexible).

b. A *decrease* in the supply of labor (assume that money wages are rigid downward and flexible upward and that full employment exists, at least initially).

c. An *improvement* in technology (assume that money wages are rigid downward and flexible upward, that less than full employment exists, at least initially, and that the demand for labor is unchanged).

d. A significant *increase* in the legal minimum wage (assume money wages are rigid downward and flexible upward and that less than full employment exists, at least initially).

14. In the model, with less than full employment, the real wage must be reduced in order to increase employment. But empirical studies have found that the real wage increases when the economy recovers from a recession (i.e., employment increases). Reconcile the two.

SUGGESTED READING

KEYNES, JOHN MAYNARD, *The General Theory of Employment, Interest, and Money*. New York: Harcourt, Brace and Company, 1936.

MODIGLIANI, FRANCO, "Liquidity Preference and the Theory of Interest and Money," *Econometrica*, 12 (January 1944), 45–88.

MUNDELL, ROBERT A., "An Exposition of Some Subtleties in the Keynesian System," *Weltwirtschaftliches Archiv*, 93 (December 1964), 301–12; and Walter L. Johnson and David R. Kamerschen (eds.) *Macroeconomics: Selected Readings*, pp. 32–38. Boston: Houghton Mifflin Company, 1970.

SMITH, WARREN L., "A Graphical Exposition of the Complete Keynesian System," *Southern Economic Journal*, 23 (October 1956), 115–25.

11

THE CLASSICAL
AND MONETARIST
VIEWS

So far, the models that we have considered have been Keynesian in nature. We now wish to examine some alternative approaches. In this chapter, we consider the views of the classical economists, and their intellectual heirs, the monetarists. In Chapter 12, we examine the rational expectations and supply-side approaches. We find that these views differ both from the Keynesian view and from each other in terms of both theory and policy. We start with the classical approach.

THE CLASSICAL APPROACH

In general, the classical period of economic thought is considered to be the time span from 1750 to 1870. The most prominent (mainstream) economists who lived during this period were Adam Smith, Thomas Robert Malthus, David Ricardo, and John Stuart Mill. In criticizing the views of the classical economists, John Maynard Keynes used the term *classical* more broadly. He included not only those who lived and wrote during the 1750–1870 period, but also virtually all the economists who wrote during the 1870–1936 time span. Thus, by Keynes's definition, Alfred Marshall, A. C. Pigou, Knut Wicksell, and Irving Fisher are classical economists. For our purpose, we shall follow Keynes's definition.

We shall now outline "the" classical theory. It must be recognized at the outset that the model may not accurately reflect the views of all or even the overwhelming majority of the classical economists. Nevertheless, the model is sufficiently general so as to encompass the classical "vision."

Aggregate Demand

The classical theory of aggregate demand is based on the *quantity theory of money*. This theory can be explained in terms of the following equation, usually called the *equation of exchange*:

(11.1a)
$$\mathrm{Ms}V = PY,$$

where Ms represents the nominal money supply, V the income velocity of money, P the price level, and Y real output.[1] The *income velocity of money* represents the average number of times money circulates through the economy during a year. Suppose the nominal money supply is $100 billion, the price level is 100 (percent), and output is $500 billion. The income velocity of money then is 5, obtained by substituting for Ms, P, and Y in equation (11.1a) and solving for V. With the money supply, $100 billion, circulating through the economy 5 times during the year, households and firms were able to buy $500 billion worth of goods and services.

As the equation stands, it is a tautology—something that is true by definition. In the example, the velocity of money must have been 5 in order for a money supply of $100 billion to purchase $500 billion worth of goods and services. To derive the quantity theory of money, we assume that the velocity of money is constant.[2]

The classical economists believed that the velocity of money depends on such factors as the number of times people are paid per year, the extent to which receipts and expenditures coincide, and the regularity of receipts and expenditures. The more often people are paid, the more rapidly money will circulate through the economy. Similarly, the greater the coincidence between receipts and expenditures, the more rapidly money will circulate. In contrast, the greater the irregularity of receipts and expenditures, the less rapidly money will circulate. With irregularity, households and firms must hold larger amounts of money in anticipation of future expenditures. If more money is held, it will circulate less rapidly through the economy.

These and the other determinants of the velocity of money were viewed by the classical economists as changing only slowly over time. Consequently, they believed that the velocity of money could be regarded as a constant in the short run. They recognized, of course, that velocity would change in the long run as financial innovations occurred and as communications improved. They also recognized that it would change during the transition, or adjustment, period following a disturbance in the economy.[3] After the adjustment period, however, they believed that it would return to its former value.

With the velocity of money constant, a change in the money supply, Ms, now alters nominal income, PY. Before analyzing the impact of a change in the money supply, however, we note that an aggregate demand curve is implied by equation (11.1a). Since V is assumed constant and since the classical economists assumed, implicitly or explicitly, that the nominal money supply is an exogenous variable, MsV is a constant. Therefore, the aggregate demand curve, a relationship between the price level P and output Y, is a rectangular hyperbola. If the nominal money supply is Ms_0 and the velocity of money, V, is constant, the aggregate demand curve in Figure 11.1 is the rectangular hyperbola $PY = Ms_0V$.

According to this formulation, a reduction in the price level causes a movement along the aggregate demand curve. We can explain this movement more easily if we rewrite equation (11.1a) and introduce some new notation. First, divide both sides of equation (11.1a) by P and V to obtain

$$\frac{Ms}{P} = \frac{1}{V}(Y).$$

Next, substitute k for $1/V$. Hence,

(11.1b) $$\frac{Ms}{P} = kY,$$

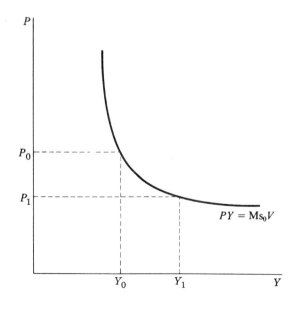

$PY = Ms_0V$

FIGURE 11.1

The classical aggregate demand curve

where k is the proportion of real income that people wish to hold in the form of real money balances. Written in this manner, the equation emphasizes the holding of money rather than its circulation through the economy. This approach, with its emphasis on the demand for money, is called the *Cambridge* (or *cash-balance*) *approach* because many of its originators, including Alfred Marshall and A. C. Pigou, were affiliated with Cambridge University.

In their discussions of the demand for money, the Cambridge economists took many factors into account, including wealth and interest rates. In formalizing the relationship, however, they emphasized that the demand for real money balances is a constant proportion, k, of real income, Y. When the money market is in equilibrium, the real amount of money supplied, Ms/P, equals the real amount of money demanded, kY, and equation (11.1b) is the result. Consequently, equation (11.1b) should be regarded as the equilibrium condition for the money market since the left side of the equation represents the real money supply and the right side represents the real demand for money.

To consider the impact of a change in the price level on aggregate demand, suppose the price level decreases. With the decrease, the real money supply increases. The money market is no longer in equilibrium; households and firms now have excess real balances. How does this affect spending? In the classical view, the excess real balances cause spending to increase. The classical economists used two different mechanisms to explain the increase in spending. The first is the *direct mechanism* whereby households spend their excess real balances directly because of the real balance effect. The classical economists believed that the demand for goods and services depends, in part, on real money balances so that an increase (a decrease) in real balances causes an increase (a decrease) in the demand for goods and services. The effect of a change in real balances upon the consumption of goods and services is called the *real balance effect*.

The second mechanism is the *indirect mechanism*, which works through the interest rate. According to the classical view, excess real balances cause the market interest rate to fall. As a result, the interest rate at which firms can borrow is less than the natural interest rate which equals the (unchanged) marginal product of capital. Consequently, firms will increase their spending on plant and equipment. Moreover, the increase in investment will continue until the market interest rate again equals the natural rate. (The determination of the natural interest rate is discussed later.)

Both mechanisms generate movements along the aggregate demand curve. Moreover, the movements continue until the excess real balances are eliminated. In terms of Figure 11.1, the increase in the aggregate amount demanded, with the reduction in the price level from P_0 to P_1, is from Y_0 to Y_1. With k constant, the increase in Y is proportional to the increase in real balances resulting from the decrease in the price level.

As just demonstrated, a change in the price level, with the nominal money supply constant, results in a movement along a given aggregate demand curve. If the nominal money supply changes, the aggregate demand curve will shift. With an increase in the nominal money supply, households and firms have excess real balances and the aggregate demand for goods and services will increase. Consumption will increase because of the real balance effect. Investment will increase because of the decrease in the market interest rate. The increase in aggregate demand is shown in Figure 11.2 as a shift in the aggregate demand curve from AD_0 to AD_1. If the price level is assumed constant at, say, the P_0 level, aggregate demand will increase from Y_0 to Y_2. At the new, higher level of aggregate demand, the real money supply will again be equal to the real demand for money.

Aggregate Supply

As just discussed, equation (11.1a) may be used to develop the classical theory of aggregate demand. With regard to aggregate supply, the classical economists believed, like Keynes, that output is a function of employment and that the demand for, and supply of, labor are functions of the real wage. Consequently, the production function and labor demand and supply functions are

(11.2)
$$Y = f(N),$$

(11.3)
$$D_N = g\left(\frac{W}{P}\right),$$

and

(11.4)
$$S_N = h\left(\frac{W}{P}\right),$$

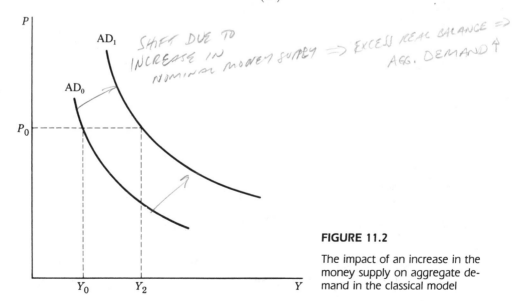

FIGURE 11.2

The impact of an increase in the money supply on aggregate demand in the classical model

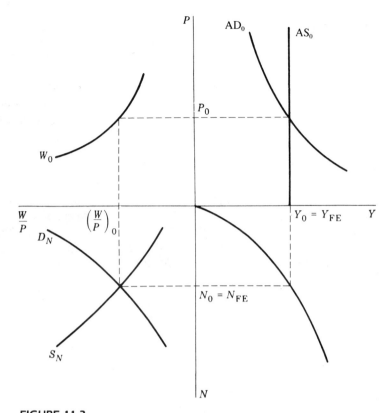

FIGURE 11.3

Aggregate supply and demand in the classical model

respectively. These functions were discussed in Chapter 10; they are plotted in Figure 11.3.

For the labor market to be in equilibrium, the amount of labor demanded must equal the amount of labor supplied. Consequently, the equilibrium condition for the labor market is

(11.5)
$$D_N = S_N.$$

As discussed in Chapter 10, full employment exists when the amount of labor demanded equals the amount of labor supplied. In Figure 11.3, the full employment levels of employment and output are N_0 and Y_0, respectively.

As shown in Chapter 10, an aggregate supply curve may be derived on the basis of equations (11.2) to (11.5); it is AS_0 in Figure 11.3. Since the classical economists assumed that money wages are flexible, the aggregate supply curve is perfectly inelastic at the full employment level of output, Y_0. If aggregate demand is AD_0 and aggregate supply is AS_0 in Figure 11.3, the equilibrium price, money wage, real wage, employment, and output levels are P_0, W_0, $(W/P)_0$, N_0, and Y_0, respectively. Since the money wage and price level are assumed to be flexible, output and employment are at their full employment levels.

Saving, Investment, and the Interest Rate

Like Keynes, the classical economists assumed that investment, I, is inversely related to the interest rate, i. The investment function,

(11.6) $$I = I(i),$$

is plotted in Figure 11.4.

Unlike Keynes, however, the classical economists assumed that saving, S, depends on the interest rate, i:

(11.7) $$S = S(i).$$

In particular, they assumed that saving is directly related to the interest rate, implying that consumption is inversely related to the interest rate. The saving function is also plotted in Figure 11.4.

For the interest rate to be at its equilibrium level, investment must equal saving. Thus, the equilibrium condition is

(11.8) $$I = S.$$

In this regard, investment may be thought of as the demand for loanable funds

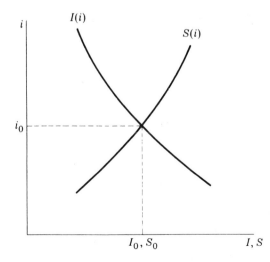

FIGURE 11.4

Investment, saving, and the interest rate in the classical model

and saving as the supply of loanable funds. In Figure 11.4, the equilibrium interest rate is i_0 since the demand for loanable funds is equal to the supply only at that interest rate. If the interest rate were less than i_0, the demand for loanable funds would exceed the supply and the interest rate would rise in response to the excess demand. Conversely, if the interest rate were greater than i_0, the supply of loanable funds would exceed the demand and the interest rate would fall.

In the classical model, the interest rate serves to equate investment and saving. At the same time, it determines the division of output into consumption and investment. Once the equilibrium level of investment, I_0 (or saving S_0), is determined, the equilibrium level of consumption can be determined by subtracting I_0 (or S_0) from the equilibrium level of income, Y_0.

If households were to save more (or less), the interest rate and the division of output into consumption and investment would be altered; however, output and the price level would remain the same. If households were to save more, the saving function in Figure 11.4 would shift to the right and, as a result, the interest rate would decrease and investment and saving would increase. Since the aggregate demand and supply curves of Figure 11.3 are not altered, output and the price level, after the adjustment period, are the same as they were originally. With output constant, the implication is that the increase in investment due to the decrease in the interest rate has been sufficient to offset the reduction in consumption. Thus, after the adjustment period, output is the same but the division of output into consumption and investment is altered. If firms were to invest more (or less), a similar result would follow.

In the classical model, the interest rate is determined by investment and saving. Consequently, the classical theory of interest rates is regarded as a *real* theory of interest rates. It is called a real theory because investment and saving are regarded as real factors. Investment reflects the productivity of capital. If technological progress, for example, were to make capital more productive, the investment function of Figure 11.4 would shift to the right and the interest rate would rise. Saving, on the other hand, reflects the thriftiness of society. If households, for example, decide to save more, the saving function of Figure 11.4 would shift to the right and the interest rate would fall.

Interest rate i_0 in Figure 11.4 is called the *natural interest rate*; it equals the marginal product of capital. As illustrated, it will be altered if the (real) factors which determine it change. On the other hand, if the money supply changes, the natural interest rate will be unaffected; the market interest rate will be altered, but only temporarily. Suppose the economy is in equilibrium initially and the money supply increases. With the influx of loanable funds, commercial banks and other lenders will have an excess of loanable funds and the market interest rate will fall. As a result, firms will borrow more and investment will increase. Since full employment already exists, the excess aggregate demand will result in a higher price level, not increased output and employment. As the price level rises, the real money supply decreases and, as a result, the market interest rate rises until it once again equals the natural rate.

The Self-Equilibrating Nature of the Classical Model

The classical economists believed that money wages and prices are flexible so that full employment is the normal state of affairs. They also believed that, as disturbances to the economy occur, money wages and prices change automatically so as to restore full employment relatively quickly. We can easily demonstrate this self-equilibrating property of the classical model.

Suppose, in Figure 11.5, aggregate demand is AD_0 and aggregate supply is AS_0 so that the equilibrium price level is P_0, the money wage W_0, the real wage $(W/P)_0$, employment N_0, and output Y_0. Employment and output are at their full employment levels. Next, suppose the nominal money supply decreases so that aggregate demand falls to AD_1. With the reduction in aggregate demand, the price level falls. As the price level falls, the real wage rises, creating an excess supply of labor. As a result, the money wage, assumed flexible by the classical economists, falls. In fact, the money wage continues to fall until the equilibrium real wage, $(W/P)_0$, is restored. Consequently, with the reduction in aggregate demand, we find that the price level and money wage fall to P_1 and W_1, respectively. Once the adjustment process has run its course, however, the real wage, employment, and output are at their original (full employment) levels. Even with a reduction in aggregate demand, no (permanent) increase in unemployment occurs.

Thus, with money wages and prices flexible, they tend to adjust to restore full employment following a disturbance to the economy. Moreover, the adjustment is automatic; no action is necessary on the part of either the central bank or government.

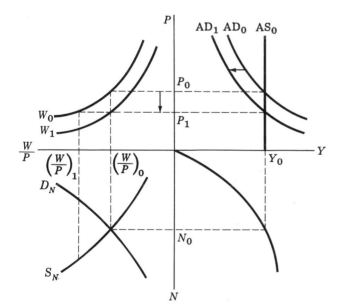

FIGURE 11.5

The impact of a reduction in aggregate demand in the classical model

Monetary and Fiscal Policy

Since the classical economists assumed wage and price flexibility, they believed full employment to be the normal state of affairs. Consequently, the scope for discretionary monetary and fiscal policy was limited. Moreover, they believed that even if unemployment existed, fiscal policy, unless accompanied by a change in the money supply, would be unable to alleviate it.

The classical economists recognized that money wages might be rigid downward and that unemployment might exist as a result. If the money wage is rigid downward at the W_0 level, the aggregate supply curve (as derived in Chapter 10) is AS_0 in Figure 11.6. If aggregate demand is AD_0, the price level will be P_0, the money wage W_0, the real wage $(W/P)_0$, employment N_0, and output Y_0. Since the

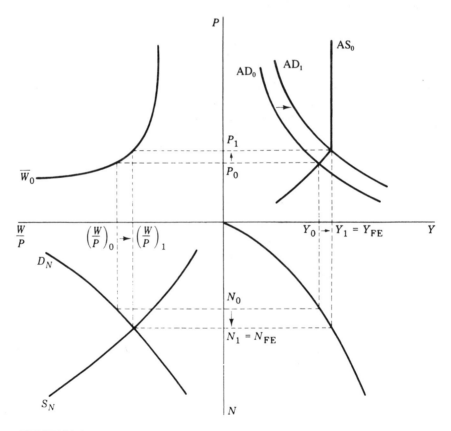

FIGURE 11.6

The impact of an increase in the money supply on output and employment in the classical model, assuming money wages rigid downward

actual level of employment, N_0, is less than the full employment level, N_1, unemployment exists.

If the money wage and price level were to fall, employment and output would increase and full employment would eventually be restored. If they cannot fall, or fall only slowly, it may be desirable for the monetary authorities to increase the money supply. If they were to do so, aggregate demand would increase to AD_1 and output and employment would increase to Y_1 and N_1, respectively, and full employment would be achieved.

If money wages and prices are rigid, the central bank has a role to play with regard to stabilization policy. If full employment is to be maintained, the central bank must supply enough money so that aggregate demand equals aggregate supply at the full employment level of output. In contrast, the classical economists believed that government is powerless to alter output and employment through the use of fiscal policy.

Suppose unemployment exists and government increases its purchases of goods and services. The classical economists emphasized that the increase in government purchases must be financed by increasing taxes, by borrowing (issuing bonds), or by increasing the money supply. Suppose the deficit is financed by a tax increase. The classical economists believed that the increase in public spending (government purchases) is completely offset by the decrease in private spending (consumption and investment) due to the tax increase. As a result, aggregate demand and, therefore, output and employment are unchanged.

Alternatively, suppose the increase in government purchases is financed by borrowing. Since the government must compete with private borrowers for funds, interest rates rise, thereby reducing investment and consumption.[4] Once again, the classical economists believed that the increase in public spending (government purchases) is completely offset by the decrease in private spending (investment and consumption). Consequently, aggregate demand, output, and employment are unaltered.

Finally, suppose the increase in government purchases is financed by increasing the money supply. The increase in the money supply does not cause an offsetting decrease in private spending. In fact the increase, as we have seen, is expansionary. Consequently, if the increase in government purchases is financed by an increase in the money supply, output and employment increase (assuming less than full employment initially). The same effect could have been achieved, however, by merely increasing the money supply; there is no reason, from the aggregate standpoint, to increase government purchases since it is a clumsy way to increase the money supply.

Thus, in the classical world, fiscal policy, unless accompanied by a change in the money supply, cannot be used to increase the nation's output and employment.[5] As a result, government, assuming an independent central bank, has no role to play in stabilizing the economy. In the classical world, the government's role is confined mainly to the enforcement of contracts, police protection, national defense, and matters of that nature.

The Keynesian Critique

Equations (11.1a) and (11.2) to (11.8), or equations (11.1b) to (11.8), form the classical model. Keynes's model, described in Chapter 10, is similar to the classical model in many ways. In fact, there are only three significant differences in assumptions. First, the classical economists assumed that consumption varies with the interest rate; Keynes assumed that it is a function of income. Second, the classical economists believed that the real demand for money depends on real income only. Keynes argued that it depends on both real income and the interest rate. Third, the classical economists assumed that money wages and prices are flexible. In contrast, Keynes asserted that money wages are rigid downward.

Although only a few differences exist between the classical and Keynesian models, the implications of the models differ significantly. Because the classical economists believed that money wages and prices are flexible, they believed full employment to be the normal state of affairs. Unemployment might exist temporarily, but as money wages and prices adjust in response to market conditions, full employment will soon be restored. Keynes assumed that money wages are rigid downward. As a result, unemployment can exist for prolonged periods or even indefinitely. To illustrate, with money wages rigid downward, the aggregate supply curve in Figure 11.6 is AS_0. If aggregate demand is AD_1, full employment prevails. If aggregate demand is AD_0, however, unemployment exists. Moreover, so long as money wages are rigid downward and aggregate demand is AD_0, unemployment will prevail.

In the situation just described, no adjustments will take place if money wages are rigid downward. If money wages are flexible but adjust only sluggishly, full employment may eventually be restored. Suppose, in Figure 11.7, aggregate demand and supply are AD_0 and AS_0, respectively. Unemployment exists since employment, N_0, is less than the full employment level, N_2. If the money wage falls to W_1 in response to the excess supply of labor, the aggregate supply curve shifts to AS_1. With the shift, the price level decreases to P_1 and employment and output increase to N_1 and Y_1, respectively. In the classical model, the increases occur because, with the reduction in money wages and prices, the real money supply increases, thereby increasing consumption and investment through the direct and indirect mechanisms described earlier. In the Keynesian model, the increase in employment occurs because the reduction in the price level results in an increase in the real money supply. Consequently, the interest rate decreases and investment increases (see Chapter 10 for a discussion of the Keynes's effect).

Thus, if money wages and prices eventually respond to market forces, a tendency exists for the economy to gravitate to full employment. But if one of the *special cases* exists, the reductions in money wages and prices will be ineffective in restoring full employment. By special cases, we mean a perfectly interest elastic demand for money function or a perfectly interest inelastic investment function. If either of those cases prevails, the adjustment mechanism envisaged by Keynes fails to achieve the desired result. If the demand for money is perfectly interest

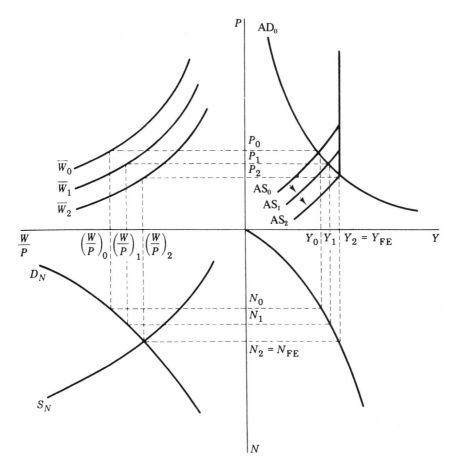

FIGURE 11.7

The impact of reductions in money wages and prices on output and employment in the classical and Keynesian models

elastic in the relevant range, the reduction in the price level and subsequent increase in the real money supply does not result in a reduction in the interest rate since the economy is in the liquidity trap. With the interest rate constant, investment and, hence, aggregate demand are unchanged. Consequently, output and employment remain constant.

This case is depicted in Figure 11.8. If the demand for money function is perfectly interest elastic over part of its range, the aggregate demand curve has a perfectly inelastic portion, which corresponds to the perfectly interest elastic portion of the demand for money function. As a result, the aggregate demand curve is, say, AD_0. If aggregate supply is AS_0, the price level is P_0, employment is N_0, and output is Y_0. Since N_0 is less than the full employment level, N_{FE}, unemployment

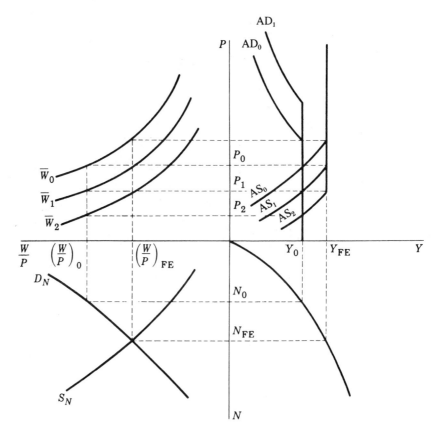

FIGURE 11.8

The impact of reductions in money wages and prices on output and employment
in the Keynesian model: the special cases

exists. If the money wage falls from W_0 to W_1, the aggregate supply curve shifts
from AS_0 to AS_1. Since the new aggregate supply curve cuts the aggregate demand
curve at the same level of output, no increases in output and employment occur.
Consequently, unemployment is not reduced. Moreover, even if money wages and
prices were to continue to decrease, unemployment would remain as the aggregate
supply curve slides down the perfectly inelastic portion of the aggregate demand
curve. Thus, in the Keynesian model, reductions in money wages and prices do
not result in higher levels of output and employment if the demand for money is
perfectly interest elastic.

The same result holds if the investment function is perfectly interest inelastic
over part of its range. Suppose unemployment exists and money wages fall in
response to the excess supply of labor. The accompanying reduction in the price
level increases the real money supply and, if the demand for money is less than
perfectly interest elastic, the interest rate decreases. If investment is perfectly

interest inelastic, however, no increase in investment occurs. Consequently, there is no change in aggregate demand and, hence, no changes in output and employment. Thus, unemployment continues.

This case is also shown in Figure 11.8. If the investment function is perfectly interest inelastic over part of its range, the aggregate demand curve has a perfectly inelastic portion, which corresponds to the perfectly inelastic portion of the investment function. This aggregate demand curve is, say, AD_0 in Figure 11.8. If aggregate supply is AS_0, the price level is P_0, employment N_0, and output Y_0; as before, unemployment exists. If money wages and prices decrease, the result is the same; the aggregate supply curve slides down the perfectly inelastic portion of the aggregate demand curve. Since employment remains at the N_0 level, unemployment continues. Thus, in the Keynesian model, reductions in money wages and prices do not result in higher levels of output and employment if investment is perfectly interest inelastic.

By arguing that money wages are rigid downward or change only slowly in response to labor market conditions, Keynesians were able to show that the tendency for the economy to gravitate to full employment was not as strong as the classical economists believed. Moreover, even if money wages and prices fall, the Keynesian model suggests that the forces driving the economy toward full employment are nonexistent (weak) if the demand for money is perfectly (highly) interest elastic and/or investment is perfectly (highly) interest inelastic.

Under these circumstances, expansionary monetary policy is a possibility. An increase in the nominal and real money supplies, through the impact on the interest rate and investment, would result in an increase in aggregate demand, thereby increasing output and employment. Unlike the classical economists, however, early Keynesians were not optimistic about the potency of monetary policy because they believed that the demand for money is relatively interest elastic and investment relatively interest inelastic. As discussed in Chapter 9, these elasticities imply a relatively ineffective monetary policy. In fact, in the special cases, monetary policy is ineffective. If the demand for money is perfectly interest elastic (the liquidity trap), the interest rate will not fall in response to the increase in the money supply. If the investment function is perfectly interest inelastic, investment won't increase even if the interest rate decreases. Either way, no increase in investment occurs; consequently, aggregate demand will be constant over the relevant range. (In terms of Figure 11.8, the aggregate demand curve shifts from AD_0 to AD_1, implying that output, Y_0, and employment, N_0, are unchanged.)

Based on the foregoing analysis, early Keynesians were pessimistic about restoring full employment through the use of monetary policy. In contrast to the classical economists, they believed that it could be done through the use of fiscal policy. Specifically, they believed that full employment could be restored by increasing government purchases and/or reducing taxes. These changes, they believed, would cause aggregate demand to increase, thereby causing output and employment to increase. (In terms of Figure 11.8, the entire aggregate demand curve will shift to the right in response to an increase in government purchases or a reduction in taxes, causing output and employment to increase.) This argument was presented in Chapters 9 and 10 and will not be repeated here other than to note that if the demand for money is perfectly interest elastic, or investment is perfectly interest inelastic, fiscal policy is at its peak in terms of effectiveness.

The Classical Rebuttal

The classical economists believed that the forces driving the economy toward full employment are strong and could be augmented, if necessary, by actions of the central bank to increase the nominal money supply. In the absence of a change in the money supply, however, neither an increase in government purchases nor a decrease in taxes would prove effective in restoring full employment. Thus, the classical analysis suggests that government has no role to play with regard to stabilization policy.

Keynes and the early Keynesians cast doubts as to the strength of the forces driving the economy toward full employment and the effectiveness of monetary policy. Moreover, their analysis strongly suggested that fiscal policy was very powerful. Under these circumstances, government has a very important role to play with regard to stabilization policy.

The Keynesian view is in sharp contrast to that of the classical economists. It is not surprising, therefore, that the Keynesian model came under heavy criticism in the late 1930s and 1940s.

A. C. Pigou lead the theoretical attack.[6] He argued that if consumption is a function of both income and real balances, the implications of Keynes's theory are altered drastically. If consumption is positively related to real balances, a reduction in the price level increases real balances, thereby stimulating consumption. Consequently, even if the economy is characterized by a perfectly interest elastic demand for money function or a perfectly interest inelastic investment function, the economy will show a tendency to gravitate to full employment because even if investment does not increase, consumption does. Moreover, expansionary monetary policy will now be effective even in the special cases because of its impact on consumption. Thus, if consumption depends on real balances, a tendency exists for the economy to gravitate to full employment. Similarly, it makes monetary policy effective in the special cases and more effective in general. Hence, we need not rely on government and fiscal policy.[7]

Despite the validity of Pigou's analysis, the Keynesian view became dominant. Indeed, it was not effectively challenged until the 1960s when Milton Friedman and other monetarists took up the attack. We now turn to the monetarist approach.

THE MONETARIST APPROACH

As we shall see, the views of the monetarists are quite similar to those of the classical economists. This section presents the distinctive elements of monetarist thought. They are: (1) the dominance of monetary impulses based on the quantity theory of money; (2) their version of the transmission mechanism; (3) belief in the inherent stability of the private sector; and (4) the irrelevance of allocative detail.[8] We start with the dominance of monetary impulses.

The Dominance of Monetary Impulses

Monetarists argue that changes in the money supply are the principal determinant of changes in nominal income. This view is based on the quantity theory of money. Recall that the relationship between the nominal money supply and nominal income can be expressed as $MsV = PY$ or, alternatively, as $Ms = kPY$. If V is constant, a change in the nominal money supply, Ms, will result in a proportional change in nominal income, PY. Keynes did not deny the validity of the relationship $MsV = PY$. Instead, he emphasized the variability of the velocity of money. In fact, he claimed that an increase in the money supply might result in such a large decrease in velocity that nominal income would be unaltered. Thus, if the monetarist proposition regarding the dominance of monetary impulses is correct, a stable relationship must exist between the nominal money supply and nominal income.

Monetarists do not claim that the velocity of money is constant. They do claim, however, that it is not highly variable. Perhaps the best illustration is offered by Milton Friedman.[9] He argues that the demand for money is a stable function of a relatively few variables. According to Friedman, money is an asset and the demand for it can be analyzed in the same manner as the demand for any other asset. In this regard, money is one way of holding wealth. Wealth can be held in other forms: bonds, equities, physical nonhuman goods, and human capital. The demand for money thus depends on the tastes and preferences of the wealth-owning units; the total amount of wealth to be held in the various forms; and the prices of, and returns to, the various forms of wealth. Specifically, the real amount of money demanded depends on wealth (defined so as to include human wealth); the ratio of nonhuman to human wealth; the expected rates of return on money, bonds, and equities; the expected inflation rate (which represents the expected rate of return on real assets); and any variables that can be expected to affect tastes and preferences.[10] If wealth increases, more money is demanded. If the expected rate of return on either bonds or equities rises, less money is demanded since bonds or equities are now relatively more attractive to hold than money. Similarly, if the inflation rate rises, it becomes relatively more expensive to hold money, because it depreciates in value with inflation. Consequently, if the expected inflation rate rises, the real amount of money demanded will be reduced.

According to Friedman, the quantity theory of money is primarily a theory of the demand for money. Even so, Friedman's demand for money function can be used to establish a stable relationship between the nominal money supply (which is presumably determined independently of the demand for money) and nominal income. If the demand for money is a stable function of a limited number of variables and if the values of these variables are known, we can calculate the amount of money demanded and, hence, the velocity of money.

Under these circumstances, a stable and predictable relationship exists between the nominal money supply and nominal income. This relationship will not be very helpful, however, if the variables which determine the amount of money demanded change appreciably, or if the amount of money demanded varies appreciably in response to small changes in those variables. To overcome this problem, monetarists assume that either the variables which determine the amount of money demanded are constant or approximately so (at least in the short run), or that the demand for money is relatively inelastic with respect to the variables that determine it. If either condition is satisfied, a stable and (approximately) constant relationship exists between the nominal money supply and nominal income so that changes in the money supply will be reflected in changes in nominal income. In this regard, monetarists argue that the empirical evidence supports the view that changes in velocity are small compared to changes in the money supply and that, rather than offsetting changes in the money supply, changes in velocity are positively correlated with them.

Monetarists do not deny that factors other than the money supply affect nominal income. They assert, however, that changes in those factors result in only small changes in income. They believe, for example, that a shift in the investment function will have a minor impact on nominal income. To illustrate, suppose firms decide to invest more. With the increase in investment, the interest rate rises and, as a result, the velocity of money increases. Even though the money supply is constant, nominal income increases because of the increase in velocity. As a consequence, it appears that a change in investment causes a change in nominal income and that the change is potentially quite large. If investment is relatively interest elastic, so that the increase in the interest rate is small, or if the demand for money is relatively interest inelastic, the change in the amount of money demanded, hence velocity of money, will be small. As a result, the change in nominal income will be small.

The same sort of analysis can be applied to the consumption, government purchases, and tax functions, implying that shifts in those functions have only a minor impact on nominal income. In contrast, a shift in the demand for money function (by altering the velocity of money) would have a major impact. Monetarists, however, believe that the demand for money function is a stable function. Thus, while monetarists do not deny that other factors affect nominal income, they claim that the money supply is the dominant influence.

One implication of the monetarist analysis is that a change in the nominal money supply will have significant impact on nominal income, implying that monetary policy is very powerful. Another implication is that fiscal policy, unless accompanied by a change in the money supply, will have a negligible impact on nominal income. Friedman, for example, believes that the main impact of an increase in government purchases is an increase in the size of the public sector.

According to Friedman, most Keynesians define investment and saving too narrowly. If investment and saving are defined more broadly, the IS curve is more interest elastic than is commonly drawn. A relatively interest elastic IS curve, IS_0, is depicted in Figure 11.9.

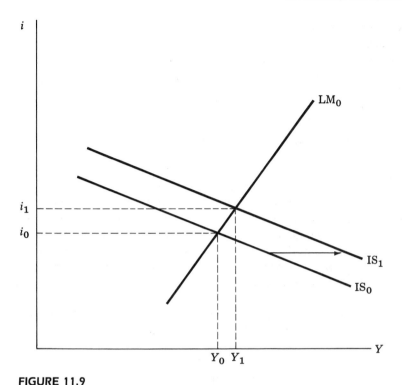

FIGURE 11.9

The impact of an increase in government purchases

If government purchases increase or taxes are reduced, the IS curve in Figure 11.9 shifts to the right to, say, IS_1, resulting in an increase in both income and the interest rate. The increase in income is relatively small, however, because, given the relatively interest elastic IS curve, the increase in the interest rate from i_0 to i_1 results in a relatively large decrease in investment.[11]

Friedman concedes that fiscal policy has some impact on income, but believes it to be small. In terms of the monetarist framework, the increase in the interest rate causes the velocity of money to rise. Because the IS curve is relatively interest elastic, however, the increase in the interest rate will be small, resulting in only small increases in the velocity of money and nominal income.

The Transmission Mechanism

In many versions of the Keynesian model, the money supply is assumed to affect income through the interest rate and investment. Monetarists claim that adjustment takes place over a broad range of assets and that the Keynesian framework is too narrow to capture the essence of the adjustment process. As a consequence, they offer an alternative view of the adjustment or transmission mechanism. The following description of the transmission mechanism is based on an outline suggested by Milton Friedman and Anna J. Schwartz.[12]

Suppose the Federal Reserve increases the money supply through open market purchases of Treasury securities. As the purchases take place, the price of these securities increases, thereby reducing the yield. Similarly, as the transactions occur, the composition of the public's portfolio (asset holdings) is altered. The public now holds more money and fewer Treasury securities. With the increase in the supply of money, its implicit yield is reduced so that wealth holders try to rearrange their portfolios to reduce their money holdings. Initially, they attempt to purchase marketable securities. As the purchases occur, the prices of these securities increase and their yields decrease. As a result, the demand for other assets, including equities and real assets such as houses and land, increases. With the increase in demand, the prices of these assets increase, thereby stimulating the production of real assets. As production rises, the demand for the various factors of production increases. Also, with the increase in the price of real assets, the price of these assets will be high relative to the price of services. For example, it will be relatively less costly to rent a house than to buy one. Consequently, the demand for services will increase.

Thus, Friedman and Schwartz argue that an increase in the money supply has its initial impact on financial markets. The impact then spreads to the various markets for goods and services, resulting in significant increases in both investment and consumption.

Based on their view of the transmission mechanism, monetarists conclude that an increase in the money supply leads to a significant increase in aggregate demand. In the short run, they believe that this increase in aggregate demand causes both output and the price level to rise. In the long run, they believe that the increase affects mainly the price level. Monetarists believe that the rate at which output increases in the long run is determined by real factors such as the rates of technological progress and saving. As a consequence, a permanent increase in the growth rate of the money supply results in a higher inflation rate, not a higher output growth rate. (The relationship between the inflation rate and the growth rate of the money supply is discussed in Chapter 13.)

In describing the transmission mechanism, Friedman and Schwartz emphasize that a change in the money supply may be viewed as operating through interest rates. But if the mechanism is described in that manner, they believe that a much broader range of interest rates must be considered than is usually the case. They also emphasize that the final result need not be a change in interest rates. This implies that interest rates are a poor indicator of the thrust of monetary policy and, indeed, monetarists strongly prefer to judge whether monetary policy is expansionary or contractionary on the basis of changes in the nominal money supply.

In the Keynesian model, an increase in the money supply (assuming less than full employment and a less than perfectly interest elastic demand for money function) causes the interest rate to decrease. Monetarists concede that the interest rate falls initially in response to the increase in the money supply, but stress that this is only the beginning of the adjustment process. With the increase in the money supply, aggregate demand increases and, as a result, both income and the price level increase. With the increase in income, the amount of money demanded increases. With the increase in the price level, the real money supply is reduced. Friedman claims that these forces will reverse the initial downward pressure on interest rates in less than a year. After a year or two, these forces will return interest rates to their original levels. He also believes that, given the tendency for the economy to overreact, the forces are likely to raise interest rates temporarily above their original levels.

So far, it has been assumed that people's expectations concerning inflation have not changed. Friedman argues that if people expect more inflation in the future, interest rates will rise above their original equilibrium levels. To substantiate his claim, he relies on a relationship between interest rates and the expected inflation rate postulated by Irving Fisher.[13] Fisher argued that the observed or nominal interest rate, i, equals the real interest rate, i_r, plus the expected inflation rate, $(\Delta P/P)^E$. In equation form, the relationship is

(11.9)
$$i = i_r + \left(\frac{\Delta P}{P}\right)^E,$$

where i represents the observed or nominal interest rate, i_r the real interest rate, and $(\Delta P/P)^E$ the expected inflation rate.

To illustrate, suppose the real interest rate is 4 percent and no inflation is expected. Based on equation (11.9), the nominal interest rate is 4 percent; borrowers and lenders are willing to borrow and make loans, respectively, at that rate. Suppose inflation occurs and society expects it to continue at 6 percent per year. Lenders will not make loans at a nominal interest rate of 4 percent since the purchasing power of money is expected to decrease by 6 percent per year. Consequently, they will insist on lending at a higher rate to compensate for the deterioration in the purchasing power of money. In this case, the nominal interest rate is 10 percent, obtained by summing the real interest rate (assumed unchanged) and the expected inflation rate. Borrowers are presumably willing to borrow at the higher rate since a 10 percent interest rate with a 6 percent inflation rate is no more burdensome for the typical borrower than a 4 percent interest rate with no inflation.

Friedman argues that changes in price expectations are slow to develop. If, however, the money supply were to increase more rapidly for a prolonged period, the inflation rate would increase. As people revise their expectations about inflation, the higher rate of monetary expansion will result in higher, not lower, nominal interest rates.

Because interest rates first fall and then rise in response to an increase in the growth rate of the money supply, monetarists believe that interest rates are a poor indicator of monetary policy. For that reason, monetarists caution against using them for that purpose because it may induce the Federal Reserve to pursue inappropriate policies. To illustrate, suppose interest rates are rising. The monetary authorities may interpret the rise in interest rates as an indication that the policies they have been pursuing have not been sufficiently expansionary. As a result, they may increase the growth rate of the money supply to keep interest rates from rising. In the short run, they may be successful. In the long run, the higher growth rate of the money supply causes both higher inflation rates and higher interest rates.

Inherent Stability of the Private Sector

A third proposition held by monetarists is their belief in the inherent stability of the private sector. Like the classical economists, they believe that the economy tends to adjust relatively quickly to disturbances so that discretionary monetary policy is not necessary. They also believe that discretionary monetary policy, on balance, is destabilizing rather then stabilizing.

If aggregate demand or supply were to change suddenly, monetarists believe that money wages, prices, and interest rates will adjust automatically so as to minimize the impact on output and employment. To illustrate, suppose aggregate demand falls. In the monetarist view, money wages, prices, and interest rates will fall, thereby stimulating investment and consumption. As a consequence, the initial reductions in output and employment will not be as large as one might expect. Moreover, as the adjustment process continues, output and employment will be restored to their full employment levels relatively quickly. Thus, monetarists believe that the forces driving the economy toward full employment are strong.

As discussed previously, Keynesians are of the opposite opinion. Early Keynesians believed that the demand for money was relatively interest elastic and investment relatively interest inelastic so that the forces driving the economy toward full employment are, at best, weak. Consequently, even if money wages and prices fall, the market mechanism cannot be relied upon to restore full employment quickly.[14] The nation's dismal economic performance during the 1930s was often cited as proof. (As discussed in Chapter 19, this evidence is not as clear as it first appears.)

Contemporary Keynesians concede that the forces driving the economy toward full employment are stronger than early Keynesians believed. Even so, they believe that the adjustment mechanism works only slowly so that unemployment can persist for long periods of time. They believe, therefore, that discretionary monetary and fiscal policy is necessary to maintain or restore full employment.

Since monetarists believe in the self-equilibrating nature of the economy, they see little need for discretionary monetary policy. They also believe that discretionary monetary policy, on balance, is destabilizing. For these reasons, monetarists such as Milton Friedman favor increasing the money supply at a constant rate, say, 3 percent. Friedman believes that a major advantage of this approach is preventing monetary changes from exerting a destabilizing influence on the economy. In Friedman's view, episodes of major instability in the United States have, in almost every case, been caused or at least greatly intensified by monetary instability. In his opinion, therefore, the central problem is to prevent money and monetary policy from being a source of instability.

Increasing the money supply at a constant rate guarantees that the money supply will not be a destabilizing element. Monetarists concede, however, that it will not eliminate fluctuations in output and employment due to other disturbances in the economy. Consequently, one might argue that the Federal Reserve should use policies designed to alter the growth rate of the money supply in order to offset the impact of these disturbances. Friedman argues against this approach because the lag associated with monetary policy is long and variable. If the growth rate of the money supply is altered, it will have an impact on the economy, but only after a number of months. Moreover, the lag is variable, ranging from, say, 6 to 18 months. Because of the long and (unpredictably) variable lag associated with monetary policy, it is very difficult to design discretionary policies which smooth the business cycle.

Furthermore, the long lag between a change in the growth rate of the money supply and its impact on the economy will impel the monetary authorities to over-react. Since there will be no immediate response to policy changes, the monetary authorities, Friedman believes, are likely to pursue policies which ultimately prove to be too strong. In a recession, they may increase the money supply by more than is necessary since, initially, nothing appears to happen when the money supply is increased. When the economy is threatened by inflation, the authorities may reduce the growth rate of the money supply by more than is necessary for the same reason.

In conclusion, monetarists believe that little need exists for discretionary policy and, if discretionary policy is used, the effect is destabilizing, rather than stabilizing. This view is in sharp contrast to the Keynesian position. For example, Franco Modigliani, a leading Keynesian, argues that the fundamental message of Keynes's *General Theory* is that a free enterprise economy needs to be stabilized and, since discretionary policy is stabilizing, monetary and fiscal policy should be used for that purpose.[15] Modigliani asserts that Keynesians have accepted this message but monetarists have not. Because of the importance of this issue, we shall explore the monetarist position and Modigliani's critique of it in detail in Chapter 19, Monetary Policy.

The (Approximate) Irrelevance of Allocative Detail

The fourth and final element of monetarist thought has to do with allocative detail. Monetarists argue that aggregate forces determine nominal income and allocative (sectoral) detail is (largely) irrelevant. This view is based on monetarist beliefs regarding the dominance of monetary impulses and the transmission mechanism. In their view, monetary impulses have a significant impact on nominal income. In contrast, changes occurring in individual sectors do not have a significant impact on nominal income. These changes do, of course, alter relative prices and the composition of output. Similarly, given the stable relationship between the money supply and nominal income, the effects of an increase in the money supply will spread through the economy in a predictable manner regardless of the characteristics of individual sectors. Consequently, there is no need to build large-scale econometric models to trace the impact of, say, an increase in the nominal money supply.

Monetarists do not believe that allocative detail is unimportant. For example, they believe that it is necessary to study allocative detail to determine the behavior of relative prices. On the other hand, they believe that more allocative detail is unlikely to be very helpful in charting movements in nominal income.

In contrast, Keynesians believe that allocative detail is important. They assert that the impact of various aggregate forces on nominal income is determined, in large part, by the characteristics of the individual sectors. To capture these characteristics, they favor the construction of large-scale econometric models. They also believe that changes in nominal income can occur because of changes in one or more of the sectors. Therefore, it is important that each sector be included in the model.

In conclusion, the monetarist position regarding allocative detail helps to explain their approach to model building and, in particular, their attitude towards the construction of large-scale econometric models. Another reason for their antipathy towards these models is their belief that these models, no matter how detailed, do not capture all of the ways in which a change in the money supply affects the economy. As a result, monetary policy will appear to be less powerful than it really is.

The Convergence of Monetarist and Keynesian Views

As we have seen, monetarists and Keynesians disagree on many issues. Over the years, however, their views on most issues have tended to converge. Monetarists now concede that fiscal policy has at least some impact on nominal income while contemporary Keynesians believe that monetary policy is more powerful than early Keynesians thought. Similarly, if sophisticated versions of the Keynesian transmission mechanism are compared to those of the monetarists, few, if any, differences will be found.

Despite the narrowing of differences in these and other areas, the gap between Keynesian and monetarist thought with regard to the stability of the private sector and the role of discretionary policy remains very wide. Although contemporary Keynesians believe that the forces driving the economy toward full employment are stronger than early Keynesians thought, they still believe that the forces are too weak to let the process run its course. Since they believe discretionary policy is stabilizing, they are strong advocates of the use of monetary and fiscal policy to stabilize the economy. Monetarists are of the opposite opinion in regard to both the inherent stability of the private sector and the effects of discretionary policy. To many, if not most, economists, these competing views on the stability of the private sector and the role of discretionary policy constitute the principal differences between monetarists and Keynesians today. Because of the importance of these issues, we shall return to them in Chapters 18 and 19.

CONCLUDING REMARKS

Prior to this chapter, various macroeconomic models were presented; these models were Keynesian in nature. In this chapter, two alternative models—classical and monetarist—were examined.[16] We found that these approaches differ from the Keynesian approach in terms of both theory and policy. In the next chapter, we consider two more models—rational expectations and supply-side. These approaches also differ from the Keynesian approach in important respects.

NOTES

1. The equation of exchange is sometimes written as $MsV_T = P_T T$. In the equation, T represents the volume of transactions and is a broader concept since it includes many transactions (purchases of intermediate goods, stocks, bonds, etc.) which are not included in GNP and the other measures of the nation's output. As before, Ms is the nominal money supply; V_T is the transactions velocity of money and P_T is the price level for the transactions in question. Over the years, the transactions approach has proved to be less popular because of the conceptual problems involved in defining total transactions and the price level associated with them and because of the paucity of data for these variables.

2. The following description of the quantity theory of money is greatly simplified. See, for example, Irving Fisher, *The Purchasing Power of Money*, New York: Macmillan, Inc., 1911.

3. The transition period may be lengthy. Irving Fisher, for example, believed it to be about ten years.

4. The difference between government spending and its revenue represents the government's demand for loanable funds and can be added to the investment function of Figure 11.4. If government purchases increase, the new function will shift to the right, resulting in a higher interest rate and, therefore, lower levels of investment and consumption.

5. The classical argument regarding the effectiveness of fiscal policy can be explained in terms of the Keynesian model in the following way. The classical economists believed that the real demand for money depends only on real income, which implies that the demand for money is perfectly interest inelastic. In terms of the IS–LM model, the classical assumption of a perfectly interest inelastic demand for money results in a perfectly interest inelastic LM curve at the prevailing level of output. If expansionary fiscal policy is employed, the IS curve shifts to the right. Since the LM curve is perfectly interest inelastic, the result is a relatively large increase in the interest rate, but no increase in output. This implies that the effect of the increase in government purchases (or tax reduction) is offset by the effect of the decrease in investment due to the higher interest rate.

6. A. C. Pigou, "Economic Progress in a Stable Environment," *Economica*, 14 (August 1947), 180–88.

7. Even with the real balance effect, Don Patinkin argued that relying on the market mechanism to achieve full employment within a reasonable period of time may be unsatisfactory. First, money wages and prices may not be very flexible. Second, the relationship between consumption and real balances may be weak; hence, the price level may have to decrease significantly in order to achieve full employment. Third, dynamic factors might make achievement of full employment more difficult than it first appears. The decline in prices may lead people to expect further declines. If it does, people may postpone their purchases, thereby increasing rather than decreasing unemployment. Moreover, if the decline in prices creates uncertainty, people may increase their demand for money, which has

adverse effects on the interest rate and investment. Don Patinkin, "Price Flexibility and Full Employment," *American Economic Review*, 38 (September 1948), 543–64.

8. Karl Brunner, a leading monetarist, believes that these are the distinctive elements of monetarist thought. Brunner, "The 'Monetarist Revolution' in Monetary Theory," *Weltwirtschaftliches Archiv*, 105, no. 1 (March 1970), 1–30. See, however, Thomas Mayer, "The Structure of Monetarism," *Kredit und Kapital*, 8 (1975), 191–218 and 293–316; and David E. W. Laidler, "Monetarism: An Interpretation and an Assessment," *Economic Journal*, 91 (March 1981), 1–28.

9. Milton Friedman, "The Quantity Theory of Money—A Restatement," in *Studies in the Quantity Theory of Money,* ed. M. Friedman (Chicago: University of Chicago Press, 1956), pp. 3–21.

10. The (nominal) rate of return on money may be positive, zero, or negative. The (nominal) rate of return on bonds and equities consists of two elements: (1) any currently paid yield, such as interest on bonds and dividends on equities; and (2) changes in their (nominal) prices. With regard to the ratio of nonhuman to human wealth, Friedman argues that it is relatively easier to borrow on the basis of tangible assets than on the basis of human wealth, which reflects the individual's prospective earnings from labor. Consequently, an increase in the ratio of nonhuman to human wealth results in a decrease in the amount of money demanded.

11. As discussed in Chapter 9, the more interest elastic the investment function, the less effective is fiscal policy.

12. Milton Friedman and Anna J. Schwartz, "Money and Business Cycles," *Review of Economics and Statistics*, 45 (February 1963), 32–64. See also Milton Friedman and David Meiselman, "The Relative Stability of Monetary Velocity and the Investment Multiplier in the United States, 1897–1958," in the Commission on Money and Credit, *Stabilization Policies* (Englewood Cliffs, N.J.: Prentice-Hall, Inc., 1963), pp. 217–22.

13. Irving Fisher, *The Theory of Interest* (New York: Macmillan, Inc., 1930).

14. Their narrow view of the transmission mechanism may have contributed to this belief. To illustrate, if consumption is positively related to real money balances and/or inversely related to the interest rate, adjustment will take place more rapidly.

15. Franco Modigliani, "The Monetarist Controversy or, Should We Forsake Stabilization Policies?" *American Economic Review*, 67 (March 1977), 1–19. For other critiques, see Abba P. Lerner, "A Review of *A Program for Monetary Stability*," *Journal of the American Statistical Association*, 57 (March 1962), 211–20; Arthur M. Okun, "Fiscal-Monetary Activism: Some Analytical Issues," *Brookings Papers on Economic Activity*, no. 1 (1972), 123–63; and James Tobin, "Stabilization Policy Ten Years After," *Brookings Papers on Economic Activity*, no. 1 (1980), 19–71.

16. We examine the classical, Keynesian, and monetarist approaches to inflation in Chapter 13.

REVIEW QUESTIONS

1. What is the equation of exchange? Why is it a tautology? How can it be used to derive an aggregate demand curve?

2. Distinguish between the direct and indirect mechanisms. Why are they important?

3. What determines the interest rate in the classical model? Why is the classical theory of interest rate determination called a real theory?

4. How do the classical and Keynesian models differ? In your opinion, what is the most important difference? Defend your answer.

5. According to the classical economists, the economy is self-equilibrating. Explain why they believed this to be the case. Give the Keynesian counterargument.

6. Explain why the classical economists believed that monetary (fiscal) policy would be effective (ineffective) in restoring full employment. Explain why early Keynesians believed that monetary policy might be ineffective.

7. The classical economists believed that government has no role to play with regard to stabilization policy. Early Keynesians believed that government has a very important role. Explain.

8. With regard to monetarist thought, what is meant by "the dominance of monetary impulses"?

9. Compare and contrast the Keynesian and monetarist views regarding the potency of fiscal policy.

10. Monetarists believe that the Keynesian view of the transmission mechanism is too narrow. Explain.

11. Why do monetarists believe that interest rates first fall and then rise in response to an increase in the growth rate of the money supply?

12. Compare and contrast the Keynesian and monetarist views regarding

   a. the stability of the private sector.

   b. the use of discretionary policy to stabilize the economy.

13. Why are monetarists less interested in allocative detail than Keynesians?

14. Keynesians and monetarists differ on many issues. What is (are) the most important difference(s)? Defend your answer.

SUGGESTED READING _____

ASCHHEIM, JOSEPH, and CHING-YAO HSIEH, *Macroeconomics: Income and Monetary Theory*. Columbus, Ohio: Charles E. Merrill Publishing Company, 1969.

BLAUG, MARK, *Economic Theory in Retrospect* (3rd ed.). New York: Cambridge University Press, 1978.

BRUNNER, KARL, "The 'Monetarist Revolution' in Monetary Theory," *Weltwirtschaftliches Archiv*, 105 (March 1970), 1–30.

———, "Has Monetarism Failed?" *Cato Journal*, 3 (Spring 1983), 23–62.

COCHRANE, JAMES, *Macroeconomics Before Keynes*, Glenview, Ill.: Scott, Foresman & Company, 1970.

FRIEDMAN, MILTON, *The Counter-Revolution in Monetary Theory*. London: Institute of Economic Affairs, 1970.

———, "Money: Quantity Theory," *International Encyclopedia of the Social Sciences*, vol. 10, pp. 432–47. New York: Macmillan, Inc., 1968.

———, "The Quantity Theory of Money—A Restatement," in Milton Friedman (ed.),

Studies in the Quantity Theory of Money, pp. 3–21. Chicago: University of Chicago Press, 1956.

———, "The Role of Monetary Policy," *American Economic Review*, 58 (March 1968), 1–17.

———, *A Theoretical Framework for Monetary Analysis*. New York: National Bureau of Economic Research, 1971.

KALDOR, NICHOLAS, *The Scourge of Monetarism* (2nd ed.). New York: Oxford University Press, 1986.

LAIDLER, DAVID E. W., "Monetarism: An Interpretation and an Assessment," *Economic Journal*, 91 (March 1981), 1–28.

MAKINEN, GAIL E., *Money, the Price Level, and Interest Rates: An Introduction to Monetary Theory*. Englewood Cliffs, N.J.: Prentice-Hall, Inc., 1977.

MAYER, THOMAS, "Some Reflections on the Current State of the Monetarist Debate," *Zeitschrift für Nationalokonomie*, 38 (1978), 61–84.

———, and others, *The Structure of Monetarism*. New York: W. W. Norton & Co., Inc., 1978.

MODIGLIANI, FRANCO, "The Monetarist Controversy or, Should We Forsake Stabilization Policies?" *American Economic Review*, 67 (March 1977), 1–19.

SOWELL, THOMAS, *Classical Economics Reconsidered*. Princeton, N.J.: Princeton University Press, 1974.

STEIN, JEROME L., (ed.), *Monetarism*. Amsterdam: North-Holland Publishing Company, 1976.

TEIGEN, RONALD L., "A Critical Look at Monetarist Economics," Federal Reserve Bank of St. Louis, *Review*, 54 (January 1972), 10–25.

TOBIN, JAMES, "How Dead Is Keynes?" *Economic Inquiry*, 15 (October 1977), 459–68.

———, "The Monetarist Counter-Revolution Today—An Appraisal," *Economic Journal*, 91 (March 1981), 29–42.

———, "Stabilization Policy Ten Years After," *Brookings Papers on Economic Activity*, no. 1 (1980), 19–71.

VANE, HOWARD R., and JOHN L. THOMPSON, *Monetarism: Theory, Evidence, and Policy*. New York: Halsted Press, 1979.

12

THE RATIONAL EXPECTATIONS
AND SUPPLY-SIDE VIEWS

In the previous chapter, we considered the views of the classical economists and the monetarists. In this chapter, we examine the rational expectations and supply-side approaches. We find that these approaches differ in important ways from those considered earlier. We start with the rational expectations approach.

THE RATIONAL EXPECTATIONS APPROACH

Expectations are very important in economics. To illustrate, firms invest in new plant and equipment only when it is expected to be profitable. Similarly, households increase their consumption when they experience increases in income, but the magnitudes of these increases depend largely upon whether the higher incomes are expected to be permanent or temporary.

Until recently, expectations were incorporated into economic models mechanically. It was often assumed, for example, that the expected price level is a weighted average of past price levels. This formulation was criticized because it ignores information that may be relevant. Indeed, the theory of rational expectations was developed to provide an alternative that incorporates all relevant information into the formation of expectations.[1] Before discussing rational expectations, we shall present the adaptive expectations hypothesis.

Adaptive Expectations

Starting in the 1950s, the adaptive expectations approach became very popular.[2] According to this view, people adjust their forecasts based on their current forecast error. In equation form, the assumption is

(12.1) $$_{t-1}P_t^e - _{t-2}P_{t-1}^e = \beta(P_{t-1} - _{t-2}P_{t-1}^e) \qquad 0 < \beta < 1,$$

where $_{t-1}P_t^e$ is the price level expected to prevail in time period t by individuals forming expectations in time period $t - 1$; $_{t-2}P_{t-1}^e$ is the price level expected to prevail in time period $t - 1$ by individuals forming expectations in time period $t - 2$; P_{t-1} is the actual price level in period $t - 1$; and β is a constant (between 0 and 1). The difference between the actual price level in time period $t - 1$ and the expected price level for period $t - 1$ is the forecast error for period $t - 1$.

Equation (12.1) has several implications. First, if people's expectations are correct, they will not revise them. In terms of equation (12.1), $_{t-2}P_{t-1}^e$ equals P_{t-1} if people's expectations are correct, implying that $_{t-1}P_t^e$ also equals $_{t-2}P_{t-1}^e$. Second, if people's expectations prove to be incorrect, they will revise them. For example, if the price level proves to be greater than expected, the forecast error, $P_{t-1} - _{t-2}P_{t-1}^e$, will be positive, and people will revise their expectations. In particular, they will forecast a higher price level for time period t. To illustrate, suppose P_{t-1} is 110, $_{t-2}P_{t-1}^e$ is 100, and β is 0.5. Substituting into equation (12.1) yields

$$_{t-1}P_t^e - 100 = 0.5(110 - 100),$$

or, $$_{t-1}P_t^e = 100 + 5 = 105.$$

Thus, with the unexpected increase in the price level, people revise their expectations upward. Note, however, that with β between 0 and 1, the new expected price level, $_{t-1}P_t^e$, will be less than the actual price level in period $t - 1$.

To show that the expected price level, $_{t-1}P_t^e$, is a weighted average of past price levels, we first rearrange equation (12.1) to obtain

(12.2) $$_{t-1}P_t^e = \beta P_{t-1} + (1-\beta)_{t-2}P_{t-1}^e.$$

Since β is assumed constant, the same relationship must hold for the previous period. Thus,

(12.3) $$_{t-2}P_{t-1}^e = \beta P_{t-2} + (1-\beta)_{t-3}P_{t-2}^e.$$

Next, we substitute the value of $_{t-1}P^e_{t-2}$ given by equation (12.3) into equation (12.2) to obtain

$$_{t-1}P^e_t = \beta P_{t-1} + (1-\beta)[\beta P_{t-2} + (1-\beta)_{t-3}P^e_{t-2}],$$

or
$$_{t-1}P^e_t = \beta P_{t-1} + \beta(1-\beta)P_{t-2} + (1-\beta)^2_{t-3}P^e_{t-2}.$$

If we continue this process, we eventually obtain

(12.4)
$$_{t-1}P^e_t = \beta P_{t-1} + \beta(1-\beta)P_{t-2} + \beta(1-\beta)2P_{t-3} + \ldots$$
$$+ \beta(1-\beta)^n P_{t-n-1} + (1-\beta)^{n+1}_{t-n-2}P^e_{t-n-1}.$$

Moreover, with β between 0 and 1, $(1-\beta)^{n+1}_{t-n-2}P^e_{t-n-1}$ approaches 0 as n approaches infinity. Consequently, we may drop the last term of equation (12.4) to obtain

(12.5) $\quad _{t-1}P^e_t = \beta P_{t-1} + \beta(1-\beta)P_{t-2} + \beta(1-\beta)^2 P_{t-3} + \ldots + \beta(1-\beta)^n P_{t-n-1}.$

Equation (12.5) indicates that the price level expected to prevail in time period t is a weighted average of past price levels. Moreover, with β between 0 and 1, the weights β, $\beta(1-\beta)$, $\beta(1-\beta)^2$, . . . , become smaller as n increases, indicating that price level P_{t-1} is weighted most heavily with prior period price levels weighted less and less heavily.

The adaptive expectations approach is appealing. The behavior implied by equation (12.1) has some plausibility. Also, because the expected price level is a weighted average of past price levels which are observable, the approach is easy to implement empirically. For these reasons, the approach was used widely.

Despite the popularity of the adaptive expectations approach, critics argue that it is deficient in a number of respects. For our purposes, the most important criticism is that it ignores information that may be relevant. Equation (12.5) implies that the expected price level depends only on past price levels. But if the growth rate of the money supply were altered significantly, it seems likely that individuals would take the event into account. The same is true for other events (war, crop failure, a change in crude oil prices, etc.) that have an impact on the price level.[3]

Rational Expectations

By *rational expectations*, we mean those based on the efficient use of all available, relevant information. This does not mean that individuals have perfect foresight; they may make errors, even large ones. It does imply, however, that these errors are not systematic and that it is not possible for persons to improve upon their predictions based on the information at hand. To make the concept operational, these expectations are generally assumed to be the same as those implied by the relevant economic theory, except for a random element. Consequently, individuals are assumed to act *as if* they knew the relevant theory.

The theory of rational expectations has three important implications for macroeconomics.[4] The first implication is that discretionary monetary and fiscal policy cannot be used to stabilize the economy. The second (which is related to the first) is that no tradeoff exists between inflation and unemployment. The third implication is that econometric models are not useful in evaluating alternative economic policies. Each of these implications is discussed in turn.

According to proponents of the rational expectations theory, discretionary monetary and fiscal policy cannot be used to stabilize the economy. Their argument is that (anticipated) changes in monetary and fiscal variables have no impact on output and employment. Therefore, they cannot be used to alter output and employment so as to offset the impact of other disturbances in the economy.

In addition to postulating that expectations are formed rationally, proponents of the theory assume that wages and prices are flexible. Furthermore, they assume that the aggregate supply function may be written as

(12.6) $$Y_t = Y_{FE} + \lambda(P_t - {}_{t-1}P_t^e) \qquad \lambda > 0,$$

where Y_t is output in time period t; Y_{FE} is the full employment level of output; P_t is the price level in time period t; ${}_{t-1}P_t^e$ is the price level expected to prevail in time period t by individuals forming expectations in time period $t - 1$; and λ is a (positive) constant.

Equation (12.6) implies that when the expected price level in time period t, ${}_{t-1}P_t^e$, equals the actual price level in that period, output in period t equals the full employment level of output. Since this is true for all price levels, the implied aggregate supply curve will be perfectly inelastic at the full employment level of output. One such curve is AS_0 in Figure 12.1.

Equation (12.6) also implies that when the expected price level in time period t, ${}_{t-1}P_t^e$, is less than the actual price level, output in time period t will be greater than the full employment level. To illustrate, suppose that the price level is P_1 in period t and P_1 exceeds the expected price level. Under these circumstances, firms will have an incentive to produce more than the full employment level of output and output will be, say, Y_1. This implies that if people's expectations are incorrect, the aggregate supply curve will be positively sloped. Aggregate supply curve AS_0' in Figure 12.1 is based upon this assumption.

We are now ready to consider the impact of an increase in the money supply upon output and the price level. Assume initially that aggregate demand is AD_0 and people's expectations are correct. Under these circumstances, output is Y_0 and the price level is P_0, given by the intersection of AD_0 and AS_0 in Figure 12.1. Next, assume that the money supply is increased so that aggregate demand increases to AD_1. If the increase in the money supply takes people by surprise or if their price forecasts are based on adaptive rather than rational expectations, the price level will rise to P_1. Since this price level is greater than expected, output will

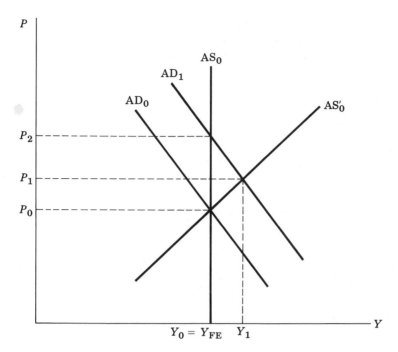

FIGURE 12.1

Rational expectations, aggregate supply, and aggregate demand

increase to Y_1 which is greater than the full employment level of output. On the other hand, if people are aware of the increase in the money supply and use this information in making their forecasts, the price level will rise to P_2 and output will remain at the Y_0 ($= Y_{FE}$) level. This result occurs because people will recognize the implications of the increase in the money supply and incorporate them into their forecasts. As a result, their expectations will prove to be correct (except for a random element) and output and employment will be unaltered.

In conclusion, the analysis just presented suggests that (anticipated) changes in the money supply have no impact on output and employment. The same argument can be extended to changes in government purchases and taxes. This proposition—that anticipated changes in the monetary and fiscal policy variables have no impact on output and employment—is called the *policy ineffectiveness proposition*. The policy ineffectiveness proposition is inconsistent with both the Keynesian and monetarist positions. It is consistent, however, with the classical position, and for this reason, the theory of rational expectations is sometimes called the "new classical economics." We shall consider criticisms of this argument in the next section.

Although anticipated changes in the monetary and fiscal policy variables have no impact on output and employment, unanticipated changes do have an impact since people are "surprised" by the changes and are, therefore, unable to incorporate the implications of the changes into their price forecasts. When people learn of the changes, however, output and employment return to their full employment levels so that the main impact of unanticipated changes in the monetary and fiscal policy variables is to increase the volatility of output and employment. To minimize the fluctuations in output and employment, rational expectations theorists favor the use of simple policy rules so as to make the actions of the monetary and fiscal authorities predictable. To illustrate, many, if not most, rational expectations theorists favor increasing the money supply at a constant rate. This rate, say 4 percent, would be sufficient to accommodate an expanding economy without causing upward pressure on the price level. This approach is, of course, the same as that advocated by monetarists.

A second implication of the theory of rational expectations is that no tradeoff exists between inflation and unemployment. The relationship between inflation and unemployment is discussed in detail in Chapters 14 and 15, but we discuss it briefly here because of the implications of the theory of rational expectations for the relationship. For years, it was argued that lower unemployment rates could be obtained at the expense of higher inflation rates through more rapid increases in aggregate demand. In the late 1960s, this view was criticized by several economists who argued that a tradeoff exists in the short run, but not in the long run. Proponents of the rational expectations theory go even further; they argue that no tradeoff exists even in the short run. Their argument is as follows: suppose that the Federal Reserve implements a new monetary policy that calls for more rapid increases in the money supply. Since people realize that an increase in the growth rate of the money supply implies a higher inflation rate, they will use this information in making their price forecasts and once again the expected price level will equal the new, higher price level and output and employment will be unchanged (see Figure 12.1). Consequently, even though the inflation rate has increased, the unemployment rate is unaltered, implying that no tradeoff exists between inflation and unemployment.

A third and final implication of the theory of rational expectations has to do with the use of econometric models. Proponents of the theory argue that these models are not very useful in evaluating alternative economic policies. At the end of Chapter 10, it was argued that policy makers must have estimates of the changes in the price level, output, and employment which will occur due, say, to a $10 billion increase in government purchases. Various econometric models have been used to obtain such estimates. Since many of these models are very detailed and their parameters have been estimated using sophisticated statistical techniques, their proponents claim that they are very helpful in assessing the impact of various policy alternatives.[5] Proponents of the rational expectations theory argue, however, that their usefulness is, at best, limited, because the parameters of the models change when new policies are introduced. They claim that the actions of households and firms are based, in part, on the monetary and fiscal policies in effect during the period in question. Should new policies be implemented, households and firms will behave differently and, as a result, the parameters of the model will change. Since the estimates of the effects of new policies are based on the original set of (estimated) parameters, the actual effects may be quite different. Consequently, econometric models are not very helpful in selecting appropriate policies.

Criticisms

Opponents of the theory of rational expectations offer four major criticisms. First, they claim that, in a complex and uncertain world where information is costly, people do not base their forecasts upon rational expectations. Instead, people use simpler approaches, such as adaptive expectations.[6] Proponents of the rational expectations approach respond to this argument by noting that households and firms have a strong economic incentive to forecast future business conditions accurately because their economic welfare depends on this ability. Thus, they will obtain the relevant information and use it efficiently. Advocates of the theory also assert that any other theory is ad hoc and implies that people make forecasts that are systematically wrong. For these reasons, proponents of the theory claim that forecasts are based on rational expectations.

A second criticism is that money wages and prices are "sticky," rather than flexible as assumed by rational expectations theorists. If this criticism is valid, it means that discretionary monetary and fiscal policy will have an impact on output and employment even if expectations are formed rationally. To illustrate, suppose that money wages are fixed and the money supply increases. As a result of the increase in the money supply, prices rise, real wages fall, and firms respond by increasing employment and output. Thus, even if the impact of the increase in the money supply is anticipated, the assumption of a fixed money wage guarantees that output will increase.

Rational expectations theorists respond to this criticism by arguing that the reasons commonly given for wage and price rigidity are not convincing. (Some of these reasons are discussed in Chapter 10.) Moreover, even if money wages and prices are "sticky," the monetary and fiscal authorities can do little to exploit this in the long run. For example, suppose money wages have been set in advance by long-term contracts and the monetary authorities increase the growth rate of the money supply. Prices will rise more rapidly than anticipated when the contracts were signed. When the contracts expire, labor will have a strong incentive to include cost-of-living adjustment clauses in the new contracts or to reduce the length of the contracts. Either way, the scope for discretionary monetary and fiscal policy will be reduced or even eliminated.

Another criticism of the rational expectations theory is that, if policy makers have more information about their policy actions or the economy than the public, policies can be devised that will alter output and employment. To illustrate, suppose, unknown to the public, the monetary authorities increase the growth rate of the money supply. Since the more rapid increase in the money supply is unanticipated, output and employment increase. But if the rational expectations view is correct, output and employment will return to their original levels after the public learns of the new policy. Under these circumstances, the new policy will be effective only during the learning process, which may be very short-lived. If policy makers have more information about the economy (and it is by no means clear that they do), it might be easier for them to disseminate the information and let the public act on it rather than implementing new policies.

Finally, critics charge that the rational expectations theory cannot explain the prolonged periods of unemployment that we sometimes observe. If expectations are formed rationally and if wages and prices are flexible, they claim that deviations from the equilibrium levels of output and employment should be short-lived. Since this implication appears to be inconsistent with actual experience, many critics reject the theory on this basis. In response, proponents of the theory have constructed theories of the business cycle based on rational expectations. These theories are capable of explaining the observed movements in output and employment, but whether these theories provide a better explanation than more conventional theories is an open question.

In conclusion, we note that debate continues regarding the merits of the theory of rational expectations. At present, only a small minority of economists supports the theory. On the other hand, support seems to be growing. Because of the theory's implications for the conduct of policy, resolution of the debate is very important.

THE SUPPLY-SIDE APPROACH

In the late 1970s, Keynesian economics was heavily criticized for neglecting aggregate supply. The critics, known as supply-side economists, argued that increasing the aggregate supply of goods and services is the best way to improve the economic performance of the United States. To increase aggregate supply, they favored sharp reductions in tax rates. These reductions, they claimed, would provide greater incentives to work, save, and invest. With the greater incentives, aggregate supply would increase and both inflation and unemployment would be reduced.

Supply-side economics is based on the view that taxes drive a "wedge" between the price a buyer must pay and the price the seller receives. With regard to the labor market, federal (and state) income and social security taxes constitute such a wedge. The effect of this wedge is to reduce both the amount of labor demanded and the amount of labor supplied. To illustrate, it is not uncommon for households to face marginal tax rates of 33 percent or more. If an individual were to work longer or harder, he would receive only 67 percent of any additional income because 33 percent of it would accrue to the government in taxes. Under these circumstances, the individual has little incentive to work longer or harder. To reduce this disincentive effect, supply-siders favor sharp cuts in marginal tax rates.

Supply-siders also believe that high marginal tax rates discourage saving. Suppose an individual is considering saving an additional $1,000, which she can lend at a 15 percent interest rate. Furthermore, suppose the individual faces a 33 percent marginal tax rate. Although the interest rate is 15 percent, the after-tax rate of return is only 10 percent, because 33 percent of the income accrues to the government in taxes. To provide a greater incentive to save, supply-siders believe that tax rates should be reduced. If the marginal tax rate were reduced from 33 percent to 20 percent in our example, the after-tax return would rise from 10 percent to 12 percent. Since the after-tax rate of return is the relevant variable, the increase in it gives the individual a greater inducement to save.

As with labor supply and saving, the after-tax rate of return is the relevant variable in the investment decision making process. Since high marginal tax rates imply low after-tax rates of return, supply-siders argue that marginal tax rates must be reduced to provide firms with a greater incentive to invest. If personal income tax rates are reduced, single proprietorships and partnerships will have a greater incentive to invest in new plant and equipment. Similarly, if corporations were to receive more favorable tax treatment (see Chapter 6), they will have a greater incentive also. (In Chapter 18, various tax policies to promote investment are discussed.)

The effects of a reduction in tax rates and their impact on aggregate supply can be analyzed in terms of the aggregate supply–aggregate demand model of Chapter 10. If the cuts result in an increase in the supply of labor, the aggregate supply of goods and services increases (see Figures 10.17 and 10.18). If saving increases as a result of an increase in the after-tax rate of return, interest rates fall, thereby increasing investment. If business were to receive a more favorable tax treatment, investment would also increase for that reason. With the increases in investment, the nation's capital stock will increase more rapidly. Moreover, as the capital stock increases, the demand for labor will increase. Both changes result in increases in the aggregate supply of goods and services. The combined effects of the increases in the supply of labor, capital stock, and demand for labor result in the shift of the aggregate supply curve from AS_0 to AS_1 in Figure 12.2.

If the tax cuts result in more work, saving, and investment, the aggregate supply of goods and services will increase, thereby increasing the nation's output. The effect on the price level depends on aggregate demand. If it were to remain constant, or increase by an amount less than the increase in aggregate supply, the result is a lower price level, but if aggregate demand were to increase by a larger amount, the price level would increase. In Figure 12.2, if aggregate demand remains at AD_0, the price level falls to P_1; if it increases to AD_2, the price level rises to P_2. Critics of the supply-side approach argue that, at least in the short run, the increase in aggregate demand will be greater than the increase in aggregate supply, resulting in higher prices. For the most part, their argument is based on the contention that households will spend most of the increase in disposable income, thereby resulting in a large increase in aggregate demand. Many, if not most, supply-siders concede the validity of this argument and stress that government spending must be reduced and a less expansionary monetary policy be followed in order for aggregate demand to be held in check. We shall return to this argument in the next section.

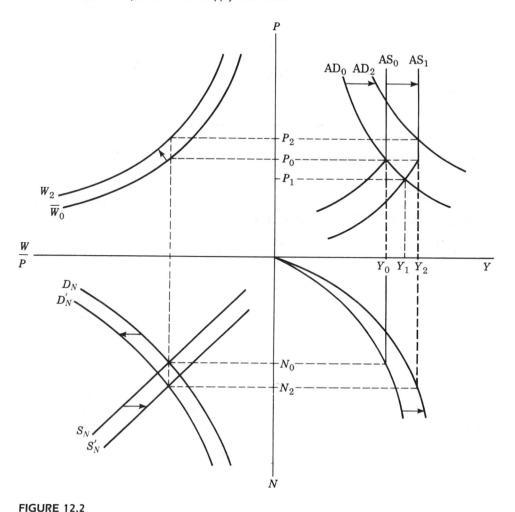

FIGURE 12.2

The supply-side effects of a reduction in personal income tax rates

Criticisms

Before turning to President Reagan's economic program (which is widely viewed as a supply-side program), let us consider some criticisms of the supply-side approach. Opponents offer three main criticisms. First, they claim that even if a relatively large decrease in tax rates were to occur, the resulting increases in labor supply, saving, and investment will be very modest, especially in the short run. Second, even if aggregate supply increases, aggregate demand will increase even more rapidly, resulting in a higher rather than lower inflation rate. Third, if contractionary monetary policy is used to reduce the rate of increase in aggregate demand, the consequent higher interest rates will discourage investment. We consider each criticism in turn.

The first criticism relates to the impact on labor supply, saving, and investment of changes in the tax structure. With regard to the supply of labor, many economists believe that the amount of labor supplied is unresponsive to changes in after-tax real wages. From a theoretical standpoint, the substitution and income effects of an increase in after-tax real wages tend to be offsetting. With a reduction in tax rates, the after-tax real wage rises and leisure becomes more costly. As a result, workers tend to substitute work for leisure, increasing the amount of labor supplied. On the other hand, with the higher after-tax real wage, workers have higher incomes and can afford more leisure. Therefore, they may work less, reducing the amount of labor supplied. Since a reduction in tax rates can lead theoretically to either an increase or decrease in the amount of labor supplied, the nature of the relationship must be determined empirically.

Until recently, it was widely held that the amount of labor supplied by prime-age males is unresponsive to changes in after-tax real wages, but that the amount of labor supplied by married females is responsive (with the amount of labor supplied by female heads of households more responsive than for males but less than for married females). Recently, however, Jerry A. Hausman found that married men (from 25 to 55 years of age) are also responsive to changes in after-tax real wages.[7] He concluded that replacing the progressive income tax by a proportional tax would lead to a significant increase in the amount of labor supplied. While Hausman's evidence is not conclusive with regard to this complex issue, it does suggest that the amount of labor supplied by males is more responsive to changes in tax rates than once thought. This new evidence with regard to males, plus the increasing importance of females in the labor force, supports the claim that the quantity of labor supplied responds positively to increases in the after-tax real wage.

As discussed in Chapter 5, the relationship between saving and the interest rate is ambiguous. Michael J. Boskin and various other economists have found evidence that a positive relationship exists between saving and the expected real after-tax rate of return. Others have found evidence to the contrary. Because of the difficulties in measuring both saving and the expected real after-tax rate of return, these conflicting views have not been reconciled. Consequently, we cannot be certain that a reduction in marginal tax rates will lead to a significant increase in saving through its effect on the real rate of return.

The relationship between investment and the cost of capital services, which reflects both interest rates and the tax treatment of business income, was discussed in Chapter 6. The conclusion was that the cost of capital is an important determinant of the desired capital stock and, therefore, investment. Consequently, a more favorable tax treatment for business income should result in a higher rate of capital accumulation. It should be emphasized, however, that even if the cost of capital is reduced the increase in the capital stock will not occur immediately. It takes time for firms to revise their plans and to obtain new equipment or build new plants. Moreover, if the economy is experiencing a recession, most firms will have excess capacity so that the new policies may not have much of an effect until the economy improves.

We may summarize the empirical evidence with regard to the first criticism. Reductions in marginal tax rates provide greater incentives to work, but the effect on saving is less certain. If the tax system were altered so as to give more favorable treatment to business income, investment would increase, but one should not expect a dramatic increase in the capital stock in the short run. Our conclusion is that reductions in marginal tax rates will increase aggregate supply, although their short-run effect is likely to be modest.

Even if Keynesian critics were to concede that aggregate supply increases, they believe that the increase will be swamped by the accompanying increase in aggregate demand. They claim that households will consume most of the increase in disposable income due to the reduction in personal income tax rates, which would increase aggregate demand significantly. To the extent that investment increases, the increase will also result in a higher level of aggregate demand. These increases in aggregate demand, they argue, will result in higher, not lower, prices.

Supply-siders are, of course, more optimistic about the impact of their policies on saving and aggregate supply. Some believe that tax cuts will result in a much higher level of economic activity, which will generate a more than offsetting increase in tax revenue. The net increase in tax revenue will help to alleviate the inflationary pressure on the economy. This argument is discussed later.

Other supply-siders respond by arguing that the effects of the increases in consumption and investment can be offset by the effects of reduced government spending and a lower rate of increase in the money supply. If the necessary reductions in government spending are forthcoming, their argument is correct. For political reasons, however, the reductions in government spending may not be made. Consequently, more reliance would have to be placed on contractionary monetary policy to keep aggregate demand in check.

If the necessary reductions in government spending do not occur and contractionary monetary policy is applied, the net effect is higher interest rates. With a tax reduction and a relatively small decrease in government spending, fiscal policy is expansionary. Monetary policy, on the other hand, is contractionary. Both policies imply higher interest rates, at least in the short run. As a result, investment will be less, which is counterproductive in terms of the supply-side approach. If the approach is followed, many Keynesians believe that the economy will stagnate because of higher interest rates.

Supply-siders respond that, if their program is enacted, inflation should fall, thereby reducing interest rates. Many of them believe that interest rates will fall quickly, because people will realize that the administration and Federal Reserve are committed to policies designed to reduce inflation and adjust their expectations accordingly. Earlier administrations and the Federal Reserve have made similar commitments in the past, however, only to abandon them. Consequently, inflationary expectations and interest rates may adjust much more slowly than supply-siders expect. (To achieve lower interest rates quickly, some supply-siders advocate a return to the gold standard, a possibility that is discussed later.)

President Reagan's Economic Program

Early in his administration, President Reagan announced a four-point economic program: lower tax rates, reduced government spending, encouragement of monetary restraint, and easing of the regulatory burden on business. If enacted, the administration claimed that the program would result in lower inflation and unemployment rates.

As part of the program, the Economic Recovery Tax Act of 1981 was passed. This act provided significant changes in the nation's tax laws. Personal income tax rates were reduced 25 percent, with a 5 percent reduction on October 1, 1981 and successive 10 percent reductions on July 1, 1982 and July 1, 1983. The maximum personal income tax rate on investment income was reduced from 70 percent to 50 percent on January 1, 1982. This reduction had the effect of reducing the maximum rate on capital gains from 28 percent to 20 percent. These reductions were designed to increase the incentives to work, save, and invest. The act contained other provisions designed for the same purpose. Under the act, any wage earner could invest up to $2,000 a year in a personal pension plan called an Individual Retirement Account (IRA). No taxes are paid on the contribution or the interest it earns until the person starts withdrawing funds from the plan. The act also provided that personal income taxes be indexed to the Consumer Price Index (CPI) starting in 1985. Under the provision, tax brackets, personal exemptions, and standard deductions are adjusted each year to take inflation into account. As a consequence, taxpayers who receive wage increases that merely keep pace with inflation will have a constant real tax payment.

The Economic Recovery Tax Act also contained a number of provisions favorable to business. Retroactive to January 1, 1981, business depreciation schedules were simplified and redesigned to accelerate the writeoff of investment in plant and equipment. In addition, firms received a 6 percent investment tax credit for the purchase of new cars, small trucks, and research equipment and a 10 percent credit for other equipment. These changes reduce the cost of capital, thereby providing an incentive for firms to invest in new plant and equipment.[8]

Despite the enactment of the Economic Recovery Tax Act of 1981, the economy experienced a severe recession in 1981 and 1982. The unemployment rate increased from 7.3 percent in April 1981 to 8.8 percent in December of that year and continued to climb in 1982. At the same time, the inflation rate dropped. As measured by the implicit price deflator for GNP, the inflation rate dropped from 10.2 percent in 1980 to 8.7 percent in 1981 and to 5.9 percent in the following year. Economists generally attribute the reduction in the inflation rate and increase in the unemployment rate to the sharp reductions in the growth rate of the money supply that occurred in 1980 and 1981. (This episode is discussed in more detail in Chapter 15.)

Prior to the recession, supply-siders claimed that it was possible to reduce the inflation and unemployment rates simultaneously and, indeed, some people optimistically predicted that passage of the Economic Recovery Tax Act would achieve those goals. Unfortunately, this was not the case; the inflation rate dropped but the unemployment rate increased. Supply-siders offer several explanations of why the economy did not respond as predicted. They note, for example, that the supply-side agenda included an immediate 30 percent across-the-board cut in personal income tax rates. Tax rates, however, were cut by only 25 percent and, more importantly, the reductions were spread over the period from October 1, 1981 to July 1, 1983, with an initial cut of only 5 percent. Given the modest initial cut (which was largely or completely offset by increases in social security and other taxes), supply-siders claim that it is not surprising that the effect of the reductions in the growth rate of the money supply overwhelmed the effect of the tax cut.[9] There is some truth to this argument; however, it is also clear that the program was "oversold," a common phenomenon in the nation's capital. The supply-side agenda should be viewed more properly as a program to increase the nation's growth rate in the long run rather than as a program aimed at reducing the inflation and unemployment rates in the short run. We shall examine this view in more detail in the next chapter.

The Laffer Curve

Over the years, politicians have been reluctant to reduce tax rates significantly because it was believed that tax revenue would be reduced, thereby creating a larger budgetary deficit. Some supply-siders, including Arthur B. Laffer, have argued that tax rates can be reduced without loss of tax revenue.[10] In fact, they claim the reduction may actually increase tax revenue by providing incentives which lead to much higher levels of economic activity. If they are correct, one serious objection to tax cuts is eliminated.

The argument may be illustrated in terms of the *Laffer curve*, a relationship between total tax revenue and tax rates. If total tax revenue is plotted on the vertical axis and tax rates on the horizontal, we may obtain the relationship shown in Figure 12.3. (The curve is assumed symmetrical for simplicity only.) At a zero tax rate, no tax revenue is raised; hence, the curve starts at the origin. With a tax rate of 100 percent, persons have no incentive to engage in economic activity since the remuneration accrues entirely to the government. Consequently, they will not do so and tax revenue is again zero, so the curve ends at the horizontal axis. Between tax rates of 0 and 100 (percent), the curve has an inverted U shape, indicating that tax revenue rises as tax rates increase over some range (to tax rate t_0) and then falls. Over the 0 to t_0 range, the effect of the increase in tax rates dominates the disincentive effect. From t_0 to 100, the opposite is true. Thus, at tax rates greater than t_0, a tax increase actually reduces tax revenue, which implies that the appropriate way to increase tax revenue is to reduce tax rates.

Few economists disagree with the notion that at a sufficiently high (greater than t_0) tax rate a tax cut will increase tax revenue. Most economists, however,

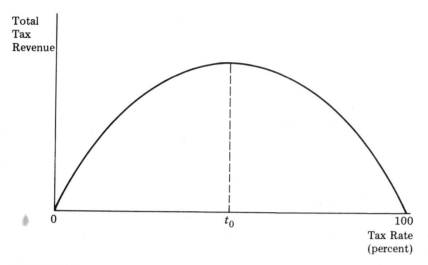

FIGURE 12.3

The Laffer curve

deny that the prevailing tax rate is that high. They believe, therefore, that tax cuts will reduce tax revenue and, if unmatched by reductions in government spending, will result in larger deficits. Even so, to the extent that the tax reductions provide incentives to work, save, and invest, the loss in tax revenue will be minimized. Also, to the extent that people shift from tax-sheltered to other activities, tax revenue will increase. Similarly, if the tax cuts result in the surfacing of part of the underground economy, tax revenue will increase. The net effect of these changes will probably still be a reduction in tax revenue, at least in the short run, but this loss may be less than expected.

As indicated earlier, not all supply-siders believe that cutting tax rates will result in increased tax revenue. Since the Reagan administration forecasted large deficits, little support apparently existed within the administration for that view. In Chapter 18, we consider the effects of deficits and a large and growing national debt upon the economy.

Restoration of the Gold Standard

A number of supply-siders favor a return to the gold standard. Essentially, a gold standard is a commitment by government to fix the price of its currency in terms of a specified amount of gold. The government maintains the fixed price by buying or selling gold to anyone at that price. For example, the United States maintained the price of gold at $20.67 per ounce over the 1834–1933 period (with the exception of 1861–78).

If the United States were to return to a gold standard, proponents claim that the growth rate of the money supply would be constrained since the supply of gold grows only slowly. The return would also restore confidence in the dollar since people would know that dollars can be exchanged for gold at a fixed rate. With the reduction in the growth rate of money supply and restoration of confidence in the dollar, both the actual and expected inflation rates would drop sharply. As a result, interest rates would drop. Lower interest rates would stimulate investment, thereby promoting more rapid economic growth. Lower interest rates would also make it less costly for the federal government to service the national debt. Finally, by constraining the Federal Reserve's ability to increase the money supply, proponents argue that it would be more difficult for the government to run budget deficits.

Other economists argue that the same results could be obtained much more easily by a commitment on the part of the Federal Reserve to increase the money supply at a slow and steady rate. In response, the supply-siders claim that the Federal Reserve is either unable or unwilling to do this for prolonged periods of time. Moreover, they believe that it is not possible to define the money supply, because of new monetary and credit instruments that serve as money. Consequently, they argue that money cannot be defined, let alone controlled. Other economists deny these claims.

Many objections to a return to the gold standard exist, but, prior to discussing them, let us compare the performance of the U.S. economy during the period from 1880 to 1914, the heyday of the gold standard, to its performance during the post-World War II period.[11] The first period was characterized by long-term price stability; in contrast, the second period is marked by inflation. Even so, the price level exhibited greater instability on a year-to-year basis during 1880–1913. Similarly, the earlier period was characterized by greater instability of output. Surprisingly enough, even the money supply showed greater instability in the first period. The average unemployment rate was also higher, 6.8 percent, during 1880–1913; the corresponding rate was 5.0 percent for the post-World War II period. The data also suggest that per capita real income grew somewhat more rapidly in the 1970s, a dismal decade in terms of modern U.S. economic performance, than during the pre-1914 period. Thus, despite the long-term price stability of the 1880–1914 period, it was not a period in which the U.S. economy's performance was exemplary.

Now, we briefly consider various objections to the gold standard. First, adherence to a gold standard may result in greater instability in the economy. A gold standard prevents or inhibits the use of discretionary monetary policy to offset disturbances arising in the economy. Even worse, the gold standard itself may become a source of instability. Suppose a country loses gold (to another country) for some reason; the country's money supply is reduced. To the extent that wages and prices are sticky, output and employment fall. The country's monetary and fiscal authorities will be under strong pressure to restore output and employment to their previous levels. Based on past experience, the country is likely to deviate from the "rules" of the gold standard (or even leave the standard) under these circumstances.

Various technical problems exist in returning to the gold standard. If the price of gold is set too high, massive amounts of gold will move to this country and the money supply will increase accordingly. If the price is set too low, the reverse will happen. Also, it would be difficult or impossible for the United States to return to a gold standard without its major international trading partners doing so. So far, they have shown no such inclination. Of course, if the various countries were to fix their currencies in terms of gold, it would be the end of flexible exchange rates (discussed in Chapter 16). Although flexible exchange rates have some disadvantages, they have worked reasonably well. They have, for example, accommodated the massive transfers of wealth resulting from successive OPEC oil shocks.

Another disadvantage is that the supply of gold may not increase rapidly enough to provide sufficient money for economic growth. In the face of insufficient growth in the money supply, money wages and prices should fall; but if they are sticky, high rates of unemployment and low rates of growth will result. Finally, a return to the gold standard is risky because the two leading gold producers, South Africa and the Soviet Union, may prove unreliable. South Africa, the leading producer, is potentially unstable because of racial tensions. In addition, the Soviet Union would have a much greater opportunity to disrupt the world's economic order under a gold standard.

In view of poor performance of the U.S. economy during the heyday of the gold standard and the many objections to it, a return to the gold standard is not desirable and not all supply-siders advocate it. If the economy is to experience less inflation, supply-siders agree that the nation's money supply must increase less rapidly. As monetarists have emphasized, this can be achieved without moving to a gold standard.

CONCLUDING REMARKS

In this chapter, we treated the theory of income determination from the rational expectations and supply-side perspectives. These views differ from the Keynesian view on many important issues. For this reason, we shall refer to them (as well as to the classical and monetarist views) in subsequent chapters.

NOTES _____

1. The theory was originated by John F. Muth in an article published in 1961, but was largely ignored until the 1970s. Muth, "Rational Expectations and the Theory of Price Movements," *Econometrica*, 29 (July 1961), 315–35.

2. Phillip Cagan, "The Monetary Dynamics of Hyperinflation," in *Studies in the Quantity Theory of Money*, ed. Milton Friedman (Chicago: University of Chicago Press, 1956), pp. 25–117.

3. The adaptive expectations hypothesis implies that individuals will revise their price expectations upward only after the higher price levels are observed. Under these circumstances, expectations will adjust only sluggishly.

4. All are discussed in Thomas J. Sargent and Neil Wallace, "Rational Expectations and the Theory of Economic Policy," *Journal of Monetary Economics*, 2 (April 1976), 169–83.

5. As discussed in Chapter 11, monetarists question the usefulness of these models, but for different reasons.

6. If this criticism is valid, it means that discretionary monetary and fiscal policy will have an impact on output and employment.

7. Jerry A. Hausman, "Labor Supply," in *How Taxes Affect Economic Behavior*, eds. Henry J. Aaron and Joseph A. Pechman (Washington, D.C.: The Brookings Institution, 1981), pp. 27–72.

8. The act contains a number of other provisions which are important but less relevant for our purposes. Some of the provisions which gave business a more favorable tax treatment were repealed or modified in 1982. For discussions of the 1981 and 1982 tax acts and their impact, see Allen Sinai, Andrew Lin, and Russell Robins, "Taxes, Saving, and Investment: Some Empirical Evidence," *National Tax Journal*, 36 (September 1983), 321–45; and Mack Ott, "Depreciation, Inflation and Investment Incentives: The Effects of the Tax Acts of 1981 and 1982," Federal Reserve Bank of St. Louis, *Review*, 66 (November 1984), 17–30.

9. Some supply-siders blame the nation's poor economic performance in 1981–82 on the Reagan administration's inability to reduce or slow the rate of increase in government spending. (According to this view, the tax cuts resulted in large budget deficits which kept real interest rates high.) Others blame it on the failure to return to the gold standard.

10. Arthur B. Laffer, "Government Exactions and Revenue Deficiencies," *Cato Journal*, 1 (Spring 1981), 1–21.

11. Michael D. Bordo, "The Classical Gold Standard: Some Lessons for Today," Federal Reserve Bank of St. Louis, *Review*, 63 (May 1981), 2–17.

REVIEW QUESTIONS

1. Why are expectations important?

2. What are adaptive expectations? What are the advantages and disadvantages of this approach?

3. What are rational expectations? If expectations are rational, can individuals make forecasting errors?

4. What implications do rational expectations have for the

   a. use of discretionary monetary and fiscal policy?

   b. tradeoff between inflation and unemployment?

   c. use of large-scale econometric models?

5. What is the policy ineffectiveness proposition? Does it hold if

   a. the change in the monetary or fiscal variable is unanticipated?

   b. expectations are formed adaptively?

   c. wages and prices are "sticky"?

6. Why do rational expectations theorists favor the use of simple policy rules?

7. Outline the main criticisms of the theory of rational expectations. How do proponents of the theory respond to these criticisms?

8. In terms of the aggregate supply–aggregate demand model, illustrate the effects supply-siders expect from reductions in personal income tax rates.

9. Critics of supply-side economics argue that reductions in personal income tax rates may not affect the supply of labor. Discuss this argument both theoretically and empirically.

10. Critically evaluate the statement that government spending must be reduced significantly if the supply-side approach is to be successful in promoting economic growth and reducing the inflation rate.

11. Outline and critically evaluate President Reagan's economic program.

12. Explain why reductions in tax rates may actually increase tax revenue. For which group in society is this most likely to be the case?

13. Some supply-siders favor a return to the gold standard. How might this be helpful in promoting economic growth and reducing the inflation rate? Outline the main arguments against it.

SUGGESTED READING

BARTLETT, BRUCE, and TIMOTHY P. ROTH (eds.), *The Supply-Side Solution*. Chatham, N.J.: Chatham House Publishers, Inc., 1983.

BOSKIN, MICHAEL J. (ed.), *The Economy in the 1980s: A Program for Growth and Stability*. San Francisco: Institute for Contemporary Studies, 1980.

BUITER, WILLEM H., "The Macroeconomics of Dr. Pangloss: A Critical Survey of the New Classical Macroeconomics," *Economic Journal*, 90 (March 1980), 34–50.

FINK, RICHARD H. (ed.), *Supply-Side Economics: A Critical Appraisal*. Frederick, Md.: University Publications of America, Inc., 1982.

GILBERT, CHARLES, "The Rational Expectations Hypothesis: Survey and Recent Research," in Thomas M. Havrilesky (ed.), *Modern Concepts in Macroeconomics*, pp. 143–65. Arlington Heights, Ill.: Harlan Davidson, Inc., 1985.

HAILSTONES, THOMAS J. (ed.), *Viewpoints on Supply-Side Economics*. Richmond, Va.: Robert F. Dame, Inc., 1982.

HOLLAND, A. STEVEN, "Rational Expectations and the Effects of Monetary Policy: A Guide for the Uninitiated," Federal Reserve Bank of St. Louis, *Review*, 67 (May 1985), 5–11.

KLAMER, ARJO, *Conversations with Economists*. Totowa, N.J.: Rowman and Allanheld, Publishers, 1984.

LAFFER, ARTHUR B., "Supply-Side Economics," *Financial Analysts Journal*, 37 (September–October 1981), 29–43.

LUCAS, ROBERT E., JR., *Studies in Business-Cycle Theory*. Cambridge, Mass.: The MIT Press, 1981.

————, and THOMAS J. SARGENT (eds.), *Rational Expectations and Econometric Practice*. Minneapolis: University of Minnesota Press, 1981.

MADDOCK, RODNEY, and MICHAEL CARTER, "A Child's Guide to Rational Expectations," *Journal of Economic Literature*, 20 (March 1982), 39–51.

MEYER, LAURENCE H. (ed.), *The Supply-Side Effects of Economic Policy*. Boston: Kluwer-Nijhoff Publishing, 1981.

PARKIN, MICHAEL, *Macroeconomics*. Englewood Cliffs, N.J.: Prentice-Hall, Inc., 1984.

SHEFFRIN, STEVEN M., *Rational Expectations*. New York: Cambridge University Press, 1983.

STONE, CHARLES F., and ISABEL V. SAWHILL, *Economic Policy in the Reagan Years*. Washington, D.C.: The Urban Institute Press, 1984.

STUBBLEBINE, WM. CRAIG, and THOMAS D. WILLETT (eds.), *Reaganomics: A Midterm Report*. San Francisco: Institute for Contemporary Studies, 1983.

TOBIN, JAMES, *Asset Accumulation and Economic Activity*. Chicago: University of Chicago Press, 1980.

———, "Are New Classical Models Plausible Enough to Guide Policy?" *Journal of Money, Credit, and Banking*, 12 (November 1980), 788–99.

WANNISKI, JUDE, *The Way the World Works*. New York: Basic Books, Inc., Publishers, 1978.

13

INFLATION

A s discussed in Chapter 1, price stability is an economic goal. In this chapter, we turn our attention to inflation, its causes and consequences, and policies designed to promote price stability. (Chapter 14 discusses the relationship between inflation and unemployment.)

Inflation is a general and continuing increase in prices. This does not imply that all prices are increasing; however, the general trend is upward. The rise in prices must also be continuing; once-and-for-all price increases are excluded. For example, suppose part of the nation's capital stock is destroyed by a natural disaster. With the decrease in the capital stock, the aggregate supply of goods and services is reduced. As a result, the price level rises. After the adjustment process is complete, however, the price level ceases to rise or at least stops rising for that reason.

The main reason for excluding once-and-for-all price increases from the definition of inflation relates to policy. If the increase in the price level is a once-and-for-all increase, no policy action is necessary. Once the adjustment period is past, the price level ceases to increase and policies designed to halt the price increases are not required. In contrast, with inflation, the price level continues to increase until some corrective action is taken.

THE MEASUREMENT OF INFLATION

The three major sources of data measuring prices or price changes are the consumer price index (CPI), the producer price indexes, and the implicit price deflator for gross national product (IPD). The *consumer price index* is based on the price of a fixed market basket of goods and services, which includes food, clothing, shelter, transportation, and entertainment. Prior to 1978, the Bureau of Labor Statistics (BLS) published a single CPI which was based on the purchases of households headed by urban wage earners and clerical workers. Since 1978, the BLS has published two CPIs, the CPI for urban wage earners and clerical workers (CPI-W) and the CPI for all urban consumers (CPI-U). The former covers the purchases of households which account for about 40 percent of the noninstitutional civilian population while the latter covers the purchases of households accounting for about 80 percent of the same population. Both indexes are based on a consumer expenditure survey conducted in major urban areas in 1972 and 1973. The CPI-U is cited more frequently by the media, but movements in the two indexes are highly correlated. These indexes, as well as those for major product categories, are published monthly.

The CPI is often referred to as the cost of living index; this is a misnomer. Even the broadly defined index is based on only the purchases of urban households. Consequently, the index may not be reliable for society as a whole. Moreover, it is an index for a *representative* urban household. For example, food and beverage items receive a weight of about 19 percent in the index. Should food prices increase relatively rapidly, households that allocate more than 19 percent of their expenditures to food and beverages will find their "cost of living" increasing more rapidly than the CPI. Conversely, those that allocate less than 19 percent of their expenditures to food and beverages will find their "cost of living" increasing less rapidly than the CPI.

A similar problem arises over time. The CPI measures the price of a fixed market basket. Over time, consumers find that some prices rise more rapidly than others. Consequently, instead of continuing to buy the same market basket of goods and services, they substitute goods which have risen relatively less in price for goods that have risen relatively more in price. For example, suppose meat prices have risen more rapidly than cheese prices. Families have a tendency to substitute cheese for meat in their diets. To the extent that they do so, their "cost of living" will increase less rapidly than the CPI, which assumes that families continue to buy the same relative amounts of meat and cheese. For these and other reasons, the CPI should not be interpreted as a cost of living index.

Despite the shortcomings of the CPI as a measure of the cost of living, it is a very important concept. It is the most familiar measure of inflation and, as a consequence, is often used as a guide to public policy. The CPI is frequently cited in labor negotiations and usually serves as the basis for cost of living adjustments in wages and salaries. It also serves as the basis for adjusting social security benefits and personal income tax brackets and personal exemptions.

Producer price indexes measure the prices of commodities at various stages of production. The indexes are published both by stage of production and by commodity. The former are divided into indexes for finished goods, intermediate materials, and crude materials. Finished goods are those that will not undergo further processing and are ready for sale to their ultimate users, either households or firms. Intermediate materials are commodities that have been processed but require further processing before they become finished goods. Crude materials include products entering the market for the first time that have not been manufactured or fabricated but will be processed before becoming finished goods. Examples are grains, livestock, crude oil, and iron and steel scrap.

In addition to the indexes just described, an index for all commodities is published. But for analysis of prices in general, the stage-of-processing indexes are more useful than the all-commodities index, because the latter exaggerates price changes. For example, suppose the price of scrap iron increases. The increase will be reflected in higher prices for steel sheets and ultimately for automobiles. The higher price would be reflected in the all-commodities index not once but three times—as scrap iron, as steel sheets, and as automobiles. Consequently, the price increase is overstated greatly.[1]

The producer price indexes have various uses, but so far as we are concerned, they are important because movements in the indexes may foreshadow or lead movements in the CPI. The producer price indexes are published monthly.

As discussed in Chapter 2, the implicit price deflator for gross national product (IPD) is a measure of the prices of all final goods and services produced in the nation's economy during a given period. It is, therefore, a measure of the general price level and is the most comprehensive of the indexes. Like the consumer and producer price indexes, subindexes are available for the IPD. Unlike the other indexes, however, IPD data are published only quarterly. Data for the CPI and IPD for the years 1929–85 are contained in Table 13.1.

THE EFFECTS OF INFLATION

The effects or consequences of inflation differ, depending upon whether inflation is anticipated or unanticipated. *Unanticipated inflation* refers to price increases which are not expected or are larger than expected. For example, suppose people expect no inflation and inflation occurs. The inflation is unanticipated inflation. By the same token, *anticipated inflation* refers to price increases which are expected. If people expect inflation to occur at a 5 percent rate and prices increase at that rate, the inflation is anticipated inflation.

Unanticipated Inflation and the Redistribution of Income and Wealth

With unanticipated inflation, a redistribution of real income occurs. Some individuals gain, because their nominal incomes increase more rapidly than prices. Others lose, because their nominal incomes increase less rapidly than prices. To

TABLE 13.1 The consumer price index and the implicit price deflator for gross national product, 1929–85 (1967 = 100)

Year	Consumer Price Index	Percentage Changes in the Consumer Price Index	Implicit Price Deflator for Gross National Product[1]	Percentage Changes in the Implicit Price Deflator for Gross National Product
1929	51.3		40.7	
1933	38.8		31.2	
1940	42.0		36.2	
1945	53.9		44.0	
1946	58.5	8.5	54.0	22.9
1947	66.9	14.4	61.3	13.9
1948	72.1	7.8	65.7	7.0
1949	71.4	−1.0	65.5	−0.5
1950	72.1	1.0	66.9	2.0
1951	77.8	7.9	69.9	4.8
1952	79.5	2.2	71.0	1.5
1953	80.1	0.8	72.1	1.6
1954	80.5	0.5	73.3	1.6
1955	80.2	−0.4	75.8	3.2
1956	81.4	1.5	78.3	3.4
1957	84.3	3.6	81.1	3.6
1958	86.6	2.7	82.7	2.1
1959	87.3	0.8	84.7	2.4
1960	88.7	1.6	86.1	1.6
1961	89.6	1.0	86.9	1.0
1962	90.6	1.1	88.9	2.2
1963	91.7	1.2	90.3	1.6
1964	92.9	1.3	91.6	1.5
1965	94.5	1.7	94.2	2.7
1966	97.2	2.9	97.5	3.6
1967	100.0	2.9	100.0	2.6
1968	104.2	4.2	105.0	5.0
1969	109.8	5.4	110.9	5.6
1970	116.3	5.9	117.0	5.5
1971	121.3	4.3	123.7	5.7
1972	125.3	3.3	129.5	4.7
1973	133.1	6.2	137.9	6.5
1974	147.7	11.0	150.4	9.1
1975	161.2	9.1	165.2	9.8
1976	170.5	5.8	175.8	6.4
1977	181.5	6.5	187.5	6.7
1978	195.4	7.7	201.1	7.3
1979	217.4	11.3	218.9	8.9
1980	246.8	13.5	238.7	9.0
1981	272.4	10.4	261.8	9.7
1982	289.1	6.1	278.6	6.4
1983	298.4	3.2	289.1	3.8
1984	311.1	4.3	301.1	4.1
1985	322.2	3.6	311.1	3.3

[1]The original data for the implicit price deflator are presented in Table 2.8 with 1982 as the base. For comparison, the data have been transformed so that 1967 equals 100.

Source: *Economic Indicators* (May 1986), p. 23; *1980 Supplement to Economic Indicators* (1980), p. 87.

illustrate, suppose workers in a particular industry accept a long-term contract stipulating 5 percent wage increases annually. The workers reached the agreement anticipating little or no inflation. Now, if inflation occurs, say, at a 10 percent rate, the workers' wages will rise less rapidly than prices.

With unanticipated inflation, a redistribution of wealth also occurs. With inflation, the prices of some assets increase more rapidly than the price level. The owners of the assets benefit, therefore, from the inflation. The prices of other assets, however, increase less rapidly than the price level. The owners of these assets are adversely affected by the inflation.

One important type of redistribution of wealth is that from creditors to debtors. To illustrate, suppose we consider two individuals, A and B, who hold two types of assets—monetary assets and real assets—and one type of liability—monetary debt. If the value of an asset is fixed in nominal terms or if the income from it is fixed in nominal terms, the asset is said to be a *monetary asset*. Monetary assets include currency, checkable deposits, time deposits, and bonds. In contrast, if the value of an asset is not fixed in nominal terms or if the income from it is not fixed in nominal terms, the asset is said to be a *real asset*. Real assets include factories and houses. If inflation occurs, the nominal values of real assets usually increase. *Monetary debt* is an obligation to pay an amount which is fixed in nominal terms now or at some date(s) in the future. Monetary debts includes obligations relating to mortgages and personal loans.

Initially, suppose individual A holds monetary assets totaling $6,000, real assets totaling $30,000, and monetary debt totaling $16,000 (as shown in the following T-account). Individual A may have borrowed, for example, to buy a house. Individual A's net wealth or net worth, the difference between A's assets and liabilities, is $20,000. Similarly, suppose individual B holds monetary assets totaling $18,000 and real assets totaling $2,000 (also shown in the following T-account). Unlike individual A, individual B is not in debt. Individual B's net wealth is also $20,000.

Individual A		Individual B	
Assets	Liabilities and Net Wealth	Assets	Liabilities and Net Wealth
Monetary assets $6,000	Monetary debt $16,000	Monetary assets $18,000	Monetary debt $ 0
Real assets $30,000	Net Wealth $20,000	Real assets $2,000	Net wealth $20,000

Initially, both A and B have the same net wealth, $20,000. Since individual A's monetary debt, $16,000, exceeds his monetary assets, $6,000, A is said to be a *net debtor*. In contrast, individual B's monetary assets, $18,000, exceed her debt, $0; consequently, B is said to be a *net creditor*. Should inflation occur, individual A gains, because A is a net debtor and individual B loses because B is a net creditor.

To illustrate, suppose the price level increases by 100 percent, that the prices of real assets increase at the same rate as prices in general, and that no other changes take place with regard to the T-accounts of the individuals. Given the assumptions, the values of the monetary assets and liabilities of the individuals are unaltered. With the increase in prices, however, the nominal value of individual A's real assets increases to $60,000, while the nominal value of individual B's real assets increases to $4,000 (as shown in the following T-accounts).

Individual A		Individual B	
Assets	Liabilities and Net Wealth	Assets	Liabilities and Net Wealth
Monetary assets $6,000	Monetary debt $16,000	Monetary assets $18,000	Monetary debt $ 0
Real assets $60,000	Net wealth $50,000	Real assets $4,000	Net wealth $22,000

With the increase in prices, individual A's net wealth is now $50,000; individual B's is $22,000. Thus, in nominal terms both experienced increases in net wealth. Individual A had a 150 percent increase (from $20,000 to $50,000); B had only a 10 percent increase (from $20,000 to $22,000). In real terms, individual A experienced an increase in wealth, since the increase in A's wealth in nominal terms, 150 percent, exceeded the increase in prices, 100 percent. In real terms, however, individual B experienced a decrease in wealth, since the increase in B's wealth in nominal terms, 10 percent, was less than the increase in prices, 100 percent.

The reasoning about the gains and losses is straightforward. Inflation reduces the real value of both monetary assets and liabilities. But since individual A is a net debtor, inflation's effect upon liabilities predominates and A gains with inflation. Since individual B is a net creditor, inflation's effect upon assets predominates and B is adversely affected by inflation.

Anticipated Inflation and the Redistribution of Income and Wealth

If inflation is anticipated, the redistribution of income and wealth is minimal. As inflation occurs, people adjust their expectations. Anticipated inflation induces people to act to protect themselves from the effects of the inflation. To illustrate, workers will attempt to include wage increases in their contracts to compensate for the higher expected inflation rate. Alternatively, they will attempt to include a cost-of-living adjustment (COLA) clause which ties their wages to the CPI. Management will accede to provisions of this nature because it anticipates higher product prices. In the short run, some redistribution may occur because of existing contractual arrangements.

Similarly, as people recognize that inflation is occurring, they will buy assets (such as land and gold) to serve as hedges against inflation. Moreover, the anticipated inflation results in increases in the nominal interest rate, thereby reducing or eliminating the redistribution of wealth from creditors to debtors. As discussed in Chapter 11, the nominal interest rate is the sum of the real interest rate and the expected inflation rate. If the real interest rate is 5 percent and the expected inflation rate is 0 percent, the nominal interest rate is 5 percent. If people expect inflation to occur at a 5 percent rate in the future, the nominal interest rate increases to 10 percent. At that rate, persons are willing to lend even though they anticipate inflation, because the higher interest rate compensates them for the loss in purchasing power of the dollar. People are also willing to borrow at that rate, because they expect their nominal income to keep pace with the inflation so that the burden of the debt is no greater than before.

Although the increase in the nominal interest rate minimizes the redistribution of wealth from creditors to debtors, some redistribution may occur in the short run because of debts incurred before the increase in the nominal interest rate. Moreover, no interest is paid on some forms of money and only a limited amount on other forms. Consequently, the increase in the interest rate does not compensate those who hold money for the increase in prices.

When people realize that inflation is occurring, they try to reduce their holdings of money.[2] To minimize their holdings, households may make more use of credit cards and charge accounts; firms may pay their employees more often and alter the frequency of their orders. In general, both households and firms will devote more resources to asset management and to nonmonetary (barter) transactions in order to minimize their holdings of money. To the extent that resources are devoted to these activities, society's output of goods and services is reduced.

Other Effects of Inflation

Inflation has other effects upon the economy. For example, the government benefits from inflation in two ways. It is a net debtor and, with inflation, wealth is redistributed from net creditors to net debtors. It also benefits because part of our nation's tax system is based on nominal rather than real income. Consequently, additional real tax revenue may be generated even if real income is constant.

Although our personal income tax system has been indexed since 1985, we may illustrate the nature of the problem in terms of the pre-1985 system. Under that system, individuals could find themselves in higher marginal tax brackets as a result of inflation even if their real incomes were constant. Under such circumstances, they experience a reduction in their real after-tax income. To illustrate, suppose an individual has a yearly (pretax) income of $20,000 with a tax liability equal to 20 percent of his income ($4,000). His after-tax or disposable income is $16,000. If the IPD is 100, his real pretax and after-tax incomes are $20,000 and $16,000, respectively.

Next, suppose, over a period of years, that the price level increases by 100 percent, and that the individual's (pretax) income increases to $40,000. Since the new IPD is 200, the individual's real (pretax) income is still $20,000. Although his real pretax income is the same, his real after-tax income is less. With the increase in nominal income, the individual is pushed into higher tax brackets. Consequently, instead of the tax liability being 20 percent, it may be 30 percent of his income, or $12,000. With the increase in tax liability, the individual's after-tax income is $28,000; but, in real terms, it is only $14,000, obtained by dividing $28,000 by the new IPD. Thus, the effect of inflation has been to reduce the individual's real after-tax income from $16,000 to $14,000.

With inflation, a larger fraction of real income accrues to the government in the form of tax revenue. The net result is a transfer of real income from individuals to the government and, ultimately, to those who benefit from government spending. The redistribution of income (and, since the government is a net debtor, wealth) may or may not be desirable. It must be recognized, however, that the transfer takes place without legislative action to increase tax rates. Voters, therefore, have no opportunity to express their approval or disapproval. Moreover, since inflation is an alternative to higher tax rates, it may reduce the government's resolve to stop it.

To prevent the redistribution of real income, personal income taxes were indexed starting January 1, 1985. The indexation links tax rates, personal exemptions, and standard deductions to the CPI. If inflation occurs, the rates, personal exemptions, and standard deductions are altered so that real tax revenue remains the same. Each year's adjustment is based on September-to-September movements in the CPI for tax returns due the following April.[3]

Although our personal income tax system is now indexed, the corporate income tax system is not. As a result, additional real tax revenue may be generated merely because of inflation. Moreover, the system is likely to discourage investment and distort its allocation during periods of inflation. To illustrate, let us consider two features of the corporate tax system which act to raise real corporate income taxes and reduce real after-tax corporate income during periods of inflation: the treatments of depreciation allowances and inventory profits.

In determining profits, firms are permitted to deduct allowances for depreciation of their plant and equipment. These allowances, however, are based on *original* costs, not *replacement* costs. When inflation is occurring, the original costs will be less than replacement costs, and the maximum depreciation allowance will be less than the true cost of replacing plant and equipment. Consequently, firms will be unable to deduct their "true" depreciation, and corporate profits will be overstated. Higher reported profits, of course, result in a greater tax liability for the firm.

The tax increase affects investment in two ways. First, by reducing real after-tax profits, it discourages investment.[4] Second, since original costs approximate more closely replacement costs in the short run than in the long run, firms tend to concentrate on short-term projects, thereby distorting the allocation of resources. Both problems are made worse by higher rates of inflation, because a higher inflation rate results in higher reported profits and, therefore, greater tax liabilities.

Profits arising from sales from inventory are taxed at the same rate as other profits. Therefore, the accounting procedure used to calculate the value of business inventories is important in determining a firm's tax liability. As discussed in Chapter 2, firms typically use either the FIFO or the LIFO method, with the FIFO method resulting in higher reported profits and therefore greater tax liabilities during periods of inflation.

Unlike depreciation, for which original costs must be used, firms need not use the FIFO method. But many firms continue to use it despite the fact that their tax liabilities are increased during periods of inflation. (Many are reluctant to change because of the costs involved in making the switch and because of the reduction in reported profits.) Because of the persistence of firms in using FIFO, the real tax burden associated with inventories is increased significantly as the inflation rate rises.

To the extent that inflation interacts with the present corporate tax system to discourage investment and distort its allocation, the system reduces the nation's growth rate.[5] For this reason, many, if not most, economists favor restructuring or indexing the corporate tax system. We shall return to this topic in Chapter 18.

Inflation also creates uncertainty, which, in turn, has adverse effects upon the economy. Uncertainty exists because inflation does not occur at a steady rate. In addition, the variability of the inflation rate increases as the inflation rate rises, thereby causing even greater uncertainty.[6] With uncertainty, resources are allocated from production to forecasting. Resources are also reallocated to searching for protection from the inflation and to speculation. For example, parties will be reluctant to enter into long-term contracts because of the uncertainty. As a result, the efficiencies associated with such contracts will be lost and additional resources will be diverted from production to handle the more frequent negotiations. To the extent that fewer resources are devoted to production, the nation's output of goods and services is reduced.

Inflation may cause balance of payments problems. If a country's rate of inflation exceeds that of the rest of the world, the country's competitive position in world markets deteriorates and a balance of payments deficit may develop. With flexible exchange rates, the likelihood of a deficit is minimized, since exchange rates tend to adjust to compensate for the inflation. The effect of an increase in the price level on the balance of payments is discussed in more detail in Chapter 16.

Finally, should the rate of inflation become sufficiently great, money may lose its traditional functions as a medium of exchange and as a unit of account. If so, exchange would proceed on the basis of barter—goods and services being directly exchanged for other goods and services. Such an arrangement is highly inefficient and is likely to be accompanied by a collapse of the economy.

THE CAUSES OF INFLATION

From a discussion of the effects of inflation, we turn to the theory of inflation. In this regard, we note that (1) inflation is a long-term phenomenon and (2) it is a monetary phenomenon. That inflation is a long-run phenomenon follows from the definition of inflation as a general and *continuing* increase in prices. To show that it is a monetary phenomenon, we consider inflation from the Keynesian and other perspectives. We start with the classical and monetarist views.

The Classical and Monetarist Views

The classical theory of inflation can be analyzed in terms of the equation of exchange, $MsV = PY$. This equation may be rewritten as

$$\frac{\Delta Ms}{Ms} + \frac{\Delta V}{V} = \frac{\Delta P}{P} + \frac{\Delta Y}{Y},$$

where $\Delta P/P$ is the inflation rate and $\Delta Ms/Ms$, $\Delta V/V$, and $\Delta Y/Y$ are the growth rates of the money supply, velocity, and output, respectively. If the velocity of money is constant, $\Delta V/V$ is 0, and the equation becomes

(13.1) $$\frac{\Delta Ms}{Ms} = \frac{\Delta P}{P} + \frac{\Delta Y}{Y}.^7$$

Equation (13.1) states that the growth rate of the money supply equals the inflation rate plus the growth rate of output.

Suppose the money supply and output are growing at the same rate, say, 3.0 percent, implying that aggregate demand and aggregate supply are also growing at that rate. Aggregate demand grows at the same rate as the money supply because an increase in the money supply causes a proportional increase in aggregate demand in the classical model (see Chapter 11). Aggregate supply increases because of technological progress, capital accumulation, and increases in the supply of labor. Since the classical economists assumed full employment to be the normal state of affairs, the only way output can grow at a 3.0 percent rate over time is for aggregate supply to grow at that rate. (Historically, the average annual increase in real GNP in the United States has been about 3.0 percent.) The increases in aggregate demand and aggregate supply are shown in Figure 13.1.

With aggregate demand and aggregate supply growing at the same rate, the price level, P_0 in Figure 13.1, is constant, implying that no inflation is occurring. This result ($\Delta P/P = 0$) may be confirmed by substituting the 3.0 percent growth rates for the money supply and output into equation (13.1).

Next, suppose the growth rate of the money supply increases to, say, 6.0 percent. With the rise in the growth rate of the money supply, aggregate demand will increase more rapidly. The growth rate of aggregate supply will be unaltered,

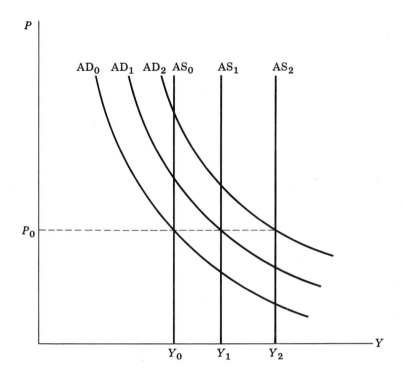

FIGURE 13.1

Aggregate demand, aggregate supply, and the price level in the classical model

however, because the factors which determine the growth rate of aggregate supply are independent of the growth rate of the money supply. With the money supply and aggregate demand growing at a 6.0 percent rate and aggregate supply at a 3.0 percent rate, the inflation rate rises from 0.0 percent to 3.0 percent (as equation (13.1) confirms).[8]

    With the growth rate of aggregate demand linked to the growth rate of the money supply, this analysis suggests that the more rapidly the money supply increases, the higher the inflation rate will be. Moreover, since the growth rate of output is constant (or approximately so), the implication is that inflation is a monetary phenomenon and the classical economists viewed it as such.

    Like the classical economists, monetarists believe that inflation is a monetary phenomenon. Indeed, the monetarist view of inflation is very similar to that of the classical economists in almost all respects. Unlike the classical economists, however, monetarists argue that an increase in the money supply causes increases in both the price level and output in the short run. Like the classical economists, they stress that an increase in the growth rate of the money supply affects the inflation rate rather than the growth rate in the long run.[9]

    The foregoing discussion suggests that inflation is a monetary phenomenon.

One implication of this view is that the Federal Reserve has an important role to play in achieving price stability. If inflation is occurring, for example, the Fed can reduce the growth rate of the money supply, thereby reducing or eliminating the inflation. We discuss the policy implications in more detail later in this chapter as well as in Chapters 14, 15, and 19.

The Keynesian View

Although the classical economists believed that inflation is a monetary phenomenon, Keynes did much, intentionally or unintentionally, to convince people otherwise.[10] Keynes emphasized that the velocity of money is a variable, not a constant, so that an increase in the money supply may, in the extreme case, leave the price level unchanged. This follows if, for example, the demand for money is perfectly interest elastic. In this situation, the additional money balances are simply absorbed into idle balances. Thus, even though the relationship $MsV = PY$ holds, the increase in the money supply, Ms, is offset by the decrease in the velocity of money, V, so as to leave the price level unchanged.

Keynes's emphasis on the variability of output and the short run also contributed to the view that inflation is not a purely monetary phenomenon. Unlike the classical economists, Keynes believed that unemployment could exist for prolonged periods of time. With unemployment, an increase in the money supply (except in extreme cases) causes both the price level and output to increase (see Chapter 10). With the increase in output, the increase in the price level will be less than proportional to the increase in the money supply, even if the velocity of money is constant.

As just illustrated, the money supply is a determinant of the price level in the Keynesian model. In the short run, however, many other variables, including consumption, investment, government purchases, and taxes, are determinants of the price level. If firms decide to invest more, for example, aggregate demand increases and the price level rises (see Chapter 10). (In the classical model, it is the interest rate, not aggregate demand and the price level, that increases.) The same sort of analysis holds for consumption, government purchases, and taxes.

The preceding analysis suggests that many variables, including the money supply, affect the price level in the short run. Even early Keynesians recognized, however, that the price level could not continue to rise in the absence of increases in the money supply. In the case of an investment boom, the increase in the interest rate (in the absence of increases in the money supply) would eventually choke off the increases in investment and, therefore, aggregate demand. The same would be true of increases in government purchases (or decreases in taxes). Without increases in the money supply, the increase in the interest rate would eventually depress private spending by amounts sufficient to offset the increases in government purchases.[11] Despite the recognition that the price level could not increase indefinitely without increases in the money supply, this aspect was frequently overlooked by early Keynesians because of their emphasis on the short run.

Like the classical economists and monetarists, contemporary Keynesians believe that inflation is a monetary phenomenon and, as a consequence, they place emphasis on reducing the growth rate of the money supply in order to reduce the inflation rate.[12] As we shall see in the next two chapters, however, Keynesians and monetarists differ with regard to several issues relating to inflation, including the costs associated with reducing the inflation rate.

Before turning to the rational expectations and supply-side views, it is convenient to note that since the money supply is only one determinant of the price level in the short run, the actual increase in the price level in the short run may deviate from the rate that is consistent with the growth rate of the money supply in the long run. In the future, we shall refer to the latter as the *underlying inflation rate*. Suppose the economy is experiencing an investment boom. In the short run, the price level will rise at a rate greater than the underlying rate. Similarly, suppose crude oil prices fall as they did in 1981 and 1982. In the short run, the price level will rise at a rate less than the underlying rate. Because the price level is determined by various factors in the short run, the actual increase in the price level may deviate from the underlying rate in the short run. If it does, policy makers and others may be misled. It may appear to them that inflation is less (greater) than it really is. As a result, they may adopt policies which are inappropriate.

The Rational Expectations and Supply-Side Views

Rational expectations theorists view inflation as a monetary phenomenon. Moreover, they believe that anticipated changes in the money supply affect only the price level. In this regard, the rational expectations view is much closer to the classical position than it is to the monetarist and Keynesian positions. Since rational expectations theorists believe inflation is a monetary phenomenon, they assert that the money supply is the key to achieving price stability.

Supply-side economists also view inflation as a monetary phenomenon. Consequently, they favor monetary restraint to reduce inflation. At the same time, they favor reducing tax rates in order to increase the growth rate of aggregate supply. By increasing the growth rate of aggregate supply, they believe that the inflation rate will be reduced. Unfortunately, supply-side policies alone cannot reduce the inflation rate significantly. To illustrate, suppose that aggregate demand is increasing at a 13 percent rate while aggregate supply is increasing at a 3 percent rate. The result is an inflation rate of 10 percent, obtained by subtracting the rate of increase in aggregate supply from the corresponding rate for aggregate demand. Suppose supply-side policies are enacted and, as a result, aggregate supply now increases at a 4 percent rate. The increase in the growth rate of aggregate supply from 3 to 4 percent represents a 33 ⅓ percent increase, a huge increase by historical standards. Even so, the resulting reduction in the inflation rate is modest. Assuming that aggregate demand continues to increase at the 13 percent rate (recall that supply-side policies alone may result in a higher rate of increase in aggregate demand), the inflation rate will drop from 10 percent to 9 percent, obtained by subtracting the new rate of increase in aggregate supply from the rate of increase in aggregate demand. This reduction in the inflation rate is small, and in a world in which inflation rates vary substantially from year to year, it would be difficult to detect in the short run. Thus, supply-side policies alone are unlikely to reduce the rate of inflation significantly; policies designed to reduce aggregate demand are necessary. This does not mean that supply-side policies are undesirable. In conjunction with a program for reducing the rate of increase in aggregate demand, they make a contribution in reducing the inflation rate. More importantly, by increasing the nation's growth rate, they make higher standards of living possible.

Monopoly Power and Inflation

Despite general agreement that inflation is a monetary phenomenon, some people argue that inflation is due to the monopolistic actions of some economic groups, labor unions and firms, in society. According to this view, inflation is caused by labor unions forcing up money wages more rapidly than they would otherwise increase. Alternatively, inflation is caused by the monopolistic practices of managers who increase prices even in the absence of increases in demand or rising costs.

Suppose unions, through the collective bargaining process, are successful in gaining wage increases greater than those implied by market forces. Assuming these increases are large enough to increase significantly the average money wage for the economy, aggregate supply will decrease relative to aggregate demand and the price level will rise. Under these circumstances, labor unions may be said to be responsible for the increase in the price level.

Despite the possibility just outlined, most economists doubt that labor unions cause inflation. First, labor unions (in the aggregate) may lack the power to influence the course of money wages for union members.[13] To be sure, some unions are powerful and have influenced the course of money wages of their members. Others, however, have little or no bargaining power. Second, even if labor unions can alter the course of money wages of their members, it is doubtful that they can alter significantly the course of money wages for the economy as a whole. Only about 19 percent of wage and salary earners belongs to unions. If unions are successful in raising money and real wages, they necessarily reduce employment in the union sector because of the negatively sloped demand curve for labor. Therefore, more workers seek employment in the nonunionized sector; this increase in labor supply reduces money and real wages in the nonunionized sector. Consequently, even if unions have enough monopoly power to alter the course of money wages for union members, the average money wage for the economy may not be affected.

Finally, even if labor unions have sufficient monopoly power to alter the course of money wages for the economy as a whole (a very doubtful proposition), the process cannot continue indefinitely without increases in the money supply. As aggregate supply falls relative to aggregate demand, unemployment rises, forcing unions to moderate their wage demands. Thus, if the increases in money wages and prices are to continue, the Federal Reserve must act to increase the money supply. Inflation is a monetary phenomenon even in this case.

We now turn to the argument that managers cause inflation through monopolistic pricing policies. Of course, if the economy were characterized by pure competition, this could not occur. Individual firms would have no control over prices; prices would be determined by the forces of demand and supply.[14] Few people, however, suggest that our economy is characterized by pure competition. Some industries are purely competitive or approximately so; others are not. Therefore, many firms have monopoly power to set prices.

Even if many (or most) industries are characterized by imperfect competition, inflation is not inevitable. Economic theory suggests that monopoly pricing has no special relevance to inflation.[15] For given demand and cost conditions, a monopolist sets a profit-maximizing price. This price is greater than the purely competitive price. In the absence of increases in demand and/or costs, however, a monopolist has no incentive to increase price. If demand and/or costs increase, the monopolist normally sets a higher price. In these circumstances, however, the monopolist is reacting to changing conditions, not initiating inflation. Thus, economic theory suggests that prices are higher under monopoly than under pure competition; it does not suggest that prices should rise more rapidly under monopoly than under pure competition.[16]

One possibility is that the economy is becoming more monopolistic. The price level would rise as firms raise their prices relative to what they had been under pure competition.[17] Although this is a possibility, there is little or no evidence to suggest that the economy as a whole is becoming more monopolistic. Although some industries are becoming more monopolistic, others are becoming less monopolistic so that little or no trend exists for the economy as a whole. In conclusion, the argument that firms cause inflation through monopolistic pricing practices has little or no theoretical and empirical support.

Although few economists believe that inflation is due to monopoly power, some do. If they are correct, the policy implications are quite different from those outlined earlier. To illustrate, if inflation is caused by the monopolistic practices of labor unions and management, the obvious solution is to make the economy more competitive so that the ability of labor unions and firms to push up money wages and prices is reduced or eliminated. If that is not possible for political or other reasons, some form of incomes policy may be necessary. By *incomes policy*, we mean governmental action—excluding monetary and fiscal measures—designed to influence or control the rate of increase of prices, money wages, and other forms of income. Incomes policy includes both wage–price guidelines and controls. These policies and the U.S. experience with them are discussed at length in Chapter 20.

CONCLUDING REMARKS

In this chapter, we considered the causes and consequences of inflation. In doing so, we emphasized the inflation is both a long-run and a monetary phenomenon. Although appropriate, the emphasis on the long run has some costs. For one thing, it obscures the impact of a change in the growth rate of the money supply on output and employment in the short run. For another, it conceals important differences among the Keynesian, monetarist, rational expectations, and supply-side theories regarding inflation. Although all agree that inflation is a monetary phenomenon, substantial disagreement exists as to the nature of the short-run tradeoff between inflation and unemployment, the costs associated with reducing inflation, and the appropriate policies to reduce the inflation rate.

In the next chapter, we consider the inflationary process with a view to determining the impact of a change in the growth rate of the money supply on output and employment in the short run. Based on this analysis, we examine alternative views regarding the short-run tradeoff between inflation and unemployment. In Chapter 15, we discuss alternative views regarding the costs associated with reducing the inflation rate and the appropriate policies for reducing inflation.

NOTES ————————————————————————————————

1. Historically, the producer price indexes have had a number of shortcomings. For discussions of these deficiencies and the steps that have been or are being taken to overcome them, see John F. Early, "Improving the Measurement of Producer Price Change," *Monthly Labor Review* (April 1978), 7–15, and "The Producer Price Index Revision: Overview and Pilot Survey Results," *Monthly Labor Review* (December 1979), 11–19.

2. With the shift from unanticipated inflation, the demand for money is reduced, which results in a higher rate of inflation. For a discussion, see Reuben A. Kessel and Armen A. Alchian, "Effects of Inflation," *Journal of Political Economy*, 70 (December 1962), 521–37.

3. For a discussion, see John A. Tatom, "Federal Income Tax Reform in 1985: Indexation," Federal Reserve Bank of St. Louis, *Review*, 67 (February 1985), 5–12.

4. For illustrations, see John A. Tatom and James E. Turley, "Inflation and Taxes: Disincentives for Capital Formation," Federal Reserve Bank of St. Louis, *Review*, 60 (January 1978), 2–8.

5. For discussions of the effects of the 1981 and 1982 tax acts, see Mack Ott, "Depreciation, Inflation and Investment Incentives: The Effects of the Tax Acts of 1981 and 1982," Federal Reserve Bank of St. Louis, *Review*, 66 (November 1984), 17–30; and Allen Sinai, Andrew Lin, and Russell Robins, "Taxes, Saving, and Investment: Some Empirical Evidence," *National Tax Journal*, 36 (September 1983), 321–45.

6. For new evidence and summaries of earlier studies, see A. Steven Holland, "Does Higher Inflation Lead to More Uncertain Inflation?" Federal Reserve Bank of St. Louis, *Review*, 66 (February 1984), 15–26.

7. In the analysis, the velocity of money need not be constant. It could, for example, be rising as it has been in the United States since World War II. On the other hand, it should not be highly variable.

8. With the increase in the inflation rate, the real amount of money demanded decreases, implying that the velocity of money increases. With the increase in velocity, the equilibrium inflation rate will be greater than 3.0 percent. For simplicity, we ignore the effect of the increase in the inflation rate on velocity.

9. For references to the classical and monetarist views, see Chapter 11.

10. See Thomas M. Humphrey, "Keynes on Inflation," in *Essays on Inflation*, 3rd ed., (Richmond, Va.: Federal Reserve Bank of Richmond, 1982), pp., 38–48.

11. Some people argue that budget deficits cause inflation. This is true if and only if the deficit is financed, in whole or in part, by increasing the money supply. As we shall see in Chapter 18, it is by no means inevitable that deficits will be financed in that manner.

12. In terms of the equation of exchange, contemporary Keynesians believe that the velocity of money shows much greater stability in the long run than in the short run. Similarly, they believe that the output growth rate is constant or approximately so in the long run despite its variability over the business cycle.

13. For discussions, see H. G. Lewis, *Unionism and Relative Wages in the United States* (Chicago: University of Chicago Press, 1963); Daniel J. B. Mitchell, *Unions, Wages, and Inflation* (Washington, D.C.: The Brookings Institution, 1980); and C. J. Parsley, "Labor Union Effects on Wage Gains: A Survey of Recent Literature," *Journal of Economic Literature*, 18 (March 1980), 1–31.

14. The same would be true of money wages if labor markets were purely competitive.

15. For a discussion, see George J. Stigler, "Administered Prices and Oligopolistic Inflation," *Journal of Business*, 35 (January 1962), 1–13. For discussions of the empirical evidence, see F. M. Scherer, *Industrial Market Structure and Economic Performance*, 2nd ed. (Chicago: Rand McNally & Company, 1980); and Steven Lustgarten, *Industrial Concentration and Inflation* (Washington, D.C.: American Enterprise Institute, 1975).

16. One could argue that firms do not set a profit-maximizing price immediately because they fear antitrust action, new entry, and so on, but rather, gradually increase prices to their profit-maximizing levels. If this is the case, prices will eventually stop rising unless there are increases in either demand or costs.

17. In aggregate terms, aggregate supply would fall relative to aggregate demand.

REVIEW QUESTIONS —————————————————————

1. Define inflation and explain why once-and-for-all increases in the price level are excluded from the definition of inflation.

2. The consumer price index, the producer price indexes, and the implicit price deflator for gross national product are price indexes. Compare and contrast them. Which index is the most relevant when discussing inflation? Defend your answer.

3. A redistribution of income and wealth occurs when inflation is unanticipated. Little or no redistribution occurs when inflation is anticipated. Are these statements correct? Why? Why not?

4. Wealth may be redistributed from creditors to debtors as the result of inflation.

Can wealth ever be redistributed from debtors to creditors? Under what circumstances?

5. Describe the impact of inflation upon

   a. government.

   b. the nation's exports and imports.

6. List and briefly discuss the various ways in which inflation may reduce the nation's output of goods and services.

7. Inflation is said to be a monetary phenomenon. Explain.

8. According to Keynesians, many variables determine the price level in the short run. List some of these variables and explain how each affects the price level in the short run.

9. Explain how the actual change in the price level in the short run may differ from the rate that is consistent with the growth rate of the money supply in the long run. How might this mislead policy makers?

10. Explain why supply-side policies alone are unlikely to reduce the inflation rate significantly. If this is true, why are supply-side policies desirable?

11. Some people argue that labor unions cause inflation. Outline and critically evaluate this argument.

12. Suppose inflation is occurring and money wages are increasing more rapidly than productivity. Does this necessarily imply that the inflation is caused by labor unions? Defend your answer.

SUGGESTED READING

ACKLEY, GARDNER, "The Costs of Inflation," *American Economic Review*, 68 (May 1978), 149–54.

FISCHER, STANLEY, and FRANCO MODIGLIANI, "Towards an Understanding of the Real Effects and Costs of Inflation," *Weltwirtschaftliches Archiv*, 114 (1978), 810–33.

FRIEDMAN, MILTON, "Money: Quantity Theory," *International Encyclopedia of the Social Sciences*, vol. 10, pp. 432–47. New York: Macmillan, Inc., 1968.

FRISCH, HELMUT, *Theories of Inflation*. New York: Cambridge University Press, 1983.

HALL, ROBERT E. (ed.), *Inflation: Causes and Effects*. Chicago: University of Chicago Press, 1982.

LAIDLER, DAVID E. W., and MICHAEL J. PARKIN, "Inflation: A Survey," *Economic Journal*, 85 (December 1975), 741–809.

U.S. Department of Labor, Bureau of Labor Statistics, *CPI Detailed Report*. Washington, D.C.: Government Printing Office, monthly.

———, *Producer Prices and Price Indexes*. Washington, D.C.: Government Printing Office, monthly.

WALLACE, WILLIAM H., and WILLIAM E. CULLISON, *Measuring Price Changes: A Study of Price Indexes* (4th ed.), Federal Reserve Bank of Richmond, Va., April 1979.

14

THE INFLATIONARY PROCESS

In the previous chapter, we emphasized that inflation is a long-run phenomenon and focused upon the effects of inflation in that context. In this chapter, we place more emphasis on the short run and examine the effects of a change in the growth rate of the money supply. In doing so, we find that a tradeoff between inflation and unemployment exists, but only in the short run. After considering the tradeoff from the Keynesian, monetarist, rational expectations, and supply-side perspectives, we consider recent U.S. experience with inflation and unemployment.

A PREVIEW OF THE ARGUMENT

In the following sections, we outline an inflationary process. This process has two phases—expansion and stabilization. During the *expansion phase*, the growth rate of the money supply and, hence, the inflation rate increase. Since labor's expectations regarding inflation are assumed to adjust slowly, the actual inflation rate exceeds the expected inflation rate and output and employment increase. The increases in output and employment, however, are only temporary. If the inflation rate remains at the new, higher level, labor's expectations adjust until the expected inflation rate equals the actual inflation rate. With the adjustment, output and employment return to their long-run equilibrium levels. During the *stabilization phase*, the growth rate of the money supply and, therefore, the inflation rate decrease. Since labor's expectations regarding inflation do not adjust immediately, the expected inflation rate exceeds the actual rate and output and employment decrease. Once again, however, the decreases are only temporary. Labor's expectations adjust until the expected inflation rate equals the actual rate and output and employment return to their long-run equilibrium levels.

Because labor's expectations do not adjust immediately, a change in the inflation rate causes a change in the unemployment rate in the opposite direction, resulting in a tradeoff between inflation and unemployment. This tradeoff is only temporary because, as labor's expectations adjust, the unemployment rate returns to its long-run equilibrium level.

INFLATION AND THE LABOR MARKET

In the previous chapters, the supply of labor was assumed to be a function of the real wage. Mathematically, the relationship is

$$S_N = h\left(\frac{W}{P}\right),$$

where S_N is the amount of labor supplied and W/P is the real wage. Implicitly, it was assumed that prospective workers know both the money wage and the price level and therefore can make the appropriate employment decisions. This assumption may not be correct. If the inflation rate increases and the increase is unanticipated, prospective workers will believe that the price level is less than the actual price level. Nevertheless, they still make their employment decisions upon what they *think* the real wage is and will be. To take into account the possibility that labor's perception of the price level may not be correct, we postulate that the supply of labor is a function of the *perceived* or *expected* real wage. Mathematically, the relationship is

$$S_N = h\left(\frac{W}{P^e}\right),$$

where S_N is the amount of labor supplied and W/P^e is the expected or perceived real wage. The expected or perceived real wage is, in turn, the ratio of the money wage, W, to the expected or perceived price level, P^e.[1] For our immediate purposes, we assume that labor forms its expectations of the price level adaptively. As discussed in Chapter 13, this means that labor's expectations are based upon past price levels with the most recent price level weighted most heavily and prior period price levels weighted less and less heavily. Because expectations are assumed to be based solely on past price levels, expectations adjust relatively slowly to changing circumstances. (We shall relax the adaptive expectations assumption later.)

In previous chapters, the demand for labor was assumed to be a function of the real wage. In equation form, the relationship is

$$D_N = g\left(\frac{W}{P}\right),$$

where D_N is the amount of labor demanded and W/P is the real wage. We shall continue to use this assumption. In doing so, we recognize that management's task is easier than labor's. In making decisions with regard to employment, a firm must take into consideration, in the short run, only the money wage (or wages) it pays and the price (or prices) that it receives for its product (or products). In contrast, workers must take into consideration the money wage they are to get and the prices of all the goods and services they buy.

Since labor may not correctly perceive the price level, we have the possibility of two labor supply curves—the labor supply curve perceived by workers and the actual labor supply curve. The *perceived labor supply curve*, S_P, shows the number of prospective job holders as a function of the perceived real wage. The *actual labor supply curve*, S_a, shows the number of prospective job holders as a function of the actual real wage. If labor correctly perceives the price level, the perceived and actual supply of labor curves are the same, as indicated by the coincidence of S_p and S_a in Figure 14.1.

On the other hand, if labor incorrectly perceives the price level, the two curves diverge because of the difference between the perceived and actual price levels. For example, suppose prices increase. If labor believes that prices are unchanged, a divergence emerges between the perceived and actual supply of labor

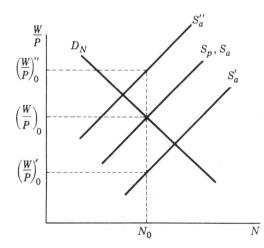

FIGURE 14.1

The relationship between the perceived and actual supply of labor curves

curves. In particular, the actual supply of labor curve, S'_a, will lie to the right of the perceived curve, S_p, as shown in Figure 14.1. Suppose, at employment level N_0, the money wage is \$20,000 per year. If the perceived price index number is 100 percent, the perceived real wage is also \$20,000 per year or $(W/P)_0$. On the other hand, if the actual price index number is 125 percent, the real wage is \$16,000 per year or $(W/P)'_0$. The first combination is represented by a point on the perceived labor supply curve S_p, and the second by a point on the actual supply curve S'_a. Consequently, if the actual price level is greater than the perceived price level, the actual labor supply curve will lie to the right of the perceived labor supply curve.

Conversely, if the actual price level is lower than the perceived price level, the relationship between the two curves will be reversed; the actual labor supply curve will lie to the left of the perceived curve. For example, suppose at employment level N_0 the money wage is \$20,000 per year. If the perceived price index number is 100, the perceived real wage is also \$20,000 per year or $(W/P)_0$. If the actual price index number is 80, the real wage is \$25,000 per year or $(W/P)''_0$. The first combination is represented by a point on the perceived labor supply curve S_p; the second, by a point on the actual supply of labor curve S''_a. Thus, if the actual price level is lower than the perceived price level, the actual labor supply curve will lie to the left of the perceived labor supply curve.

We shall now trace the adjustment to unexpected inflation in the labor market. To do so, we need to follow the market over a number of market periods, with a *market period* being defined as a length of time during which the demand and supply curves do not change. In each period, the equilibrium levels of the real wage and employment are given by the intersection of the period's actual labor demand and supply curves.[2] For example, suppose the price level has been constant for a number of periods. If labor expects no inflation and none occurs, the perceived and actual price levels are equal and the perceived labor supply curve, S_p, and actual labor supply curve, S_a, coincide, as shown in Figure 14.2. The equilibrium real wage is $(W/P)_0$ and the equilibrium level of employment is N_0.

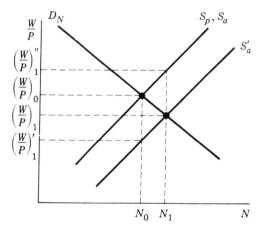

FIGURE 14.2

An unexpected increase in the inflation rate and the labor market

Next, suppose the growth rate of the money supply and, hence, the inflation rate increase. If labor fails to perceive the increase in the inflation rate, the perceived and actual labor supply curves diverge with the actual curve, S'_a, lying to the right of the perceived curve, S_p. Initially, the real wage is $(W/P)_0$ and employment is N_0. With the increase in the price level, the real wage decreases to $(W/P)'_1$. At real wage $(W/P)'_1$, however, more labor is demanded than supplied, and the money wage increases. As a result, the new equilibrium real wage is $(W/P)_1$, which is less than the original equilibrium level $(W/P)_0$. With the reduction in the real wage, firms are willing to hire N_1 workers. Since labor did not perceive the increase in the price level, workers believe, with the increase in the money wage, that the real wage has increased to $(W/P)''_1$. As a consequence, N_1 workers are willing to accept employment. Thus, employment increases from N_0 to N_1.

With the unanticipated increase in the inflation rate, employment increases, but only temporarily. As the price level rises (or rises more rapidly), labor will adjust its expectations and the actual labor supply curve will shift to the left, thereby reducing employment. Assuming the inflation rate remains constant, labor's expectations will eventually prove to be correct. When that happens, the actual and perceived labor supply curves will again coincide and employment will be N_0, the original equilibrium level.

Suppose the monetary authorities believe that the inflation rate is too high and reduce the growth rate of the money supply. As a result, the inflation rate drops. If the reduction in the inflation rate takes labor by surprise, the perceived and actual labor supply curves diverge, as shown in Figure 14.3, with the actual curve, S''_a, lying to the left of the perceived curve, S_p. Since the actual inflation rate is less than the expected rate, the actual real wage, $(W/P)'_2$, is greater than the perceived real wage, $(W/P)_0$, at employment level N_0. At real wage $(W/P)'_2$, more labor is supplied than demanded, and the money wage falls, at least in relative terms. As a result, a new equilibrium real wage, $(W/P)_2$, is established. This real wage is greater than the original equilibrium real wage $(W/P)_0$.

With the increase in the real wage, employment decreases from N_0 to N_2. Firms have an incentive to reduce employment because of the increase in the real wage. In addition, fewer people have an incentive to work because labor believes, erroneously as it turns out, that the real wage has decreased from $(W/P)_0$ to $(W/P)''_2$. They hold this belief because they observe the reduction in the money wage and because they fail to recognize that the inflation rate has decreased.

With the unexpected reduction in the inflation rate, employment decreases, but, once again, the change is only temporary. As the price level increases less rapidly, labor adjusts its expectations to reflect the new reality. As a result, the actual labor supply curve shifts to the right and employment increases. The expected inflation rate will eventually equal the actual rate and the actual and perceived labor supply curves will coincide. In that situation, employment will be N_0, the original equilibrium level.

In conclusion, we note that when the expected inflation rate equals the actual inflation rate, the actual and perceived labor supply curves coincide and employ-

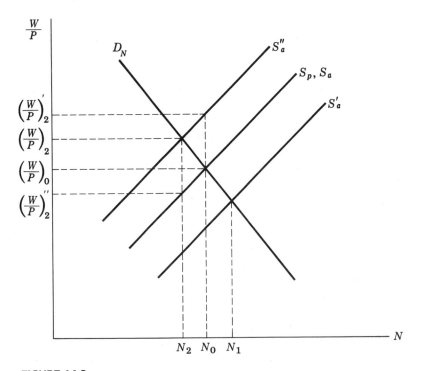

FIGURE 14.3

An unexpected decrease in the inflation rate and the labor market

ment is N_0. Although the expected inflation rate may not equal the actual rate in the short run, the two rates are equal in the long run because labor will, sooner or later, adjust its expectations to reflect reality. Since labor's expectations are correct in the long run, we may regard N_0 as the long-run equilibrium level of employment.[3]

In the short run, employment may deviate from its long-run equilibrium level, N_0, because of unanticipated changes in the inflation rate. If an unanticipated increase (decrease) in the inflation rate occurs, the actual labor supply curve lies to the right (left) of the perceived labor supply curve and employment increases (decreases) to N_1 (N_2). The increase (decrease) in employment is only a temporary, or short-run, phenomenon because, in the long run, labor's expectations will adjust to reflect the new reality. As that happens, employment returns to its long-run equilibrium level, N_0.

INFLATION AND AGGREGATE SUPPLY

The new labor supply function, $S_N = h(W/P^e)$, may be used to derive the aggregate supply curve. The result is two versions of the aggregate supply curve, the long run and the short run. In the long run, labor's perceptions of the price level are correct and the *long-run aggregate supply curve* is vertical. In the short run, labor's perceptions of the price level may be incorrect. As a consequence, the *short-run aggregate supply curve* may be positively sloped.

To derive the long-run aggregate supply curve, we proceed as follows: suppose no inflation is occurring and none is expected so that the perceived and actual labor supply curves coincide, as shown in Figure 14.4. The level of employment is N_0 and the corresponding level of output is Y_0. If the price level is P_0, then (Y_0, P_0) represents a point on the long-run aggregate supply curve, AS_{lr}. Similarly, if the price level is P_1, then (Y_0, P_1) is another point on the long-run aggregate supply curve. In fact, so long as labor's perceptions are correct (and they are assumed correct in the long run), employment and output are N_0 and Y_0, respectively. Consequently, output is Y_0 whatever the price level, and the long-run aggregate supply curve is a vertical line.

In the short run, labor's perceptions may not be correct. Suppose, in Figure 14.5, the initial price level is P_0. Assuming that labor correctly perceives the price level to be P_0, the actual and perceived labor supply curves (S_a and S_p, respectively) coincide, and Y_0 represents the equilibrium level of income. Thus, (Y_0, P_0) represents a point on the short-run aggregate supply curve, AS_{sr}, as well as on the long-run aggregate supply curve (not shown, see Figure 14.4). Next, suppose the price level increases to P_1. If labor does not perceive the increase in the price level, the actual and perceived labor supply curves differ. Based upon the analysis of the previous section, the actual labor supply curve, S'_a, lies to the right of the perceived labor supply curve. The increase in the price level creates an excess demand for labor, and the money wage increases to W_1. Since labor is assumed not to perceive the increase in the price level, workers believe, with the increase in the money wage, that the real wage has increased. As a consequence, N_1 persons are willing to accept jobs at the new real wage. Since the real wage has actually decreased, firms are willing to hire N_1 workers. Thus, the new level of employment is N_1 and

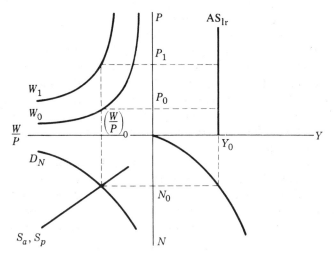

FIGURE 14.4

The derivation of the long-run aggregate supply curve

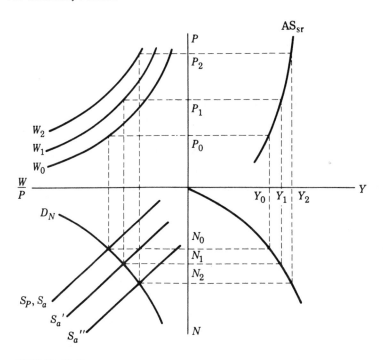

FIGURE 14.5

The derivation of the short-run aggregate supply curve

the new level of output is Y_1. Consequently, (Y_1, P_1) constitutes a point on the short-run aggregate supply curve, AS_{sr}.

Initially, the price level was assumed to be P_0. The price level was then assumed to increase to P_1. Suppose the price level had increased to P_2. Since price level P_2 is greater than P_1, the increase in the price level is greater than before. If labor fails to perceive the increase in the price level, a discrepancy exists between the actual and perceived labor supply curves. With the greater price increase, the discrepancy between the new actual labor supply curve, S_a'', and the perceived labor supply curve, S_p, is greater than before. Since the level of employment is given by the intersection of the demand for labor curve, D_N, and the actual supply of labor curve, S_a'', employment is N_2. As a consequence, output is Y_2, and (Y_2, P_2) represents another point on the short-run aggregate supply curve, AS_{sr}. Other points on the aggregate supply curve may be derived in the same manner. The short-run aggregate supply curve is positively sloped.

The long- and short-run aggregate supply curves are derived from the various relationships in the model. If these relationships change, the aggregate supply curves shift. In the following section, two types of shifts are important. First, technological progress, capital accumulation, and increases in the supply of labor shift both the long- and short-run aggregate supply curves to the right. Second, an increase in the expected inflation rate shifts the short-run aggregate supply curve to the left (a decrease in the expected inflation rate has the opposite effect) because that curve is derived on the basis of a given expected inflation rate. In contrast, the long-run aggregate supply curve is unaltered because it is derived by assuming that the expected and actual inflation rates are equal, but not necessarily constant.

THE INFLATIONARY PROCESS

We now proceed to describe the inflationary process. In period one, assume that no inflation is expected and none is occurring and that the relevant aggregate demand and aggregate supply curves in Figure 14.6 are AD_1 and AS_1, respectively, The short-run equilibrium combination of output and price level is (Y_1, P_1), given by the intersection of AD_1 and AS_1. Since the expected and actual inflation rates are equal, the long-run equilibrium combination is also (Y_1, P_1).

In period two, suppose aggregate demand increases to AD_2 because of growth in the supply of money, and aggregate supply increases to AS_2 because of tech-

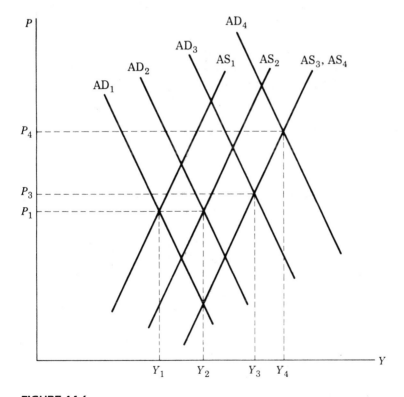

FIGURE 14.6

The inflationary process: the expansion phase

nological progress, etc. The new short-run equilibrium combination of output and price level is (Y_2, P_1). With no inflation expected and none occurring, the new long-run equilibrium combination is also (Y_2, P_1). As in period one, the economy is in both short- and long-run equilibrium.

In period three, assume that the growth rate of the money supply increases. This implies that aggregate demand grows more rapidly; in period three, aggregate demand increases to, say, AD_3. If aggregate supply continues to increase at the same rate, aggregate supply rises to AS_3. The new short-run equilibrium combination of output and price level is (Y_3, P_3), indicating that both output and the price level increase. Employment also increases and is now greater than its long-run equilibrium level. This is because labor failed to anticipate the increase in the price level. With the actual increase in the price level exceeding the expected increase, the actual labor supply curve lies to the right of the perceived labor supply curve and employment is greater than its long-run equilibrium level (see Figure 14.2). With the increases in the price level, output, and employment, the economy is in the expansion phase of the inflationary process.

Suppose, in period four, the money supply and aggregate demand grow at the new, higher rate; the new aggregate demand curve is AD_4. Aggregate supply tends to increase for the same reasons as before. By period four, however, labor will realize that the price level is increasing and revise its expectations regarding inflation. As the expected inflation rate rises, aggregate supply tends to decrease. For simplicity, we assume the latter tendency exactly offsets the former so that the aggregate supply curve for period four coincides with the aggregate supply curve for period three. The new short-run equilibrium combination of output and price level is (Y_4, P_4). As before, output increases, but by a smaller amount.[4] On the other hand, the price level increases by an even larger amount.

With the price level rising more rapidly, the monetary authorities might respond by reducing the growth rate of the money supply. Consequently, we now wish to turn our attention to the stabilization phase of the inflationary process. Before doing so, we must note that it is not inevitable that the monetary authorities will react by reducing the growth rate of the money supply. They may, for example, continue to increase the money supply at the higher rate. If they do, the price level will eventually rise at the rate consistent with the growth rate of the money supply in the long run. Since labor will eventually expect that rate to prevail, the expected inflation rate will equal the actual rate and employment will be at its long-run equilibrium level.

Although not inevitable, the U.S. experience suggests that the monetary authorities, in fact, will react by reducing the growth rate of the money supply. For simplicity, we shall assume that the growth rate is cut to 0.0 percent.[5] With no increase in the money supply in period five, aggregate demand is constant and aggregate demand curve AD_5 coincides with aggregate demand curve AD_4 in Figure 14.7.

Despite the constancy of aggregate demand, there is no guarantee that the

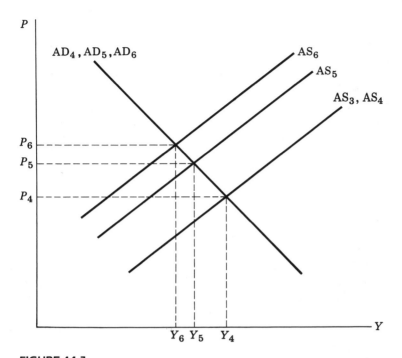

FIGURE 14.7

The inflationary process: the stabilization phase

price level will be constant. In fact, it is likely to continue to rise. In period four, the tendency for aggregate supply to increase because of technological progress, etc., was assumed to be exactly offset by the tendency for aggregate supply to decrease because of the increase in the expected inflation rate. In period four, however, labor was reacting to the increase in the price level from P_1 to P_3. In period five, labor is reacting to the much larger increase in the price level (from P_3 to P_4) which took place in period four. Consequently, in period five, the tendency for aggregate supply to decrease because of the increase in the expected inflation rate will dominate the tendency for aggregate supply to increase, and AS_5 will lie to the left of AS_4. Under these circumstances, the price level continues to rise.

Despite the increase in the price level, output and employment decline. With the reduction in the growth rate of money supply and the constancy of aggregate demand, the price level is now increasing less rapidly than before and the expected inflation rate exceeds the actual rate. Consequently, the actual supply of labor curve lies to the left of the perceived supply of labor curve and employment is less than its long-run equilibrium level (see Figure 14.3).

The monetary authorities now face a dilemma. If they continue with the stabilization program, output and employment may continue to decline. If they increase the growth rate of the money supply, aggregate demand will increase, thereby increasing output and employment. At the same time, the price level will increase more rapidly and the inflation will resume.

Suppose the monetary authorities continue to hold the money supply and aggregate demand constant. For a time, the price level may continue to increase and output and employment to decrease. With aggregate demand constant, however, the increases in the price level become smaller and smaller. As that happens, labor adjusts its expectations. Eventually, the expected inflation rate will equal the actual rate and long-run equilibrium will be restored. In that situation, the price level will change at the rate consistent with the growth rate of the money supply in the long run. With the expected inflation rate equal to the actual rate, employment will be at its long-run equilibrium level and output will grow at its long-run equilibrium rate.

In summary, the inflationary process has two distinct phases: the expansion phase and the stabilization phase. During the expansion phase, the increase in the inflation rate takes labor by surprise. As a result, output and employment increase to levels greater than their long-run equilibrium levels. As time passes, however, labor adjusts its expectations regarding inflation and output and employment return to their long-run equilibrium levels. During the stabilization phase, the monetary authorities react to the rising price levels by reducing the growth rate of the money supply. The reduction in the inflation rate takes labor by surprise and output and employment decrease to levels less than their long-run equilibrium levels. Once again, however, labor's expectations regarding inflation adjust and output and employment return to their long-run equilibrium levels. Finally, we note that the changes in output and employment that occur during the inflationary process are due to labor's inability to forecast the actual inflation rate accurately. This has important implications for the analysis that follows.

THE TRADEOFF BETWEEN INFLATION AND UNEMPLOYMENT

The relationship between the inflation and unemployment rates implied by the discussion of the inflationary process can be depicted geometrically. Suppose the actual and expected inflation rates are plotted on the vertical axis of Figure 14.8 and the unemployment rate on the horizontal. The negatively sloped lines, E, E', and E'', each drawn for a different expected inflation rate, depict the short-run tradeoff between inflation and unemployment, while the vertical line depicts the long-run tradeoff. To illustrate, suppose that no inflation is occurring and none is expected. The actual and perceived labor supply curves coincide and employment will be at its long-run equilibrium level. The unemployment rate which corresponds to this employment level is called the *natural rate of unemployment* and is depicted in Figure 14.8 as u_0. With no inflation and an unemployment rate of u_0, we are at point a in Figure 14.8. If the monetary authorities increase the growth rate of the

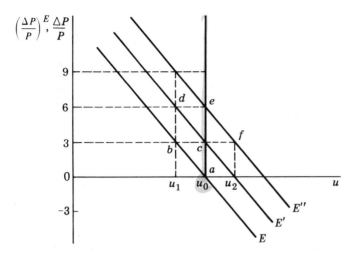

FIGURE 14.8

The short- and long-run relationships between the inflation and unemployment rates

money supply, aggregate demand increases more rapidly and the inflation rate increases to, say, 3 percent. If labor fails to anticipate the inflation, the actual and perceived labor supply curves diverge and employment increases. As a consequence, the unemployment rate drops to u_1 as shown by a movement along E from point a to point b.

The reduction in the unemployment rate from u_0 to u_1 is, however, only a short-run phenomenon. As time passes, workers revise their expectations regarding inflation. If the inflation rate continues to be 3 percent, labor will expect that rate to continue. Since the actual and expected inflation rates are the same, the actual and perceived labor supply curves will coincide, and the unemployment rate will return to the natural rate, u_0. This combination of inflation and unemployment rates (3 percent, u_0) is shown as point c in Figure 14.8, which suggests that E depicts only a short-run relationship between inflation and unemployment rates.[6]

The line E is drawn on the assumption that the expected inflation rate is zero. As labor revises its expectations with regard to inflation, the curve shifts; in this case, the relevant curve becomes E', which is based on an expected inflation rate of 3 percent. If the expected inflation rate is 3 percent and the monetary authorities increase the growth rate of the money supply so that the inflation rate rises to, say, 6 percent, the unemployment rate is reduced to u_1 as shown by a movement along E' from point c to point d. But, as workers revise their expectations, the curve shifts and the unemployment rate returns to u_0.

The analysis suggests that only a short-run tradeoff exists between inflation and unemployment. It also suggests that the unemployment rate will equal the natural rate u_0 in the long run regardless of the inflation rate. This implies that the long-run relationship is depicted by the vertical line in Figure 14.8, a result that follows from our assumption that, in the long run, the actual and expected inflation rates are equal, so that the actual and perceived labor supply curves coincide and employment is at its long-run equilibrium level.

Our analysis suggests that attempts to reduce the unemployment rate below the natural rate will be successful in the short run but not in the long run. It also suggests that attempts to reduce the inflation rate will, in the short run, increase the unemployment rate. For example, suppose the inflation rate is 6 percent and labor expects the price level to increase at that rate in the future. This means that the actual and expected inflation rates are equal and that the unemployment rate equals the natural rate. In terms of Figure 14.8, this combination of unemployment and inflation rates is depicted by point e. If the monetary authorities reduce the growth rate of the money supply, the inflation rate will decline to, say, 3 percent. If labor fails to perceive the decrease in the inflation rate, the expected inflation rate will continue to be 6 percent. With the discrepancy between the actual and expected inflation rates, the actual and perceived labor supply curves diverge and the unemployment rate increases to u_2, as shown by a movement along E'' (the relevant short-run relationship with an expected inflation rate of 6 percent) from point e to point f. The new unemployment rate, u_2, exceeds the natural rate, because labor expects inflation to continue at the 6 percent rate and the actual inflation rate is only 3 percent.

If the money supply continues to grow at a rate which maintains the 3 percent inflation rate, labor will eventually expect that rate to prevail. As a consequence, the short-run relationship will shift from E'' to E', and the unemployment rate will fall to the natural rate. This new combination of inflation and unemployment rates is shown by point c in Figure 14.8.

To sum up, if policy makers attempt to reduce the unemployment rate to a level less than the natural rate, they may be successful for a time. But as workers adjust their expectations in response to the new, higher rate of inflation, the short-run relationship shifts, and the tradeoff between inflation and unemployment evaporates. Similarly, if policy makers attempt to reduce the inflation rate, they will be successful, but the unemployment rate will temporarily exceed the natural rate. As workers adjust their expectations in respect to the new, lower rate of inflation, the short-run relationship shifts and the unemployment rate declines to the natural rate.

DIFFERENT VIEWS ON THE INFLATION–UNEMPLOYMENT TRADEOFF

Despite the widespread view that no long-run tradeoff exists between inflation and unemployment, opinions differ about the nature of the short-run tradeoff. For the most part, Keynesians do not believe in the existence of a long-run tradeoff. They do believe, however, in a short-run tradeoff. Moreover, they believe that the relevant time period is lengthy so that the unemployment rate can be held below the natural rate for several years or more through the use of expansionary monetary policy. Similarly, they believe that if contractionary monetary policy is used to reduce the inflation rate, the unemployment rate will be above the natural rate for a prolonged period of time. Consequently, they believe that it is very costly in terms of output and employment to use contractionary monetary policy alone to reduce the inflation rate. As we shall see in Chapter 15, this has led many Keynesians to favor the use of other policies, such as wage–price controls or guidelines, in conjunction with contractionary monetary policy.

Monetarists also believe in the existence of a short-run tradeoff and that the adjustment period is lengthy, although not as long as that postulated by many Keynesians. Monetarists do not favor the use of a more expansionary monetary policy to force the unemployment rate below the natural rate, nor do they advocate the use of wage–price guidelines or controls to reduce the inflation rate.

Proponents of the rational expectations view deny that even a short-run tradeoff exists. As discussed in Chapter 12, this view assumes that households and firms anticipate the effects of, say, an increase in the growth rate of the money supply. As a consequence, money wages and prices increase, not output and employment. Output and employment change if the policy changes are unanticipated or if the economy experiences a shock. Presumably, however, households and firms will learn of the implementation of a new policy quickly, so that for all practical purposes no tradeoff exists. Since no tradeoff exists and since policy changes create uncertainty, which has adverse effects on the economy, most proponents of the rational expectations view favor increasing the money supply at a constant rate.

Supply-side economists also deny that a short-run tradeoff exists. Unlike rational expectations theorists, however, they believe that both inflation and unemployment can be reduced in the short run. For this to occur, aggregate supply must increase relative to aggregate demand during the stabilization phase. As discussed in Chapter 12, supply-siders favor increasing the money supply at a slower rate and reducing tax rates. If workers were to dampen their expectations regarding inflation quickly and the tax cuts were to cause people to work, save, and invest more, aggregate supply might increase relative to aggregate demand. In such a situation, both inflation and unemployment would be reduced. This and other possibilities are discussed in Chapter 15.

THE UNITED STATES EXPERIENCE

Before examining policies to reduce inflation and unemployment, let us consider the U.S. experience over the 1966–85 period. This experience is summarized in Figure 14.9, which shows combinations of inflation (as measured by the IPD) and unemployment rates for 1966–85. For very short periods, the data show some evidence of a tradeoff (example: 1966–69), but for the period as a whole, the data do not support the view that a tradeoff exists. In fact, it appears that higher inflation rates are associated with higher rather than lower unemployment rates.[7] We now consider the period in more detail.

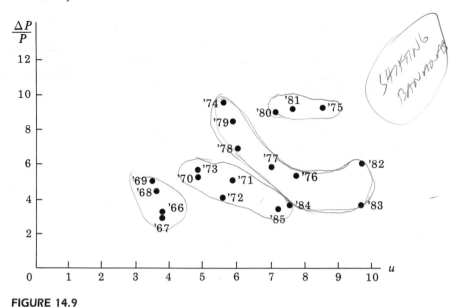

FIGURE 14.9

Inflation and unemployment in the United States: 1966–85

In 1966, the unemployment rate was 3.8 percent, suggesting that the economy was at full employment. Before 1966, the rate of inflation was relatively modest, averaging less than 2 percent per year in terms of the IPD. With the subsequent increases in government spending and in the money supply, the price level increased more rapidly. In 1966, the IPD increased at a 3.6 percent rate. In 1967 and 1968, the increases were 2.6 and 5.0 percent, respectively. The unemployment rate remained at 3.8 percent in 1967 and declined to 3.6 percent in 1968. Real GNP increased each year. The GNP increase in 1966 was 5.8 percent; the subsequent increases were 2.9 and 4.2 percent.

With the inflation, the monetary and fiscal authorities acted to restrain aggregate demand. From December 1968 to December 1969, the money supply increased by only 3.0 percent. In contrast, the money supply had increased at an average annual rate of approximately 7.5 percent from December 1966 to December 1968. Government purchases, after increasing rapidly in 1967 and 1968, decreased in 1969. Government transfer payments increased in 1969 but at a lower rate. An income tax surcharge was imposed in 1968.

With the application of contractionary monetary and fiscal policy, aggregate demand grew less rapidly. The economy, however, was not affected immediately. In 1969, the average unemployment rate was 3.5 percent and real GNP increased by 2.4 percent. The price level increased more rapidly; in 1969, the IPD increased by 5.6 percent.

In 1970, the effects of the stabilization program were widespread. The unemployment rate increased from 3.5 percent in December 1969 to 5.0 percent in

May. For the year, real GNP decreased slightly; the price level increased rapidly. As measured by the IPD, it increased by 5.5 percent.

The price level continued to rise in 1971. The IPD increased by 5.7 percent over the course of the year. To curtail the inflation, a wage-price freeze was imposed in August of that year. During 1971, real GNP increased by 2.8 percent. Even so, the unemployment rate increased.

From August 1971 to April 1974, the economy was subject to wage and price controls of varying degrees of severity. The experience with wage-price controls during this period is discussed at length in Chapter 20. To anticipate that discussion, we note that the controls were relatively ineffective in reducing the rate of inflation. In 1972, the IPD increased by 4.7 percent; in 1973, by 6.5 percent. At the same time, the economy was experiencing a business expansion. The unemployment rate decreased from 5.9 percent in 1971 to 5.6 percent in 1972 and 4.9 percent in 1973. Over the same period; real GNP increased rapidly. In 1972, real GNP increased by 5.0 percent and, in 1973, it increased by 5.2 percent. The rapid expansion in the economy is generally attributed to expansionary monetary and fiscal policy. For example, from the end of 1971 to mid-1973, the money supply increased at an average annual rate of 7.6 percent.

By mid-1973, inflation was the primary concern of the monetary and fiscal authorities. As a consequence, they pursued policies designed to slow the rate of increase in aggregate demand. For example, the rate of increase in the money supply during the second half of 1973 was very modest, only about 3.0 percent on an annual basis. At the same time, the economy was undergoing a "growth recession." Real GNP was increasing, but at a rate less than the average increase in the long run.

In 1974, the economy, already experiencing a "growth recession," was hard hit by the effects of the sharp increase in crude oil prices and the oil embargo. For the year, the IPD increased by 9.1 percent while GNP decreased by 0.5 percent.[8] By December 1974, the unemployment rate was 7.2 percent. In December 1973, the unemployment rate had been only 4.8 percent. The recession continued in 1975. The unemployment rate increased until it peaked at 8.9 percent in May, the highest rate since the Great Depression. For the year, real GNP decreased by 1.3 percent. The price level, however, continued to rise with the IPD increasing at a 9.8 percent rate.

Although the economy did not perform well during the year, 1975 did mark the beginning of the recovery. The unemployment rate declined after May and reached 8.3 percent in December 1975. Real GNP also increased significantly during the third and fourth quarters of 1975. The recovery continued in 1976 and 1977. By December 1976, the unemployment rate had fallen to 7.8 percent; by December 1977, it had dropped to 6.4 percent. At the same time, real GNP increased by 4.9 percent in 1976 and by 4.7 percent in 1977. The IPD increased significantly during both 1976 and 1977. In 1976, the IPD went up at a 6.4 percent rate; in 1977, it increased at a 6.7 percent rate.

The economic expansion continued in 1978 and 1979. By June 1978, the unemployment rate had dropped to 5.9 percent and remained very close to that rate through December 1979. As discussed in the next chapter, this rate is very close to the natural rate for the period. Real GNP increased by 5.3 percent in 1978 and by 2.5 percent in 1979. At the same time, the price level as measured by the IPD began to increase more rapidly; in 1978, it increased at a 7.3 percent rate and, in 1979, it increased at an 8.9 percent rate. The CPI showed even greater increases. In view of the price increases, 1978 and 1979 may be seen as years in which the inflation rate accelerated.

The main reason for the acceleration in the inflation rate was more rapid increases in the nation's money supply. It increased at an average annual rate of 7.9 percent from December 1976 to December 1979. In contrast, it had increased at an average annual rate of only 5.3 percent in the four preceding years. Fiscal policy remained expansionary, but it tended to become less expansionary over the period. The big increase in crude oil prices in 1979 also contributed significantly to the inflation.

In 1980, the economy experienced a recession, one of the shortest in the nation's history. In fact, real GNP decreased in only one quarter, the second. For the year, real GNP decreased by 0.2 percent, a very small decrease. The unemployment rate increased from 5.9 percent in December 1979 to 7.6 percent in May 1980 and then declined gradually to 7.0 percent in July 1981. Despite the recession, the IPD increased by 9.0 percent and the CPI increased by an even greater amount, 13.5 percent. The main reason for the recession was a sharp reduction in the growth rate of the money supply. From December 1979 to December 1980, it increased at a 7.4 percent rate, only half a percentage point less than during the three preceding years. From October 1979 to June 1980, however, the money supply showed virtually no change, marking an abrupt deceleration in the rate of growth of the money supply. The crude oil price increases that occurred during the period also had an adverse effect on output and employment, as well as the price level.

Following resumption of a more normal expansion in the money supply, economic activity increased during the last two quarters of 1980 and the first quarter of 1981. Even so, the increase in activity was short-lived. Real GNP decreased in the second and fourth quarters of 1981 and, for the year, real GNP increased by only 1.9 percent, despite a very strong first quarter showing. The unemployment rate increased from 7.3 percent in April to 8.8 percent in December. Despite the increase in the unemployment rate, the price level, as measured by the IPD, continued to increase at a rapid rate. For the year, the increase was 9.7 percent.

The primary reason for the recession which began in 1981 was a sharp reduction in the growth rate of the money supply. From April 1980 to April 1981, the money supply increased at a 10.9 percent rate. But from April 1981 to December 1981, it increased at only a 2.6 percent rate.

The recession continued in 1982. The unemployment rate increased from 8.8 percent in December 1981 to 10.8 percent in November, a new post-World War

II high. For the year, real GNP decreased by 2.5 percent, a large decrease by historical standards. With the reduction in the level of economic activity, the price level increased by a smaller amount. In 1982, the IPD increased at a 6.4 percent rate, as compared to 9.7 percent in 1981.

Despite the economy's dismal performance in 1982, recovery began in November of that year. The unemployment rate dropped steadily in 1983 and 1984. From a high of 10.8 percent in November 1982, the (average) unemployment rate declined to 9.6 percent in 1983 and to 7.5 percent in 1984. At the same time, real GNP increased by 3.5 percent in 1983 and by 6.5 percent in 1984. Inflation was moderate by recent standards; the IPD increased by 3.8 percent in 1983 and by 4.1 percent in 1984.

For the most part, the increase in economic activity in 1983–84 was due to the more expansionary policy followed by the Federal Reserve. For example, from December 1982 to December 1983, the money supply increased at a 9.8 percent rate, a relatively rapid rate. Various changes in the tax laws, including the reductions in personal income tax rates which occurred on October 1, 1981, July 1, 1982, and July 1, 1983, were contributing factors as were the reductions in crude oil prices which took place in the early 1980s.

In 1985, the economy grew less rapidly, particularly during the first part of the year. For the year, real GNP increased at a 2.3 percent rate. The unemployment rate dropped to 7.2 percent, a slight decline. The IPD increased at a lower rate, 3.3 percent, than it did in 1983 and 1984.

The economy continued to grow in 1986. The expansion, however, was more in line with U.S. experience in 1985, rather than the more robust expansion that took place in 1983 and 1984. To illustrate, real GNP increased at a 2.9 percent rate during the first quarter of 1986. Owing to the significant reduction in crude oil prices that took place during that quarter, the IPD increased at only a 2.9 percent rate.

CONCLUDING REMARKS

In reviewing our discussion of the inflationary process, we see that it is very difficult to stop inflation once the process starts. During the stabilization process, output and employment are likely to be below their long-run equilibrium levels for prolonged periods of time, which makes it very costly to reduce the inflation rate. In the next chapter, we consider various policies to slow the inflation rate. We also consider indexation as an alternative to these policies.

Even after the stabilization phase ends and output and employment are at their long-run equilibrium levels, the unemployment rate may still be too high from society's viewpoint. For this reason, we also consider microeconomic policies designed to reduce the natural unemployment rate.

NOTES

1. Prospective workers are assumed to know the current money wage. If they do not, the equation must be modified so as to include the expected or perceived money wage, W^e.

2. In the following analysis, money wages are assumed flexible because inflation is a long-run phenomenon and money wages are more flexible in the long run. Also, money wages need not fall in the inflation context in order for real wages to fall; the same result is obtained if money wages increase less rapidly than prices.

3. It may, of course, take a long time for the economy to reach its long-run equilibrium level of employment. In fact, it may never be reached if the monetary authorities follow erratic policies. Nevertheless, long-run equilibrium is a useful concept even if it is never achieved.

4. Employment will still be greater than its long-run equilibrium level, but by a smaller amount. Since labor now recognizes that some inflation is occurring, the divergence of the actual and perceived supply of labor curves will be less, implying that the divergence of employment from its long-run equilibrium level will be less.

5. Most stabilization programs are more gradual.

6. The relationship between the inflation and unemployment rates is often referred to as a *Phillips curve*, although the relationship postulated by A. W. Phillips was between the rate of change of money wages and the unemployment rate. Phillips, "The Relation Between Unemployment and the Rate of Change of Money Wage Rates in the United Kingdom, 1861–1957," *Economica*, 25 (November 1958), 283–99.

7. For a discussion as to why the relationship between inflation and unemployment rates may be positive, see Milton Friedman, "Nobel Lecture: Inflation and Unemployment," *Journal of Political Economy*, 85 (June 1977), 451–72.

8. The increase in the price level was also owing in part to an increase in world demand for agricultural products and the accompanying increase in agricultural prices.

REVIEW QUESTIONS

1. How is the supply of labor function modified in this chapter? How are labor's expectations with regard to inflation formed?

2. Distinguish between the perceived and actual supply of labor curves.

3. Based on the analysis of this chapter:

   a. Derive the short-run aggregate supply curve.

   b. Suppose the capital stock increases. Show how the short- and long-run aggregate supply curves are modified.

4. In terms of the inflationary process, how is long-run equilibrium defined? Distinguish between the expansion and stabilization phases.

5. In terms of the inflationary process, what sort of patterns of changes in the price level, output, and employment would you expect during the process? Does the United States experience conform to these patterns? Defend your answer.

6. What is meant by the natural rate of unemployment? Can the natural rate be altered through discretionary monetary and fiscal policy? Defend your answer.

7. Suppose the relationship between the actual inflation rate, the expected inflation rate, and the unemployment rate is expressed mathematically as

$$\frac{\Delta P}{P} = 18 - 3a + \left(\frac{\Delta P}{P}\right)^{E}.$$

   a. Determine the natural rate of unemployment.

   b. Suppose the expected inflation rate is 3 percent and the actual inflation rate is 6 percent. Determine the unemployment rate.

   c. Suppose the expected inflation rate is 6 percent and the actual inflation rate is 3 percent. Determine the unemployment rate.

8. How do Keynesians, monetarists, rational expectations theorists, and supply-side economists differ in their views with regard to the tradeoff between inflation and unemployment?

9. Does the U.S. experience over the 1966–85 span support the view that a tradeoff exists between inflation and unemployment in the long run? In the short run? Defend your answers.

SUGGESTED READING

BLINDER, ALAN S., *Economic Policy and the Great Stagflation*. New York: Academic Press, Inc., 1979.

ECKSTEIN, OTTO, *Core Inflation*. Englewood Cliffs, N. J.: Prentice-Hall, Inc., 1981.

Economic Report of the President. Washington, D.C.: Government Printing Office, annually.

FRIEDMAN, MILTON, "The Role of Monetary Policy," *American Economic Review*, 58 (March 1968), 1–17.

FRISCH, HELMUT, *Theories of Inflation*. New York: Cambridge University Press, 1983.

GORDON, ROBERT J., "Recent Developments in the Theory of Inflation and Unemployment," *Journal of Monetary Economics*, 2 (1976), 185–219.

HALL, ROBERT E. (ed.), *Inflation: Causes and Effects*. Chicago: University of Chicago Press, 1982.

LAIDLER, DAVID E. W., and MICHAEL J. PARKIN, "Inflation: A Survey," *Economic Journal*, 85 (December 1975), 741–809.

PHELPS, EDMUND S., "Money-Wage Dynamics and Labor-Market Equilibrium," *Journal of Political Economy*, 76 (July–August 1968), 678–711.

————, and others, *Microeconomic Foundations of Employment and Inflation Theory*. New York: W. W. Norton & Co., Inc., 1970.

SANTOMERO, ANTHONY M., and JOHN J. SEATER, "The Inflation-Unemployment Tradeoff: A Critique of the Literature," *Journal of Economic Literature*, 16 (June 1978), 499–544.

15

POLICIES
TO REDUCE INFLATION
AND UNEMPLOYMENT

During the 1970s and now the 1980s, the U.S. economy has experienced high rates of inflation and unemployment. In this chapter, we consider various policies aimed at reducing these rates. Policies to reduce the inflation rate are considered first, followed by a discussion of indexation, which is really an attempt to cope with inflation rather than to reduce it. As we shall see, even if these policies are successful, the long-run equilibrium unemployment rate may be too high. For this reason, we conclude the chapter by considering various policies designed to reduce it.

POLICIES TO REDUCE THE INFLATION RATE

Economists agree that a less expansionary monetary policy will reduce the inflation rate. Beyond that, very little agreement exists; consequently, various viewpoints—Keynesian, monetarist, rational expectations, and supply-side—will be considered.

The Keynesian Perspective

Keynesians believe contractionary monetary policy can reduce the inflation rate. But they also believe that it will take a very long time to do it and that output and employment will be substantially below their long-run equilibrium levels during this period. From this, they conclude that it is very costly to reduce inflation through the use of contractionary monetary policy.

According to Keynesians, the prices of most goods are closely linked to costs of production, and, of the various costs of production, by far the largest is labor costs. They believe, therefore, that price changes primarily reflect changes in money wages. These wage changes depend in part on the nation's level of economic activity, rising less rapidly or falling in a recession and rising more rapidly when the level of economic activity is higher. Past trends in wages and prices are even more important in determining wage changes. Since wage changes depend heavily on past changes, it is very difficult to alter the course of money wages and prices through demand management policies. If wage changes depend primarily on past trends in wages and prices, workers will be slow in adjusting their expectations concerning inflation and, thus, their wage demands. In terms of the inflationary process discussed in Chapter 14, this implies that the stabilization phase will be prolonged and that output and employment will be below their long-run equilibrium levels for an extended period.

Various estimates of the costs associated with reducing the inflation rate are available. George L. Perry, for example, has estimated that if contractionary monetary policy is used to keep the unemployment rate a percentage point above the natural rate, the resulting decrease in the inflation rate will be less than one percentage point even after three years.[1] Output, on the other hand, would be $50 to $60 billion less in each of the three years. Arthur M. Okun, after surveying six different studies, arrived at a similar conclusion.[2] Based on the studies, he estimated that, if the unemployment rate were kept one percentage point higher for a year, the inflation rate would decline by only three-tenths of a percentage point. He also estimated the cost of a one percentage point reduction in the inflation rate to be about 10 percent of a year's GNP. Based on these estimates, it would be extremely costly to achieve price stability.

Because of the high costs associated with reducing inflation through contractionary monetary policy, many, if not most, Keynesians advocate the use of other policies in conjunction with a less expansionary monetary policy. For example, the wage–price guidelines program that existed during part of the Carter administration was enacted in an attempt to achieve a lower inflation rate and to reduce the costs associated with the use of contractionary monetary policy alone. Other suggestions include wage–price controls and various programs which would work through the tax system to promote wage and price stability.[3] These programs are designed to encourage or force workers and firms to accept lower rates of increase in money wages, which would shorten the stabilization phase and minimize the costs associated with reducing the inflation rate.

The Monetarist Perspective

With regard to reducing inflation, monetarists differ from Keynesians on two issues: (1) costs and (2) the efficacy of wage–price guidelines and similar programs.

With regard to the costs associated with reducing the inflation rate, monetarists argue that, although substantial, the costs are not as great as postulated by most Keynesians. By and large, monetarists believe that a steady reduction in the growth rate of the money supply will reduce the inflation rate and dampen labor's expectations with regard to the price level. As a consequence, labor will adjust its wage demands and the unemployment rate will return to the natural rate. To minimize the costs associated with reducing inflation, monetarists favor a gradual reduction in the rate of growth of the money supply, since sharp reductions have very adverse effects on the economy.

Monetarists oppose wage–price guidelines and similar programs which many Keynesians believe will minimize the costs associated with reducing the inflation rate. These programs are examined in detail in Chapter 20, but we may list some objections to them. Many believe these programs are ineffective in restraining wages and prices; much evidence exists to support this view. To the extent that these programs are effective in slowing the rates of increase of wages and prices, critics charge that they cause misallocation of resources and inequities. Finally, the administration of these programs is costly to both taxpayers and business. For these reasons, monetarists, as well as many other economists, are opposed to such programs.

The Rational Expectations Perspective

The rational expectations view contrasts sharply with the views of Keynesians and monetarists. As discussed in Chapter 12, rational expectations theorists believe that no tradeoff between inflation and unemployment exists even in the short run. Suppose the Federal Reserve announces that it is implementing a less expansionary monetary policy. Since expectations are formed rationally, people will realize that less inflation will occur in the future and wages and prices will adjust, but output and employment will remain the same.

Since no tradeoff between inflation and unemployment exists, the inflation rate can be reduced without cost. Rational expectations theorists are critical of studies which purport to show that the costs are high. As discussed in Chapter 12, adherents of the rational expectations theory claim that the parameters of the models upon which the results are based change when new policies are introduced. Consequently, the actual effects of, say, a less expansionary monetary policy will be quite different from the effects estimated on the basis of the original set of parameters. To reduce the inflation rate, rational expectations theorists favor a less expansionary monetary policy. (For criticism of the theory, see Chapter 12.)

The rational expectations view is extreme in that it suggests that reducing inflation involves no costs. A less extreme version of the rational expectations theory is offered by William Fellner.[4] Fellner's position, called the *credibility hypothesis*, is that people will change their expectations regarding inflation more rapidly if policy makers follow firm and credible policies. For example, if policy makers were to pursue a policy of consistent demand disinflation, people would expect less inflation in the future and the adjustment process would take much less time than postulated by Keynesians. Fellner concedes that it would take time to establish credibility, but he believes that this period would take at most three to five years. This estimate, he believes, is consistent with experience abroad as well as in this country. Thus, Fellner's view is that reducing the inflation rate is, contrary to the standard rational expectations view, time consuming and costly but not nearly as time consuming and costly as suggested by Keynesians.

The Supply-Side Perspective

Like rational expectations theorists, supply-siders believe that no short-run tradeoff between inflation and unemployment exists. In fact, many, if not most, supply siders go further and claim that it is possible to reduce both inflation and unemployment in the short run. They claim that if the policies they recommend are enacted, aggregate supply will increase, resulting in higher levels of output and employment and a lower price level. This implies that, during the stabilization phase of the inflationary process discussed in Chapter 14, aggregate supply must increase relative to aggregate demand. This might happen if workers were to dampen their expectations regarding inflation quickly and tax cuts were to increase the incentive for people to work, save, and invest. In general, supply-siders believe that people's expectations will be altered quickly as the supply-side program is implemented. As a consequence, wages and prices will increase less rapidly and interest rates will fall. As Fellner and others have warned, however, it may be years before a new policy approach becomes credible. Supply-siders also believe that tax cuts will stimulate work, saving, and investment. As noted in Chapter 12, critics charge that the effects are much smaller than claimed by supply-siders and they are probably correct regarding the short-run effects. In the long run, the effects are likely to be larger.

It appears unlikely that the supply-side approach will reduce both inflation and unemployment in the short run, but we have little direct evidence. It is true that the nation entered a recession in 1981, the year in which much of President Reagan's economic program was enacted. This recession was due, however, to the less expansionary monetary policy followed by the Federal Reserve and would have occurred with or without the implementation of the rest of the program. Moreover, the reduction in personal income tax rates, the cornerstone of the supply-side agenda, was phased in only gradually. Consequently, the 1981–82 recession does not prove that it is impossible to reduce inflation and unemployment simultaneously. An appropriate test would require a more rapid implementation of the program. Of course, those supply-siders that believe restoration of the gold standard is necessary would insist that the appropriate test involves both tax cuts and a return to the gold standard.

TABLE 15.1 A summary of views regarding the inflation–unemployment tradeoff and policies to reduce inflation

Issue	Keynesian	Monetarist	Rational Expectations Theorists	Supply-side Advocates
Long-run tradeoff between inflation and unemployment?	No	No	No	No
Short-run tradeoff between inflation and unemployment?	Yes	Yes	No	No[1]
Costs associated with reducing inflation?	Very high	Substantial	None	None[1]
Policies to reduce inflation?	Less expansionary monetary policy plus wage–price guidelines or other programs	Less expansionary monetary policy	Less expansionary monetary policy	Less expansionary monetary policy plus reductions in marginal tax rates

[1]Supply-siders believe that if the policies they recommend are implemented, both inflation and unemployment will be reduced in the short run, which implies that reducing inflation will be beneficial rather than costly.

Summary

As we have seen, the views of Keynesians, monetarists, rational expectations theorists, and supply-side advocates differ regarding the existence of an inflation-unemployment tradeoff, the costs associated with reducing the inflation rate, and appropriate policies to reduce inflation. These views are summarized in Table 15.1. The reader should be aware that this summary represents a simplification. For example, not all Keynesians support the use of wage–price guidelines or other programs aimed at reducing wage and price increases directly. Nevertheless, the summary is helpful in keeping track of the relevant views.

INDEXATION

Because of the high costs that most economists associate with reducing inflation, some have recommended indexation, an approach aimed at coping with inflation rather than reducing it. With *indexation*, money payments are linked or tied to some specified price index in order to preserve the purchasing power of the payments. For example, union contracts often include a cost-of-living adjustment (COLA) clause which links money wages to the CPI. With the clause, money wages increase automatically as the CPI rises. With a complete system, indexation would be widespread. Wages, salaries, and pensions would be covered, as well as loans and insurance policies. Government transfer payments and the tax system would also be covered.[5] Profits would not be indexed since they are a residual.

To an extent, our economy is indexed. Many long-term union contracts contain COLA clauses. Social security and other benefits are indexed and so is our personal income tax system. Nevertheless, the overwhelming majority of workers are not covered by COLAs. In addition, loan contracts are rarely, if ever, written to guarantee repayment in real dollars. Finally, even though part of our tax system is indexed, the rest is not.

The main argument in favor of indexation is that it minimizes the redistribution effects of unanticipated inflation.[6] As discussed in Chapter 13, redistribution of income and wealth occurs with unanticipated inflation. With indexation, money wages, social security benefits, and so on adjust automatically. Creditors are also protected, since loans are indexed.

The main arguments against indexation are three-fold. First, it is argued that indexation reduces support for anti-inflationary policies. After all, indexation is a way to "live with" inflation, not a way to prevent it. This argument assumes, explicitly or implicitly, that price stability is inherently desirable. This is not so; inflation is undesirable because of its side effects. If these can be overcome, there is no reason to insist that prices be stabilized. Moreover, as Milton Friedman and others have argued, indexation may indirectly promote price stability.[7] In itself, indexation neither increases nor decreases the rate of inflation. By reducing or eliminating the revenue that the government gains from inflation, indexation of taxes reduces the government's incentive to enact inflationary policies. At the same time, indexation reduces the side effects associated with unanticipated deflation. If a restrictive monetary policy is pursued, the rate of inflation is reduced. If the actual rate of inflation is less than the anticipated rate, a redistribution of income and wealth occurs. If the economy is indexed, however, the redistribution is reduced or eliminated.

Similarly, if the actual rate of inflation is less than the anticipated rate and wage contracts are not indexed, money wages will increase rapidly relative to prices. As a result, output and employment will be less than their long-run equilibrium levels. With indexed wage contracts, however, money wages will increase less rapidly, and the real wage will adjust so as to minimize the impact on output and employment. Since wage indexation minimizes the side effects associated with reducing inflation, policy makers may be more willing to pursue the monetary policy necessary to reduce the inflation rate.

The second argument against indexation is that it may lead to greater instability in the economy.[8] Previously, we said that if less expansionary monetary and fiscal policies were pursued, wage indexation would result in smaller changes in output and employment than would otherwise occur. More generally, any change in aggregate demand is likely to result in smaller changes in output and employment with wage indexation, since money wages will tend to adjust so as to minimize the impact on output and employment. This is not the case for changes in aggregate supply. Suppose, for example, the economy experiences a supply shock; in particular, assume that it is a large increase in crude oil prices. As a consequence, the aggregate supply curve shifts to the left, resulting in a higher price level and lower levels of output and employment. With wage indexation, the higher price level will lead to higher money wages and, as a consequence, higher real wages. As a result, output and employment will be even less than they would be in the absence of wage indexation.

The foregoing analysis suggests that wage indexation yields greater stability when aggregate demand changes and less when aggregate supply changes. Consequently, it is not clear that the *net* result will be greater instability. Moreover, the issue is complicated when indexation of the personal income tax system is considered. In that case, the preceding results are reversed, with indexation of the tax system leading to greater instability when aggregate demand changes and less when aggregate supply changes.[9] To illustrate, suppose that aggregate demand increases. The resulting increase in the price level will, in the absence of indexation, lead to higher (real) tax revenue, which will result in smaller increases in output and employment. If the personal income tax system is indexed, the system will be adjusted so that the higher price level will not affect real tax revenue. As a consequence, the increases in output and employment will be greater.

In the foregoing case (a change in aggregate demand), indexation of the personal income tax system leads to larger changes in output and employment. If aggregate supply changes, indexation results in smaller changes in output and employment. Suppose the economy experiences a supply shock consisting of a large increase in crude oil prices. The aggregate supply curve shifts to the left, causing the price level to increase and output and employment to decrease. Because of the increase in the price level, the personal income tax system will be adjusted to keep real tax revenue from increasing. As a consequence, aggregate demand will be higher than it would otherwise be. The changes in output and employment due to the shift in the aggregate supply curve will, therefore, be smaller than they would otherwise be. Thus, with indexation of the personal income tax system, changes in output and employment due to changes in aggregate supply are minimized.

In conclusion, it is not clear that indexation will result in greater fluctuations in output and employment.[10] It depends on various factors, including the degrees to which money wages and taxes are indexed and whether the economy is subjected mainly to supply or demand shocks.

The third argument against indexation relates to the practical problems associated with moving to such a system. To illustrate, at any point in time, many contracts exist which do not contain escalator clauses. It is not clear whether these contracts would be renegotiated or allowed to stand. Similarly, the task of selecting the appropriate price index is not as easy as it first appears. Should it be the CPI, IPD, or one of the subindexes of the CPI or IPD? This and other issues related to establishing indexation are not easy to resolve.[11]

Thus the arguments regarding indexation are inconclusive. In fact, the case for or against indexation may depend on the inflation rate. If inflation is occurring at a moderate rate (say 5 percent or less), indexation may not be desirable because of its costs. It takes resources to incorporate the necessary provisions in wage and other contractual arrangements and the tax system; it also takes resources to administer such a system. At higher rates of inflation, indexation becomes more desirable because of the relatively high costs associated with high and variable inflation rates. Moreover, indexation is likely to make it easier for policy makers to pursue a less expansionary monetary policy, which will reduce the inflation rate.

POLICIES TO REDUCE THE UNEMPLOYMENT RATE

Even if price stability and the long-run equilibrium level of employment are achieved, the corresponding unemployment rate may be too high from society's viewpoint. In the remainder of the chapter, we shall consider the unemployment rate and various policies to reduce it.

The Unemployment Rate

One of the most frequently cited statistics in economics is the unemployment rate. Simply stated, the unemployment rate is the number of persons unemployed as a percentage of the civilian labor force. In April 1986, this rate was 7.1 percent.

To obtain the data necessary to compile the unemployment rate, interviewers from the Bureau of the Census visit approximately 60,000 households each month.[12] These households are scattered throughout the 50 states and the District of Columbia. The interviewers try to get information on the employment status of each member of the household 16 years of age or over for the calendar week including the twelfth of the month.

In the survey, a person is classified as employed if the person worked as a paid employee or worked 15 hours or more as an unpaid worker in an enterprise operated by a member of the family. A person is also classified as employed if the person is not working but has a job or business from which the person is temporarily absent because of illness, bad weather, vacation, labor-management dispute, or personal reasons.

In contrast, a person is classified as unemployed if the person did not work during the survey week, was available for work during the survey week (except for temporary illness), and had made specific efforts to find a job within the past four weeks. A person is also classified as unemployed if the person did not work at all, was available for work, and (1) was waiting to be called back to a job from which the person had been laid off or (2) was waiting to report to a new job within 30 days.

The civilian labor force is comprised of persons classified as employed or unemployed. Given the Bureau of Labor Statistics definitions, some persons are classified as neither employed nor unemployed and, therefore, not in the civilian labor force. All persons under 16 years of age fall into this category. Individuals confined to various types of institutions, as well as members of the armed forces, are also excluded from the civilian labor force.

Even civilians aged 16 or over may be classified as not in the civilian labor force. For example, many of the elderly are retired; hence, they are not classified as employed. Since they are not actively seeking employment, they are not classified as unemployed either. Since they are neither employed nor unemployed, they are classified as not in the labor force. Similarly, persons who have searched for employment in the past, but have become discouraged and discontinued job search, are classified as not in the civilian labor force.

As indicated, the unemployment rate is the number of persons unemployed as a percentage of the civilian labor force. Since the civilian labor force is composed of those persons classified as employed or unemployed, the unemployment rate is obtained by dividing the number of persons unemployed by the total number of persons employed or unemployed and expressing the result in percentage terms. For example, in April 1986, unemployment was 8,342,000 and employment was 108,892,000.[13] This means that the unemployment rate was 7.1 percent, obtained by dividing 8,342,000 by 117,234,000, the total number of persons employed or unemployed.

In addition to the overall unemployment rate, unemployment rates are calculated within the labor force by sex, age, marital status, race, and so on. These rates often differ substantially from the overall rate. Until recently, the employment rate for women was usually much higher than for men; they are now about the same. To illustrate, in April 1986, the unemployment rate for women, aged 20 and over, was 6.4 percent; the corresponding rate for men was 6.0 percent. The unemployment rate for teenagers is always substantially greater than for older persons. The unemployment rate of teenagers was 19.6 percent in April 1986, about three times the rate for those 20 and over. The unemployment rate for Blacks and other nonwhite persons is usually about twice that of whites. In April 1986, the unemployment rate of the former was 13.6 percent; of the latter, 6.1 percent.

Table 15.2 contains U.S. data on employment, unemployment, and the unemployment rate for 1929–85. The unemployment rate reached a peak of 24.9 percent in 1933 and remained at relatively high levels during the rest of the 1930s. The unemployment rate reached its low point, 1.2 percent, in 1944. During the post-World War II period, the unemployment rate (on a yearly basis) ranged between 3.5 and 9.7 percent.

At first glance, it might appear that full employment requires that the unemployment rate be zero. Given the Bureau of Labor Statistics definition of unemployment, a zero unemployment rate is, for all practical purposes, unattainable. Persons classified as unemployed include those that have been temporarily laid off and are waiting to be called back to work and those temporarily between jobs during the survey week. Since there are always some persons in those categories, there is inevitably some unemployment. Even during World War II, the unemployment rate did not drop below 1.2 percent (on a yearly basis).

TABLE 15.2 Employment, unemployment, and the unemployment rate, 1929–85[1]

Year	Employment (thousands)	Unemployment (thousands)	Unemployment Rate (percent)
1929	47,630	1,550	3.2
1933	38,760	12,830	24.9
1940	47,520	8,120	14.6
1944	53,960	670	1.2
1945	52,820	1,040	1.9
1946	55,250	2,270	3.9
1947	57,038	2,311	3.9
1948	58,343	2,276	3.8
1949	57,651	3,637	5.9
1950	58,918	3,288	5.3
1951	59,961	2,055	3.3
1952	60,250	1,883	3.0
1953	61,179	1,834	2.9
1954	60,109	3,532	5.5
1955	62,170	2,852	4.4
1956	63,799	2,750	4.1
1957	64,071	2,859	4.3
1958	63,036	4,602	6.8
1959	64,630	3,740	5.5
1960	65,778	3,852	5.5
1961	65,746	4,714	6.7
1962	66,702	3,911	5.5
1963	67,762	4,070	5.7
1964	69,305	3,786	5.2
1965	71,088	3,366	4.5
1966	72,895	2,875	3.8
1967	74,372	2,975	3.8
1968	75,920	2,817	3.6
1969	77,902	2,832	3.5
1970	78,678	4,093	4.9
1971	79,367	5,016	5.9
1972	82,153	4,882	5.6
1973	85,064	4,365	4.9
1974	86,794	5,156	5.6
1975	85,846	7,929	8.5
1976	88,752	7,406	7.7
1977	92,017	6,991	7.1
1978	96,048	6,202	6.1
1979	98,824	6,137	5.8
1980	99,303	7,637	7.1
1981	100,397	8,273	7.6
1982	99,526	10,678	9.7
1983	100,834	10,717	9.6
1984	105,005	8,539	7.5
1985	107,150	8,312	7.2

[1]The 1929–46 data are for persons 14 years of age and over; the 1947–85 data are for persons 16 years of age or over.

Source: *Economic Report of the President, 1982* (Washington, D.C.: Government Printing Office, 1982), p. 266; *Economic Indicators* (May 1986), pp. 11–12.

The full employment rate of unemployment is the lowest unemployment rate consistent with a stable price level or, in the inflation context, a constant inflation rate. Thus, the full employment rate of unemployment is the same as the natural or long-run equilibrium unemployment rate. For years, this rate was considered to be 4.0 percent, and the Humphrey-Hawkins Full Employment and Balanced Growth Act lists an unemployment rate of 4.0 percent (3.0 percent for adults) as the interim goal. The full employment rate is likely to be much higher. For example, the 1983 *Economic Report of the President* expressed the view that the full employment rate of unemployment is between 6 and 7 percent, with the inflation rate accelerating as the unemployment rate approaches 6 percent.[14] Much evidence exists to support this view.

In the *Report* and elsewhere, the increase in the full employment rate of unemployment is attributed, in whole or in part, to changes in the composition of the labor force. For example, in 1955, teenagers and young adults accounted for 15 percent of the labor force. In 1976, they accounted for 24 percent of the labor force. Since the unemployment rate for this group is greater than the overall rate, increased participation in the labor force by this group raises the overall rate.

Since attempts to reduce the unemployment rate below the natural rate through expansionary monetary and fiscal policies lead to an acceleration in the inflation rate, other policies are necessary to reduce the natural unemployment rate.[15] We now turn to a discussion of some of these policies. It should be emphasized that these policies are microeconomic rather than macroeconomic in nature.

Manpower Training Programs

Manpower training programs have been advocated as a means to reduce the unemployment rate since the late 1950s and early 1960s. In the late 1950s, the unemployment rate increased to levels exceeding those that had prevailed earlier in the decade. Most economists argued that the unemployment was due to inadequate aggregate demand. This view was challenged by a group of economists who claimed that it was the result of structural changes in the economy. When technology changes or when the composition of final demand for goods and services changes, the economy is said to be undergoing *structural change*. When the economy experiences structural change, old jobs are destroyed and new ones are created. If the displaced workers are able to meet the educational and skill requirements of the new jobs and are willing to relocate if necessary, no special problems are created, except during the adjustment period. If the displaced workers cannot meet the educational or skill requirements or are unwilling to relocate, they will remain unemployed for long periods of time. This type of unemployment is called *structural unemployment*.

Proponents of the structural unemployment thesis conceded that some unemployment had always occurred because of structural changes in the economy. However, they claimed that structural change was occurring more rapidly in the 1950s, thereby causing more unemployment. For example, Charles C. Killingsworth, one of the proponents of the structural unemployment thesis, argued that technological progress had speeded up during the 1950s.[16] Moreover, he claimed that technological progress in the 1950s differed from the progress in earlier years because many of the displaced workers in the 1950s lacked the education or skills necessary to fill the new jobs.

Under the structural unemployment thesis, the problem is a mismatch between the educational and skill requirements associated with job vacancies and the educational and skill levels of unemployed workers. Since the problem is not inadequate aggregate demand, policies designed to increase aggregate demand will, according to proponents of the structural unemployment thesis, be relatively ineffective in reducing unemployment. To illustrate, suppose expansionary monetary and/or fiscal policy is used to increase aggregate demand. If the unemployment is due to inadequate aggregate demand, unemployment decreases with a relatively small increase in the price level. If the unemployment is the result of structural change, however, little or no decrease in unemployment occurs, while a significant increase in the price level takes place, for the jobs created with the increase in aggregate demand are similar to vacancies already in existence. Consequently, firms will compete for the limited number of workers qualified to fill those jobs, causing money wages and prices to increase. In short, since the problem is one of a mismatch between vacancies and unemployed workers, it does little good to create additional jobs.

Proponents of the structural unemployment thesis contend that it is necessary to take different measures to reduce the unemployment rate. For example, Killingsworth argued that manpower training programs should be expanded to provide the unemployed with new job skills. He also advocated new ways to finance college education, since more education is necessary to meet the job requirements of a technologically advanced society.

Critics of the structural unemployment thesis argue that unemployment due to structural change is not new and that little or no evidence exists to suggest that technological progress in the 1950s was more rapid than in the past or that it was fundamentally different from earlier technological progress in the United States.[17] Expansionary fiscal and monetary policies, these critics assert, can be effective in combating structural unemployment. Increased aggregate demand would give employers an incentive to hire additional workers and, if necessary, train them on the job. Furthermore, in many cases, a college education is not necessary for satisfactory job performance. When substantial unemployment exists, firms may use educational levels as a screening device. If unemployment decreases, firms will tend to lower their formal requirements rather than compete for the limited number of college-trained persons. Also, as money wages increase, workers will have greater incentive to relocate. Finally, unless there are jobs available, there is little point in expanding manpower programs.

In retrospect, much of the unemployment of the late 1950s and early 1960s was due to inadequate aggregate demand rather than to structural change. Even so, there is little doubt that the mismatch between the educational and skill levels of unemployed workers and the educational and skill requirements associated with job vacancies is a problem. Attempts to reduce the unemployment rate below the natural rate by increasing aggregate demand will, under these circumstances, result in higher and higher rates of inflation with little or no reduction in the unemployment rate.

Since the passage of the Manpower Development and Training Act of 1962, the federal government has been involved, at one time or another, in numerous training programs. These have included the Job Corps, Job Opportunities in the Business Sector (JOBS), and the Work Incentive Program (WIN), as well as many other programs.[18] These programs vary in that some involve classroom instruction, while others involve on-the-job training (OJT).

Despite the potential of these programs as a means to reduce the natural unemployment rate, the results have been mixed. About a third of the trainees (depending on the type of program) drop out for one reason or another. Moreover, the placement record varies. For example, for those in the WIN program, only about one-half find jobs within 30 days after completion of the program. As expected, the placement record is better during periods of prosperity than during recessions. In view of these and other problems, most experts conclude that the training programs have yet to fulfill their potential.

The Legal Minimum Wage

In the previous section, it was argued that one of the reasons for a high natural unemployment rate is that many prospective workers lack the education and skills necessary to fill the existing job vacancies. This problem is compounded by the existence of minimum wage laws.[19] These laws discourage firms from hiring persons with minimal skills. As a consequence, many economists favor abolishing or modifying these laws.

Following the passage of the Fair Labor Standards Act of 1938, a federal minimum wage, 25 cents per hour, was imposed for workers engaged in interstate commerce. Over the years, the minimum wage has been increased and its coverage broadened. In addition, many states have passed minimum wage legislation of their own.

The impact of the minimum wage varies considerably. Since the minimum wage is usually set well below the average wage, it has little or no impact on most workers. The impact on persons with minimal job skills is more serious. In the absence of a minimum wage, firms will hire the young and inexperienced as well as others with minimal skills despite their low productivity. With a minimum wage, firms have no incentive to hire them.

Because of their impact on the employment of persons with minimal job skills, many economists believe that the minimum wage should be abolished. Others believe that teenagers, the main group adversely affected by the minimum wage, should be excluded. If this were done, more teenagers would obtain jobs that provide valuable experience.

The Public Employment Service

Improving the public employment service is advocated as another means to reduce the natural unemployment rate. It is claimed, for example, that a more efficient employment service would speed job placement and reduce the mismatching of workers and jobs, which tends to increase labor turnover. This view is based on the notion that workers and firms lack information.

Just as workers differ in terms of the education and skills that they possess, jobs differ in terms of wages and working conditions. In view of this heterogeneity, it is unlikely that workers will have complete information about wage rates and working conditions elsewhere. Moreover, while they continue to be employed, they may have difficulty in obtaining the relevant information. Consequently, it is rational for workers to quit in order to devote full time to job search. It is also rational for them to refuse the first job offer since they may find better jobs by continuing their search. Workers, however, will not search indefinitely, because as time passes they will scale down their expectations if they cannot find jobs that meet those expectations. Persons engaged in full-time job search are, of course, counted as unemployed.

Unemployment of this type cannot be eliminated permanently by increasing aggregate demand. With an increase in aggregate demand, money wages and prices increase and unemployment is reduced, because at least some of the unemployed find jobs that now fulfill their expectations in terms of wages and working conditions. But as workers realize that real wages have decreased because of inflation rather than increased, the unemployment rate will return to the natural rate. Consequently, other types of policies are necessary to reduce the unemployment rate.[20]

Our present employment service system was established by the Wagner-Peyser Act of 1933. This act provided that states establishing employment services would receive matching funds from the federal government. In return, the federal government reserved the right to prescribe minimum standards. Thus, the present public employment system represents a joint effort by federal and state governments.

Most towns and cities with populations of 10,000 or more have local employment service offices. These offices provide information about job openings to job-seekers and information about job applicants to prospective employers. In addition, they are supposed to match prospective workers and job vacancies through recruitment, interviews, and tests of job applicants.

Despite the widespread availability of these services, only a small proportion of placements (probably less than one-fourth) in private industry is through the employment service. The main reason is that employers can usually fill good jobs easily without listing them with the service. Another reason is that, historically, the employment service has been associated with the unemployment compensation program. This has discouraged skilled and white-collar workers from using the service and also discouraged employers from listing jobs, because they believe the service is more interested in placing those drawing unemployment compensation than in meeting their job requirements.

Many believe that an expanded and improved employment service could reduce the unemployment rate significantly by speeding up job placement and improving the quality of the matches.[21] By speeding up job placement, the unemployment rate will be reduced since fewer workers will be recorded as unemployed each month. By improving the matches, the unemployment rate will be reduced since labor turnover will be less. Specific recommendations include encouragement of employers to list jobs, elimination of administration of unemployment compensation programs, and increased use of computers. With regard to the latter, some believe that a nationwide computerized system for matching workers and jobs would be advantageous.

Critics of this approach do not deny that the proposed changes are desirable.[22] They argue, however, that the reduction in the unemployment rate will be much less than claimed. For one thing, many employers have no incentive to participate because they have a sufficient number of good applicants. For another, if the service does speed job placement, it may have adverse effects on quits and layoffs. If it is easier to find a job, workers may be more likely to quit. Similarly, the easier it is to fill a position, the more likely an employer will be to fire. Consequently, increased quits and layoffs will tend to offset the faster placement of workers. In view of these and other criticisms, it is not clear that an expanded and improved public employment service will reduce the natural unemployment rate significantly.

Unemployment Compensation

In the previous section, it was argued that an improved public employment service would speed job placement and reduce labor turnover. We now consider the nation's unemployment compensation (insurance) system. This system, it is claimed, unduly prolongs job search and promotes temporary layoffs. As a consequence, the natural unemployment rate is increased.

Among other things, the Social Security Act of 1935 provided for a federal-state system of unemployment insurance. Although state laws vary, workers are usually eligible for unemployment compensation if they have had sufficient employment and earnings during the preceding year, are unemployed through no fault of their own, are willing and able to work, and are available for work. Benefits are usually 50 percent or less of a person's weekly earnings. The benefits are, however, tax-free, so they are a higher percentage of a person's net earnings. For the most part, benefits are payable for a maximum of 26 weeks.

A number of economists, including Martin S. Feldstein, have argued strongly that the present system of unemployment compensation increases the natural unemployment rate.[23] According to Feldstein, unemployment insurance replaces approximately two-thirds of lost net earnings for covered workers. Consequently, unemployed workers may continue to search for jobs until their unemployment insurance benefits are exhausted. Also, with the present system, firms have a greater incentive to lay off workers in response to temporary changes in demand because they can be relatively confident of rehiring them when demand increases. By prolonging job search and providing firms with a greater incentive for temporary layoffs, the unemployment compensation system results in a higher unemployment rate.[24]

Among other things, Feldstein has proposed that unemployment compensation be taxed at the same rate as other income and that it be made more costly for firms to lay off workers temporarily. He believes that these changes would reduce the unemployment rate significantly. It must be recognized, however, that the system does provide important benefits to the unemployed. Consequently, the problem is to restructure the system so as to continue the benefits while removing the disincentive effects.

Public Service Employment

Over the years, public service employment (PSE) has been recommended as a means for reducing the natural unemployment rate.[25] The basic argument is that public service employment programs can focus on segments of the labor force and geographical regions with high unemployment rates, thereby reducing the overall unemployment rate.

There have been several major PSE programs. The first began in 1971 under the Emergency Employment Act (EEA); the second began in 1974–75 under the Comprehensive Employment and Training Act (CETA) of 1973. Under these programs, state and local governments received subsidies from the federal government to hire workers who had previously been unemployed. These funds were not to be used to employ workers in jobs that local funds would otherwise have paid for.

To reduce the natural unemployment rate, PSE programs must hire those that have difficulty in finding jobs in the private sector. Evidence exists, however, that CETA employees are better qualified than the unemployed population in general. In fact, many had jobs immediately prior to accepting public service employment. Moreover, the net increase in employment is likely to be less than anticipated because state and local governments have an incentive to substitute CETA employees for regular employees. It has been estimated that up to 60 percent of those hired under PSE programs in the first year merely replace regular hires. Over time, the substitution percentage rises; in the long run, it may be as high as 90 percent.

The federal government could, of course, attempt stricter enforcement. As just indicated, however, state and local governments have an incentive to substitute CETA for other employees. In addition, the officials that do the hiring have little incentive to hire the most disadvantaged persons since their primary interest is getting work done. Finally, even if the disadvantaged are hired, there is no guarantee that they will receive training which will qualify them for better jobs or promotion. In view of their shortcomings, it is not surprising that the various PSE programs have been abolished (example: CETA) or reduced in size under the Reagan administration.

In conclusion, it appears that an expansion of public service employment is unlikely to reduce the natural rate of unemployment. In the past, the net increase in jobs has been small, and no evidence exists to support the view that public service employment is concentrated on disadvantaged workers. Given the incentive structure, one cannot be optimistic about restructuring the program along the lines necessary to reduce the natural unemployment rate.

CONCLUDING REMARKS

In this chapter, we considered policies to reduce the inflation rate. For the most part, these policies are macroeconomic in nature. If these policies are successful, price stability will be achieved and the natural unemployment rate will prevail. Society, however, may view the natural unemployment rate as too high. If so, other policies, microeconomic in nature, must be used, since a more expansionary monetary policy will result in a higher inflation rate. Unfortunately, much disagreement exists as to which is the most appropriate set of policies to reduce the natural rate.

NOTES

1. George L. Perry, "Slowing the Wage–Price Spiral: The Macroeconomic View," *Brookings Papers on Economic Activity*, no. 2 (1978), 259–91. See also Edward M. Gramlich, "Macro Policy Responses to Price Shocks," *Brookings Papers on Economic Activity,* no. 1 (1979), 125–66.

2. Arthur M. Okun, "Efficient Disinflationary Policies," *American Economic Review*, 68 (May 1978), 348–52.

3. As an example, see Okun, ibid., pp. 350–52.

4. William Fellner, *Towards a Reconstruction of Macroeconomics* (Washington, D.C.: American Enterprise Institute, 1976). See also Fellner, "The Credibility Effect and Rational Expectations: Implications of the Gramlich Study," *Brookings Papers on Economic Activity*, no. 1 (1979), 167–78; and "The Valid Core of Rationality Hypotheses in the Theory of Expectations," *Journal of Money, Credit, and Banking*, 12 (November 1980), 762–87.

5. In a completely indexed world, money would also be indexed so as to maintain its purchasing power.

6. If money were indexed, it would also reduce the costs associated with anticipated inflation.

7. Milton Friedman, "Monetary Correction," in Herbert Giersch and others, *Essays on Inflation and Indexation* (Washington, D.C.: American Enterprise Institute, 1974), pp. 25–61; and "Using Escalators to Help Fight Inflation," *Fortune Magazine* (July 1974), 94–97, 174, and 176.

8. For discussions, see Jo Anna Gray, "Wage Indexation: A Macroeconomic Approach," *Journal of Monetary Economics*, 2 (April 1976), 221–35; Stanley Fischer, "Wage Indexation and Macroeconomic Stability," in *Stabilization of the Domestic and International*

Economy, eds. Karl Brunner and Allan Meltzer, (Amsterdam: North-Holland, 1977), pp. 107–47; and Alex Cukierman, "The Effects of Wage Indexation on Macroeconomic Fluctuations," *Journal of Monetary Economics*, 6 (April 1980), 147–70.

9. For a discussion, see Neil Bruce, "Some Macroeconomic Effects of Income Tax Indexation," *Journal of Monetary Economics*, 8 (September 1981), 271–75.

10. James L. Pierce and Jared J. Enzler have suggested that indexing of the personal income tax system will have a negligible impact on economic stability. Pierce and Enzler, "The Implication for Economic Stability of Indexing the Individual Income Tax," in *Inflation and the Income Tax*, ed. Henry J. Aaron, (Washington, D.C.: The Brookings Institution, 1976), pp. 173–88.

11. For a discussion, see Jai-hoon Yang, "The Case For and Against Indexation: An Attempt at Perspective," Federal Reserve Bank of St. Louis, *Review*, 56 (October 1974), 2–11.

12. For a description of the procedure and the various definitions, see Department of Labor, Bureau of Labor Statistics, *Employment and Earnings* (Washington, D.C.: Government Printing Office), various issues.

13. The data have been seasonally adjusted to eliminate changes which can be ascribed to the normal pattern of seasonal variation. This makes it possible to observe cyclical and other nonseasonal changes in the data.

14. *Economic Report of the President, 1983* (Washington, D.C.: Government Printing Office, 1983), pp. 38–39.

15. The unemployment which exists at full employment is usually referred to as *frictional unemployment*.

16. See, for example, Charles C. Killingsworth, "Automation, Jobs, and Manpower," in *Nation's Manpower Revolution, Part 5*, Hearings before the Subcommittee on Employment and Manpower, Senate Committee on Labor and Public Welfare, 88th Cong., 1st Sess. (Washington, D.C.: Government Printing Office, 1963), pp. 1461–83. See also Eleanor G. Gilpatrick, *Structural Unemployment and Aggregate Demand* (Baltimore, Md.: Johns Hopkins University Press, 1966); and Richard Perlman, *Labor Theory* (New York: John Wiley & Sons, Inc., 1969), pp. 167–96.

17. *Higher Unemployment Rates, 1957–60: Structural Transformation or Inadequate Demand*, Subcommittee on Economic Statistics of the Joint Economic Committee, Congress of the United States (Washington, D.C.: Government Printing Office, 1961).

18. For a discussion, see Lloyd G. Reynolds, Stanley H. Masters, and Colletta H. Moser, *Labor Economics and Labor Relations*, 9th ed. (Englewood Cliffs, N.J.: Prentice-Hall, Inc., 1986).

19. For an introduction to the literature, see Douglas Adie, "Teenage Unemployment and Real Federal Minimum Wages," *Journal of Political Economy*, 81 (March–April 1973), 435–41; Finis Welch, "Minimum Wage Legislation in the United States," *Economic Inquiry*, 12 (September 1974), 285–318; Jacob Mincer, "Unemployment Effects of Minimum Wages," *Journal of Political Economy*, 84 (August 1976), S87–S104; Edward M. Gramlich, "Impact of Minimum Wages on Other Wages, Employment, and Family Incomes," *Brookings Papers on Economic Activity*, no. 2 (1976), 409–51; and Charles Brown, Curtis Gilroy, and Andrew Kohen, "The Effect of the Minimum Wage on Employment and Unemployment," *Journal of Economic Literature*, 20 (June 1982), 487–528.

20. Manpower training programs will not be successful in reducing this type of unemployment since the problem is lack of information, not lack of job skills or education.

21. See, for example, Charles C. Holt, C. Duncan MacRae, Stuart O. Schweitzer, and Ralph E. Smith, "Manpower Proposals for Phase III," *Brookings Papers on Economic Activity*, no. 3 (1971), 703–22.

22. See, for example, Robert E. Hall, "Prospects for Shifting the Phillips Curve through Manpower Policy," *Brookings Papers on Economic Activity*, no. 3 (1971), 659–701.

23. Martin S. Feldstein, "The Economics of the New Unemployment," *Public Interest*, 33 (Fall 1973), 3–42; and *Lowering the Permanent Rate of Unemployment*, a study prepared for the use of the Joint Economic Committee, Congress of the United States (Washington, D.C.: Government Printing Office, 1973).

24. Much disagreement exists about the magnitude. For surveys of the evidence, see Daniel S. Hamermesh, *Jobless Pay and the Economy*, (Baltimore, Md.: Johns Hopkins University Press, 1977); and Finis Welch, "What Have We Learned from Empirical Studies of Unemployment Insurance?" *Industrial and Labor Relations Review*, 30 (July 1977), 451–61.

25. It has also been recommended as a means to (1) restructure the economy so that it has a larger public sector and (2) reduce unemployment during recessions. It is not clear that a larger public sector is desirable and, even if it is, that public service employment is the best way to achieve that goal. With regard to reducing unemployment during recessions, policy makers have other means at their disposal. Also, both capital and labor are idle during recessions. Since the idle capital is concentrated in the private sector, it is better to create jobs in the private sector than in the public sector.

REVIEW QUESTIONS

1. Why do many Keynesians favor using wage–price guidelines or controls (in conjunction with a less expansionary monetary policy) to reduce the inflation rate? Why are other economists opposed to their usage?

2. Compare and contrast the views of monetarists, rational expectations theorists, and supply-siders regarding the costs associated with reducing the inflation rate.

3. What is indexation? Outline the arguments for and against it.

4. How might indexation lead to greater instability in the economy?

5. Suppose 90 million workers are employed and 10 million are unemployed. If the total number of persons aged 16 and over is 120 million, calculate the unemployment rate.

6. Explain why unemployment exists even at full employment.

7. Suppose part of the unemployment which exists at full employment is due to mismatches between the educational and skill levels of the unemployed and the educational and skill levels associated with existing job vacancies. Explain why more expansionary monetary and fiscal policies are unlikely to reduce or eliminate this type of unemployment. What policies would you recommend to reduce or eliminate it?

8. Suppose part of the unemployment which exists at full employment is due to lack of information on the part of workers and firms. Explain why more expansionary monetary and fiscal policies are unlikely to permanently reduce

or eliminate this type of unemployment. What policies would you recommend to reduce or eliminate it?

9. What is public service employment (PSE)? How might PSE programs be used to reduce the natural rate of unemployment? Based on past experience, do you believe such programs will be successful? Defend your answer.

10. Discuss the roles of microeconomic and macroeconomic policies with regard to unemployment.

SUGGESTED READING

ARAK, MARCELLE V., "Indexation of Wages and Retirement Income in the United States," Federal Reserve Bank of New York, *Quarterly Review*, 3 (Autumn 1978), 16–23.

FELDSTEIN, MARTIN S., "The Economics of the New Unemployment," *Public Interest*, 33 (Fall 1973), 3–42.

FELLNER, WILLIAM, *Towards a Reconstruction of Macroeconomics.* Washington, D.C.: American Enterprise Institute, 1976.

GIERSCH, HERBERT, and others, *Essays on Inflation and Indexation.* Washington, D.C.: American Enterprise Institute, 1974.

HALL, ROBERT E., "Why Is the Unemployment Rate So High at Full Employment?" *Brookings Papers on Economic Activity*, no. 3 (1970), 369–402.

HAMERMESH, DANIEL S., *Jobless Pay and the Economy.* Baltimore, Md.: Johns Hopkins University Press, 1977.

HORRIGAN, BRIAN, "Indexation: A Reasonable Response to Inflation," Federal Reserve Bank of Philadelphia, *Business Review* (September–October 1981), 3–11.

PALMER, JOHN L. (ed.), *Creating Jobs: Public Employment Programs and Wage Subsidies.* Washington, D.C.: The Brookings Institution, 1978.

PHELPS, EDMUND S., and others, *Microeconomic Foundations of Employment and Inflation Theory.* New York: W. W. Norton & Co., Inc., 1970.

REYNOLDS, LLOYD G., STANLEY H. MASTERS, and COLLETTA H. MOSER, *Labor Economics and Labor Relations* (9th ed.). Englewood Cliffs, N.J: Prentice-Hall, Inc., 1986.

SMITH, SHARON P., "The Changing Composition of the Labor Force," Federal Reserve Bank of New York, *Quarterly Review*, 1 (Winter 1976), 24–30.

16

INTERNATIONAL TRADE
AND STABILIZATION POLICY

According to the national income accounts, exports of goods and services totaled $370.2 billion (in current dollars) in 1985, 9.3 percent of gross national product. Imports of goods and services equaled $447.0 billion, equivalent to 11.2 percent of gross national product. Thus, although exports are a smaller fraction of gross national product for the United States than for many other countries, the fraction is not negligible for the economy as a whole and certainly not negligible for various sectors of the economy, such as agriculture. The same is true for imports.

In this chapter, we incorporate the foreign trade sector into the earlier macroeconomic models. Before doing so, we consider the U.S. balance of payments and define what is meant by equilibrium in the balance of payments. After incorporating the foreign trade sector into the various models of income determination, we consider policy implications.

THE BASIS FOR INTERNATIONAL TRADE

International trade is based on the principle of comparative advantage. Consider two countries, the United States and the United Kingdom, and two types of products, agricultural and manufactured goods. Suppose that both types of products can be produced in the United States with fewer resources than in the United Kingdom. At first glance, there appears to be no basis for mutually advantageous trade between the countries, since the United States is more efficient in the production of both types of goods. If, however, the United States is relatively more efficient in the production of one type of good, a basis for mutually advantageous trade exists.

To illustrate, suppose only labor is necessary to produce agricultural and manufactured goods. Assume that an hour of labor is required to produce 20 units of agricultural goods or 5 units of manufactured goods in the United States. Assume also that an hour of labor produces only 8 units of agricultural goods or 4 units of manufactured goods in the United Kingdom. Although the United States is more efficient in producing both goods, it is relatively more efficient in the production of agricultural goods, whereas the United Kingdom is relatively more efficient in the production of manufactured goods. Under the circumstances, the United States should specialize in producing agricultural goods and the United Kingdom in producing manufactured goods. If the United States produces agricultural goods, it may export those goods to the United Kingdom in exchange for manufactured goods. Assuming that the exchange ratio is, say, three units of agricultural goods per unit of manufactured goods, both countries benefit. If the United States were to reallocate labor from agriculture to manufacturing, agricultural production would decline by four units for each additional unit of manufacturing goods produced. By specializing in agricultural production and exporting agricultural goods in exchange for manufactured goods, the United States can get a unit of manufactured goods for only three units of agricultural products. Similarly, by specializing in manufacturing and exporting manufactured goods in exchange for agricultural goods, the United Kingdom can get three units of agricultural goods for each unit of manufactured goods. If the United Kingdom were to reallocate labor from manufacturing to agriculture, it could obtain only two additional units of agricultural goods for each unit of manufacturing production lost.

In the foregoing example, the countries benefit from international trade because it allows them to specialize in relatively efficient productive activities. Should international trade be interrupted, the countries would be forced to engage in a wide range of activities, including those in which they are relatively inefficient.[1]

THE BALANCE OF PAYMENTS

The *balance of payments* is a summary of all economic transactions between households, firms, and government agencies of one country and the rest of the world during a given period of time. The transactions include exports, imports, and various capital flows. The transactions are divided into two categories: those giving rise to dollar inpayments (plus items) and those resulting in dollar outpayments (minus items). The U.S. balance of payments for 1985 is shown in Table 16.1.

In 1985, exports of goods (line 1) amounted to $214.0 billion; imports (line 2) equaled $338.3 billion. Since exports give rise to dollar inpayments, exports are recorded as a plus item. Since imports require dollar outpayments, they are recorded as a minus item. In 1985, merchandise imports exceeded merchandise exports by $124.3 billion. This excess of imports over exports is indicated by the merchandise trade balance (line 3).

Net expenditures on travel and transportation are denoted in line 4. When U.S. citizens travel abroad, what they spend for meals, hotel accommodations, and transportation represents outpayments. When foreigners visit this country, the amount they spend for meals, hotels, and transportation constitutes inpayments. Similarly, the shipping charges for goods transported by foreign vessels are recorded as outpayments; similar charges for goods transported by U.S. ships are listed as

TABLE 16.1 Summary of U.S. international transactions in 1985[1] (millions of dollars)

Line	Item	Plus	Minus	Balance
	Merchandise:			
1	Exports	213,990		
2	Imports		338,279	
3	*Balance on Merchandise Trade*			− 124,289
	Services:			
4	Travel and transportation, net		11,741	
5	Investment income, net	24,684		
6	Other services, net[2]	8,467		
7	*Balance on Goods and Services*			− 102,880
8	Unilateral transfers, net		14,784	
9	*Balance on Current Account*			− 117,664
	Capital flows:			
10	Net change in U.S. government assets other than official reserve assets		2,628	
11	Net change in U.S. private assets		31,697	
12	Net changes in foreign private assets in the United States	125,016		
13	Statistical discrepancy	32,739		
14	*Official Reserve Transactions Balance*			5,764
	Official short-term capital, net			
15	Net changes in U.S. reserve assets		3,858	
16	Net changes in foreign official assets in the United States		1,908	

[1]Preliminary. Small discrepancies exist because of rounding.
[2]Includes military transactions.

Source: U.S. Department of Commerce, *Survey of Current Business*, 66 (March 1986), 36.

inpayments. In 1985, net travel and transportation payments amounted to $11.8 billion. Since outpayments exceeded inpayments by that amount, the entry is recorded as a minus item.

Net investment income is shown on line 5. Investment income arises from interest and dividend payments. United States citizens own stocks and bonds of foreign companies. These holdings produce income which is recorded as a plus item in the balance of payments. By the same token, foreigners own stocks and bonds of U.S. corporations. These holdings result in payments which are recorded as a minus item. According to Table 16.1, net investment income (line 5) was $24.7 billion in 1985. Since investment income from abroad exceeded that paid to foreigners, the amount enters as a plus item. Fees and royalties from direct investment abroad or from foreign direct investment in the United States are included in "other services" rather than "investment income." In 1985, (net) inpayments from other services (line 6) amounted to $8.5 billion.

The balance on goods and services (line 7) was $102.9 billion in 1985. This balance differs from net exports of goods and services in the national income accounts in that the former includes special military sales and U.S. government interest payments.

Unilateral transfers are shown on line 8. They include foreign aid, as well as private gifts of money to persons or organizations in foreign countries. Net unilateral transfers totaled $14.8 billion in 1985. Since outpayments exceeded inpayments by that amount, the entry is a minus item.

The entries discussed so far (lines 1, 2, 4, 5, 6, and 8) constitute the *current account.* In 1985, the balance on current account was $117.7 billion.

We now turn to the *capital account* (lines 10 to 12). Capital outpayments (minus items) are denoted in lines 10 and 11. They include government loans (less repayments of loans) to foreign countries, direct private investment abroad by U.S. corporations (including the establishment of foreign subsidiaries), and purchases of foreign securities (such as stocks and bonds) and deposits in foreign banks by U.S. citizens. These outpayments increase U.S. asset holdings. Corresponding to these outpayments are inpayments resulting from direct private investment in the United States by foreign corporations and the purchases of U.S. securities and deposits in U.S. banks by foreigners. The total of these inpayments (plus items) is shown on line 12.

The statistical discrepancy entry (line 13) is included as a balancing entry and serves the same function as the statistical discrepancy in the national income accounts (see Chapter 2). Note that in 1985 it was relatively large, $32.7 billion.

The official reserve transactions balance (line 14) shows the balance for the preceding entries. In 1985, it was $5.8 billion.

The net change in U.S. reserve assets is shown in line 15. These assets consist mainly of gold and foreign currencies. Since an increase in these assets can be obtained by an outpayment of dollars, an increase is shown as a minus item. In 1985, the United States experienced an increase in reserve assets of $3.9 billion. The net change in foreign official assets is shown in line 16. These assets include

U.S. Treasury bills held by foreign central banks. Since a decrease in these assets may involve a dollar outpayment, an increase is shown as a minus item. In 1985, foreign official assets in the United States decreased by $1.9 billion.

The data in Table 16.1 represent a summary of international transactions for the United States. The data are recorded in terms of plus and minus items. Since the table is based on a double-entry accounting system, the sum of the plus entries must equal the sum of the minus entries. In other words, the balance of payments must balance. For example, in 1985, merchandise imports exceeded merchandise exports by $124.3 billion. This excess of imports over exports must have been financed somehow in order for it to have occurred. The remaining entries in the table indicate how it was financed.

Before 1976, the U.S. Department of Commerce published various balances, such as the balance on goods and services. Since these balances were based on only part of the balance of payments, the balances could be classified as surpluses or deficits. For example, if the sum of the plus items for goods and services is greater (less) than the sum of the minus items, a *surplus (deficit)* is said to exist. By this definition, the balance of goods and services showed a deficit of $103.9 billion in 1985.

Several of these balances (called *overall balances*) were held to useful in discussing equilibrium in the balance of payments. With regard to balance of payments equilibrium, two types of transactions must be distinguished: autonomous and accommodating. *Autonomous transactions* are those determined by such factors as domestic and foreign incomes, domestic prices relative to foreign prices, and interest rate differentials. In contrast, *balancing or accommodating transactions* are those determined by the state of the balance of payments. To illustrate, suppose the transactions listed above line 14 in Table 16.1 are regarded as autonomous, while those below line 14 are accommodating. Since the sum of the plus items exceeds the sum of the minus items above line 14, the official reserve transactions balance, $5.8 billion, suggests that the United States had a balance of payments surplus of that amount in 1985. This surplus was determined by the autonomous transactions (assumed in the example to be those transactions listed above line 14) and accommodated by those transactions listed below line 14. In this case, the surplus has been financed by an increase in U.S. reserve assets and by a decrease in foreign official assets in the United States.

From a statistical standpoint, it is difficult or impossible to classify transactions in terms of autonomous and accommodating. For this reason, the Advisory Committee on the Presentation of Balance of Payments Statistics emphasized in its 1976 report that a meaningful picture of U.S. international transactions can be obtained only by studying all categories of transactions, rather than one or several balances.[2] They recommended, therefore, that the publication of various balances (such as the official reserve transactions balance) be discontinued.

The committee did recommend continuation of two balances—the goods and services and current account balances—largely because of their relationships to other economic accounting systems. For example, the balance on goods and services is closely related to net exports in the national income accounts. In addition, the committee recommended that the words *surplus* and *deficit* be avoided since situations described by these words are often interpreted as *good* and *bad*, respectively. According to the committee, this interpretation is often incorrect. For the most part, the committee's recommendations have been accepted.

Although the Department of Commerce no longer publishes overall balances because of difficulties in distinguishing between autonomous and accommodating transactions, the distinction is important conceptually. In fact, *equilibrium* in the *balance of payments* requires that the sum of the outpayments associated with the autonomous transactions equal the sum of the inpayments associated with the autonomous transactions. If the sum of the outpayments exceeds the sum of the inpayments, the country is experiencing a *balance of payments deficit*. If the opposite is true, the country is experiencing a *balance of payments surplus*. A country may run a balance of payments deficit for a time. Its ability to do so depends upon the size of its international reserves and the willingness of other countries to accept its currency. Eventually, however, the country must take corrective action to eliminate the deficit. The United States has been fortunate in this regard. It has had a balance of payments deficit more or less continuously since 1950. The dollar, however, is an international currency and other countries have been willing to accept dollars. Most countries are not so fortunate.

A country experiencing a surplus is in much the same position. Sooner or later it must adjust, because a surplus on the part of one country implies a deficit for at least one other country. In many cases, it is easier for a surplus country to take corrective action than for a deficit country.

In the next section, for simplicity, we assume that exchange rates are fixed. An *exchange rate* is the number of units of one currency exchangeable for a unit of another. A U.S. citizen planning to visit the United Kingdom may, before the trip, wish to trade dollars for pounds. If a British pound is worth $2.00 in U.S. currency, the person will be able to swap dollars for pounds at that exchange rate. Later, we shall assume that exchange rates are free to fluctuate.

INTERNATIONAL TRADE AND THE DOMESTIC ECONOMY

In 1985, exports of goods and services accounted for 9.3 percent of gross national product; imports were equivalent to 11.2 percent of gross national product. To a degree, the percentages understate the importance of exports and imports to our economy. For example, should exports increase, the impact will spread throughout the economy rather than being confined to the export sector. To examine the impact of, say, an increase in exports, we shall incorporate the foreign sector into the earlier models of income determination.

Initially, suppose exports, X, are exogenous, so that

(16.1)
$$X = X_0.$$

Similarly, assume that imports, M, are positively related to income, Y. This implies that as income increases, imports also increase. This assumption is plausible, since as income increases both households and firms purchase more from abroad. For simplicity, suppose imports are a linear function of income so that

(16.2)
$$M = M_0 + mY \quad (0 < m < 1).$$

In the equation, m represents the marginal propensity to import, the change in imports associated with a change in income.

The export and import functions can now be incorporated into the model of Chapter 4 to obtain

$$C = a + bY_d \quad (\text{where } Y_d = Y - T),$$

$$I = I_0,$$

$$G = G_0,$$

$$T = T_0 + tY,$$

$$X = X_0,$$

$$M = M_0 + mY.$$

The equilibrium condition is

$$I + G + X = S + T + M.$$

Exports have the same impact on aggregate demand as investment and government purchases. Consequently, exports are added to the left side of the equilibrium condition. In contrast, imports have the same impact as saving and taxes. Therefore, imports are added to the right side of the equilibrium condition.

The equilibrium level of income may be determined algebraically by substituting the various relationships into the equilibrium condition. The equilibrium level of income may also be determined by plotting the $I + G + X$ and $S + T + M$ functions and finding the intersection of the two functions. These functions are plotted in Figure 16.1.[3] If the initial level of exports is X_0, the equilibrium level of income is Y_0, given by the intersection of the $S + T + M$ and $I_0 + G_0 + X_0$ curves.

Suppose the level of exports increases from X_0 to X_1. With the increase in exports, the $I + G + X$ function shifts upward, thereby increasing the equilibrium level of income. The amount of the increase in income can be determined with the

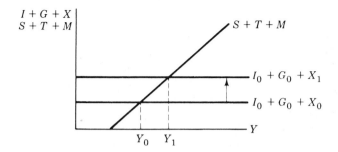

FIGURE 16.1

Exports, imports, and the equilibrium level of income

aid of the export multiplier. In Chapters 3 and 4, multipliers were derived for investment, government purchases, and taxes. Based on the foregoing model, it is possible to derive multipliers for exports and imports. In the case of exports, the multiplier is $1/(1 - b + bt + m)$. If b is 0.75, t is 0.20, and m is 0.10, the export multiplier is

$$\frac{1}{1 - 0.75 + 0.75\,(0.20) + 0.10} = \frac{1}{0.50} = 2.$$

This implies that an increase in exports of \$20 billion will ultimately result in a \$40 billion increase in income. Thus, an increase in exports is beneficial not only to the export sector of the economy but also to the economy as a whole, because as exports increase, income increases. The recipients of the increase in income respond by increasing their consumption. This, in turn, also increases income and, therefore, consumption. Like an increase in investment or government purchases, an increase in exports results, through the multiplier process, in an increase in income which is greater than the initial increase in exports.

With the increase in exports and income, imports also increase. If the marginal propensity to import is 0.10 and the change in income is \$40 billion, imports increase by \$4 billion, obtained by multiplying the marginal propensity to import by the change in income. This increase in imports occurs because, as income increases, households and firms purchase more from abroad. Consequently, despite the \$20 billion increase in exports, net exports (exports minus imports) increase by only \$16 billion.

If society decides to import more, the $S + T + M$ curve shifts upward and the equilibrium level of income decreases. If the new $S + T + M$ curve is parallel to the original curve, the change in income can be determined with the assistance of the import multiplier, $-1/(1 - b + bt + m)$.[4] The import multiplier is identical to the export multiplier except for sign. The minus sign indicates that an increase in imports results in a decrease in income.

Multipliers for investment, government purchases, and taxes may be derived from the preceding model. These multipliers are smaller (in absolute terms) than the corresponding multipliers of Chapter 4, because, as government purchases (investment) increase (increases) or taxes decrease, income increases, resulting in an increase in imports. With part of the increase in income being spent on imports rather than domestically produced goods, the ultimate increase in income is less.

In the preceding analysis, exports have been assumed exogenous. But U.S. exports depend, in part, on income in the rest of the world. Consequently, if income in the rest of the world were to increase, exports would increase, thereby increasing income in the United States through the multiplier effect. As income increases, however, imports increase. Since goods and services imported into the United States are exports of other countries, the increase in imports has a stimulating effect on income abroad. The resulting increase in income induces those countries to import more from other countries, including the United States. As a consequence, exports increase once again. It is possible to construct a model of income determination which allows for these foreign repercussions. Since these models are more often covered in textbooks on international economics, we omit them and proceed to incorporate the foreign sector into the models of Chapters 9 and 10.[5]

The IS–LM Model

The export and import functions just postulated can be incorporated into the IS–LM model of Chapter 9 and the aggregate supply–aggregate demand model of Chapter 10. With prices assumed variable in the aggregate supply–aggregate demand model, it seems more reasonable to asume that exports and imports depend, in part, on domestic prices relative to foreign prices. For example, if prices in the United States rise relative to prices abroad, exports become less attractive to foreign buyers and imports become more attractive. We shall also assume that exports depend, in part, on income abroad. In equation form, the export function is

$$\textbf{(16.3)} \qquad\qquad X = X\!\left(Y_0^F, \frac{P}{P_0^F} \right),$$

where X represents exports, Y_0^F foreign income, which is assumed to be exogenous, and P/P_0^F the ratio of domestic prices to foreign prices, with foreign prices assumed to be exogenous. Should income abroad increase, exports increase. If domestic prices rise relative to foreign prices, however, exports decline.[6]

The corresponding import function is

$$\textbf{(16.4)} \qquad\qquad M = M\!\left(Y, \frac{P}{P_0^F} \right),$$

where M represents imports, Y domestic income, and P/P_0^F the ratio of domestic prices to foreign prices, with foreign prices assumed to be exogenous. Should income increase, imports increase. Imports also increase if domestic prices rise relative to foreign prices.

To obtain IS and LM curves, we assume initially that prices are constant. With prices and foreign income constant, exports are also constant so that exports may be added to the $I + G$ function in the same manner as government purchases were added to the investment function in Chapter 6. The $I + G + X$ function is plotted in Figure 16.2.

With prices assumed constant, imports are a function of income as postulated in equation (16.2) and the $S + T + M$ curve is the same as the curve plotted in Figure 16.1. The $S + T + M$ curve is plotted, with axes reversed, in Figure 16.2. The IS curve is derived in the same manner as in Chapter 6.[7]

Should income abroad increase, exports increase and the $I + G + X$ curve shifts to the left. As a result, the IS curve shifts to the right. If domestic prices rise relative to foreign prices, imports increase and exports decrease. The increase in imports shifts the $S + T + M$ curve to the left; the decrease in exports shifts the $I + G + X$ function to the right. In both cases, the IS curve shifts to the left.

The LM curve is derived from the supply of, and demand for, money functions in the same manner as in Chapter 8. It must be recognized, however, that the balance of payments may have an impact on the money supply. Suppose, for example, a country is importing more than it is exporting. If the deficit is financed by increased holdings of its currency abroad, the country's money supply decreases. For the present, we assume that the monetary authorities take action to offset changes in the money supply due to balance of payments surpluses or deficits. By assumption, therefore, the money supply is independent of the balance of payment situation.

In addition to the IS and LM curves, we can now add a third curve, the BP curve. We have indicated that imports are a function of income. Capital flows are, in part, a function of domestic interest rates relative to foreign interest rates. If interest rates are higher in the United States than abroad, funds flow to the United

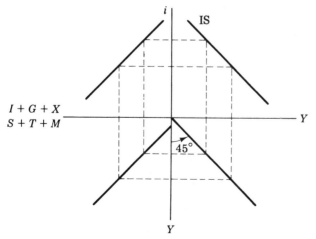

FIGURE 16.2

Exports, imports, and the IS curve

States. If interest rates are higher abroad than in the United States, funds flow to other countries.

These flows in response to interest rate differentials may serve to offset a deficit in the merchandise trade balance. For example, suppose a country is importing more than it is exporting. If its interest rate is sufficiently high relative to the rest of the world, the capital inflow will offset the deficit. As a result, equilibrium will prevail in the balance of payments.

Consequently, a third equilibrium relationship between income and the interest rate can be derived. As income increases, imports increase. Since exports are constant, the increases in imports result in greater and greater discrepancies between imports and exports. On the other hand, as interest rates increase, the inflow of funds becomes greater and greater. Thus, for every level of income and corresponding level of imports, there is an interest rate sufficiently high to provide a flow of funds to offset the difference between imports and exports. These combinations of income and interest rates constitute the BP curve. The BP curve is shown in Figure 16.3.

The BP curve consists of combinations of income and interest rates which provide for equilibrium in the balance of payments. At income level Y_0 and interest rate i_0, the balance of payments is in equilibrium. In contrast, at income level Y_0 and interest rate i_1, there is a balance of payments surplus because, at income level Y_0, imports are unchanged. The interest rate, i_1, is now higher than the equilibrium rate, i_0, and the corresponding capital inflow is greater than the equilibrium level. Consequently, the economy is experiencing a balance of payments surplus. By the same token, the economy has a balance of payments deficit at income level Y_0 and interest rate i_2.

To sum up, combinations of income and interest rates on the BP curve provide for equilibrium in the balance of payments. Combinations of income and interest rates to the left of the BP curve yield balance of payments surpluses; those to the right produce deficits. The BP curve itself is positively sloped since higher levels of income yield higher levels of imports. As a result, the interest rate must be

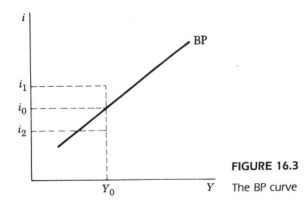

FIGURE 16.3

The BP curve

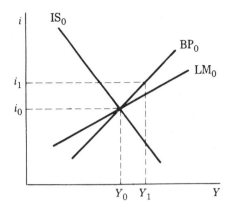

FIGURE 16.4

Internal and external equilibrium

higher in order to produce a greater capital inflow and maintain equilibrium in the balance of payments.

Given the BP curve, it is now possible to consider balance of payments equilibrium within the IS-LM context. Initially, suppose the relevant curves are IS_0, LM_0, and BP_0 in Figure 16.4. Suppose also that the economy's income is Y_0 and interest rate is i_0. The IS and LM curves intersect at income Y_0 and interest rate i_0. Consequently, the product and money markets are in equilibrium. Income Y_0 and interest rate i_0 are a combination of income and interest rates on the BP curve. Hence, the balance of payments is in equilibrium.

At income Y_0, the economy may be at full employment. But if the full employment level of income is Y_1, unemployment prevails at income Y_0. If unemployment exists at income Y_0, full employment and balance of payments equilibrium may be achieved through the appropriate mix of monetary and fiscal policies.[8] Since full employment prevails at income Y_1 and balance of payments equilibrium at income Y_1 and interest rate i_1, the authorities should undertake monetary and fiscal policies to achieve that combination of income and interest rates. In this case, expansionary fiscal policy should be used to shift the IS curve to the right so that it passes through the point (Y_1, i_1). Contractionary monetary policy should be used to shift the LM curve to the left so that it passes through the same point. Since the BP curve already passes through the point, the balance of payments remains in equilibrium. Since income is now Y_1, full employment also prevails.[9]

At income Y_1 and interest rate i_1, full employment and balance of payments equilibrium prevail. This combination of income and interest rate was achieved through expansionary fiscal policy and contractionary monetary policy. Even if it were technically feasible to achieve that combination of income and interest rate, it may not be possible to do so for political reasons. For example, interest rate i_1 may be viewed as "unreasonably high."[10] If it is not possible to use the appropriate combination of monetary and fiscal policies to achieve full employment and balance of payments equilibrium, policies designed to shift the BP curve must be used. These policies are discussed later.

Next, consider an economy with a balance of payments deficit. Suppose the relevant IS, LM, and BP curves are IS_0, LM_0, and BP_0, respectively, in Figure 16.5. If income is Y_0 and the interest rate is i_0, the product and money markets are in equilibrium. Since (Y_0, i_0) is a combination of income and interest rates off the BP curve, there is disequilibrium in the balance of payments. For the balance of payments to be in equilibrium at income Y_0, the interest rate must be i_1 in order to attract sufficient funds to equilibrate the balance of payments. Since the interest rate is only i_0, there is a balance of payments deficit.

Earlier, it was assumed that the monetary authorities take action to offset changes in the money supply due to balance of payments surpluses or deficits. For the moment, we assume that they do not. With a balance of payments deficit, the money supply declines and the LM curve shifts to the left. As income decreases, imports decrease. Moreover, as the money supply decreases and the interest rate increases, there is a greater inflow of capital. Both changes help to eliminate the balance of payments deficit. Adjustment will continue until income Y_2 and interest rate i_2, given by the intersection of the IS_0, LM_2, and BP_0 curves, are reached. At income Y_2 and interest rate i_2, the balance of payments is in equilibrium.[11]

In the example, adjustment continues until balance of payments equilibrium is achieved. The adjustment process is triggered by the response of the money supply to the balance of payments deficit. The monetary authorities may, however, act to offset the monetary effects of the balance of payments deficit. In fact, they are likely to do so since the nation's income and, hence, employment decrease as a result of the adjustment process. If offsetting action is taken, there will be no adjustment and the balance of payments deficit will remain.[12]

Rather than allow the adjustment process to continue and income to decrease, officials may use some other policy. For example, they may try to achieve full employment and balance of payments equilibrium through a combination of mon-

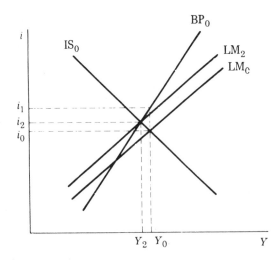

FIGURE 16.5

Adjustment to a balance of payments deficit

etary and fiscal policies. But this approach may fail for the reasons just given. Consequently, they may undertake policies designed to shift the BP curve. We now turn to those policies.

If a country is experiencing a balance of payments deficit, its leaders may decide to devalue the currency. The term *devaluation* refers to a decrease in the value of a currency in terms of other currencies. For example, the British pound was devalued from $4.00 to $2.80 in 1949.

With a devaluation, a country's exports appear cheaper to foreign purchasers. For example, after the British devaluation in 1949, British goods were cheaper in terms of dollars. A consumer in the United States could buy for $2.80 what he had previously bought for $4.00. Consequently, there was a tendency for British exports to increase.[13] Foreign goods appeared to be more expensive to the British. Before the devaluation, consumers in the United Kingdom could buy $4.00 worth of U.S. goods for a pound. After the devaluation, the same pound bought only $2.80 worth of U.S. goods. Hence, the British tended to purchase more from domestic sources and less from abroad. Thus, following a devaluation, the country's exports tend to increase and its imports to decrease. Both changes help to alleviate the country's balance of payments deficit, thereby shifting the BP curve to the right. With the increase in exports and decrease in imports, the IS curve also shifts to the right.

Because of its expansionary impact, devaluation is particularly attractive to countries experiencing both unemployment and a balance of payments deficit. Devaluation, however, has some disadvantages. It invites retaliation. When a country devalues its currency, its exports increase and its imports decrease. Its trading partners experience decreases in exports and increases in imports. The changes produce reductions in income and employment in those countries. As a result, they may devalue their currencies, thus frustrating the attempt of the first country to improve its balance of payments.

Rather than devaluing the currency, officials may impose tariffs or other trade restrictions. A *tariff* is a tax levied upon a good when it crosses a national boundary. An import tariff raises the price of the good to purchasers in the country levying the duty, thereby discouraging the importation of the good and encouraging its domestic production.

Assuming the country is at less than full employment, the reduction in imports results in an improvement in the balance of payments. To the extent that domestic production is encouraged, employment and output increase. This does not, however, suggest that imposing tariffs is the best solution to a balance of payments deficit. Again, foreign countries may retaliate by imposing tariffs on their imports. This means that exports from the initial country decline, implying that there may be no net improvement in its balance of payments. Tariffs also reduce international trade and, therefore, the gains from trade. For this reason, some other approach is desirable.

Rather than imposing tariffs, a country may erect other barriers to international trade. For example, it may impose *import quotas*. With an import quota, imports of a good are limited to a certain maximum level. Since a quota restricts the volume of imports, quotas raise the domestic price of a commodity in much the same manner as tariffs. But there is an important difference. With a tariff, more goods can be imported provided that buyers are willing to pay the price. Consequently, if domestic demand for the product increases, the domestic price cannot rise above the world price plus the tariff. This is not the case with a quota. If the domestic demand for the product increases, the domestic price can rise without limit since no more can be imported under a quota. As a consequence, quotas are even less desirable than tariffs.

Various other devices, such as voluntary export quotas (for foreign countries) and exchange controls are also used to reduce imports. Since they serve to limit international trade, they are subject to the same criticism as tariffs and quotas.

The Aggregate Supply–Aggregate Demand Model

Based on the IS-LM model of the previous section, it is possible to derive an aggregate demand curve by conceptually varying the price level. For price level P_0, there will be a level of income Y_0, which will equilibrate the product and money markets. Should the price level be reduced to P_1, the real money supply increases. As a consequence, the real money supply curve and, hence, the LM curve shift to the right (as indicated in Chapter 10). With the price reduction, however, domestic prices fall relative to foreign prices. As a result, exports increase and imports decrease. With the increase in exports, the $I + G + X$ curve shifts to the left, and with the decrease in imports, the $S + T + M$ curve shifts to the right. Both shifts result in movements of the IS curve to the right. With both the IS and LM curves shifting to the right, there is a greater increase in the equilibrium level of income than previously. This implies that the new aggregate demand curve is more elastic than the aggregate demand curve of Chapter 10.[14]

The new aggregate demand curve may be superimposed on the aggregate supply curve of Chapter 10 in order to determine the equilibrium levels of prices, money wages, employment, and output. For example, suppose aggregate demand is AD_0 and aggregate supply is AS_0 in Figure 16.6. This implies that the equilibrium levels of prices, money wages, real wages, employment, and output are P_0, W_0, $(W/P)_0$, N_0 and Y_0, respectively.

Suppose income abroad increases so that the imports of those countries increase. This means that exports of the country under consideration increase. With the increase in exports, the $I + G + X$ curve shifts to the left; hence, the IS curve shifts to the right. This implies that the aggregate demand curve shifts to the right, to, say, AD_2. With the increase in aggregate demand, the price level, output, and employment increase and the real wage decreases. Of course, had full employment prevailed initially, money wages and prices would have increased with output and employment constant at their full employment levels.

Suppose prices abroad fall relative to prices in the country under consideration. The result is a decrease in exports and an increase in imports. The $I + G + X$ curve shifts to the right, and the $S + T + M$ curve shifts to the left. These shifts cause the IS curve to shift to the left, thereby reducing aggregate demand.

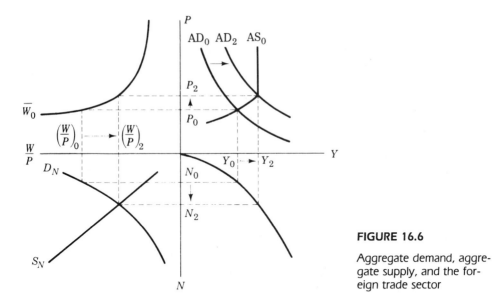

FIGURE 16.6

Aggregate demand, aggregate supply, and the foreign trade sector

As a consequence, the price level, output, and employment decrease and the real wage increases.

So far, it has been assumed that changes in exports and imports alter only the aggregate demand curve. It is possible that the aggregate supply curve may be altered. From October 1973 to March 1974, the United States experienced an oil embargo. From the discussion in Chapter 10, we know that the production function assumes given levels of the economy's capital stock and natural resources. The embargo had the same effect on the production function as a significant reduction in U.S. oil reserves. Consequently, the production function in Figure 16.7 shifts to the left. Since the demand for labor function is derived from the production function, the demand for labor function also shifts; in this case the demand for labor function shifts to the right since the demand for labor decreases.

With the shifts in the production and demand for labor functions, aggregate supply decreases. As a consequence, the price level increases, whereas employment and output decrease.[15] In other words, the oil embargo, through its effect on aggregate supply, resulted in higher prices and lower output. Of course, the price and output changes which occurred during the period were not entirely due to the oil embargo.

The "supply shock" associated with the oil embargo and increase in crude oil prices provides an illustration of the problem created for discretionary monetary and fiscal policy when aggregate supply is reduced.[16] If the monetary and fiscal authorities pursue policies designed to minimize the increase in the price level, the reductions in output and employment are greater than they would otherwise be. If the authorities pursue policies designed to increase output and employment, the increase in the price level is even greater than it would otherwise be.

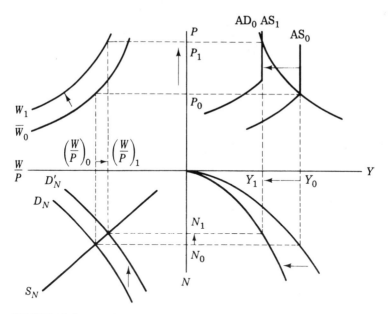

FIGURE 16.7

Aggregate demand, aggregate supply, and the oil embargo

It has been argued that the monetary authorities should have pursued a more expansionary policy during 1974, so as to have prevented the large decrease in output which occurred during the 1974–75 period. In retrospect, this view is probably correct. But with the reduction in aggregate supply (see Figure 16.7), expansionary monetary (and/or fiscal) policy could not have prevented some reduction in output.

STABILIZATION POLICY

We have examined the effects of changes in exports and imports on the price level, output, and employment. We now return to the problems of unemployment and balance of payments disequilibrium. Suppose, in Figure 16.6, aggregate demand is AD_0 and aggregate supply is AS_0. As indicated previously, the equilibrium levels of prices, employment, and output are P_0, N_0, and Y_0, respectively. Since output is less than the full employment level, the monetary and fiscal authorities may wish to pursue expansionary policies in order to increase aggregate demand and, hence, output. If the country is experiencing a balance of payments surplus, an increase in aggregate demand will reduce or eliminate the balance of payments surplus, since exports decrease owing to the increase in domestic prices relative to foreign prices, and imports increase owing to the increases in output and domestic prices relative to foreign prices.[17]

Thus, if the country is experiencing unemployment and a balance of payments surplus, expansionary policies are desirable. Similarly, if the country is experiencing inflation and a balance of payments deficit, contractionary monetary policy is desirable. If the country is experiencing unemployment and a balance of payments deficit or if it is experiencing inflation and a balance of payments surplus, the appropriate policy for solving the domestic problem conflicts with the appropriate policy for solving the international problem. For example, if the country is experiencing unemployment and a balance of payments deficit, the appropriate policy for curing the unemployment is expansionary policy, but the appropriate policy for curing the balance of payments deficit is contractionary policy.[18]

Since it may not be possible to achieve both full employment and balance of payments equilibrium with a single set of policies, it may be necessary to use two sets of policies. For example, expansionary policies may be needed to achieve full employment and devaluation may be needed to achieve balance of payments equilibrium.

FLEXIBLE EXCHANGE RATES

Rather than devaluing the currency and retaining fixed exchange rates, a system of flexible exchange rates could be adopted. An exchange rate is said to be *freely fluctuating, floating,* or *flexible* if the exchange values of the currencies are allowed to vary according to conditions in the market for foreign exchange. Under these circumstances, the exchange values of the currencies will be determined by demand and supply conditions in the foreign exchange market. To illustrate, suppose we consider two countries, the United States and West Germany, and assume the countries trade exclusively with each other.

From the German standpoint, there exists both a demand for and a supply of dollars in terms of the mark (the West German currency). These are shown in Figure 16.8. The demand for dollars is based on the German desire to purchase goods from the United States, to travel in this country, and so on. As the price of the dollar falls in terms of marks, the amount of dollars demanded by Germans increases. For example, if the price of the dollar falls from 4 marks to 3 marks, the quantity of dollars demanded increases, since Germans can now buy a dollar's worth of goods from the United States for 3 marks rather than 4 marks.

The supply of dollars is based on the desire of people in the United States to purchase German goods, to travel in West Germany, and so on. As the price of the dollar rises in terms of marks, the amount of dollars supplied increases. For instance, if the price of the dollar rises from 3 marks to 4 marks, the amount of dollars supplied increases, since Americans can now buy 4 marks' (rather than 3 marks') worth of German goods for a dollar.

In terms of Figure 16.8, the equilibrium exchange rate is 2.5 marks per dollar. At that exchange rate, there is neither an excess supply of dollars nor an excess demand. Suppose, however, the exchange rate were 3 marks per dollar. At that

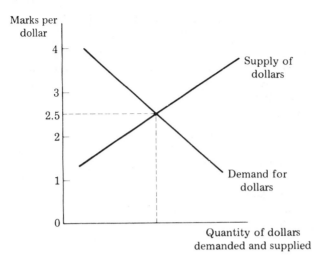

FIGURE 16.8

The demand for and the supply of dollars in West Germany

rate, there is an excess supply of dollars, which means that the United States is running a balance of payments deficit. The balance of payments deficit may be eliminated by allowing the exchange rate to depreciate.[19] It must be emphasized, however, that the deficit will disappear only gradually.

A freely fluctuating exchange rate system offers a number of advantages.[20] First, since exchange rates are determined by supply and demand, they will change automatically with changes in supply and demand. These changes in exchange rates serve to minimize balance of payments problems. Since March 1973, the dollar and a number of other major currencies have been floating. As a consequence, the problems associated with the oil embargo and quadrupling of crude oil prices during 1973–75 were much less serious than they would have been under a system of fixed exchange rates.

Second, by relying on fluctuations in the exchange rate to provide for balance of payments equilibrium, the authorities may concentrate on the appropriate stabilization policies for full employment. We have noted that at times the appropriate policies for full employment and balance of payment equilibrium conflict. For example, a country with unemployment and a balance of payments deficit may be reluctant to pursue expansionary monetary and fiscal policies in order to achieve full employment because of the adverse effects of the policies on the deficit. Under a system of floating exchange rates, the exchange rate will decline automatically. The decline will serve to eliminate the deficit, thereby removing the constraint on domestic stabilization policies.[21]

Third, with floating exchange rates, the need for international reserves is minimized. For example, suppose a country is experiencing a balance of payments deficit. It can continue to run a deficit at the existing exchange rate only if other countries are willing to hold increasing amounts of its currency or if it has international reserves which it may use to finance its transactions. For most countries, the first alternative is not possible. With floating exchange rates, the exchange rate will adjust automatically to eliminate the deficit. Thus, the country has little or no reason to hold reserves.

Floating exchange rates may have some disadvantages. First, it is claimed that floating rates introduce considerable risk into international transactions and, as a consequence, discourage international trade. Contracts are often signed well in advance of actual payments. If floating exchange rates prevail, the exchange rate may vary and make a profitable transaction unprofitable for one of the parties. Proponents of flexible exchange rates argue that the parties have several ways to protect themselves. They also argue that the fluctuations in the exchange rate are likely to be small.

Second, it is claimed that speculation is destabilizing and likely to lead to appreciable fluctuations in exchange rates. A fall in the exchange value of a currency is likely to lead speculators to expect a further decline. Hence, they will sell the currency in question, thereby producing the decline. Proponents of flexible exchange rates argue that speculation is unlikely to be destabilizing in the long run. They also argue that speculation can be highly destabilizing with fixed exchange rates. If a currency is weak, speculators know that the exchange rate, if it is altered, can move in only one direction. Consequently, they have a strong incentive to sell the currency and buy other currencies. If the currency is not devalued, speculators lose very little; if it is, they may gain considerably. Speculation of this type puts the currency in question under heavy pressure.

The case for floating exchange rates is strong. Yet it should not be taken for granted that the present system will prevail in the future. Many people, for various reasons, favor returning to fixed exchange rates.[22]

THE APPRECIATION OF THE DOLLAR: 1980–85

From its low in 1980 to its high in 1985, the dollar appreciated by approximately 50 percent relative to such important currencies as the mark and pound. Various reasons are given for this appreciation. First, it is claimed that expansionary fiscal policy in the United States combined with contractionary fiscal policy in many other countries produced relatively high interest rates in the United States.[23] With higher interest rates in the United States, the demand for dollars increased, causing the dollar to appreciate. Second, it is asserted that the real after-tax rate of return increased in the United States because of changes in the tax laws, financial deregulation, and the sharp reduction in the inflation rate. With the increase in the rate of return, the demand for dollars increased. Finally, the United States is viewed as a "safe haven." Compared to most countries, the United States is politically and economically stable, especially after the reduction in the inflation rate in the early 1980s. Because it is safe, many people prefer to hold dollars, thereby increasing the demand for dollars. In general, economists attribute most of the dollar's appreciation during 1980–85 to the relatively high interest rates in the United States which resulted from the application of expansionary fiscal policy. The other factors are important, but less so.

With the appreciation of the dollar, goods produced in the United States became more expensive when viewed from abroad. As a result, it became more difficult for the United States to export. At the same time, goods produced in other countries became less expensive when viewed from the United States. Consequently, it became more difficult for domestic industries to compete with imports. Indeed, the appreciation of the dollar contributed significantly to the record balance of payments deficits which occurred during the period. In 1980, the U.S. balance on current account was near zero. In 1985, it was $117.7 billion.

Despite the difficulties encountered by the export and import-competing industries because of the appreciation of the dollar, the appreciation did have some positive effects. For one thing, it kept the price level from rising by as much as it would have otherwise. With the appreciation of the dollar, imports became less expensive, thereby relieving some of the upward pressure on the price level. For another, the capital flows to this country (which contributed heavily to the appreciation of the dollar) helped finance the record federal budget deficits, thereby keeping interest rates lower than they would have been otherwise.

In light of the impact of the dollar's appreciation on the export and import-competing sectors of the economy and on the balance of payments, many people advocated policies which would result in the dollar's depreciation. In general, these people favored altering the mix of fiscal and monetary policies. In particular, they favored a less expansionary fiscal policy and a more expansionary monetary policy. As discussed earlier, this combination of policies will result in lower interest rates. With (relatively) lower interest rates in this country, the demand for dollars will drop and the dollar will depreciate.

Some people advocated the imposition of protectionist measures, including tariffs and quotas. As discussed earlier (and in the next section), such policies are disadvantageous. In this situation, they are particularly inappropriate because they would tend to alleviate the pressure on the dollar to depreciate. All other things equal, a deficit in the current account will lead to the dollar's depreciation. If imports are curtailed, the pressure on the dollar is reduced and the more fundamental problem will remain.

Finally, many people viewed the appreciation of the dollar during 1980–85 as a failure of the flexible exchange rate system. Some, therefore, favored a return to fixed exchange rates, including the gold standard. The advantages and disadvantages of fixed exchange rates were discussed in the previous section and will not be repeated here. Others favored moving to a system of managed flexible exchange rates. Under such a system, the Federal Reserve and other central banks would buy or sell foreign exchange so as to prevent movements in exchange rates which they believe are inappropriate. Unfortunately, central bankers rarely, if ever, know what exchange rates are appropriate. Consequently, their policies may cause exchange rates to deviate from the equilibrium rates.

RISING PROTECTIONISM

In recent years, calls for protectionist measures have become increasingly common. One reason for this is the increasing importance of international trade to the United States. In 1960, real imports (exports) totaled $102.4 billion ($98.4 billion), equal to 6.1 percent (5.9 percent) of real GNP. In 1985, real imports (exports) were $466.8 billion ($360.1 billion), equal to 13.1 percent (10.1 percent) of real GNP. Another reason has to do with the appreciation of the dollar during 1980–85 which affected both export and import-competing industries and made the balance of payments deficit much worse than it would have been otherwise. Finally, the recession in 1981–82, the lagging recovery of other nations, and the belief that other countries are engaging in unfair trading practices were contributing factors.

Economists agree that, in general, free trade is best for society. They concede, however, that it is not necessarily best for all groups, particularly for firms and workers in import-competing industries. Even so, economists do not, in general, favor protectionist measures, such as tariffs and quotas, to help those industries. If imposed, these measures would increase prices to consumers. To illustrate, an agreement was reached with Japan in 1981 regarding the exportation of Japanese cars to the United States. Under this agreement, the Japanese "volunteered" to limit Japanese automobile exports to the United States to 1.68 million cars per year, beginning in April. (This agreement was later modified.) It has been estimated that this agreement increased the average price of a Japanese car (in the United States) by about $1,000. By limiting the supply of Japanese cars, the arrangement also increased the demand for U.S. cars. The increase in demand, in turn, caused the price of U.S. cars to rise by approximately $400 per car.

In addition to raising prices, protectionist measures impede the reallocation of resources. As time passes, resources tend to shift from industries that have lost their comparative advantage to other industries. If tariffs or quotas are imposed to protect industries that can no longer compete, the reallocation process will be slowed and a misallocation of resources will occur. This misallocation can be very costly. For example, the cost to society of saving a job in the automobile industry under the "voluntary" arrangement with Japan has been placed at $160,000 per year.

Finally, protectionist measures on the part of the United States invite retaliation from other countries. Suppose the United States were to impose trade barriers to protect its automobile, steel, and textile industries. Other countries may react by imposing barriers to protect their agricultural, aerospace, and chemical industries, adversely affecting U.S. exports. Moreover, even if they do not retaliate, those countries will experience a reduction in export earnings if the United States imposes trade barriers. Consequently, they will be less able to buy U.S. exports.

With dwindling U.S. and world trade, many of the gains from international trade would be lost.

The foregoing analysis indicates that measures designed to protect import-competing industries are disadvantageous for society as a whole. If no action is taken, however, pockets of unemployment may develop as workers are displaced by imports. If those displaced are qualified for other jobs and are able and willing to relocate, if necessary, no particular problem exists. On the other hand, if those displaced lack the necessary jobs skills or are unable to relocate, they may remain unemployed or underemployed for long periods of time. Consequently, it may be appropriate to provide adjustment assistance in the form of temporary retraining and relocation subsidies. Such a policy would permit society to reap the benefits of free trade and, at the same time, minimize the costs borne by specific groups.

The United States has had some experience with adjustment assistance. Under the Trade Expansion Act of 1962, workers displaced by imports which resulted from a reduction in trade barriers qualified for certain benefits. Although the intent was to help displaced workers retrain or relocate, the payments, as a rule, were not closely tied to those activities. For the most part, they served as a supplement to unemployment compensation, which may have unintentionally slowed the adjustment process. Even so, the program served to moderate the demands for protection.

CONCLUDING REMARKS

In this chapter, we integrated foreign trade into our earlier models of income determination. We found that changes originating abroad have a significant impact upon the domestic economy. We also found that changes in the domestic economy have a significant impact on both the foreign trade sector and the world economy. With the growing U.S. involvement in the world economy, this interaction will be even more important in the future.

In the next chapter, we turn our attention from short-run theories of income determination to long-run theories. These long-run theories are called growth theories or models.

NOTES _____

1. For a detailed examination of the basis for international trade, see Mordechai E. Kreinin, *International Economics: A Policy Approach*, 4th ed. (New York: Harcourt Brace Jovanovich, Inc., 1983), Chap. 11, pp. 206–44.

2. U.S. Department of Commerce, Bureau of Economic Analysis, *Survey of Current Business*, 56 (June 1976), 18–27.

3. To obtain the $S + T + M$ function, substitute $-a + (1 - b)(Y - T)$ for S, $T_0 + tY$ for T, and $M_0 + mY$ for M. After simplifying, the $S + T + M$ function becomes $-a$

$+ bT_0 + M_0 + (1 - b + bt + m)Y$, with $1 - b + bt + m$ the slope of the function. Since m is positive and the slope of the $S + T$ function is $1 - b + bt$, the $S + T + M$ function is steeper than the $S + T$ function of Chapter 4.

4. The import multiplier $-1/(1 - b + bt + m)$ is based on a change in the M_0 term in the import function $M = M_0 + mY$. If M_0 changes, the new $S + T + M$ curve is parallel to the original $S + T + M$ curve. It is also possible to derive an import multiplier based on a change in the marginal propensity to import, m.

5. See, for example, Kreinin, *International Economics*, pp. 389–91.

6. Strictly speaking, exports (imports) depend on prices in the export (import) sector rather than the overall domestic (foreign) price level. We shall assume that changes in export (import) prices parallel those of other prices so that disaggregation is not necessary.

7. The new IS curve is more inelastic than the previous IS curve. As the interest rate decreases and investment increases, income increases. Since imports increase, however, the ultimate increase in income will be less than before.

8. For a more detailed discussion, see Robert A. Mundell, "The Appropriate Use of Monetary and Fiscal Policy for Internal and External Stability," International Monetary Fund, *Staff Papers*, 9 (March 1962), 70–79; or Marina V. N. Whitman, *Policies for Internal and External Balance* (Princeton, N.J.: Princeton University Press, 1970).

9. If prices are assumed variable, the price level increases since the net effect of the combination of monetary and fiscal policies is expansionary. With the increase in the price level, exports decrease and imports increase. As a consequence, the BP curve shifts to the left, since interest rates must be higher in order to maintain balance of payments equilibrium. Final equilibrium may still be achieved at income Y_1. The interest rate must be greater than i_1 in order that balance of payments equilibrium be maintained.

10. David J. Ott and Attiat F. Ott, "Monetary and Fiscal Policy: Goals and the Choice of Instruments," *Quarterly Journal of Economics*, 82 (May 1968), 313–25.

11. If prices are assumed variable, the decrease in the money supply reduces aggregate demand, hence, the price level. The decrease in the price level tends to mitigate the movement of the LM curve. As the price level decreases, exports increase and imports decrease. As a result, the IS curve shifts to the right. With the increase in exports and decrease in imports, the BP curve also shifts to the right, since interest rates no longer need to be as high in order to maintain balance of payments equilibrium. The net result is still a reduction in income; but because of the shifts in the IS and BP curves, income does not decline by as much.

12. The classical economists believed that balance of payments deficits (and surpluses) would be eliminated automatically. During the nineteenth century, the major trading nations of the world adhered to the gold standard. Each country's currency was fixed in terms of gold and, therefore, in relation to the currencies of other countries. Since countries were willing to buy or sell gold at the official price, exchange rates did not vary except within narrow limits determined by the cost of shipping gold. In addition, the money supplies of the countries were tied to gold.

Suppose a country was experiencing a balance of payments deficit. Gold would flow from the deficit country to the surplus countries. With the gold outflow, the deficit country's money supply decreases. According to the quantity theory of money, prices decrease proportionately. Similarly, with the gold inflow, the surplus countries experience money supply increases. With fixed exchange rates and prices falling in the deficit country and rising in the surplus countries, the exports of the deficit country increase and its imports decrease. Similarly, the surplus countries experience a decrease in exports and an increase in imports. According to the classical view, the adjustment process continues until the deficits and surpluses are eliminated.

With the advent of the Keynesian revolution, economists became skeptical of the classical view of the adjustment process. Among other things, Keynes emphasized that a reduction in aggregate demand is likely to reduce both output and prices. Consequently, when the money supply of the deficit country decreases, income and prices decrease. The reduction in income results in fewer imports, thereby reinforcing the price effects. With the reduction in the money supply and aggregate demand, employment also decreases. Thus, although the balance of payments deficit is reduced or eliminated, the country experiences a recession. Under these circumstances, the monetary authorities are tempted to act to offset the effect of the gold outflow on the money supply. Some evidence suggests that they did so long before the publication of Keynes's *General Theory*.

13. The volume of British exports will increase. But the value of British exports will increase if, and only if, the foreign demand for British exports is elastic. This seems to be so. See, for example, H. S. Houthakker and Stephen P. Magee, "Income and Price Elasticities in World Trade," *Review of Economics and Statistics*, 51 (May 1969), 111–25.

14. For convenience, we assume that the monetary authorities act to offset changes in the money supply due to balance of payments surpluses or deficits.

15. With the oil embargo, oil imports decreased. Total imports continued to increase, however, so there was probably little or no change in aggregate demand during the period due to the oil embargo.

16. For a discussion, see Chapter 13. For a discussion with special reference to a reduction in food supplies, see Robert J. Gordon, "Alternative Responses of Policy to External Supply Shocks," *Brookings Papers on Economic Activity*, no. 1 (1975), 183–204.

17. Much, however, depends on the interest rate. If the increase in aggregate demand is due to expansionary fiscal policy, the interest rate increases and there will be a capital inflow and the surplus may continue. If the increase in aggregate demand is due to expansionary monetary policy, the interest rate decreases and there will be a capital outflow. This will increase the likelihood that the surplus will be eliminated.

18. As discussed earlier, it may not be possible to use the appropriate mix of monetary and fiscal policies to achieve both full employment and balance of payments equilibrium.

19. A floating currency is said to *depreciate* when its exchange value decreases and to *appreciate* when its exchange value increases. Under a system of fixed exchange rates, a decrease in the exchange value of a currency is termed a *devaluation* and an increase in the exchange value a *revaluation*.

20. Milton Friedman, "The Case for Flexible Exchange Rates," in his *Essays in Positive Economics* (Chicago: University of Chicago Press, 1953), pp. 157–203; and Egon Sohmen, *Flexible Exchange Rates*, 2nd ed. (Chicago: University of Chicago Press, 1969). For more recent discussions, see John F. O. Bilson and Richard C. Marston, eds., *Exchange Rate Theory and Practice* (Chicago: University of Chicago Press, 1984); and Maurice Obstfeld, "Floating Exchange Rates: Experience and Prospects," *Brookings Papers on Economic Activity*, no. 2 (1985), 369–450.

21. The decline in the exchange rate increases exports and decreases imports. Both changes are beneficial in terms of the domestic economy.

22. For example, some supply-siders favor a return to the gold standard (see Chapter 12). Actually, the United States does not have a freely fluctuating exchange rate. The Federal Reserve has intervened on many occasions to support the dollar. In April 1981, however, the United States adopted a minimal intervention approach. Even so, the Federal Reserve has intervened in behalf of other central banks since that time. For a discussion, see Scott E. Pardee, "Treasury and Federal Reserve Foreign Exchange Operations: Interim Report," *Federal Reserve Bulletin*, 67 (June 1981), 486–87.

23. For a discussion of the effects of the policy mix on interest rates, see Chapter 9. The contractionary monetary policy pursued by the Federal Reserve during the first part of the period also contributed to the higher interest rates.

REVIEW QUESTIONS _____

1. Why is international trade advantageous?

2. What is the balance of payments? Why does the balance of payments always balance?

3. Distinguish between autonomous and accommodating items and define equilibrium in the balance of payments.

4. Suppose we have the following model:

$$C = 50 + 0.75Y_d,$$

$$I = 20,$$

$$G = 80,$$

$$T = 16 + 0.2Y,$$

$$X = 40,$$

$$M = 8 + 0.1Y.$$

   a. Determine the equilibrium value of each of the following variables: income, consumption, taxes, and imports.

   b. Determine the impact upon income and net exports of each of the following changes:

   (1) A $10 billion increase in investment.

   (2) A $10 billion increase in exports.

   (3) A $10 billion increase in M_0.

5. Show how to incorporate exports and imports into the IS–LM diagram. How is the aggregate demand curve of Chapter 10 altered by the inclusion of the foreign trade sector?

6. What is the BP curve? Why is it positively sloped? Explain how various policies may be used to shift the BP curve.

7. Can the appropriate monetary and fiscal policies for domestic purposes conflict with the appropriate monetary and fiscal policies for equilibrium in the balance of payments? If so, indicate how the conflict may be resolved.

8. Discuss the advantages and disadvantages of a system of freely fluctuating exchange rates relative to a system of

   a. fixed exchange rates.

   b. managed flexible exchange rates.

9. Explain how an increase in the demand for dollars leads to an appreciation of the dollar. What impact will the appreciation have on the United States? On other countries? Should officials intervene to keep the dollar from appreciating? Defend your answer.

10. Outline and critically evaluate the case for protectionism from the viewpoint of

   a. society.

   b. the import-competing sector.

SUGGESTED READING

BILSON, JOHN F. O., and RICHARD C. MARSTON (eds.), *Exchange Rate Theory and Practice.* Chicago: University of Chicago Press, 1984.

DORNBUSCH, RUDIGER, *Open Economy Macroeconomics.* New York: Basic Books, Inc., Publishers, 1980.

FRIEDMAN, MILTON, "The Case for Flexible Exchange Rates," in M. Friedman, *Essays in Positive Economics*, pp. 157–203. Chicago: University of Chicago Press, 1953.

KREININ, MORDECHAI E., *International Economics: A Policy Approach* (4th ed.). New York: Harcourt Brace Jovanovich, Inc., 1983.

MASKUS, KEITH E., "Rising Protectionism and U.S. International Trade Policy," Federal Reserve Bank of Kansas City, *Economic Review*, 69 (July–August 1984), 3–17.

MUNDELL, ROBERT A., "The Appropriate Use of Monetary and Fiscal Policy for Internal and External Stability," International Monetary Fund, *Staff Papers*, 9 (March 1962), 70–79.

OBSTFELD, MAURICE, "Floating Exchange Rates: Experience and Prospects," *Brookings Papers on Economic Activity*, no. 2 (1985), pp. 369–450.

U.S. Department of Commerce, Bureau of Economic Analysis, *Survey of Current Business.* Washington, D.C.: Government Printing Office, monthly.

WHITMAN, MARINA V. N., *Policies for Internal and External Balance.* Princeton, N.J.: Princeton University Press, 1970.

17

ECONOMIC GROWTH

I n this chapter, we consider economic growth and some theories which purport to explain economic growth or the lack of it. Several theories are pessimistic about the possibility of long-term economic growth. One theory predicts that the limits of growth will be reached within the next hundred years with catastrophic results. At the end of the chapter, we discuss the desirability of economic growth.

ECONOMIC GROWTH DEFINED

Economic growth is usually defined as secular (long-run) increases in per capita real income. If per capita income increases as the economy recovers from a recession, the increase is cyclical rather than secular and is not considered to be economic growth. Growth is defined in per capita terms. Even if income is rising, it must be increasing faster than population for growth to occur.

It is common to distinguish between *economic growth* and *economic development*. Both terms imply secular increases in per capita income. When per capita

355

income increases in developed countries, such as the United States, we say economic growth is occurring. On the other hand, when per capita income rises in less developed countries, we label the increases economic development. Economic development implies more than increases in per capita income; it implies transformation of a society. For the most part, economic growth is institutionalized in developed countries. No sharp changes in values or institutions are necessary. In fact, growth occurs more or less automatically if employment is at, or near, the full employment level. Such is not true in less developed countries. For per capita income to increase in such countries, it may be necessary for values to change and new institutions to replace old ones. In practice, of course, the distinction between economic growth and economic development is not as sharp as stated here. Nevertheless, the distinction is useful since apparently developed countries grow more easily than less developed countries. The rest of the chapter deals with economic growth, not economic development, since the latter is beyond the scope of this book.

THE CLASSICAL THEORY OF ECONOMIC GROWTH

The classical economists, Adam Smith, Thomas Robert Malthus, David Ricardo, John Stuart Mill, and others, were very much concerned with economic growth.[1] They thought that economic growth would eventually cease. With the cessation of growth, the economy would enter a stationary state. In that state, population growth would be zero, and investment would be for replacement only. Real wages would be constant and at a low level.

Classical theory was based, in part, on the theory of population associated with Thomas Robert Malthus. In simplest terms, Malthus assumed that population increases geometrically: 1, 2, 4, 8, 16, ... Food production, on the other hand, is capable of increasing only arithmetically: 1, 2, 3, 4, 5, ... Consequently, difficulties will arise in the long run as population outstrips the food supply. At that point, mortality rates increase owing to starvation and malnutrition.

In the short run, the classical economists assumed that economic growth would occur. Profits would be high and capital accumulation would take place. As the capital stock increased, it was assumed that real wages would rise above the minimum subsistence level, thereby inducing population growth.

The classical economists stressed land as a factor of production and emphasized the law of diminishing returns. They argued that land was essentially a nonaugmentable factor of production; therefore, as population increased and capital accumulated, diminishing returns would prevail. Consequently, real wages and profits would fall until only investment for replacement would be profitable. To be sure, the classical economists conceded that technological progress might postpone the stationary state, but not indefinitely. The prognosis of the classical economists was, therefore, gloomy. Small wonder that some nineteenth-century people called economics the *dismal science*.

Later economists were less pessimistic. The Malthusian theory of population has been widely criticized and largely discredited. Later economists also deemphasized the role of land as a factor of production. For example, in the neoclassical model to be considered, land does not even enter the production function as a factor. Later economists stressed the possibility and even likelihood that technological progress would overcome the law of diminishing returns.

Moreover, even if the economy enters a stationary state, real wages need not be at a biological subsistence level. Malthus himself appeared to concede that the subsistence level might be culturally determined, thereby implying that birth rates might decline before real wages fall to the biological subsistence level. If so, real wages in the stationary state might be above the minimum level necessary for subsistence.

HARROD'S THEORY OF ECONOMIC GROWTH

With the Great Depression of the 1930s and the publication of Keynes's *General Theory* in 1936, economists turned their attention to short-run theories of income determination. Keynes himself was predominantly interested in the short run. As we have seen, his analysis assumed that the economy's capital stock and technology were constant. These assumptions are justifiable for short-run theories of income determination, but not for long-run theories. Consequently, Keynes left the development of long-run theories of income determination, called *growth theories* or models, to others.

Following Keynes, R. F. Harrod and E. Domar were among the first to develop theories of economic growth.[2] Their theories are similar and Keynesian in nature. Since Harrod's theory has received the most attention, we shall concentrate on it.

Harrod's theory is based on a number of assumptions. First, he assumes that saving, S, is a constant fraction, s, of income, Y. This implies that saving in time period t, S_t, equals the fraction of income saved, s, multiplied by income in time period t, Y_t, or

(17.1) $$S_t = sY_t \qquad (0 < s < 1).$$

Since s is assumed constant, the same relationship holds for other time periods as well. The saving function, $S_t = sY_t$, corresponds to the long-run consumption function discussed in Chapter 5. In the saving function, s, or $(1 - b)$ in terms of the earlier notation, represents both the marginal and average propensities to save.

Second, Harrod assumes that investment is a function of changes in the level of income. In particular, he assumes that investment in time period t equals v, a positive constant, multiplied by the change in income from time period $t - 1$ to time period t, $Y_t - Y_{t-1}$, or

(17.2) $$I_t = v(Y_t - Y_{t-1}) \qquad (v > 0).$$

Thus, if income is increasing, investment is positive. This is a particularly simple version of the accelerator principle discussed in Chapter 6. In the investment function, v represents the accelerator coefficient.

Third, Harrod's simplest model excludes the government and foreign trade sectors. To concentrate on the basic model, we shall also exclude them.

If investment in time period t, I_t, equals saving in time period t, S_t, we have

$$I_t = S_t.$$

Since I_t equals $v(Y_t - Y_{t-1})$ and S_t equals sY_t, we obtain, by substitution,

$$v(Y_t - Y_{t-1}) = sY_t.$$

If both sides of the equation are divided by Y_t and v, we get

$$\frac{Y_t - Y_{t-1}}{Y_t} = \frac{s}{v}.$$

The expression $(Y_t - Y_{t-1})/Y_t$ represents the growth rate of income. Harrod calls this rate of growth the *warranted growth rate*. This rate, denoted as G_w, equals the saving rate, s, divided by the accelerator coefficient, v, or

(17.3) $$G_w = \frac{s}{v}.$$

For example, if s equals 0.1 and v equals 1, the warranted rate of growth is 0.1/1 or 10 percent.

In a sense, the warranted rate of growth represents an equilibrium growth rate. According to equation (17.1), the amount that households intend to save depends on the level of income. The amount that households actually save also depends on the level of income. Since both depend on the level of income, intended and actual or realized saving are equal. Since realized saving is always equal to realized investment (with no government and foreign trade sectors), the level of income and corresponding level of saving determine the amount of realized investment. For example, if s equals 0.10 and Y equals $500 billion, realized saving is $50 billion. With no government and foreign trade sectors, realized investment must also equal $50 billion.

Although intended and realized saving are determined by the level of income, intended investment is determined by changes in the level of income in accordance with equation (17.2). As discussed in Chapter 3, intended investment is the amount that firms wish or intend to invest. If v equals 1 and income increases from $450 billion to $500 billion, intended investment is $50 billion, the product of v and the change in income, $Y_t - Y_{t-1}$. With s equal to 0.10 and income equal to $500 billion, realized saving and investment equal $50 billion. Intended and realized investment are, therefore, equal and managers are satisfied with their production and invest-ment decisions. Consequently, if income is growing at the warranted rate, managers have no incentive to change their behavior. Thus, for managers the warranted rate of growth represents an equilibrium rate.

Suppose income does not grow at the warranted rate. Intended and realized investment are no longer equal, and managers think that they have increased production either too rapidly or too slowly. Suppose the *actual growth rate*, G, is less than the warranted rate, G_w. If income grows at a rate less than the warranted rate, intended investment is less than realized saving and investment. This occurs because intended investment depends on changes in the level of income and income is growing at a rate less than the warranted rate, whereas intended and realized saving depend on the level of income. Since intended investment is less than realized investment, there is an unintended increase in inventories or, in terms of Chapter 3, positive unintended investment. The unintended increase in inventories implies that managers cannot sell their entire output. Thus, although the actual growth rate of output is less than the warranted rate, it will appear to managers that they have increased production too rapidly.

To illustrate, suppose s equals 0.1 and v equals 1, which implies that the warranted rate of growth, G_w, is 10 percent. If income is $450 billion in time period $t - 1$, income must increase to $500 billion in period t for the warranted rate of growth to be maintained. Suppose, however, that income increases to only $480 billion. The actual rate of growth, G, is only 6.25 percent, obtained by dividing the difference between incomes in time period t and time period $t - 1$ by income in time period t. If income is $480 billion in time period t, realized saving is $48 billion, the product of $s = 0.1$ and $Y_t = $480 billion. Since realized investment must equal realized saving, realized investment is also $48 billion. Intended in-vestment, however, is only $30 billion, obtained by multiplying v by the change in income from time period $t - 1$ to time period t. The excess of realized over intended investment represents the unintended increase in inventories which occurs because managers cannot sell their entire output.

Since managers believe that they have increased production too rapidly, Har-rod argues that they will increase production by a smaller amount in the next period or even decrease production. Consequently, there will be an even greater discrep-ancy between the warranted and actual rates of growth in the next period and, by implication, an even greater discrepancy between intended and realized investment. Therefore, managers will believe that they have overproduced by a greater amount, and they will respond by increasing production by an even smaller amount in the next period or by decreasing production by an even greater amount, whichever the case may be. Thus, if the actual rate of growth is less than the warranted rate, there is a tendency for the situation to become cumulatively worse.

The same tendency exists if the actual rate of growth exceeds the warranted rate. If the actual growth rate exceeds the warranted rate, intended investment exceeds realized investment, since the former is based on changes in income and the latter on the level of income. Thus, it will appear to managers that they have not increased production rapidly enough to meet the various demands for goods and services.[3] Hence, they will increase production even faster in the next period, which will cause an even greater discrepancy between intended and realized investment. In their attempts to increase production more rapidly, managers will soon encounter shortages in productive capacity. As a result, inflation will occur and become progressively worse as managers try to increase production even more rapidly.

In summary, if income grows at the warranted rate, intended and realized investment are equal. Managers are, therefore, satisfied with their production decisions. If income fails to grow at the warranted rate, however, managers will believe that they have increased production either too rapidly or too slowly. According to Harrod, they will react by altering production and the actual growth rate will deviate farther from the warranted rate. Thus, unemployment or inflation will become progressively worse. Moreover, once the actual growth rate deviates from the warranted rate, Harrod believes that it is very difficult to reestablish their equality.

Harrod considers a third growth rate, the *natural growth rate*. The natural growth rate, denoted by G_n, represents the full employment growth rate. That is, it is the maximum rate of growth permitted by increases in the labor force, capital accumulation, and technological progress, assuming full employment.

According to Harrod, it is desirable for the warranted and natural growth rates to be equal and for the actual growth rate to equal the warranted and natural rates. If the warranted and actual growth rates are equal, managers are satisfied with their production decisions. Moreover, if the warranted and natural growth rates are equal, there is no tendency for unemployment or inflation to develop.

Suppose the warranted rate is less than the natural rate. Even if the actual rate equals the warranted rate, unemployment will increase since the actual and warranted rates are less than the natural rate. On the other hand, suppose the warranted rate is greater than the natural rate. Temporarily, the actual and warranted rates may be equal. But the actual growth rate cannot exceed the natural growth rate indefinitely, since the natural rate represents the maximum rate. Thus, once full employment is achieved, the actual growth rate will drop to the natural rate. Of course, once the actual growth rate becomes less than the warranted rate, the actual rate tends to decline and unemployment tends to develop.

Thus, unemployment tends to develop unless the actual and warranted growth rates equal the natural rate. Consequently, Harrod suggests that the monetary and fiscal authorities undertake policies to equate the warranted and natural rates. He is, however, rather pessimistic about the ability of the authorities to achieve equality of the rates.

Criticisms of Harrod's Theory of Economic Growth

Harrod's model has been criticized from various viewpoints. First, his saving and investment functions have been criticized as being unduly simplistic. Harrod is aware of their limitations. He has argued, however, that essentially the same conclusions emerge even if more complex saving and investment functions are utilized.

Second, William J. Baumol has argued that managers may view a deviation between the actual and warranted rates of growth as temporary. Consequently, the tendency for a deviation between the actual and warranted rates to become progressively larger may not be as strong as postulated by Harrod. For example, suppose income has been growing at the warranted rate for a number of periods. If in a particular period the rates diverge, managers may regard the discrepancy as temporary and continue to increase their output at the same rate as in the past. As a result, there will be no tendency, at least in the period in question, for the actual and warranted rates to diverge further. Of course, should the discrepancy prevail for a number of periods, managers will be forced to adjust their production. Even so, there will be less instability than postulated by Harrod.

Third, Robert Solow and others have criticized Harrod's model because it does not allow for factor substitution.[4] These critics claim that if factor prices are flexible and that if factor substitution is possible, full employment will prevail. Since these assumptions form the cornerstone of neoclassical growth theory, we shall postpone further discussion of Harrod's model until we have considered the neoclassical theory.

NEOCLASSICAL GROWTH THEORY

Neoclassical growth theory is based on a number of assumptions.[5] First, it is assumed that investment is always equal to the full employment level of saving. Thus, full employment is assumed at the outset. Second, it is assumed that saving is a constant fraction, s, of output. Thus,

(17.4) $$S = sY \quad (0 < s < 1).$$

The neoclassical saving function is, therefore, the same as Harrod's.

Third, it is assumed that the labor force and population grow at a constant rate, n. This rate is independent of the real wage and other economic variables. Fourth, a production function is postulated which allows for factor substitution. Thus, firms may substitute capital for labor, and vice versa, in the production process.

Rather than postulating a general production function, we shall assume that the economy is characterized by a particular type of production function called the *Cobb–Douglas production function*. A Cobb–Douglas production function has the form

(17.5) $$Y = Ae^{rt}K^\alpha N^{1-\alpha} \quad (0 < \alpha < 1),$$

where Y represents output, K the capital stock, and N the number of workers employed. The expression Ae^{rt} represents the effect of technology, with A representing a positive constant, e the natural e from mathematics (2.718. . .), r the growth rate of technology, and t time. Thus, we are assuming that technology improves at the constant rate r. The terms α and $1 - \alpha$ represent the partial elasticities of production with respect to capital and labor, respectively. If α equals 0.25, a 1 percent increase in the capital stock results in a 0.25 percent increase in output. If α equals 0.25, $1 - \alpha$ equals 0.75 and a 1 percent increase in employment results in a 0.75 percent increase in output. Assuming pure competition, α and $1 - \alpha$ also represent the shares of national income accruing to capital and labor, respectively. For example, if α equals 0.25 and the return to capital equals the marginal product of capital (the case under pure competition), the owners of the capital stock receive one-fourth of the economy's output. If $1 - \alpha$ equals 0.75 and the real wage equals the marginal product of labor (the case under pure competition), labor receives three-fourths of the economy's output.

The Cobb–Douglas production function has several characteristics which are important in the following analysis. First, the production function exhibits constant returns to scale. If the factors of production, capital and labor, are increased in the same proportion, output also increases by that proportion. For example, if the capital stock and labor force both increase by 10 percent, output also increases by 10 percent. Second, the production function displays diminishing returns to the factors of production. Thus, if one factor of production increases with the other factor (and technology) constant, output will increase but at a diminishing rate. For example, if the capital stock increases, with the labor force constant, output increases, but the increases in output become smaller and smaller as the capital stock increases.

From the production function, it is possible to derive the growth rate of output.[6] The growth rate of output, q, is given by

$$(17.6) \qquad q = r + \alpha h + (1 - \alpha)n,$$

where q, r, h, and n represent the growth rates of output, technology, capital, and labor, respectively. Thus, equation (17.6) suggests that the growth rate of output is positively related to the rate of technological progress and the growth rates of the factors of production, capital and labor.

For the economy to be in equilibrium in this context, the variables must be constant or growing at constant exponential rates. This does not imply that all variables must be constant or that all variables must grow at constant rates. Some variables may be constant, with the others growing at constant exponential rates. This definition of equilibrium is the growth theory counterpart of the usual definition of equilibrium. If the economy is in equilibrium in the growth theory context, the economy is said to be in a *golden age*.[7] Alternatively, the economy is said to be experiencing steady-state growth or to be in a steady state.

For an economy to be in a golden age, the following variables must be growing at constant exponential rates: output, the capital stock, investment, and the labor supply. We have already assumed that the labor supply is growing at a constant exponential rate, n. We know that (net) investment, I, equals the change in the capital stock, ΔK, and that investment equals a constant fraction, s, of output, Y; hence,

$$I = \Delta K = sY.$$

If we divide ΔK and sY by K, we obtain

$$\frac{\Delta K}{K} = s\frac{Y}{K}$$

or

(17.7)
$$h = s\frac{Y}{K}.$$

Since s is a constant, the ratio of Y to K must also be a constant for the capital stock to grow at the constant rate, h. For this to occur, income, Y, must grow at the same rate, h, as the capital stock, K, in a golden age.

Since the growth rate of income, q, equals the growth rate of the capital stock, h, in a golden age, we may replace those rates by g, the *golden age growth rate*. Thus, equation (17.6) becomes

$$g = r + \alpha g + (1 - \alpha)n$$

by substitution. After rearranging terms and dividing by $(1 - \alpha)$, we obtain

(17.8)
$$g = \frac{r}{1 - \alpha} + n,$$

where g represents the golden age growth rates of output and the capital stock, r the growth rate of technology, and n the growth rate of the labor supply. Since investment is a constant fraction of income and since income is growing at the golden age growth rate, investment is also growing at that rate.

This result suggests that the golden age, or equilibrium, growth rate depends on the growth rates of technology and the labor supply. Should either rate increase, the golden age growth rate increases. This result also implies that it is impossible for per capita income to increase in the absence of technological progress. If technology is constant, r equals zero and the golden age growth rate, g, equals the growth rate of the labor force (and population), n. If income and population are growing at the same rate, per capita income is constant. For example, suppose income and population are growing at 3 percent per year. Per capita income will be unchanged.

In the absence of technological progress, it is relatively easy to rationalize this particular result. If technology is constant, r equals zero, and the golden age growth rate, g, equals the growth rate of the labor force, n. Since the capital stock must be growing at the same rate as output for the economy to be in a golden age, the capital stock and the labor force are growing at the same rate. Since the Cobb–Douglas production function is characterized by constant returns to scale, output must be growing at the same rate. For example, if the labor force and the capital stock are growing at 3 percent per year, output must also be growing at 3 percent per year. If technological progress is occurring, output and the capital stock will be growing at the same rate, but their growth rate will exceed that of labor. As a result, per capita income will increase.

The implications of neoclassical growth theory are quite different from those of Harrod's theory. For one thing, unemployment is not a problem in neoclassical theory because full employment is assumed to prevail. As a consequence, there can be no divergence of, in Harrod's terms, the natural and warranted rates.

In the neoclassical model, increases in the growth rates of the labor force and technology increase the golden age growth rate. In Harrod's model, increases in the growth rates of the labor force and technology increase the natural rate of growth, but not necessarily the actual and warranted growth rates. In fact, in Harrod's model, it is likely that an increase in the growth rate of the labor supply will result in increased unemployment.

Finally, in Harrod's model, an increase in the fraction, s, of income saved and invested results in an increase in the warranted growth rate, s/v. This is not so in the neoclassical model, since in that model the golden age or equilibrium growth rate is independent of the saving rate. True, if society saves and invests a larger fraction of its income, the capital stock and income will grow more rapidly. Since the capital stock is growing more rapidly than the labor supply, however, diminishing returns will, in the long run, reduce the growth rate of income until it equals the original golden age growth rate.

Although the saving rate, s, does not determine the golden age growth rate of output, it helps to determine the level of output and, hence, per capita consumption. In fact, it is possible to determine the saving rate which maximizes per capita consumption.

Since the saving rate that maximizes per capita consumption at time $t = 0$ is the same rate that maximizes consumption at all other points in time, we shall be concerned with only time $t = 0$. If t equals zero, the Cobb-Douglas production function becomes

(17.9) $$Y = AK^\alpha N^{1-\alpha},$$

since the term e^{rt} equals 1 when t equals 0. Next, since we are interested in maximizing per capita consumption, we divide both sides of the equation by N to obtain

$$\frac{Y}{N} = \frac{AK^\alpha N^{1-\alpha}}{N} = AK^\alpha N^{-\alpha}$$

or

(17.10)
$$\frac{Y}{N} = A\left(\frac{K}{N}\right)^\alpha,$$

where Y/N represents per capita output and K/N the capital–labor ratio. Equation (17.10) suggests that per capita output is a function of the capital–labor ratio. Graphically, this relationship is plotted in Figure 17.1. It is assumed that per capita output increases as the capital–labor ratio increases. It is also assumed, however, that there are diminishing returns as the capital–labor ratio increases.

Since investment is the change in the capital stock, golden age investment equals the golden age growth rate multiplied by the capital stock or

$$I = gK.$$

For example, if the golden age growth rate is 3 percent and the capital stock is $100 billion, golden age investment is $3 billion. If both sides of the equation are divided by N, we obtain

(17.11)
$$\frac{I}{N} = g\frac{K}{N}.$$

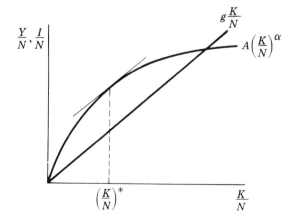

FIGURE 17.1

Per capita output and investment as functions of the capital–labor ratio

This relationship is also plotted in Figure 17.1; it has a slope equal to g, the golden age growth rate. The relationship indicates that per capita investment (or saving) is positively related to the capital–labor ratio.

Since Y/N represents per capita output and I/N represents per capita investment (or saving), the vertical distance between the two curves represents per capita consumption. The problem is to find the capital–labor ratio which maximizes per capita consumption. Graphically, this ratio is $(K/N)^*$, where the slope of the line tangent to the Y/N curve equals the slope of the I/N curve. Since the slope of the Y/N curve equals $\alpha g/s$ and the slope of the I/N curve equals g, we obtain

$$\frac{\alpha g}{s} = g$$

or

(17.12) $$s = \alpha,$$

where s represents the saving rate and α represents the fraction of income received by the owners of capital.[8]

This result suggests that per capita consumption will be maximized provided that society saves and invests an amount equal to profits (the income accruing to the owners of capital) and consumes an amount equal to labor income. This proposition is called the *golden rule*. Thus, the saving rate, s is important in determining per capita consumption even though it does not determine the golden age growth rate.

Neoclassical growth theory has been extended in a number of directions. Rather than pursuing the discussion, however, we turn to the criticisms of neoclassical growth theory.[9]

Criticisms of Neoclassical Growth Theory

The neoclassical growth model has been vigorously criticized. Among the most persistent critics have been Joan Robinson and Nicholas Kaldor; both are members of the *Cambridge school of economists*, a group of economists associated although not necessarily affiliated with Cambridge University. Criticism of the neoclassical model is not, however, confined to members of the Cambridge school.

Perhaps the most important criticism concerns the neoclassical assumption of full employment. Neoclassical theory assumes that factor prices are sufficiently flexible to provide full employment. Consequently, investment is always equal to the full employment level of saving. Thus, by assumption, neoclassical theorists eliminate one of the major problems with which Keynes and Harrod were concerned. Critics of neoclassical growth theory question whether factor prices are sufficiently flexible to provide full employment.[10]

Responses to this criticism have generally taken two forms. First, factor price rigidity is essentially a short-run phenomenon and in the long run there is sufficient flexibility to guarantee full employment. Second, monetary and fiscal authorities can provide the appropriate set of policies to achieve and maintain full employment. In either case, full employment prevails and the growth path of the economy can be approximated by the neoclassical model. These responses have not proved convincing to the critics of neoclassical theory.

Critics have also claimed that in the neoclassical model adjustment may take a very long time. For example, suppose the saving rate, s, increases. Neoclassical growth theory suggests that in the short run there will be an increase in the economy's growth rate, but not in the long run. Therefore, if the short run consists of a relatively short time span, policies designed to increase the saving rate are less desirable than if the short run consists of a relatively long time span. Ryuzo Sato has argued that it may take as long as 100 years for the growth rate to return to 90 percent of its former level in response to an increase in the saving rate.[11] This suggests that policies designed to increase the saving rate will be successful in increasing the economy's growth rate for an extended period of time. The length of the adjustment process implied by the neoclassical model impels Sato to argue that the Harrod model may serve as a better approximation to the economy than the neoclassical model.

Other economists have argued that the estimated time required for adjustment is very sensitive to the specification of the neoclassical model.[12] They contend that had Sato considered alternative versions of the neoclassical model he would have found the necessary adjustment time much shorter. Hence, they believe that the neoclassical model may be a good approximation to reality even for a relatively short time span.

Neoclassical growth theory has also been criticized because it contains no explicit investment function and because it ignores expectations, both important elements of Harrod's model. Of course, if full employment prevails, no investment function is necessary, as full employment saving determines investment.

Finally, members of the Cambridge school generally object to the aggregation of the capital stock and use of the aggregate production function. They claim that the capital stock consists of many heterogeneous items and that the standard methods of aggregation are invalid. For example, it is common to discount the future income stream associated with the capital stock in order to find its value. To discount the income stream, however, it is necessary to determine the market rate of interest. The critics claim that it is impossible to determine the market rate of interest without first determining the value of the capital stock. They also object to the use of the aggregate production function because of the aggregation problems and because of the difficulties in incorporating technological progress into them.

The validity of neoclassical growth theory has been widely disputed. Many of its proponents, nevertheless, think it is a useful approximation to reality or, at least, more useful than alternative models.[13] Other economists think Harrod's model is a more useful approximation to reality, at least in the short run. Still others offer alternative models.[14] We now turn to a much different type of theory, which suggests that economic growth will soon stop.

THE CLUB OF ROME MODEL (OR THE CLASSICAL THEORY OF ECONOMIC GROWTH REVISITED)

In 1972, *The Limits to Growth* appeared.[15] Its principal conclusion was that, if the present growth trends in population, food production, industrialization, pollution, and resource depletion continue, the limits to economic growth on a global basis will be reached within the next 100 years. This conclusion was based on a study directed by Dennis Meadows and conducted at the Massachusetts Institute of Technology (MIT). Since the study was initiated by the Club of Rome, an informal international association of individuals, it is generally referred to as the *Club of Rome study* or *model*.

The study considered five basic growth elements: population, food production, industrialization, pollution, and depletion of resources. It claims that each grows at an exponential rate. The research group noted that not only is population growing exponentially but that the growth rate has increased, thereby adding to the population problem. In 1650, world population was growing at a rate of about 0.3 percent per year, which implies that it would take approximately 250 years for world population to double. In contrast, the rate of growth of world population was 2.1 percent in 1970, implying a doubling time of only 33 years.

The study group expects population to continue to grow at an exponential rate, but it is pessimistic about future growth in the world's food supply. Much of the world's population is inadequately nourished now; the best land is already under cultivation. Furthermore, the study states that inadequate supplies of fresh water may also limit the growth of the food supply. They doubt that improvements in technology will be sufficient to offset the increasing relative scarcity of land and water.

The study group concedes that, in the past, industrial output has grown even more rapidly than population. They believe, however, that the growth rate of industrial production is likely to be reduced in the future. They cite various factors for the decline, the most important being depletion of the world's nonrenewable resources. These resources—aluminum, copper, mercury, natural gas, petroleum, and so on—will be exhausted relatively soon. Furthermore, if pollution continues to increase unabated, the ecological limits will soon be reached.

The study group dealt with the interaction of the five variables, population, food production, industrialization, pollution, and depletion of resources, by computer simulation. The group concluded that the limits of growth will be reached within the next 100 years, with the exact time span depending upon the assumptions made about the discovery of new deposits of natural resources, the rate of technological progress, and the like. The study finds that the end will come within a century even if it makes relatively optimistic projections about the discovery of new resource deposits.

Once the limits of growth are reached, the effects are catastrophic. With population outstripping the food supply, starvation will be widespread; death rates will increase dramatically. The very high levels of pollution will also increase death rates. The net effect is a large reduction in the world's population. Industrial output will also decline dramatically with the exhaustion of the world's natural resources, the high levels of pollution, and the problems associated with a declining population.

The study group claims that such a collapse can be avoided only if action is taken now or in the near future. For example, policies designed to reduce birth rates and, therefore, population growth appear desirable although insufficient to completely eliminate a collapse. To prevent the collapse, it is necessary to stabilize both population and industrial output. If both are stabilized, there will be relatively high levels of industrial output and food on a per capita basis although, eventually, resource shortages will reduce the per capita levels. The research group offers a more detailed program which it claims would prevent such a deterioration.

Thus, the study group finds only two possibilities: either we impose limits to growth or nature will. The latter leads to collapse. Consequently, the group claims that the only reasonable alternative is the former and, given the nature of exponential growth, we must undertake policies designed to limit growth soon.

The study has been widely criticized. Since its conclusions are derived from its assumptions, most of the criticism has been aimed at the assumptions, explicit and implicit. Perhaps the most crucial assumption has to do with technological progress. It is assumed that population, resource needs, and pollution grow exponentially. Yet, technological progress is assumed to be limited. The result is inevitable; industrial and food production will eventually be outstripped by population. Based on past experience, it appears that technological progress does occur at an exponential rate. Although technology may not improve at an exponential rate in the future, the study group does not offer any reasons for technological advance to take place more slowly.

The study group also assumes that population will continue to expand rapidly. But considerable evidence, casual and otherwise, suggests that as per capita income increases, birth rates decline, thereby alleviating the population problem.

The model also ignores, for the most part, the price mechanism. The price system provides incentives to economize on scarce resources and to seek additional supplies.[16] For example, suppose the demand for a particular natural resource is increasing more rapidly than supply. The price of the resource increases, providing an incentive for firms to economize on its use and to consider the use of alternative resources, either natural or synthetic. On the supply side, higher prices make it profitable to search for new deposits and to exploit deposits which were unprofitable to exploit in the past. Higher prices will also promote research designed to circumvent the shortages. Hence, shortages of a particular natural resource may not be as critical as thought by the study group. Moreover, even if the limits of growth are reached, the process is likely to be much more gradual than postulated by the group.

These and other considerations make it risky to assume that the end is in sight so far as economic growth is concerned. Yet it may be that further growth is not desirable. We consider this issue in the following section.

IS ECONOMIC GROWTH DESIRABLE?

In Chapter 1, economic growth was listed as an economic goal, but it was indicated that many people, particularly in the late 1960s and early 1970s, have questioned the desirability of further economic growth. The view contrasts sharply with that held over most of this nation's history. The change in attitude may, in part, be due to awareness that material abundance and happiness are not necessarily correlated. Per capita output has increased over the years, but it is not clear that today's people are happier than those who lived before them. The change in attitude may also be attributed to greater awareness of the costs associated with economic growth. Critics of economic growth argue that the benefits are outweighed by the costs.[17] Among the most commonly cited of these costs are more rapid depletion of natural resources, pollution, urban problems like congestion, noise pollution, and crime, and problems of the countryside, such as strip mining and the indiscriminate clear cutting of timber.

In regard to the more rapid depletion of natural resources, it is not clear that the current growth rate should be reduced for the sake of future generations. As discussed in the last section, if the demand for a particular natural resource is growing rapidly relative to its supply, the price of the resource increases. Firms respond to the higher price by substituting other resources and by employing technologies which minimize the use of the resource. Moreover, as the prices of commodities utilizing the natural resource increase, households buy less of those commodities and more of other commodities.

Pollution is alleged to be another cost associated with economic growth. As growth occurs, more pollutants are dumped into the nation's air and water. This is not inevitable; it depends on the nature of the growth process. In the past, we have overpolluted because of an important flaw in the price system. The flaw is that firms, governments, drivers of automobiles, and others are allowed to pollute without paying the full cost of what they do. Firms dispose of waste by discharging it into rivers or through their smokestacks. Municipal governments dump sewage into rivers. People drive automobiles which emit pollutants. The list is long.

The flaw in the price system can be corrected by regulation of the discharge of wastes into the environment either by direct control or by taxing those who pollute. There are good reasons for preferring the latter approach.[18] The main point, however, is that the flaw can be corrected and the cost of doing so is not prohibitive. Thus, the economy can grow without adding to the pollution problem.

In fact, some contend that growth is necessary to pay the costs of reducing the current level of pollution.

Many of the other costs associated with economic growth, such as urban sprawl, congestion, noise pollution, and crime in the streets, appear to be problems whether economic growth is occurring or not. Perhaps accelerating economic growth intensifies these problems. But it is possible to reduce the magnitude of the problems without eliminating economic growth. In fact, if economic growth were eliminated, it is not clear that society would be willing to pay the costs necessary to alleviate the problems, since to do so would reduce society's material well-being.

Economic growth increases the amount of goods and services available to society. It does not necessarily mean that a more equitable distribution of income will result. Some have argued that the redistribution of income is more pressing than continued economic growth. With economic growth, however, it should be easier to redistribute income since, in a growing economy, no one's income has to be reduced in order to increase the incomes of others. This does not guarantee that such a redistribution will take place. In the less developed countries of the world, economic development is the only hope of achieving higher standards of living, since the developed countries of the world are unwilling to allocate even 1 percent of their gross national products to assist the less developed countries.

To sum up, there seems little or no reason to take an extreme position in regard to economic growth. To advocate growth with no regard for the environment appears unreasonable. To forsake economic growth completely also appears unreasonable, since it is possible to grow and reduce pollution at the same time. The best course seems to be a middle position. That is, we should advocate continued economic growth but at the same time insist on policies prohibiting ecologically dangerous activities and forcing producers and consumers to pay for using the environment as a dump.

CONCLUDING REMARKS

Economic growth is the subject of controversy. We have presented four models of economic growth. Two of them suggest that growth is not possible in the long run. The others suggest that long-run growth is possible, but they differ in almost all other respects.

Even if economic growth is possible, people disagree about its desirability. Some argue that the costs associated with economic growth are so great that policies should be undertaken to check or halt such growth. The view expressed here is that such an extreme position is not necessary. It is possible for the economy to grow without the abuses of the environment that have accompanied growth in the past. Such growth will not be easy to achieve because firms and individuals have an economic incentive to continue to pollute the environment. As a consequence, government must act to prohibit certain actions or to force firms and individuals to bear the costs of their actions. Whether legislators do so in the face of vested interests depends ultimately on the electorate.

NOTES

1. For a survey, see William J. Baumol, *Economic Dynamics: An Introduction*, 3rd ed. (New York: The Macmillan Company, 1970), pp. 13–21.

2. R. F. Harrod, *Towards a Dynamic Economics* (London: MacMillan and Co. Ltd., 1948). E. Domar, *Essays in the Theory of Economic Growth* (New York: Oxford University Press, Inc., 1957).

3. In terms of the previous example, suppose *s* equals 0.1 and *v* equals 1, which implies that the warranted rate of growth is 10 percent. If income in time period $t - 1$ is \$450 billion, income must increase to \$500 billion in period *t* for the warranted rate to be maintained. Suppose income increases to \$520 billion. This implies that the actual growth rate is 13.5 percent, obtained by dividing the difference between \$520 billion and \$450 billion by \$520 billion, so that the actual growth rate exceeds the warranted rate. Realized saving equals \$52 billion, which implies that realized investment equals \$52 billion. Intended investment, however, equals \$70 billion. Since intended investment is greater than realized investment, there is an unintended reduction in inventories, and managers will try to increase production even more rapidly in the next period.

4. Robert Solow, "A Contribution to the Theory of Economic Growth," *Quarterly Journal of Economics*, 70 (February 1956), 65–94.

5. For early expositions of the neoclassical theory, see Solow, ibid., and T. W. Swan, "Economic Growth and Capital Accumulation," *Economic Record*, 32 (November 1956), 334–61.

6. First, the production function is differentiated with respect to time, *t*, to obtain

$$\frac{dY}{dt} = rAe^{rt}K^{\alpha}N^{1-\alpha} + \alpha Ae^{rt}K^{\alpha-1}N^{1-\alpha}\frac{dK}{dt} + (1 - \alpha)Ae^{rt}K^{\alpha}N^{-\alpha}\frac{dN}{dt}.$$

Since $K^{\alpha-1}$ equals K^{α}/K and $N^{-\alpha}$ equals $N^{1-\alpha}/N$, we obtain, by substitution,

$$\frac{dY}{dt} = rAe^{rt}K^{\alpha}N^{1-\alpha} + \alpha Ae^{rt}K^{\alpha}N^{1-\alpha}\left(\frac{1}{K}\frac{dK}{dt}\right) + (1 - \alpha)Ae^{rt}K^{\alpha}N^{1-\alpha}\left(\frac{1}{N}\frac{dN}{dt}\right).$$

Since $Ae^{rt}K^{\alpha}N^{1-\alpha}$ equals Y, we obtain, by substitution,

$$\frac{dY}{dt} = rY + \alpha Y\left(\frac{1}{K}\frac{dK}{dt}\right) + (1 - \alpha)Y\left(\frac{1}{N}\frac{dN}{dt}\right).$$

Finally, by dividing both sides of the equation by Y, we get

$$\frac{1}{Y}\frac{dY}{dt} = r + \alpha\left(\frac{1}{K}\frac{dK}{dt}\right) + (1 - \alpha)\left(\frac{1}{N}\frac{dN}{dt}\right),$$

where $(1/Y)(dY/dt)$ represents the growth rate of output, *r* the growth rate of technology, $(1/K)(dK/dt)$ the growth rate of capital stock, and $(1/N)(dN/dt)$ the growth rate of the labor supply. To simplify the notation, let us replace $(1/Y)(dY/dt)$ by *q* and $(1/K)(dK/dt)$ by *h*. Since $(1/N)(dN/dt)$ equals *n*, we obtain $q = r + \alpha h + (1-\alpha)\,n$.

7. The term *golden age* was coined by Joan Robinson. See Robinson, *The Accumulation of Capital*, 2nd ed. (New York: St. Martin's Press, Inc., 1966), p. 99. In the Harrod

model, the actual, warranted, and natural rates of growth must be equal for the economy to be in a golden age.

8. The slope of the Y/N curve is found by differentiating equation (17.10) with respect to K/N. Thus,

$$\frac{d(Y/N)}{d(K/N)} = \alpha A(K/N)^{\alpha-1} = \alpha AK^{\alpha-1}N^{1-\alpha} = \frac{\alpha AK^\alpha N^{1-\alpha}}{K} = \alpha\,\frac{Y}{K},$$

where Y/K represents the output-capital ratio. To obtain the golden age output-capital ratio, substitute the golden age growth rate g for h in equation (17.7) in order to obtain

$$g = s\,\frac{Y}{K}.$$

If we rearrange terms and divide both sides of the equation by s, we get

$$\frac{Y}{K} = \frac{g}{s}.$$

Thus, in a golden age, the output-capital ratio equals the golden age growth rate, g, divided by the saving rate, s. If g/s is substituted for Y/K in the expression $\alpha(Y/K)$, we obtain

$$\frac{d(Y/N)}{d(K/N)} = \frac{\alpha g}{s}.$$

9. A number of books deal with growth theory. See, for example, Hywel G. Jones, *An Introduction to Modern Theories of Economic Growth* (New York: McGraw-Hill Book Company, 1976).

10. Moreover, factor price flexibility is not sufficient to guarantee full employment if factor substitution is not possible. Critics of neoclassical growth theory often stress that little or no factor substitution is possible, especially after capital is in place. The neoclassical model has, however, been extended to show that it is not necessary to have factor substitution at all stages. The results of neoclassical growth theory hold even if there is factor substitution only at the planning stage.

11. Ryuzo Sato, "Fiscal Policy in a Neo-Classical Growth Model: An Analysis of Time Required for Equilibrating Adjustment," *Review of Economic Studies*, 30 (February 1963), 16–23; and "The Harrod-Domar Model vs. the Neo-Classical Growth Model," *Economic Journal*, 74 (June 1964), 380–87.

12. See John Conlisk, "Unemployment in a Neoclassical Growth Model: The Effect on Speed of Adjustment," *Economic Journal*, 76 (September 1966), 550–66; and Kazuo Sato, "On the Adjustment Time in Neoclassical Growth Models," *Review of Economic Studies*, 33 (July 1966), 263–68.

13. See, for example, Hans Brems, "Reality and Neoclassical Theory," *Journal of Economic Literature*, 15 (March 1977), 72–83.

14. For Cambridge models, see Joan Robinson, *The Accumulation of Capital* and *Essays in the Theory of Economic Growth* (London: MacMillan and Company Ltd., 1962), as well as Nicholas Kaldor and J. S. Mirrlees, "A New Model of Economic Growth," *Review of Economic Studies*, 29 (June 1962), 174–92.

15. Donella H. Meadows, Dennis L. Meadows, Jorgen Randers, and William W. Behrens III, *The Limits to Growth*, 2nd ed. (New York: Universe Books, 1974). For references to other doomsday models and critiques, see Richard T. Gill, *Great Debates in Economics*, I (Santa Monica, Calif.: Goodyear Publishing Co., Inc. 1976), pp. 125–80.

16. For a discussion of the issues and an extensive bibliography, see Frederick M. Peterson and Anthony C. Fisher, "The Exploitation of Extractive Resources: A Survey," *Economic Journal*, 87 (December 1977), 681–721.

17. For example, see Ezra J. Mishan, *The Costs of Economic Growth* (New York: Praeger Publishers, Inc., 1967). For a contrary view, see Wilfred Beckerman, *Two Cheers for the Affluent Society: A Spirited Defense of Economic Growth* (New York: St. Martin's Press, Inc., 1975).

18. Walter W. Heller, *Economic Growth and Environmental Quality: Collision or Coexistence?* (Morristown, N.J.: General Learning Press, 1973); and Robert M. Solow, "Is the End of the World at Hand?" *Challenge*, 16 (March–April, 1973), 39–50.

REVIEW QUESTIONS _____

1. Distinguish between economic growth and economic development.

2. Discuss the roles of population, the law of diminishing returns, land, and technological progress in the classical theory of economic growth.

3. In terms of Harrod's theory, define the actual, warranted, and natural rates of growth. Explain why, according to Harrod, it is so difficult for the economy to grow at the natural rate.

4. Suppose the marginal propensity to consume is 0.9 and the accelerator coefficient is 0.5. Determine the warranted rate of growth. How is the warranted rate altered if

   a. the marginal propensity to consume increases.

   b. the accelerator coefficient increases.

5. How do the assumptions underlying Harrod's theory differ from those underlying the neoclassical theory of economic growth?

6. Suppose that technological progress is occurring at a rate of 2 percent per year, that 80 percent of national income accrues to labor, and that the labor supply (and population) is growing at 2.5 percent per year. Determine

   a. the golden age growth rate of output.

   b. the golden age growth rate of per capita output.

7. Explain why increases in per capita output are not possible in the neoclassical model without technological progress.

8. Compare and contrast the roles of the saving rate in the Harrod and neoclassical models.

9. Critically evaluate the neoclassical theory of economic growth.

10. Suppose, over time, our natural resources are depleted. What will be the effect on aggregate supply? Explain in terms of the model of Chapter 10. Can

the depletion of natural resources be overcome by increasing aggregate demand? Explain. What sorts of policies are necessary to deal with the problem?

11. The Club of Rome model suggests that economic growth is likely to come to an end suddenly, with catastrophic results. Explain why, if economic growth does cease, it may do so gradually.

12. Is economic growth desirable? Defend your answer.

SUGGESTED READING

BARNEY, GERALD O. (Study Director). *The Global 2000 Report to the President of the U.S. Entering the 21st Century. Volume I: The Summary Report*. New York: Pergamon Press, 1980.

BAUMOL, WILLIAM J., *Economic Dynamics: An Introduction* (3rd ed.). New York: The MacMillan Company, 1970.

BECKERMAN, WILFRED, *Two Cheers for the Affluent Society: A Spirited Defense of Economic Growth*. New York: St. Martin's Press, Inc., 1975.

HARROD, R. F., *Towards a Dynamic Economics*. London: Macmillan and Co. Ltd., 1948.

JONES, HYWEL G., *An Introduction to Modern Theories of Economic Growth*. New York: McGraw-Hill Book Company, 1976.

MEADOWS, DONELLA H., DENNIS L. MEADOWS, JORGEN RANDERS, and WILLIAM W. BEHRENS III, *The Limits to Growth* (2nd ed.). New York: Universe Books, 1974.

MISHAN, EZRA J., *The Costs of Economic Growth*. New York: Praeger Publishers, Inc., 1967.

PETERSON, FREDERICK M., and ANTHONY C. FISHER, "The Exploitation of Extractive Resources: A Survey," *Economic Journal*, 87 (December 1977), 681–721.

SOLOW, ROBERT, "A Contribution to the Theory of Economic Growth," *Quarterly Journal of Economics*, 70 (February 1956), 65–94.

18

FISCAL POLICY

Government serves a number of functions: (1) the allocation function, (2) the distribution function, and (3) the stabilization function. The *allocation* function relates to the government's role in providing goods for which the net social benefits differ from the net private benefits. Such goods include national defense, elementary education, and enforcement of contracts. The government may be able to provide these goods more efficiently than the private sector. The *distribution* function relates to the distribution of income and wealth. A market economy may fail to provide an equitable distribution of income and wealth. If it does, governmental action may be taken to achieve a more equitable distribution.

The *stabilization* function relates to the use of budget policy to achieve full employment, price stability, an appropriate rate of economic growth, and balance of payments equilibrium. This chapter deals with government and its stabilization function. The other functions are beyond the scope of this book. Furthermore, we concentrate on the federal government. State and local governments influence the level of economic activity by their actions. However, only the federal government has responsibility for the conduct of fiscal policy.

In this chapter, we first consider various budget concepts and the budgetary process. Next, the measurement of fiscal restraint is discussed. After dealing with the effectiveness of various fiscal policy actions and the time lags associated with them, we consider the selection of the appropriate fiscal tool or tools. Finally, we cover two issues related to fiscal policy, the use of tax policy to stimulate investment and the impact of budget deficits and the public debt on the economy.

THE FEDERAL BUDGET

There are three important budget concepts: the unified budget, the national income accounts budget, and the high employment budget. The unified budget is the official budget of the U.S. government. It is a summary statement of the receipts and expenditures of the goverment, except for certain federal agencies, and of trust funds, such as social security. The receipts and expenditures are generally recorded on a cash basis, with receipts recorded at the time the cash is collected and expenditures at the time checks are issued. The unified budget is on a fiscal year basis, with the fiscal year running from October 1 through September 30.

Although the unified budget is the official budget of the federal government, it does not include the outlays of all federal agencies. Some agencies are *off-budget*, which means their receipts and expenditures are not included in the unified budget.[1] The Postal Service, for example, is an off-budget agency. Although the outlays of these agencies are small compared to total outlays in the unified budget, some evidence suggests that off-budget outlays are increasing more rapidly than outlays in general. Consequently, the unified budget is becoming less reliable as a measure of the government's true budgetary position.

The national income accounts budget summarizes the receipts and expenditures of the federal government as they affect the national income accounts. In the national income accounts budget, receipts are, for the most part, recorded when the tax liability is incurred; expenditures are recorded when delivery is made to the government. The national income accounts budget is based on the calendar year; however, quarterly estimates are available. As indicated in Table 18.1, the federal government had a deficit in the national income accounts budget of $200.0 billion in 1985.

The high employment budget, or cyclically adjusted budget as it is often called, is an estimate of the national income accounts budget which would prevail at a high level of resource utilization. To calculate the high employment budget, the high employment level of output is estimated. Expenditures and tax receipts are then estimated on the assumption that output is at the high employment level. In 1982, the high employment budget deficit was $88.9 billion, much less than the actual national income accounts deficit of $145.9 billion. The main reason for the difference was that the actual level of output in 1982 was appreciably less than the high employment level of output. Consequently, tax receipts were much less and

TABLE 18.1 *The national income accounts budget in 1981 (billions of current dollars)*

Receipts			784.7
Personal tax and nontax receipts		350.7	
Income taxes	343.7		
Estate and gift taxes	6.5		
Nontaxes	0.5		
Corporate profits tax accruals		67.1	
Indirect business tax and nontax accruals		57.0	
Contributions for social insurance		309.9	
Expenditures			984.7
Purchases of goods and services		355.4	
National defense	261.9		
Nondefense	93.6		
Transfer payments		379.8	
To persons	366.3		
To foreigners	13.4		
Grants-in-aid to state and local governments		99.0	
Net interest paid		129.2	
Subsidies less current surplus of government enterprises		21.1	
Wage accruals less disbursements		−0.2	
Surplus (+) or deficit (−), national income and product accounts			−200.0

Source: U.S. Department of Commerce, *Survey of Current Business*, 66 (April 1986), 14.

transfer payments greater than they would have been at the high employment output level.

Although the unified budget is the official budget of the federal government, the national income accounts budget is more useful for our purposes since it is tied to the national income accounts. As will be discussed, the high employment budget provides a better measure of fiscal restraint than does the national income accounts budget.

THE BUDGETARY PROCESS

In an attempt to reform the budgetary process, the Congressional Budget and Impoundment Control Act was passed in 1974. Widespread dissatisfaction with the budgetary process existed before the act was passed. Many people believed that Congress had no effective means to limit federal spending. Moreover, many appropriation bills were passed only after a new fiscal year had begun. In some instances, the delay was as long as six months.

The act created House and Senate Budget Committees and a Congressional Budget Office "to improve the Congress's informational and analytical resources with respect to the budgetary process."[2] In addition, the act established new procedures and a new timetable for the congressional budget (see Table 18.2).

According to the timetable, the president submits an official budget on or before the fifteenth day after Congress convenes (about January 30).

On or before March 15, committees in the House and Senate submit reports to their respective budget committees. These reports give the budget committees an early indication of committee legislative plans and proposed outlays for the next fiscal year. In addition, the Congressional Budget Office is required to submit a report to the budget committees no later than April 1. The report deals primarily with alternative budget levels and national budget priorities and is used by the budget committees to prepare the first concurrent resolution on the budget.

April 15 is the deadline for the budget committees' report of the first concurrent resolution on the budget to their respective houses. The first concurrent resolution is a preliminary budget; it includes the appropriate outlays for the next

TABLE 18.2 *The Congressional budget timetable*

On or Before	Action To Be Completed
Fifteenth day after Congress convenes	President submits an official budget.[1]
March 15	Committees and joint committees submit reports to Budget Committees.
April 1	Congressional Budget Office submits report to budget committees.
April 15	Budget committees report first concurrent resolution on the budget to their houses.
May 15	Committees report bills authorizing new budget authority.
May 15	Congress completes action on first concurrent resolution on the budget.
Seventh day after Labor Day	Congress completes action on bills and resolutions providing new budget authority and new spending authority.
September 15	Congress completes action on second required concurrent resolution on the budget.
September 25	Congress completes action on reconciliation bill or resolution, or both, implementing second required concurrent resolution.
October 1	Fiscal year begins.

[1]Along with the budget, the president is required to submit current services estimates. These estimates are projections of the expenditures necessary to continue existing programs during the next fiscal year.

Source: George Cross, *The Congressional Budget and Impoundment Control Act of 1974: A General Explanation*, U.S. House of Representatives Committee on the Budget (Washington, D.C.: Government Printing Office, 1975).

fiscal year in terms of each major functional category of the budget, as well as the aggregate. It also includes the appropriate budget surplus or deficit for the next fiscal year and the recommended level of federal revenues to achieve that surplus or deficit. At this stage, the budgeted amounts are to be regarded as targets rather than ceilings.

Between April 15 and May 15, the first concurrent resolution is debated and ultimately passed by both houses. If differences exist between the House and Senate versions, the differences must be resolved in conference. By May 15, the final conference report is passed by both houses. May 15 is also the deadline for the reporting of bills authorizing new budget authority.

During the next few months, the various committees continue to work on bills within their jurisdictions. These bills must be passed by Congress on or before the seventh day after Labor Day. On or before September 15, both houses must complete action on the second concurrent resolution on the budget. The second resolution fixes the final totals for spending, revenues, and the resulting surplus or deficit. If differences exist between the House and Senate versions, they must be resolved so that the second concurrent resolution can be implemented no later than September 25. The new fiscal year begins October 1.

The budget may be revised later. Such action would require an additional concurrent resolution.

Until 1980, the new budget process worked reasonably well.[3] Beginning with the fiscal 1981 budget, however, Congress has had difficulty in finalizing budgets. The 1981 budget, for example, was never completed because of the inability of Congress and President Carter to agree on a budget.

The main reasons for the breakdown in the budget process are differences in philosophies concerning spending levels and priorities both between and within our political parties. While the budget process itself might be improved, it is unlikely that it will work much better until a greater consensus on the role of the federal government emerges in Congress.

THE BUDGETARY PROCESS
AND THE GRAMM–RUDMAN–HOLLINGS ACT

Growing dissatisfaction with the budgetary process and the mounting federal budget deficit led to the passage and signing, in December 1985, of the Balanced Budget and Emergency Deficit Control Act of 1985, better known as the Gramm–Rudman–Hollings Act. Under this act, the federal budget deficit is to be reduced by at least $36 billion each fiscal year so that the deficit will be eliminated by fiscal 1991. Specifically, the maximum allowable deficit would be $172 billion in fiscal 1986, followed by $144 billion for fiscal 1987, $108 billion for fiscal 1988, $72 billion for fiscal 1989, $36 billion for fiscal 1990, and zero for fiscal 1991.

Prior to the beginning of the fiscal year, both the Congressional Budget Office (CBO) and the Office of Management and Budget (OMB) must calculate whether and by how much the proposed budget will overshoot the deficit target. The General Accounting Office (GAO), an arm of Congress, then reviews the reports of the CBO and OMB. If the GAO determines that the deficit goal has not been met, it specifies the necessary cuts and formally notifies the president. If Congress and the president cannot agree on spending cuts and/or tax increases sufficient to meet the goal, the act requires that the president institute across-the-board reductions in government spending. Not all government programs would be subjected to these automatic cuts. Social security, interest on the national debt, some military spending, food stamps, and other items are exempt. Of the remaining programs, some can be cut by limited amounts only. In fact, more than 70 percent of all government spending and about 85 percent of nondefense spending is either exempt from the automatic cuts or limited as to the amounts that can be cut. If the automatic cuts are triggered, the reductions in spending must be equally divided between military and nonmilitary spending (after exclusions).

Various members of Congress and others claimed that the provision relating to the automatic cuts is unconstitutional and, after the act was passed and signed into law, they filed a lawsuit to that effect. On February 7, 1986, a special three-judge federal court agreed. In their decision, the judges ruled that the provision "vested executive power in the comptroller general, an officer removable by Congress," and is, therefore, unconstitutional. Under the act, the comptroller general, head of the GAO, is given the authority to determine the size of the automatic spending cuts that would be triggered. The court found the rest of the act, including a "fallback" system in which the GAO report containing the budget cuts would be submitted to Congress for a vote, to be constitutional.

The lower court's ruling was appealed to the Supreme Court. On July 7, 1986, the Supreme Court announced that it was upholding the lower court's decision regarding the unconstitutionality of the role of the comptroller general and the constitutionality of the rest of the act. The Supreme Court's decision means that failure to meet the deficit goal will no longer result in automatic reductions in government spending. Instead, Congress must vote on the cuts.

Despite the desirability of reducing or eliminating the budget deficit, various objections may be raised to the Gramm–Rudman–Hollings Act. First, it will virtually eliminate fiscal policy as a means to stabilize the economy over the life of the act. This objection is not as serious as it first appears because more reliance may be placed on monetary policy and because the act may be suspended during a recession or wartime. A second and more serious objection has to do with the act's lack of flexibility, at least in its original form. Very little flexibility exists regarding the overall reduction in the deficit. Moreover, if Congress and the president cannot agree on a deficit reduction plan, the act, at least in its original form, requires across-the-board cuts in government spending. Because most government spending is excluded, the cuts will fall across a narrow range of programs, thereby making the cuts much deeper than would otherwise be the case. Furthermore, the programs would be cut by the same percentage regardless of the desirability of supporting such government agencies as the Federal Aviation Administration (which hires safety inspectors and air traffic controllers), the Federal Bureau of Investigation, and the U.S. Customs Service (which helps enforce the nation's drug laws). Finally, equal amounts must be cut from military and nonmilitary spending.

THE MEASUREMENT OF FISCAL RESTRAINT

A deficit in the national income accounts budget is often interpreted as proof that the government is pursuing an expansionary fiscal policy; a surplus is seen as evidence that the government is pursuing a contractionary policy. For example, if a $20 billion deficit occurred during a particular year the deficit is regarded as evidence that the government was pursuing an expansionary fiscal policy. The deficit may have been caused by expansionary fiscal policy; it may, however, have resulted from a recession. As discussed in Chapter 4, taxes decrease and transfer payments increase as the economy enters a recession. These automatic changes in spending and tax receipts cause a larger deficit (or smaller surplus) in the government's budget. Because of the impact of the economy on the government's budget, a deficit cannot be regarded as proof that the government is actually pursuing an expansionary policy.

To obtain a more reliable measure of fiscal restraint, the high or full employment budget concept was developed.[4] As discussed earlier, the high employment budget is calculated on the assumption that there is a high degree of resource utilization. By assuming high employment, the impact of the economy on the government's budget is eliminated. As a result, the high employment budget deficit or surplus measures only the exogenous impact of the budget on the economy. A deficit in the high employment budget is evidence that the government is pursuing expansionary fiscal policy. Similarly, a surplus is evidence that the government is following contractionary fiscal policy. The size of the deficit (surplus) is also considered important because a larger high employment budget deficit (surplus) implies that fiscal policy is more expansionary (contractionary).

At times, both the actual and high employment budgets may be in deficit. In such cases, the appropriate interpretation of the government's fiscal posture could be based on either the actual or high employment budgets. At other times, the actual budget will show a deficit, suggesting an expansionary fiscal policy, and the high employment budget will show a surplus, implying a contractionary fiscal policy. Since the actual deficit is due to a low level of income, not expansionary fiscal policy, the high employment budget is the appropriate measure of fiscal restraint. Concentration on the actual budget deficit can be highly misleading. The government budget during the 1930s provides a good illustration. It consistently showed deficits, suggesting to the uninitiated that the government pursued expansionary fiscal policy during the Great Depression. The high employment budget reveals that the federal government actually pursued contractionary policies during some of the Great Depression years.[5]

To summarize, the actual budget surplus fails to distinguish between the influence of the budget on the economy and the influence of the economy on the budget. In contrast, the influence of the economy on the budget is eliminated by the high employment surplus concept since it measures government spending and tax receipts at their high employment levels, thereby revealing the influence of the budget on the economy.

Although the high employment budget surplus is an improvement over the actual budget surplus as a measure of fiscal restraint, the concept has a number of shortcomings.[6] One shortcoming is that it gives equal weight to government purchases and taxes. As discussed in Chapter 4, an equal increase in government purchases and taxes is expansionary. With an equal increase in government purchases and taxes, the high employment surplus will be unchanged, indicating incorrectly that there has been no change in the degree of fiscal restraint. Consequently, government purchases and taxes must be weighted in some manner to reflect the different multipliers associated with them.

A second shortcoming arises because the high employment surplus will change if the high employment level of output changes. Over time, real output increases. Given the progressive nature of the tax system, real tax receipts will grow more rapidly than real output and real government spending. The resulting increase in the high employment surplus suggests, incorrectly, that the government has intentionally made fiscal policy less expansionary.

Third, even if real output is unchanged, the full employment surplus increases if inflation occurs. Tax receipts depend, in part, upon nominal income. Given the nature of the tax system, inflation will result in a higher fraction of real income accruing to the government in terms of tax revenue. As a consequence, the high employment surplus will increase even in the absence of fiscal policy changes.

Fourth, if the economy is experiencing high rates of unemployment, changes in the high employment surplus may be misleading. For example, suppose there is an increase in the corporate income tax rate combined with a reduction in personal income tax rates. Since profits are low when unemployment is high, the net effect may be a tax cut which is expansionary. Since the high employment surplus is calculated on the basis of the high employment output and profits are high at full employment, the high employment surplus may increase, indicating that the policy is contractionary.[7]

These and other considerations give the high employment surplus only limited usefulness as a measure of fiscal restraint.[8] The high employment surplus is more reliable than the actual budget surplus in that it attempts to eliminate the influence of the economy on the budget. But it must be supplemented by other budget information to provide an adequate picture of governmental policy.

THE EFFECTIVENESS OF FISCAL POLICY[9]

With regard to stabilization policy, Keynesians believe fiscal policy to be potent; monetarists believe it to be impotent. The theoretical issues were examined in earlier chapters. In this chapter, we examine and critically evaluate the empirical evidence relating to the effectiveness of fiscal policy.

Many of the studies relating to the effectiveness of fiscal policy are based on single-equation models rather than large-scale econometric models of the economy. In 1968, Leonall C. Andersen and Jerry L. Jordan published a study of the relative effectiveness of monetary and fiscal policies.[10] They postulated that the level of economic activity depends upon various factors, including monetary and fiscal actions. In equation form the relationship is

$$Y = f(E, R, M, Z),$$

where Y represents the level of economic activity, E summarizes government spending policies, R summarizes government tax policies, M summarizes monetary policy, and Z summarizes all other determinants of the level of economic activity. The level of economic activity was measured by nominal gross national product. Several measures of fiscal policy were used, including the high employment budget surplus. Two measures of monetary policy were used, the nominal money supply and the monetary base. Because of the impossibility (they believe) of quantifying all the determinants of the level of economic activity, Andersen and Jordan did not explicitly include the Z variable in their model.

In their empirical work, Andersen and Jordan used regression analysis to establish a relationship between changes in GNP and changes in the various monetary and fiscal variables. The data covered the period from the first quarter of 1952 to the second quarter of 1968 and were on a quarterly basis.

The empirical results obtained by Andersen and Jordan do not support the view that fiscal policy is effective in the absence of a change in the money supply. If fiscal policy were effective, a significant, inverse relationship should exist between the level of economic activity and the high employment budget surplus. For the first two quarters following a change in the high employment budget surplus, Andersen and Jordan found the expected inverse relationship, but it was not statistically significant. They also found, contrary to expectation, that the relationship was positive (but not statistically significant) for the next two quarters and the entire four-quarter period. The absence of a significant, inverse relationship between economic activity and the high employment budget surplus supports the view that fiscal policy is ineffective.

Andersen and Jordan conducted similar tests by considering high employment expenditures and receipts separately. The results were similar to those obtained by using the high employment surplus. Consequently, they concluded that either the fiscal variables do not accurately reflect the influence of fiscal policy or fiscal policy is ineffective.

Andersen and Jordan also tested the relationship between the level of economic activity and the money supply and found that the money supply was very influential in determining total spending. With an increase in the money supply, there should be an increase in economic activity; hence, there should be a significant, positive relationship between nominal GNP and the nominal money supply. Andersen and Jordan found that the hypothesized relationship held for each of the four quarters and for the entire four-quarter period.

Andersen and Jordan found that the evidence is consistent with the view that the response of economic activity to monetary actions is much greater than the response to fiscal actions.[11] As a consequence, they advocated greater reliance upon monetary policy.

The publication of the Andersen-Jordan study resulted in a series of articles critical of it. In one of the early critiques, Frank de Leeuw and John Kalchbrenner raised the question of *reverse causation*.[12] They noted that to obtain an estimate of the true relationship between the level of economic activity and the monetary and fiscal variables the latter variables must be exogenous. If the level of economic activity influences the monetary and fiscal variables, the estimated relationship will not be the true relationship. De Leeuw and Kalchbrenner claim that the monetary and fiscal variables utilized by Andersen and Jordan do not satisfy this requirement and suggest alternative variables which they believe to be satisfactory.[13] Utilizing these variables, they tested the relative effectiveness of monetary and fiscal policies by the same methodology as Andersen and Jordan used. Their results supported the view that monetary policy is effective. Contrary to the Andersen–Jordan study, however, the results of de Leeuw and Kalchbrenner suggested that fiscal policy is effective.

In response to de Leeuw and Kalchbrenner, Andersen and Jordan argued that the variable they employed to measure monetary policy (the monetary base) is superior to the alternative measure suggested by de Leeuw and Kalchbrenner on both theoretical and empirical grounds.[14] Andersen and Jordan conceded that the fiscal policy variable suggested by de Leeuw and Kalchbrenner is superior to their own, but they note that their results on the relative effectiveness of monetary and fiscal policies are unaltered if the new fiscal variable is used in conjunction with their original monetary policy variable.[15]

Rather than pursue the reverse causation and other arguments relating to the statistical properties of the Andersen–Jordan model, suppose we assume that the fiscal and monetary policy variables are measured properly and that no other variables systematically influence the level of economic activity.[16] Under these assumptions, the level of economic activity is determined by fiscal and monetary actions plus purely random forces. Thus, the changes in the level of economic activity (ΔY) can be written as a function of the change in fiscal policy (ΔF), the change in monetary policy (ΔM), and purely random forces:

(18.1) $\Delta Y = a_1 \Delta F + a_2 \Delta M + \text{random forces},$

where a_1 and a_2 are constants.

Suppose the monetary authorities do not try to stabilize the level of economic activity or that their attempts are unsuccessful. On the other hand, suppose the fiscal authorities are successful in stabilizing the level of economic activity by undertaking fiscal action to offset the influence of the random forces. This implies that the government is changing fiscal policy so that the impact of fiscal actions, $a_1 \Delta F$, is equal and opposite to the impact of the random forces. Thus, $a_1 \Delta F +$

random forces equals zero and the equation becomes

$$\Delta Y = a_2 \Delta M.$$

The equation suggests, contrary to our initial assumption, that the fiscal variable has no impact on the level of economic activity, whereas the monetary variable explains changes in the level of economic activity very well. Given our model, this result, essentially that obtained by Andersen and Jordan, is wrong. Paradoxically, the more effective fiscal policy is in stabilizing the level of economic activity, the less effective it will appear in terms of equation (18.1). Similarly, the less effective monetary policy is in stabilizing the level of economic activity, the more effective it will appear in terms of equation (18.1). As a consequence, the Andersen–Jordan study could be interpreted as providing support for the view that fiscal policy is effective.

Besides the objections raised earlier, which cast doubt on the results obtained by Andersen and Jordan, the empirical evidence based on large-scale econometric models is inconsistent with the results obtained by Andersen and Jordan. In a comparison of various econometric models, Gary Fromm and Lawrence R. Klein list multipliers for government nondefense expenditures and personal taxes.[17] Except for the St. Louis Federal Reserve Bank model, the multipliers suggest that fiscal policy is effective. The St. Louis model (which is not a large-scale econometric model) indicates that an increase in government nondefense expenditures causes an increase in real GNP during the first four quarters, but after four quarters the increase in real government expenditures causes a decrease in real GNP. Even during the first four quarters, the multipliers never exceed 1, which implies that the increase in real GNP never exceeds the increase in real government expenditures.

In the other nine models, an increase in real government nondefense expenditures results in an increase in real GNP in the initial quarter greater than the initial increase in real government expenditures. The first-quarter multipliers range from 1.1 to 1.8. The multipliers gradually increase in value until, after one year, the multipliers range from 1.5 to 2.8. After reaching a peak in a year or two, the multipliers decline.[18] These multipliers suggest that a change in real government nondefense expenditures has a significant short-run impact on real GNP.

The personal tax multipliers show a similar pattern except that the tax multipliers are less (in absolute terms) than the corresponding government nondefense expenditure multipliers. For the seven models for which tax multipliers are available, the first-quarter multipliers range from −0.4 to −1.0. After one year, the multipliers range from −1.2 to −1.6, indicating that a change in real personal taxes has a significant short-run impact on real GNP.

The evidence from large-scale econometric models suggests that fiscal policy is effective. In view of this evidence, the deficiencies of the Andersen–Jordan study, and the evidence from single-equation models which contradicts the Andersen-Jordan results, we conclude that changes in government purchases and taxes do have a significant impact upon the level of economic activity.

POLICY LAGS

Even though fiscal policy is effective, it may not be stabilizing. The time lags for fiscal policy might be long or variable enough to make fiscal policy destabilizing. There are three time lags: the recognition lag, the implementation lag, and the response lag. The *recognition lag* is the period between the time at which the need for action arises and the time at which the need for action is recognized. The *implementation lag* is the period between the time when the need for action is recognized and the time of the actual policy change. The *response lag* is the period between the time of the actual policy change and the time at which the new policy actually affects the economy. The problem of time lags is common to fiscal and monetary policy. In this chapter, we concentrate on the problem with regard to fiscal policy.

The recognition lag arises because it takes time to collect and process data on the economy and to analyze their implications. For example, suppose GNP increased less rapidly (or even decreased) in a particular quarter. Does this mean that the economy is headed for a recession? Similarly, suppose the CPI increases more rapidly over a two-or three-month time span. Does this imply that the economy is entering a new era in terms of inflation? Perhaps one can answer these questions on the basis of existing data; however, it may be necessary for more time to elapse before the true direction of the economy can be determined. As a consequence, it may take several quarters between the time a need for action arises and the time that the authorities realize that action is necessary. The recognition lag is presumably the same for both fiscal and monetary policies.

The implementation lag is relevant once the need for a policy change has been recognized. The president has little or no discretion with regard to fiscal policy since Congress must approve programs designed to alter government spending and/or taxes. The implementation lag can be a month or less; in general, it is much longer.[19] Perhaps the best-known cases are the tax cut of 1964 and the income-tax surcharge of 1968. President Kennedy's economic advisers had recommended a tax cut in 1961. But he did not request a tax reduction until the summer of 1962, and it was not approved until 1964. Similarly, the request for the income-tax surcharge became law in mid-1968, some eighteen months after it was proposed by President Johnson, who may have initially delayed the proposal for political reasons.

There are many reasons for the long implementation lag for fiscal policy. Most important perhaps are the economic and political implications of changes in government spending and tax programs. For example, before elections, it may be very difficult for Congress and the president to cut popular spending programs or to raise taxes, even if those actions are desirable from the standpoint of the economy.

To reduce the implementation lag, it has been suggested that the president be given limited authority to change tax rates. The discretionary changes could be limited to, say, a 10 percent change in existing liabilities, with a provision for subsequent approval by Congress. Although various proposals have been introduced in Congress, none has been close to passage. Many congressmen contend that such action would weaken Congress's constitutional responsibilities in regard to the budget. At present, there appears to be little chance of achieving much in the way of flexibility in regard to fiscal policy. Consequently, in the absence of a national emergency, the implementation lag associated with fiscal policy is likely to be long. As discussed in Chapter 19, the implementation lag associated with monetary policy is much shorter.

Unlike the implementation lag, the response lag is likely to be short for some forms of fiscal action. In general, the multipliers for government nondefense expenditures suggest that an increase in government expenditures has a stimulating effect on the economy immediately and that most of the impact occurs during the first year. This evidence is misleading, however, since a long lag between the time increases in government purchases are authorized and the time the purchases actually take place is likely. In their study of fiscal policy lags, Albert Ando and E. Cary Brown concluded that changes in government purchases have an impact on the economy only after long lags.[20] Thus, the picture is not encouraging if changes in government expenditures are to be used to smooth or eliminate short-run fluctuations in output and employment. If the increases in government expenditures are to be used to bring the economy from a deep recession or depression, time lags are not a serious problem.

The picture is somewhat brighter in regard to tax changes. The tax multipliers for the various econometric models suggest that a change in personal taxes has an immediate effect on GNP. They also indicate that most of the impact occurs in the first year. Unlike changes in government purchases, changes in personal taxes can take effect almost immediately since withholding rates can be altered quickly.

To recapitulate, the implementation lag is likely to be long for fiscal policy. The response lag varies by type of fiscal action, with the lag for expenditure changes generally longer than the lag for tax changes. With the lags, it is possible that by the time the new policy has an impact on the economy, it may no longer be necessary. Even worse, by the time the new policy has an impact on the economy, the policy may be inappropriate. To illustrate, suppose unemployment is the problem. By the time new spending or tax legislation is enacted and has an impact on the economy, inflation may be the problem, not unemployment. If so, the effect of the new program will be to produce even more inflation.

Because discretionary policy may be destabilizing, it is important to be able to predict the future course of the economy. Given the long time lags, it is not enough for policy makers to know the current state of the economy. They must have some idea of what is likely to prevail in the next few years. Economists have made considerable progress in constructing large-scale econometric models of the economy. These models are used to predict the state of the economy in the future. If the predictions are accurate, the models will be valuable to policy makers. If the predictions are inaccurate, policies based on those predictions will be unsatisfactory. Economists disagree on how useful large-scale econometric models are as a predictive device. Some believe the models are reasonably accurate and can be used in conjunction with policymaking. If they are right, the time-lag problem is not too serious and discretionary policy is likely to prove to be stabilizing. If they are wrong, as some economists believe, the time-lag problem is serious and discretionary policy may prove to be destabilizing. This question is considered at greater length in Chapter 19.

THE CHOICE OF FISCAL POLICY TOOLS

If changes in both government spending and taxes alter aggregate demand, which method should be used? Generally, a change in government purchases has a greater multiplier effect than the corresponding change in personal income taxes. If personal income taxes are changed by a larger amount, government can compensate for the smaller multiplier associated with changes in those taxes. As a result, the difference in the sizes of the multipliers should not be a major factor in the selection of the appropriate fiscal tool.

Another consideration is the time lags associated with changes in government purchases and taxes. As discussed earlier, the lag associated with tax changes is likely to be shorter than the lag associated with changes in government purchases. Thus, tax changes may be favored on those grounds.

Besides differences in multipliers and time lags, there is another policy problem, the appropriate size of the public sector. To some, this issue is of paramount importance. Increases in government purchases enlarge the size of the public sector, whereas tax reductions do not. Proponents of a larger public sector favor increases in government purchases during recessions and tax increases during inflationary periods. This accords with their view that society's greatest needs are in the public sector—better schools, improved public transportation, safer streets, and the like.[21]

Proponents of a smaller public sector assert that the private sector can do many things cheaper and more efficiently than the government. They also claim that government is interfering unduly in the lives of citizens and abridging their freedoms. Since they believe in the desirability of a small public sector, they favor tax cuts during recessions and reductions in government purchases during inflationary periods.

TAX POLICY AND INVESTMENT

In addition to its general powers to spend and tax, the federal government may alter the tax structure so as to affect consumption and investment. For example, policy makers might raise personal tax rates and lower corporate tax rates, which would discourage consumption and encourage investment. In fact, many economists have argued that the tax structure should be altered so as to stimulate investment. In this section, we consider various tax policies that might be used for this purpose. Before doing so, however, we shall consider several proposals which would eliminate some of the distortions caused by inflation.

Inflation and Investment

As discussed in Chapter 13, firms are permitted to deduct depreciation allowances in calculating taxable income. These allowances, however, are based on original costs rather than replacement costs. When inflation occurs, original costs will be less than replacement costs, and depreciation allowances will be less than those based on replacement costs. Consequently, profits will be overstated, resulting in a greater tax liability for firms. This aspect of the tax system has the effect of discouraging investment. It also has the effect of distorting the allocation of resources. Since original costs approximate more closely replacement costs in the short run, firms tend to concentrate on short-term projects.

Economists have proposed various changes in the tax system to eliminate the effects of inflation on investment. One solution is to index depreciation allowances.[22] With indexation, each year's depreciation allowance would be adjusted for the inflation which occurred during the year. As a consequence, the real value of the allowance would be preserved and the real after-tax profit rate would not be reduced because of the inflation.

Another solution is to permit firms to deduct the present value of economic depreciation from taxable income in the year in which the asset is purchased.[23] Like indexation, this method would prevent the erosion of the real value of depreciation allowances over time.

A third solution is to permit accelerated depreciation. This could take several forms. For example, firms might be permitted to write off plant and equipment over shorter time spans. If this were done, original costs would more closely approximate replacement costs, and the tendency for inflation to reduce the real after-tax profit rate would be reduced. Although accelerated depreciation has some merit as a means to stimulate investment, it is not a very satisfactory way to inflation-proof the tax system. The first two solutions overcome the effects of inflation regardless of the prevailing inflation rate. For any specific depreciation scheme, this is not the case. Consider a scheme that permits firms to write off investment over a shorter time span. Corresponding to this scheme is some inflation rate such that the effects of inflation on depreciation are just offset by the effects of the more rapid writeoff. At higher inflation rates, the acceleration will not be sufficient to offset the effects of inflation whereas at lower rates, the opposite is true.

Stimulating Investment

Policy makers can institute various tax policies to stimulate investment. Three such policies are to reduce corporate tax rates, provide investment tax credits, and allow firms to accelerate depreciation. The maximum corporate tax rate is 34 percent. If this rate were reduced, real after-tax profits would increase and firms would have a greater incentive to invest in new plant and equipment.

Investment tax credits allow a firm to deduct a proportion of the purchase price of equipment from its federal tax liability. For example, if a firm purchases

$10,000 worth of equipment and the investment tax credit is 10 percent, the firm's tax liability is reduced by $1,000. Thus, for a profitable firm, an investment tax credit effectively reduces the purchase price of equipment. As a consequence, investment tax credits stimulate investment.

For the most part, accelerated depreciation involves changing the depreciation formulas or the time span over which plant and equipment may be written off. Unlike investment tax credits, which reduce a firm's tax liability, accelerated depreciation simply shifts tax deductions from the later years of an asset's life to earlier years. Consequently, the firm's total liability is not reduced; the firm benefits, however, because the deductions can be taken earlier, which increases the present value of the deductions. By writing off investment in plant and equipment more quickly, the present value of the profits associated with the investment increases. Thus, firms have an incentive to invest more.

Evidence exists that all three policies can stimulate investment.[24] If the policies are evaluated in terms of loss in tax revenue, however, investment tax credits and accelerated depreciation are much more effective than reductions in corporate tax rates. The main reason why a tax cut is more costly to the Treasury is that it reduces the tax revenues on income accruing to capital already in place, whereas investment tax credits and accelerated depreciation need not have an effect on tax revenue from previously installed capital. Since investment tax credits and accelerated depreciation can be limited to new investment and since it is the profitability of new investment that is important for incentive purposes, investment tax credits and accelerated depreciation are preferred to reductions in corporate tax rates.

One disadvantage with investment tax credits and accelerated depreciation is that neither is neutral with respect to types of investment. Investment tax credits tend to favor short-lived assets, while accelerated depreciation favors long-lived assets. With short-lived assets, the assets may be replaced more often so as to permit more frequent use of the investment tax credit. With accelerated depreciation, investment is written off more quickly so that much of the firm's tax liability is deferred to later years. Since it is advantageous for a firm to defer its tax liability as long as possible, accelerated depreciation is more advantageous for long-lived assets.

In conclusion, if the policies are judged in terms of lost tax revenue, the investment tax credit and accelerated depreciation approaches are more efficient than corporate tax reductions. With regard to the allocation of resources, however, neither is neutral.

BUDGET DEFICITS AND THE PUBLIC DEBT

In recent years, much concern has been expressed regarding deficits in the federal budget and the large and growing public debt. In this section, we examine the basis for this concern.

Budget Deficits

Deficits in the federal budget have been a fact of life for years. Starting in 1966, the national income accounts budget has shown a deficit in every year except one, 1969. In recent years, the deficits have become larger and larger. Many people believe that these deficits should be reduced or eliminated because they have an adverse impact on the economy. Specifically, they believe that deficits (1) cause inflation, (2) reduce economic growth because they result in higher interest rates, which discourage investment, and (3) reduce exports and increase imports because of the impact of higher interest rates on the value of the dollar. Since the latter was discussed in Chapter 16, we shall concentrate on the first two arguments in this chapter.

It is generally agreed that the method of financing is important in determining the impact of deficits on the economy. As discussed at the end of Chapter 7, the federal government may finance a deficit by issuing government debt (selling Treasury securities to the private sector) or by issuing high-powered money (selling Treasury securities to the Federal Reserve). Since agreement exists with regard to the effects of the latter, we shall begin with it.

Suppose the federal government is running a deficit and sells Treasury securities. As it sells the securities, bond prices fall and interest rates rise. If the Federal Reserve buys Treasury securities to keep interest rates from rising, high-powered money (the monetary base) increases and, as a consequence, the money supply increases. (For a discussion, see Chapter 7.) So long as the deficit exists and the Federal Reserve continues to buy Treasury securities, the money supply will increase. With the increase in the money supply, aggregate demand increases. If the economy is at less than full employment, the price level, output, and employment increase. Once full employment is reached, however, only the price level will increase. Thus, a budget deficit financed by a more rapid increase in the money supply has an expansionary effect on the economy. While this effect may be desirable when the economy is in a recession, it is undesirable at full employment.

A budget deficit financed by a more rapid increase in the money supply also has an impact on interest rates. At less then full employment, the more rapid increase in the money supply may reduce interest rates temporarily. But as full employment is reached and the inflation rate rises, nominal interest rates increase.

Now suppose the federal government is running a deficit, but the Federal Reserve does not accommodate the Treasury by buying Treasury securities. Assuming that government debt is part of the nation's wealth and that both consumption and the demand for money are positively related to wealth, we can analyze the impact of the increase in government debt.[25] As the Treasury issues government debt, wealth increases and, as a result, both consumption and the demand for money increase (see Figure A3-2 in Appendix 3). Both changes cause the interest rate to increase, thereby decreasing investment. The net effect, however, is expansionary. Consequently, output and employment increase until full employment is achieved. The full employment level of output, however, increases less rapidly because the decrease in investment reduces the rate of capital accumulation. As a consequence, aggregate supply will be growing less rapidly, causing more inflation, even though the deficit has not been financed by the creation of high-powered money.

In the last case, it was assumed that government debt is part of the nation's wealth. This assumption has been criticized by a number of economists, including Robert J. Barro.[26] Basically, the argument is that an increase in government debt means that the federal government is obligated to pay interest on this debt and, ultimately, to pay off the debt. These payments represent an additional tax liability. The present value of these payments equals the increase in government debt. As a consequence, an increase in government debt does not constitute an increase in wealth because it implies an equal and offsetting increase in tax liabilities. If this argument is correct, a budget deficit will have, according to this model, no effect on the economy. Government debt would increase, but since it is not part of the nation's wealth, neither consumption nor the demand for money would increase.

Various economists have attempted to test the hypothesis that taxpayers regard an increase in government debt as generating an equal and offsetting increase in tax liabilities.[27] The evidence is conflicting, however, so that it is not possible to resolve the issue at this time.

To summarize, if a budget deficit is financed by issuing high-powered money, the deficit is expansionary if unemployment exists and inflationary if full employment prevails. If the deficit is financed by issuing government debt, the deficit is also expansionary (assuming that taxpayers do not regard the increase in debt as equivalent to a tax increase), but the main effect is to raise interest rates, which discourages investment. As a consequence, the rate of capital accumulation is reduced, which has an adverse impact on the nation's growth rate.

Many people believe that deficits are highly inflationary. They are correct provided that the economy is at or near full employment and the deficit is financed by increasing high-powered money. Some people argue that the Federal Reserve is very likely to buy Treasury securities when the Treasury is borrowing because, as the latter borrows, interest rates rise, and the Federal Reserve may be committed to stabilizing interest rates. While the Federal Reserve has supported the Treasury in the past, it has not always done so. In fact, the empirical evidence suggests that it is by no means inevitable that the Federal Reserve will respond by increasing the money supply more rapidly.[28]

Similarly, many people believe that deficits result in higher interest rates and much—but not all—of the empirical evidence supports this view. In a recent study, Gregory Hoelscher found evidence to support the linkage between deficits and long-term interest rates.[29] Hoelscher estimates that the average annual deficit over the 1980–84 period raised the ten-year Treasury bond rate by (about) 1 to 2 percentage points. (His estimates vary depending upon which measure of the deficit is used).

For the most part, the foregoing analysis suggests that deficits are undesirable. Some argue that policies designed to reduce or eliminate the deficit may, under some circumstances, be even more undesirable. They claim that reducing government spending and/or increasing taxes to reduce or eliminate a deficit may cause a recession. Their analysis, however, assumes that monetary policy will be unaltered despite the change in fiscal policy and this is not necessarily the case. As discussed in Chapter 9, the monetary and fiscal authorities may alter the policy mix so as to maintain the desired level of aggregate demand.

The Public Debt

Even if the current budget deficit were eliminated, a large public debt would remain. As of December 1, 1985, the gross federal government debt was almost 2 trillion dollars, $1,937.4 billion to be exact. The debt increased significantly during World War II and also during the Korean and Vietnam wars, but it is no longer true that most of the debt is due to war finance.

The public debt is composed of various instruments: U.S. Treasury bills, notes, and bonds, U.S. government savings bonds, and the like. Most of the debt is marketable; some of it (government savings bonds) is not. On December 31, 1985, approximately 27 percent of the debt was held by federal agencies and trust funds and by Federal Reserve Banks. Private investors held the other 73 percent. Foreign investors, classified as private investors, held approximately 15 percent of the privately held debt.

Given the size of the debt and its rate of increase, concern is often registered when large government deficits are projected. Concern is warranted, but not for some of the reasons commonly cited. Often, people draw an analogy between an individual and the federal government. If an individual goes into debt too deeply, he may become bankrupt. Hence, it is sometimes feared that the federal government faces bankruptcy. Since the federal government has the power to tax and print money, there is little to fear on this basis. Similarly, it is argued that public debt, like private debt, must ultimately be repaid. This is true in the sense that part of the debt falls due each year. The Treasury, however, typically borrows to pay the holders of the obligations as they mature. Thus, the public debt need not be repaid in the sense of being ultimately reduced to zero.

It is claimed that the public debt imposes a burden upon the present and future generations. In this regard, it must be recognized that the public debt is largely owed to ourselves. As just shown, most of the debt is held internally—by Federal agencies and trust funds, Federal Reserve Banks, and private investors in this country. This portion of the debt represents a liability to taxpayers and an asset to public debt holders in the United States. With interest payments on the debt, income is redistributed from taxpayers to holders of the public debt. Although the redistribution may not be equitable, it does not directly reduce the nation's productive capacity, output, or the goods and services available to our society.

As matters now stand, interest on the public debt is the third largest single item in the federal budget after defense and social security. If high tax rates are necessary to pay this interest, those high rates may dampen incentives to work, save, invest, and innovate. If they do, the nation's productive capacity and output are reduced. Reduction in output represents a burden to the present generation. Moreover, with the reduction in productive capacity, output will be less in the future, representing a burden to future generations.

As mentioned earlier, part of the public debt is held by foreigners. We do not, therefore, owe the entire debt to ourselves. In real terms, interest payments and repayments of principal involve the transfer of real output to other nations. The reduction in output available to our society also represents a burden to present and future generations.

In conclusion, grounds do exist for concern about the size of the public debt.[30] Even so, few economists believe that the federal government should run surpluses so as to reduce the debt. Instead, they favor reducing or eliminating the deficit so that the debt grows slowly, if at all. With economic growth, debt as a percentage of GNP would decline. Similarly, with the growth of private debt, public debt as a percentage of total debt would decrease. Both changes imply that the public debt would become less of a problem over time.

CONCLUDING REMARKS

In this chapter, we have considered fiscal policy and its impact on the economy. We found, contrary to monetarist claims, that fiscal policy is effective at least in the short run. We reached no conclusion in regard to the question as to whether fiscal policy is stabilizing. This question is dealt with more thoroughly in Chapter 19.

NOTes

1. For discussions, see Andrew S. Carron, "Fiscal Activities Outside the Budget," in *Setting National Priorities: The 1982 Budget*, ed. Joseph A. Pechman (Washington, D.C.: The Brookings Institution, 1981), pp. 261–69; Herman B. Leonard and Elisabeth H. Rhyne, "Federal Credit and the 'Shadow Budget'," *Public Interest*, no. 65 (Fall 1981), 40–58; and Stephen H. Pollock, "Off-budget Federal Outlays," Federal Reserve Bank of Kansas City, *Economic Review* (March 1981), 3–16.

2. George Cross, *The Congressional Budget and Impoundment Control Act of 1974: A General Explanation*, U.S. House of Representatives Committee on the Budget (Washington, D.C.: Government Printing Office, 1975), p. 4.

3. Allen Schick, *Congress and Money: Budgeting, Spending, and Taxing* (Washington, D.C.: Urban Institute, 1980). For discussions of the budgetary process and possible reforms, see Lisa E. Rockoff, "The Federal Budget Process: How It Works," Federal Reserve Bank of Atlanta, *Economic Review*, 70 (May 1985), 34–40; Alice M. Rivlin, "Reform of the Budget Process," *American Economic Review*, 74 (May 1984), 133–37; and *Strengthening the Federal Budget Process: A Requirement for Effective Fiscal Control* (New York: Committee for Economic Development, 1983).

4. The concept has a long history. For references, see Arthur M. Okun and Nancy H. Teeters, "The Full Employment Surplus Revisited," *Brookings Papers on Economic Activity*, no. 1 (1970), 77–110; and Alan S. Blinder and Robert M. Solow, "Analytical Foundations of Fiscal Policy," in Alan S. Blinder and others, *The Economics of Public Finance* (Washington, D.C.: The Brookings Institution, 1974), pp. 11–36.

5. E. Cary Brown, "Fiscal Policy in the 'Thirties: A Reappraisal," *American Economic Review*, 46 (December 1956), 857–79.

6. For a more thorough discussion, see Blinder and Solow, "Analytical Foundations."

7. For a measure of fiscal restraint which is not subject to these criticisms, see Blinder and Solow, ibid., pp. 21–27. For other criticisms and another proposed measure, see Robert Eisner and Paul J. Pieper, "A New View of the Federal Debt and Budget Deficits," *American Economic Review*, 74 (March 1984), 11–29.

8. Moreover, calculating the high employment surplus presents a number of problems. See George L. Perry, "Potential Output and Productivity," *Brookings Papers on Economic Activity*, no. 1 (1977), 11–47; Joseph A. Pechman, "The Full-Employment Budget," in Pechman, *Setting National Priorities*, pp. 419–24; and Keith M. Carlson, "Estimates of the High-Employment Budget and Changes in Potential Output," Federal Reserve Bank of St. Louis, *Review*, 59 (August 1977), 16–22.

9. The following discussion of the effectiveness of fiscal policy ignores the government's budget constraint. (For a discussion of the implications of the budget constraint, see Appendix 3.) The changes in government purchases and taxes are to be regarded as permanent. (For a discussion of temporary changes, see Chapter 5.)

10. Leonall C. Andersen and Jerry L. Jordan, "Monetary and Fiscal Actions: A Test of Their Relative Importance in Economic Stabilization," Federal Reserve Bank of St. Louis, *Review*, 50 (November 1968), 11–24.

11. Andersen and Jordan, ibid., p. 22. They also argued that the response of economic activity to monetary actions is faster and more predictable.

12. Frank de Leeuw and John Kalchbrenner, "Monetary and Fiscal Actions: A Test of Their Relative Importance in Economic Stabilization—Comment," Federal Reserve Bank of St. Louis, *Review*, 51 (April 1969), 6–11.

13. For the fiscal policy variable, de Leeuw and Kalchbrenner used the high employment surplus adjusted for price changes. For the monetary policy variable, they used two measures; the monetary base minus borrowed reserves (reserves obtained by member banks borrowing from Federal Reserve Banks) and the monetary base minus the sum of borrowed reserves and currency.

14. Leonall C. Andersen and Jerry L. Jordan, "Monetary and Fiscal Actions: A Test of Their Relative Importance in Economic Stabilization—Reply," Federal Reserve Bank of St. Louis, *Review*, 51 (April 1969), 12–16. See also Leonall C. Andersen, "Additional Empirical Evidence on the Reverse-Causation Argument," Federal Reserve Bank of St. Louis, *Review*, 51 (August 1969), 19–23.

15. Many found the response by Andersen and Jordan unsatisfactory and various attempts were made to replicate the Andersen–Jordan study using alternative measures of fiscal and monetary policy. These studies typically show that both fiscal and monetary policies are effective. See, for example, E. Gerald Corrigan, "The Measurement and Importance of Fiscal Policy Changes," Federal Reserve Bank of New York, *Monthly Review*, 52 (June 1970), 133–45.

16. The statistical properties of the Andersen–Jordan model have been examined in various studies. See, for example, Richard G. Davis, "How Much does Money Matter? A Look at Some Recent Evidence," Federal Reserve Bank of New York, *Monthly Review*, 51 (June 1969), 119–31. The following argument is based on Blinder, *Fiscal Policy*, p. 17.

See also Blinder and Solow, "Analytical Foundations," pp. 67–71. For other arguments, see Franco Modigliani, "The Monetarist Controversy or, Should We Forsake Stabilization Policies?" *American Economic Review*, 67 (March 1977), 9–11.

17. Gary Fromm and Lawrence R. Klein, "A Comparison of Eleven Econometric Models of the United States," *American Economic Review*, 63 (May 1973), 385–93.

18. In some of the models, the multipliers become negative in the long run. For example, in the BEA model, the multipliers become negative after six years. Thus, it might be argued that in the long run an increase in real government nondefense expenditures has no effect or even a negative effect on real gross national product. The money multipliers derived from various econometric models display a similar pattern. Nurun N. Choudhry, "Integration of Fiscal and Monetary Sectors in Econometric Models: A Survey of Theoretical Issues and Empirical Findings," International Monetary Fund, *Staff Papers*, 23 (July 1976), 395–440.

19. Albert Ando and E. Cary Brown, "Lags in Fiscal Policy," in Commission on Money and Credit, *Stabilization Policies* (Englewood Cliffs, N.J.: Prentice-Hall, Inc., 1963), pp. 8–9.

20. Ibid., pp. 11–12. For a supporting view in regard to public works, see Ronald L. Teigen, "The Effectiveness of Public Works as a Stabilization Device," in *Readings in Money, National Income, and Stabilization Policy*, 2nd ed., eds. Warren L. Smith and Ronald L. Teigen (Homewood, Ill.: Richard D. Irwin, Inc., 1970), pp. 333–39.

21. John Kenneth Galbraith is an eloquent spokesman for this position. See, for example, his *The Affluent Society* (Boston: Houghton Mifflin Company, 1958). The opposing viewpoint is ably espoused by Milton Friedman. See, for example, his *Capitalism and Freedom* (Chicago: University of Chicago Press, 1962).

22. For a discussion, see Martin Feldstein, "Adjusting Depreciation in an Inflationary Economy: Indexing versus Acceleration," *National Tax Journal*, 34 (March 1981), 29–43.

23. Allan J. Auerbach and Dale W. Jorgenson, "Inflation-Proof Depreciation of Assets," *Harvard Business Review,* 58 (September–October 1980), 113–18.

24. For evidence, see the studies cited in the two previous notes as well as various studies in *Public Policy and Capital Formation* (Washington, D.C.: Board of Governors of the Federal Reserve System, 1981); and George M. von Furstenberg, ed., *The Government and Capital Formation* (Cambridge, Mass.: Ballinger Publishing Co., 1980). For discussions of the 1981 and 1982 tax acts and their impact, see Allen Sinai, Andrew Lin, and Russell Robins, "Taxes, Saving, and Investment: Some Empirical Evidence," *National Tax Journal*, 36 (September 1983), 321–45; and Mack Ott, "Depreciation, Inflation and Investment Incentives: The Effects of the Tax Acts of 1981 and 1982," Federal Reserve Bank of St. Louis, *Review*, 66 (November 1984), 17–30.

25. For a formal analysis, see Appendix 3.

26. Robert J. Barro, "Are Government Bonds Net Wealth?" *Journal of Political Economy,* 82 (November—December 1974), 1095–1117.

27. For references, see Chapter 5, notes 14 and 15.

28. As examples, see William A. Niskanen, "Deficits, Government Spending, and Inflation," *Journal of Monetary Economics*, 4 (August 1978), 591–602; Michael J. Hamburger and Burton Zwick, "Deficits, Money, and Inflation," *Journal of Monetary Economics,* 7 (1981), 141–50; Scott E. Hein, "Deficits and Inflation," Federal Reserve Bank of St. Louis, *Review*, 63 (March 1981), 3–10; Daniel L. Thornton, "Monetizing the Debt," Federal Reserve Bank of St. Louis, *Review*, 66 (December 1984), 30–43; and Richard G. Sheehan, "The Federal Reserve Reaction Function: Does Debt Growth Influence Monetary Policy?" Federal Reserve Bank of St. Louis, *Review*, 67 (March 1985), 24–33.

29. Gregory Hoelscher, "New Evidence on Deficits and Interest Rates," *Journal of*

Money, Credit, and Banking, 18 (February 1986), 1–17. Hoelscher's study contains discussions of, and references to, earlier studies.

30. There are other arguments concerning the public debt. For example, James M. Buchanan has argued that the public debt is a burden to future generations. In simplest terms, he believes that an increase in public debt is not a burden to the current generation since its members have voluntarily exchanged money for bonds. Future generations will not have a choice; they must pay higher taxes to support interest payments on the debt. James M. Buchanan, *Public Principles of Public Debt* (Homewood, Ill.: Richard D. Irwin, Inc., 1958).

REVIEW QUESTIONS

1. Compare and contrast the unified, national income accounts, and high employment budgets.

2. Explain:

   a. why surpluses (or deficits) in the national income accounts budget may be misleading as a measure of fiscal restraint and

   b. why surpluses (or deficits) in the high employment budget are a better measure of fiscal restraint.

   c. why the latter may be misleading as a measure of fiscal restraint.

3. Outline and critically evaluate the Andersen–Jordan study of the relative effectiveness of monetary and fiscal policy. Is their evidence consistent with that based on large-scale econometric models and other single-equation models?

4. Although fiscal policy may be effective, it may not be stabilizing. Explain.

5. With regard to fiscal policy, explain why the implementation lag may be long. What sorts of changes might be made to reduce the implementation lag?

6. Discuss the role of forecasting with regard to policymaking.

7. Outline the advantages and disadvantages of changes in personal income tax rates as a stabilization device.

8. Inflation is said to discourage investment. Explain why this is the case. How might the tax system be changed so as to alleviate the problem?

9. How might the tax system be modified so as to encourage investment? Explain the pros and cons of each approach.

10. A budget deficit is said to have different effects depending on whether the deficit is financed by issuing government debt or by issuing high-powered money. Explain.

11. Suppose an increase in government purchases is financed by issuing government debt. If the increase in debt is regarded as equivalent to a tax increase, what are the implications for fiscal policy?

12. Some argue that the government should not engage in deficit spending. Others argue that it is sometimes advantageous to do so. Outline the arguments for and against deficit spending.

SUGGESTED READING _____

ANDERSEN, LEONALL C., and JERRY L. JORDAN, "Monetary and Fiscal Actions: A Test of Their Relative Importance in Economic Stabilization," Federal Reserve Bank of St. Louis, *Review,* 50 (November 1968), 11–24.

BLINDER, ALAN S., *Fiscal Policy in Theory and Practice.* Morristown, N.J.: General Learning Press, 1973.

———, and others, *The Economics of Public Finance.* Washington, D.C.: The Brookings Institution, 1974.

BUCHANAN, JAMES M., and RICHARD E. WAGNER, *Democracy in Deficit: The Political Legacy of Lord Keynes.* New York: Academic Press, Inc., 1977.

COURANT, PAUL N., and EDWARD M. GRAMLICH, *Federal Budget Deficits: America's Great Consumption Binge.* Englewood Cliffs, N.J.: Prentice-Hall, Inc., 1986.

Economic Report of the President. Washington, D.C.: Government Printing Office, annually.

EISNER, ROBERT, and PAUL J. PIEPER, "A New View of the Federal Debt and Budget Deficits," *American Economic Review*, 74 (March 1984), 11–29.

Fighting Federal Deficits: The Time for Hard Choices. New York: Committee for Economic Development, 1984.

LEE, DWIGHT R. (ed.) *Taxation and the Deficit Economy: Fiscal Policy and Capital Formation in the United States.* San Francisco: Pacific Institute for Public Policy Research, 1986.

MILLS, GREGORY B., and JOHN L. PALMER (eds.), *Federal Budget Policy in the 1980s.* Baltimore: The Urban Institute Press, 1984.

SCHICK, ALLEN, *Congress and Money: Budgeting, Spending, and Taxing.* Washington, D.C.: The Urban Institute, 1980.

VON FURSTENBERG, GEORGE M. (ed.), *The Government and Capital Formation.* Cambridge, Mass.: Ballinger Publishing Co., 1980.

WAGNER, RICHARD E., and ROBERT D. TOLLISON, *Balanced Budgets, Fiscal Responsibility, and the Constitution.* San Francisco: Cato Institute, 1980.

19

MONETARY POLICY

This chapter deals with monetary policy, its impact upon the economy, and its potential as a stabilization tool. At one time, many economists believed monetary policy to be ineffective. Although they still disagree about the potency of monetary policy, few believe it to be ineffective. In this chapter, we examine the current conduct of monetary policy. We consider evidence relating to the effectiveness of monetary policy and the time lags associated with it. We discuss the arguments for and against the use of discretionary monetary policy and the arguments for and against an independent Federal Reserve.

THE CONDUCT OF MONETARY POLICY[1]

Monetary policy is determined mainly by the Federal Open Market Committee (FOMC). The FOMC, a part of the Federal Reserve System, consists of twelve members: the seven Federal Reserve Board members and the presidents of five of the twelve Federal Reserve Banks.[2] The president of the Federal Reserve Bank

400

of New York is always a member of the FOMC; the other presidents alternate as committee members. All twelve presidents attend the meetings in Washington and take part in the discussion, but only committee members can vote.

Although the FOMC determines open market policy, the actual purchase or sale of government securities is handled by the Federal Reserve Bank of New York. After deciding upon a course of action, the FOMC issues a directive to the manager of the Federal Reserve System's Open Market Account, a vice-president of the Federal Reserve Bank of New York. As will be discussed, the directive does not order the timing or amounts of open market purchases or sales. The manager must make these specific decisions within the general framework of the directive.

At its meetings, the committee members (and others) discuss alternative monetary policies. After the discussion, the committee adopts the monetary position which the majority of the members believe to be most appropriate. Usually, this involves a specification of the desired rates of growth of the money supply and other monetary aggregates for the long run (a year or more). Because the growth rate of the money supply is hard to control, the targeted rate of increase in the money supply is specified as a range rather than a single number. For example, at the February 11–12, 1986, FOMC meeting, the committee established the monetary growth ranges for 1986.[3] For M1, the range was 3 percent to 8 percent. The ranges for the monetary aggregates are included in a directive to the manager of the Open Market Account.

To implement the desired increase in the money supply, the FOMC also specifies a particular range for the Federal Funds rate. The *Federal Funds rate* is the interest rate at which member bank deposits at Federal Reserve Banks are borrowed from, or loaned to, other member banks.[4] The Federal Reserve does not have complete control of the Federal Funds rate. By modifying the reserve position of the banking system, however, it can alter the Federal Funds rate.

After the appropriate range for the Federal Funds rate is determined by the FOMC, it is included in the directive to the manager of the Open Market Account along with the ranges for the monetary aggregates. Prior to October 6, 1979, the range for the Federal Funds rate was very important because the manager of the Open Market Account usually acted to hold the Federal Funds rate within the specified range, even if it meant that the growth rates of the monetary aggregates fell outside their specified ranges. Many economists criticized this emphasis on the Federal Funds rate (and interest rates in general).[5]

On October 6, 1979, the Federal Reserve announced that in the future greater emphasis would be placed on the use of reserve aggregates in the day-to-day conduct of monetary policy and less emphasis would be placed on limiting short-term fluctuations in the Federal Funds rate. Since that time, the FOMC has continued to specify a range for the Federal Funds rate, but it is much wider than those specified prior to October 6, 1979.

The new operating procedure remained in effect through September 1982. At its October 1982 meeting, the FOMC altered the procedure so as to place less emphasis on monetary aggregates, including the temporary suspension of the short-run objectives for M1. In many respects, the change marked a return to the pre-October 1979 operating procedure.

Financial Innovations and Monetary Policy[6]

Although financial innovations have always occurred, the rate at which they occur increased significantly in the United States during the 1970s. As a result, numerous analysts claim that these innovations have altered the relationship between the money supply (M1) and nominal income and made it more difficult for the Federal Reserve to control the money supply. We now wish to examine these claims.

Most economists attribute the burst of innovative activity in the 1970s to (1) the high inflation and interest rates which prevailed during the period and (2) the technological advances in computers and communications. With rising inflation and interest rates, firms and households were under strong pressure to economize on money holdings and they responded by becoming much more sophisticated with regard to cash management. With the technological advances in computers and communications, the real cost of processing and transmitting data decreased dramatically. This, in turn, made it profitable for financial institutions to offer new services. At the same time, it made it profitable for firms and households to use these services and to implement new cash management techniques.

In addition to the development and spread of NOW, Super NOW, and ATS accounts (see Chapter 7), other innovations took place in the 1970s and 1980s. To illustrate, banks and various thrift institutions introduced *money market deposit accounts* (MMDAs) in December 1982. They were introduced, in part, to compete with money market mutual funds. The accounts are not subject to an interest rate ceiling, but do require a $1,000 minimum balance. MMDAs are similar to Super NOW accounts in both respects. Unlike Super NOW accounts, however, limits exist as to the number of third-party transactions that can be made with a money market deposit account. Because of this limit, MMDAs are considered savings deposits, and are not subject to reserve requirements.

For monetary policy to be successful, a stable and predictable relationship must exist between the money supply and nominal income (see Chapters 8 and 11). Various analysts have claimed that recent innovative activity and deregulation have altered this relationship and made it less predictable. As discussed in Chapter 8, the activity may have caused the demand for money to decrease in the mid-1970s and to increase in 1982–83.

In addition, the innovative activity has made it more difficult to define the money supply. In the past, the definition of the money supply (M1) was based on the view that it is the medium through which economic transactions are made. As a result, currency and demand deposits are defined as money, but time deposits are not. With the proliferation of accounts, the line between transactions and other accounts has become blurred. NOW and Super NOW deposits are counted as part of the money supply; however, part of these deposits may be held for nontransactions purposes. Conversely, money market mutual funds and MMDAs are not counted as part of the money supply; yet, part of these deposits may be held for transactions purposes.

Finally, some analysts claim that efforts of the Federal Reserve to reduce the growth rate of the money supply in order to restrain the economy will prove unsuccessful because it leads to the development of money substitutes. Thus, even if the growth rate of the money supply is reduced, it will have little impact on the economy. In such cases, it will do little good to revise the definition of the money supply.

In view of the (alleged) problems created by financial innovations, a variety of solutions have been offered. One is to pay less attention to M1 and more attention to broader monetary aggregates such as M2 and M3. Unfortunately, the relationship between these aggregates and nominal income does not appear to be as stable and predictable as the relationship between M1 and money income.

Another suggestion is to weight the various components of the money supply prior to summing them. Proponents of this approach argue that the various assets have different degrees of "moneyness." In this context, *moneyness* refers to the monetary services provided by the asset. By weighting the various assets, the new aggregate would reflect the different degrees of moneyness. Consequently, the new monetary aggregate would be expected to exhibit a closer and more predictable relationship with nominal income. Moreover, it might be less sensitive to financial innovation. Several weighted aggregates have been constructed. Unfortunately, none has proved to be unambiguously superior to M1.[7] Research in this area continues and may prove fruitful in the future.

Still another suggestion involves focusing on interest rates (or other variables) rather than M1 or other monetary aggregates. As discussed earlier, focusing on interest rates has a number of disadvantages. Finally, some analysts believe that returning to the gold standard is the only feasible solution. As discussed in Chapter 12, the arguments against such a move are overwhelming.

In conclusion, financial innovations have the potential for causing serious problems for the monetary authorities and the authorities must be alert for such changes since they are not easy to recognize at the outset. Fortunately, the relationship between M1 and nominal income is fairly robust. Consequently, it appears that the money authorities can concentrate on M1 in conducting monetary policy.

THE EFFECTIVENESS OF MONETARY POLICY

An impressive amount of evidence has been accumulated which supports the view that a change in the money supply (monetary policy) has a significant impact upon the economy. The evidence is based on an examination of the historical record, as well as on single-equation and large-scale econometric models. We begin by looking at the historical record.

Milton Friedman has argued that the money supply and its rate of growth have a significant impact on nominal income and its rate of growth. Often in conjunction with Anna J. Schwartz, he has amassed a wide range of statistical and other evidence to support this argument.[8] To illustrate, Friedman and Schwartz believe a causal relationship exists between the money supply and economic activity over the business cycle. They note that the money supply increased steadily over the period 1867–1960 with only a few exceptions.[9] The money supply did fall appreciably during six periods, with decreases ranging from 2.4 percent to 35.2 percent. These periods corresponded to economic contractions (depressions) which were more severe than any of the other contractions experienced by the United States during the period.

In other contractions, the money supply increased. If the trend effect is eliminated, however, there appears to be a relationship between the cyclical behavior of the money supply and the business cycle. Peaks in the growth rate of the money supply precede peaks in the business cycle; similarly, troughs in the growth rate of the money supply precede business cycle troughs. Based on the National Bureau of Economic Research (NBER) dating procedure, the average lead for all business cycles is 18 months for peaks and 12 months for troughs. To be sure, one finds considerable variability in lead time between cycles. Friedman and Schwartz concluded that, although there is a fairly strong relationship between the money supply and business activity over the business cycle, the relationship is not perfect. The imprecision may result from inadequacies in the indexes of economic activity or statistical errors in the measurement of the money supply. They also concede that the imprecision may be due to the existence of only a weak relationship between the money supply and business activity.[10]

Although the historical evidence suggests a fairly close relationship between the cyclical behavior of the money supply and the cyclical behavior of the economy, that evidence does not necessarily demonstrate causality. Changes in the growth rate of the money supply may cause the cyclical behavior of the economy. On the other hand, the behavior of the money supply might be largely the result of the cyclical behavior of the economy. To determine the direction of the causal relationship, Friedman and Schwartz examined the historical record to ascertain the circumstances underlying the changes in the money supply. They concluded that, in general, the changes in the money supply were not attributable to changes in business activity. Instead, these changes were the result of specific historical circumstances, such as the discovery of gold, which were independent of the level of economic activity. Therefore, Friedman and Schwartz believe that the causal relationship runs from the money supply to business activity.

Examination of the historical record made Friedman and Schwartz conclude that a substantial change in the growth rate of the money supply causes a substantial change in the growth rate of money income both secularly and over the business cycle. They aver that a change in the long-run rate of growth of the money supply will manifest itself mainly in a different rate of change in prices. In contrast, a change in the short-run rate of growth of the money supply will alter the growth rates of both output and prices.

In spite of the Friedman and Schwartz evidence, one can say that it converted relatively few nonbelievers to the Friedman–Schwartz position.[11] Nonbelievers argue that the changes in the money supply may have been caused by changes in the level of economic activity; thus, the causal relationship runs from the level of economic activity to the money supply.[12] In the context of the Friedman-Schwartz study, the causality issue can be resolved only by detailed study of the historical evidence. This is unnecessary for our purposes, since other evidence supports the contention that changes in the money supply have a significant impact on the level of economic activity.

The additional evidence on money's influence is based on both single-equation and large-scale econometric models. As discussed in Chapter 18, Andersen and Jordan's results indicate a strong relationship between the nominal money supply and/or the monetary base and nominal GNP.[13] For reasons discussed in the previous chapter, those results are suspect. Nevertheless, economists have replicated the Andersen-Jordan study using alternative assumptions and have obtained similar results on the effectiveness of monetary policy. Thus, evidence from the single-equation models supports the view that monetary policy has a significant impact on the economy.

The evidence from large-scale econometric models reported by Gary Fromm and Lawrence R. Klein also supports the view that monetary policy is effective.[14] Unlike the results for fiscal policy, however, the effects of a sustained increase in the monetary variable vary widely among the models. In the Bureau of Economic Analysis (BEA) and the Anticipations Version of the Wharton models, the effect of an increase in the monetary variable is relatively slight. For example, the BEA model shows no measurable increase in real GNP in the first two quarters after a $1 billion increase in unborrowed reserves (reserves less member bank borrowing from Federal Reserve Banks). After four quarters, the increase in real GNP is only $0.2 billion; the maximum increase is $0.7 billion, occurring after three years.[15] The pattern for the Anticipations model is similar, except that the indicated increase in real GNP is greater during each time period. The results indicate that a $1 billion increase in unborrowed reserves causes a $0.4 billion increase in real GNP during the first quarter. Real GNP continues to increase until, after four quarters, the total increase is $0.8 billion. The maximum increase is $1.3 billion, occurring after two years. The remaining models show much larger increases in real GNP. To illustrate, in the Data Resources Incorporated (DRI) and the Wharton Mark III models, real GNP increases by over $4 billion at the end of four quarters in response to an increase of $1 billion in unborrowed reserves. The maximum increases for the models are $8.3 billion (after two years) and $8.6 billion (after three years), respectively, for the DRI and Mark III models.[16]

On the whole, evidence from the various econometric models suggests that monetary policy is effective. Since this evidence is consistent with the evidence provided by Friedman and by the various single-equation models, the weight of the evidence suggests that monetary policy is effective.[17]

MONETARY POLICY AND TIME LAGS

Although monetary policy is effective, it may be destabilizing because of the time lags associated with it. As discussed in Chapter 18, the recognition lag, presumably the same for both monetary and fiscal policy, may last several quarters. The implementation lag for monetary policy is short, much shorter than for fiscal policy. Once the need for a policy change has been recognized, a new monetary policy can be implemented almost immediately. On the other hand, it has been argued that the response lag is relatively long, longer in fact than the corresponding lag for fiscal policy. For that reason, much attention has been focused on the response lag.

In their study, Friedman and Schwartz found that peaks (troughs) in the growth rate of the money supply precede peaks (troughs) in the business cycle by an average of 18 (12) months. There is, however, considerable variability, with ranges of 13 to 29 months at the peaks and 4 to 21 months at the troughs.[18] Based on these results, Friedman has argued that the lag associated with monetary policy is long and variable.[19]

Friedman's view has been criticized by J. M. Culbertson and by John Kareken and Robert M. Solow.[20] Culbertson raised three issues relating to the empirical evidence cited by Friedman. First, he noted that Friedman and Schwartz compared the peaks (troughs) of the *growth rate* of the money supply with peaks (troughs) in the *absolute levels* of business activity. He believes that this procedure is invalid. Second, Culbertson disagreed with Friedman's definition of the lag. Culbertson argued that the appropriate definition is the period between the time of the change in monetary policy and the time at which the behavior of the economy is altered. If a different definition is used, Friedman's results are likely to be modified. Third, Culbertson raised the question of reverse causation. He argued that although increases in the money supply cause increases in economic activity, an increase in economic activity also causes an increase in the money supply. Because of the interaction between the money supply and economic activity, Culbertson contended that it was very difficult to estimate the lags accurately. Although he cited no empirical evidence to support his view, Culbertson claimed that the predominant direct effects of monetary policy occur within three to six months; that suggests to him that monetary policy is not destabilizing provided that it is pursued rather early in the business expansion or contraction.[21]

John Kareken and Robert M. Solow have also criticized Friedman's conclusions. They raised some of the same objections as Culbertson and claimed that the lag is shorter and less variable than Friedman and Schwartz found. In particular, Kareken and Solow asserted that a change in monetary policy has some effect quickly; the effects build over time, so that a change in monetary policy has a significant impact upon the economy within six to nine months.[22]

Thomas Mayer has countered that the conclusions of Kareken and Solow do not follow from their results and, thus, are misleading.[23] According to Mayer, Kareken and Solow fail, in general, to present data which permit calculation of the total lag. On the response of inventories, they do present sufficient data, but this lag is much longer than Friedman's lag. On the response of producers' durable equipment, the data are insufficient, but even the data available suggest that the lag is longer than Friedman's lag. Mayer claimed that Kareken and Solow should have criticized Friedman for underestimating the lag, not overestimating it.[24] He concluded that if Kareken and Solow's estimates are correct, monetary policy is probably destabilizing rather than stabilizing.

Mayer claimed that all empirical studies of the response lag suggest that it is substantial. Particularly, he noted that, although considerable diversity exists among the results of the various studies, all show a lag of two quarters or more. If the response lag is added to the recognition and implementation lags, Mayer avers that the total lag may greatly reduce or even eliminate the effectiveness of monetary policy as a stabilization tool.[25]

Even if the lag is long, it may be possible to develop forecasting models so as to permit the use of discretionary monetary policy. But if the lag is also variable and unpredictably so, better forecasting models are not the solution to the lag problem. Mayer contends that the existing estimates of the variability of the lag are poor. More recent studies have tended to confirm the view that the time lags associated with monetary policy are variable.[26]

The evidence from the various single-equation and large-scale econometric models is mixed. In the Andersen-Jordan model, nominal GNP responds very quickly to a change in the nominal money supply. For example, a $1 billion increase in the money supply results in a $1.57 billion increase in nominal GNP in the first quarter. The increase in GNP in the second quarter ($1.94 billion) is even greater. The third- and fourth-quarter increases ($1.80 and $1.28 billion, respectively) are smaller. Few economists believe that monetary policy acts so quickly.[27] Certainly, the evidence from large-scale econometric models does not support this view. For example, in the DRI model, real GNP increases by $0.3 billion in the first quarter in response to increases in unborrowed reserves of $1.0 billion.[28] In the second quarter, the corresponding increase in real GNP is $0.5 billion. After four quarters, the increase is $4.1 billion. Real GNP continues to increase so that after eight quarters the total increase is $8.3 billion. The experience for the other models varies. The BEA model shows a greater immediate response. In general, real GNP is less responsive to changes in monetary policy than to changes in fiscal policy during the first few quarters.

In summary, the evidence from several sources suggests that the lag associated with monetary policy is long and possibly variable. Consequently, discretionary monetary policy may be destabilizing.

RULES VERSUS DISCRETION

At present, the Federal Reserve employs discretionary monetary policy. That is, it attempts to alter the growth rate of the money supply so as to stabilize the economy. If the economy is entering a recession, the Federal Reserve uses policies designed to increase the growth rate of the money supply. If the economy is threatened by inflation, the Federal Reserve uses policies designed to reduce the growth rate of the money supply. Over the years, some economists have suggested that the Federal Reserve abandon discretionary monetary policy and undertake to increase the money supply at a constant rate.[29]

Milton Friedman, for example, has suggested that the money supply be increased at a constant rate, from 3 to 5 percent. This rate, if sustained, is consistent with a reasonably constant price level in the long run since output increases over time.[30] Friedman believes that the major advantage of this approach is preventing monetary changes from exerting a destabilizing influence on the economy. In Friedman's opinion, episodes of major instability in the United States have, in almost every case, been caused or at least greatly intensified by monetary instability. To illustrate, the money supply decreased by approximately one-third from 1929 to 1933. Friedman believes that this decrease in the money supply resulted in much larger reductions in output and employment than would have occurred if the money supply had not shrunk. Similarly, the Federal Reserve doubled reserve requirements in 1936 and 1937. The increase in reserve requirements had an adverse effect on the money supply and, hence, the economy. Friedman concedes that the contraction of 1937–38 might have occurred without the increase in reserve requirements. He contends, however, that it would not have been as severe. Thus, in Friedman's view, the central problem is to prevent money and monetary policy from being a source of instability.

Increasing the money supply at a constant rate almost guarantees that the money supply will not be a destabilizing element. The policy does not eliminate cyclical movements in the economy caused by other factors. Consequently, one might argue that the Federal Reserve should use policies designed to alter the growth rate of the money supply in order to offset the influence of other factors on the economy. Friedman argues against this approach because the lag associated with monetary policy is long and variable. If the growth rate of the money supply is altered, it will have an impact on the economy, but only after a number of quarters. Moreover, the lag is variable, ranging from, say, 6 to 18 months. Because of the long and variable lag associated with monetary policy, it is very difficult to design discretionary policies which smooth the business cycle.

Furthermore, the long lag between a change in the growth rate of the money supply and its impact on the economy will impel the monetary authorities to overreact. Since there will be no immediate response to policy changes, the monetary authorities, Friedman believes, are likely to pursue policies which ultimately prove to be too strong. In a recession, they may increase the money supply by more than is necessary since, initially, nothing appears to happen when the money supply is increased. When the economy is threatened by inflation, the authorities may reduce the growth rate of the money supply by more than is necessary for the same reason. In this regard, Friedman cites a number of examples, including the "credit crunch" in 1966. The Federal Reserve, he argued, acted appropriately in early 1966 when it undertook a less expansionary policy. In doing so, however, the Federal Reserve pursued the policy too vigorously, resulting in the "credit crunch". To alleviate the crunch, the Federal Reserve pursued the correct policy in late 1966 when it followed a more expansionary policy. Once again, however, the Federal Reserve overreacted; the growth rate of the money supply exceeded the earlier growth rate, which was, in Friedman's view, excessive.[31]

Friedman concedes that in theory it is desirable to vary the growth rate of the money supply in order to offset other factors. In practice, however, we do not know when, or by how much, to alter the growth rate of the money supply. Consequently, changes in the growth rate of the money supply are destabilizing, rather than stabilizing. Friedman also concedes that some day it may become possible to carry out discretionary monetary policy to offset other changes in the economy. But given our present state of knowledge, that is not possible now.

To summarize, Friedman usually lists three advantages for the rules approach. First, it would prevent the money supply from becoming a source of instability. Second, by increasing the money supply at a steady rate, monetary policy can minimize the effects of disturbances arising from other sources. For example, suppose government spending is increasing rapidly. The monetary authorities may use policies designed to increase the money supply more rapidly in order to minimize the increase in interest rates. Yet increasing the money supply more rapidly makes a higher rate of inflation likely. If the monetary authorities are restrained by a rule, the money supply will increase less rapidly and a lower rate of inflation will result. To be sure, interest rates will be higher in the short run. With a lower rate of inflation, however, lower nominal interest rates should prevail in the long run.

Third, by increasing the money supply at a constant rate, the price level will, in the long run, be constant or approximately so. According to Friedman, our economy functions best when the price level behaves in a predictable manner. Since the growth rate of output depends, in the long run, upon such factors as the growth rate of the labor supply and the rate of capital accumulation, rapid growth can occur with either rising or falling price levels provided that the changes in the price level are moderate and reasonably predictable. On the other hand, erratic and unpredictable changes in the price level are, in Friedman's view, injurious to the growth process.

The suggestion for increasing the money supply at a constant rate has been widely criticized. One of the most penetrating critiques has been offered by Franco Modigliani. He argues that the fundamental practical message of Keynes's *General Theory* is that the economy needs to be stabilized, and, since discretionary policy is stabilizing, that discretionary policy should be used.[32] Modigliani argues that nonmonetarists have accepted this message. In contrast, Friedman and other monetarists contend that there is no serious need to stabilize the economy. Even if the need exists, discretionary policy would make matters worse since it is destabilizing.

In terms of the model of Chapter 10, stabilization policy is not necessary provided that money wages and prices are flexible. If aggregate demand falls, money wages and prices fall. With a decrease in prices, the real money supply increases, thereby reducing interest rates. The resulting increases in investment and aggregate demand eventually restore the full employment levels of output and employment. The length of time necessary for the adjustment process to run its course depends on a number of factors: (1) the degree of wage and price flexibility, (2) the interest elasticity of the demand for money, and (3) the interest elasticity of investment. The greater the degree of wage and price flexibility, the shorter will be the time needed to restore full employment. Similarly, the greater the interest inelasticity (elasticity) of the demand for money (investment), the shorter will be the length of time. Even if money wages and prices are rigid downward, interest rates will still decline (although by a smaller amount) as output and, hence, the amount of money demanded decrease. But the reduction in interest rates and subsequent increase in investment will not be sufficient to restore full employment.

Since early Keynesians believed that the demand for money was highly interest elastic and investment was highly interest inelastic, they believed that, even if money wages and prices were flexible, unemployment could exist for very long periods. Therefore, stabilization policy was necessary to restore full employment.

Many contemporary economists do not regard the demand for money as highly interest elastic and investment as highly interest inelastic, but they still believe that unemployment can exist for prolonged periods. In contrast, Friedman and other monetarists appear to believe that the adjustment mechanism works rather quickly to restore output and employment to their full employment levels provided that the money supply itself does not become a source of instability. Consequently, if the money supply is increased at a constant rate, any deviation from full employment will be small and temporary. Thus, there is no need for discretionary policy.

Since discretionary policy has been used, it is difficult or even impossible to determine how rapidly the economy would return to full employment without using such a policy after a reduction in aggregate demand. In discussions of the tendency for the economy to gravitate to full employment, the United States experience in the 1930s is often mentioned. In the 1930s, the United States experienced very high unemployment rates, almost 25 percent in 1933. Moreover, the unemployment rate declined slowly, reaching only 14.6 percent in 1940. Thus, the experience is often cited as evidence that, although the economy may have a tendency to gravitate to full employment, the process is too slow to be of practical importance.

Michael R. Darby has uncovered a major error in the unemployment estimates for 1930–43.[33] His corrected data show a stronger movement toward full employment following 1933 than that just reported. Darby discovered that, during the period, workers employed in emergency government programs, such as the Works Progress (Projects after 1939) Administration (WPA) and the Civilian Conservation

Corps (CCC), were counted as unemployed rather than employed. The practice, common at the time, is inconsistent with the definition currently employed by the Bureau of Labor Statistics, as well as with other definitions of unemployment. If the workers in those programs are reclassified, employment is much greater than originally reported. For each of the years 1933–41, employment was 2 million or more greater, and in 1936 employment was actually 3.5 million greater. The reclassification also significantly alters the unemployment rates for the 1933–41 period. For each of the years, the corrected unemployment rate is 4 to 7 percentage points less than the reported rate. Darby concluded that the misclassification of workers obscured the decreases in the unemployment rate which occurred during the 1934–41 period.[34] Thus, the tendency for the economy to gravitate toward full employment may be stronger than originally thought.

Despite present views concerning the interest elasticities of the demand for money and investment and Darby's evidence, nonmonetarists believe, according to Modigliani, that the adjustment mechanism works only slowly. Thus, although the economy is not as unstable as once thought, it is not highly stable; therefore discretionary policy is required.

Even if a need for stabilization policy exists, Modigliani claimed that monetarists would oppose its use because such policies would, in practice, be destabilizing.[35] Modigliani argued on various grounds that discretionary policy has, on balance, been stabilizing in the post-World War II period. He noted that, until 1974, the United States had experienced only relatively mild recessions since 1937. The recession of 1974 was more severe; Modigliani claimed that it was caused by a supply shock (the quadrupling of crude oil prices, the oil embargo, and so on), not mismanagement of the money supply.

To determine the impact of a constant rate of increase in the money supply, Modigliani found two periods (and only two) during the post-Korean war era where the money supply grew at a relatively constant rate. The first period ran from early 1953 to the first half of 1957, approximately four years. The second period began with the first quarter of 1971 and continued until 1974, a span of almost four years. Although the growth rate of the money supply was relatively constant, the economy was marked by instability during both periods. The 1953–57 period or, allowing for lags, the 1954–58 period was characterized by instability with a recession in 1954, a sharp recovery in 1955, and another recession in 1958. The period 1971–74 (or 1972–75) was also characterized by sharp fluctuations in output and employment, as well as the rate of increase in prices. In fact, the period was characterized by greater instability than any other in recent U.S. history. This evidence is not, of course, conclusive. In both cases, the time span is relatively short, approximately four years, and the economy was subject to wage and price controls for most of 1971–74.

In another experiment to determine whether a constant increase in the money supply would have stabilized the economy, Modigliani, in conjunction with L. Papademos, simulated the U.S. economy with the aid of a computer and the MPS model.[36] The simulations covered the period from the beginning of 1959 to the middle of 1971. Modigliani and Papademos found, provided that the major shocks were eliminated, that a 3 percent increase in the money supply stabilized the economy. On the other hand, if the shocks that actually occurred are incorporated into the experiment, a steady 3 percent increase in the money supply is destabilizing. That is, the constant increase in the money supply resulted in greater instability than those policies actually followed. On the basis of the U.S. experience (and that of other Western nations) in the post-World War II period, of his tests, and of other studies, Modigliani believes that discretionary policy is stabilizing.[37]

To summarize, Modigliani believes that the economy is slow in adjusting to shocks, and since it is likely to be subjected to shocks in the future, stabilization policy is desirable. Moreover, he believes that discretionary policy is stabilizing. Thus, given the need (and stabilizing properties of discretionary policy), he believes that discretionary policy should be used.

Modigliani's views about discretionary policy are in sharp contrast to those of Friedman's. Since both cite evidence which supports their position, it is difficult to determine which is correct. Substantial support exists among professional economists for the continued use of discretionary policy. Also, various steps could be taken to make discretionary policy more effective. For example, as discussed earlier in this chapter, the conduct of monetary policy might be improved if the monetary authorities were to concentrate on monetary aggregates in the short as well as the long run. Given political realities and the present state of the art, the use of discretionary policy is unlikely to eliminate completely fluctuations in employment, output, and the rate of increase in prices. But many economists believe that discretionary policy can moderate these fluctuations.

INDEPENDENCE OF THE FEDERAL RESERVE

From time to time, the question of the Federal Reserve's independence arises. For example, during the autumn of 1977, some members of President Carter's administration said that the Federal Reserve's monetary policy was not sufficiently expansionary.[38] The statement implied that the interests of the country would be best served if the Federal Reserve were to pursue policies consistent with those followed or advocated by the executive branch of the government.

The Federal Reserve is an independent agency of the federal government. The president does appoint the members of the board of governors of the Federal Reserve. They are appointed for fourteen-year terms, however, and since the appointments are staggered, there is only one appointment, unless resignations occur, every two years. Thus, the president has only limited authority to appoint new members to the board. The president does select the board chairman from among the members of the board, but the chairman's term of office, four years, does not coincide with the president's.

Legally, the Federal Reserve is an agent of Congress. Consequently, it must submit an annual report to that body. Congress has delegated authority to the

Federal Reserve to supervise the monetary system and to conduct monetary policy. Moreover, Congress has little or no budgetary control with regard to the Federal Reserve since it operates at a profit.

The case for an independent Federal Reserve rests on several grounds. First, it is argued that independence is essential in order to minimize inflation. Government spending would increase more rapidly (with the resulting deficit financed by increases in the money supply) if the legislative and executive branches of the government had control of the money supply.[39] Second, an independent Federal Reserve, it is argued, can prevent the president or other members of the executive branch from manipulating the money supply for political purposes. For example, before an election, the money supply might be increased more rapidly to stimulate output and employment. Since prices respond less rapidly to an increase in the money supply, the increase in prices will occur only after the election. The increases in output and employment will benefit the incumbents; the long-run effects on the economy are undesirable because of the ensuing price increases. Third, if the Federal Reserve were to lose its independence, it might also lose some of its flexibility in terms of monetary policy. Presumably, one advantage of discretionary monetary policy is its short implementation lag. If the Federal Reserve were to become part of the executive branch or subservient to Congress, the implementation lag might become appreciably longer and countercyclical monetary policy would be less likely to be stabilizing.

The case against an independent Federal Reserve is also based upon a number of arguments. First, those opposed to independence stress that the present arrangement is elitist; they assert that economic policy should be formulated by elected officials who may be replaced if they act in a manner contrary to the wishes of the electorate. Second, monetary policy should be consistent with other governmental policies designed to promote the various economic goals of society. Since the Fed is an independent agency, there is no guarantee of consistency. In fact, opponents argue that, given the position of the Federal Reserve as controller of the money supply, the monetary authorities tend to be biased in favor of policies designed to maintain the value of money.[40] Thus, they favor policies designed to promote price stability over those designed to promote full employment. Third, opponents of an independent Fed argue that the monetary authorities are not insensitive to political pressure. The monetary authorities, they claim, have used policies designed to benefit incumbent administrations.[41]

Various recommendations have been made to reduce the independence of the Federal Reserve. In 1975, Congress passed House Concurrent Resolution 133.[42] Under the resolution, the Federal Reserve must report to Congress quarterly and specify the projected rates of growth in the major monetary and credit aggregates for the next year. The procedure is useful since it provides information about future action by the Federal Reserve and stimulates discussion of the appropriateness of its targets. The resolution also forces the Fed to plan at least a year in advance and to focus its attention on monetary aggregates rather than interest rates. Yet it is doubtful that the Federal Reserve has lost much of its independence.[43] For one thing, it projects rates of growth in terms of a range rather than a specific number. For another, the Fed is allowed to deviate from the range if it cannot meet the targeted increase or if conditions change.

In closing, several words of caution are appropriate. The independence of the Federal Reserve should not be exaggerated. The monetary authorities know that Congress established the Federal Reserve and that Congress can pass new legislation to change its status at any time. Moreover, evidence exists that the Federal Reserve tends to adopt policies favored by the president.[44] Since the Federal Reserve's independence is, to some degree, illusory, the benefits (or costs) associated with a change in its status are not as great as they may first appear.

CONCLUDING REMARKS

In this chapter, we considered monetary policy, its impact on the economy, and some of the problems associated with the conduct of monetary policy. In the previous chapter, we did the same for fiscal policy. In the next chapter, we turn our attention to incomes policy. By *incomes policy*, we mean governmental action—excluding monetary and fiscal measures—designed to influence or control the rate of increase of prices, money wages, and other forms of income. Examples include wage and price guidelines and controls.

Proponents of incomes policy claim that fiscal and monetary policies by themselves are inadequate to achieve price stability and a socially acceptable unemployment rate. For this reason, they argue that an incomes policy must be used in conjunction with the appropriate fiscal and monetary policies to achieve those admirable goals.

NOTES

1. For discussions of the formulation of monetary policy, see Stephen M. Axilrod, "U.S. Monetary Policy in Recent Years: An Overview," *Federal Reserve Bulletin*, 71 (January 1985), 14–24; Alton R. Gilbert, "Operating Procedures for Conducting Monetary Policy," Federal Reserve Bank of St. Louis, *Review*, 67 (February 1985), 13–21; and Henry C. Wallich, "Recent Techniques of Monetary Policy," Federal Reserve Bank of Kansas City, *Economic Review* (May 1984), 21–30.

2. The FOMC determines open market policy; the Federal Reserve Board has responsibility for the other instruments of monetary policy. Since the latter are rarely used to implement monetary policy (see Chapter 7), the FOMC emerges as the Federal Reserve's principal policymaking unit. Of course, the seven Federal Reserve Board members constitute a majority of the FOMC, with the chairman of the board serving as chairman of the FOMC. The FOMC schedules eight meetings per year; however, the committee can meet more often.

3. The record of FOMC policy actions for each meeting is released about a month after the meeting. The record is published in the *Federal Reserve Bulletin* several months

after the meeting and in the board's *Annual Report* at the end of the year. A statement on the financial position of the 12 Federal Reserve Banks is published weekly. Selected data from the statement are printed each Friday in major newspapers. Although the Federal Reserve does not include a discussion of the changes that occurred during the week, it is possible to determine the changes by comparing the weekly statements.

4. On a particular day, some member banks have excess reserves and other banks have reserve deficiencies. Banks with deficiencies can borrow reserves (deposits at Federal Reserve Banks) from banks with excess reserves. The interest rate at which they borrow is the Federal Funds rate. The Federal Funds rate is sensitive to changes in the reserve position of the banking system.

5. As discussed in Chapters 9 and 11, using interest rates as an indicator may result in destabilizing changes in the money supply. Suppose, for example, that the economy is expanding and, as a result, interest rates are rising. If the Federal Reserve employs policies designed to restrain interest rates, those policies will be expansionary and increase the likelihood of inflation.

6. For recent discussions, see Alfred Broaddus, "Financial Innovation in the United States—Background, Current Status and Prospects," Federal Reserve Bank of Richmond, *Economic Review,* 71 (January–February 1985), 2–22; Lyle E. Gramley, "Financial Innovation and Monetary Policy," *Federal Reserve Bulletin,* 68 (July 1982), 393–400; and Thomas D. Simpson, "Changes in the Financial System: Implications for Monetary Policy," *Brookings Papers on Economic Activity,* no. 1 (1984), 249–65.

7. In this regard, see William A. Barnett, "Economic Monetary Aggregates: An Application of Index Number and Aggregation Theory," *Journal of Econometrics,* 14 (September 1980), 11–48; Paul A. Spindt, "Money Is What Money Does: Monetary Aggregation and the Equation of Exchange," *Journal of Political Economy,* 93 (February 1985), 175–204; and Dallas S. Batten and Daniel L. Thornton, "Are Weighted Monetary Aggregates Better Than Simple-Sum M1?" Federal Reserve Bank of St. Louis, *Review,* 67 (June–July 1985), 29–40.

8. Milton Friedman and Anna Jacobson Schwartz, *A Monetary History of the United States 1867–1960* (New York: National Bureau of Economic Research, 1963). For reviews, see Robert W. Clower, "Monetary History and Positive Economics," *Journal of Economic History,* 24 (September 1964), 364–80; and James Tobin, "The Monetary Interpretation of History," *American Economic Review,* 55 (June 1965), 464–85.

9. Friedman and Schwartz, ibid., or Friedman and Schwartz "Money and Business Cycles," *Review of Economics and Statistics,* 45 (February 1963), 33–34. The money supply was defined so as to include time deposits held by the nonbank public.

10. Friedman and Schwartz, "Money and Business Cycles," ibid., pp. 39–40. They offer additional evidence to support the view that there is a close relationship between the money supply and money income.

11. The same is true of the evidence supplied by Friedman and David Meiselman. Friedman and Meiselman, "The Relative Stability of Monetary Velocity and the Investment Multiplier in the United States, 1897–1958," in Commission on Money and Credit, *Stabilization Policies* (Englewood Cliffs, N.J.: Prentice-Hall, Inc., 1963), pp. 165–268.

12. For a discussion, see James Tobin, "Money and Income: Post Hoc Ergo Propter Hoc?" *Quarterly Journal of Economics,* 84 (May 1970), 301–17; and Friedman, "Comment on Tobin," *Quarterly Journal of Economics,* 84 (May 1970), 318–27. See also Richard G. Davis, "The Role of the Money Supply in Business Cycles," Federal Reserve Bank of New York, *Monthly Review,* 50 (April 1968), 63–73.

13. Leonall C. Andersen and Jerry L. Jordan, "Monetary and Fiscal Actions: A Test of Their Relative Importance in Economic Stabilization," Federal Reserve Bank of St. Louis, *Review,* 50 (November 1968), 11–24.

14. Gary Fromm and Lawrence R. Klein, "The NBER/NSF Model Comparison Seminar: An Analysis of Results," in *Econometric Model Performance: Comparative Simulation Studies of the U.S. Economy,* eds. Lawrence R. Klein and Edwin Burmeister (Philadelphia: University of Pennsylvania Press, 1976), pp. 380–407. See also Carl F. Christ, "Judging the Performance of Econometric Models of the U.S. Economy," ibid., pp. 322–42.

15. According to Fromm and Klein, more recent versions of the model suggest that the response of real GNP is much stronger, ibid., p. 400.

16. The results differ for many reasons, including differences in periods over which the multipliers are calculated. For a discussion, see Fromm and Klein, ibid., pp. 395–96.

17. For supporting views, see W. C. Brainard and R. N. Cooper, "Empirical Monetary Macroeconomics: What Have We Learned in the Last 25 Years?" *American Economic Review,* 65 (May 1975), 167–75; and Gordon Fisher and David Sheppard, *Effects of Monetary Policy on the United States Economy: A Survey of Econometric Evidence* (Organization for Economic Co-operation and Development, December 1972).

18. Based on an alternative approach, Friedman and Schwartz found that peaks (troughs) in the growth rate of the money supply precede peaks (troughs) in the business cycle by an average of seven (four) months. Although the average lag is less, its variability is almost the same. Friedman and Schwartz, "Money and Business Cycles," p. 38. For a comprehensive review of the literature relating to the time lags associated with monetary policy, see Mary Susan Rosenbaum, "Lags in the Effect of Monetary Policy," Federal Reserve Bank of Atlanta, *Economic Review,* 70 (November 1985), 20–33.

19. See Friedman, "The Role of Monetary Policy," *American Economic Review,* 58 (March 1968), 16; and *A Program for Monetary Stability* (New York: Fordham University Press, 1959).

20. J. M. Culbertson, "Friedman on the Lag in Effect of Monetary Policy," *Journal of Political Economy,* 68 (December 1960), 617–21; and John Kareken and Robert M. Solow, "Lags in Monetary Policy," in *Stabilization Policies,* pp. 1–96.

21. Culbertson, ibid., p. 621. For Friedman's response and Culbertson's reply, see Friedman, "The Lag in Effect of Monetary Policy," and Culbertson, "The Lag in Effect of Monetary Policy: Reply," *Journal of Political Economy,* 69 (October 1961), 447–77.

22. Kareken and Solow, "Lags," p. 2. Kareken and Solow asserted that the lag between the time a need for policy action arises and the time a policy change occurs is eight months for switches to expansionary policies and three months for switches to contractionary policies. They also believe that the Federal Reserve can alter the reserves of the banking system in less than a month. Kareken and Solow found the lag between the change in reserves and the resulting change in interest rates to be long, and they suggested that monetary policy may work through the availability of credit as well as interest rates.

23. Thomas Mayer, "The Lag in the Effect of Monetary Policy: Some Criticism," *Western Economic Journal,* 5 (September 1967), 324–42.

24. Mayer, ibid., p. 328. In a comment on the Kareken–Solow study, Friedman stated that their estimate of the response lag (six to nine months) is not inconsistent with his own. "Note on Lag in Effect of Monetary Policy," *American Economic Review,* 54 (September 1964), 759–61.

25. Mayer, ibid., pp. 330–31. In an earlier study, Franco Modigliani found that discretionary monetary policy is superior to steady increases in the money supply as a stabilization policy. According to Mayer, however, if a lag is introduced, the results are less favorable to discretionary policy. He thinks, therefore, that Modigliani's claim about the superiority of discretionary policy must be rejected, ibid., p. 334.

26. As examples, see Thomas F. Cargill and Robert A. Meyer, "The Time Varying Response of Income to Changes in Monetary and Fiscal Policy," *Review of Economics and*

Statistics, 60 (February 1978), 1–7; and J. Ernest Tanner, "Are the Lags in the Effects of Monetary Policy Variable?" *Journal of Monetary Economics,* 5 (January 1979), 105–21.

27. See, for example, the comments of Richard G. Davis in "How Much Does Money Matter? A Look at Some Recent Evidence," Federal Reserve Bank of New York, *Monthly Review,* 51 (June 1969), 122–23.

28. For these and other results, see Fromm and Klein, "The NBER/NSF Model Comparison," p. 405. Since these results are in terms of real GNP, they are not comparable to those of Andersen and Jordan. For additional evidence and discussions of the various problems associated with estimating the lag, see Michael J. Hamburger, "The Lag in the Effect of Monetary Policy: A Survey of Recent Literature," Federal Reserve Bank of New York, *Monthly Review,* 53 (December 1971), 289–98; and Fisher and Sheppard, *Effects of Monetary Policy,* pp. 81–84.

29. Henry C. Simons, "Rules Versus Authorities in Monetary Policy," *Journal of Political Economy,* 44 (February 1936), 1–30; Friedman, "The Supply of Money and Changes in Prices and Output," in U.S. Congress Joint Economic Committee, *The Relationship of Prices to Economic Stability and Growth: Compendium of Papers Submitted by Panelists* (Washington, D.C.: Government Printing Office), pp. 241–56; Friedman, *A Program for Monetary Stability;* Friedman, "The Role of Monetary Policy," and Edward S. Shaw, "Money Supply and Stable Economic Growth," in *United States Monetary Policy,* ed. N. H. Jacoby (New York: The American Assembly, 1958), pp. 49–71.

30. The rationale may be expressed in terms of the equation of exchange. In terms of growth rates, the equation of exchange, $MsV = PY$, is written

$$\frac{\Delta Ms}{Ms} + \frac{\Delta V}{V} = \frac{\Delta P}{P} + \frac{\Delta Y}{Y},$$

where $\Delta Ms/Ms$, $\Delta V/V$, $\Delta P/P$, and $\Delta Y/Y$ represent the growth rates of the nominal money supply, income velocity of money, price level, and output, respectively. If the velocity of money is constant ($\Delta V/V = 0$), the equation becomes

$$\frac{\Delta Ms}{Ms} = \frac{\Delta P}{P} + \frac{\Delta Y}{Y}.$$

If output grows at a 3 percent rate, the money supply must also grow at that rate in order to provide for price stability ($\Delta P/P = 0$). If the income velocity of money were to decrease (increase), the money supply would have to grow more (less) rapidly to provide for price stability. According to Friedman, the necessary rate of increase depends upon the definition of the nominal money supply. It is not the specific rate that is important, however; it is the constancy of the rate. Some critics of Friedman's rule have argued that the Federal Reserve does not have complete control of the money supply and, therefore, cannot increase the money supply at a constant rate. The same criticism, however, applies to discretionary monetary policy.

31. Friedman, "The Role of Monetary Policy," pp. 15–16. Many of Friedman's examples are drawn from before World War II. Hence, some critics have argued that, since the Fed was in its infancy during that period, it will not make the same mistakes in the future. It is relatively easy to find examples of monetary mismanagement after World War II. This does not necessarily imply that discretionary monetary policy was, on balance, destabilizing. For examples from the postwar period, see Friedman, "The Role of Monetary Policy," and "Statement on the Conduct of Monetary Policy," in *Second Meeting on the*

Conduct of Monetary Policy, Hearings before the Committee on Banking, Housing, and Urban Affairs, U.S. Senate, 94th Cong., 1st Sess., November 4, 6 (Washington, D.C.: Government Printing Office, 1975), pp. 42–48.

32. Franco Modigliani, "The Monetarist Controversy or, Should We Forsake Stabilization Policies?" *American Economic Review,* 67 (March 1977), 1–19. For other critiques, see Abba P. Lerner, "A Review of *A Program for Monetary Stability*", *Journal of the American Statistical Association,* 57 (March 1962), 211–20; and Arthur M. Okun, "Fiscal-Monetary Activism: Some Analytical Issues," *Brookings Papers on Economic Activity,* no. 1 (1972), 123–63.

33. Michael R. Darby, "Three-and-a-Half Million U.S. Employees Have Been Mislaid: Or, an Explanation of Unemployment, 1934–1941," *Journal of Political Economy,* 84 (February 1976), 1–16.

34. For example, Darby noted that the reported reduction in employment from 1932 to 1936 was only about half of the actual reduction. For comments on Darby's views, see Robert J. Gordon, "Recent Developments in the Theory of Inflation and Unemployment," *Journal of Monetary Economics,* no. 2 (1976), pp. 195–96.

35. Since Friedman and other monetarists believe that fiscal policy is ineffective, they are concerned only with the possible destabilizing effects of monetary policy. As a non-monetarist, Modigliani is concerned with the possible effects of both monetary and fiscal policy.

36. The experiment is reported in Modigliani, "The Monetarist Controversy," p. 12.

37. For references to the other studies, see Modigliani, ibid.

38. The claim was presumably based on increasing interest rates at the time. The money supply had increased at a 9.7 percent annual rate in the third quarter of 1977 and at an 8.7 percent rate in the second quarter. Both are relatively rapid increases and evidence that the Fed was pursuing an expansionary monetary policy. Whether the expansion was "sufficiently" rapid is another question.

39. Arthur F. Burns, former Chairman of the Federal Reserve Board, argued repeatedly along this line. See, for example, "The Independence of the Federal Reserve System," Address by Arthur F. Burns, Chairman, Board of Governors of the Federal Reserve System, at the One Hundred and Thirteenth Commencement Exercises of Bryant College, Smithfield, Rhode Island, May 22, 1976. Reprinted in *Federal Reserve Bulletin,* 62 (June 1976), 493–96.

40. Harry G. Johnson, "Should There Be an Independent Monetary Authority?" in *The Federal Reserve System after Fifty Years,* Hearings before the Subcommittee on Domestic Finance, Committee on Banking and Currency, House of Representatives, 88th Cong., 2nd Sess. (Washington, D.C.: Government Printing Office, 1964), pp. 970–73.

41. For evidence on the "political" business cycle, see William D. Nordhaus, "The Political Business Cycle," *Review of Economic Studies,* 42 (April 1975), 169–90; and C. Duncan MacRae, "A Political Model of the Business Cycle," *Journal of Political Economy,* 85 (April 1977), 239–63.

42. With regard to recommendations, see, for example, those of the Commission on Money and Credit in their report, *Money and Credit* (Englewood Cliffs, N.J.: Prentice-Hall, Inc., 1961). For a discussion of the commission's recommendations, see G. L. Bach, "Economics, Politics, and the Fed," *Harvard Business Review,* 40 (January–February 1962), 81–91.

43. For a discussion, see Edward J. Kane, "New Congressional Restraints and Federal Reserve Independence," *Challenge,* 18 (November–December 1975), 37–44.

44. Robert E. Weintraub, "Congressional Supervision of Monetary Policy," *Journal of Monetary Economics,* 4 (April 1978), 341–62. Also, John Gildea, "A Survey of Federal Reserve Policymaking Behavior: Strategy and Tactics," in *Modern Concepts in Macroeco-*

nomics, pp. 347–67, ed. Thomas M. Havrilesky (Arlington Heights, Ill.: Harlan Davidson, Inc., 1985).

REVIEW QUESTIONS _____

1. Explain how monetary policy is formulated.
2. How did the conduct of monetary policy change after October 6, 1979? Do you believe that this change was desirable? Defend your answer.
3. It is said that financial innovations have the potential for causing serious problems for the monetary authorities. What are these problems? How might these problems be solved? Defend your answer.
4. Outline the Friedman–Schwartz evidence with regard to
   a. the relationship between the money supply and the level of economic activity over the business cycle.
   b. the length and variability of the time lag associated with monetary policy. Why did the evidence fail to win widespread support for the view that monetary policy is potent?
5. Outline the case for the effectiveness of monetary policy based on the evidence from single-equation and large-scale econometric models.
6. With regard to monetary policy, explain why the response lag may be long.
7. Monetarists claim that monetary policy is very potent. Yet they do not recommend the use of discretionary monetary policy. Why?
8. Suppose, in the long run, the money supply were to remain constant rather than increase. What would be the impact on the economy?
9. Explain how the argument for the use of discretionary policy depends upon the economy's reaction to shocks.
10. Based on the current economic situation, what sorts of monetary and fiscal policies would you recommend? Defend your answer.
11. Explain the relationship between the Federal Reserve and the legislative and administrative branches of the federal government. Outline and critically evaluate the arguments for an independent Federal Reserve.

SUGGESTED READING _____

AXILROD, STEPHEN H., "U.S. Monetary Policy in Recent Years: An Overview," *Federal Reserve Bulletin*, 71 (January 1985), 14–24.

BROADDUS, ALFRED, "Financial Innovation in the United States—Background, Current Status and Prospects," Federal Reserve Bank of Richmond, *Economic Review*, 71 (January–February 1985), 2–22.

FRIEDMAN, MILTON, "Monetary Policy: Theory and Practice," *Journal of Money, Credit, and Banking,* 14 (February 1982), 98–118.

———, "The Role of Monetary Policy," *American Economic Review,* 58 (March 1968), 1–17.

———, and ANNA JACOBSON SCHWARTZ, *A Monetary History of the United States 1867–1960.* New York: National Bureau of Economic Research, 1963.

———, "Money and Business Cycles," *Review of Economics and Statistics,* 45 (February 1963), 32–64.

GILBERT, ALTON R., "Operating Procedures for Conducting Monetary Policy," Federal Reserve Bank of St. Louis, *Review,* 67 (February 1985), 13–21.

MODIGLIANI, FRANCO, "The Monetarist Controversy or, Should We Forsake Stabilization Policies?" *American Economic Review,* 67 (March 1977), 1–19.

OKUN, ARTHUR M., "Fiscal-Monetary Activism: Some Analytical Issues," *Brookings Papers on Economic Activity,* no. 1 (1972), 123–63.

ROSENBAUM, MARY SUSAN, "Lags in the Effect of Monetary Policy," Federal Reserve Bank of Atlanta, *Economic Review,* 70 (November 1985), 20–33.

WALLICH, HENRY C., "Recent Techniques of Monetary Policy," Federal Reserve Bank of Kansas City, *Economic Review* (May 1984), 21–30.

20

INCOMES POLICY

Since World War II, the United States and many Western European countries have experimented with incomes policy. *Incomes policy* in general is governmental action—excluding monetary and fiscal measures—designed to influence or control the rate of increase of prices, money wages, and other forms of income. The policies actually adopted range from exhortation (jawboning) by public officials to statutory regulation of money wages and prices. Until 1971, U.S. experience with such policies was mainly limited to wartime controls. An important exception was the use of explicitly stated wage and price guidelines by the Kennedy and Johnson administrations from 1962 to 1966. Since these guidelines were not legally enforceable, compliance was encouraged by publicizing the guidelines and by exhortation. In August 1971, however, President Nixon imposed a 90-day wage–price freeze, which was followed by a series of programs designed to control wages and prices.

Incomes policies are usually based on the belief that much, or perhaps most, of the economy is characterized by imperfect competition. Under such circumstances, money wages and prices are determined by the monopolistic practices of unions and firms. Prices and money wages may increase even in the face of under-utilized productive capacity and unemployment.[1] Presumably, a high level of unemployment would moderate the wage and price increases; but proponents of the incomes approach argue that the necessary level of unemployment is socially unacceptable. Consequently, an incomes policy is allegedly required to slow the rate of increase of money wages and prices while expansionary fiscal and monetary policies are pursued to reduce the unemployment rate.

This chapter outlines the arguments for and against the incomes policy approach. After a review of the history of incomes policies in the United States, the arguments are evaluated with special reference to U.S. experience. Several recent proposals are then outlined and critically evaluated.

THE CASE FOR AN INCOMES POLICY

The case for an incomes policy or, more specifically, wage–price controls rests mainly on the view that firms and labor unions have the power to "administer" prices and money wages and use this power to increase them even during recessions. Consequently, attempts to achieve full employment through expansionary fiscal and monetary policies will cause inflation. Fiscal and monetary policies can achieve price stability only if socially undesirable amounts of excess capacity and unemployment are maintained. Thus, an incomes policy is necessary to restrain money wages and prices while expansionary monetary and fiscal policies are used to increase income and employment.[2]

The inflation process may be viewed in different ways. Gardner Ackley sees the process as the result of a struggle over income distribution occurring in an economy characterized by imperfect competition.[3] Firms and unions use their market power both to obtain increases in real income and to maintain their real incomes in the face of inflation. Once inflation begins, Ackley asserts, most increases in prices and money wages are made to maintain the real incomes of the parties involved. These increases, however, threaten the real incomes of others, thereby prompting additional increases in prices and money wages. The main consequence of the struggle over income distribution is higher prices and money wages. Ackley concludes that the inflationary process can be controlled only by incomes policy.

Ackley argues that both labor and management contribute to the inflationary process. Henry C. Wallich and Sidney Weintraub stress the impact of inflationary wage settlements.[4] The problem, they say, is that labor unions possess enough monopoly power to obtain inflationary wage increases. Wallich and Weintraub propose an incomes policy designed to stiffen the resistance of management to inflationary wage settlements.

Since proponents of the incomes approach allege the incompatibility of full employment and price stability to be due to the monopoly power of firms and/or labor unions, the problem could be dealt with by policies designed to make the economy more competitive. Basically, these policies involve (1) enforcing the antitrust laws more effectively, (2) weakening labor unions, and (3) removing impediments to international trade in order to promote international competition. Proponents of the incomes approach do not deny that making the economy competitive is desirable. They assert, however, political reasons make that approach unrealistic.[5]

Advocates of the incomes approach contend that the approach is more urgently needed today than it ever has been, for firms and unions are more likely to use their monopoly power now than previously. For example, Ackley argues that the social norms regulating group behavior now permit or even encourage the use of monopoly power, that management and union leadership are more sophisticated, and that better measures of relative position are now available. Given these factors and recent experience with inflation, Ackley claims that price and wage increases are likely to occur more quickly and to be greater.

With the more aggressive use of monopoly power, the (short-run) Phillips curve shifts to the right, indicating that there is a higher rate of inflation associated with each unemployment rate. Advocates of the incomes policy approach also cite other reasons for the (short-run) Phillips' curve shift to the right, including changes in the composition of the labor force. With the shift in the Phillips curve, monetary and fiscal policies designed to promote full employment (price stability) will result in a higher rate of inflation (unemployment).

Finally, they claim that society has become less willing to tolerate unemployment. Thus, the monetary and fiscal authorities have no choice; they must follow expansionary policies in order to promote employment. This means that without an incomes policy inflation will be even greater than in the past.

THE CASE AGAINST AN INCOMES POLICY

Since the argument for an incomes policy or, more explicitly, wage–price controls is based largely on the view that firms and labor unions possess monopoly power and use it to raise prices and money wages, opponents of the incomes policy approach have directed much of their attack to this view. Since this view was discussed in Chapter 13, this chapter does not deal with it. Instead, we outline and critically evaluate other arguments: (1) controls are ineffective; (2) they distort the allocation of resources and result in inequities; (3) they are costly to administer; and (4) they are inconsistent with basic economic and political freedoms.

Controls are likely to be ineffective, critics charge, since firms and labor unions have many ways to evade them. Firms may reduce the standard sizes of their products. Candy bars, for example, may become smaller. Similarly, firms may cheapen the quality of their products. Both practices amount to price increases but are difficult or impossible to police. With regard to wages, new job classifications may be created in order to increase the wages of newly "promoted" workers by amounts in excess of those permitted under controls.

If controls are effective, critics of the incomes approach argue that they will distort the allocation of resources. One function of the price system is the allocation of resources. If the demand for a product increases, its price rises. The rise is an incentive for firms to increase production. In their efforts to produce more, they hire more labor and purchase additional raw materials. They may also invest in new plant and equipment so as to increase their productive capacity. To the extent that profits in the industry increase, other firms may enter the industry.

If the controls are not sufficiently flexible to allow for price (and wage) increases in industries experiencing increases in demand, there will be a misallocation of resources. An increase in demand should call forth an increase in the quantity produced. With no increase in price, however, firms have no incentive to increase output. Hence, too few resources will be allocated to making the product. With price constant, moreover, the increase in demand will cause shortages; some people will be unable to buy the desired amounts. As a result, some system other than the price system will develop to allocate the scarce good. The possibilities include standing in line, bribery, black markets, and rationing.

Proponents of the incomes policy approach concede that controls may alter the allocation of resources. They claim, however, that, in an economy characterized by imperfect competition, the initial allocation of resources could hardly have been optimal. They argue, too, that distortions are most likely to occur when the economy is at full employment. Until full employment is achieved, therefore, they believe there is little reason to worry about distortions. Proponents of this argument fail to recognize that recovery takes place at different rates in different industries. There may be shortages in certain industries (such as the lumber and oil industries in 1972) even when the economy is operating at less than full employment.

In general, the more effective the controls in restraining inflation, the greater the likelihood of a misallocation of resources. Hence, to foster efficiency, it is preferable to allow prices to increase rather than risk the consequences of suppressed inflation. If shortages develop, a new system must be instituted to replace the price system. Since the price system is very efficient in allocating resources, the substitute system is likely to be less efficient.[6] Inflation, if it is to exist, should be open rather than suppressed.

Opponents of the incomes approach assert that controls will produce inequities. For example, firms and unions in "visible" industries will be more strictly supervised than corresponding firms and unions in other industries. Stricter supervision is likely in those industries because the resources necessary to supervise all industries are unlikely to be forthcoming and because it is important for the public to retain confidence in the program (and those responsible for the program). The stricter supervision is likely to result in lower price and wage increases in the "visible" industries, regardless of conditions in those industries. The result is a misallocation of resources and inequities.[7]

Opponents of the incomes policy approach also note that administration of a controls program consumes resources which could be used in the production of goods and services. In World War II, some 60,000 persons were employed by the Office of Price Administration; during the Korean War, 15,000 persons worked for the Office of Price Stabilization. The staff for the program which began in 1971 (the Economic Stabilization Program) totaled approximately 1,000 persons.[8] In addition, the equivalent of about 3,000 man-years of services was provided by the Internal Revenue Service. The primary reason for the smaller staff was that the program was viewed as temporary; its cost is discussed in more detail later.

Finally, opponents of the incomes policy approach regard governmental intervention into the decision-making process as a threat to freedom. Milton Friedman, for example, has argued that power delegated to persons for the "good" purpose of restraining money wages and prices may be used by those in office for other "good" purposes, such as keeping themselves in power.

THE WAGE–PRICE GUIDEPOSTS OF THE 1960s[9]

When President Kennedy took office in January 1961, the unemployment rate was high, 6.6 percent, but inflation was minimal, approximately 1 percent per year. Policies were proposed to reduce the unemployment rate to 4 percent; the administration was concerned that economic expansion might rekindle the inflation which occurred in the 1950s. Thus, the problem was to devise a set of policies which would lead to increased output and employment and, at the same time, restrain money wages and prices.

The Kennedy administration responded by introducing formal wage–price guidelines or guideposts. The guideposts first appeared in the 1962 *Economic Report of the President*. They were as follows:

> The general guide for noninflationary wage behavior is that the rate of increase in wage rates (including fringe benefits) in each industry be equal to the trend rate of over-all productivity increase. General acceptance of this guide would maintain stability of labor cost per unit of output for the economy as a whole— though not of course for individual industries.
>
> The general guide for noninflationary price behavior calls for price reduction if the industry's rate of productivity increase exceeds the overall rate— for this would mean declining unit labor costs; it calls for an appropriate increase in price if the opposite relationship prevails; and it calls for stable prices if the two rates of productivity increase are equal.

Thus, the rate of increase in money wages in each industry was to equal the rate of increase in overall productivity. For example, if output per person increased by 3 percent, money wages were to increase at the same rate. If labor productivity and money wages increase at the same rate, the increase in money wages will not exert any pressure on prices.

An industry's prices were to remain constant if the industry's rate of productivity increase equaled the productivity increase for the entire economy. On the other hand, an industry's prices were to fall if the industry's rate of productivity increase exceeded the overall rate. Since money wages were to increase at the overall rate, an industry experiencing more rapid productivity increases would have declining per unit labor costs. The guideposts suggested that the benefits of the lower per unit labor costs be passed on to the industry's customers in terms of lower prices. By the same token, an industry experiencing less rapid productivity increases would have increasing per unit labor costs. Therefore, based on the guideposts, such an industry was justified in increasing its prices more rapidly.

In addition to the general guideposts, a number of exceptions were permitted:

(1) Wage rate increases would exceed the general guide rate in an industry which would otherwise be unable to attract sufficient labor; or in which wage rates are exceptionally low compared with the range of wages earned elsewhere by similar labor, because the bargaining position of workers has been weak in particular local labor markets.

(2) Wage rate increases would fall short of the general guide rate in an industry which could not provide jobs for its entire labor force even in times of generally full employment; or in which wage rates are exceptionally high compared with the range of wages earned elsewhere by similar labor, because the bargaining position of workers has been especially strong.

(3) Prices would rise more rapidly, or fall more slowly, than indicated by the general guide rate in an industry in which the level of profits was insufficient to attract the capital required to finance a needed expansion in capacity; or in which costs other than labor costs had risen.

(4) Prices would rise more slowly, or fall more rapidly, than indicated by the general guide in an industry in which the relation of productive capacity to full employment demand shows the desirability of an outflow of capital from the industry; or in which costs other than labor costs have fallen; or in which excessive market power has resulted in rates of profit substantially higher than those earned elsewhere on investments of comparable risk.

Compliance was voluntary. It was hoped that the force of public opinion would keep labor and management in line.

In such general form, the guideposts and accompanying list of exceptions failed to provide specific answers for individual cases.[10] Gradually, however, the guideposts became more specific. In 1964, for example, a specific figure, 3.2 percent, was introduced to serve as a basis for acceptable wage increases.[11]

Output and employment increased with little or no inflation during the early 1960s. By 1966, the economy was at, or close to, full employment. Nevertheless, government spending and the money supply continued to increase rapidly. As a result, money wages and prices started to increase more rapidly. These increases were in clear violation of the guideposts and signaled their demise for all practical purposes.

THE EFFECTIVENESS OF THE GUIDEPOSTS

A number of studies on the effectiveness of the guideposts have been published. In one such study, George L. Perry concluded that they were successful in moderating wage increases during the 1962–66 period.[12] In his study, Perry developed an equation for estimating wage changes in manufacturing based on quarterly data for the 1947–60 period. He then used the equation to predict wage changes for the 1962–66 period. He found that the actual wage changes were less than those predicted on the basis of his equation and attributed the differences to the guideposts.

As an additional test, Perry considered the effects of the guideposts on "visible" and "invisible" industries. He did not define "visible" and "invisible" industries other than to suggest that visible industries are more susceptible to public pressure and, therefore, are more likely to follow the guidelines. When compared to the mid-1950s, Perry found, during the mid-1960s, that money wages in visible industries increased less rapidly relative to those in invisible industries. He interpreted the results as support for the view that the guideposts were effective.

In separate comments, Paul S. Anderson, Michael L. Wachter, and Adrian W. Throop criticized Perry's study.[13] They noted that the equation which Perry used to predict wage changes for the 1962–66 period is unstable. Consequently, it cannot be used to obtain accurate estimates of wage changes. They also noted that the division of industries into visible and invisible is arbitrary and that the results Perry obtained in regard to the test can be explained on other grounds. Perry, however, does not think that these criticisms invalidate his results.[14]

In conclusion, the evidence on the impact of the guideposts on money wages is mixed. The same is true with regard to prices. John Sheahan, in *The Wage–Price Guideposts*, concluded that the guideposts did slow the rate of increase in money wages and prices. He conceded, however, that the data are consistent with other explanations. For example, the smaller increases in money wages and prices may have been due to a reduction in inflationary expectations following the recessions of 1957–58 and 1960.[15] At any rate, the guideposts broke down in 1966 when inflationary pressures in the economy became intense.

THE ECONOMIC STABILIZATION PROGRAM

When President Nixon took office in January 1969, the unemployment rate was much lower, 3.3 percent, than at the beginning of the Kennedy administration. Prices, however, were increasing much more rapidly. In 1969, the first year of the new administration, consumer prices rose 6.1 percent. In 1970, the increase was less, 5.5 percent, but not appreciably so. To counter the inflation, the administration embarked on a program of "gradualism," involving fiscal and monetary restraint. By applying the brakes gradually, it hoped to check the inflation with little or no increase in the unemployment rate.

The program showed mixed results. Unemployment reached 6.2 percent in December 1970 and fluctuated within a narrow range around 6 percent during the first seven months of 1971. Consumer prices increased at a slower rate from December 1970 to July 1971; on an annual basis, the rate of increase was 3.9 percent. The decline in the rate of increase in consumer prices was not matched by a decline in the rate of increase of wholesale prices. In fact, wholesale prices increased more rapidly from December 1970 to July 1971 (5.6 percent on an annual basis) than in 1970, 2.3 percent. Despite the moderation of the rate of increase of consumer prices, however, criticism of the Nixon administration's economic policies intensified.

Initially, much of the criticism came from organized labor and Congress. Spokesmen for organized labor and many congressmen stressed that the administration's policies were causing unemployment with little or no reduction in the inflation rate. They also emphasized the desirability of more drastic action, including the imposition of wage and price controls. By summer, 1971, criticism was also forthcoming from the business community, the press, and Arthur Burns, chairman of the board of governors of the Federal Reserve System. Given the mounting criticism of the administration's policies and its fear that more drastic fiscal and monetary restraint would result in higher unemployment, the administration moved closer to direct controls on money wages and prices. Perhaps the final straw was the deterioration of the U.S. balance of payments. The United States deficit increased significantly in the second and third quarters of 1971; by the summer of 1971 the dollar was under heavy pressure abroad.

The Ninety-Day Wage-Price Freeze (Phase 1)

On August 15, 1971, President Nixon announced the imposition of a comprehensive freeze on prices, wages, and rents. The freeze constituted the first peacetime attempt at direct control of prices and wages in the United States. It was also the first (Phase I) in a series of programs designed to control prices and wages. Arnold Weber has argued that the decision to impose the freeze was based upon the same factors which led other Western countries to take similar actions.[16] The factors were inflation, a balance of payments deficit, and unwillingness (or inability) to pursue restrictive monetary and fiscal policies because of their impact upon output and employment.

The Economic Stabilization Act of 1970, as amended, gave the president power "to issue such orders and regulations as he may deem appropriate to stabilize prices, rents, wages, and salaries." The president could not exercise this power "with respect to a particular industry or segment of the economy" unless "prices or wages in that industry or segment of the economy have increased at a rate which is grossly disproportionate to the rate at which prices or wages have increased in the economy generally." This provision almost guaranteed that the coverage would be comprehensive.[17]

Although prices, rents, wages, and salaries were to be controlled, certain exceptions were made, including raw agricultural products, exports, and imports. Raw agricultural products were excluded for a number of reasons. First, those markets are basically competitive (in the absence of government intervention). Second, agricultural products were generally abundant in supply so that their prices had been relatively stable. It was hoped that these conditions would persist during the freeze period. Third, given the nature of agricultural markets, attempts to regulate agricultural prices would have been an administrative nightmare. Fourth, raw agricultural products had been excluded from controls during World War II and the Korean War. Fifth, many of those products were subject to price support and other programs established by Congress.

In addition to raw agricultural products, exports and imports were excluded. Exports were excluded because of the difficulty or impossibility of controlling transactions abroad. The treatment of import prices was more controversial. If import prices were to rise, the cost of living would increase. On the other hand, if import prices were frozen, imports would tend to maintain their competitive edge. It was finally decided that imports were to be exempted; the price of finished goods sold in the United States could increase without limit. If the price of imports used in the production of domestic goods increased, however, the price increase could not be passed on to the purchasers of the final product.

Following the initial announcement, the Cost of Living Council (CLC) was given overall responsibility for administering the freeze. The Cost of Living Council was composed of the secretaries of agriculture, commerce, housing and urban development, labor, and treasury, the directors of the Office of Emergency Preparedness and the Office of Management and Budget, the chairman of the Council of Economic Advisers, and the president's special assistant for consumer affairs. In addition, the chairman of the board of governors of the Federal Reserve System served as an adviser.

The general formula for determining the ceilings on prices, wages, and rents was specified August 16, in Executive Order 11615:

> (a) Prices, rents, wages, and salaries shall be stabilized for a period of 90 days from the date hereof at levels not greater than the highest of those pertaining to a substantial volume of actual transactions by each individual, business, firm, or other entity of any kind during the 30-day period ending August 14, 1971, for like or similar commodities or services. If no transactions occurred in that period, the ceiling will be the highest price, rent, salary or wage in the nearest preceding 30-day period in which transactions did occur. No person shall charge, assess, or receive directly or indirectly in any transaction prices or rents in any form higher than those permitted hereunder, and no person shall, directly or indirectly, pay or agree to pay in any transaction wages or salaries in any form, or to use any means to obtain payment of wages and salaries in any form, higher than those permitted hereunder, whether by retroactive increase or otherwise.

Despite the formula, the Cost of Living Council had considerable scope in defining the terms of the freeze.[18] Wages were defined to include all forms of compensation; thus, fringe benefits were included in the freeze. Ceiling prices were determined with reference to actual transaction prices rather than list prices. Rent ceilings were established in a similar manner. The maximum rent assumed the maintenance of services and included discounts previously allowed renters.

Within any specified base period, the ceiling price, wage, or rent was to be "the highest of those pertaining to a substantial volume of transactions." The Cost of Living Council ruled that "a substantial volume" meant 10 percent or more of total transactions, with transactions on a delivered basis. Companies could not use newly announced prices if they had shipped less than 10 percent of their goods at the new price during the relevant base period.[19]

For the most part, the administration relied on voluntary compliance. Indeed, it had little choice, given the magnitude of the task and the limited resources of the various agencies charged with administering the freeze. The administration also resorted to jawboning. In the case of interest and dividends, voluntary compliance and jawboning were particularly important since these forms of income were not covered by the Economic Stabilization Act.

When voluntary compliance and jawboning failed, legal sanctions could be applied.[20] Under the Economic Stabilization Act, as amended, violators of the freeze were subject to both civil and criminal penalties. Court action was initiated in only a few cases because of the program's possible vulnerability to legal tests and because of the time-consuming nature of legal proceedings. The threat of legal action was used much more often than legal action itself.

Phase II

On November 14, 1971, the wage-price freeze ended and a new program of wage and price controls was initiated. The expressed goal was to reduce the rate of inflation, as measured by the consumer price index, to 2 to 3 percent by the end of 1972. As during the wage-price freeze, the Cost of Living Council had primary responsibility for administering the program. During Phase II, the Council was assisted by the Price Commission and the Pay Board. The Price Commission was responsible for developing standards and implementation procedures with regard to the stabilization of prices and rents. The Pay Board had a similar responsibility with regard to wages and salaries. The Cost of Living Council, Price Commission, and Pay Board were assisted by various committees, as well as by the Internal Revenue Service.[21]

To facilitate administration of the program, firms and employee bargaining units were divided into three groups or tiers. All tiers were subject to the same standards in terms of permissible price and wage increases; however, the tiers differed in terms of the degree of reporting required. The largest firms and employee bargaining units (companies with sales of $100 million and over and employee units with 5,000 or more workers) constituted the first tier and were required to obtain prior approval for price and wage adjustments. A group of smaller firms and employee bargaining units (companies with sales between $50 million and $100 million and employee units with 1,000 to 5,000 workers) comprised the second tier. These economic units were not required to obtain prior approval for price and wage adjustments; however, they were expected to report any adjustments. A group of still smaller economic units (companies with sales less than $50 million and employee bargaining units of less than 1,000 workers) made up the third tier.

These units were not required to report price and wage adjustments but were expected to maintain records which could be audited.

The Pay Board. The Pay Board initially established 5.5 percent as the standard for permissible wage increases. This standard was viewed as consistent with the administration's goal of reducing the rate of inflation to the 2 to 3 percent range. Based on a long-term productivity increase of 3 percent, wage increases of 5.5 percent imply that per unit labor costs will increase at a 2.5 percent rate, necessitating a price increase of only 2.5 percent.

The general standard was qualified in several respects.[22] A catch-up provision allowed additional increases of up to 1.5 percent for employee units which had signed contracts before 1969 in anticipation of moderate future wage and price increases. Congress also exempted several types of fringe benefits from controls. This had the effect of raising the permissible wage increase by 0.7 percent (to 6.2 percent or, with the catch-up provision, 7.7 percent). Congress also exempted the "working poor" from wage controls. A subsequent definition of this group excluded about 40 percent of all private nonfarm workers from wage controls.

The Price Commission. The Price Commission attempted to control prices on a firm-by-firm basis. Manufacturing firms were permitted to raise prices provided that they could justify the increases in terms of cost increases. For example, if money wages increased at a 5.5 percent rate and productivity increased at a 3 percent rate, firms were allowed to increase prices by 2.5 percent. In raising prices, firms were subject to the additional constraint that such increases could not increase a firm's profits as a percentage of sales relative to the base period (the average of the best two of the three fiscal years preceding August 1971).

To ease the administrative load with regard to multiproduct firms, the commission negotiated "term limit pricing" agreements with 185 firms with sales totaling approximately $124 billion. Under the original agreements, firms were permitted to increase the prices of individual items without limit provided that the weighted average of the increases did not exceed 2 percent. The individual price increases were eventually limited to 8 percent and, finally, to 6 percent; the permissible weighted average increase was also reduced (to 1.8 percent). The term limit pricing agreements significantly eased the administrative burden. By allowing firms more discretion, however, it may have significantly reduced the effectiveness of the Phase II controls.

Firms engaged in wholesale and retail trade were subject to a different set of regulations. Under the regulations, firms were not allowed to exceed their customary (based upon the prefreeze period) percentage markups over invoice costs. Thus, firms could increase their prices if they paid higher prices for goods received. Since price increases were not permitted to cover higher operating costs, however, firms engaged in wholesale and retail trade were subject to a greater degree of restraint than firms in manufacturing.

Treatment of the other sectors of the economy varied. For the most part, authority to regulate utilities was returned to existing federal and state regulatory agencies. The health services industry was subject to a set of special regulations.

The maximum increase in fees for physicians and dentists was 2.5 percent and then only if cost justified. Hospitals and other institutions had to cost justify fee increases; their limit was 6 percent, with exceptions permitted for special hardships. Farm products, exports, and imports were exempt from controls. About half of the rental units in the country were exempt. Interest rates were not subject to controls although voluntary restraint was sought in regard to various rates.

Phases III and IV

On January 11, 1973, the administration modified its controls program. The new program, known as Phase III, differed markedly from the previous set of controls.

> To reduce the mounting delays and costs entailed in submitting requests for price increases, having them reviewed, and seeking detailed interpretations of increasingly complex rules, the basic principles of regulation developed during Phase II were to be self-administered in Phase III. Report-filing requirements were maintained only for the largest economic units. The Price Commission and Pay Board were absorbed into the staff of the Cost of Living Council; and this staff, together with the Internal Revenue Service (IRS) enforcement staff, was reduced. The Cost of Living Council retained authority, and subsequently used it, to impose specific, mandatory regulations where restraint seemed lacking, but in most sectors of the economy the system was not mandatory without further action by the CLC.[23]

Wage and price regulations were substantially modified during Phase III. On February 26, 1973, the newly formed Labor–Management Advisory Committee to the CLC announced that "no single standard of wage settlement can be expected to apply throughout the economy," thereby effectively removing the upper limit on wage increases.

> The profit margin regulations were also modified in Phase III. The basis for calculating the profit margin limitation was changed to increase the number of fiscal years from which a firm could choose the 2 years they used in calculating their base. To permit firms to benefit from productivity increases if they practiced price restraint, the profit margin limit was waived if a firm's average price increase was no more than 1.5 per cent in a year. A third change was to permit price increases "necessary for efficient allocation of resources or to maintain adequate levels of supply." Price changes were thus allowed in instances where economic growth led to exceptional demand pressures in particular markets and the alternative was shortages.[24]

During the first quarter of 1973, prices increased sharply. The increase was due to several factors, including, no doubt, relaxation of the controls.[25] Food and import prices increased more rapidly than expected. The economic expansion was also more rapid than expected, thereby subjecting the economy to more inflationary pressure. Also, anticipation of a return to stricter controls may have prompted some price increases.

In response to the acceleration in the rate of inflation, the administration, on March 6, 1973, required cost justification of the major producers of crude oil and petroleum products who sought price increases yielding more than a 1 percent yearly addition to their revenues, with prenotification from those seeking increases greater than 1.5 percent. On March 29, ceilings on prices of red meats at all levels of processing and distribution were announced. Finally, on May 2, prenotification requirements were reinstated, but only for large firms that proposed weighted average price increases 1.5 percent above price levels either authorized or in effect on January 10, 1973.

The high rate of inflation during the first five months of 1973 and the dismal prospects for the last half of 1973 put further pressure on the administration to take more drastic action. On June 13, the president announced another price freeze. During the freeze, most prices (but not wages) were prohibited from rising above their June 1–8 levels. Rents and agricultural products at the first sale were excluded from the freeze. Dividends and interest rates were subject to voluntary controls. The freeze, sometimes called Phase III½, was to last no more than 60 days and was to be followed by a new set of controls.

On August 12, 1973, Phase IV of the controls began for the manufacturing, wholesale, retail, and service sectors.[26] For workers, the general standard was an annual 5.5 percent increase in money wages with an additional 0.7 percent for fringe benefits. The emphasis was on flexibility rather than "rigid adherence to a simple standard." For most manufacturing and service industries, price increases were limited to dollar-for-dollar pass-through of allowable cost increases incurred since the last fiscal quarter of 1972. Prenotification of price increases was required of Tier 1 firms with implementation after 30 days unless disallowed by the CLC. Tier I and II firms were required to file quarterly reports with the CLC.

An important element of Phase IV was progressive decontrol of the economy. By gradually decontrolling the economy, the administration hoped to avoid or reduce the adverse effects of controls on the supply of products and to avoid a "bulge" in prices at the end of Phase IV. Decontrol began in 1973 and accelerated until, on April 30, 1974, Phase IV ended with the expiration of the Economic Stabilization Act.

THE EFFECTIVENESS OF THE ECONOMIC STABILIZATION PROGRAM

One primary goal of the Economic Stabilization Program was reducing inflation. During Phase I (the wage-price freeze), both money wages, as measured by the average hourly earnings for the private nonfarm economy, and prices increased less rapidly than in previous years (see Table 20.1).[27] Average hourly earnings increased at an annual rate of 3.1 percent during the August 1971–November 1971

TABLE 20.1 Price and wage changes before, during, and after the Economic Stabilization Program[1]

| | Pre-Phase I | | Dec. 1970 to Aug. 1971 | Phase I Freeze Aug.–Nov. 1971 | Phase II | | Phase I and Phase II Aug. 1971 to Jan. 1973 | Phase III Jan.–June 1973 | Second Freeze and Phase IV June 1973 to Apr. 1974 | Post-Phase IV | |
	Dec. 1968 to Dec. 1969	Dec. 1969 to Dec. 1970			Bulge Nov. 1971 to Feb. 1972	Post-Bulge Feb.–Dec. 1972				Apr.–Aug. 1974	Aug.–Dec. 1974
Consumer Price Index:											
All items	6.1	5.5	3.8	1.9	4.8	3.0	3.3	8.3	10.7	12.7	11.8
Food	7.2	2.2	5.0	1.7	9.7	3.6	5.6	20.3	16.2	7.0	17.0
All items less food	5.7	6.5	3.4	2.3	2.9	3.0	2.7	5.0	8.7	15.3	9.7
Wholesale Price Index:											
All commodities	4.8	2.2	5.2	-0.2	6.9	6.5	5.7	24.4	15.2	31.8	10.2
Farm products and processed foods and feeds	7.5	-1.4	6.5	1.1	14.7	14.7	13.3	49.8	6.3	24.5	9.5
Industrial commodities	3.9	3.6	4.7	-0.5	4.0	3.4	2.9	14.4	19.6	35.5	9.4
Average hourly earnings, private nonfarm economy[2]	—[3]	—[3]	—[3]	3.1	9.5	5.6	6.1	6.3	7.6	6.3	6.7

[1]Measured in seasonally adjusted annual percentage rates.
[2]Adjusted for overtime (in manufacturing only) and interindustry shifts.
[3]Average hourly earnings for private nonfarm workers increased 6.9 percent August 1969–August 1970, and an additional 6.9 percent, August 1970–August 1971.

Source: Economic Report of the President (Washington, D.C.: Government Printing Office), various issues.

period as compared to 6.9 percent in each of the two previous years. The CPI increased at an annual rate of 1.9 percent during the same period. In contrast, it had increased at an annual rate of 3.8 percent during December 1970–August 1971, and even more rapidly during 1969 and 1970. The rate of increase in the WPI also slowed; in fact, the WPI actually declined during the freeze.

During the first part of Phase II (November 1971 to February 1972), money wages and prices increased more rapidly. The "bulge" was due in part to the implementation of wage increases originally scheduled for the Phase I period. For the remainder of Phase II (February 1972 to December 1972), the increases in money wages and prices (except for wholesale prices) were more moderate. For the entire Phase I–Phase II period, the CPI increased at an annual rate of 3.3 percent, 0.5 percent less than during the December 1970–August 1971 period and 2.2 percent less than during the December 1969–December 1970 period. Money wages increased less rapidly, 6.1 percent, during the Phase I–Phase II period than during the previous two years, 6.9 percent, but not appreciably so. Wholesale prices actually increased more rapidly during the Phase I–Phase II period than during the previous years.

Money wages and prices increased more rapidly during Phase III (January 1973–June 1973) and even more rapidly (except for wholesale prices) during the second freeze–Phase IV period (June 1973–April 1974). Because of the relaxation of controls during Phase III and the acceleration of inflation in Phases III and IV, most of the empirical studies relating to the effectiveness of controls have centered on Phases I and II.

In a series of studies, Robert J. Gordon has examined the impact of controls on money wages and prices. Using an approach similar to Perry's, Gordon constructed a model based on data for the precontrol period in order to predict the behavior of money wages and prices in the absence of controls. Actual and predicted values were then compared to determine the impact of the controls. In his first study, which covered the period from the third quarter of 1971 through the second quarter of 1972 (Phase I plus part of Phase II), he reported that the controls reduced the rate of increase of money wages slightly (by a maximum of 0.68 percentage points) and the rate of increase in prices more significantly (by a maximum of 1.85 percentage points).[28]

Gordon's results are, for the most part, consistent with the findings of others. A. Bradley Askin and John Kraft used three different models to determine the impact of the Economic Stabilization Program on money wages and prices.[29] In regard to money wages, the results are mixed. One model (that originally developed by Gordon) suggested that the program reduced the rate of increase in money wages. The other two models suggested that the rate of increase of money wages actually accelerated during the Phase I–Phase II period.[30] All three models indicate that the program was successful in reducing the rate of increase of prices, although the estimated reduction varied by model. Askin and Kraft concluded that the controls appeared to have reduced the inflation rate by more than 1 percentage point and perhaps by more than 2 percentage points during the Phase I–Phase II period.

To assess the impact of the controls on the CPI and the WPI, the Price Commission developed two monthly models. Results based on the models suggest that the controls slowed the rate of increase in the CPI by approximately 2 percentage points.[31] The reduction in the rate of increase in the WPI was much less. In fact, the results for one of the models suggested that the WPI increased more rapidly during the Phase I–Phase II period.[32]

In regard to individual industries, Robert F. Lanzillotti, Mary T. Hamilton, and R. Blaine Roberts compared the performance of 16 manufacturing industries during the Phase I–Phase II period with their performance before that period. On the basis of this comparison, they concluded that the controls program had little effect on those industries. They did find evidence of a modest reduction in the rate of increase in prices in other industries; manufacturing of leather products, petroleum refining, the service industries, construction, and wholesale and retail trade.

In a more recent study, Gordon considered both the Phase I–Phase IV period and the period from the termination of the program in 1974 through 1976.[33] He concluded that the controls did not reduce the rate of increase of money wages; if anything, they had a perverse effect. In regard to prices, he found that the controls reduced inflation but only temporarily. With the relaxation of controls in 1973, prices began to increase more rapidly. These price increases offset or more than offset the effects of the price controls during the Phase I–Phase II period.

To summarize, the empirical evidence suggests that the Economic Stabilization Program had little or no effect on money wages even during the Phase I–Phase II period.[34] Most of the evidence suggests that the program was successful in slowing the rate of increase of prices, as measured by the private nonfarm deflator and the CPI, during the Phase I–Phase II period. The amount of the estimated reduction varies, with the maximum possible reduction approximately 2 percentage points. In contrast, the WPI increased more rapidly during the Phase I–Phase II period. After Phase II, prices increased more rapidly, thereby eroding the gains made during the Phase I–Phase II period. Thus, the program, considered as a whole, was ineffective in restraining money wages and prices.

Some proponents of the incomes policy approach have argued that the Phase II controls were abandoned prematurely, thereby causing a price explosion. Had Phase II been extended, they claim, prices would have risen less rapidly in 1973. By 1973, however, conditions in the economy had changed. Most of the inflation was due to rising agricultural and import prices. For example, Barry Bosworth has estimated that three-fourths of the 8.1 percent annual rate of increase of consumer prices in the first half of 1973 was due to the rise in agricultural and import prices.[35] Neither sector is amenable to controls of the Phase II type. Moreover, prices were increasing in other sectors of the economy. In August 1971, an appreciable amount of excess capacity and unemployment existed in the economy. In 1973, there was still excess general capacity; in a number of sectors, however—paper, rubber, and petroleum refining, for example—there was none. Hence, the increases in aggregate demand which occurred during the period resulted in price increases in those sectors.[36] Considering these situations, it is doubtful that inflation would have been appreciably less even if the Phase II controls had been maintained.

THE CARTER ADMINISTRATION'S PAY
AND PRICE STANDARDS

During the Carter administration, the inflation rate began to accelerate. In 1976, the IPD increased at a 6.4 percent rate. In 1977, the first year of the Carter administration, the IPD increased at a 6.7 percent rate. In 1978, the increase was even greater, 7.3 percent. The administration responded to the acceleration in the inflation rate by introducing a program designed to alleviate the inflation problem. As part of this program, President Carter announced a voluntary program of pay and price standards. More specific standards appeared in later months.[37]

Initially, the basic price standard suggested that a firm should limit its average price increase to an amount 0.5 percentage points less than its average price increase during 1976 and 1977. Numerous exceptions were permitted. To illustrate, the prices of agricultural goods, industrial raw materials, and internationally traded goods were not subject to the standard. Alternative standards were also specified for firms that experienced large, uncontrolled cost increases (examples: energy and raw materials costs).

The basic first-year pay standard suggested that the average annual increase in compensation (which included fringe benefits) should not exceed 7 percent. Once again, however, numerous exceptions were permitted. For example, legally mandated labor costs, such as employer contributions to social security, were exempt from the pay standard. Workers earning less than $4.00 per hour on October 1, 1978, were also exempt.

Although these standards were supposed to be voluntary, the government announced that firms that failed to comply would be punished in various ways, ranging from publication of a list of noncomplying firms to the withholding of large federal contracts.[38]

Despite the implementation of the program, the inflation rate continued to accelerate. In 1979, the IPD increased at an 8.9 percent rate. In 1980, the increase was even greater, 9.0 percent. Members of the administration claimed that inflation would have been even worse in the absence of the program.[39] Even so, support of the program on the part of the administration waned. In the last *Economic Report of the President* issued by the Carter administration, it is stated that after two years of operation "there seems to be general agreement that the current pay and price standards could not continue to be effective if simply extended in their present form. Workers and firms no longer appear to be willing to moderate wage and price rises in the expectation that the standards will restrain inflation."[40] With the advent of the Reagan administration in 1981, the program died quietly.

INCOMES POLICY AND THE U.S. EXPERIENCE

Attempts to restrain money wages and prices through the incomes policy approach have not been very successful in the United States. There is some evidence to support the opinion that the wage–price guideposts of the 1960s slowed the rates of increase of money wages and prices. There is also evidence to the contrary. Consequently, we cannot be certain as to the effects of the guideposts on money wages and prices. We do know, however, that the guideposts broke down when inflationary pressure became more intense. The experience with the pay and price standards of the Carter administration was similar. It may be, as the administration claimed, that the standards initially kept the inflation rate from rising as rapidly as it otherwise would have. Even so, the inflation rate accelerated throughout the period and the program collapsed.

In regard to the wage–price controls of the early 1970s, most of the evidence suggests that controls reduced the rates of increase of the CPI and the private nonfarm deflator during the Phase I–Phase II period. These reductions, however, were offset by increases during the Phase III–Phase IV period. Even during the Phase I–Phase II period, little or no evidence suggested that the controls reduced the rates of increase of money wages and the WPI. United States experience is not atypical. Other countries have had, at best, limited success with the incomes policy approach.

Although the Economic Stabilization Program was generally ineffective, distortions occurred in the lumber, oil, and several other industries.[41] During Phase II, the lumber industry was experiencing large increases in demand for its products. It was subject to controls, however, and prices were not allowed to increase to their equilibrium levels. To a large extent, the lumber industry managed to evade the controls. The controls did, however, have an undesirable effect on the allocation of resources.

According to "unconfirmed reports," lumber producers used a number of devices to evade the controls.[42] First, the dimensions of lumber products were reduced as a means to obtain disguised price increases. Second, since the regulations permitted normal markups at each stage of distribution, lumber was shipped from one wholesaler to another in order to obtain higher prices. Third, the regulations also permitted higher prices to be charged when additional services were performed. Plywood manufacturers reportedly performed the "service" of cutting 1/8 inch off plywood sheets, thereby enabling them to sell the sheets at substantially higher prices. Fourth, since imports were not subject to controls, producers in the Pacific Northwest exported lumber to Canada and reimported it, enabling them to charge much higher prices. Finally, under the regulations, some products were more profitable to produce than others. Consequently, producers concentrated their efforts on the more profitable items while curtailing their production of other items. For example, based upon the regulations, it was, at least for a time, more profitable to make two-by-fours and less profitable to make boards. Thus, a shortage of boards developed.

From December 1971 to December 1972, the lumber and wood products component of the WPI increased by about 13 percent. The actual price increase, however, may have been much greater. The WPI is based on price information obtained from firms. Under the circumstances, producers had little incentive to report prices accurately to a government agency.

The degree to which inequities arose under the Economic Stabilization Program is hard to gauge because the phases were short and evasion was possible. Nevertheless, inequities may have existed under the provisions of the program. There was differential treatment of firms and industries. Manufacturing firms were subject to a different set of regulations than firms engaged in wholesale and retail trade, with the latter subjected to greater restraint. Regulations applying to other sectors varied also. Perhaps the differential regulations were justified on economic grounds. Lanzillotti, Hamilton, and Roberts charge, however, that the Cost of Living Council made a number of politically motivated decisions. One may doubt whether regulations were based entirely on economic analysis.

Inequities may have arisen from other sources. Because of the term limit pricing agreements, multiproduct firms had a better opportunity to exploit monopoly positions during Phase II than single product firms. Inequities may also have arisen owing to the differential requirements for requesting and reporting price and wage increases. Presumably firms and unions were subject to the same regulations governing price and wage increases (within the various sectors). The largest firms and unions, however, had to obtain prior approval for price and wage increases. In contrast, medium-sized firms and unions had to report price and wage increases; smaller firms and unions were expected only to maintain records which could be audited. Given the differential requirements, differential responses in terms of price and wage increases may have occurred. To the degree that size and monopoly power are positively correlated, a differential response may be desirable. It is unlikely, however, that the correlation is perfect.

As mentioned earlier, the government used fewer people to administer the Economic Stabilization Program than it had employed for similar purposes during World War II and the Korean War. In terms of dollars, direct outlays by the federal government for the Economic Stabilization Program amounted to $56.3 million in fiscal 1972 and $68.8 million in fiscal 1973. The fiscal years 1972 and 1973 covered Phases I and II plus part of Phase III. "Other" governmental costs were estimated to be less than $2 million for the controls period.[43] To these costs must be added those incurred by firms and unions in complying with the program. Lanzillotti, Hamilton, and Roberts estimated this at approximately $700 million.

In total, the explicit and implicit outlays for the program (approximately $800 million) appear modest when compared to gross national product.[44] On the other hand, so were the accomplishments. The reductions in the rate of increase in the CPI and private nonfarm deflator during the Phase I–Phase II period were not dramatic and proved to be temporary. Proponents of the incomes policy approach claim that one reason for the lack of success of the program was the administration's lack of commitment to controls. That may be true; had the commitment been greater, however, the costs of administering the program would have been greater. As supervision increases, moreover, firms will spend more on attempting to evade the controls. Similarly, if controls are to be so administered as to avoid a misallocation of resources and inequities, more resources must be devoted to the program.

Various provisions of the Economic Stabilization Program infringed upon what many persons consider the rights of citizens.[45] Labor, management, and the public at large had no opportunity to register their views concerning the design of the program before the imposition of the Phase I freeze. When the freeze was imposed in August 1971, wage increases previously negotiated in good faith and included in presumably legal and binding contracts were prohibited from going into effect. Also, although the general provisions of the program were specified in various executive orders, the Cost of Living Council had considerable discretion. As previously indicated, some of its decisions may have been politically motivated.

To sum up, the Economic Stabilization Program was not very effective in restraining money wages and prices. Therefore, the distortions and inequities resulting from the program were less serious than they would have been under a more effective program. Because the program was seen as temporary, the costs of administering it were not large, at least compared to GNP. In light of the problems associated with the program, including its effectiveness, the Economic Stabilization Program died quietly on April 30, 1974.

OTHER INCOMES POLICY APPROACHES

The previous sections dealt almost exclusively with wage–price guideposts and controls. Recently, several other approaches have received attention, at least in part, because of disenchantment with the guideposts-controls approaches.

The Wallich–Weintraub Proposal

As discussed earlier, Wallich and Weintraub attribute inflation to excessive wage settlements.[46] To discourage such settlements, they propose a *tax-based incomes policy* (TIP). Under this policy, the corporate income tax would be increased for firms granting wage increases deemed to be excessive.

Wallich and Weintraub argue that the basic problem is the monopoly power of labor unions. Since labor unions are part of the institutional framework of society, they argue, little can be done directly to reduce their monopoly power. Consequently, these economists propose measures designed to stiffen management resistance to inflationary wage settlements. As matters now stand, they claim, management prefers to accept those settlements and pass on the costs in the form of higher prices rather than to endure costly strikes. They suggest that the corporate tax rate be increased for firms which agree to inflationary wage settlements. This approach would not prohibit such settlements. It would make them more costly.

To illustrate, suppose a firm's corporate tax liability under ordinary circumstances is $5 million. To determine whether the firm's tax liability is to be increased, the average wage must be determined and compared to the average wage in the previous year. The average wage may be calculated by dividing the firm's wage bill (total amount paid in wages and salaries) by the number of workers employed by the firm. Assume, for the moment, that it is $10,500 for the year. If the average wage for the previous year was $10,000, the new wage is 5 percent greater than last year's. If a 5 percent increase in wages is permissible, no additional taxes would be levied upon the firm. Suppose, however, the average wage was $11,000. Assuming the wage was $10,000 in the previous year, the wage increase is now 10 percent. As a consequence, a 10 percent tax, say, would be levied upon the firm, making its tax liability $5.5 million rather than $5 million.

Wallich and Weintraub believe the TIP approach offers a number of advantages. First, they think it would be effective in combating inflation. Second, they claim that it is less likely to result in a misallocation of resources than wage and price controls. With this plan, the market system is retained. Firms are not prohibited from granting wage increases greater than the norm, although it would be more costly for them to do so. Third, they argue that it would be simple and relatively inexpensive to administer. Weintraub, for example, claims that it would require only a few more calculations by firms based upon data already available. Similarly, only a few extra lines need be added to IRS forms.

Although the TIP approach is interesting, it may be criticized on various grounds. First, the approach is based upon the notion that labor unions cause inflation. As discussed in Chapter 13, this is questionable. Even if it is conceded that unions do cause inflation, they are not the only source of inflation. Second, the TIP approach may be less easy to administer than Wallich and Weintraub think.[47] For example, some distinction must be made between full-time and part-time employees. If the average wage is computed by dividing the wage bill by the number of employees, firms have an incentive to hire part-time employees in place of full-time employees so as to reduce the average wage.

Third, the TIP approach is unlikely to get either labor or management support. Labor is likely to oppose TIP because it discourages large wage settlements but does not discourage increases in other forms of income. On the other hand, management may be opposed because firms must pay the tax. Experience with incomes policy in Western Europe suggests that such policies break down when one or more of the parties withdraws its support. Based on that experience, it is unlikely that the TIP approach would be successful.

Okun's Proposal

Arthur M. Okun has also offered a plan based on the tax system.[48] Under the plan, firms and workers would receive benefits through the tax system if they participated in the anti-inflationary program. To qualify, a firm must agree at the beginning of the year not to increase the average wage of its employees by more than 6 percent and not to increase the average of its prices by more than 4 percent (a dollar-for-dollar pass-through of nonlabor costs would be permitted). In return, the firm would get a tax rebate equal to 5 percent of its tax liability on domestic operating profits. Employees of the firm would get a tax rebate equal to 1.5 percent of their wage income, with a maximum of $225 per person. Participation in the program would be voluntary. At the end of the year, each participating firm would file a statement of compliance with the IRS.

For various reasons, Okun's plan may be more palatable to labor and management than that of Wallich and Weintraub. It emphasizes rewards through the tax system rather than penalties. It offers benefits to both labor and management. Finally, participation in the program is voluntary.

Although labor and management may find the program more acceptable, it does have some disadvantages. First, since only a single cutoff exists with regard to permissible rates of increase in wages and prices, there is no reward for minimizing the rates of increase and no penalty attached for missing them badly. Thus, there is nothing to prevent a firm from granting large wage and price increases in one year and small ones the next year in order to qualify for the program during the second year. Also, from an administrative standpoint, the plan presents many problems.[49] There is, for example, the previously discussed problem of part-time workers. Other problems include those related to the pass-through of nonlabor costs and fringe benefits. Finally, this plan, like the Wallich–Weintraub plan, will break down if inflationary pressure becomes intense. For example, if the money supply increases rapidly, few firms will be willing to participate in the program recommended by Okun.

CONCLUDING REMARKS

Wage–price guideposts and controls have not worked very well in this country. Similar programs in other countries have not been very successful either. Yet the advocates of this approach are not deterred. They assert that if new programs, free of the defects of previous programs, were put into effect, full employment and price stability could both be achieved with little or no cost to society in terms of distortions and inequities. Others claim that more innovative forms of incomes policy (example, TIP) are necessary to achieve full employment and price stability.

In the author's opinion, the various forms of incomes policy are unlikely to achieve those admirable goals. In the terminology of earlier chapters, a fundamental problem exists; the natural rate of unemployment is greater than the rate which the proponents of the incomes policy approach deem socially acceptable. To achieve a "socially acceptable" unemployment rate, they propose expansionary fiscal and monetary policies. To restrain prices, they advocate an incomes policy approach. If the unemployment rate falls below the natural rate, however, inflation tends to accelerate and it becomes increasingly difficult to restrain prices. Moreover, insofar as the authorities do succeed in suppressing inflation, they will cause distortions in the allocation of resources and inequities. Eventually, the controls will be abandoned.

The only satisfactory way to deal with the problem is by policies designed to reduce the natural rate of unemployment. These policies were outlined in Chapter 15. Proponents of the incomes policy approach will object because they promise relief only in the long run. Given the theoretical objections to, and past experience with, incomes policies, however, policies designed to reduce the natural rate of unemployment appear to be the only way to achieve a "socially acceptable" rate of unemployment and price stability.

NOTES

1. Much of the impetus for wage and price guideposts stemmed from the inflation the United States experienced from 1955 through 1957. Prices increased in spite of excess productive capacity and unemployment. Some economists attributed the inflation to monopolistic practices by firms and unions; others argued that other factors were responsible. Whatever the cause, members of the Kennedy administration became convinced that monopolistic practices by business and labor would thwart attempts to achieve full employment and price stability through expansionary fiscal and monetary policies.

2. Robert Lekachman, "The Inevitability of Controls," *Challenge,* 17 (November–December 1974), 6–8. Henry C. Wallich has argued that without an incomes policy we have only one instrument—the management of aggregate demand—to achieve two goals: full employment and price stability. Hence we cannot reach these goals without a second instrument—an incomes policy. Henry C. Wallich, "Alternative Strategies for Price and Wage Controls, *Journal of Economic Issues,* 6 (December 1972), 89–104.

3. Gardner Ackley, "An Incomes Policy for the 1970's," *Review of Economics and Statistics,* 54 (August 1972), 218.

4. Henry C. Wallich, "Alternative Strategies for Price and Wage Controls"; Sidney Weintraub, "An Incomes Policy to Stop Inflation," *Lloyds Bank Review,* no. 99 (January 1971), 1–12; and Henry C. Wallich and Sidney Weintraub, "A Tax-Based Incomes Policy," *Journal of Economic Issues,* 5 (June 1971), 1–19. See also Sidney Weintraub, *Capitalism's Inflation and Unemployment Crisis: Beyond Monetarism and Keynesianism* (Reading, Mass.: Addison-Wesley Publishing Co., Inc., 1978).

5. See, for example, Lekachman, "The Inevitability of Controls," p. 7. Gottfried Haberler is a noteworthy exception. He agrees that the monopoly power of labor unions is an important source of inflation, but rather than relying on incomes policy, he proposes to reduce their power. Gottfried Haberler, "Incomes Policy and Inflation: Some Further Reflections," *American Economic Review,* 62 (May 1972), 240.

6. Milton Friedman, "What Price Guideposts?" in *Guideposts, Informal Controls, and the Market Place*, eds. George P. Shultz and Robert Z. Aliber (Chicago: University of Chicago Press, 1966), pp. 17–39.

7. So far as "visible" industries are monopolistic and "invisible" ones are not, the stricter supervision may be desirable. The correlation between degree of visibility and degree of monopoly power is not perfect.

8. Robert F. Lanzillotti, Mary T. Hamilton, and R. Blaine Roberts, *Phase II in Review: The Price Commission Experience* (Washington, D.C.: The Brookings Institution, 1975), p. 52. Lanzillotti and Hamilton were members of the Price Commission; Roberts was an economist on its staff.

9. For a discussion of U.S. wage–price controls during World War II, see Colin D. Campbell, ed., *Wage–Price Controls in World War II, United States and Germany* (Washington, D.C.: American Enterprise Institute, 1971). For discussions of incomes policies under the Truman and Eisenhower administrations, see Craufurd D. Goodwin and R.

Stanley Herren, "The Truman Administration: Problems and Policies Unfold," and H. Scott Gordon, "The Eisenhower Administration: The Doctrine of Shared Responsibility," in *Exhortation and Controls: The Search for a Wage–Price Policy 1945–1971*, ed. Craufurd D. Goodwin (Washington, D.C.: The Brookings Institution, 1975), pp. 9–134.

10. John Sheahan has argued that the guideposts were not a radical innovation, since President Eisenhower and members of his administration frequently appealed to business and labor for responsible behavior. John Sheahan, *The Wage–Price Guideposts* (Washington, D.C.: The Brookings Institution, 1967), p. 16.

11. For a more detailed discussion, see Sheahan, ibid., or Thomas G. Moore, *U.S. Incomes Policy, Its Rationale and Development* (Washington, D.C.: American Enterprise Institute, 1971).

12. George L. Perry, "Wages and the Guideposts," *American Economic Review*, 57 (September 1967), 897–904.

13. Paul S. Anderson, "Wages and the Guideposts: Comment," *American Economic Review*, 59 (June 1969), 351–54; Michael L. Wachter, "Wages and the Guideposts: Comment," ibid., 354–58; Adrian W. Throop, "Wages and the Guideposts: Comment," ibid., 358–65.

14. George L. Perry, "Wages and the Guideposts: Reply," *American Economic Review*, 59 (June 1969), 365–70. Perry's results were also questioned by N. J. Simler and Alfred Tella. If Perry's model were modified to take account of unreported labor reserves, they argued, and if data on wages and salaries per man-hour for the private nonfarm sector were utilized, there was no evidence to show that the guideposts had an effect on money wages. N. J. Simler and Alfred Tella, "Labor Reserves and the Phillips Curve," *Review of Economics and Statistics*, 50 (February 1968), 32–49.

15. In a study which included price expectations as an independent variable, Robert J. Gordon concluded that the guideposts were ineffective in restraining money wages. Robert J. Gordon, "Inflation in Recession and Recovery," *Brookings Papers on Economic Activity*, no. 1 (1971), 105–58.

16. Arnold R. Weber, *In Pursuit of Price Stability: The Wage–Price Freeze of 1971* (Washington, D.C.: The Brookings Institution, 1973), p. 9. Weber was executive director of the Cost of Living Council, the body charged with overall responsibility for administering the freeze.

17. The act did not specifically cover interest, dividends, and profits. It was assumed, therefore, that the president had no power to control those forms of income. Nevertheless, financial institutions were urged not to raise interest rates during the freeze period; corporations were asked to limit their dividends to the levels existing immediately before the freeze. Corporations which did not cooperate were strongly urged to comply. No attempt was made to deal with profits either through direct controls or exhortation. This decision was apparently taken because the freeze was temporary and profits hard to handle.

18. Ceilings were to be determined using the 30-day period immediately before the freeze or, if no transactions had occurred in that period, the nearest preceding period in which transactions did occur. This formula was modified in several instances: first, for a product with seasonal characteristics, the ceiling price could be determined by using either a 30-day base period or the last relevant seasonal period. Second, in certain cases, use of a truncated period was allowed. If an increase in wages or published prices occurred within the 30-day base period, a new base period was defined as the time between the establishment of the new wage structure or the publication of the new price list and August 15. For example, if wages increased on August 11, the higher wages would prevail during the freeze period although there was no "substantial volume of transactions" for the normal 30-day period.

19. To aid in enforcement, Executive Order 11615 specified: "Each person engaged in the business of selling or providing commodities or services shall maintain available for public inspection a record of the highest prices or rents charged for such or similar commodities or services during the 30-day period ending August 14, 1971."

20. In applying the 10 percent rule, the relevant unit was generally defined as the most limited unit (example, a single plant) that could be identified on the basis of established practices as of August 15, 1971. For a discussion, see Weber, *In Pursuit of Price Stability,* pp. 58–59.

21. The Cost of Living Council was composed of high-level administration officials; Price Commission and Pay Board members were drawn from outside the administration. The Price Commission consisted of a chairman and six members. Membership of the Pay Board was originally set at fifteen, with equal representation from labor, management, and the public.

22. For more detail, see Daniel J. B. Mitchell, "Phase II Wage Controls," *Industrial and Labor Relations Review*, 27 (April 1974), 351–61.

23. *Economic Report of the President, 1974* (Washington, D.C.: Government Printing Office, 1974), p. 90.

24. Ibid.

25. For discussions, see Barry Bosworth, "The Current Inflation: Malign Neglect?" *Brookings Papers on Economic Activity*, no. 1 (1973), 263–83; William Poole, "Wage–Price Controls: Where Do We Go from Here?" *Brookings Papers on Economic Activity,* no. 1 (1973), 285–99.

26. New regulations had previously been implemented for farm products (July 18) and the health industry (July 19).

27. Since data for the IPD are available only on a quarterly basis, most of the ensuing discussion is in terms of the CPI and wholesale price index (WPI).

28. Money wages were measured by hourly earnings for workers in the private non-farm economy; prices were measured by the private nonfarm deflator. His model was estimated on the basis of quarterly data. Robert J. Gordon, "Wage–Price Controls and the Shifting Phillips Curve," *Brookings Papers on Economic Activity,* no. 2 (1972), 385–421. For a summary of the early studies of the effectiveness of the program, see John Kraft, "The Effectiveness of the Economic Stabilization Program: A Summary of the Evidence," in *Analysis of Inflation*, ed. Paul H. Earl (Lexington, Mass.: D. C. Heath & Co., 1975), pp. 197–209. For other studies, see *Analysis of Inflation: 1965–1974,* Studies in Income and Wealth, 42, ed. Joel Popkin (New York: National Bureau of Economic Research, 1977).

29. In the Askin–Kraft study, the relevant time span was from the third quarter of 1971 through the fourth quarter of 1972. Their money wage and price variables are the same as Gordon's. A. Bradley Askin and John Kraft, *Econometric Wage and Price Models* (Lexington, Mass.: D. C. Heath & Co., 1974).

30. Daniel J. B. Mitchell, among others, has argued that studies based on aggregate data suffer from a number of deficiencies. For example, relatively few major union contracts expired during 1972. Hence, many of the wage increases which occurred during 1972 were based on settlements reached before the imposition of controls. Mitchell is not surprised, therefore, that the studies, based on aggregate data show little or no reduction in the rate of increase of money wages during the Phase I–Phase II period. He claims that the Phase II controls had a significant impact on new settlements. Mitchell, "Phase II Wage Controls," pp. 351–75.

31. Lanzillotti and others, *Phase II in Review*, p. 111. The authors also reported on the quarterly models developed by the Price Commission. These models formed the basis of the Askin–Kraft study.

32. In still another study of the effectiveness of the controls program, Edgar L. Feige and Douglas K. Pearce estimated the increases in money wages, the CPI, and the WPI for the Phase I–Phase II period based entirely on the past history of the variables. They then compared the actual and estimated values and concluded that the rates of increase in money wages and the CPI were reduced by about 1 and 1.3 percentage points, respectively, during the Phase I–Phase II period. But the rate of increase in the WPI rose by almost 2 percentage points during the period. Edgar L. Feige and Douglas K. Pearce, "The Wage–Price Control Experiment—Did it Work?" *Challenge,* 16 (July–August 1973), 40–44.

33. Robert J. Gordon, "Can the Inflation of the 1970s Be Explained?" *Brookings Papers on Economic Activity,* no. 1 (1977), 253–77.

34. For additional support based on an alternative approach, see Michael L. Wachter, "Phase II, Cost-Push Inflation, and Relative Wages," *American Economic Review,* 64 (June 1974), 482–91.

35. Barry Bosworth, "The Inflation Problem during Phase III," *American Economic Review,* 64 (May 1974), 98.

36. For discussions, see Bosworth, "The Current Inflation: Malign Neglect?"; and Poole, "Wage–Price Controls" David Laidler has argued that the inflation in 1973 was predictable, given the large increases in the money supply in earlier years. David Laidler, "The 1974 Report of the President's Council of Economic Advisers: The Control of Inflation and the Future of the International Monetary System," *American Economic Review,* 64 (September 1974), 535–43.

37. See, for example, Council on Wage and Price Stability, *Pay and Price Standards: A Compendium* (Washington, D.C.: U.S. Government Printing Office, June 1979).

38. For discussions of the program, see Paul Bennett and Ellen Greene, "Effectiveness of the First-Year Pay and Price Standards," Federal Reserve Bank of New York, *Quarterly Review,* 4 (Winter 1979–80), 50–53; Robert Higgs, "Carter's Wage–Price Guidelines: A Review of the First Year," *Policy Review,* 11 (Winter 1980), 97–113; and Jack A. Meyer, "Wage and Benefit Trends under the Carter Administration Guidelines," in *Contemporary Economic Problems 1980,* ed. William Fellner (Washington D.C.: American Enterprise Institute, 1980), pp. 193–226; as well as various issues of the *Economic Report of the President.*

39. Some evidence exists to support this view. For example, see John B. Hagens and R. Robert Russell, "Testing for the Effectiveness of Wage–Price Controls: An Application to the Carter Program," *American Economic Review,* 75 (March 1985), 191–207.

40. *Economic Report of the President 1981* (Washington, D.C.: U.S. Government Printing Office, 1981), p. 59.

41. For examples of distortions during the guideposts and standards eras, see Friedman, "What Price Guideposts?" and Higgs. "Carter's Wage–Price Guidelines."

42. Poole, "Wage–Price Controls," p. 292. For discussions of the impact of controls on the allocation of resources in the oil industry and the difficulties of devising a flexible system of wage and price controls, see pp. 292–99.

43. Lanzillotti and others, *Phase II in Review,* p. 191.

44. The costs do not include those associated with shortages and anticipated shortages. For example, with regulation of gasoline prices, consumers in many localities were forced to wait in line for gasoline and/or fill their tanks more often in anticipation of shortages.

45. For discussions of various infringements during the wage–price guideposts era, see Shultz and Aliber, eds., *Guideposts, Informal Controls and the Market Place.*

46. The following discussion is largely based on Weintraub, *Capitalism's Inflation and Unemployment Crisis.* (For additional references, see note 4.)

47. For a discussion, see Gardner Ackley, "Okun's New Tax-Based Incomes-Policy

Proposal," *Economic Outlook USA,* 5 (Winter 1978), 8–9. Weintraub, *Capitalism's Infla-tion,* addresses some of the points.

48. In addition, Okun suggested several other policies designed to promote full em-ployment and price stability. Arthur M. Okun, "The Great Stagflation Swamp," *Challenge,* 20 (November–December 1977), 6–13. For still another approach, see Abba P. Lerner, "Stagflation—Its Cause and Cure," *Challenge,* 20 (September–October 1977), 14–19.

49. For a discussion, see Ackley, "Okun's New Tax-Based Incomes-Policy Proposal."

REVIEW QUESTIONS

1. It is claimed that the case for incomes policy is based on the view that firms and labor unions have the power to "administer" prices and money wages. Discuss.

2. Why do proponents of the incomes policy approach feel that it is more urgent to adopt these policies now than in the past?

3. Outline the case against wage and price controls.

4. In the 1960s, the United States experimented with wage–price guideposts. Outline the major elements of this approach. Do you believe it would work today? Defend your answer.

5. Outline the advantages and disadvantages of a wage–price freeze in terms of an approach to incomes policy.

6. Discuss, in general terms, the effects of the Economic Stabilization Program upon the rates of increase of money wages and prices.

7. Suppose the Economic Stabilization Program had been more successful in restraining money wages and prices. What problems would this have created for the economy?

8. Outline and critically evaluate the Wallich–Weintraub approach to incomes policy.

9. List the advantages and disadvantages of Okun's proposal.

10. Suppose it is not possible to achieve price stability with a "socially acceptable" rate of unemployment with either monetary and fiscal policy or incomes policy. What policies would you recommend to achieve the goals? Defend your answer.

SUGGESTED READING

CLAUDON, MICHAEL P., and RICHARD R. CORNWALL, (eds.), *An Incomes Policy for the United States: New Approaches.* Boston: Martinus Nijhoff Publishing, 1981.

COLANDER, DAVID C., (ed.), *Incentive-Based Incomes Policies.* Cambridge, Mass.: Ballin-ger Publishing Co., 1986.

FRIEDMAN, MILTON, "What Price Guideposts?" in *Guidelines, Informal Controls, and the Market Place*, eds. George P. Shultz and Robert Z. Aliber, pp. 17–39. Chicago: University of Chicago Press, 1966.

GOODWIN, CRAUFURD D., (ed.), *Exhortation and Controls: The Search for a Wage–Price Policy 1945–1971*. Washington, D.C.: The Brookings Institution, 1975.

LANZILLOTTI, ROBERT F., MARY T. HAMILTON, and R. BLAINE ROBERTS, *Phase II in Review: The Price Commission Experience*. Washington, D.C.: The Brookings Institution, 1975.

LERNER, ABBA P., and DAVID C. COLANDER, *MAP: A Market Anti-Inflation Plan*. New York: Harcourt Brace Jovanovich, Inc., 1980.

MOORE, THOMAS G., *U.S. Incomes Policy, Its Rationale and Development*. Washington, D.C.: American Enterprise Institute, 1971.

OKUN, ARTHUR M., and GEORGE L. PERRY, (eds.), Special Issue on Innovative Policies to Slow Inflation, *Brookings Papers on Economic Activity*, no. 2 (1978).

ROCKOFF, HUGH, *Drastic Measures: A History of Wage and Price Controls in the United States*. New York: Cambridge University Press, 1984.

SHEAHAN, JOHN, *The Wage–Price Guideposts*. Washington, D.C.: The Brookings Institution, 1967.

WEBER, ARNOLD R., *In Pursuit of Price Stability: The Wage–Price Freeze of 1971*. Washington, D.C.: The Brookings Institution, 1973.

———, and DANIEL J. B. MITCHELL, *The Pay Board's Progress: Wage Controls in Phase II*. Washington, D.C.: The Brookings Institution, 1978.

WEINTRAUB, SIDNEY, *Capitalism's Inflation and Unemployment Crisis: Beyond Monetarism and Keynesianism*. Reading, Mass.: Addison-Wesley Publishing Co., Inc., 1978.

THE INDEX
NUMBER PROBLEM

T o illustrate the compilation of real GNP, Chapter 2 presented a simple example. In that example, the production of both shirts and sweaters doubled between 1975 and 1985 and the prices of both goods increased by 50 percent. By assuming that 1975 prices prevailed in both 1975 and 1985, estimates of real GNP were obtained which showed that production doubled from 1975 to 1985. The same indicated increase in production is obtained by assuming that 1985 prices prevailed in both 1975 and 1985. Since 1985 prices are higher than 1975 prices, real GNP appears to be greater in both years, $16.5 million in 1975 and $33 million in 1985; as before, however, the estimates suggest that production doubled.

Since the change in production is the same, there is no problem in estimating real GNP in the example or, for that matter, any example, provided that the production and prices of the various goods change in the same proportions. If production and prices fail to change in the same proportions, a problem exists, *the index number problem*. To illustrate, suppose the example in Chapter 2 is modified so as to allow differential rates of change in production and prices. The data are shown in Table A1-1. In the example, shirt production doubles from 1975 to 1985,

TABLE A1-1 Hypothetical data for the computation of real gross national product

	1975 Output	1975 Prices	1985 Output	1985 Prices
Shirts	1 million	$10	2 million	$10
Sweaters	50,000	20	50,000	40

whereas sweater production is unchanged. Shirt prices are unchanged and sweater prices double.

Suppose GNP is measured in 1975 prices. According to Table A1-2, GNP in 1975 prices is $11 million in 1975 and $21 million in 1985. To facilitate the comparison of real GNP in the two years, the data are expressed in index form by dividing the $11 million and $21 million by $11 million and multiplying the results by 100. The index numbers are 100 for 1975 and 191 for 1985, indicating that production increased by 91 percent between 1975 and 1985.

Instead of using 1975 prices, suppose 1985 prices are used. The results are shown in Table A1-3. In terms of 1985 prices, GNP is $12 million in 1975 and $22 million in 1985. The corresponding index numbers are 100 and 183, suggesting that production increased only 83 percent rather than 91 percent. Which answer is correct? Did production increase by 91 percent or 83 percent? Either answer may be regarded as correct; different weighting procedures produce different results. In the example, use of 1975 prices as weights results in a higher indicated increase in production than use of 1985 prices because 1975 prices place more emphasis on shirt production and shirt production increased more rapidly. This can be seen by examining the ratio of shirt to sweater prices in the two years. In 1975 the ratio was $10 to $20 (or 1 to 2); in 1980 it was $10 to $40 (or 1 to 4). Hence, selection of 1975 prices as weights puts more emphasis on shirts, the good whose production increased more rapidly over the period. Such a selection produces a higher measured increase in real output. Selection of 1985 prices as weights puts more emphasis on sweaters, the good whose production did not increase and results in a lower indicated increase in real output.

TABLE A1-2 Computation of gross national product as measured in 1975 prices

	1975 Output	1975 Prices	1975 Output Measured In 1975 Prices	1985 Output	1975 Prices	1985 Output Measured In 1975 Prices
Shirts	1 million	$10	$10 million	2 million	$10	$20 million
Sweaters	50,000	20	1 million	50,000	20	1 million
Total			$11 million			$21 million
Index			100			191

TABLE A1-3   Computation of gross national product as measured in 1985 prices

	1975 Output	1985 Prices	1975 Output Measured In 1985 Prices	1985 Output	1985 Prices	1985 Output Measured In 1985 Prices
Shirts	1 million	$10	$10 million	2 million	$10	$20 million
Sweaters	50,000	40	2 million	50,000	40	2 million
Total			$12 million			$22 million
Index			100			183

An index with base period prices as weights (1975 in the example) is called a *Laspeyres index*; an index with terminal period prices as weights (1985 in the example) is referred to as a *Paasche index*. In equation form, the Laspeyres index is

$$100 \, \frac{\Sigma p_{i1} q_{i2}}{\Sigma p_{i1} q_{i1}},$$

whereas the Paasche index is

$$100 \, \frac{\Sigma p_{i2} q_{i2}}{\Sigma p_{i2} q_{i1}},$$

where p_i represents the price of the ith commodity, q the quantity of the ith commodity, the subscripts 1 and 2 represent the base and terminal periods, respectively, and i equals 1, 2, . . ., n. In terms of the example, the Laspeyres and Paasche indexes are

$$100 \left[\frac{\$10(2,000,000) \, + \, \$20(50,000)}{\$10(1,000,000) \, + \, \$20(50,000)} \right] = 100 \left[\frac{\$21,000,000}{\$11,000,000} \right] = 191$$

and

$$100 \left[\frac{\$10(2,000,000) \, + \, \$40(50,000)}{\$10(1,000,000) \, + \, \$40(50,000)} \right] = 100 \left[\frac{\$22,000,000}{\$12,000,000} \right] = 183,$$

respectively.

In general (and in the example above), the Laspeyres index shows a greater measured increase in real output than does the Paasche index because the prices of goods experiencing rapid increases in production typically decrease *relative* to the prices of other goods.

As indicated, different weighting schemes result in different measured increases in real output. The same problem exists in the construction of price index numbers since either base or terminal period quantities may be used as weights. As before, the index with base period weights is called a Laspeyres index, while the index with terminal period weights is referred to as a Paasche index. In equation form, the Laspeyres and Paasche price indexes are

$$100 \, \frac{\Sigma p_{i2} q_{i1}}{\Sigma p_{i1} q_{i1}}$$

and

$$100 \, \frac{\Sigma p_{i2} q_{i2}}{\Sigma p_{i1} q_{i2}},$$

respectively. In terms of the example, the Laspeyres and Paasche price indexes are

$$100 \left[\frac{\$10(1,000,000) + \$40(50,000)}{\$10(1,000,000) + \$20(50,000)} \right] = 100 \left[\frac{\$12,000,000}{\$11,000,000} \right] = 109$$

and

$$100 \left[\frac{\$10(2,000,000) + \$40(50,000)}{\$10(2,000,000) + \$20(50,000)} \right] = 100 \left[\frac{\$22,000,000}{\$21,000,000} \right] = 105,$$

In the example, the measured increase in prices is greater when base period quantities are used as weights, as the use of 1975 quantities as weights places more emphasis on sweaters, and sweater prices increased more rapidly than shirt prices. This can be seen by examining the ratio of sweater to shirt production in the two years. In 1975, the ratio was 50,000 sweaters to 1 million shirts, a ratio of 1 to 20; in 1985, it was 50,000 to 2 million or 1 to 40. Hence, selection of 1975 quantities as weights places more emphasis on sweaters, the good whose price increased more rapidly over the period. Such a selection produces a higher indicated increase in prices over the period. Selection of 1985 quantities as weights places more emphasis on shirts, the good whose price did not increase, and results in a lower indicated increase in prices.

In general (and in the foregoing example), the Laspeyres index shows a greater indicated increase in prices than the Paasche index, since demand or consumption usually increases less rapidly for goods which have risen *relatively* more in price over the period.

There is no satisfactory theoretical solution to the index number problem.[1] Different weighting procedures yield different results. Base period weights are generally used because using terminal period weights requires recalculating the index numbers for all previous periods. Since the indexes have base period weights, the indicated increase in output or prices is likely to be greater than if the indexes were based on terminal period weights. A case in point is the consumer price index. That index utilizes base period weights. As prices increase, consumers substitute goods whose prices have increased less rapidly for goods whose prices have increased more rapidly. Since base period weights are utilized, however, the substitution is not reflected in the indexes. Consequently, the consumer price index shows a greater indicated increase in prices than if terminal period weights (which would reflect the substitution) were utilized. For this and other reasons, the consumer price index is not a good measure of cost of living. The consumer price index is discussed in more detail in Chapter 13.

NOTES

1. A third index is the *Fisher ideal index*; it is the geometric average of the Laspeyres and Paasche indexes. This index has a number of desirable properties, but it is rarely used because it requires computation of both the indexes. For a discussion of the index number problem, see Roy G. D. Allen, *Index Numbers in Theory and Practice* (Chicago: Aldine Publishing Company, 1975).

appendix 2
MULTIPLIER ANALYSIS, STABILITY, AND THE IS–LM MODEL

In this appendix, the government purchases and money supply multipliers are derived within the context of the IS–LM model.[1] The stability condition for the IS–LM model is also derived and its relationship to the multipliers discussed.

The model is as follows:

(A2-1) $$C = C(Y) \qquad (0 < C_y < 1),$$

(A2-2) $$I = I(Y, i) \qquad (I_y > 0, I_i < 0),$$

(A2-3) $$G = G_0,$$

(A2-4) $$\frac{Ms}{P} = \frac{Ms_0}{P_0},$$

(A2-5) $$\frac{Md}{P} = L(Y, i) \qquad (L_y > 0, L_i < 0).$$

The equilibrium conditions are

(A2-6) $$I + G = S,$$

(A2-7) $$\frac{Ms}{P} = \frac{Md}{P}.$$

This version of the IS–LM model differs from the version presented at the beginning of Chapter 9 in two respects. First, in accordance with the discussion in Chapter 6, investment is assumed to be a function of both income and the interest rate. Second, taxes have been omitted from the model. By deleting taxes, the analysis is simplified without altering the main thrust of the argument. In order to simplify the notation, partial derivatives such as $\partial I/\partial Y$ and $\partial I/\partial i$ are written as I_y and I_i, respectively.

THE GOVERNMENT PURCHASES AND MONEY SUPPLY MULTIPLIERS

To derive the government purchases and money supply multipliers, the behavioral equations, equations (A2-1) to (A2-5), are first substituted into the equilibrium conditions, equations (A2-6) and (A2-7), so that

(A2-8) $$I(Y, i) + G_0 = Y - C(Y),$$

and

(A2-9) $$\frac{Ms_0}{P_0} = L(Y, i).$$

Treating government purchases and the real money supply as variables, we now take the total differential of each equation to obtain

$$I_y dY + I_i di + dG = dY - C_y dY,$$

or, after rearranging terms and factoring,

(A2-10) $$(1 - C_y - I_y)dY - I_i di = dG,$$

and

(A2-11) $$L_y dY + L_i di = d(Ms/P).$$

In matrix notation, we have

$$\begin{pmatrix} (1 - C_y - I_y) & -I_i \\ L_y & L_i \end{pmatrix} \begin{pmatrix} dY \\ di \end{pmatrix} = \begin{pmatrix} dG \\ d(\text{Ms}/P) \end{pmatrix}.$$

Next, we solve for dY using Cramer's Rule

(A2-12) $\qquad dY = \dfrac{\begin{vmatrix} dG & -I_i \\ d(\text{Ms}/P) & L_i \end{vmatrix}}{\begin{vmatrix} (1 - C_y - I_y) & -I_i \\ L_y & L_i \end{vmatrix}} = \dfrac{L_i dG + I_i d(\text{Ms}/P)}{L_i(1 - C_y - I_y) + I_i L_y}.$

The coefficients for dG and $d(\text{Ms}/P)$ are the government purchases and real money supply multipliers, respectively. If $d(\text{Ms}/P)$ equals 0 and we divide by dG, we obtain

(A2-13) $\qquad \dfrac{dY}{dG} = \dfrac{L_i}{L_i(1 - C_y - I_y) + I_i L_y},$

the government purchases multiplier. Similarly, if dG equals 0 and we divide by $d(\text{Ms}/P)$, we obtain

(A2-14) $\qquad \dfrac{dY}{d(\text{Ms}/P)} = \dfrac{I_i}{L_i(1 - C_y - I_y) + I_i L_y},$

the real money supply multiplier.

Examination of the individual terms in the expression dY/dG suggests that the government purchases multipliers may be either positive or negative. In the multiplier, L_i is negative since an increase in the interest rate is assumed to reduce the amount of money demanded, whereas L_y is positive, since an increase in income is assumed to increase the amount of money demanded. Since C_y, the marginal propensity to consume, is assumed to be between 0 and 1, $1 - C_y$, the marginal propensity to save, is also between 0 and 1. The marginal propensity to invest, I_y, is also assumed to be positive. Finally, I_i is negative, since an increase in the interest rate is assumed to reduce investment. Since L_i is negative, the numerator of dY/dG is negative. For dY/dG to be positive, the denominator must also be negative. Since $I_i L_y$ is negative, and $(1 - C_y - I_y)$ may be either positive or negative, the denominator is negative, provided that $I_i L_y$ exceeds $L_i(1 - C_y - I_y)$ in absolute terms. As discussed later, the denominator is negative provided that the stability condition is met, and so we assume that dY/dG is positive.

Like the government purchases multiplier, the real money supply multiplier (see equation (A2-14)) may be either positive or negative. As before, the multiplier is positive provided I_iL_y exceeds $L_i(1 - C_y - I_y)$ in absolute terms; we assume this to be the case.

The magnitudes of the multipliers depend on each of their terms. To illustrate, if either the marginal propensity to consume, C_y, or the marginal propensity to invest, I_y, increases, the denominators are reduced and, therefore, the multipliers are increased. On the other hand, if L_y, a measure of the strength of the relationship between the amount of money demanded and income, increases, the denominators increase and the multipliers decrease.

In the cases just discussed, a change in one of the terms altered the magnitudes of the multipliers in the same direction. That is, both multipliers either increased or decreased. This is not the case when L_i, a measure of the strength of the relationship between the amount of money demanded and the interest rate, and I_i, a measure of the strength of the relationship between investment and the interest rate, change. A change in either L_i or I_i reduces one of the multipliers and increases the other. Consequently, L_i and I_i may be said to be the determinants of the relative effectiveness of fiscal and monetary policy. We argued that this was the case in Chapter 9, but, after deriving the government purchases and money supply multipliers, we can demonstrate it more formally.[2] Suppose we take the ratio of the government purchases multiplier to the real money supply multiplier. This ratio is L_i/I_i, obtained by dividing the right side of equation (A2-13) by the right side of equation (A2-14). An increase in L_i (in absolute terms) increases the ratio of the government purchases multiplier, indicating that fiscal policy is now relatively more effective. In contrast, an increase in I_i (in absolute terms) decreases the ratio, indicating that monetary policy is now relatively more effective.

STABILITY

We now wish to consider stability within the context of the IS–LM model. Equation (A2-8) represents the equation for the IS curve. The slope of the IS curve may be determined by first totally differentiating the equation to obtain

$$I_i di + I_y dY = dY - C_y dY.$$

After rearranging terms and dividing both sides of the equation by I_i and dY, we find

(A2-15)
$$\frac{di}{dY} = \frac{1 - C_y - I_y}{I_i}.$$

Thus, the slope of the IS curve is $(1 - C_y - I_y)/I_i$. Since $(1 - C_y - I_y)$ may be either positive or negative, the slope of the IS curve may be either positive or negative. If the marginal propensity to invest, I_y, equals 0, the slope of the IS curve is negative, since $1 - C_y$ is assumed to be positive and I_i is assumed to be negative.

The marginal propensity to invest was assumed to be 0 in Chapter 9, and so the IS curve was drawn with a negative slope in that chapter.

The slope of the LM curve may be obtained in a similar manner. Equation (A2-9) represents the equation for the LM curve. If equation (A2-9) is totally differentiated, we obtain

$$0 = L_i di + L_y dY$$

or, after rearranging terms and dividing both sides of the equation by L_i and dY, we have

(A2-16)
$$\frac{di}{dY} = -\frac{L_y}{L_i}.$$

Thus, the slope of the LM curve, di/dY, is $-L_y/L_i$. Since L_y/L_i is preceded by a minus sign and since L_y is assumed to be positive and L_i negative, the slope of the LM curve is positive.

Since the IS curve may be either positively or negatively sloped, three possibilities exist with regard to the slope of the IS curve vis-à-vis the slope of the LM curve (excluding the case where the slopes are equal). (1) The IS curve has a negative slope, which implies that the slope of the IS curve is less than the slope of the LM curve. (2) The IS curve has a positive slope, but its slope is less than that of the LM curve. (3) The IS curve has a positive slope and its slope is greater than that of the LM curve. Each possibility is now considered in order to determine the stability condition for the IS–LM model. For convenience, they are referred to as Cases I, II, and III, respectively.

Case I

In Case I, the IS curve is negatively sloped and the LM curve is positively sloped, as shown in Figure A2-1. If the initial LM curve is LM_0, the equilibrium levels of income and the interest rate are Y_0 and i_0, respectively. Next, suppose the money supply increases. With the increase in the money supply, the LM curve shifts to the right, and the new equilibrium levels of income and the interest rate are Y_1 and i_1, respectively. However, as discussed in Chapter 1, we cannot be certain that income and the interest rate gravitate to their new equilibrium levels until the underlying adjustment process is examined. For simplicity, we assume that the interest rate adjusts immediately to a discrepancy between the real amount of money supplied and the real amount of money demanded. Thus, if the real amount of money supplied is greater (less) than the real amount of money demanded, the interest rate decreases (increases) so as to eliminate the excess supply (demand). With regard to the product market, we assume that income increases (decreases) whenever investment plus government purchases, $I + G$, is greater (less) than saving, S.

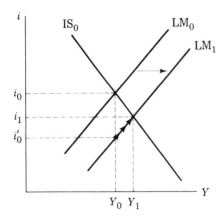

FIGURE A2-1

Stability and the IS–LM model: Case I

Given these assumptions, we are ready to trace the movements of income and the interest rate. Since the interest rate is assumed to adjust immediately, the initial effect of an increase in the money supply is a decrease in the interest rate to i_0' (see Figure A2-1). With the reduction in the interest rate to i_0', investment increases and $I + G$, originally equal to S at income Y_0 and interest rate i_0, now exceeds S. As a result, income increases. With the increase in income, more money is demanded and the interest rate increases. Since, however, the interest rate is assumed to adjust immediately to a disturbance in the money market, adjustment takes place along the LM curve. Eventually, income and the interest rate increase until they reach their new equilibrium levels. Thus, given the assumptions with regard to the adjustment process, income and the interest rate eventually gravitate to their new equilibrium levels and so a stable equilibrium exists.

Case II

In Case II, the IS curve is positively sloped, but its slope is less than the slope of the LM curve. This situation is depicted in Figure A2-2. Assuming the initial LM curve is LM_0, the equilibrium levels of income and the interest rate are Y_0 and i_0, respectively. If the money supply increases, the LM curve shifts to the right and the new equilibrium levels of income and the interest rate are Y_1 and i_1, respectively. To determine whether income and the interest rate gravitate to their new equilibrium levels, we trace the movements of income and the interest rate in the same manner as before. With the increase in the money supply and shift in the LM curve, the interest rate drops immediately to i_0'. With the reduction in the interest rate, investment increases and $I + G$ now exceeds S. Consequently, income increases. As before, the increase in income gives rise to an increase in the amount of money demanded, and so the interest rate increases. The adjustment continues along the LM curve until the new equilibrium combination of income and the interest rate, (Y_1, i_1), is attained. Since income and the interest rate eventually gravitate to their new equilibrium levels, a stable equilibrium exists.

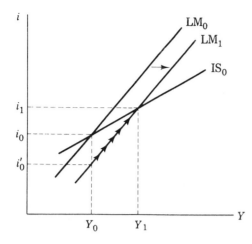

FIGURE A2-2

Stability and the IS–LM model: Case II

Thus, a stable equilibrium exists in both Cases I and II. Before examining Case III, we note several differences between Cases I and II. In Case I, the interest rate decreases from i_0 to i_1 in response to an increase in the money supply. In Case II, however, the interest rate, despite an initial decrease, increases from i_0 to i_1. The reason for the increase is related to the size of the marginal propensity to invest, I_y. The stronger the relationship between investment and income, the greater is the marginal propensity to invest and, therefore, the greater is the value of the money multiplier. Since the marginal propensity to invest is relatively large (greater than the marginal propensity to save) in Case II, there is a relatively large increase in income and, therefore, a relatively large increase in the amount of money demanded. In fact, the increase in the amount of money demanded is large enough to result in an equilibrium rate of interest which is greater than the initial equilibrium level. In contrast, the marginal propensity to invest is relatively small (smaller than the marginal propensity to save) in Case I; hence, there is a relatively small increase in income and, therefore, a relatively small increase in the amount of money demanded. As a result, the ultimate effect of an increase in the supply of money is a reduction in the equilibrium rate of interest.

Case III

In Case III, the IS curve is positively sloped and its slope exceeds that of the LM curve. This situation is depicted graphically in Figure A2-3. Assuming the original LM curve is LM_0, the original equilibrium levels of income and the interest rate are Y_0 and i_0, respectively. If the money supply increases, the LM curve shifts to the right and the new equilibrium levels of income and the interest rate are Y_1 and i_1, respectively. To determine whether income and the interest rate gravitate to their new equilibrium levels, we proceed as before. With the increase in the money supply and the shift in the LM curve, the interest rate drops immediately

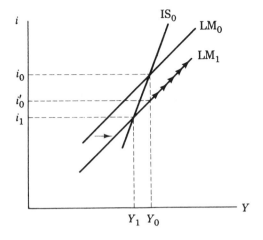

FIGURE A2-3

Stability and the IS–LM model: Case III

to i_0'. With the reduction in the interest rate, investment increases and $I + G$ now exceeds S. As a result, income increases. As income increases, more money is demanded and the interest rate increases. Moreover, given the initial assumptions, income and the interest rate increase indefinitely. Thus, instead of income and the interest rate decreasing to their new equilibrium levels, they increase. As a consequence, an unstable equilibrium is said to exist.

Thus, if the slope of the IS curve is less than that of the LM curve (Cases I and II), a stable equilibrium exists. In contrast, if the slope of the IS curve is greater than that of the LM curve (Case III), an unstable equilibrium exists.[3] It follows, therefore, that the stability condition—the condition necessary for a stable equilibrium to exist—is that the slope of the IS curve must be less than the slope of the LM curve. Since the slope of the IS curve is $(1 - C_y - I_y)/I_i$ and the slope of the LM curve is $-L_y/L_i$, the stability condition may be written

(A2-17)
$$\frac{(1 - C_y - I_y)}{I_i} < \frac{-L_y}{L_i}.$$

After multiplying both sides of the equation by $I_i L_i$ and rearranging terms, we obtain

(A2-18)
$$L_i(1 - C_y - I_y) + I_i L_y < 0.$$

Thus, for a stable equilibrium to exist, $L_i(1 - C_y - I_y) + I_i L_y$ must be less than 0. If this condition is satisfied, the government purchases and money multipliers derived earlier are positive, since $L_i(1 - C_y - I_y) + I_i L_y$, the denominator in both multipliers, must be negative for the multipliers to be positive.

NOTES

1. The money supply multiplier of this appendix is a relationship between a change in the real money supply and the resulting change in real income. This multiplier should not be confused with the money multiplier of Chapter 7, which is a relationship between a change in the monetary base and the resulting change in the nominal money supply.

2. In Chapter 9, the demonstration was in terms of interest elasticities rather than partial derivatives. The general principle, however, is the same.

3. The existence of an unstable equilibrium is related to the size of the marginal propensity to invest, I_y. In Cases I and II, I_y was assumed to be small relative to the other terms, and the slope of the IS curve was less than the slope of the LM curve. In Case III, I_y is larger than $1 - C_y$; hence, $1 - C_y - I_y$ is negative. Moreover, $1 - C_y - I_y$ is large enough in absolute terms to cause $L_i (1 - C_y - I_y)$ to be greater than the absolute value of $I_i L_y$, which implies that the slope of the IS curve exceeds that of the LM curve. Since I_y is relatively large, investment increases significantly as income increases, and the effect of the increase in income on investment more than offsets the effect of the increase in the interest rate (unlike Case II). Consequently, income and the interest rate tend to increase indefinitely.

appendix 3

THE IS–LM MODEL
WITH A GOVERNMENT
BUDGET CONSTRAINT

In Chapters 4 and 9, the effects of an increase in government purchases were considered. In doing so, we ignored the fact that the government must finance an increase in spending by increasing taxes, by borrowing from (selling Treasury securities to) the private sector, or by borrowing from (selling Treasury securities to) the Federal Reserve.

As discussed in Chapter 7, no changes in the money supply occur if the increase in spending is financed by a tax increase or by borrowing from the private sector. If the increase is financed by borrowing from the Federal Reserve, the monetary base, H, increases by an amount equal to the bond sales. The increase in the monetary base, or *high-powered money* as it is often called, has the same effect on the money supply as any other increase in the monetary base. Since the government is, in effect, issuing high-powered money, the three methods of financing a government deficit may be said to be (1) increasing taxes, (2) issuing government debt (selling Treasury securities to the private sector), and (3) issuing high-powered money (selling Treasury securities to the Federal Reserve).

Government spending is constrained, or limited, to the revenue that it can obtain from the various sources. The budget constraint may be written

(A3-1) $$PG = PT + \Delta B + \Delta H,$$

where PG represents the nominal value of government spending, PT the nominal value of tax receipts, ΔB the change in the nominal value of government debt, and ΔH the change in high-powered money. The equation indicates that government spending must be financed by tax revenue, by issuing government debt, or by issuing high-powered money (or some combination). This constraint may be incorporated into the IS–LM model in order to consider the impact of the alternative ways to finance a government deficit.

Before proceeding, we shall modify the IS–LM model in two ways. First, consumption is assumed to depend, in part, on wealth. As a consequence, wealth, defined so as to include the money supply and government debt, is included in the consumption function. (As discussed earlier, consumption is positively related to wealth.) Second, the demand for money is assumed to depend, in part, on wealth. Economists argue that money is one form of wealth, and should wealth increase, people will desire to hold more money (as well as other forms of wealth). Based on their argument, wealth is included in the demand for money function. With an increase in wealth, the amount of money demanded increases, but by an amount less than the increase in wealth.

THE ISSUANCE OF HIGH-POWERED MONEY

We can now examine the effects of the various means of financing a budgetary deficit. Suppose, initially, government purchases increase and the increase in spending is financed by an increase in high-powered money. The impact of the changes may be traced in Figure A3-1. With the increase in government purchases, the IS curve shifts from IS_0 to IS_1. If the increase in government purchases is financed by an increase in high-powered money, the money supply increases and the LM curve shifts from LM_0 to LM_2.[1] With the increase in the money supply, wealth and, hence, consumption increase, causing the IS curve to shift from IS_1 to IS_2.[2] The new equilibrium level of income is Y_2, given by the intersection of IS_2 and LM_2.

Income level Y_2 is greater than the initial level of income Y_0; it is also greater than income level Y_1, the level of income obtained in Figure 9.2 where the government budget constraint is ignored. Income level Y_2 is greater than Y_1 because the increase in the money supply served to reduce the magnitude of the increase in the interest rate and, thus, to reduce the magnitude of the decrease in investment, which partially offsets the increase in government purchases. Income level Y_2 is also greater than Y_1 because we have assumed that the increase in wealth causes an increase in consumption.

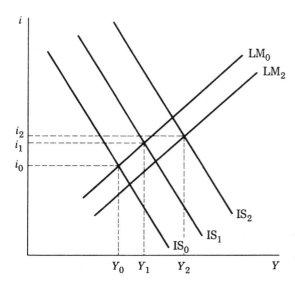

FIGURE A3-1

The impact of an increase in government purchases financed by an increase in high-powered money

Although income level Y_2 represents the new equilibrium level of income, it represents only the short-run equilibrium level. At income level Y_2, government spending is likely to exceed tax receipts, and the government must issue additional high-powered money to finance the deficit. Consequently, high-powered money and the money supply increase once more and the LM curve shifts to the right. As wealth increases, consumption increases and the IS curve also shifts to the right. These shifts continue over a number of periods until income reaches its long-run equilibrium level.

For income to be at its long-run equilibrium level, government spending must equal tax receipts. If government spending exceeds tax receipts, the government must continue to finance the deficit by issuing high-powered money. So long as the government continues to issue high-powered money, income continues to increase. Income will reach its long-run equilibrium level only when income has increased enough to generate sufficient tax revenue to support the new, higher level of government spending. Thus, for income to be at its long-run equilibrium level, ΔH must equal zero.

In the long run, the increase in income due to the increase in government purchases and high-powered money equals the long-run government purchases multiplier times the change in government purchases. In this model, the long-run government purchases multiplier equals the reciprocal of the marginal tax rate. Thus, if the tax function is $T = T_0 + tY$, the long-run government purchases multiplier is $1/t$. For example, if the marginal tax rate, t, is 0.20, the government purchases multiplier is $1/0.20$ or 5. This implies that a \$10 billion increase in government purchases will, in the long run, generate a \$50 billion increase in income. Without resorting to mathematics, we can see the logic of the argument.

To be at long-run equilibrium, the change in high-powered money must equal zero. Consequently, in the long run, income will continue to increase until tax revenue equals the new, higher level of government spending. In the example, if government purchases increase by $10 billion and the marginal tax rate is 0.20, income must increase by $50 billion in order for tax revenue to increase by $10 billion.

THE ISSUANCE OF GOVERNMENT DEBT

Suppose the increase in government purchases is financed by issuing bonds rather than by issuing high-powered money. What will be the short-run impact? As before, with the increase in government purchases, the IS curve in Figure A3-2 shifts from IS_0 to IS_1. As the government issues bonds to finance the deficit, wealth and, hence, consumption increase; as a consequence, the IS curve shifts from IS_1 to IS_2. As wealth increases, the demand for money increases and the LM curve shifts from LM_0 to LM_2. The new equilibrium level of income is Y_2, given by the intersection of the new IS curve IS_2 and the new LM curve LM_2.

Even though income increases, the increase is less than when the deficit was financed by an increase in high-powered money. In the previous case, the increase in high-powered money, and hence the money supply, caused the LM curve to shift to the right, reducing the magnitude of the increase in the interest rate and therefore the magnitude of the decrease in investment. In the present case, the increase in bonds, hence wealth, increases the demand for money without a corresponding increase in the money supply. As a consequence, the LM curve shifts to the left and the increase in the interest rate is accentuated. Investment decreases by a greater amount, thereby offsetting to a greater degree the increase in government purchases and producing a smaller increase in income. Thus, in the short

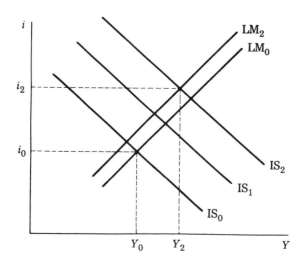

FIGURE A3-2

The impact of an increase in government purchases financed by issuing bonds run, an increase in government purchases financed by issuing high-powered money provides a greater stimulus to the economy than an equal increase in government purchases financed by issuing bonds.

As before, government spending is likely to exceed tax receipts at income level Y_2. Therefore, the government must issue additional bonds to finance the deficit. As wealth and consumption increase, the IS curve shifts to the right. On the other hand, as wealth and the demand for money increase, the LM curve shifts to the left. Presumably, the shift in the IS curve predominates and the equilibrium level of income increases.[3] So long as a government deficit exists, the government must continue to issue government debt. As a result, the IS and LM curves continue to shift, and income increases until it has generated sufficient tax revenue to support the new, higher level of government spending. Since tax revenue equals government spending at the long-run equilibrium level of income, ΔB and ΔH equal zero and no tendency exists for the IS and LM curves to shift.

In the long run, the increase in government purchases financed by issuing bonds results in a greater increase in income than if the increase had been financed by issuing high-powered money. As in the previous case, income must increase so as to generate sufficient tax revenue to support the new, higher level of government purchases. But if the deficit is financed by issuing debt, the government is obligated to make additional interest payments. Consequently, income must increase by a greater amount to support the new, higher level of government purchases and interest payments.

In the short run, an increase in government purchases financed by high-powered money provides a greater stimulus to the economy than an equal increase in government purchases financed by issuing debt. In the long run, the converse is true. Should the fiscal authorities use the short-run results or the long-run results as their primary guide to policy? Since the economic situation changes in the long run, and policies must be revised to meet the new conditions, the short-run results offer a better guide for policy makers.

TAX INCREASES

If the increase in government purchases is financed by a change in the tax structure, income increases in the short run but is either constant or decreases in the long run. With the increase in government purchases, the IS curve in Figure A3-3 shifts from IS_0 to IS_1. If the deficit is financed by an equal increase in the T_0 term of the tax function, the IS curve shifts from IS_1 to IS_2. Consequently, the new short-run equilibrium level of income is Y_2. As discussed in Chapter 4, income level Y_2 is greater than Y_0 since consumption does not decrease by the full amount of the tax increase. As discussed in Chapter 9, however, the increase in income is less than the increase in government purchases.

At income level Y_2, tax receipts exceed government spending. We assumed initially that the increase in government purchases was matched by an increase in

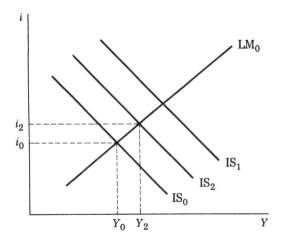

FIGURE A3-3

The impact of an increase in government purchases financed by a tax increase

taxes. As income increases, additional tax revenue is generated and a budget surplus develops. Assuming government purchases constant, the government has two choices: it may impound the surplus or retire government debt. If it impounds the surplus, the money supply declines and the LM curve shifts to the left. As the money supply decreases, wealth and, hence, consumption decrease and the IS curve shifts to the left. Both shifts reduce the equilibrium level of income; these shifts continue until income reaches its long-run equilibrium level. In this case, the long-run equilibrium level of income is Y_0 because, with the postulated change in the tax structure, it is the only level of income where government spending equals tax revenue at the new, higher level.

If the government retires debt, wealth and, hence, consumption decrease, and the IS curve shifts to the left. Also, with the decrease in wealth, the demand for money decreases and the LM curve shifts to the right. Presumably, the shift in the IS curve predominates and income decreases until it reaches its long-run equilibrium level. The long-run equilibrium level of income will be less than the original equilibrium level of income Y_0 because the debt retirement reduces the government's interest payments. With the reduction in interest payments, income must decline to a level less than the original equilibrium level of income for taxes to equal the new level of government spending.

When the government's budget constraint is considered, we find that the long-run balanced budget multiplier is either zero or negative. But even in the absence of a budget constraint, it is unlikely that fiscal authorities would choose to finance an increase in government purchases by increasing taxes during a recession. In Chapter 9, we found the balanced budget multiplier to be less than 1. Consequently, it would take a relatively large increase in government purchases and taxes to provide much of an increase in the equilibrium level of income. An increase in government purchases financed by issuing high-powered money or debt would provide a much greater increase in income. Also, if the economy were in a recession, it might be difficult politically to explain the desirability of a tax increase. Consequently, if the economy is in a recession, it is much more likely that expansionary fiscal policy will involve an increase in government purchases financed by issuing high-powered money or debt rather than by altering the tax structure.

We have seen that when the government budget constraint is considered, the multipliers are different from those that result when the constraint is ignored. Since the government must finance an increase in government purchases in some manner, the constraint must be considered. Consequently, the relevant multipliers are those derived with the budget constraint.

NOTES

1. With the increase in the money supply, wealth increases. Since wealth increases, the demand for money also increases and a tendency exists for the LM curve to shift to the left. Since the demand for money increases by an amount less than the increase in wealth, the tendency is more than offset by the tendency for the LM curve to shift to the right as a result of the increase in the money supply.

2. As discussed in Chapter 6, an increase in wealth reduces saving. As a consequence, the $S + T$ function shifts to the right. With the shift, the IS curve also shifts to the right, indicating that the equilibrium level of income is greater at each interest rate.

3. Bond financing may result in a lower level of income (lower than Y_0) in the long run. Alan S. Blinder and Robert M. Solow argue that this is unlikely. Blinder and Solow, "Analytical Foundations of Fiscal Policy," in Alan S. Blinder and others, *The Economics of Public Finance* (Washington, D.C.: The Brookings Institution, 1974), pp. 52–54.

appendix 4
PRODUCTIVITY GROWTH: PROBLEMS AND PROSPECTS

RONALD L. MOOMAW*

Labor productivity, or output per worker (Y/N), derives its importance from its relationship to economic well-being. For increased output to result in a higher standard of living, output (Y) must grow faster than the labor force (N) (or more precisely, population), which, with a constant ratio of employment to population, implies that labor productivity must grow. In short, the growth rate of labor productivity is an important determinant of the growth rate of the standard of living.

In the post-World War II period, the growth rate of labor productivity in the United States has been comparatively low; furthermore, sometime after 1965 this growth rate declined. This slowdown in productivity growth has influenced and been influenced by macroeconomic and microeconomic instability. It contributed to the dislocations that have occurred in the automobile, steel, apparel, and other manufacturing industries. On the other hand, relatively low saving and investment

---

*This appendix was written expressly for this text by Ronald L. Moomaw, Oklahoma State University.

rates, inflation, wage and price controls, and other macroeconomic shocks have contributed to the slowdown.

In this appendix, the U.S. productivity level and growth are described over time and relative to other countries. Next, two components of labor productivity are defined. The causes of the slowdown in the productivity growth rate are then discussed and related to the two components of labor productivity. The appendix concludes with a brief policy discussion.

LAGGING PRODUCTIVITY GROWTH

Three elements of productivity performance in the United States are important. One, labor productivity in the United States may be no higher than the average for the industrialized world. Two, labor productivity has been growing less rapidly in the post-World War II period in the United States than in most other industrial countries. Three, sharp reductions in the growth rate of labor productivity occurred in the United States and other industrialized countries after 1965.

The Level of Labor Productivity

Output per hour of work in the United States is no longer unequivocally higher than in other countries at a comparable level of development. As Table A4-1 shows, gross domestic product per employee-hour in the United States in

TABLE A4-1 A comparison of productivity levels: selected countries

Nation	Real Gross Domestic Product Per Employee Hour[1]			Output Per Hour Of Work In Manufacturing
	1870	1950	1977	1983
Canada	89[2]	78	88	93
France	62	41	79	109
Germany	63	35	84	111
Italy	59	31	68	97
Japan	24	14	52	97
United Kingdom	122	55	61	62
United States	100	100	100	100

[1]Real GDP is measured in 1970 U.S. prices and exchange rates.

[2]Productivity levels are given in index form with that of the United States equal to 100.

Source: Gross domestic product per employee hour is from Angus Maddison, "Long Run Dynamics of Productivity Growth," *Banca Nacionale del Lavoro Quarterly Review*, March 1979. Productivity levels in manufacturing are calculated from data in Lester Thurow, "A Time to Dismantle the World Economy," *The Economist*, November 9, 1985.

1950 was approximately 2 to 7 times greater than in the war-ravaged economies of Europe and Japan. By 1977, these countries had closed much of the productivity gap. U.S. labor productivity had dropped to somewhere between 1.5 and 1.25 times that of the European economies, excluding the United Kingdom. Labor productivity in Japan had moved from about 15 percent to about 50 percent of the U.S. level.

Table A4-1 also shows that, by 1983, labor productivity in the manufacturing sector of the U.S. economy had dropped below that of the German and French economies. Although the small differences could be due to measurement error, it is evident that a continuation of past trends will result in labor productivity (both in the manufacturing sector and in the entire economy) falling substantially behind that of other economies, including those of Germany, France, Italy, and Japan.

Although considerations of national pride may be at stake, other less nebulous considerations are more relevant. As we shall see, the productivity advantage of the United States relative to these other countries diminished or disappeared, in part, because of the absolutely slow growth of labor productivity in the United States. A slow growth in productivity implies a slow growth in the standard of living in an economy. In the U.S. economy from 1960 to 1969, real GNP per capita grew at a 2.9 percent rate; from 1970 to 1979, its growth rate was somewhat less, 2.4 percent. Although this difference in growth rates is large enough to have a substantial effect in the long run, it is not troublesome in the short run. Inauspiciously, much of the per capita GNP growth of the 1970s occurred because of increases in the proportion of the population employed. Indeed, a comparison of the growth rates of GNP per employee reveals a sharp difference in the growth experience of the two decades. In the 1960s, GNP per employee grew at an annual rate of 2.3 percent; in the 1970s, it grew at an annual rate of only 0.9 percent. We can gain perspective on these different growth rates by noting that GNP per employee would double in about 30 years with the growth rates of the 1960s; the doubling time with the growth rates of the 1970s is about 80 years. In conclusion, to maintain a growth rate of real GNP per capita comparable to that of the first 8 decades of this century, either the productivity growth rate must increase or the proportion of the population employed must continue to increase. Natural limits to the latter option exist.

International Comparisons

The productivity growth record of the United States compares unfavorably with that of other industrialized nations in the post-World War II period. For instance, U.S. productivity growth rates, after exceeding those of most industrialized countries throughout the first half of this century, fell below the gains achieved in those countries between 1963 and 1979. Nevertheless, the productivity slowdown is international in scope. In Canada, Germany, France, Italy, Japan, and the United Kingdom, productivity growth slowed from an average annual rate of 4.6 percent between 1963 and 1973 to an average rate of 1.9 percent over the period 1973–

79. For the United States the slowdown was greater; the annual growth rate fell from 1.9 percent to 0.1 percent.[1]

Labor productivity also grew more slowly in the manufacturing sector of the United States than in that of any of ten other major industrial countries (see Table A4-2). The U.S. average growth was about 50 percent lower than that of France, Sweden, Italy, Germany, The Netherlands, Belgium, and Denmark; and about 67 percent lower than that of Japan.

In addition, the manufacturing productivity growth rates for the 1960s, 1970s, and 1980–84 demonstrate a changing pattern of U.S. productivity performance. These comparisons are preliminary because they ignore cyclical differences and the effects of different currencies, both of which should be controlled before final judgments are made. With this caveat, we observe that the United States had a lower rate of productivity growth than the other countries for both the 1960s and the 1970s. A productivity growth slowdown in the 1970s relative to the 1960s occurred for all countries considered, except Belgium. Many of the other countries, however, had larger precentage drops in their growth rates than did the United States. Moreover, in the first part of the 1980s, the average annual growth rates of productivity increased for the United Kingdom, Sweden, and the United States. During this period, the U.S. manufacturing productivity growth rate exceeded that of three of the other countries. This turnaround for the United States, however, may be a cyclical event due to the strong recovery in the U.S. economy that began late in 1982.

TABLE A4-2 Average annual rates of productivity growth in manufacturing: selected countries (percent)

Country	1960–84	1960–70	1970–80	1980–84
United States	2.7	2.8	2.5	3.2
United Kingdom	3.4	3.7	2.6	5.2
Canada	3.3	4.2	2.8	2.3
France	5.5	6.5	4.8	4.6
Sweden	4.8	6.5	3.3	4.5
Italy	5.4	6.9	4.7	3.5
West Germany	4.7	5.6	4.5	3.0
Netherlands[1]	6.1	6.9	5.9	4.3
Belgium[1]	6.2	6.0	6.9	4.5
Denmark	5.1	5.8	5.2	2.0
Japan	8.5	10.3	7.4	6.6

[1]Time period is 1960–83.

Source: Calculated from Table 47, *Monthly Labor Review*, 109 (January 1986) and Table 129, *Handbook of Labor Statistics*, Bulletin 2217, 1985, p. 425, both from U.S. Bureau of Labor Statistics, U.S. Department of Labor.

The comparison of manufacturing productivity growth rates among various developed countries is particularly pertinent to the concern that the U.S. economy is becoming less competitive in international markets. Among others, the U.S. automobile and steel industries have declined partly because of foreign competition. Concern is sometimes expressed that disappearance of the U.S. productivity advantage will drive U.S. products from the international marketplace. Another concern is that the United States will experience large and continuing balance of payments deficits. Finally, there is a concern that the U.S. unemployment rate will rise as more workers are displaced from its manufacturing industries. According to W. J. Baumol, these concerns are misplaced.[2]

As previously stated, the major consequence of low or zero productivity growth is a low or zero growth in a country's standard of living. If productivity levels in other countries overtake the level in the United States, U.S. exporting will continue. As was demonstrated in Chapter 16, even if a country has an absolute disadvantage in the production of all goods, it necessarily has a comparative advantage in the production of some goods. If balance of payments deficits arise because of these productivity changes, exchange rates will adjust to restore equilibrium. If certain industries lose their comparative advantage, comparative advantage emerges in other industries. The adjustments to the new equilibrium will require that workers who lose their jobs in declining industries acquire jobs in rising industries. In many cases, these adjustments are painful. They are, however, no more painful than other adjustments that must be made in a dynamic economy; nor will they lead to large increases in unemployment.

As Baumol shows, however, there are adverse consequences to this chain of events. Suppose that the productivity gap results in a balance of payments deficit. Equilibrium might be restored by a decrease in the value of the dollar. Thus, the Swedes, for instance, can buy more dollars and hence more U.S. goods with a krona, and U.S. workers receive fewer krona and hence fewer Swedish goods for a dollar. As a result, the average price level for all goods—domestic and imported—goes up for U.S. workers and down for Swedish workers. In other words, the real wage in the United States goes down relative to the real wage in other countries, allowing the United States to compete in international markets on the basis of cheap labor rather than superior productivity. Once again, lagging productivity means a lagging standard of living.

THE SLOWDOWN IN THE UNITED STATES

One careful study of the slowdown of the growth rate of labor productivity in the private business sector of the U.S. economy examined the period 1948 to 1978.[3] Within this time span, labor productivity growth averaged 3.32 percent per year. This rate of increase declined to 2.32 percent from 1965 to 1973; a further decline to 1.20 percent occurred from 1973 to 1978. To appreciate the extent of the decline, note that the growth rate dropped by approximately 30 percent in the period 1965–

73 compared to 1948–65; then in the period 1973–78, it dropped by 50 percent compared to 1965–73. For the period 1965–78, the growth rate of labor productivity was approximately 65 percent lower than in the period 1948–65.

This decline in the growth of labor productivity was not confined to any one sector of the United States economy. Its full extent is apparent when we emphasize comparisons between the first and third periods. Of the eight major sectors for which reliable data exist, only the communications sector had a higher productivity growth rate in 1973–78 than in 1948–65. Mining, manufacturing, transportation, and electric, general, and sanitary services all experienced declines in their labor productivity growth rates in 1965–73, followed by another decline in 1973–78. Indeed, the productivity growth rate declined almost to zero in the utilities sector in the 1973–78 period, with the experience in the transportation sector being almost as severe. The slowdown in mining in the 1973–78 period actually translated into an absolute drop in the level of labor productivity. Finally, the severity of the situation in the 1973–78 period is further evidenced by the emergence of a slowdown in sectors that escaped it in the 1965–73 period, namely, agriculture, trade, and government enterprise.

Recently, two studies have questioned whether or not such a sharp change in productivity growth did, in fact, take place. On the basis of econometric tests, A. E. Blakemore and D. E. Schlagenhauf conclude that the annual productivity growth rate, adjusted for cyclical effects, did not drop sharply in the latter part of the 1953–80 period. Rather they find that the productivity growth rate trended downward during the entire period.[4] In an iconoclastic paper that disputes the now conventional wisdom about recent productivity growth, M. R. Darby contends that there was no slowdown; rather productivity growth from 1965–79 mirrored the productivity growth of the period 1900–1929.[5] Moreover, both periods experienced rapid employment growth and reductions in the growth rate of labor quality (as measured by experience and education) due, in the first period, to substantial immigration and, in the second period, to the maturation of the baby boom generation and the increased labor force participation rate of women. In other words, the proportion of inexperienced workers in the labor force increased in both periods. Adjusting for these demographic factors, Darby finds that the average annual productivity growth rate is almost identical for the periods 1900–1929, 1929–65, and 1965–79. Differences in the demographically-adjusted growth rates do exist, however, among the subperiods in his study.

According to Darby, the above-normal productivity growth rate from 1948 to 1965 is explained, almost completely, by a rapid growth rate of capital relative to labor, which, in turn, was in response to the below-normal capital stock that emerged as a result of the Great Depression and World War II. He also contends that the productivity growth rate of the 1965–73 period, as measured, was biased upward by the Nixon wage and price controls. As explained in Chapter 20, firms in the face of price controls have an incentive to allow the quality of their products to deteriorate, while maintaining their prices. Increases in output, as measured, are large because the quality of the output is not held constant. Thus, productivity growth during 1965–73, as measured, was artificially enhanced. Then, with the elimination of price controls, increases in real output were underestimated; and measured productivity growth was biased downward. In short, Darby contends that no significant slowdown in productivity growth occurred. Before considering this contention and before discussing some of the policy proposals related to the productivity performance of the U.S. economy, two productivity concepts are developed.

PRODUCTIVITY: TWO CONCEPTS

It is helpful to use the Cobb–Douglas production function (introduced in Chapter 17) to develop the productivity concepts. Rewriting equation (17.5) gives

(A4-1)
$$Y = A'K^\alpha N^{1-\alpha} \quad (0 < \alpha < 1),$$

where Y represents output, K the capital stock, and N the number of workers employed. In equation (A4-1), $A' = Ae^{rt}$ represents the effect of technology, with A representing a positive constant, e the natural e from mathematics, r the growth rate of technology, and t time. The partial elasticities of output with respect to capital and labor are α and $1 - \alpha$, respectively. These parameters are also the shares of capital and labor in total income.

Divide equation (A4-1) by N to get

(A4-2)
$$\frac{Y}{N} = \frac{A'K^\alpha N^{1-\alpha}}{N} = A'K^\alpha N^{-\alpha} = A'\left(\frac{K}{N}\right)^\alpha.$$

The equation states that output per unit of labor, *labor productivity*, is determined by the level of technology (A') and by the level of capital intensity (K/N).

In productivity analysis the level of technology is sometimes referred to as *total factor productivity*. To see why, divide equation (A4-1) by $K^\alpha N^{1-\alpha}$ to obtain

(A4-3)
$$\frac{Y}{K^\alpha N^{1-\alpha}} = A'.$$

In words, A' is output divided by a weighted average of all inputs or by the total factor; thus $Y/K^\alpha N^{1-\alpha}$ is denoted as total factor productivity, just as Y/N is denoted as labor productivity. Total factor productivity is a measure of the overall efficiency of the economy's operation. It depends on much more than technology. It reflects the allocation of resources, the diligence of labor, the skill of management, and more. Clearly, if the overall efficiency of the economy increases, labor productivity will increase (see equation (A4-2)).

The other determinant of labor productivity is capital intensity, K/N. Capital intensity is the amount of capital equipment available per worker. A worker using more capital equipment can produce more (see equation (A4-2)).

The implication of these production relationships for the growth of labor productivity is found by taking the differential of equation (A4-2). It is

(A4-4)
$$\Delta\left(\frac{Y}{N}\right) = \Delta A' + \alpha\Delta\left(\frac{K}{N}\right).$$

Equation (A4-4) states that any change in labor productivity can be broken down into a change in total factor productivity and a weighted change in capital intensity. Alternatively, the change in total factor productivity can be computed as the difference between the change in labor productivity and the change in capital intensity (weighted by capital's share in total output). We now use this framework to examine the sources of the productivity growth slowdown in the United States.

SOURCES OF THE SLOWDOWN IN PRODUCTIVITY GROWTH

Disagreement still exists concerning the sources of the slowdown in productivity growth. Table A4-3 presents average annual productivity growth rates broken down into changes due to the growth in capital intensity (the substitution of capital for labor), and changes due to the growth of total factor productivity as in equation (A4-4). From 1960 to 1984 labor productivity for the private business sector grew at an annual rate of 2.1 percent. Over this period, the growth in capital intensity added 0.8 percent to the growth rate of labor productivity and the growth in total factor productivity added the remaining 1.3 percent of the 2.1 percent annual growth rate.

TABLE A4-3 Average annual rates of productivity growth: selected time periods for the private business sector of the U.S. economy (percent)

	1960–84	1960–73	1973–80	1980–84
Labor productivity growth	2.1	2.9	0.5	2.0
The contribution of:				
Total factor productivity growth[1]	1.3	2.0	0.1	1.5
Capital intensity growth	0.8	0.9	0.4	0.5

[1]The Bureau of Labor Statistics refers to this as multifactor productivity.

Source: Calculated from the *Monthly Labor Review*, 108 (November 1985), 99.

Annual average productivity growth rates are also presented for the periods 1960–73 (which spans the peaks of two business cycles), 1973 to 1980 (which spans the peaks of one business cycle), and 1980–84 (which begins at the peak year for one business cycle and ends in a recovery year for another cycle). Subperiod analysis shows that the 0.5 percent average annual labor productivity growth in the middle period represents an 83 percent drop from the 2.9 percent rate of the previous period. This is the productivity growth slowdown. The growth rate increased in the 1980s to 2 percent. The degree to which previous productivity growth rates will be restored as the economic recovery continues is, of course, unknown.

Examining Table A4-3, we see that the productivity growth slowdown of the middle period resulted in large part because total factor productivity growth almost ceased. In the final period, however, it returned to 75 percent of the first period rate. Its reduction accounted for about 80 percent of the slowdown. In turn, the increased labor productivity growth observed thus far in the 1980s results, almost entirely, from the acceleration of total factor productivity growth to an annual rate of 1.5 percent.

The reduction of the growth of capital intensity in the middle period accounted for only 20 percent of the middle period slowdown. In the 1980s, however, capital intensity growth continues to contribute to labor productivity growth at its low middle period rate. Table A4-3 shows that, in contrast to total factor productivity growth, capital intensity growth gives no indication of contributing to labor productivity growth at its 1960s rate. Relatedly, J. R. Norsworthy and D. H. Malmquist find that the substantially faster Japanese labor productivity growth is due almost entirely to a more rapid accumulation of capital.[6]

Thus, the disadvantage of the United States relative to Japan, and perhaps other countries, is due in large part to a slower accumulation of capital. In comparison with the European economies, in particular, a substantially more rapid rate of growth in employment in the United States also contributes to its slower growth of capital intensity. The slower rate of capital accumulation can be traced to a U.S. saving rate only one-half that of the European economies and one-third that of Japan. Although the relatively slow rate of labor productivity growth in the United States may be related to saving and investment behavior, the causes of its absolutely low rate of total factor productivity growth in the 1970s and perhaps beyond are in dispute.

Blakemore and Schlagenhauf aver that no sharp slowdown in productivity growth occurred in the 1970s. The steady downward trend that they find would be related to some gradually occurring factor like resource depletion, a growing void in great innovations, or economic arteriosclerosis.[7] Darby goes farther and suggests that no productivity growth slowdown has occurred. He argues that adjusting observed labor productivity growth for demographic changes eliminates or accounts for the lower observed growth.

W. D. Nordhaus has summarized what is perhaps the consensus of many economists with regard to the 1970s slowdown.[8] It is noteworthy that he refers to his dissection of the slowdown as being based on his best guesses. He compares the annual growth rate in labor productivity (gross product originating in the private sector per hour worked) for the period 1973–79 to the growth rate for the period 1948–65. The comparison shows that the annual growth declined from 2.3 percent per year in the early period to 0.2 percent in the later period.

He attributes 12 percent of this decline to slower economic growth in the 1973–79 period. Since greater aggregate output increases efficiency due to the existence of economies of scale, slower economic growth retards productivity growth. From this perspective, an increase in the overall growth rate would stimulate productivity growth.

Nordhaus concludes that the other sources of the slowdown in the 1973–79 period are reductions in the growth of capital intensity and the growth of total factor productivity, in about the same proportions we found earlier. He attributes 12 percent of the slowdown to a reduced rate of growth of capital intensity and 76 percent of the slowdown to a reduced growth rate of total factor productivity. Of the 76 percent, about one-half (36 percent) is related to such specific influences as labor quality, energy problems, federal government regulatory activities, reduced research and development activity, and resource reallocations among sectors of the economy. The remaining 40 percent is not accounted for; that is, Nordhaus (along with many other economists) concludes that almost one-half of the entire productivity slowdown cannot be attributed to one specific source or to a small number of sources.

The reduction in the rate of growth in capital intensity occurred in association with an acceleration in the rate of growth of the labor force and employment. As labor becomes relatively more abundant, relatively more labor will be used per unit of capital; hence, the growth rate of labor productivity will fall. Part of the slowdown that is attributed to decreased capital intensity is simply an appropriate market response to changing conditions in the labor market. In addition, investment and, hence, capital intensity may have been depressed by high and variable inflation, high unemployment, and the supply shocks of the 1970s.

The influence of changes in the growth of labor quality on productivity growth is also an expected and appropriate market response to labor market changes. Nordhaus attributes 4 percent of the slowdown to these changes in labor quality growth. The reduction of the rate of growth of labor quality was due to an increase in the proportion of inexperienced workers in the labor force. This, in turn, was due to the coming of age of the children of the baby boom and an accelerated growth in female labor force participation. This increase in inexperienced workers was partially offset by continuing increases in educational levels. Although the absorption of inexperienced workers reduced productivity growth, the absorption itself was an important economic achievement. The effect on productivity was unfortunate but necessary, and is being reversed in the 1980s with a slower rate of entrance into the labor market of young people and women.

Another 12 percent of the slowdown was due to what Nordhaus calls sectoral shifts. Some of the productivity growth of the past was due to the shift of resources from low-productivity sectors like agriculture, to higher-productivity sectors like manufacturing. This source of productivity increase is no longer available because agriculture is not a particularly low-productivity sector and because the oversupply of resources in agriculture is smaller. Combined with the elimination of this source of productivity gain has been a productivity loss, because certain low-productivity parts of the service sector have been growing more rapidly than other parts of the economy. Nevertheless, given the increased demand for the output of these sectors, the rapid growth in low-productivity sectors of the economy is an appropriate response to changing market conditions. Unfortunately, this appropriate response leads to a retardation of productivity growth.

Nordhaus attributes 8 percent of the slowdown to the economy's response to higher energy prices. Increased energy prices may have resulted in a substitution of labor for capital and energy and may have reduced the efficiency of the existing capital stock. Both events can be appropriate responses to higher energy prices; yet they, too, lower productivity. Moreover, energy price shocks may have reduced the rate of capital formation and thus contributed to the slowdown via the capital intensity route. It remains to be seen how the reduction in oil prices will affect productivity growth. Presumably, it will have a positive effect.

Environmental regulation, according to Nordhaus, accounts for 8 percent of the slowdown, largely because of the diversion of capital equipment from the production of goods to the production of environmental quality by, for instance, using scrubbers to reduce the emission of pollutants into the atmosphere. Since the services of the improved environment are not measured in the national income accounts, this diversion results in a reduction of measured labor productivity. The fact that this reduces measured labor productivity growth is largely irrelevant to an evaluation of the regulations. Careful benefit-cost analyses are necessary to evaluate environmental regulations.

Finally, Nordhaus attributes 4 percent of the slowdown to decreased intensity and effectiveness of research and development (R&D) activities. A declining intensity of R&D can be reversed through government policy; a declining effectiveness, on the other hand, is more difficult to reverse.

POLICY DISCUSSION

These identified sources of productivity growth—capital intensity, labor quality, sectoral shifts, energy prices, regulations, and research and development—account for roughly 60 percent of the 1970s slowdown. The demographic factors that reduced capital intensity and labor quality are unlikely to have these same effects in the remaining years of this century. Rather, changing demographic factors may increase productivity growth. Energy price changes and the reduction in the growth rate of regulatory activity may also stimulate productivity growth.

Indeed, the data in Table A4-3 hint at the possibility that the slowdown in total factor productivity growth has been reversed. Data for only four years, however, cannot be conclusive. Furthermore, the total factor productivity growth rate of the 1980s is still twenty-five percent below the rate of 1960–73. The growth rate of capital intensity, however, shows no sign of increasing. Perhaps a continuation of steady economic growth with stable inflation in tandem with tax reform can increase the rate of saving and investment, stimulating the growth rate of capital intensity and total factor productivity. Lessons learned from the 1970s slowdown may be helpful in understanding the causes of the slowdown in the growth of total factor productivity and of capital intensity.

Unfortunately, about one-half of the 1970s slowdown is unaccounted for. One explanation is that high tax rates, cumbersome regulations (not captured in the regulation effect discussed previously), and variable and increasing rates of inflation combined to reduce the initiative and incentive of workers and managers. If the assertion that U.S. labor no longer works effectively is valid, it is, according to this explanation, because high marginal tax rates reduce the incentive to work effectively.

Furthermore, it is often asserted that managers in the United States make decisions using a very short-term horizon. As a result, long-term productivity-enhancing investments in plant and equipment or research and development are shunted aside in favor of short-term investments with a quick payoff. Many observers have commented on this alleged phenomenon, often blaming it on the quantitative approach to management taught in many business schools. In contrast, this explanation suggests that variable rates of inflation and regulatory zeal make the future uncertain so that future profits are heavily discounted.

Finally, the low saving rate and oft-cited decline in the U.S. entrepreneurial spirit are also taken to be the result of the excessively high marginal tax rates on unearned income. If most of the returns to entrepreneurial activity are taxed away at the margin, so this scenario goes, then entrepreneurial activity will diminish.

A corollary of this supply-side explanation of lagging productivity growth is that the supply-side policies of the Reagan administration, as discussed in Chapter 12, combined with an effective anti-inflation policy, should be providing an important impetus to productivity growth.

Other economists, while agreeing with some of the supply-side critique, maintain that generalized pro-saving policies are not appropriate pro-productivity policies or appropriate policies in general. This may be because they attribute the unexplained portion of the slowdown to a series of specific events such as the energy situation and a tax system tilted toward "nonproductive" asset accumulation. Nordhaus, for instance, agrees that anti-inflation policy and, more potently, policies designed to stimulate aggregate demand or to avoid deficient aggregate demand can stimulate productivity growth. It would be consistent for him to believe that the fiscal stimulus provided by the Reagan administration is promoting more rapid productivity growth. His emphasis, however, is on aggregate demand, rather than on anti-inflation policy, which sets him apart from the supply side. In addition, rather than using generalized tax policy, he would target tax policy so as to (1) channel resources into research and more particularly to specific types of research, (2) encourage foreign direct investment, (3) encourage corporate investment, (4) channel more resources into academia, and (5) channel investment away from low-productivity areas like housing, gold, art, and land. Finally, he too would undertake regulatory reform.

Many similarities exist between the two sets of policy recommendations. The main differences are in the area of macroeconomic policy, the scope of regulation, and the use of tax cuts. The supply-side approach is to increase incentives with generalized tax cuts. The alternative approach is to use specific tax policy to channel resources into and away from certain areas.

Regardless of viewpoint, many economists would agree that policies designed specifically to deal with labor productivity are unnecessary. Policies that promote macroeconomic stability and microeconomic efficiency can be expected to improve productivity performance. Such policies, as Nordhaus suggests, are not evoked by the productivity slowdown. They simply are sound economic policy.

NOTES

1. See C. R. Hulten, "Why Do Growth Rates Vary? An International Comparison," *The Wharton Magazine*, 5 (Summer 1981), 42–47.

2. W. J. Baumol, "On Productivity Growth in the Long Run," *Atlantic Economic Journal*, 12 (September 1984), 5–10.

3. J. R. Norsworthy, M. J. Harper, and R. Kunze, "The Slowdown in Productivity Growth: Analysis of Some Contributing Factors," *Brookings Papers on Economic Activity*, no. 2 (1979), 387–471.

4. A. E. Blakemore and D. E. Schlagenhauf, "Estimation of the Trend Rate of Growth of Productivity," *Applied Economics* 15, (December 1983), 887–914.

5. M. R. Darby, "The U.S. Productivity Slowdown," *American Economic Review*, 74, (June 1984), 301–22.

6. J. R. Norsworthy and D. H. Malmquist, "Recent Productivity Growth in Japanese and U.S. Manufacturing," in *Productivity Growth and U.S. Competitiveness*, W. J. Baumol and K. McLennan, eds., New York: Oxford University Press, 1985 as discussed in W. J. Baumol, op. cit.

7. See also M. Olson, *The Rise and Decline of Nations: Economic Growth, Stagflation, and Social Rigidities*, New Haven: Yale University Press, 1982, for a discussion of the effects of an aging economy.

8. W. D. Nordhaus, "Policy Responses to the Productivity Slowdown," in *The Decline in Productivity Growth*, Conference Series, (Federal Reserve Bank of Boston, 1980).

INDEX